# THE COLONIAL IMAGE
## Origins of American Culture

*By John C. Miller*

# THE COLONIAL IMAGE

## Origins of American Culture

**SELECTED AND EDITED WITH INTRODUCTION AND NOTES BY**

*John C. Miller*

GEORGE BRAZILLER

NEW YORK 1962

# Preface

No sooner had the first settlers established precarious footholds on the strange shores than some of them began to record their thoughts and experiences. In so doing they began to create a new literature. American writing is as old as Jamestown, Plymouth, and Massachusetts Bay; well before the American Revolution it had become as rich and varied as the colonial culture it represented. The years between 1607 and 1776 span almost half the total era of American experience. They were formative years, the seed beds for much that is traditionally and characteristically American.

The first Englishmen to settle in the New World demonstrated an optimistic expansiveness that has never been lost—not only Captain John Smith chronicling his adventures but even a Massachusetts Bay Puritan who penned apostrophes to the salubrious, healing climate, and promptly died a victim of it. There is much that is serious and thought-provoking in the long panorama of colonial writers: William Bradford and his stark, impressive history of Plymouth; John Winthrop, the Mathers and a host of Puritans, leaving their mark upon American government and character as well as theology; the brilliant Jonathan Edwards proclaiming the Great Awakening. There is much that is light and entertaining as well: Thomas Morton's record of the bacchanalian festivities at Merrymount; the great diaries of two worldly colonials, Samuel Sewall of Boston and William Byrd of Westover, Virginia, and the mock-epic poem by Ebenezer Cook, *The Sot-Weed Factor*. There is adventure in the personal narratives of those who had been captured by the Indians. There is Benjamin Franklin's "Poor Richard" guide to business success, and the contrasting philosophy of the serene Quaker, John Woolman, putting material possessions behind him so he could better testify against social injustice. And in the writings of a Frenchman, Michel-Guillaume Jean de Crèvecoeur, is a classic analysis of the American character as it had already developed by the eve of the Revolution.

The remarkable breadth of colonial writing will delight readers for whom this book will serve as an introduction. Those long familiar with

5

the period will appreciate the judiciousness with which John C. Miller has selected these representative and significant writings. The felicitous introductions are added evidence of his distinction as a historian of early America.

FRANK FREIDEL

*. . . all great and honorable actions are accompanied with great difficulties and must be both enterprised and overcome with answerable courages. It was granted the dangers were great, but not desperate. The difficulties were many, but not invincible. For though there were many of them likely, yet they were not certain. It might be sundry of the things feared might never befall; others by provident care and the use of good means might in a great measure be prevented; and all of them, through the help of God, by fortitude and patience, might either be borne or overcome.*

WILLIAM BRADFORD, 1630

# Contents

Head and Ears in cold Water, and then to bind it naked to a
convenient Board.

It is a solemn sight to see so many Christians lying in their blood,
some here and some there, like a company of sheep torn by wolves,
all of them stripped naked by a company of hellhounds, roaring,
singing, ranting, and insulting, as if they would have torn our very
hearts out.

Some people have been so ill inform'd, as to say, that Virginia is
full of toads, though there never yet was seen one Toad in it.

Our hunters killed a large doe and two bears, which made all other
misfortunes easy. Certainly no Tartar ever loved horseflesh, or Hottentot guts and garbage, better than woodsmen do bear. The truth
of it is, it may be proper food perhaps for such as work or ride
it off, but, with our chaplain's leave, who loved it much, I think it
not a very proper diet for saints, because 'tis apt to make them a
little too rampant.

Then while we live, in love let's so persevere,
That when we live no more, we may live ever.

But Adam's guilt our souls hath split,
    His fault is chargéd on us,
And that alone hath overthrown
    And utterly undone us.

Lord, make my Faith thy golden Quill wherethrough
    I vital Spirits from thy blood may suck.

If it be sin to think Death brib'd can be
We must be guilty: say 'twas bribery
Guided the fatal shaft.

I met a Quaker, Yea and Nay:
A Pious Conscientious Rogue,
As e'er wore Bonnet or a Brogue,

Who neither Swore nor kept his Word
But cheated in the Fear of God;
And when his Debts he would not pay,
By Light within he ran away.

I never saw an oft-removéd tree,
Nor yet an oft-removéd family,
That throve so well as those that settled be.

A Pennsylvanian will tell a lie with a sanctified, solemn face; a
Marylander, perhaps, will convey his fib in a volley of oaths.

So I sold some of my books to raise a little money, and was taken
on board privately, and, as we had a fair wind, in three days I found
myself in New York, near three hundred miles from home, a boy
of but seventeen, without the least recommendation to, or knowledge
of, any person in the place, and with very little money in my pocket.

My employer, having a negro woman, sold her, and desired me to
write a bill of sale . . . through weakness I gave way and wrote it;
but at the executing of it I was so afflicted in my mind, that I said
before my master . . . that I believed slave-keeping to be a practise
inconsistent with the Christian religion.

*He* is an American who, leaving behind him all his ancient prejudices
and manners, receives new ones from the new mode of life he
embraces, the new government he obeys, the new rank he holds.

# Introduction

## *John C. Miller*

American literature was born when Englishmen began to write about their experiences in the trans-Atlantic colonies. It was the offspring of the marriage between the English language and the American environment. In the beginning, it took the form of descriptions of the new land and its inhabitants, accounts of the hardships met with by the settlers, and narratives of their relations with the Indians. Few of the men who produced this body of literature would have written anything worthy of a place in literary history had they remained in England; they were primarily men of action in whose lives writing played a secondary part. By providing them with a theme, setting and incidents—a whole new range of experience—America helped to create a fresh, virile branch of literature.

Because the overriding need of the colonies was for people, many of the early American writers were publicists who made it their business to persuade Englishmen and others to pull up stakes and settle in the New World. The techniques of modern advertising originated in this effort to "sell" America to prospective immigrants. To promote the growth of the newly founded colonies, the Virginia and Massachusetts Bay companies enlisted the services of poets, pamphleteers, ship captains, preachers and returned travelers. As a result, there was such an outpouring of tracts, ballads, and sermons devoted to America that the colonizing companies virtually became publishing houses. After the Indian Massacre in Virginia in 1622, the Reverend John Donne, the eminent poet and dean of St. Paul's, preached a sermon in which he declared that continued support of the colony would advance both the interests of England and the Kingdom of God. For services rendered, the Reverend Dr. Donne was paid by the Virginia Company in stock.

The importance of creating a favorable image of America was made the more necessary by the reports detrimental to the colonies that found ready credence in the Old World. It was rumored that the country was infested with "Devills or Lyons"; that once they crossed the Atlantic, women could not bear children; that New England rattlesnakes were

able to fly and to kill a man with their breath; that the settlers starved
miserably and that there was nothing to drink but water; that bloodthirsty
savages were constantly on the prowl for scalps; that the sun turned all
people black and that Englishmen quickly learned to treat their wives as
the Indians did their squaws, compelling them "to sit on the lower hand,
and to carrie water, and the like drudgerie."

As a result of these and other "such prodigious Phantasms," said John
Hammond, the author of *The Two Fruitful Sisters of Virginia and Mary-
Land* (1656), "many deceived Souls, chose rather to Beg, Steal, rot in
Prison, and come to shameful deaths, than to better their being by going
thither, wherein is plenty of all Things Necessary for Human subsistence."

If Englishmen preferred to endure privation at home rather than partake of the plenty that awaited them in the New World, it was not the
fault of American writers. They portrayed the colonies as a country
blessed by an abundance of cheap land, a healthy climate and high wages
—everything, in short, necessary for the good life, including sport. The
Reverend Alexander Whitaker, who went to Virginia in 1611 to minister
to the souls of the Jamestown settlers, assured his readers in *Good Newes
from Virginia* (published in 1613 by the Virginia Company) that the
fishing, with which his clerical duties apparently did not interfere, was
excellent. Citing the text, "Cast thy bread upon the waters: for after
many days thou shalt find it," the Reverend Mr. Whitaker predicted that
investors in the Virginia Company would profit both in soul and pocket-
book. As the event proved, the investors would have been better off fi-
nancially if they, too, had gone fishing: not one recovered his capital.

New England writers likewise dwelt upon the lush soil, indulgent
climate and other felicities that awaited immigrants. William Wood, the
author of *New England's Prospect* (1634), asserted that the climate
was so salubrious that "in publick assemblies it is strange to heare a
man sneeze or cough as ordinarily they do in old England." After spending a few months in Boston in 1630, the Reverend Francis Higginson portrayed the new land as a vast health resort: "there is hardly a more
healthful place to be found in the World that agreeth better with our
English Bodies," he reported. "Many that have been weak and sickly
in old England, by coming hither have been thoroughly healed and
grown Healthful and strong. . . . A sup of New England's air is better
than a whole draught of Old England's ale." Suiting his actions to his
words, he cast off his cap and heavy clothing and exposed himself to the
invigorating, health-restoring air. Six months later he was dead of
tuberculosis. His tribute to the tonic effects of the New England climate,
*New England's Plantation* (1630), appeared posthumously.*

---

* In 1608, Captain Peter Wynne wrote from Virginia that he had found the
most pleasant country in the world. "I am now willing here to end my dayes."
And six months later, end them he did.

Instead of lamenting their virginity at home, spinsters were urged to come to the colonies where the shortage of women was so acute and the demand so brisk that it was said that "if any Maid or single Woman . . . be but Civil and under 50 years of age, some honest Man or other, will purchase them for their Wives." Except "some wenches that are nasty, beastly, and fit only to labor in the fields," women who went to the colonies as indentured servants could be sure of being courted by lusty, full-blooded planters, eager to carry them off to their plantations where they were treated like gentlewomen. And, in fact, some of them did: Daniel Defoe's niece, an indentured servant, married her owner's son. But this was merely the beginning of domestic happiness: according to Gabriel Thomas, the author of *Newes from Pennsylvania* (1698), children born overseas were "generally well-favored, and beautiful to behold: I never knew any come into the World with the least blemish on any part of its Body, being in the general, observ'd to be *better Natur'd, Milder and more tender Hearted* than those born in England."

In the course of their efforts to lure immigrants to the colonies, these writers were led to examine the deeper significance America held for the Old World. They found this meaning in the opportunity offered the common man to attain freedom, dignity and economic well-being: "those which Fortune hath frown'd upon in *England,* to deny them an inheritance amongst their Brethren, or such as by their utmost labors can scarcely procure a living" could make a fresh start in America with the assurance that here labor would meet with its due reward. Indentured servants were said to live better in the colonies than free laborers in England; and the servants, unlike the laborers, could look forward to becoming respected landowners and full-fledged citizens when their term of service expired. In short, the first picture of America presented to Europeans was of a land designed by providence for the common man weary of the social and economic inequities of Europe.

But it was recognized that it took a special breed of men to seize the opportunities offered by the American colonies. From the beginning, there was a winnowing and sifting process that left behind the timid, the satisfied and the indolent. The ingredients of success in early America were optimism, courage, determination and willingness to work hard. As the Reverend Francis Higginson said, "Those that love their own chimney-corner, and dare not go beyond their own town's end, shall never have the honor to see these wonderful works of Almighty God."

Of this special breed of men, Captain John Smith was a conspicuous example. A swashbuckling, devil-may-care, but at the same time devout and patriotic Elizabethan, Smith found in America a stage upon which to display his heroism, endurance and powers of command. It was his thirst for fame and his ardent desire for England to become the seat of a great empire rivaling that of Spain—when Smith lived, it was the Spaniards' boast that "the Sunne never sets in the Spanish dominions"—that spurred him into action. He became the first Englishman to be directly associated with the major continental colonies established by England in the early seventeenth century: Virginia and New England. Of the first he was the self-styled "governor"; and for his services in charting the coast of New England he received from the Prince of Wales the title of "Admirall of New England."

Smith owes his place in American history not only to his actual achievements in the New World, for there were few among his contemporaries to give him credit, but to the skill and persistence with which he trumpeted his own fame. His purpose in writing the history of the settlement of Virginia, he said, was the "eternizing of the memory of those that effected it." In practice, this became self-commemoration. Although he made no pretense of literary ability—his "rude military hand," he said, was more adept in wielding the pikestaff than the pen—he knew how to tell a story, particularly when the story had to do with Indian surprise attacks, ambushes, exploring trips into the interior and his efforts to instill spirit and discipline into the gold-crazed settlers at Jamestown.

From the turmoil of early Virginia, John Smith emerged as the dominant figure; from the bleak settlement at Plymouth, William Bradford, an equally forceful personality and Smith's superior as a literary artist, took a commanding place. Both men found their true being in the world of advancing a great cause: Smith dedicated himself almost wholly to the expansion of English dominion overseas while Bradford devoted his life to the establishment of the Kingdom of God upon earth. One sought to remake America in the image of England; the other took heaven as his model of the good society.

Bradford's pre-eminence in the Pilgrim community was not owing to any superiority in education. Like most Pilgrims, he came from plain yeoman stock whose educational opportunities were severely restricted. Nevertheless, he was not a rustic: before he came to Plymouth he had been a weaver and small businessman in Leyden. What set Bradford apart from his companions was his passionate love of learning. He taught himself Latin, Greek and—in order to read the Bible in the original— Hebrew. In Plymouth he collected a library of four hundred volumes, many of which were Latin and Greek classics.

Besides playing an active part at Plymouth in business and politics— he was elected governor thirty times—Bradford wrote the best history produced in seventeenth-century America: *The History of Plymouth Plantation*. Here he captured the epic quality of the second heroic age of Protestantism—the courage and idealism that actuated a handful of English men and women to brave the casualties of the sea, "sore sickness and grievous diseases," hunger, cold and want in order that truth might prevail and that "the churches of God recover their primitive order, liberty and beauty." If Americans find it easier to respond emotionally to Plymouth Rock than to Boston or Jamestown, it is in large measure owing to Bradford's *History*.

The grandeur and solemnity that distinguish *The History of Plymouth Plantation* are largely derived from Bradford's reading of the Bible and the classical historians. It owes its effect also to his "plain style"—the direct, simple, unadorned language of the Geneva Bible. By the same token that he believed that religious truth lay in simplicity, in stripping off accretions and nonessentials, he considered that thought was best expressed in a spare, functional style which is all the more moving because it is not consciously "literary." Yet he did not avoid all literary artifice: he used effectively such devices as antithesis, alliteration and the balanced sentence. His purpose was not to delight the ear but to convey truth: like the great historians of every age he tried to describe exactly how things happened.

We know John Smith for his *History of Virginia;* we know the Pilgrims for William Bradford's *History of Plymouth Plantation.* Whereas Smith was a flamboyant soldier of fortune, fond of excess to self-dramatization, Bradford was unwilling to speak of his personal achievements lest he seem to detract from the honor due God. As a result, the personal pronoun is as conspicuous by its absence from Bradford's *History* as it is by its presence in the writings of John Smith. For example, Bradford made no mention of the death of his wife, Dorothy, at Cape Cod. This omission may be owing, however, to the probability that she committed suicide after looking for several weeks at the desolate sand dunes in the vicinity of Provincetown. Even the stoutest hearts aboard the *Mayflower* experienced a sinking feeling as they surveyed the unpromising site of the New Jerusalem.

Despite his natural kindliness and long-suffering patience, Bradford could be pushed too far. Thomas Morton went well beyond Bradford's limits of endurance but, then, Morton's idea of sport was baiting Puritans. Among Englishmen, this was a popular pastime, but Morton made the mistake of playing the game among the Puritans themselves: he settled down at Merrymount, not far from Plymouth, and proceeded to make himself as offensive as possible to the Pilgrim Fathers.

Morton was the kind of Englishman the Pilgrims had come three thousand miles to get away from: the hard-drinking, Sabbath-breaking, Maypole-dancing, bear-baiting, roistering type—in short, the Englishman in his natural state, which James I and Charles I much preferred to the product refined and sanctified by Puritanism. In his trading post at Merrymount, Morton held high carnival, feasting and frolicking with the Indian "damsels." Morton insisted that it was good clean fun in the time-honored English way: a maypole, some stout fellows harmonizing around a barrel of beer and fifes, drums and guns to enliven the occasion. The maypole, he announced, stood as a beacon to the whole country "how to find out the way to mine host of Mare-Mount." It became a well-beaten trail: large numbers of Indians joined the revels and the color line was quickly washed away by the Flowing Bowl. Morton got on famously with the Indians: he thought that their language contained Greek and Latin words—which indicated to him that they were refugees from Troy. He gladly supplied the descendants of such renowned warriors with firearms as well as firewater in exchange for beaver skins.

The "Strangers" among the Pilgrims, oppressed by the grim austerity of Plymouth, began to yearn for the gay, carefree life of Merrymount; and even the Pilgrim sons and daughters were not immune to Morton's siren song. Moreover, by selling arms and ammunition to the Indians, Morton posed an even greater danger to Plymouth: there was no telling when the Indians might decide to act on the maxim that the only good Pilgrim was a dead Pilgrim.

While Morton and his crew were whooping it up at Merrymount, the Pilgrims were taking steps to remove this "excrescence" from New England. The aid of the Puritan settlements as far north as Cape Ann was enlisted—the first instance of co-operative action among the English colonies—and an army of nine men under the command of Captain Myles Standish (Morton dubbed him "Captain Shrimp") marched on Merrymount. Although Morton and his men, when properly primed with liquor, were as brave as lions, some of them overdid this phase of their preparation for battle—with the result that the outnumbered garrison fell almost without resistance to Standish and his army. John Endicott immortalized himself by cutting down the maypole at Merrymount.

Although the population of the various English colonies upon the North American continent was relatively homogeneous and the colonists shared a common experience in wresting homes and farms from what William Bradford called "a hideous and desolate wilderness, full of wild beasts and wild men," New Englanders and Virginians did not view the significance of their labors in the same light. The English colonies were small communities, each with its own church, hierarchy, social organization and sense of mission. In the early period of settlement, there were many points of similarity between Virginia and Massachusetts—in Jamestown, attendance at religious services was compulsory and even as hard-bitten a character as John Smith declared that the settlement was a work "most acceptable to God"—but the two colonies soon became distinct entities, separated by profound differences in their ways of life as well as by hundreds of miles of wilderness. Virginia became the "Old Dominion," "the happy Retreat of true *Britons* and true *Churchmen*," while New

England became a "City upon a Hill," consecrated, spiritually aloof, dedicated to the lofty mission of regenerating Christendom.

From the beginning, it was made plain that New England was not simply a refuge for the poor and downtrodden in search of economic betterment. Since New England was to be "a fit abode for Saints," the Puritans felt that they were doing God's work by establishing immigration restrictions. For admission to this haven of righteousness, it was said, only those who were prepared to make "His Glory as a principal, and all other outward things but as accessories," need apply. The mesh was fine: "God sifted a whole nation," said William Stoughton in 1668, "that He might send choice grain into this wilderness." Thus, to the Puritans, America did not represent an opportunity for the average man to get a fresh start; rather, it afforded the godly man a chance to attain true godliness.

English Puritanism was distinguished by a strong intellectual strain—the first Puritans were scholars in the English universities—and this quality did not disappear in the New World. Besides their seeds, tools and other implements, the Puritans carried heavy intellectual baggage. Their leaders, many of whom were graduates of Oxford and Cambridge, were resolved to advance learning as an indispensable adjunct of religion. For that purpose they established a college and a printing press at Cambridge; and the clergy helped to keep the flame alive by putting in a twelve-hour day at their studies. The Reverend John Cotton loved to sweeten his mouth before retiring with a juicy bit of Calvin's *Institutes*. The Reverend Richard Mather died lamenting that he could not breathe his last in his library among his beloved books.

With men of such considerable intellectual endowments, the New World had a galvanizing effect upon the literary impulse. Never has so much and so erudite writing been done by men engaged in a struggle for survival, precariously clinging to a beachhead in the American wilderness. When the Puritans arrived in New England, they fell upon their knees to thank God and then reached for their pens to record their impressions.

The orientation of the books and pamphlets that streamed from the printing presses at Cambridge and Boston was mostly heavenward. Puritans were mad about sermons; despite the frigid temperature of the meetinghouses, they insisted upon sitting through two sermons on the Sabbath and many churchgoers made it a practice to bring notebooks in order to preserve a record of their pastor's words. In Puritan New England, the publication of a sermon was a literary event. As a result, a whole literature of sermons came into being. Give a parson a text he could ride and he was certain to come back with a book in his saddlebag.

This preoccupation with the intellectual side of religion helped to prevent the New England mind from succumbing to frontier influences

hostile to things of the mind. The Puritan mind was narrow but it loved
to probe deeply; and by probing, it kept the edge of the intellect sharp.
It is highly improbable that the idea of mental activity for its own sake or
of art for art's sake could have taken the place of the concern with religion that kept learning and literary activity alive in New England.

The question asked by Puritans of every book was: Did it promote
the cause of religion, morality and learning? Amusement and pleasure
were of no consequence; indeed, Puritans could not tolerate light, diver-
sionary reading: it took the mind off holy things and was therefore evil.
The theater and even the reading of plays was put under the ban (no
copies of Shakespeare or Jonson have been found in the libraries of the
early settlers) and had they had their way, the theaters in England would
have been closed and, instead of marking a great age of English drama,
the Elizabethan and early Stuart periods would have produced little more
than didactic sermons and religious tracts. As for humor, if met with in
a Puritan it was wholly unintentional: they were grave, humorless men
to whom levity had no place in the all-absorbing business of glorifying
God and getting to heaven.

Unlike Virginians, the New England Puritans were under a religious
compulsion to write history. Having embarked upon a holy errand to the
wilderness and believing themselves to be under the direct guidance of
the Almighty, the Puritans were far removed from the mundane sphere of
everyday events: in their own eyes, they were a Chosen People whom
God had commissioned to erect the New Jerusalem. Viewed in this light,
the history of New England became a series of Illustrious Providences
in which God demonstrated his approval and love of His Saints. And so,
when the Puritans dedicated themselves to the task of recording these
providences, they glorified God and celebrated His ordinances. Thus the
writing of history took the form of a devotional exercise: God was exalted
by an account of His doings.

Accordingly, the history of New England came to be written mainly in
the form of a chronicle: a day-by-day account of the benefactions of the
Almighty, the tribulations and joys of His Chosen People. Since history
was conceived to be the study of an unfolding of a Divine Plan already
laid down in heaven, nothing could be omitted from the record: even
seemingly trivial events might have significance in the over-all plans of
Jehovah. If the mind of God could not be read in events as they occurred,
the pattern was certain to emerge later on. The safest course for a historian, therefore, was to interpret wherever possible but to record everything, however inscrutable, that occurred. Because the settlement of New
England was thought to be the culminating event of human history (the
Apocalypse could not be far distant), the Puritan historians often began
with Genesis. Fortunately for the purposes of chronology, the date of

that event had been fixed by the researches of Archbishop Ussher at 4004 B.C.

The most detailed and inclusive account of the Puritan period is John Winthrop's *The History of New England from 1630 to 1649*. Written in the form of a journal, the *History* records the affairs of the entire community and its dominant theme is the triumph of God's People and God's Work rather than the intimate personal affairs of the author. Dry, factual and austere, it succeeds in conveying a sense of the Puritan mind and it is a prime source for the history of New England. The more human, almost charming, side of Winthrop's character is revealed by the love letters he wrote his wife during 1629–1630.

The Puritans regarded themselves as soldiers of Christ engaged in an all-out struggle with the Powers of Darkness. This military analogy provided the inspiration for Edward Johnson's *Wonder-Working Providence of Sion's Savior in New England* (1654). Johnson was an uneducated farmer, ship carpenter and militia captain who made a spirited effort to write a Puritan masterpiece. (It was the great American epic, not the great American novel that first captivated the imagination of American writers.) Johnson violated all the canons of grammar and orthography, yet his work has a rude, rhetorical vigor that occasionally approaches the rhapsodical. He was militant, fanatical, intolerant and superstitious, but he wore his Puritanism proudly: it is the Puritanism of the relatively uneducated rank and file. Unlike many of the leaders of Massachusetts Bay, Johnson was not an unhappy, self-tortured man; instead, he achieved a rare happiness by expressing his ideals in action. A man of immense vitality he found in religion an outlet and a goal for his energy.

In Johnson's blood and iron epic, Jehovah, delighting in war and carnage, commissioned "the select Bands of Saints" as soldiers in His ever-conquering army and took personal command of the host. Not the smallest detail of equipment, logistics and strategy escaped His omniscience: He changed the climate for the special benefit of the "soldiers of Christ"; He steadied Myles Standish's arm when that doughty captain drew a bead on a redskin; and He supervised the arrangements in the commissariat. When the Puritan army was hungry, Johnson related, "Christ caused abundance of very good Fish to come to their Nets and Hookes, and as for such as were unprovided with the meanes, they caught them with their hands." After a few experiences such as this, the soldiers were convinced that "Christ will rather raine bread from Heaven than his people should want." As further evidence of God's benevolence, Johnson cited the "fearfull Desolations" among the Indians caused by smallpox— a "wondrous worke of the Great Jehovah" that proved to Johnson's satisfaction that the Puritans were divinely commissioned to conquer the wilderness and dispossess the natives. Here theology sanctified land hunger: the Puritans being God's people, it followed, to Johnson's way of thinking, that the Indians were creatures of the devil.

The triumphant saints of Johnson's *Wonder-Working Providence* are not lowly and downtrodden: Puritanism had proved itself a success; the Puritans had demonstrated that they were worthy of God's favor; and the City on the Hill was solidly established. As between the Puritanism of Old and New England, Johnson unhesitatingly pronounced the American brand superior.

This superiority provided the subject matter of the Reverend Nathaniel Ward's *The Simple Cobbler of Aggawam in America* (1647). Ward was a Cambridge graduate who came to New England in 1634. After serving for several years as minister to the congregation at Ipswich (then called Aggawam), he was compelled by ill health to resign his post. But illness and retirement did not diminish the ascerbity of his temper or weaken the force of his prejudices. As the "Simple Cobbler" he undertook to nail down "all the devils in Britannia," among them the "blasphemous" doctrine of religious toleration. Because the English Puritans had grown soft and tolerant, Ward declared that England had become a bear garden of conflicting opinions, extravagant fashions in thought and dress, and of depraved manners. True religion, he held, did not permit dissent: there was but one truth and its name was orthodoxy. The objective of church and state, by Ward's reckoning, ought to be to "preserve unity of spirit, faith and ordinances, to be all like-minded, or one accord; every man to take his brother into his Christian care." He thanked the God of Mercies that thus far New England had escaped the contagion of the tolerating spirit that had spread such havoc in England.

While there was nothing distinctive about Ward's opinions—the Baptists and Quakers who ventured into Massachusetts learned that the only right they enjoyed in that jurisdiction was the right to be damned—Ward stated the case against toleration in the extravagantly baroque style that had been fashionable among the Elizabethans. Few men have proclaimed their prejudices with more zest, self-assurance and truculence. He was a conservative who sincerely believed that it was his duty to save mankind from the evils it was certain to bring upon itself by tolerating error.

Nathaniel Ward, a Puritan, carried intolerance to its utmost limit; Roger Williams, also a Puritan, was one of the foremost exponents of the principle of religious freedom. Both men derived their convictions and their arguments from the Bible, and each insisted that his creed was truly Christian. In support of toleration, Williams invoked the right of free inquiry; Ward based his case against toleration upon the necessity of uniformity of belief in a community such as Massachusetts where absolute "truth" had become the established law.

Williams was a devout Puritan who wished to go beyond the leaders of the colony in purifying the church. He insisted upon a complete and irrevocable severance of all ties between the Congregational churches and the Church of England. Because he believed that the church ought to be composed solely of true believers, holy and apart from the rest of the community, he strove to separate church and state completely and to deny the civil authorities any control over the consciences of citizens. This was radical doctrine, indeed, for it was an article of faith among the Puritans that the state must safeguard the interests of the established church, punish nonconformists and root out heresy.

Being an arch-individualist, Williams proposed to make New England safe for other individualists. To the Puritan leaders, Williams' doctrine portended the downfall of God's work in New England, for in a chaos of conflicting opinions they saw no hope of restoring primitive Christianity. They had come to New England to build a City upon a Hill, not to erect a Tower of Babel. After much searching of conscience, for Williams was liked by many of those who deplored his opinions, he was excommunicated and banished to Rhode Island.

Although Williams' theological premises were discarded by the leaders of the American Enlightenment of the eighteenth century, their goal was the same as his: the complete separation of church and state and the establishment of the principle of religious liberty.

The intellectual side of Puritanism found expression in sermons, moralizing biographies and history, and polemical tracts dealing with "God's controversy with New England and New England's controversy with everybody else." Its more imaginative aspect was realized in poetry. Puritanism was a deeply felt religion and the holy fire touched many unknown and unsung minor Miltons in New England. Only a small fraction of the poetry written during the Puritan period was published or, indeed, publishable. In general, the Puritan addressed his poetic raptures to God; it was a private domain of the spirit from which outsiders were excluded. Since poetry was regarded as an approved way of rendering homage to God, there was no need to put it in print—presumably, the message had already reached its destination. The highest reward to which the Puritan poet looked forward was not to have his work read here below but to have it rendered by a heavenly choir in the form of a hosanna.

The first book published in the English colonies, the Bay Psalm Book, was poetry or, more precisely, versified scholarship. Intent upon achieving a literal translation of the Psalms, the leading ministers of New England succeeded in putting them into rhyme and meter, although the English language took a severe beating in the process. Indeed, the battered, clumsy verses seem to have been "hammered out on an anvil by blows from the blacksmith's sledge." The Reverend Richard Mather, one of the

principal blacksmiths on the job, justified in the preface the rough handling to which he and his heavy-handed colleagues had subjected the
King's English: "If the verses are not always so smooth and elegant as
some may expect or desire," said Mather, "let them consider that God's
altar needs not our polishings, for we have respected rather a plain translation than to smooth our verses with the sweetness of any paraphrase;
and so have attended conscience rather than elegance, fidelity rather than
poetry." The Psalm of David, as rendered by the ministers, represents
the triumph of fidelity over poetry:

> The Lord to mee a shepheard is,
>     want therefore shall not I.
> Hee in the fold of tender-grasse,
>     doth cause mee downe to lie;
> To waters calme me greatly leads
>     restore my soule doth hee;
> He doth in paths of righteousness;
>     for his names sake leade mee.

Of all the versifiers of religious dogma in colonial New England,
Michael Wigglesworth achieved the greatest acclaim. *The Day of Doom*,
Wigglesworth's masterpiece, may be described as the poor man's Dante.
Considered as popular poetry, however, it does not suffer unduly from
comparison with the best-selling poetry of a later period of mass culture.
What gives it distinction is its harsh and repellent theology—a theology
which has become a stick with which to beat the Puritans. With perfect
unconsciousness, it has been observed, Wigglesworth "attributes to the
Divine Being a character the most execrable and loathsome to be met
with, perhaps, in any literature, Christian or pagan." And yet, Wigglesworth actually softened the stern lineaments of the Puritan Jehovah: in
His Infinite Mercy, the God of the *Day of Doom* consigns infant repro-
bates to the easiest room in hell when, according to the canons of strict
justice, being the corrupt seed of Adam, they had no right whatever to
preferential treatment. Furthermore, the poem takes the advanced
ground that mankind was free to choose between eternal bliss and eternal
damnation and that salvation was assured to all who truly believed.

At best, *The Day of Doom* is a literary curiosity. Fortunately for the
Puritans, their reputation in poetry does not rest solely upon Michael
Wigglesworth.

In Anne Bradstreet, New England Puritanism produced "the earliest
significant woman poet of the English language." Daughter of a Massachusetts governor and wife to another governor, she wrote poetry besides
managing her household and rearing seven children. Around 1650 her
brother-in-law brought some of her manuscripts to England, where they
were published under the title, apparently not of Anne's choosing, *The*

*Tenth Muse lately sprung in America. Or Severall Poems, compiled with great Variety of Wit and Learning.* Although much of her poetry was written in the form of a private colloquy with God, she attempted, among other things, to paraphrase in verse Sir Walter Raleigh's *History of the World.*

The Reverend Edward Taylor, today acclaimed the greatest of the New England writers of devotional verse, printed nothing during his lifetime and even enjoined his heirs against publishing his manuscripts. He almost succeeded in consigning his work to oblivion: it was not until 1937 that fragments of his poetry began to appear in print.

Taylor was born in England, studied at Cambridge and came to New England in 1668 at the age of twenty-six. He became a clergyman and settled down in a quiet country pastorate. His strong religious and poetic nature found release in composing "Sacramental Meditations"—poems expressive of his thoughts as he prepared to administer the Lord's Supper to his congregation. Virtually all of Taylor's poetry is derived from religious rapture—the ecstasy of knowing God and of finding favor in His eyes. He was both a mystic and a poet: his poetry sprang from his religion and his religion was based upon the sense of being one with the Creator.

But he was also an orthodox Calvinist. His theology does not differ essentially from that of Michael Wigglesworth: mankind lives in a fallen world, the many are condemned to damnation, the remnant is to be saved and this, in view of the transgressions of the original pair, is as it should be. He lamented his sinfulness, acknowledged his utter loathsomeness, quailed at the thought of hell and rejoiced in the prospect of heaven—the conventional gamut run by the Puritan conscience.

It was not America but the Bible and his intense religious fervor that inspired Taylor's poetry. The external world was of little moment to him; America did not even provide a background for his poetry. What mattered to him was the journey of his soul toward immortality; hence he deliberately insulated himself from outward things in order to concentrate his attention more fully upon his spiritual state. As a result of his immersion in the Bible, Jerusalem was far more real to him than the ordinary sights and sounds of a New England village: he felt a closer affinity to the apostles, patriarchs and prophets of the Bible than to his neighbors.

Limited as was Taylor's experience, his poetic range was even more severely demarcated. He belonged to the "metaphysical" school of poets popular in England during his early manhood. Together with the flamboyant metaphors, baroque analogies and sensuous allusions favored by the members of that school, he embellished his poetry with Biblical allegory and imagery. Bread, for example, is always "manna"; congregations are "flocks" and the sacrament is "Heaven's sugar cake." Satan appears "with Griping Paws, and Goggling Eyes. . . . Like some fierce Shagg'd Red Lion, belching Fire." He pictures souls bent double with stomach pains, and Jesus Christ the Vine bears raisins as well as grapes.

Over a period of forty years, Taylor did not alter either the form or the content of his poetry: his last "Meditation" is hardly distinguishable from his first. It was as though the world of poetry had stood still: Dryden and Pope came and went, leaving their impress upon English poetry, yet Taylor remained oblivious to the new ideas and modes of expression. In the meantime, of course, metaphysical poetry went wholly out of fashion. Taylor, it is true, was a poet in a wilderness, but most American writers did not permit themselves to be shut off so entirely from the currents of English thought and literary fashion. Yet Taylor deliberately sought intellectual isolation because to him the only important thing was the relationship of his soul to God. Neither Pope nor Dryden could tell him anything about that.

Just as the purpose of the Puritan historians was to record God's dealings with a whole people, so the Puritan diarist undertook to set down God's dealings with a single individual. Like history, the diary was a work of piety, edification and divination—for the diarist hoped, by putting into words his thoughts, acts and spiritual experiences, to unravel the mystery of his fate: whether his ultimate destination was heaven or hell. In this sense, the diary was a testimonial to the Puritan's unremitting quest for personal holiness. Finally, the diary served as a therapeutic device to relieve the intolerable tensions generated by introspection. The traumatic experience of looking into the pit of hell—a favorite Puritan vista—often had the effect of turning the mind of the beholder into a chamber of horrors. In the absence of a confessional, the Puritan found some measure of relief in pouring out his soul on paper.

Samuel Sewall, the most indefatigable of the New England diarists, kept a diary from 1673 to 1729, a period longer than that covered by Pepys or Evelyn. In its printed form, Sewall's journal runs to three bulky volumes. In addition to being a revelation of character unsurpassed among Puritan diaries, it furnishes an intimate view of the social life of New England for over half a century. Sewall was well placed to provide such an over-all view: he had an active career as businessman, magistrate, member of the Massachusetts Council, Judge of Probate and, finally, Chief Justice of Massachusetts.

Living during a period of declining religious fervor, Sewall was eager to restore the zeal and sense of dedication to an ideal that had characterized the early Puritans. His diary leaves little doubt that he himself failed to recapture that spirit; he succeeded only in preserving Puritanism's outward forms and its superstitions. Sewall's real significance is not as a frustrated would-be restorer of the past but as a reformer. In 1700, he wrote the *Selling of Joseph,* one of the first antislavery tracts published in America; he protested against the injustice done the Indians by the whites and he was a pioneer in the cause of women's rights. Thus Sewall touched upon three of the most important crusades of the nineteenth century: slavery, the rights of women and the Indian problem.

It was natural that Cotton Mather, the most morbidly introspective of Puritans, should have kept a diary. As one who not only walked with but, on occasion, talked with God, Mather felt it to be his duty to keep a record for the benefit of posterity of his "sweet conversation" and "extraordinaryly Intimate Communion" with the Almighty. At one juncture, God told Mather: "Go into your Great Chamber and I will speak with you." He did as directed and had the gratification of receiving "unutterable Communications from the Holy Ghost." In 1705, on a truly memorable day, he "conversed with each of the three Persons in the Eternal Godhead."

Unfortunately for Mather's fame as a mystic and man of letters, the diary is more revelatory of Mather's personality than of the nature of the Almighty. Apparently the cosmos revolved round Cotton Mather; at least his diary leaves the impression that the Deity was as much concerned with Mather's doings, the state of his soul and the welfare of his family as was Cotton himself. Repeatedly he was assured that God wished him well, that mercies for himself and his family were being stored up in heaven pending his arrival and that everything Mather did had the wholehearted approval of heaven. But in none of the revelations vouchsafed Mather was there anything of interest to mankind in general. Seldom has a ravished soul looked into heaven and hell and emerged with a more banal description of those places.

The theme of the diary is the titanic struggle between God and Satan to determine if Cotton Mather should be permitted to further the Lord's work on earth or if his efforts should end in barrenness and negation. In part, Mather's war with the Powers of Darkness took the form of an effort to preserve the old ways of Puritanism against the corroding effects of prosperity and worldliness. He complained, however, that when he wrestled with the devil, "a carnal, giddy, rising Generation" cheered loudly whenever Satan seemed on the point of pinning down the Man of God. By way of rebuke, he wrote a book entitled *Ungodly Children,* calculated, he hoped, to make adolescents "serious, and prayerful and afraid of Sin." Seemingly, its only effect was to make them afraid of Cotton Mather.

Reared in an atmosphere of pervasive piety, Cotton Mather revered his father, the Reverend Increase Mather, as a paragon of all that was holy. From childhood he made it his study to emulate his father. He could have seen little of that distinguished gentleman, however, for the Reverend Doctor Mather made it his practice to spend sixteen hours a day in his study, poring over Latin, Greek, Hebrew and English authors, writings scores of books and sermons and, on rare occasions, speaking intimately with God.

When other boys were at play, Cotton was at prayer, reading omnivorously and writing sermons. A censorious and priggish youth, he reproved his schoolmates for their unedifying pastimes—"and sometimes," he recounted, "I suffered from them the persecution of not only *Scoffs* but Blows *also*, for my Rebukes." He entered Harvard at the age of eleven and began to preach at seventeen. The most erudite man in America, he spoke and read seven languages and he wrote more books than any other American of the colonial period. Four hundred and sixty-eight books, many of them sermons, are included in his bibliography. He set himself a stint of a book a month, but in 1702–1703 he broke all records by publishing six books in a little over two months.

The book which Mather hoped would crown his reputation, the *Biblia Americana,* a vast compendium of church history, was never published. Yet he did bring to partial completion one of the most ambitious undertakings in American literary history—a task which, he admitted, required the services of thirty men. The *Magnalia Christi Americana* consisted of seven books devoted to eulogistic biographies of the governors, ministers and Harvard graduates; "remarkable providences" in the history of New England; the history of the Congregational churches and all other matters pertaining to "the triumphs of Christ in the New World." The immense scope of this work and the prefatory reference to the *Aeneid,* indicate that Mather believed that he was writing the great American epic.

The good life, as Mather defined it, consisted in doing good. His was an active, purposeful Christianity; he always strove to be both holy and useful. He described himself as "a man whose Business it is to do good unto all." Setting his words to action, he aided the poor, widows, orphans, prisoners, seamen, Indians and Negroes. At his own expense, he maintained for many years a charity school for Negroes in Boston. A considerable part of his salary went to charitable and humanitarian causes. By 1721, he did not own a foot of land, his entire estate having been expended in philanthropy.

At the end of a long life devoted to uplifting and regenerating the spirit of early Puritanism, Cotton Mather felt that his labors had been wasted upon a heedless, pleasure-loving, worldly generation. Religion seemed everywhere to be in abeyance, and even the spirit of the times— the Age of Reason—appeared hostile to its resurrection. Yet within a decade of Mather's death, the American colonies were swept by the Great Awakening, the first of a succession of religious revivals that brought religious fervor to fever pitch.

In the early history of this revival, the Reverend Jonathan Edwards was one of the most successful of the evangelical preachers. Edwards was as much of a heaven-directed man as was Roger Williams. Like Williams, he was primarily a theologian who accepted the Bible as the principal repository of such truths as God had seen fit to reveal to mankind. The questions always uppermost in Edwards' and Williams' minds were: What was man's relation to his Creator and how could mortal, sinful man assure himself of immortality?

But Jonathan Edwards lived in a very different intellectual atmosphere from that which had prevailed in Puritan Boston. The eighteenth-century Enlightenment with its emphasis upon reason, scientific method and distrust of emotionalism inevitably exerted a deep influence upon Edwards' thought. While he remained a Calvinist—he has been called the first genuinely consistent Calvinist in America—he buttressed his theology with the new science and philosophy. God was still the Jehovah of the Old Testament, full of wrath against mankind; and mankind itself was depraved and wormlike in the eyes of God. The truth of these postulates of Calvinistic theology Jonathan Edwards attempted to prove by calling upon reason and science as well as upon the Bible. The course of events in the twentieth century has given fresh relevance to Edwards' ideas. "The terror he imparted was the terror of modern man, the terror of insecurity," says Perry Miller. ". . . Edwards brought mankind face to face, without mitigation, protection, or indulgence, with a cosmos fundamentally inhuman."

While New Englanders were turning their attention increasingly to trade, commerce and politics, a class of leisured aristocrats was rising in the South. Owners of great plantations, these grandees were, for the most part, second or third generation Virginians who owed their wealth to the hard work, good fortune and business acumen of their fathers. Many were educated in England, where they acquired the cultural and intellectual interests of the governing class. When they returned to Virginia they leavened the social life of the Old Dominion with the courtly manners and knowledge of men and books they had obtained in England and on the Continent. In contrast to the clerical intellectuals of New England, the Virginians carried their learning lightly: they were primarily men of the world to whom politics, society, gambling, horseracing and polite literature were essential parts of the good life.

From these opulent, pleasure-loving, public-spirited aristocrats came the political leadership and the literary output of Virginia and Maryland. Although many of them were imbued with English ideals, nevertheless, constituting a powerful political group, they engaged in a contest for political power with the royal governor—a contest that did not end until the American Revolution. With few exceptions, they were conspicuously loyal to their native province. Their literary efforts were in part the result of a determination, plainly evident in the political sphere, to demonstrate that Virginia was not an outlandish spot upon the periphery of the empire but the home of educated, literate citizens of the world, every whit the equal of their counterparts in England.

By the end of the seventeenth century, the sense of identification with England and the monarchy that had won for Virginia the name of the "Old Dominion" had perceptibly weakened. Virginians were becoming increasingly aware that they were not simply transplanted Englishmen and that they had a unique history and destiny. It was not claimed that Virginia was a new heaven—that was left to the New England Puritans —but it began to be regarded as part of a new earth. In the history of their own "country," Virginians found ample justification for their conviction that a new society that owed precedence to none had been created in the New World.

After the first ordeal of settlement was over, Virginians almost wholly neglected to write their history. No colonist troubled to publish an account of Bacon's Rebellion—the two contemporary pamphlets which describe the insurrection were written by a Londoner—partly, no doubt, for the reason that there was no permanent printing press in Virginia until 1730. Even so, one poem written in seventeenth-century Virginia, an elegy addressed to Nathaniel Bacon, is the most glowing tribute paid any leader of the colonial period.

After a long period of neglect, the writing of history in Virginia was revived by Robert Beverley. Born in Virginia, the son of one of the leading planters, Beverley was sent to England for his education. When he returned to Virginia to manage his estate he married the sister of William Byrd and was elected to the House of Burgesses. In 1705, he published in London *The History and Present State of Virginia,* the most readable and informative account of the Old Dominion written during the colonial period. Beverley wrote his book in order to dispel the dismal "Phantasms" regarding Virginia that still held sway in England; to expose the oppressive and arbitrary acts of the royal governors; to attract settlers to the colony and to remove the suspicion that Virginians harbored "Republican Notions and Principles" and were therefore hostile to the mother country.

As every page of the *History* attests, Beverley took pride in being a Virginian. "I am an *Indian,*" he said, "and don't pretend to be exact in my Language." In actuality, he was neither an Indian nor even a frontiersman and his was the kind of language spoken in the politest circles in England. Nor was Beverley merely trying to make the best of a remote and uncomfortable colonial world by calling the grapes of the Old World sour. On the contrary, his whole purpose was to assert the equality of the Virginia gentleman with his Old World counterpart in such matters as culture, good manners and devotion to the traditional liberties of

Englishmen. Beverley himself wrote with the wit, urbanity and sarcasm that were the hallmarks of the fashionable writing of his day.

Yet his affection for his "country" did not blind him to its shortcomings. He deplored Virginians' "slothful Indolence" and their habit of sponging upon "the blessings of a warm sun and fruitful soil: Where God Almighty is so Merciful as to work for People," he concluded, "they never work for themselves." If Virginians were more energetic, he was persuaded, they would make the country an earthly paradise. As matters stood, however, Virginians seemed capable of doing little more than gathering the bounties nature lavished upon them. Pleasant as this existence was, it did not produce the kind of progress a local booster like Beverley advocated.

Although Beverley's devotion to Virginia was too exclusive to be called American, he was a prototype of a new kind of man who was to play a decisive role in later American history—the Virginia aristocrat. A landed proprietor who consciously modeled his life upon that of the English gentry, he was nevertheless a stanch upholder of provincial liberty when it came into conflict with the authority of the English government. As the American Revolution was to show, the Virginia aristocracy was capable of admiring to excess English society and manners and yet rebelling against the English government.

The fame of Robert Beverley has been overshadowed by that of his brother-in-law, William Byrd II, the First Gentleman of Virginia. Like Beverley, Byrd was a second-generation Virginian, the son of a London goldsmith who had grown rich and respectable in the colony. Educated in England (he studied law in the Middle Temple), William Byrd II spent most of his early life in London as a man-about-town, equipped with those indispensable adjuncts of gentility, a carriage and a mistress; he was a member of the select circle of wits, writers and dilettantes that held forth in the London coffeehouses and clubs.

Byrd's character and literary interests were molded by the company he kept in London: when he returned to Virginia, he was a model of an urbane, exquisitely mannered gentleman with a literary bent. His *Secret Diary* reveals, however, that he lived a Dr. Jekyll and Mr. Hyde existence: among the bordellos and streetwalkers of London he displayed a lubricity that makes James Boswell appear continent by comparison. Boswell took refuge in alcohol as well as in street drabs; Byrd was temperate in everything except his need for an endless succession of women. Nevertheless, he lived by a code of honor: a gentleman, he said, never attempted to seduce his friend's wife or daughter. In these instances, he remarked, if he committed sin it was only in his mind.

Although he wrote intermittently while in England, Byrd's literary reputation rests almost wholly upon the books he wrote, but did not publish, during the last eighteen years of his life in Virginia: *The History of the Dividing Line, A Journey to the Land of Eden* and *A Progress to the Mines.* The most readable, witty and amusing of colonial writers, he wrote as though he were addressing himself to an audience of English coffeehouse *literati.* An earthy, hearty man under his veneer of gentility, Byrd had an unerring eye for the absurd, the pretentious and the bizarre in the human comedy. While he was quick to see human frailty and to hold it up to laughter, Byrd had none of the mordant qualities of Jonathan Swift nor did he share the Puritans' view that man was vile: instead of execrating his fellow men he poked fun at them. The character sketches in which he excelled reveal his wit at its most devastating: "He has an infinite fondness for his own person," he remarked of one of his acquaintances, "without having any Rival but his mother."

A member of the Royal Society, Byrd contributed a description of an albino Negro which appeared in the Society's *Transactions*—one of the few pieces Byrd published during his lifetime. In Virginia he busied himself with the management of his plantation, searching for coal, iron and copper deposits, building his mansion at Westover, collecting specimens of plants for the Royal Society, serving as Receiver General of the royal revenues and as a member of the Virginia Council. Despite the heavy demands upon his time, he never allowed his intellectual interests to lapse: throughout his life he devoted his attention to painting, drama, botany, divinity, medicine and languages. Besides English, he read Hebrew, Greek, Latin, French, Italian and Dutch. In the realm of intellectual curiosity and versatility, William Byrd rivaled even Thomas Jefferson.

The news from America was not wholly of good living, high wages and cheap land. Indeed, in their eagerness to persuade Europeans to emigrate to the colonies, the publicists painted too rosy a picture of conditions in America—with the inevitable result that many newcomers suffered severe disillusionment.

Among the most vocal of the disenchanted settlers was Ebenezer Cook, who, having come to Maryland with high hopes, returned a few years later to England a sadder and a wiser man, lamenting the day that he had ever set foot on that benighted shore. He commemorated his monumental wrath in a poem published in London in 1708: *The Sot-Weed Factor: Or, a Voyage to Maryland. A Satyr. In which is describ'd, the Laws, Government, Frolicks, Entertainments and Drunken Humours of the Inhabitants of that Part of America. In Burlesque Verse. By Eben. Cook, Gent.* This marks the high-water mark in America of the "Hudibrastic" comic verse associated with the name of Samuel Butler. A "Hudibrastic" poem is a mock epic in which everything is made to serve the main objective—ridicule.

A more serious critic of America—indeed, there is no lightness of touch whatever in his work—was Gottlieb Mittelberger. Born in Württemberg, Germany, Mittelberger was invited in 1750 to serve as organist to a Lutheran church in Pennsylvania. He was a pious, earnest, sensitive man who, when he embarked for America, was wholly unprepared for the appallingly harsh conditions he encountered on board the immigrant ships and the lack of refinement that prevailed in America, particularly on the frontier. His first duty to his countrymen, he believed, was to warn them of the hardships experienced by the redemptioners—immigrants who secured passage to America on condition that upon their arrival in the colonies they consented to enter into servitude for a term of years. In effect, their labor was put up for auction and sold to the highest bidder. His second duty, as he saw it, was to inform would-be German settlers of the true state of affairs they could expect to find in Pennsylvania. He did not paint a pleasant picture: the price of land was high and rising rapidly; the country abounded with sectarians and manners were deplorably lax. While he liked the equality and amity that prevailed in Pennsylvania, he was of the opinion that Americans abused their freedom. Pennsylvania, he concluded, was "a paradise for women, a purgatory for men, and a hell for horses."

With respect to subject matter, the most distinctively American writing produced during the colonial period was the narratives of the Indian wars and Indian captures. The historians of the Indian wars were for the most part participants in those struggles who wrote from personal experience. In these histories and in the accounts of Indian captivity are contained the raw material of the novels of James Fenimore Cooper and his successors and the "Western" screenplay. During the colonial period, over five hundred narratives of Indian captivity were published, some of which achieved the status of best-sellers. They helped provide the thrill of vicarious violence and suffering to a society far less preoccupied with violence than is that of the twentieth century. They were also valued as testimonials to the durability of the Protestant faith under the tortures of savages; in that respect, they are a continuation of the *Book of Martyrs*, which celebrated the heroism of the Protestant victims of the sixteenth-century religious persecutions. Although Jesuits and other missionary priests wrote the story of their sufferings at the hands of the Indians, their courage and dedication did not elicit sympathy in the English colonies, where the people generally regarded Roman Catholic priests as emissaries of France whose religious ministrations thinly disguised their efforts to incite the tribesmen to attack the English frontier. Finally, since most of the captures of whites by Indians took place during the wars between England and France, these narratives have strong patriotic overtones. Even though they were assured of being acclaimed as heroes or heroines and virtually guaranteed a reading public for their memoirs, not all the captives were eager to return to civilization. As Benjamin Franklin said, "When white persons, of either sex, have been taken prisoners by the Indians, and lived awhile with them, though ransomed by their friends, and treated with all imaginable tenderness to prevail with them to stay among the English, yet in a short time they become disgusted with our manner of life, and the care and pains that are necessary to support it, and take the first opportunity of escaping again into the woods, from whence there is no redeeming them." During the colonial period, especially on the frontier, civilization had to compete with the undeniable attractions of "going native."

By the middle of the eighteenth century, Philadelphia had become the most active commercial and intellectual center in the English colonies. Of all the colonial towns, Philadelphia took the lead in civic improvements, journalism, literary, scientific and artistic pursuits, and in establishing societies for the promotion of useful knowledge.

The winds of change began to blow through Philadelphia with unwonted briskness after Benjamin Franklin's arrival in the City of Brotherly Love. For his own and all succeeding generations, Franklin has epitomized the self-made man. Born in humble circumstances and denied all but the most rudimentary education, he became an international celebrity who ranked with the greatest philosophers and scientists of his day, who stood before kings and who helped to dispossess one unlucky monarch of his transatlantic dominions. He was the typical American cast in a more heroic mold who exemplified all the qualities his countrymen most deeply cherished. He was Everyman, American style, embodying some of the characteristics of Thomas Jefferson, Abraham Lincoln, Thomas A. Edison and George F. Babbitt. A firm believer in the transmigration of souls, he expected to appear in many more and, he hoped, improved versions. But there was only one Franklin and the original model has not yet been brought to a higher pitch of perfection.

Franklin began his career as one of the Angry Young Men of Puritan Boston. He was in rebellion against the entire Establishment: the magistrates, the clergy and Harvard College, all aroused his ire. (Too many Harvard students, he complained, were congenital blockheads whom education merely made "more proud and self-conceited.") Nevertheless, after his removal to Philadelphia he became one of the most persuasive exponents of the Puritan virtues of hard work, thrift and strict observance of the moral code. Throughout his life, Franklin tried to live by these ideals, but he admitted that it ran much against the grain. As he said in his *Autobiography*, his moral bookkeeping produced such discouraging results that he abandoned it, contenting himself with the similitude of virtues that remained beyond his reach. Nothing succeeded, he concluded, like virtue, but failing the real thing, an outward show could be made to pay off handsomely. By his reckoning, the Way to Wealth was paved with bright and shining moral virtues—some of which might be slightly cracked on the underside.

As "Poor Richard," Franklin helped establish the conviction among his countrymen that the pursuit of happiness led directly to the Way to Wealth. This view has been repeatedly challenged in America, most notably by Henry David Thoreau. In the colonial period, the most eloquent counterstatement to Benjamin Franklin came from a Quaker mystic, John Woolman.

A tailor, shopkeeper and itinerant Quaker minister, John Woolman was a simple, pious man whose life was a long search for spiritual purity. For him, outward events were of secondary importance: hence his *Journal*, first published in 1774, was a spiritual autobiography. God, to Woolman, was Infinite Goodness and Love. It was therefore the duty of man to cultivate to the full the divine garden within him. "The true felicity of man in this life and in that which is to come," he said, "is in being inwardly united to the Fountain of universal love and bliss."

To Woolman's way of thinking, this supreme felicity was attainable only by those who had emancipated themselves from the tyranny of material possessions, ambition and selfishness. The craving for wealth, he believed, became so insatiable that it ended by devouring the whole man; to those who sought happiness and peace of mind in luxuries and self-indulgence, life became a burden and a misery; ambition served only to take men's minds away from God; and the spirit of selfishness, "the greatest of all tyrants," was the cause of war, oppression and most of the calamities that befell mankind.

Confronted by all these evils, Woolman saw no hope of opening up the human soul to the purifying influences of the Divine Spirit except by leading a life of simplicity, meekness, patience, justice, goodness and love of all men. He himself renounced business success and superfluity of every kind lest they destroy the contact he had established with God. Moreover, his conscience gave him no rest until he had testified against social injustice. Slavery and other forms of the exploitation of labor, the neglect of the poor, the mistreatment of Indians—every manifestation, in short, of man's inhumanity to man aroused his concern. He was not content until he had acquainted himself by personal experience with the hardships and difficulties of his fellow men—hence he went to live among the Indians and talked familiarly with Negro slaves. Yet so filled was he with universal love that he could not bring himself to hate slaveholders or other men he regarded as wrongdoers. Always, he sought to offset the love of power by the power of love. He reverenced all life because he regarded it as a manifestation of God's love. "To say we love God, and, at the same time exercise Cruelty toward the least Creature," he said, "is a Contradiction in itself."

Possessed of the bare essentials of life and free to bear witness against oppression and wrong, Woolman did not ask for more. He had good reason to be content: he had reached the complete serenity of mind and the "quiet, calm, and happy way intended for us to walk in."

In his life and thought, Benjamin Franklin provided the best answer given by colonial America to the question: What is this new man, the American? But it remained for a Frenchman, Michel-Guillaume Jean de Crèvecoeur, to describe fully the unique type of human being that was emerging from the American environment, and, by so describing, to interpret the whole meaning of the American experience during the colonial period.

Born in Normandy, Crèvecoeur traveled widely in Canada and the English colonies before settling down in 1769 as a farmer under the name of John Hector St. John. While he was intimately acquainted with the frontier and the farming areas of the colonies, he knew little of the towns. Nor did they much concern him: in his eyes, the true American was a farmer and it was the agricultural way of life, together with the qualities it developed in human beings, that he believed would prevail in America.

Living on a farm in Orange County, New York, and surrounded by people of diverse national origins and religious creeds, Crèvecoeur became one of the first proponents of the "melting-pot" theory. The American story, as recounted by Crèvecoeur in the *Letters From an American Farmer* is a success story: from penury to prosperity by means of hard work and plain living. As depicted by Crèvecoeur, the American farmer resembles man just before the Fall: innocent, happy, simple, honest, industrious and just. The earth supplied in abundance all his needs, and liberty, equality, democracy and religious freedom were his birthright. In short, here is the agrarian Elysium of the American Dream—the lost Paradise, the regaining of which became one of the principal objectives of later American liberalism.

Yet Crèvecoeur admitted that there was a darker side to American life. Not every immigrant succeeded—it was "only the sober, the honest and industrious," he observed, who made good—and in his later book, *A Voyage to Pennsylvania and New York* (1801), he dwelt upon the hardships experienced by American farmers. Few observers have described frontiersmen with less romanticism and sentimentality than did Crèvecoeur.

The *Letters From an American Farmer* are evidence of Americans' extraordinary preoccupation with their national character. No people have been more engrossed in looking into a mirror and asking if it is not the fairest of them all. Nor has any nation shown equal sensitivity to the criticisms of foreign observers. This highly developed self-consciousness first appeared during the colonial period in the efforts of American writers to explain and analyze America. From the earliest publicists and promoters of immigration to Crèvecoeur, these writers generally saw in the English colonies the best hope of realizing one of mankind's most persistent, but elusive dreams: liberty, plenty and a chance for every man to better his condition. Early American literature affirmed the promise of American life; one of the central themes of American history is the story of the efforts to fulfill that promise.

# PART I

# ARRIVALS

# The Plymouth Plantation

## William Bradford

*Bradford began to write the* History of Plymouth Plantation *about 1630. It is the first section, carrying the story down to 1621, that recaptures in artistic form the sweep and majesty of the Pilgrim experience. Although he succeeded in bringing the account of events at Plymouth down to 1647, in its later stages the* History *peters out into a mere chronicle.*

*The manuscript of Bradford's* History *was used by several generations of New England historians. During the War of Independence, it was lost to view and did not reappear until 1855, when it was discovered in the library of the Bishop of London. Presumably the manuscript had been brought to England by a Massachusetts Loyalist and deposited with the Bishop of London, under whose jurisdiction all American communicants of the Church of England lay.*

*After much searching of conscience on the bishop's part, the manuscript was returned to the United States in 1897. The* History of Plymouth Plantation *was first published by the Massachusetts Historical Society in 1856.*

### OF THEIR DEPARTURE INTO HOLLAND AND THEIR TROUBLES THEREABOUT, WITH SOME OF THE MANY DIFFICULTIES THEY FOUND AND MET WITHAL. ANNO 1608

Being thus constrained to leave their native soil and country, their lands and livings, and all their friends and familiar acquaintance, it was much; and thought marvelous by many. But to go into a country they knew not but by hearsay, where they must learn a new language and get their livings they knew not how, it being a dear place and subject to the miseries of war, it was by many thought an adventure almost desperate; a case intolerable and a misery worse than death. Especially seeing they were not acquainted with trades nor traffic (by which that country doth subsist) but had only been used to a plain country life and the innocent

William Bradford: *Of Plymouth Plantation.* Edited by Samuel Eliot Morison.

trade of husbandry. But these things did not dismay them, though they did sometimes trouble them; for their desires were set on the ways of God and to enjoy His ordinances; but they rested on His providence, and knew Whom they had believed. Yet this was not all, for though they could not stay, yet were they not suffered to go; but the ports and havens were shut against them, so as they were fain to seek secret means of conveyance, and to bribe and fee the mariners, and give extraordinary rates for their passages. And yet were they often times betrayed, many of them; and both they and their goods intercepted and surprised, and thereby put to great trouble and charge, of which I will give an instance of two and omit the rest.

There was a large company of them purposed to get passage at Boston in Lincolnshire, and for that end had hired a ship wholly to themselves and made agreement with the master to be ready at a certain day, and take them and their goods in at a convenient place, where they accordingly would all attend in readiness. So after long waiting and large expenses, though he kept not day with them, yet he came at length and took them in, in the night. But when he had them and their goods aboard, he betrayed them, having beforehand complotted with the searchers and other officers so to do; who took them, and put them into open boats, and there rifled and ransacked them, searching to their shirts for money, yea even the women further than became modesty; and then carried them back into the town and made them a spectacle and wonder to the multitude which came flocking on all sides to behold them. Being thus first, by these catchpoll officers rifled and stripped of their money, books and much other goods, they were presented to the magistrates, and messengers sent to inform the Lords of the Council of them; and so they were committed to ward. Indeed the magistrates used them courteously and showed them what favour they could; but could not deliver them till order came from the Council table. But the issue was that after a month's imprisonment the greatest part were dismissed and sent to the places from whence they came; but seven of the principal were still kept in prison and bound over to the assizes.

The next spring after, there was another attempt made by some of these and others to get over at another place. And it so fell out that they light of a Dutchman at Hull, having a ship of his own belonging to Zealand. They made agreement with him, and acquainted him with their condition, hoping to find more faithfulness in him than in the former of their own nation; he bade them not fear, for he would do well enough. He was by appointment to take them in between Grimsby and Hull, where was a large common a good way distant from any town. Now against the prefixed time, the women and children with the goods were sent to the place in a small bark which they had hired for that end; and the men were to meet them by land. But it so fell out that they were there a day before the ship came, and the sea being rough and the women very sick, prevailed with the seamen to put into a creek hard by where they lay on ground at low water. The next morning the ship came but they were fast and could not stir until about noon. In the meantime, the shipmaster, perceiving how the matter was, sent his boat to be getting the men aboard whom he saw ready, walking about the shore. But after the first boatful was got aboard and she was ready to go for more, the master espied a great company, both horse and foot, with bills and guns and other weapons, for the country was raised to take them. The Dutchman, seeing that, swore his country's oath *sacremente*, and having the wind fair, weighed his anchor, hoised sails, and away.

But the poor men which were got aboard were in great distress for their wives and children which they saw thus to be taken, and were left destitute of their helps; and themselves also, not having a cloth to shift them with, more than they had on their backs, and some scarce a penny about them, all they had being aboard the bark. It drew tears from their eyes, and anything they had they would have given to have been ashore again; but all in vain, there was no remedy, they must thus sadly part. And afterward endured a fearful storm at sea, being fourteen days or more before they arrived at their port; in seven whereof they neither saw sun, moon nor stars, and were driven near the coast of Norway; the mariners themselves often despairing of life, and once with shrieks and cries gave over all, as if the ship had been foundered in the sea and they sinking without recovery. But when man's hope and help wholly failed, the Lord's power and mercy appeared in their recovery; for the ship rose again and gave the mariners courage again to manage her. And if modesty would suffer me, I might declare with what fervent prayers they cried unto the Lord in this great distress (especially some of them) even without any great distraction. When the water ran into their mouths and ears and the mariners cried out, "We sink, we sink!" they cried (if not with miraculous, yet with a great height or degree of divine faith), "Yet Lord Thou canst save! Yet Lord Thou canst save!" with such other expressions as I will forbear. Upon which the ship did not only recover, but shortly after the violence of the storm began to abate, and the Lord filled their afflicted minds with such comforts as everyone cannot understand, and in the end brought them to their desired haven, where the people came flocking, admiring their deliverance; the storm having been so long and sore, in which much hurt had been done, as the master's friends related unto him in their congratulations.

But to return to the others where we left. The rest of the men that were in greatest danger made shift to escape away before the troop could surprise them, those only staying that best might be assistant unto the women. But pitiful it was to see the heavy case of these poor women in this distress; what weeping and crying on every side, some for their husbands that were carried away in the ship as is before related; others not knowing what should become of them and their little ones; others again melted in tears, seeing their poor little ones hanging about them, crying for fear and quaking with cold. Being thus apprehended, they were hurried from one place to another and from one justice to another, till in the end they knew not what to do with them; for to imprison so many women and innocent children for no other cause (many of them) but that they must go with their husbands, seemed to be unreasonable and all would cry out of them. And to send them home again was as difficult; for they alleged, as the truth was, they had no homes to go to, for they had either sold or otherwise disposed of their houses and livings. To be short, after they had been thus turmoiled a good while and conveyed from one constable to another, they were glad to be rid of them in the end upon any terms, for all were wearied and tired with them. Though in the meantime they (poor souls) endured misery enough; and thus in the end necessity forced a way for them.

But that I be not tedious in these things, I will omit the rest, though I might relate many other notable passages and troubles which they endured and underwent in these their wanderings and travels both at land and sea; but I haste to other things. Yet I may not omit the fruit that came hereby, for by these so public troubles in so many eminent places their cause became famous and occasioned many to look into the same, and their godly carriage and Christian behaviour was such as left a deep impression in the minds of many. And though some few shrunk at these first conflicts and sharp beginnings (as it was no marvel) yet many more came on with fresh courage and greatly animated others. And in the end, notwithstanding all these storms of opposition, they all gat over at length, some at one time and some at another, and some in one place and some in another, and met together again according to their desires, with no small rejoicing.

#### SHOWING THE REASONS AND CAUSES OF THEIR REMOVAL

After they had lived in this city about some eleven or twelve years (which is the more observable being the whole time of that famous truce between that state and the Spaniards) and sundry of them were taken away by death and many others began to be well stricken in years (the grave mistress of Experience having taught them many things), those prudent governors with sundry of the sagest members began both deeply to apprehend their present dangers and wisely to foresee the future and think of timely remedy. In the agitation of their thoughts, and much discourse of things hereabout, at length they began to incline to this conclusion: of removal to some other place. Not out of any new-fangledness of other such like giddy humor by which men are oftentimes transported to their great hurt and danger, but for sundry weighty and solid reasons, some of the chief of which I will here briefly touch.

And first, they saw and found by experience the hardness of the place and country to be such as few in comparison would come to them, and fewer that would bide it out and continue with them. For many that came to them, and many more that desired to be with them, could not endure that great labour and hard fare, with other inconveniences which they underwent and were contented with. But though they loved their persons, approved their cause and honoured their sufferings, yet they left them as it were weeping, as Orpah did her mother-in-law Naomi, or as those Romans did Cato in Utica who desired to be excused and borne with, though they could not all be Catos. For many, though they desired to enjoy the ordinances of God in their purity and the liberty of the gospel with them, yet (alas) they admitted of bondage with danger of conscience, rather than to endure these hardships. Yea, some preferred and chose the prisons in England rather than this liberty in Holland with these afflictions. But it was thought that if a better and easier place of living could be had, it would draw many and take away these discouragements. Yea, their pastor would often say that many of those who both wrote and preached now against them, if they were in a place where they might have liberty and live comfortably, they would then practice as they did.

Secondly. They saw that though the people generally bore all these difficulties very cheerfully and with a resolute courage, being in the best and strength of their years; yet old age began to steal on many of them; and their great and continual labours, with other crosses and sorrows, hastened it before the time. So as it was not only probably thought, but apparently seen, that within a few years more they would be in danger to scatter, by necessities pressing them, or sink under their burdens, or both. And therefore according to the divine proverb, that a wise man seeth the plague when it cometh, and hideth himself, Proverbs xxii. 3, so they like skillful and beaten soldiers were fearful either to be entrapped or surrounded by their enemies so as they should neither be able to fight nor fly. And therefore thought it better to dislodge betimes to some place of better advantage and less danger, if any such could be found.

Thirdly. As necessity was a taskmaster over them so they were forced to be such, not only to their servants but in a sort to their dearest children, the which as it did not a little wound the tender hearts of many a loving father and mother, so it produced likewise sundry sad and sorrowful effects. For many of their children that were of best dispositions and gracious inclinations, having learned to bear the yoke in their youth and willing to bear part of their parents' burden, were oftentimes so oppressed with their heavy labours that though their minds were free and willing, yet their bodies bowed under the weight of the same, and became decrepit in their early youth, the vigour of nature being consumed in the very bud as it were. But that which was more lamentable, and of all sorrows most heavy to be borne, was that many of their children, by these occasions and the great licentiousness of youth in that country, and the manifold temptations of the place, were drawn away by evil examples into extravagant and dangerous courses, getting the reins off their necks and departing from their parents. Some became soldiers, others took upon them far voyages by sea, and others some worse courses tending to dissoluteness and the danger of their souls, to the great grief of their parents and dishonour of God. So that they saw their posterity would be in danger to degenerate and be corrupted.

Lastly (and which was not least), a great hope and inward zeal they had of laying some good foundation, or at least to make some way thereunto, for the propagating and advancing the gospel of the kingdom of Christ in those remote parts of the world; yea, though they should be but even as stepping-stones unto others for the performing of so great a work.

These and some other like reasons moved them to undertake this resolution of their removal; the which they afterward prosecuted with so great difficulties, as by the sequel will appear.

The place they had thoughts on was some of those vast and unpeopled countries of America, which are fruitful and fit for habitation, being devoid of all civil inhabitants, where there are only savage and brutish men which range up and down, little otherwise than the wild beasts of the same. This proposition being made public and coming to the scanning of all, it raised many variable opinions amongst men and caused many fears and doubts amongst themselves. Some, from their reasons and hopes conceived, laboured to stir up and encourage the rest to undertake and prosecute the same; others again, out of their fears, objected against it and sought to divert from it; alleging many things, and those neither unreasonable nor unprobable; as that it was a great design and subject to many unconceivable perils and dangers; as, besides the casualties of the sea (which none can be freed from), the length of the voyage was such as the weak bodies of women and other persons worn out with age and travail (as many of them were) could never be able to endure. And yet if they should, the miseries of the land which they should be exposed unto, would be too hard to be borne and likely, some or all of them together, to consume and utterly to ruinate them. For there they should be liable to famine and nakedness and the want, in a manner, of all things. The change of air, diet and drinking of water would infect their bodies with sore sicknesses and grievous diseases. And also those which should escape or overcome these difficulties should yet be in continual danger of the savage people, who are cruel, barbarous and most treacher-

ous, being most furious in their rage and merciless where they overcome;
not being content only to kill and take away life, but delight to torment
men in the most bloody manner that may be; flaying some alive with the
shells of fishes, cutting off the members and joints of others by piecemeal
and broiling on the coals, eat the collops of their flesh in their sight whilst
they live, with other cruelties horrible to be related.

And surely it could not be thought but the very hearing of these things
could not but move the very bowels of men to grate within them and
make the weak to quake and tremble. It was further objected that it
would require greater sums of money to furnish such a voyage and to fit
them with necessaries, than their consumed estates would amount to; and
yet they must as well look to be seconded with supplies as presently to be
transported. Also many precedents of ill success and lamentable miseries
befallen others in the like designs were easy to be found, and not forgotten to be alleged; besides their own experience, in their former
troubles and hardships in their removal into Holland, and how hard a
thing it was for them to live in that strange place, though it was a neighbour country and a civil and rich commonwealth.

It was answered, that all great and honourable actions are accompanied
with great difficulties and must be both enterprised and overcome with
answerable courages. It was granted the dangers were great, but not
desperate. The difficulties were many, but not invincible. For though
there were many of them likely, yet they were not certain. It might be
sundry of the things feared might never befall; others by provident care
and the use of good means might in a great measure be prevented; and all
of them, through the help of God, by fortitude and patience, might either
be borne or overcome. True it was that such attempts were not to be
made and undertaken without good ground and reason, not rashly or
lightly as many have done for curiosity or hope of gain, etc. But their
condition was not ordinary, their ends were good and honourable, their
calling lawful and urgent; and therefore they might expect the blessing of
God in their proceeding. Yea, though they should lose their lives in this
action, yet might they have comfort in the same and their endeavours
would be honourable. They lived here but as men in exile and in a poor
condition, and as great miseries might possibly befall them in this place;
for the twelve years of truce were now out and there was nothing but
beating of drums and preparing for war, the events whereof are always
uncertain. The Spaniard might prove as cruel as the savages of America,
and the famine and pestilence as sore here as there, and their liberty less
to look out for remedy.

After many other particular things answered and alleged on both sides,
it was fully concluded by the major part to put this design in execution
and to prosecute it by the best means they could.

OF THEIR VOYAGE, AND HOW THEY PASSED THE SEA;
AND OF THEIR SAFE ARRIVAL AT CAPE COD

*September 6.* These troubles being blown over, and now all being compact together in one ship, they put to sea again with a prosperous wind,
which continued divers days together, which was some encouragement
unto them; yet, according to the usual manner, many were afflicted with
seasickness. And I may not omit here a special work of God's providence.
There was a proud and very profane young man, one of the seamen, of a
lusty, able body, which made him the more haughty; he would alway be
contemning the poor people in their sickness and cursing them daily with
grievous execrations; and did not let to tell them that he hoped to help to
cast half of them overboard before they came to their journey's end, and
to make merry with what they had; and if he were by any gently reproved, he would curse and swear most bitterly. But it pleased God
before they came half seas over, to smite this young man with a grievous
disease, of which he died in a desperate manner, and so was himself the
first that was thrown overboard. Thus his curses light on his own head,
and it was an astonishment to all his fellows for they noted it to be the
just hand of God upon him.

After they had enjoyed fair winds and weather for a season, they were
encountered many times with cross winds and met with many fierce
storms with which the ship was shroudly shaken, and her upper works
made very leaky; and one of the main beams in the midships was bowed
and cracked, which put them in some fear that the ship could not be able
to perform the voyage. So some of the chief of the company, perceiving
the mariners to fear the sufficiency of the ship as appeared by their mut-
terings, they entered into serious consultation with the master and other
officers of the ship, to consider in time of the danger, and rather to return
than to cast themselves into a desperate and inevitable peril. And truly
there was great distraction and difference of opinion amongst the mariners
themselves; fain would they do what could be done for their wages' sake
(being now near half the seas over) and on the other hand they were loath
to hazard their lives too desperately. But in examining of all opinions, the
master and others affirmed they knew the ship to be strong and firm under
water; and for the buckling of the main beam, there was a great iron
screw the passengers brought out of Holland, which would raise the beam
into his place; the which being done, the carpenter and master affirmed
that with a post put under it, set firm in the lower deck and otherways
bound, he would make it sufficient. And as for the decks and upper works,
they would caulk them as well as they could, and though with the working of the ship they would not long keep staunch, yet there would otherwise be no great danger, if they did not overpress her with sails. So they
committed themselves to the will of God and resolved to proceed.

In sundry of these storms the winds were so fierce and the seas so high, as they could not bear a knot of sail, but were forced to hull for divers days together. And in one of them, as they thus lay at hull in a mighty storm, a lusty young man called John Howland, coming upon some occasion above the gratings was, with a seele of the ship, thrown into sea; but it pleased God that he caught hold of the topsail halyards which hung overboard and ran out at length. Yet he held his hold (though he was sundry fathoms under water) till he was hauled up by the same rope to the brim of the water, and then with a boat hook and other means got into the ship again and his life saved. And though he was something ill with it, yet he lived many years after and became a profitable member both in church and commonwealth. In all this voyage there died but one of the passengers, which was William Butten, a youth, servant to Samuel Fuller, when they drew near the coast.

But to omit other things (that I may be brief) after long beating at sea they fell with that land which is called Cape Cod; the which being made and certainly known to be it, they were not a little joyful. After some deliberation had amongst themselves and with the master of the ship, they tacked about and resolved to stand for the southward (the wind and weather being fair) to find some place about Hudson's River for their habitation. But after they had sailed that course about half the day, they fell amongst dangerous shoals and roaring breakers, and they were so far entangled therewith as they conceived themselves in great danger; and the wind shrinking upon them withal, they resolved to bear up again for the Cape and thought themselves happy to get out of those dangers before night overtook them, as by God's good providence they did. And the next day they got into the Cape Harbor where they rid in safety.

A word or two by the way of this cape. It was thus first named by Captain Gosnold and his company, Anno 1602, and after by Captain Smith was called Cape James; but it retains the former name amongst seamen. Also, that point which first showed those dangerous shoals unto them they called Point Care, and Tucker's Terrour; but the French and Dutch to this day call it Malabar by reason of those perilous shoals and the losses they have suffered there.

Being thus arrived in a good harbour, and brought safe to land, they fell upon their knees and blessed the God of Heaven who had brought them over the vast and furious ocean, and delivered them from all the perils and miseries thereof, again to set their feet on the firm and stable earth, their proper element. And no marvel if they were thus joyful, seeing wise Seneca was so affected with sailing a few miles on the coast of his own Italy, as he affirmed, that he had rather remain twenty years on his way by land than pass by sea to any place in a short time, so tedious and dreadful was the same unto him.

But here I cannot but stay and make a pause, and stand half amazed at this poor people's present condition; and so I think will the reader, too, when he well considers the same. Being thus passed the vast ocean, and a sea of troubles before in their preparation (as may be remembered by that which went before), they had now no friends to welcome them nor inns to entertain or refresh their weatherbeaten bodies; no houses or much less towns to repair to, to seek for succour. It is recorded in Scripture as a mercy to the Apostle and his shipwrecked company, that the barbarians showed them no small kindness in refreshing them, but these savage barbarians, when they met with them (as after will appear) were readier to fill their sides full of arrows than otherwise. And for the season it was winter, and they that know the winters of that country know them to be sharp and violent, and subject to cruel and fierce storms, dangerous to travel to known places, much more to search an unknown coast. Besides, what could they see but a hideous and desolate wilderness, full of wild beasts and wild men—and what multitudes there might be of them they knew not. Neither could they, as it were, go up to the top of Pisgah to view from this wilderness a more goodly country to feed their hopes; for which way soever they turned their eyes (save upward to the heavens) they could have little solace or content in respect of any outward objects. For summer being done, all things stand upon them with a weatherbeaten face, and the whole country, full of woods and thickets, represented a wild and savage hue. If they looked behind them, there was the mighty ocean which they had passed and was now as a main bar and gulf to separate them from all the civil parts of the world. If it be said they had a ship to succour them, it is true; but what heard they daily from the master and company? But that with speed they should look out a place (with their shallop) where they would be, at some near distance; for the season was such as he would not stir from thence till a safe harbor was discovered by them, where they would be, and he might go without danger; and that victuals consumed apace but he must and would keep sufficient for themselves and their return. Yea, it was muttered by some that if they got not a place in time, they would turn them and their goods ashore and leave them. Let it also be considered what weak hopes of supply and succour they left behind them, that might bear up their minds in this sad condition and trials they were under; and they could not but be very small. It is true, indeed, the affections and love of their brethren at Leyden was cordial and entire towards them, but they had little power to help them or themselves; and how the case stood between them and the merchants at their coming away hath already been declared.

What could now sustain them but the Spirit of God and His grace? May not and ought not the children of these fathers rightly say: "Our fathers were Englishmen which came over this great ocean, and were ready to perish in this wilderness; but they cried unto the Lord, and He heard their voice and looked on their adversity," etc. "Let them therefore

praise the Lord, because He is good: and His mercies endure forever."
"Yea, let them which have been redeemed of the Lord, shew how He
hath delivered them from the hand of the oppressor. When they wandered
in the desert wilderness out of the way, and found no city to dwell in,
both hungry and thirsty, their soul was overwhelmed in them. Let them
confess before the Lord His lovingkindness and His wonderful works
before the sons of men."

### SHOWING HOW THEY SOUGHT OUT A PLACE OF HABITATION; AND WHAT BEFELL THEM THEREABOUT

Being thus arrived at Cape Cod the 11th of November, and necessity
calling them to look out a place for habitation (as well as the master's
and mariners' importunity); they having brought a large shallop with
them out of England, stowed in quarters in the ship, they now got her out
and set their carpenters to work to trim her up; but being much bruised
and shattered in the ship with foul weather, they saw she would be long
in mending. Whereupon a few of them tendered themselves to go by land
and discover those nearest places, whilst the shallop was in mending; and
the rather because as they went into that harbor there seemed to be an
opening some two or three leagues off, which the master judged to be a
river. It was conceived there might be some danger in the attempt, yet
seeing them resolute, they were permitted to go, being sixteen of them
well armed under the conduct of Captain Standish, having such instructions given them as was thought meet.

They set forth the 15th of November; and when they had marched
about the space of a mile by the seaside, they espied five or six persons
with a dog coming towards them, who were savages; but they fled from
them and ran up into the woods, and the English followed them, partly
to see if they could speak with them, and partly to discover if there might
not be more of them lying in ambush. But the Indians seeing themselves
thus followed, they again forsook the woods and ran away on the sands
as hard as they could, so as they could not come near them but followed
them by the track of their feet sundry miles and saw that they had come
the same way. So, night coming on, they made their rendezvous and set
out their sentinels, and rested in quiet that night; and the next morning
followed their track till they had headed a great creek and so left the
sands, and turned another way into the woods. But they still followed
them by guess, hoping to find their dwellings; but they soon lost both
them and themselves, falling into such thickets as were ready to tear their
clothes and armor in pieces; but were most distressed for want of drink.
But at length they found water and refreshed themselves, being the first
New England water they drunk of, and was now in great thirst as
pleasant unto them as wine or beer had been in foretimes.

Afterwards they directed their course to come to the other shore, for they knew it was a neck of land they were to cross over, and so at length got to the seaside and marched to this supposed river, and by the way found a pond of clear, fresh water, and shortly after a good quantity of clear ground where the Indians had formerly set corn, and some of their graves. And proceeding further they saw new stubble where corn had been set the same year; also they found where lately a house had been, where some planks and a great kettle was remaining, and heaps of sand newly paddled with their hands. Which, they digging up, found in them divers fair Indian baskets filled with corn, and some in ears, fair and good, of divers colours, which seemed to them a very goodly sight (having never seen any such before). This was near the place of that supposed river they came to seek, unto which they went and found it to open itself into two arms with a high cliff of sand in the entrance but more like to be creeks of salt water than any fresh, for aught they saw; and that there was good harborage for their shallop, leaving it further to be discovered by their shallop, when she was ready. So, their time limited them being expired, they returned to the ship lest they should be in fear of their safety; and took with them part of the corn and buried up the rest. And so, like the men from Eshcol, carried with them of the fruits of the land and showed their brethren; of which, and their return, they were marvelously glad and their hearts encouraged.

After this, the shallop being got ready, they set out again for the better discovery of this place, and the master of the ship desired to go himself. So there went some thirty men but found it to be no harbor for ships but only for boats. There was also found two of their houses covered with mats, and sundry of their implements in them, but the people were run away and could not be seen. Also there was found more of their corn and of their beans of various colours; the corn and beans they brought away, purposing to give them full satisfaction when they should meet with any of them as, about some six months afterward they did, to their good content.

And here is to be noted a special providence of God, and a great mercy to this poor people, that here they got seed to plant them corn the next year, or else they might have starved, for they had none nor any likelihood to get any till the season had been past, as the sequel did manifest. Neither is it likely they had had this, if the first voyage had not been made, for the ground was now all covered with snow and hard frozen; but the Lord is never wanting unto His in their greatest needs; let His holy name have all the praise.

The month of November being spent in these affairs, and much foul weather falling in, the 6th of December they sent out their shallop again with ten of their principal men and some seamen, upon further discovery, intending to circulate that deep bay of Cape Cod. The weather was very cold and it froze so hard as the spray of the sea lighting on their coats, they were as if they had been glazed. Yet that night betimes they got down into the bottom of the bay, and as they drew near the shore they saw some ten or twelve Indians very busy about something. They landed about a league or two from them, and had much ado to put ashore any-where—it lay so full of flats. Being landed, it grew late and they made themselves a barricado with logs and boughs as well as they could in the time, and set out their sentinel and betook them to rest, and saw the smoke of the fire the savages made that night. When morning was come they divided their company, some to coast along the shore in the boat, and the rest marched through the woods to see the land, if any fit place might be for their dwelling. They came also to the place where they saw the Indians the night before, and found they had been cutting up a great fish like a grampus, being some two inches thick of fat like a hog, some pieces whereof they had left by the way. And the shallop found two more of these fishes dead on the sands, a thing usual after storms in that place, by reason of the great flats of sand that lie off.

So they ranged up and down all that day, but found no people, nor any place they liked. When the sun grew low, they hasted out of the woods to meet with their shallop, to whom they made signs to come to them into a creek hard by, the which they did at high water; of which they were very glad, for they had not seen each other all that day since the morning. So they made them a barricado as usually they did every night, with logs, stakes and thick pine boughs, the height of a man, leaving it open to lee-ward, partly to shelter them from the cold and wind (making their fire in the middle and lying round about it) and partly to defend them from any sudden assaults of the savages, if they should surround them; so being very weary, they betook them to rest. But about midnight they heard a hideous and great cry, and their sentinel called "Arm! arm!" So they bestirred them and stood to their arms and shot off a couple of muskets, and then the noise ceased. They concluded it was a company of wolves or such like wild beasts, for one of the seamen told them he had often heard such a noise in Newfoundland.

So they rested till about five of the clock in the morning; for the tide, and their purpose to go from thence, made them be stirring betimes. So after prayer they prepared for breakfast, and it being day dawning it was thought best to be carrying things down to the boat. But some said it was not best to carry the arms down, others said they would be the readier, for they had lapped them up in their coats from the dew; but some three or four would not carry theirs till they went themselves. Yet as it fell out, the water being not high enough, they laid them down on the bank side and came up to breakfast.

But presently, all on the sudden, they heard a great and strange cry, which they knew to be the same voices they heard in the night, though they varied their notes; and one of their company being abroad came running in and cried, "Men, Indians! Indians!" And withal, their arrows came flying amongst them. Their men ran with all speed to recover their arms, as by the good providence of God they did. In the meantime, of those that were there ready, two muskets were discharged at them, and two more stood ready in the entrance of their rendezvous but were commanded not to shoot till they could take full aim at them. And the other two charged again with all speed, for there were only four had arms there, and defended the barricado, which was first assaulted. The cry of the Indians was dreadful, especially when they saw their men run out of the rendezvous toward the shallop to recover their arms, the Indians wheeling about upon them. But some running out with coats of mail on, and cutlasses in their hands, they soon got their arms and let fly amongst them and quickly stopped their violence. Yet there was a lusty man, and no less valiant, stood behind a tree within half a musket shot, and let his arrows fly at them; he was seen to shoot three arrows, which were all avoided. He stood three shots of a musket, till one taking full aim at him and made the bark or splinters of the tree fly about his ears, after which he gave an extraordinary shriek and away they went, all of them. They left some to keep the shallop and followed them about a quarter of a mile and shouted once or twice, and shot off two or three pieces, and so returned. This they did that they might conceive that they were not afraid of them or any way discouraged.

Thus it pleased God to vanquish their enemies and give them deliverance; and by His special providence so to dispose that not any one of them were either hurt or hit, though their arrows came close by them and on every side of them; and sundry of their coats, which hung up in the barricado, were shot through and through. Afterwards they gave God solemn thanks and praise for their deliverance, and gathered up a bundle of their arrows and sent them into England afterward by the master of the ship, and called that place the First Encounter.

From hence they departed and coasted all along but discerned no place likely for harbor; and therefore hasted to a place that their pilot (one Mr. Coppin who had been in the country before) did assure them was a good harbor, which he had been in, and they might fetch it before night; of which they were glad for it began to be foul weather.

After some hours' sailing it began to snow and rain, and about the middle of the afternoon the wind increased and the sea became very rough, and they broke their rudder, and it was as much as two men could do to steer her with a couple of oars. But their pilot bade them be of good cheer for he saw the harbor; but the storm increasing, and night drawing on, they bore what sail they could to get in, while they could see. But herewith they broke their mast in three pieces and their sail fell overboard in a very grown sea, so as they had like to have been cast away. Yet by God's mercy they recovered themselves, and having the flood with them, struck into the harbor. But when it came to, the pilot was deceived in the place, and said the Lord be merciful unto them for his eyes never saw that place before; and he and the master's mate would have run her ashore in a cove full of breakers before the wind. But a lusty seaman which steered bade those which rowed, if they were men, about with her or else they were all cast away; the which they did with speed. So he bid them be of good cheer and row lustily, for there was a fair sound before them, and he doubted not but they should find one place or other where they might ride in safety. And though it was very dark and rained sore, yet in the end they got under the lee of a small island and remained there all that night in safety. But they knew not this to be an island till morning, but were divided in their minds; some would keep the boat for fear they might be amongst the Indians, others were so wet and cold they could not endure but got ashore, and with much ado got fire (all things being so wet); and the rest were glad to come to them, for after midnight the wind shifted to the northwest and it froze hard.

But though this had been a day and night of much trouble and danger unto them, yet God gave them a morning of comfort and refreshing (as usually He doth to His children) for the next day was a fair, sunshining day, and they found themselves to be on an island secure from the Indians, where they might dry their stuff, fix their pieces and rest themselves; and gave God thanks for His mercies in their manifold deliverances. And this being the last day of the week, they prepared there to keep the Sabbath.

On Monday they sounded the harbor and found it fit for shipping, and marched into the land and found divers cornfields and little running brooks, a place (as they supposed) fit for situation. At least it was the best they could find, and the season and their present necessity made them glad to accept of it. So they returned to their ship again with this news to the rest of their people, which did much comfort their hearts.

On the 15th of December they weighed anchor to go to the place they had discovered, and came within two leagues of it, but were fain to bear up again; but the 16th day, the wind came fair, and they arrived safe in this harbor. And afterwards took better view of the place, and resolved where to pitch their dwelling, and the 25th day began to erect the first house for common use to receive them and their goods.

## THE STARVING TIME

But that which was most sad and lamentable was, that in two or three months' time half of their company died, especially in January and February, being the depth of winter, and wanting houses and other comforts; being infected with the scurvy and other diseases which this long voyage and their inaccommodate condition had brought upon them. So as there died some times two or three of a day in the foresaid time,

that of 100 and odd persons, scarce fifty remained. And of these, in the
time of most distress, there was but six or seven sound persons who to
their great commendations, be it spoken, spared no pains night nor day,
but with abundance of toil and hazard of their own health, fetched them
wood, made them fires, dressed them meat, made their beds, washed their
loathsome clothes, clothed and unclothed them. In a word, did all the
homely and necessary offices for them which dainty and queasy stomachs
cannot endure to hear named; and all this willingly and cheerfully,
without any grudging in the least, showing herein their true love unto
their friends and brethren; a rare example and worthy to be remembered.
Two of these seven were Mr. William Brewster, their reverend Elder,
and Myles Standish, their Captain and military commander, unto whom
myself and many others were much beholden in our low and sick condition. And yet the Lord so upheld these persons as in this general calamity
they were not at all infected either with sickness or lameness. And what
I have said of these I may say of many others who died in this general
visitation, and others yet living; that whilst they had health, yea, or any
strength continuing, they were not wanting to any that had need of them.
And I doubt not but their recompense is with the Lord.

But I may not here pass by another remarkable passage not to be forgotten. As this calamity fell among the passengers that were to be left
here to plant, and were hasted ashore and made to drink water that the
seamen might have the more beer, and one in his sickness desiring but a
small can of beer, it was answered that if he were their own father he
should have none. The disease began to fall amongst them also, so as
almost half of their company died before they went away, and many of
their officers and lustiest men, as the boatswain, gunner, three quarter-
masters, the cook and others. At which the Master was something strucken
and sent to the sick ashore and told the Governor he should send for beer
for them that had need of it, though he drunk water homeward bound.

But now amongst his company there was far another kind of carriage
in this misery than amongst the passengers. For they that before had been
boon companions in drinking and jollity in the time of their health and
welfare, began now to desert one another in this calamity, saying they
would not hazard their lives for them, they should be infected by coming
to help them in their cabins; and so, after they came to lie by it, would
do little or nothing for them but, "if they died, let them die." But such of
the passengers as were yet aboard showed them what mercy they could,
which made some of their hearts relent, as the boatswain (and some
others) who was a proud young man and would often curse and scoff at
the passengers. But when he grew weak, they had compassion on him and
helped him; then he confessed he did not deserve it at their hands, he had
abused them in word and deed. "Oh!" (saith he) "you, I now see, show

your love like Christians indeed one to another, but we let one another lie and die like dogs." Another lay cursing his wife, saying if it had not been for her he had never come this unlucky voyage, and anon cursing his fellows, saying he had done this and that for some of them; he had spent so much and so much amongst them, and they were now weary of him and did not help him, having need. Another gave his companion all he had, if he died, to help him sport with, and used them worse than slaves. Of which the aforesaid Mr. Dermer redeemed two of them; and they conceived this ship was now come to revenge it.

Also, as after was made known, before they came to the English to make friendship, they got all the Powachs of the country, for three days together in a horrid and devilish manner, to curse and execrate them with their conjurations, which assembly and service they held in a dark and dismal swamp.

But to return. The spring now approaching, it pleased God the mortality began to cease amongst them, and the sick and lame recovered apace, which put as it were new life into them, though they had borne their sad affliction with much patience and contentedness as I think any people could do. But it was the Lord which upheld them, and had beforehand prepared them; many having long borne the yoke, yea from their youth. Many other small matters I omit, sundry of them having been already published in a journal made by one of the company, and some other passages of journeys and relations already published, to which I refer those that are willing to know them more particularly.

And being now come to the 25th of March, I shall begin the year 1621.

### ANNO 1621 MAYFLOWER DEPARTS AND CORN PLANTED

They now began to dispatch the ship away which brought them over, which lay till about this time, or the beginning of April. The reason on their part why she stayed so long, was the necessity and danger that lay upon them; for it was well towards the end of December before she could land anything here, or they able to receive anything ashore. Afterwards, the 14th of January, the house which they had made for a general rendezvous by casualty fell afire, and some were fain to retire aboard for shelter; then the sickness began to fall sore amongst them, and the weather so bad as they could not make much sooner any dispatch. Again, the Governor and chief of them, seeing so many die and fall down sick daily, thought it no wisdom to send away the ship, their condition considered and the danger they stood in from the Indians, till they could procure some shelter; and therefore thought it better to draw some more charge upon themselves and friends than hazard all. The master and seamen likewise, though before they hasted the passengers ashore to be gone, now many of their men being dead, and of the ablest of them (as is before noted), and of the rest many lay sick and weak; the master durst not put to sea till he saw his men begin to recover, and the heart of winter over.

Afterwards they (as many as were able) began to plant their corn, in which service Squanto stood them in great stead, showing them both the manner how to set it, and after how to dress and tend it. Also he told them, except they got fish and set with it in these old grounds it would come to nothing. And he showed them that in the middle of April they should have store enough come up the brook by which they began to build, and taught them how to take it, and where to get other provisions necessary for them. All which they found true by trial and experience. Some English seed they sowed, as wheat and pease, but it came not to good, either by the badness of the seed or lateness of the season or both, or some other defect.

### BRADFORD SUCCEEDS CARVER; CIVIL MARRIAGE

In this month of April, whilst they were busy about their seed, their Governor (Mr. John Carver) came out of the field very sick, it being a hot day. He complained greatly of his head and lay down, and within a few hours his senses failed, so as he never spake more till he died, which was within a few days after. Whose death was much lamented and caused great heaviness amongst them, as there was cause. He was buried in the best manner they could, with some volleys of shot by all that bore arms. And his wife, being a weak woman, died within five or six weeks after him.

Shortly after, William Bradford was chosen Governor in his stead, and being not recovered of his illness, in which he had been near the point of death, Isaac Allerton was chosen to be an assistant unto him who, by renewed election every year, continued sundry years together. Which I here note once for all.

May 12 was the first marriage in this place which, according to the laudable custom of the Low Countries, in which they had lived, was thought most requisite to be performed by the magistrate, as being a civil thing, upon which many questions about inheritances do depend, with other things most proper to their cognizance and most consonant to the Scriptures (Ruth iv) and nowhere found in the Gospel to be laid on the ministers as a part of their office. "This decree or law about marriage was published by the States of the Low Countries Anno 1590. That those of any religion (after lawful and open publication) coming before the magistrates in the Town, or State house, were to be orderly (by them) married one to another."—Petit's History, fol. 1029. And this practice hath continued amongst not only them, but hath been followed by all the famous churches of Christ in these parts to this time—Anno 1646.

INDIAN DIPLOMACY

Having in some sort ordered their business at home, it was thought meet to send some abroad to see their new friend Massasoit, and to bestow upon him some gratuity to bind him the faster unto them; as also that hereby they might view the country and see in what manner he lived, what strength he had about him, and how the ways were to his place, if at any time they should have occasion. So the second of July they sent Mr. Edward Winslow and Mr. Hopkins, with the foresaid Squanto for their guide; who gave him a suit of clothes and a horseman's coat, with some other small things, which were kindly accepted; but they found but short commons and came both weary and hungry home. For the Indians used then to have nothing so much corn as they have since the English have stored them with their hoes, and seen their industry in breaking up new grounds therewith.

They found his place to be forty miles from hence, the soil good and the people not many, being dead and abundantly wasted in the late great mortality, which fell in all these parts about three years before the coming of the English, wherein thousands of them died. They not being able to bury one another, their skulls and bones were found in many places lying still above the ground where their houses and dwellings had been, a very sad spectacle to behold. But they brought word that the Narragansetts lived but on the other side of that great bay, and were a strong people and many in number, living compact together, and had not been at all touched with this wasting plague.

About the latter end of this month, one John Billington lost himself in the woods, and wandered up and down some five days, living on berries and what he could find. At length he light on an Indian plantation twenty miles south of this place, called Manomet; they conveyed him further off, to Nauset among those people that had before set upon the English when they were coasting whilst the ship lay at the Cape, as is before noted. But the Governor caused him to be inquired for among the Indians, and at length Massasoit sent word where he was, and the Governor sent a shallop for him and had him delievered. Those people also came and made their peace; and they gave full satisfaction to those whose corn they had found and taken when they were at Cape Cod.

Thus their peace and acquaintance was pretty well established with the natives about them. And there was another Indian called Hobomok come to live amongst them, a proper lusty man, and a man of account for his valour and parts amongst the Indians, and continued very faithful and constant to the English till he died. He and Squanto being gone upon business among the Indians, at their return (whether it was out of envy to them or malice to the English) there was a sachem called Corbitant, allied to Massasoit but never any good friend to the English to this day, met with them at an Indian town called Namasket, fourteen miles to the west of this place, and began to quarrel with them and offered to stab Hobomok. But being a lusty man, he cleared himself of him and came running away all sweating, and told the Governor what had befallen him. And he feared they had killed Squanto, for they threatened them both; and for no other cause but because they were friends to the English and serviceable unto them. Upon this the Governor taking counsel, it was conceived not fit to be borne; for if they should suffer their friends and messengers thus to be wronged, they should have none would cleave to them, or give them any intelligence, or do them serivce afterwards, but next they would fall upon themselves. Whereupon it was resolved to send the Captain and fourteen men well armed, and to go and fall upon them in the night. And if they found that Squanto was killed, to cut off Corbitant's head, but not to hurt any but those that had a hand in it.

Hobomok was asked if he would go and be their guide and bring them there before day. He said he would, and bring them to the house where the man lay, and show them which was he. So they set forth the 14th of August, and beset the house round. The Captain, giving charge to let none pass out, entered the house to search for him. But he was gone away that day, so they missed him, but understood that Squanto was alive, and that he had only threatened to kill him and made an offer to stab him but did not. So they withheld and did no more hurt, and the people came trembling and brought them the best provisions they had, after they were acquainted by Hobomok what was only intended. There was three sore wounded which broke out of the house and assayed to pass through the guard. These they brought home with them, and they had their wounds dressed and cured, and sent home. After this they had many gratulations from divers sachems, and much firmer peace; yea, those of the Isles of Capawack sent to make friendship; and this Corbitant himself used the mediation of Massasoit to make his peace, but was shy to come near them a long while after.

After this, the 18th of September they sent out their shallop to the Massachusetts, with ten men and Squanto for their guide and interpreter, to discover and view that Bay and trade with the natives. The which they performed, and found kind entertainment. The people were much afraid of the Tarentines, a people to the eastward which used to come in harvest time and take away their corn, and many times kill their persons. They returned in safety and brought home a good quantity of beaver, and made report of the place, wishing they had been there seated. But it seems the Lord, who assigns to all men the bounds of their habitations, had appointed it for another use. And thus they found the Lord to be with them in all their ways, and to bless their outgoings and incomings, for which let His holy name have the praise forever, to all posterity.

## FIRST THANKSGIVING

They began now to gather in the small harvest they had, and to fit up their houses and dwellings against winter, being all well recovered in health and strength and had all things in good plenty. For as some were thus employed in affairs abroad, others were exercised in fishing, about cod and bass and other fish, of which they took good store, of which every family had their portion. All the summer there was no want; and now began to come in store of fowl, as winter approached, of which this place did abound when they came first (but afterward decreased by degrees). And besides waterfowl there was great store of wild turkeys, of which they took many, besides venison, etc. Besides they had about a peck a meal a week to a person, or now since harvest, Indian corn to that proportion. Which made many afterwards write so largely of their plenty here to their friends in England, which were not feigned but true reports.

### THE FORT BUILT; VISITORS FROM VIRGINIA RECEIVED

This summer they built a fort with good timber, both strong and comely, which was of good defense, made with a flat roof and battlements, on which their ordnance were mounted, and where they kept constant watch, especially in time of danger. It served them also for a meeting house and was fitted accordingly for that use. It was a great work for them in this weakness and time of wants, but the danger of the time required it; and both the continual rumors of the fears from the Indians here, especially the Narragansetts, and also the hearing of that great massacre in Virginia, made all hands willing to dispatch the same.

Now the welcome time of harvest approached, in which all had their hungry bellies filled. But it arose but to a little, in comparison of a full year's supply; partly because they were not yet well acquainted with the manner of Indian corn (and they had no other), also their many other employments; but chiefly their weakness for want of food, to tend it as they should have done. Also, much was stolen both by night and day before it became scarce eatable, and much more afterward. And though many were well whipped, when they were taken for a few ears of corn; yet hunger made others, whom conscience did not restrain, to venture. So as it well appeared that famine must still ensue, the next year also if not some way prevented, or supply should fail, to which they durst not trust. Markets there was none to go to, but only the Indians, and they had no trading commodities.

Behold, now, another providence of God. A ship comes into the harbor, one Captain Jones being chief therein. They were set out by some mer-chants to discover all the harbors between this and Virginia, and the shoals of Cape Cod, and to trade along the coast where they could. This ship had store of English beads (which were then good trade) and some knives; but would sell none but at dear rates and also a good quantity together. Yet they were glad of the occasion and fain to buy at any rate; they were fain to give after the rate of cento per cento, if not more; and yet pay away coat-beaver at 3s per pound, which in a few years after yielded 20s. By this means they were fitted again to trade for beaver and other things, and intended to buy what corn they could.

### MORE SEMI-STARVATION

These passengers, when they saw their low and poor condition ashore were much daunted and dismayed, and according to their divers humors were diversely affected. Some wished themselves in England again; others fell a-weeping, fancying their own misery in what they saw now in others; other some pitying the distress they saw their friends had been long in, and still were under. In a word, all were full of sadness. Only some of their old friends rejoiced to see them, and that it was no worse with them, for they could not expect it should be better, and now hoped they should enjoy better days together. And truly it was no marvel they should be thus affected, for they were in a very low condition; many were ragged in apparel and some little better than half naked, though some that were well stored before were well enough in this regard. But for food they were all alike, save some that had got a few pease of the ship that was last here. The best dish they could present their friends with was a lobster or a piece of fish without bread or anything else but a cup of fair spring water. And the long continuance of this diet, and their labours abroad, had something abated the freshness of their former complexion; but God gave them health and strength in a good measure, and showed them by experience the truth of that word, (Deuteronomy viii.3) "That man liveth not by bread only, but by every word that proceedeth out of the mouth of the Lord doth a man live."

When I think how sadly the Scripture speaks of the famine in Jacob's time, when he said to his sons, "Go buy us food, that we may live and not die," (Genesis xlii.2 and xliii.1) that the famine was great or heavy in the land. And yet they had such great herds and store of cattle of sundry kinds, which, besides flesh, must needs produce other food as milk, butter and cheese, etc. And yet it was counted a sore affliction. Theirs here must needs be very great, therefore, who not only wanted the staff of bread but all these things, and had no Egypt to go to. But God fed them out of the sea for the most part, so wonderful is His providence over His in all ages; for His mercy endureth for ever.

I may not here omit how, notwithstand all their great pains and industry, and the great hopes of a large crop, the Lord seemed to blast, and take away the same, and to threaten further and more sore famine unto them. By a great drought which continued from the third week in May, till about the middle of July, without any rain and with great heat for the most part, insomuch as the corn began to wither away though it was set with fish, the moisture whereof helped it much. Yet at length it began to languish sore, and some of the drier grounds were parched like withered hay, part whereof was never recovered. Upon which they set apart a solemn day of humiliation, to seek the Lord by humble and fervent prayer, in this great distress. And He was pleased to give them a gracious and speedy answer, both to their own and the Indians' admiration that lived amongst them. For all the morning, and greatest part of the day, it was clear weather and very hot, and not a cloud or any sign of rain to be seen; yet toward evening it began to overcast, and shortly after to rain with such sweet and gentle showers as gave them cause of rejoicing and blessing God. It came without either wind or thunder or any violence, and by degrees in that abundance as that the earth was thoroughly wet and soaked and therewith. Which did so apparently revive and quicken the decayed corn and other fruits, as was wonderful to see, and made the Indians astonished to behold. And afterwards the Lord sent them such seasonable showers, with interchange of fair warm weather as, through His blessing, caused a fruitful and liberal harvest, to their no small comfort and rejoicing. For which mercy, in time convenient, they also set apart a day of thanksgiving.

On the other hand, the Old Planters were afraid that their corn, when it was ripe, should be imparted to the newcomers, whose provisions which they brought with them they feared would fall short before the year went about, as indeed it did. They came to the Governor and besought him that as it was before agreed that they should set corn for their Particular (and accordingly they had taken extraordinary pains thereabout) that they might freely enjoy the same; and they would not have a bit of the victuals now come, but wait till harvest for their own and let the newcomers enjoy what they had brought; they would have none of it except they could purchase any of it of them by bargain or exchange. Their request was granted them, for it gave both sides good content; for the newcomers were as much afraid that the hungry Planters would have ate up the provisions brought, and they should have fallen into the like condition.

This ship was in a short time laden with clapboard by the help of many hands. Also they sent in her all the beaver and other furs they had, and Mr. Winslow was sent over with her to inform of all things and procure such things as were thought needful for their present condition. By this time harvest was come, and instead of famine now God gave them plenty, and the face of things was changed, to the rejoicing of the hearts of many, for which they blessed God. And the effect of their particular planting was well seen, for all had, one way and other, pretty well to bring the year about; and some of the abler sort and more industrious had to spare, and sell to others; so as any general want or famine hath not been amongst them since to this day.

# A Description of New England

## Captain John Smith

*A few weeks' sailing along the coast of New England was enough to
transfer Smith's loyalty from Virginia to the more northern latitudes of
America. But whether Englishmen turned their attention to the North
or to the South, Smith urged them to act before the Spaniards—whose
prowess as conquistadores he never underestimated—pre-empted all of
North America. Smith's writings had one cardinal objective: to persuade
Englishmen and the English government to join without delay in the
westward march of empire.*

In the month of April, 1614, with two Ships from London, belonging to a
few Merchants, I chanced to arrive in New England, a part of America, at
the Isle of Monahigan, in 43½ of Northern latitude. Our plan was there to
take Whales and make trials of a Mine of Gold and Copper. If those
failed, Fish and Furs was then our refuge, to make our selves savers
howsoever. We found this Whale-fishing a costly undertaking: we saw
many, and spent much time in chasing them but could not kill any, they
being a kind of Jubartes, and not the Whale that yields Fins and Oil as
we expected. As for our Gold, it was rather the Master's device to get a
voyage that projected it than any knowledge he had at all of any such
matter. Fish and Furs was now our guard: and by our late arrival and
long lingering about the Whales, the prime of both those seasons were
past before we perceived it. We thought that their seasons served at all
times but we found it otherwise for, by the midst of June, the fishing
failed. Yet in July and August some was taken, but not sufficient to defray
so great a charge as our stay required. Of dry fish we made about 4000,
of Cod fish about 7000.

While the sailors fished, my self with eight or nine others of them that
might best be spared, ranged the coast in a small boat. We got for trifles
near 1100 Beaver skins, 100 Martin skins and nearly as many Otters, and
most of them within the distance of twenty leagues.

*Travels and Works of Captain John Smith.* Edited by Edward Arber.

We ranged the Coast both East and West much further; but Eastwards our commodities were not esteemed, they were so near the French who sell them cheaper. Right against us in the mainland was a Ship of Sir Francis Popham, that had there such acquaintance, having many years used only that port, that the most part of the furs there was had by him. And forty leagues westwards were two French Ships, that had made there a great voyage by trade during the time we made these explorations, not knowing the Coast nor the Savages' habitation.

With these Furs, the train oil and Cod-fish, I returned to England in the Bark. Within six months after our departure from the Downs, we safe arrived back. The best of this fish was sold for five pounds the hundred weight, the rest because of ill usage between three pound and fifty shillings.

The other ship stayed to fit herself for Spain with the dry fish. This was sold by the Sailors' report that returned, at twenty shillings the quintal, each hundred weight weighing two quintals and a half.

New England is that of America in the Ocean Sea opposite to Nova Albion [California] in the South Sea, discovered by the most memorable Sir Francis Drake in his voyage about the world. In regard whereto this is styled New England, being in the same latitude as Nova Albion. New France, off it, is Northward; Southwards is Virginia and all the adjoining Continent, with New Granada, New Spain, New Andalusia and the West Indies.

Now because I have been so oft asked such strange questions about the goodness and greatness of those spacious Tracts of land, how they can be thus long unknown, or not possessed by the Spaniards and many such like demands, I entreat your pardons if I chance to be too plain or tedious in relating my knowledge for plain mens' satisfaction.

Florida is the next adjoining to the Indies, which unprosperously was attempted to be planted [colonized] by the French. A country far bigger than England, Scotland, France, and Ireland, yet little known to any Christian but by the wonderful endeavours of Ferdinando de Soto, a valiant Spaniard whose writings in this age is the best guide known to search those parts.

Virginia is no Isle (as many do imagine) but part of the Continent adjoining to Florida. Virginia's bounds may be stretched to the magnitude of Florida without offense to any Christian inhabitant. For from the degrees of 30 to 45 his Majesty hath granted his Letters patent, the Coast extending South-west and North-east about 1500 miles. But to follow it aboard ship, the shore may well be 2000 miles at the least, of which 20 miles is the most that gives entrance into the Bay of Chesapeake where is the London plantation. Within this entrance is a Country (as you may perceive by the description in a Book and Map printed in my name of that little I there discovered) that may well suffice 300,000 people to inhabit.

And southward adjoineth that part discovered at the charge of Sir Walter Raleigh, by Sir Ralph Lane, and that learned Mathematician Master Thomas Heriot.

Northward six or seven degrees is the River Sadagahock where was planted the Western Colony by that Honourable Patron of virtue, Sir John Popham, Lord Chief Justice of England.

There is also a relation printed by Captain Bartholomew Gosnold, of the Elizabeth Islands and another by Captain Weymouth, of Pemmaquid.

From all these diligent observers, posterity may be bettered by the fruits of their labours. But for divers others that, long before and since, have ranged those parts, within sight sometimes of the shore, some touching in one place, some in another, I must entreat them to pardon me for omitting them; or if I offend in saying that their true descriptions are concealed or were never well observed or died with the Authors: so that the Coast is yet still but even as a Coast unknown and undiscovered.

I have had six or seven different maps of those Northern parts, so unlike each to other, and most so differing from any proportion or resemblance of the Country, they did me no more good than so much waste paper, though they cost me more. It may be it was not my fortune to see the best: but lest others may be deceived as I was or through dangerous ignorance hazard themselves as I did, I have drawn a Map from Point to Point, Island to Island, and Harbour to Harbour, with the Soundings, Sands, Rocks, and Land-marks as I passed close along the Shore in a little Boat. There may be many things to be observed which the haste of other affairs did cause me to omit. For being sent more to get present commodities than knowledge by discoveries for any future good, I had not power to search as I would. Yet it will serve to direct any that should go that way to safe Harbours and the Savages' habitations. What merchandize and commodities for their labour they may find, this following discourse shall plainly demonstrate.

Thus you may see, of this 2000 miles, more than half is yet unknown to any purpose; no, not so much as the borders of the Sea are yet certainly discovered. As for the goodness and true substances of the Land, we are for the most part yet altogether ignorant of them, unless it be those parts about the Bay of Chesapeake and Sagadahock. But only here and there have we touched or have seen a little of the edges of those large dominions which stretch themselves into the Main, God doth know how many thousand miles, whereof we can yet no more judge, than a stranger that saileth between England and France can describe the Harbors and dangers, by landing here or there in some River or Bay, tell thereby the goodness and substances of Spain, Italy, Germany, Bohemia, Hungary and the rest. By this you may perceive how much they err, that think every one which hath been at Virginia understandeth or knows what Virginia is. Or that the Spaniards know one half quarter of those Territories they possess; no, not so much as the true circumference of Terra Incognita, whose large dominions may equalize the greatness and goodness of America, for any thing yet known. It is strange with what small power the Spaniard hath reigned in the East Indies; and few will understand the truth of his strength in America where, he having so much to keep with such a pampered force, they need not greatly fear his fury in the Bermudas, Virginia, New France or New England. Beyond whose bounds, America doth stretch many thousand miles: into the frozen parts whereof, one Master Hudson, an English Mariner, did make the greatest discovery of any Christian I know of, where he unfortunately died. For Africa, had not the industrious Portugales ranged her unknown parts, who would have sought for wealth among those fried Regions of black brutish Negers; where, notwithstanding all the wealth and admirable adventures and endeavours of more than 140 years, they know not one third of those black habitations.

But it is not a work for every one, to manage such an affair as makes a discovery and plants a Colony. It requires all the best part of Art, Judgment, Courage, Honesty, Constancy, Diligence and Industry, to do but near well. Some are more proper for one thing than another, and therein are to be employed; and nothing breeds more confusion than misplacing and misimploying men in their undertakings. Columbus, Cortez, Pizarro, de Soto, Magellan, and the rest served more than an apprenticeship to learn how to begin their most memorable attempts in the West Indies, which to the wonder of all ages successfully they effected when many hundreds of others, far above them in the world's opinion, being instructed but by relation, came to shame and confusion in actions of small moment, who doubtless in other matters, were both wise, discreet, generous, and courageous. I say not this to detract any thing from their incomparable merits, but to answer those questionless questions that keep us back from imitating the worthiness of their brave spirits that advanced themselves from poor Soldiers to great Captains, their posterity to great Lords, their King to be one of the greatest Potentates on earth, and the fruits of their labours, the greatest glory, power and renown.

Who can desire more content, that hath small means or but only his merit to advance his fortune, than to tread and plant that ground he hath purchased by the hazard of his life? If he have but the taste of virtue and magnanimity, what to such a mind can be more pleasant, than planting and building a foundation for his Posterity, got from the rude earth, by God's blessing and his own industry, without prejudice to any? If he have any grain of faith or zeal in Religion, what can he do less hurtful to any or more agreeable to God, than to seek to convert those poor Savages to know Christ and humanity, whose labors with discretion will triple requite thy charge and pains? What so truly suits with honour and honesty as the discovering things unknown, erecting Towns, peopling Countries, informing the ignorant, reforming things unjust, teaching virtue, and gain to our Native mother country a kingdom to attend her and find employment for those that are idle, because they know not what to do? So far from wronging any as to cause Posterity to remember thee, and remembering thee, ever honour that remembrance with praise?

Consider: what were the beginnings and endings of the Monarchies of the Chaldeans, the Syrians, the Greeks and Romans, but this one rule: What was it they would not do for the good of the commonwealth or their Mother-city? For example: Rome. What made her such a Monarchy but only the adventures of her youth, not in riots at home but in dangers abroad and the justice and judgment out of their experience when they grew aged? What was their ruin and hurt but this: The excess of idleness, the fondness of Parents, the want of experience in Magistrates, the admiration of their undeserved honours, the contempt of true merit, their unjust jealousies, their indifference to statesmanship, their hypocritical seeming goodness, and their deeds of secret lewdness? Finally, in short, growing only devoted to worldly things, all that their predecessors got in many years, they lost in a few days. Those by their pain and virtue became Lords of the world; they by their ease and vices became slaves to their servants. This is the difference between the use of Arms in the field and on the monuments of stones; the gold age and the leaden age, prosperity and misery, justice and corruption, substance and shadows, words and deeds, experience and imagination, making Commonwealths, the fruits of virtue and the results of vice.

Then who would live at home idly (or think in himself any worth to live) only to eat, drink, and sleep, and so to die? Or by consuming that carelessly, his friends got worthily? Or by using that miserably, that maintained virtue honestly? Or for being descended nobly, pine with the vain taunt of great kindred, in penury? Or (to maintain a silly show of bravery) toil out thy heart, soul, and time, basely; by shifts, tricks, cards and dice? Or by relating news of others' actions, shark here and there for a dinner or supper; deceive thy friends by fair promises and dissimulation, in borrowing where thou never intendest to pay; offend the laws, become surfeit with excess, burden thy Country, abuse thyself, despair in want, and then couzen thy kindred, yea even thy own brother, and wish thy parent death (I will not say damnation) to have their estates, thou seest what honours and rewards the world yet hath for them who will seek them and worthily deserve them?

I would be sorry to offend or that any should mistake my honest meaning: for I wish good to all, hurt to none. But rich men for the most part are grown to that dotage, through their pride in their wealth, as though there were no accident could end it or their life.

And what hellish care do such take to make it their own misery and their Country's spoil, especially when there is most need of the employment? . . . May not the miserable ruin of Constantinople, their impregnable walls, riches and pleasures at last taken by the Turk (which are but a bit, in comparison of their present mightiness) remind us of the effects of private covetousness? . . . Let this lamentable example remind them that are rich (seeing there are such great thieves in the world to rob you) not to grudge to lend some proportion to breed them that have little yet are willing to learn how to defend you; for it is too late when the deed is a-doing.

The Romans' estate hath been worse than this: for, the meer covetousness and extortion of a few of them, so moved the rest, that not having any employment but contemplation, their great judgments grew to so great malice, as themselves were sufficient to destroy themselves by faction. Let this move you to embrace employment for those whose education, spirits and judgments want but your purses, not only to prevent such accustomed dangers but also to gain more thereby than you have.

And you fathers, that are either so foolishly fond or so miserably covetous or so willfully ignorant or so negligently careless so that you will rather maintain your children in idle wantonness till they grow your masters; or become so basely unkind as they wish nothing but your deaths, so that both sorts grow dissolute. And although you would wish them any where to escape the gallows and ease your cares; though they spend you here one, two, or three hundred pounds a year, you would grudge to give half so much in adventure with them, to obtain an estate which in a small time, but with a little assistance of your providence, might be better than your own. But if an Angel should tell you that any place yet unknown can afford such fortunes you would not believe him, no more than Columbus was believed there was any such Land as is now the well known abounding America, much less such large Regions as are yet unknown, as well in America as in Africa and Asia and Terra incognita, where were courses for gentlemen (and them that would be so reputed) more suiting their qualities than begging from their Prince's generous disposition, the labours of his subjects and the very marrow of his maintenance.

I have not been so ill bred but I have tasted of Plenty and Pleasure, as well as Want and Misery. Nor doth necessity yet, or occasion of discontent, force me to these endeavors; nor am I ignorant what small thank I shall have for my pains; or that many would have the World imagine them to be of great judgment that can but blemish these my designs by their witty objections and detractions. Yet I hope my reasons with my deeds will so prevail with some that I shall not want employment in these affairs, to make the most blind see his own senselessness and incredulity, hoping that gain will make them affect that, which Religion, Charity and the Common good cannot. . . . I fear not want of company sufficient were it but known what I know of those Countries and by the proof of that wealth I hope yearly to return, if God please to bless me from such accidents as are beyond my power in reason to prevent. For I am not so simple to think that ever any other motive than wealth will ever erect there a Commonweal or draw company from their ease and humours at home to stay in New England to effect my purposes.

And lest any should think the toil might be insupportable, though these things may be had by labor and diligence, I assure myself there are men who delight extremely in vain pleasure that take much more pains in England to enjoy it than I should do here to gain wealth sufficient. And yet I think they should not have half such sweet content, for our pleasure here is still gains—in England charges and loss. Here nature and liberty affords us that freely which in England we want or it costeth us dearly. Being tired with any occasion ashore in planting vines, fruits, or herbs, in contriving their own grounds to the pleasure of their own minds, their fields, gardens, orchards, buildings, ships, and other works, etc., what pleasure can be more than to recreate themselves before their own doors in their own boats upon the sea where man, woman, and child, with a small hook and line, by angling, may take diverse sorts of excellent fish at their pleasures! And is it not pretty sport to pull up two pence, six pence, and twelve pence as fast as you can haul and veer a line! He is a very bad fisher who cannot kill in one day with his hook and line one, two, or three hundred cods which, dressed and dried, if they be sold there for ten shillings the hundred—though in England they will give more than twenty—may not both the servant, the master, and merchant be well content with this gain? If a man work but three days in seven, he may get more than he can spend unless he will be excessive. Now that carpenter, mason, gardner, tailor, smith, sailor, forgers, or what other, may they not make this, a pretty recreation, though they fish but an hour in a day to take more than they eat in a week? Or if they will not eat it because there is so much better choice, yet sell it or change it with the fishermen or merchants for anything they want. And what sport doth yield a more pleasing content and less hurt or charge than angling with a hook and crossing the sweet air from isle to isle over the silent streams of a calm sea, wherein the most curious may find pleasure, profit and content?

Thus, though all men be not fishers, yet all men, whatsoever, may in other matters do as well. For necessity doth in these cases so rule a commonwealth and catch in their several functions as their labors in their qualities may be as profitable, because there is a necessary mutual use of all.

For gentlemen, what exercise should more delight them than ranging daily those unknown parts, using fowling and fishing for hunting and hawking? And yet you shall see the wild hawks give you some pleasure in seeing them stoop, six or seven after one another, an hour or two together at the schools of fish in the fair harbors as those ashore at a fowl. And never trouble nor torment yourselves with watching, mewing, feeding, and attending them; nor kill horse and man with running and crying, See you not a hawk? For hunting also: the woods, lakes and rivers afford not only chase sufficient for any that delights in that kind of toil or pleasure, but such beasts to hunt that, besides the delicacy of their bodies for food, their skins are so rich as may well recompense thy daily labor with a captain's pay.

For laborers, if those that sow hemp, rope, turnips, carrots, cabbage, and the like give 20, 30, 40, 50 shillings yearly for an acre of ground, and meat, drink, and wages to use it, and yet grow rich, which better—at least as good—ground may be had and cost nothing but labor, it seems strange to me than such should there grow poor.

My purpose is not to persuade children from their parents, men from their wives, nor servants from their masters—only such as with free consent may be spared; but that each parish or village in city or country that will but apparel their fatherless children of thirteen or fourteen years of age, or young married people that have small wealth to live on, here by their labor may live exceeding well, provided always that first there be a sufficient power to command them, houses to receive them, means to defend them, and proper provisions for them. For any place may be overlain, and it is most necessary to have a fortress, ere this grow to practice, and sufficient masters—as carpenters, masons, fishers, fowlers, gardeners, husbandmen, sawyers, smiths, spinsters, tailors, weavers, and such like—to take ten, twelve, or twenty, or as there is occasion, for apprentices. The masters by this may quickly grow rich; the apprentices may learn their trades themselves to do the like to a general and an incredible benefit for King and country, master and servants.

It would be an history of a large volume to recite the adventures of the Spaniards and Portugals, their affronts and defeats, their dangers and miseries which, with such incomparable honour and constant resolution, so far beyond belief, they have attempted and endured in their discoveries and plantations, as may well condemn us of too much imbecility, sloth and negligence. Yet the Authors of those new inventions were held as ridiculous for a long time, as now are others, that do but seek to imitate their unparalleled virtues. And though we see daily their mountains of wealth (sprung from the plants of their generous endeavours) yet is our sensuality and untowardness such, and so great, that we either ignorantly believe nothing or so curiously contest to prevent we know not what future events that we either so neglect or oppress and discourage the present, as we spoil all in the making, crop all in the blooming, and building upon fair sand, rather than rough rocks, judge that we know not, govern that we have not, fear that which is not and for fear some should do too well, force such against their wills to be idle or as ill. And who is he that hath judgment, courage and industry or quality with understanding will leave his Country, his hopes at home, his certain estate, his friends, pleasures, liberty and the preferment sweet England doth afford to all degrees, were it not to advance his fortunes by enjoying his desserts? His prosperity once appearing will encourage others but it must be cherished as a child, till it be able to go and understand itself, and not corrected nor oppressed above its strength, ere it know wherefore.

. . . If twenty years be required to make a child a man, seven years limited to an apprentice for his trade, if scarce an age be sufficient to make a wise man a Statesman and commonly a man dies ere he hath learned to be discreet; if perfection be so hard to be obtained, as of necessity there must be practice as well as theory, let no man much condemn this paradox opinion, to say, that half seven years is scarce sufficient for a good capacity to learn in these affairs how to carry himself. And whoever shall try in these remote places the erecting of a Colony shall find at the end of seven years occasion enough to use all his discretion. And, in the interim, all the content, rewards, gains and hopes will be necessarily required to be given to the beginning, till it be able to creep, to stand and go, yet time enough to keep it from running. For there is no fear it will grow too fast or ever to any thing except if liberty, profit, honor and prosperity there found, more bind the planters of those affairs in devotion to effect it, than bondage, violence, tyranny, ingratitude and such double dealing as binds freemen to become slaves and honest men to turn knaves—which hath ever been the ruin of the most popular commonwealths and is very unlikely ever well to begin in a new.

Who seeth not what is the greatest good of the Spaniard but these new achievements in searching those unknown parts of the unknown world? . . . Now he knows little, that knowest not England may well spare many more people than Spain and is as well able to furnish them with all manner of necessaries. And seeing, for they have, they cease not still to search for that they have not and know not. It is strange we should be so dull as not to maintain that which we have and pursue that we know.

Surely I am sure many would taste it ill to be abridged of the titles and honours of their predecessors. When if but truly they would judge themselves, look how inferior they are to their noble virtues, so much they are unworthy of their honours and livings which never were ordained for shows and shadows to maintain idleness and vice but to make them more able to abound in honor by heroical deeds of action, judgment, piety and virtue. What was it they would not do both in purse and person for the good of the Commonwealth—which might move them presently to set out their spare kindred in these generous designes?

Religion, above all things, should move us (especially the Clergy) if we were religious to share our faith by our works in converting those poor savages to the knowledge of God, seeing what pains the Spaniards take to bring them to their adulterated faith. Honor might move the Gentry, the valiant and industrious and all those drawn by the hope and assurance of wealth, if we were that we would seem and be accounted. Or be we so far inferior to other nations or our spirits so far dejected from our ancient predecessors, or our minds so set upon spoil, piracy and such villainy as to serve the Portugall, Spaniard, Dutch, French or Turk (as to the cost of Europe, too many do) rather than our God, our King, our Country and ourselves? Why should we excusing our idleness and our base complaints by want of employment when here is such choice of all sorts and for all degrees, in the planting and discovering these North parts of America.

# The New English Canaan

## *Thomas Morton*

In the Month of June, 1622, it was my chance to arrive in the parts of New England with 30 Servants and provisions of all sorts fit for a plantation. While our houses were building, I did endeavor to take a survey of the Country. The more I looked, the more I liked it. And when I had more seriously considered of the beauty of the place, with all her fair endowments, I did not think that in all the known world it could be paralleled for so many goodly groves of trees, dainty fine round rising hillocks, delicate fair large plaines, sweet crystal fountains, and clear running streams that twine in fine meanders through the meads, making so sweet a murmuring noise to hear as would even lull the sense with delight asleep, so pleasantly do they glide upon the pebble stones, jetting most jocundly where they meet and hand in hand run down to Neptune's Court, to pay the yearly tribute which they owe to him as sovereign Lord of all the springs. Continued within the volume of the Land, Birds in Abundance, Fish in multitude; and discovered, besides, Millions of Turtle-doves on the green boughs, which sat pecking of the full ripe pleasant grapes that were supported by the lusty trees, whose fruitful load did cause the arms to bend. While here and there dispersed, you might see Lilies and the Daphne-tree which made the Land to me seem paradise, for in my eye it was Nature's Masterpiece: Her chief Magazine of all where lives her store. If this Land be not rich, then is the whole world poor.

Thomas Morton: *New English Canaan, or New Canaan.* Edited by Charles Francis Adams.

# Letters

## *John and Margaret Winthrop*

Most dear and loving Husband,

I cannot express my love to you, as I desire, in these poor lifeless lines; but I do heartily wish you did see my heart, how true and faithful it is to you, and how much I do desire to be always with you, to enjoy the sweet comfort of your presence, and those helps from you in spiritual and temporal duties, which I am so unfit to perform without you. It makes me to see the want of you, and wish myself with you. But I desire we may be guided by God in all our ways, who is able to direct us for the best; and so I will wait upon him with patience, who is all-sufficient for me. I shall not need to write much to you at this time. My brother Gostling can tell you any thing by word of mouth. I praise God, we are all here in health, as you left us, and are glad to hear the same of you and all the rest of our friends at London. My mother and myself remember our best love to you, and all the rest. Our children remember their duty to you. And thus, desiring to be remembered in your prayers, I bid my good husband good night. Little Samuel thinks it is time for me to go to bed; and so I beseech the Lord to keep you in safety, and us all here. Farewell, my sweet husband.

*[England, late in 1627?]*                    Your obedient wife,

MARGARET WINTHROP

My most sweet Husband,

How dearly welcome thy kind letter was to me, I am not able to express. The sweetness of it did much refresh me. What can be more pleasing to a wife, than to hear of the welfare of her best beloved, and how he is pleased with her poor endeavors! I blush to hear myself commended, knowing my own wants. But it is your love that conceives the best, and makes all things seem better than they are. I wish that I may be always pleasing to thee, and that those comforts we have in each other may be daily increased, as far as they be pleasing to God. I will use that speech to thee, that Abigail did to David, I will be a servant to wash the feet of my lord. I will do any service wherein I may please my good husband. I

*Some Old Puritan Love-Letters.* Edited by Joseph H. Twichell.

confess I cannot do enough for thee: but thou art pleased to accept the will for the deed, and rest contented.

I have many reasons to make me love thee, whereof I will name two: First, because thou lovest God; and, secondly, because that thou lovest me. If these two were wanting, all the rest would be eclipsed. But I must leave this discourse, and go about my household affairs. I am a bad house-wife to be so long from them; but I must needs borrow a little time to talk with thee, my sweet heart. The term is more than half done. I hope thy business draws to an end. It will be but two or three weeks before I see thee, though they be long ones. God will bring us together in his good time; for which time I shall pray. I thank the Lord, we are all in health. We are very glad to hear so good news of our son Henry. The Lord make us thankful for all his mercies to us and ours. And thus, with my mother's and my own best love to yourself and all the rest, I shall leave scribbling. The weather being cold, makes me make haste. Farewell, my good husband; the Lord keep thee.

Your obedient wife,<br>MARGARET WINTHROP

*Groton [England], November 22 [1628]*

[P.S.] I have not yet received the box; but I will send for it. I send up a turkey and some cheese. I pray send my son Forth such a knife as mine is. Mrs. Hugen would pray you to buy a cake for the boys.

I did dine at Groton Hall yesterday; they are in health, and remember their love. We did wish you there, but that would not bring you, and I could not be merry without thee. Mr. Lee and his wife were there; they remember their love. Our neighbor Cole and goodman Newton have been sick, but somewhat amended again. I fear thy cheese will not prove so good as thou didst expect. I have sent it all, for we could not cut it.

My good Wife,

Although I wrote to thee last week by the carrier of Hadleigh, yet, having so fit opportunity, I must needs write to thee again; for I do esteem one little, sweet, short letter of thine (such as the last was) to be well worthy two or three from me. How it is with us, these bearers can inform thee, so as I may write the less. They were married on Saturday last, and intend to stay with thee till towards the end of the term; for it will be yet six weeks before they can take their voyage. Labor to keep my son at home as much as thou canst, especially from Hadleigh. I began this letter to thee yesterday at two of the clock, thinking to have been large, but was so taken up by company and business, as I could get but hither by this morning. It grieves me that I have not liberty to make better expression of my love for thee, who art more dear to me than all earthly things; but I will endeavor that my prayers may supply the defect of my pen, which will be of best use to us both, inasmuch as the favor and blessing of our

God is better than all things besides. My trust is in his mercy, that, upon the faith of his gracious promise, and the experience of his fatherly goodness, he will be our God to the end, to hurry us along through this course of our pilgrimage, in the peace of a good conscience, and that, in the end of our race, we shall safely arrive at the haven of eternal happiness. We see how frail and vain all earthly good things are. There is no means to avoid the loss of them in death, nor the bitterness which accompanyeth them in the cares and troubles of this life. Only the fruition of Jesus Christ and the hope of heaven can give us true comfort and rest. The Lord teach us wisdom to prepare for our change, and to lay up our treasure there, where our abiding must be forever. I know thou lookest for troubles here, and, when one affliction is over, to meet with another; but remember what our Saviour tells us: BE OF GOOD COMFORT, I HAVE OVERCOME THE WORLD. See his goodness; He hath conquered our enemies beforehand, and, by faith in him, we shall assuredly prevail over them all. Therefore, (my sweet wife,) raise up thy heart, and be not dismayed at the crosses thou meetest with in family affairs or otherwise; but still fly to him, who will take up thy burden for thee. Go thou on cheerfully, in obedience to his holy will, in the course he hath set thee. Peace shall come. Thou shalt rest as in thy bed; and, in the mean time, he will not fail nor forsake thee. But my time is past; I must leave thee. So I commend thee and all thine to the gracious protection and blessing of the Lord. All our friends here salute thee; salute thou ours from me. Farewell, my good wife. I kiss and love thee with the kindest affection, and rest

Thy faithful husband,<br>Jo. Winthrop

*April 28, 1629*

My faithful and dear Wife,

It pleaseth God, that thou shouldst once again hear from me before our departure, and I hope this shall come safe to thy hands. I know it will be a great refreshing to thee. And blessed be his mercy, that I can write thee so good news, that we are all in very good health, and, having tried our ship's entertainment now more than a week, we find it agree very well with us. Our boys are well and cheerful, and have no mind of home. They lie both with me, and sleep as soundly in a rug (for we use no sheets here) as ever they did at Groton; and so I do myself, (I praise God). The wind hath been against us this week and more; but this day it has come fair to the north, so as we are preparing (by God's assistance) to set sail in the morning. We have only four ships ready, and some two or three Hollanders go along with us. The rest of our fleet (being seven ships) will not be ready this sennight. We have spent now two Sabbaths on shipboard very comfortably, (God be praised,) and are daily more and more encouraged to look for the Lord's presence to go along with us. Henry

Kingsbury hath a child or two in the Talbot sick of the measles, but like to do well. One of my men had them at Hampton, but he was soon well again. We are, in all our eleven ships, about seven hundred persons, passengers, and two hundred and forty cows, and about sixty horses. The ship, which went from Plimouth, carried about one hundred and forty persons, and the ship, which goes from Bristowe, carrieth about eighty persons. And now (my sweet soul) I must once again take my last farewell of thee in Old England. It goeth very near to my heart to leave thee; but I know to whom I have committed thee, even to him who loves thee much better than any husband can, who hath taken account of the hairs of thy head, and puts all thy tears in his bottle, who can, and (if it be for his glory) will bring us together again with peace and comfort. Oh, how it refresheth my heart, to think, that I shall yet again see thy sweet face in the land of the living!—that lovely countenance, that I have so much delighted in, and beheld with so great content! I have hitherto been so taken up with business, as I could seldom look back to my former happiness; but now, when I shall be at some leisure, I shall not avoid the remembrance of thee, nor the grief for thy absence. Thou hast thy share with me, but I hope the course we have agreed upon will be some ease to us both. Mondays and Fridays, at five of the clock at night, we shall meet in spirit till we meet in person. Yet, if all these hopes should fail, blessed be our God, that we are assured we shall meet one day, if not as husband and wife, yet in a better condition. Let that stay and comfort thy heart. Neither can the sea drown thy husband, nor enemies destroy, nor any adversary deprive thee of thy husband or children. Therefore I will only take thee now and my sweet children in mine arms, and kiss and embrace you all, and so leave you with my God. Farewell, farewell. I bless you all in the name of the Lord Jesus. I salute my daughter Winth. Matt. Nan. and the rest, and all my good neighbors and friends. Pray all for us. Farewell. Commend my blessing to my son John. I cannot now write to him; but tell him I have committed thee and thine to him. Labor to draw him yet nearer to God, and he will be the surer staff of comfort to thee. I cannot name the rest of my good friends, but thou canst supply it. I wrote, a week since, to thee and Mr. Leigh, and divers others.

Thine wheresover,

Jo. WINTHROP

*From aboard the* Arbella, *riding at the Gowes, March 28, 1630*

I would have written to my brother and sister Gostling, but it is near midnight. Let them excuse; and commend my love to them and all theirs.

My dear Wife,

I wrote to thee by my brother Arthur, but I durst write no more than I need not care though it miscarried, for I found him the old man still; yet I would have kept him to ease my brother, but that his own desire to return, and the scarcity of provisions here, yielded the stronger reason to let him go. Now (my good wife) let us join in praising our merciful God, that (howsoever he hath afflicted us, both generally and particularly mine own family in his stroke upon my son Henry) yet myself and the rest of our children and family are safe and in health, and that he upholds our hearts that we faint not in all our troubles, but can yet wait for a good issue. And howsoever our fare be but coarse in respect of what we formerly had, (pease, puddings and fish, being our ordinary diet,) yet he makes it sweet and wholesome to us, that I may truly say I desire no better. Besides in this, that he begins with us thus in affliction, it is the greater argument to us of his love, and of the goodness of the work which we are about; for Satan bends his forces against us, and stirs up his instruments to all kind of mischief, so that I think here are some persons who never showed so much wickedness in England as they have done here. Therefore be not discouraged (my dear Wife) by anything thou shalt hear from hence, I see no cause to repent of our coming hither, and thou seest (by our experience) that God can bring safe hither even the tenderest women and the youngest children (as he did many in diverse ships, though the voyage were more tedious than formerly hath been known in this season). Be sure to be warm clothed, and to have store of fresh provisions, meal, eggs put up in salt or ground malt, butter, oat meal, pease, and fruits, and a large strong chest or 2: well locked, to keep these provisions in; and be sure they be bestowed in the ship where they may be readily come by, (which the boatswain will see to and the quarter masters, if they be rewarded beforehand), but for these things my son will take care. Be sure to have ready at sea 2 or 3 skillets of several sizes, a large frying pan, a small stewing pan, and a case to boil a pudding in; store of linen for use at sea, and sack to bestow among the sailors; some drinking vessels, and peuter and other vessels: and for physic you shall need no other but a pound of Doctor Wright's *Electuariu lenitivu,* and his direction to use it, a gallon of scurvy grass to drink a little 5 or 6 mornings together, with some saltpeter dissolved in it, and a little grated or sliced nutmeg.

Thou must be sure to bring no more company than so many as shall have full provision for a year and half, for though the earth here be very fertile yet there must be time and means to raise it; if we have corn enough we may live plentifully. Yet all these are but the means which God hath ordained to do us good by: our eyes must be towards him, who as he can withhold blessings from the strongest means, so he can give sufficient virtue to the weakest. I am so straitened with much business, as can no way satisfy myself in writing to thee. The Lord will in due time let us see the faces of each other again to our great comfort. Now the Lord in mercy bless, guide and support thee: I kiss and embrace thee my dear wife. I kiss and bless you all my dear children; Forth, Mary, Deane, Sam, and the other: the Lord keep you all and work his true fear in your hearts. The blessing of the Lord be upon all my servants, whom salute from me, Jo. Samford, Amy etc., Goldston; Pease, Chote etc.: my good friends at Castlins and all my good neighbors, goodman Cole and his good wife, and all the rest.

Remember to come well furnished with linen, woollen, some more bedding, brass, peuter, leather bottles, drinking horns etc.: let my son provide 12 axes of several sorts of the Braintree Smith, or some other prime workman; whatever they cost, and some augers great and small, and many other necessaries which I can't now think of, as candles, soap, and store of beef suet, etc.: once again farewell my dear wife.

Thy faithful husband,

Jo. Winthrop

*Charlton in N. England, July 23, 1630*

# The Crossing to Pennsylvania

## Gottfried Mittelberger

*Conditions such as those described by Mittelberger were not uncommon on board immigrant ships. But even worse ordeals were experienced by other human beings in getting to America: the plight of the Negro aboard the slave ships which followed the Middle Passage to North America far exceeded in sheer misery anything encountered by Mittelberger.*

In the month of May 1750 I left my birthplace Enzweihingen in the district of Vaihingen for Heilbronn, where an organ was waiting for me, ready to be shipped to Pennsylvania. With this organ I took the usual route down the Neckar and the Rhine to Rotterdam in Holland. From Rotterdam I sailed with a transport of approximately 400 souls—Württemberger, Durlacher, Palatines, and Swiss, etc.—across the North Sea to Cowes in England; and, after a nine-day stopover there, across the Atlantic, until at last on the tenth of October 1750 I landed in Philadelphia, the capital of Pennsylvania.

The trip from home to Rotterdam including the sojourn there, took fully seven weeks because of the many delays encountered both in going down the Rhine and in Holland. Without these one could have completed the journey more quickly. The voyage from Rotterdam to Philadelphia took fifteen weeks. I spent nearly four years in America and, as my testimonials show, held the post of organist and schoolteacher in the German St. Augustine's Church in Providence. Besides that I gave private music and German lessons in the house of Captain von Diemer, as attested by the following certificate:

> Whereas the bearer Mr. Mittelberger, music master, has resolved to return from this province to his native land, which is in the Duchy of Württemberg in Germany, I have at his request granted these lines to certify that the above named Mr. Mittelberger has behaved himself honestly, diligently, and faithfully in the offices of schoolmaster and organist

Gottfried Mittelberger: *Journey to Pennsylvania.* Edited and translated by Oscar Handlin and John Clive.

during the space of three years in the Township of New-Providence, County of Philadelphia and Province of Pennsylvania, &c. So that I and all his employers were entirely satisfied, and would willingly have him to remain with us. But as his call obliges him to proceed on his long journey, we would recommend the said Mr. Mittelberger to all persons of dignity and character; and beg their assistance, so that he may pass and repass until he arrives at his respective abode; which may God grant, and may the benediction of Heaven accompany him in his journey. Deus benedicat susceptis ejus ferat eum ad amicos suos maxima prosperitate.

Dabam, Providentiae Philadelphiae
    Comitatu Pennsylvania in America,
    die 25. Apr. A.D. 1754

JOHN DIEMER, Cap.
SAM. KENNEDY, M.D.
HENRY PAWLING, Esqr.

T.
Henry Marsteller
Matthias Gmelin.

I made careful inquiries into the conditions of the country. And what I am going to describe in this book I partly found out for myself, and partly heard from reliable people who know what they were talking about. I should no doubt have been able to report and to recount more if, at the time, I had ever considered publishing anything about Pennsylvania. But I always thought myself far too feeble to do that sort of thing. It was only the misfortunes I encountered on my voyage to and fro (for in the country itself things went well with me, because I was able to earn a living right away, and could easily support myself well) and the nasty tricks the Newlanders wanted to play on me and my family, as I shall relate further on, that first gave me the idea not to keep what I knew to myself.

But what really drove me to write this little book was the sad and miserable condition of those traveling from Germany to the New World, and the irresponsible and merciless proceedings of the Dutch traders in human beings and their man-stealing emissaries—I mean the so-called Newlanders. For these at one and the same time steal German people under all sorts of fine pretexts, and deliver them into the hands of the great Dutch traffickers in human souls. From this business the latter make a huge profit, and the Newlanders a smaller one.

This, as I say, is the principal reason for my publishing this little book. In fact, I had to take a solemn oath to write it. For before I left Pennsylvania, when it became known that I wanted to return to Württemberg, numerous Württemberger, Durlacher, and Palatines (a great many of whom live there and spend their days moaning and groaning about ever having left their native country) begged me with tears and uplifted hands, and even in the name of God, to publicize their misery and sorrow in Germany. So that not only the common people but even princes and lords might be able to hear about what happened to them; and so that innocent souls would no longer leave their native country, persuaded to do so by the Newlanders, and dragged by them into a similar kind of slavery. And so I vowed to the great God, and promised those people to reveal the entire truth about it to people in Germany, according to the best of my knowledge and ability.

I hope, therefore, that my dear countrymen and indeed all of Germany will be no less concerned to get news and factual information about how far it is to Pennsylvania and how long it takes to get there; about what the journey costs, and what discomforts and dangers one has to undergo in the bargain; about what happens when the people arrive in America well or ill; about how they are sold and scattered around; and, finally, about what conditions in general are like. I conceal neither good nor bad aspects; and thus I hope that the world, liking an honest man, will look on me as impartial and truthful. Once people have read all this I have no doubt that those who might still have some desire to go over there will stay at home and will carefully avoid this long and difficult voyage and the misfortunes connected with it; since such a journey will mean for most who undertake it the loss of all they possess, of freedom and peace, and for some the loss of their very lives and, I can even go so far as to say, of the salvation of their souls.

To travel from Durlach or Wüttemberg as far as Holland and the open sea one must reckon on a trip of 200 hours. From there across the sea to England as far as Cowes, where all ships drop anchor before they finally begin the great ocean crossing, another 150 hours. From there over 100 hours until one completely loses sight of England. Then across the Atlantic, that is from land to land, as the sailors put it, 1,200 hours. Finally from the first sight of land in Pennsylvania to Philadelphia, over 40 hours. Altogether such a journey adds up to 1,700 hours or 1,700 French miles.

This journey lasts from the beginning of May until the end of October, that is, a whole six months, and involves such hardships that it is really impossible for any description to do justice to them. The reason for this is that the Rhine boats must pass by thirty-six different customs houses between Heilbronn and Holland. At each of these all the ships must be examined, and these examinations take place at the convenience of the customs officials. Meanwhile, the ships with the people in them are held up for a long time. This involves a great deal of expense for the passengers; and it also means that the trip down the Rhine alone takes from four to six weeks.

When the ships with their passengers arrive in Holland they are there held up once again for from five to six weeks. Because everything is very expensive in Holland the poor people must spend nearly all they own during this period. In addition various sad accidents are likely to occur here. I have, for instance, seen with my own eyes two of the children of a man trying to board ship near Rotterdam meet sudden death by drowning.

In Rotterdam, and to some extent also in Amsterdam, the people are packed into the big boats as closely as herring, so to speak. The bedstead of one person is hardly two feet across and six feet long, since many of the boats carry from four to six hundred passengers, not counting the immense amount of equipment, tools, provisions, barrels of fresh water, and other things that also occupy a great deal of space.

Because of contrary winds it sometimes takes the boats from two to four weeks to make the trip from Holland to Cowes. But, given favorable winds, that voyage can be completed in eight days or less. On arrival everything is examined once more and customs duties paid. It can happen that ships have to ride at anchor there from eight to fourteen days, or until they have taken on full cargoes. During this time everyone has to spend his last remaining money and to consume the provisions that he meant to save for the ocean voyage, so that most people must suffer tremendous hunger and want at sea where they really feel the greatest need. Many thus already begin their sufferings on the voyage between Holland and England.

When the ships have weighed anchor for the last time, usually off Cowes in Old England, then both the long sea voyage and misery begin in earnest. For from there the ships often take eight, nine, ten, or twelve weeks sailing to Philadelphia, if the wind is unfavorable. But even given the most favorable winds, the voyage takes seven weeks.

During the journey the ship is full of pitiful signs of distress—smells, fumes, horrors, vomiting, various kinds of sea sickness, fever, dysentery, headaches, heat, constipation, boils, scurvy, cancer, mouth-rot, and similar afflictions, all of them caused by the age and the highly-salted state of the food, especially of the meat, as well as by the very bad and filthy water, which brings about the miserable destruction and death of many. Add to all that shortage of food, hunger, thirst, frost, heat, dampness, fear, misery, vexation, and lamentation as well as other troubles. Thus, for example, there are so many lice, especially on the sick people, that they have to be scraped off the bodies. All this misery reaches its climax when in addition to everything else one must also suffer through two to three days and nights of storm, with everyone convinced that the ship with all aboard is bound to sink. In such misery all the people on board pray and cry pitifully together.

In the course of such a storm the sea begins to surge and rage so that the waves often seem to rise up like high mountains, sometimes sweeping over the ship; and one thinks that he is going to sink along with the ship. All the while the ship, tossed by storm and waves, moves constantly from one side to the other, so that nobody aboard can either walk, sit, or lie down and the tightly packed people on their cots, the sick as well as the healthy, are thrown every which way. One can easily imagine that these hardships necessarily affect many people so severely that they cannot survive them.

I myself was afflicted by severe illness at sea, and know very well how I felt. These people in their misery are many times very much in want of solace, and I often entertained and comforted them with singing, praying, and encouragement. Also, when possible, and when wind and waves permitted it, I held daily prayer meetings with them on deck, and, since we had no ordained clergyman on board, was forced to administer baptism to five children. I also held services, including a sermon, every Sunday, and when the dead were buried at sea, commended them and our souls to the mercy of God.

Among those who are in good health impatience sometimes grows so great and bitter that one person begins to curse the other, or himself and the day of his birth, and people sometimes come close to murdering one another. Misery and malice are readily associated, so that people begin to cheat and steal from one another. And then one always blames the other for having undertaken the voyage. Often the children cry out against their parents, husbands against wives and wives against husbands, brothers against their sisters, friends and acquaintances against one another.

But most of all they cry out against the thieves of human beings! Many groan and exclaim: "Oh! If only I were back at home, even lying in my pig-sty!" Or they call out: "Ah, dear God, if I only once again had a piece of good bread or a good fresh drop of water." Many people whimper, sigh, and cry out pitifully for home. Most of them become homesick at the thought that many hundreds of people must necessarily perish, die, and be thrown into the ocean in such misery. And this in turn makes their families, or those who were responsible for their undertaking the journey, oftentimes fall almost into despair—so that it soon becomes practically impossible to rouse them from their depression. In a word, groaning, crying, and lamentation go on aboard day and night; so that even the hearts of the most hardened, hearing all this, begin to bleed.

One can scarcely conceive what happens at sea to women in childbirth and to their innocent offspring. Very few escape with their lives; and mother and child, as soon as they have died, are thrown into the water. On board our ship, on a day on which we had a great storm, a woman about to give birth and unable to deliver under the circumstances, was pushed through one of the portholes into the sea because her corpse was far back in the stern and could not be brought forward to the deck.

Children between the ages of one and seven seldom survive the sea voyage; and parents must often watch their offspring suffer miserably, die, and be thrown into the ocean, from want, hunger, thirst, and the like. I

myself, alas, saw such a pitiful fate overtake thirty-two children on board
our vessel, all of whom were finally thrown into the sea. Their parents
grieve all the more, since their children do not find repose in the earth,
but are devoured by the predatory fish of the ocean. It is also worth
noting that children who have not had either measles or smallpox usually
get them on board the ship and for the most part perish as a result.

On one of these voyages a father often becomes infected by his wife
and children, or a mother by her small children, or even both parents by
their children, or sometimes whole families one by the other, so that many
times numerous corpses lie on the cots next to those who are still alive,
especially when contagious diseases rage on board.

Many other accidents also occur on these ships, especially falls in which
people become totally crippled and can never be completely made whole
again. Many also tumble into the sea.

It is not surprising that many passengers fall ill, because in addition to
all the other troubles and miseries, warm food is served only three times
a week, and at that is very bad, very small in quantity, and so dirty as to
be hardly palatable at all. And the water distributed in these ships is often
very black, thick with dirt, and full of worms. Even when very thirsty, one
is almost unable to drink it without loathing. It is certainly true that at
sea one would often spend a great deal of money just for one good piece
of bread, or one good drink of water—not even to speak of a good glass
of wine—if one could only obtain them. I have, alas, had to experience
that myself. For toward the end of the voyage we had to eat the ship's
biscuit, which had already been spoiled for a long time, even though in
no single piece was there more than the size of a thaler that was not full
of red worms and spiders' nests. True, great hunger and thirst teach one
to eat and drink everything—but many must forfeit their lives in the
process. It is impossible to drink sea water, since it is salty and bitter as
gall. If this were not the case, one could undertake such an ocean voyage
with far less expense and without so many hardships.

When at last after the long and difficult voyage the ships finally approach land, when one gets to see the headlands for the sight of which
the people on board had longed so passionately, then everyone crawls
from below to the deck, in order to look at the land from afar. And people
cry for joy, pray, and sing praises and thanks to God. The glimpse of land
revives the passengers, especially those who are half-dead of illness. Their
spirits, however weak they had become, leap up, triumph, and rejoice
within them. Such people are now willing to bear all ills patiently, if only
they can disembark soon and step on land. But, alas, alas!

When the ships finally arrive in Philadelphia after the long voyage only
those are let off who can pay their sea freight or can give good security.
The others, who lack the money to pay, have to remain on board until
they are purchased and until their purchasers can thus pry them loose

from the ship. In this whole process the sick are the worst off, for the healthy are preferred and are more readily paid for. The miserable people who are ill must often still remain at sea and in sight of the city for another two or three weeks—which in many cases means death. Yet many of them, were they able to pay their debts and to leave the ships at once, might escape with their lives.

Before I begin to describe how this commerce in human beings takes place I must report what the voyage to Philadelphia or Pennsylvania costs. Any one older than ten years has to pay £10, or 60 florins, for the passage from Rotterdam to Philadelphia. Children between five and ten pay half fare, that is to say £5, or 30 florins. All children under the age of five get free passage. In return the passengers are transported across the ocean; and as long as they are at sea, they get their board, however bad it is (as I reported above).

All this covers only the sea voyage; the cost of land transportation from home to Rotterdam, including the Rhine passage, comes to at least 40 florins no matter how economically one tries to live on the way. This does not include the expenses of any extraordinary contingencies. I can assure readers of this much—that many travelers on the journey from their homes to Philadelphia spent 200 florins, even with all possible thrift.

This is how the commerce in human beings on board ship takes place. Every day Englishmen, Dutchmen, and High Germans come from Philadelphia and other places, some of them very far away, sometime twenty or thirty or forty hours' journey, and go on board the newly arrived vessel that has brought people from Europe and offers them for sale. From among the healthy they pick out those suitable for the purposes for which they require them. Then they negotiate with them as to the length of the period for which they will go into service in order to pay off their passage, the whole amount of which they generally still owe. When an agreement has been reached, adult persons by written contract bind themselves to serve for three, four, five, or six years, according to their health and age. The very young, between the ages of ten and fifteen, have to serve until they are twenty-one, however.

Many parents in order to pay their fares in this way and get off the ship must barter and sell their children as if they were cattle. Since the fathers and mothers often do not know where or to what masters their children are to be sent, it frequently happens that after leaving the vessel, parents and children do not see each other for years on end, or even for the rest of their lives.

People who arrive without the funds to pay their way and who have children under the age of five, cannot settle their debts by selling them. They must give away these children for nothing to be brought up by strangers; and in return these children must stay in service until they are twenty-one years old. Children between five and ten who owe half-fare, that is, thirty florins, must also go into service in return until they are twenty-one years old, and can neither set free their parents nor take their debts upon themselves. On the other hand, the sale of children older than ten can help to settle a part of their parents' passage charges.

A wife must be responsible for her sick husband and a husband for his sick wife, and pay his or her fare respectively, and must thus serve five to six years not only for herself or himself, but also for the spouse, as the case may be. If both should be ill on arrival, then such persons are brought directly from the ship into a hospital, but not until it is clear that no purchaser for them is to be found. As soon as they have recovered, they must serve to pay off their fare, unless they have the means immediately to discharge the debt.

It often happens that whole families—husband, wife, and children—being sold to different purchasers, become separated, especially when they cannot pay any part of the passage money. When either the husband or the wife has died at sea, having come more than halfway, then the surviving spouse must pay not only his or her fare, but must also pay for or serve out the fare of the deceased.

When both parents have died at sea, having come more than halfway, then their children, especially when they are still young and have nothing to pawn or cannot pay, must be responsible for their own fares as well as those of their parents, and must serve until they are twenty-one years old. Once free of service, they receive a suit of clothing as a parting gift, and if it has been so stipulated the men get a horse and the women a cow.

When a servant in this country has the opportunity to get married he has to pay £5 to £6, that is, 30 to 36 florins for every year that he would still have had to serve. But many who must purchase and pay for their brides in this manner come to regret their purchases later. They would just as soon surrender their damnably expensive wares again and lose their money into the bargain.

No one in this country can run away from a master who has treated him harshly and get far. For there are regulations and laws that ensure that runaways are certainly and quickly recaptured. Those who arrest or return a fugitive get a good reward. For every day that someone who runs away is absent from his master he must as a punishment do service an extra week, for every week an extra month, and for every month a half year. But if the master does not want to take back the recaptured runaway, he is entitled to sell him to someone else for the period of as many years as he would still have had to serve.

Occupations vary, but work is strenuous in this new land; and many who have just come into the country at an advanced age must labor hard for their bread until they die. I will not even speak of the young people. Most jobs involve cutting timber, felling oak trees, and levelling, or as one says there, clearing, great tracts of forest, roots and all. Such forest land, having been cleared in this way, is then laid out in fields and meadows. From the best wood that has been felled people construct railings or fences around the new fields. Inside these, all meadows, all lawns, gardens, and orchards, and all arable land are surrounded and enclosed by thickly cut wood planks set in zigzag fashion one above the other. And thus cattle, horses, and sheep are confined to pasture land.

Our Europeans who have been purchased must work hard all the time. For new fields are constantly being laid out and thus they learn from experience that oak tree stumps are just as hard in America as they are in Germany. In these hot regions there is particularly fulfilled in them that with which the Lord God afflicted man in the first book of Moses, on account of his sin and disobedience, namely: "Thou shalt eat thy bread in the sweat of thy brow." Thus let him who wants to earn his piece of bread honestly and in a Christian manner and who can only do this by manual labor in his native country stay *there* rather than come to America.

For, in the first place, things are no better in Pennsylvania. However hard one may have had to work in his native land, conditions are bound to be equally tough or even tougher in the new country. Furthermore the emigrant has to undertake the arduous voyage, which means not only that he must suffer more misery for half a year than he would have to suffer doing the hardest labor, but also that he must spend approximately two hundred florins which no one will refund to him. If he has that much money, he loses it; if he does not have it, he must work off his debt as a slave or as a miserable servant. So let people stay in their own country and earn their keep honestly for themselves and their families. Furthermore, I want to say that those people who may let themselves be talked into something and seduced into the voyage by the thieves of human beings are the biggest fools if they really believe that in America or Pennsylvania roasted pigeons are going to fly into their mouths without their having to work for them.

How sad and miserable is the fate of so many thousand German families who lost all the money they ever owned in the course of the long and difficult voyage, many of whom perished wretchedly and had to be buried at sea and who, once they have arrived in the new country, saw their old and young separated and sold away into places far removed one from the other! The saddest aspect of all this is that in most instances parents must give away their young children getting nothing in return. For such children are destined never to see or recognize parents, brothers, and sisters again, and, after they have been sold to strangers, are not brought up in any sort of Christian faith.

In Pennsylvania there exist so many varieties of doctrines and sects that it is impossible to name them all. Many people do not reveal their own particular beliefs to anyone. Furthermore there are many hundreds of adults who not only are unbaptized, but who do not even want baptism.

Many others pay no attention to the Sacraments and to the Holy Bible, or even to God and His Word. Some do not even believe in the existence of a true God or Devil, Heaven or Hell, Salvation or Damnation, the Resurrection of the Dead, the Last Judgment and Eternal Life, but think everything visible is of merely natural origin. For in Pennsylvania not only is everyone allowed to believe what he wishes; he is also at liberty to express these beliefs publicly and freely.

Thus when young people not raised in the fundamentals of religion must go into service for many years with such freethinkers and unbelievers and are not permitted by these people to attend any church or school, especially when they live far away from them, then such innocent souls do not reach a true knowledge of the Divine and are brought up like heathen or Indians.

The ocean voyage is sometimes dangerous for those people who bring money and effects with them from home, because at sea much is often spoiled by inrushing water. And sometimes they are robbed on board by dishonest people. Thus such once-wealthy folk are to have really unhappy experiences.

As an example, let me tell the sad story of a man from Württemberg. Late in the year 1753 Bailiff Daser, well known to us at home, arrived in Philadelphia in a miserable and unhappy state, having come from Nagold with his wife and eight children. Not only had he been robbed on sea to the tune of 1,800 florins, but on account of these thefts he and the English ship's captain got involved in a great law-suit at Philadelphia. Litigation brought him no gain. On the contrary, he had to pay costs and thus lost a great deal more. Mr. Daser had to pay 600 florins to cover the passage for himself and his family. Since, however, he had been robbed of his money, all his effects, including his boxes, were publicly auctioned off for a trifling sum at a *vendue*, or public auction. Thus he and his family found themselves in even more miserable circumstances.

When at this point he wanted to borrow some money in order to buy a plantation, he was shamefully cheated by his creditor. He had made an agreement with this man, to pay him back the borrowed sum within two years. But the person who drew up the *Obligation*, or bond, as it is known there, wrote, as the result of an intentional slip of the tongue by the unscrupulous creditor, "two days" instead of "two years." Mr. Daser signed the agreement not realising that he was signing his own doom, since he knew no English. The game was played in such a way that since he did not repay the money within two days, all he owned was sold, even the shirt from his very back. Actually he had not even received the money in the first place thanks to the creditor's negligence and his various subterfuges.

Indeed, he would probably have ended up in prison, or been forced to sell his children, if, through my intercession, he had not been saved by

Captain von Diemer, who always showed great and laudable concern for Germans. The same Captain von Diemer out of charity then supplied Daser and his family with food, money, beds, and living quarters until the end of the trial. He also gave security for him, so that Mr. Daser did not have to go to debtors' prison. When I departed Captain von Diemer promised Mr. Daser and me, with hand and mouth, to help take care of the Daser family and their needs as long as he lived. During a period of eight weeks, Mr. Daser took his meals in our house, and slept there, too. But, in truth, because of the many sad misfortunes he had suffered, he became very despondent and half lost his mind. His two oldest unmarried daughters and his oldest son were forced to go into service shortly before my departure, each bound by written contract for three years.

I want to take this opportunity to relate some curious and most unfortunate instances of shipwreck. On St. James's Day in 1754, a ship with some 360 souls on board, mainly Württemberger, Durlacher, and Palatines, was driven onto a rock at night by a storm between Holland and Old England. It received three shocks, each time accompanied by loud crashes. Finally it came apart lengthwise underneath. So much water rushed in that the ship started to sink early the next morning.

When the peril was at its greatest and people tried to save themselves, sixty-three persons jumped into one boat. Since this boat was already overloaded, and since yet another person swam to it and held on, it was impossible to drive him off in any other way than by chopping off his hands; so that he had to drown. Another person is supposed to have jumped onto a barrel which had fallen out of the great ship, in order to save himself in that way. But the barrel capsized at once and sank with him.

The people who remained on board the great ship, however, held on some to the rigging, some to the masts. Many stood deep in water, clapping their hands together over their heads, and crying together in an undescribably piteous manner. From the boat one could eventually see the great ship sink with three hundred souls aboard before one's very eyes. However, merciful God sent help, in the form of an English ship in the vicinity, to the rest who had saved themselves in the boat. This took them aboard in their great peril after their shipwreck, and brought them back to land. This great misfortune would not even have become known in Germany, had the ship perished during the night with all aboard.

The following unfortunate sea voyage involving many Germans has hardly or not at all become known in Germany. In 1752 a ship arrived in Philadelphia from Holland which had taken an entire half year to make the crossing. This ship had been battered by many storms during the entire winter and was unable to land, until at last another better ship came to help it in its miserable, starved-out, and half-wrecked state. This ship was able to bring 21 out of approximately 340 persons to Phila-

delphia. Not only had these been at sea for a full half year, and driven
by the storm onto the coast of Ireland, but most people aboard had died
of starvation. They had lost mast and sails, captain and mates. And the
rest would never have reached land, if God had not come to their aid
with another ship and had thus guided them here.

Another unfortunate sea voyage has probably also not become known
in Germany. Some years ago an entire ship full of Germans is supposed to
have been lost at sea. These people, too, were reported to have come to
Philadelphia. But no one ever heard anything about them except that a
description of this same ship was sent from Holland to the merchants of
Philadelphia. News of such totally lost and wrecked ships is not publicized
in Germany lest people be frightened away from the voyage, and prevented from making it.

I find it impossible to hold back what I heard from a reliable source in
Pennsylvania by means of a bundle of letters posted at sea on the tenth
of December 1754 that reached me on the first of September 1755. In
these letters I am told in piteous fashion that in the autumn of the year
just past (1754), once again more than 22,000 souls arrived in Philadelphia alone, a great burden to the country. Most of them were Württemberger, for at that time there took place a big emigration from Württemberg. The rest were Palatines, Durlacher, and Swiss. They were so
miserably sick and wretched that once again most people had to sell their
children on account of great poverty. Such a great mass of people imposed
a great burden on the land, especially the multitude of the sick, of whom
many daily continue to fill the graves.

While I was in the country, twenty to twenty-four ships full of people
arrived in Philadelphia alone during the autumn of every year. Within
the space of four years the city was invaded by more than 25,000 souls.
This figure is in addition to those who died at sea or during the voyage,
and does not count those ships full of people that sailed to other English
colonies, that is, to New York, Boston, Maryland, Nova Scotia, and
Carolina. Thus these colonies were filled up and people as people in the
city of Philadelphia became worthless.

But the fact that so many still go to America and especially to Pennsylvania is to be blamed on the swindles and persuasions practised by
so-called Newlanders. These thieves of human beings tell their lies to
people of various classes and professions, among whom may be found
many soldiers, scholars, artists, and artisans. They abduct people from
their Princes and Lords and ship them to Rotterdam or Amsterdam for
sale. There they get three florins, or one ducat, from the merchant, for
each person ten years or older. On the other hand the merchants get from
sixty to seventy or eighty florins for such a person in Philadelphia, depending on the debts that said person has incurred on the voyage.

If such a Newlander has gathered together a transport and does not want to go to America himself, he stays behind, and spends the winter in Holland or elsewhere. In the spring he once more collects money in advance from his merchants, for the purchase of human beings. Then he begins to travel again, pretending to have come from Pennsylvania in order to buy all kinds of merchandise and to export it back there.

Often the Newlanders claim to have the authorization of the American government and of their fellow-countrymen in America to collect legacies belonging to these people. They also say that they want to take this certain and good opportunity to invite the friends, brothers and sisters, and even the fathers and mothers of those in America to join them. And it frequently happens that such old people follow their relatives, persuaded into the hope of finding better living conditions.

The Newlanders try to make these old people leave the country so that they can lure other people to go along with them. And so they pull the wool over the eyes of many who say that if such and such relatives would only come along, then they would be willing to risk the trip. This sort of enticement takes various forms. A favorite method is for these thieves of human beings to show the poor people money that, however, turns out to be nothing more than bait from Holland for human beings, and thus accursed blood-money.

Sometimes these thieves of human beings are able to talk persons of special rank, such as nobles or skilled or learned people, into making the trip. If these folk are able neither to pay their passage nor to give security, then they, just like the common poor folk, are not allowed to leave the ship, and must stay aboard until somebody comes and buys them from the ship's captain. And when they are finally let off, then they have to serve the lords and masters who purchased them, just as if they were common wage-laborers.

Their rank, skill and learning does not help them at all. For in America only workmen and artisans are needed. And the worst of it is that such people, not used to this kind of work, are beaten like cattle until they have learned hard labor. For this reason several people, finding themselves so wretchedly cheated by the Newlanders, have committed suicide. Others have fallen into such a state of despair that no one could any longer be of help to them. Still others have run away and have subsequently fared even worse than before.

It often happens that the merchants in Holland make a secret agreement with the captain and the Newlanders. This stipulates that the latter sail the fully-loaded ships not to Pennsylvania where these people want to go but to another place in America where they calculate they can sell their human cargo for a better price. In this way many who already have acquaintances or even perhaps friends, brothers, and sisters in Pennsylvania, to whose help and care they had been looking forward, are painfully hurt by being separated from their families and friends whom because of such godless misrouting they will never get to see again, either in this or that country. Thus both in Holland and at sea one has to put oneself into the hands of the wind and the captain; since at sea no one knows for certain just where the ship is proceeding. The blame for this rests with the Newlanders, and with a few unscrupulous dealers in human flesh in Holland.

Many people going to Philadelphia entrust the remains of the money they are able to bring away from home to these Newlanders. These thieves, however, often remain in Holland along with the money. Or they proceed from Holland on board another ship to a different English colony; so that the poor defrauded people, when they get to America, have no other recourse but to go into service, or to sell their children, if they have any, in order to get away from the ship.

Let me illustrate this by a curious example. In 1753 a noble lady, N. N., arrived in Philadelphia with two half-grown daughters and a young son. In the course of the Rhine journey this lady had made a loan of more than 1,000 reichsthaler to a Newlander otherwise well known to her. This villain remained in Holland along with the money after the departure of the lady's ship. Thus she was put into a position of such great want and need that her two daughters were forced to go into service. The same poor lady sent her son back across the ocean in the spring of the following year in order to locate the man who had stolen her money. But by the time of my departure in 1754 no one had heard anything of this man. Indeed, it was said that the young man looking for him had lost his life in the course of his search.

It is, by the way, impossible to touch on all the circumstances here. Besides, I am absolutely certain that those Newlanders or thieves of human beings who return never tell others the whole story and the real truth about such a miserable, difficult, and in the bargain highly dangerous voyage. When the Newlanders leave Pennsylvania or one of the other English colonies they are often given many letters to take along. When they get to Holland with these letters they have them broken open, or break them open themselves. And if someone has written in lamentation and told the truth, then such a letter is either rewritten or even thrown away.

In Pennsylvania I heard from the very lips of such thieves of human beings that in Holland there are many Jews who for a small fee are able to reproduce all seals and who can perfectly imitate all handwritings on demand. They are able to reproduce all strokes and letters, all signs and special features so faithfully that the person whose handwriting they have imitated must himself admit that it is indeed his own hand. Using such tricks they are able to cheat even people who are not gullible; and on those they practice their evil tricks all the more covertly. They themselves tell their intimates that this sort of thing is the best way of easily persuading people to leave for America.

They almost succeeded in deceiving me. For in Holland they tried to see to it that I should not leave America for good; and they attempted to use trickery and force in order to talk me into returning to England and America. These same merchants tried to convince me verbally in Rotterdam, as well as in writing from Amsterdam, that my wife and child with my sister-in-law and many of my countrymen had embarked for Philadelphia last summer with the year's final transport. In the course of this attempt they told me in great detail the names of my wife, my child and myself, as well as their height and their age. They also said that my wife had stated that her husband had been an organist in Pennsylvania for four years. They also showed me my wife's name in a letter and told me with what ship and captain they had sailed from Amsterdam; and how my wife had been accommodated in berth Number Twenty-Two with four other women.

All of this made me extraordinarily confused and irresolute. I showed them my wife's letters in which she clearly indicated that she would never go to America without me; that on the contrary she was expecting me with longing; and that she had once again received news from me to the effect that I had decided, God willing, to return to Germany during the next year. For all those reasons I could not possibly believe what they were telling me. This put me into such a state of consternation that I did not know what I ought to believe or do. At last, after mature deliberation, and without a doubt of the intent of Divine direction, I decided to complete my journey, in God's name, especially since I had already carried out the major part of it, that is, 1,400 hours, and had reached Germany.

In this I succeeded, and thus, thanks be to God, I escaped this great temptation. For I found that what these people had tried to tell and show me about my family in Holland was not true, since I encountered my wife and child happily at home. Had I believed these seducers of the people and returned by sea to England and America instead of coming home, this news might perhaps not have become so quickly known. In fact, my family and I would hardly or not at all have met again in this world.

The above mentioned thieves of human beings, as I found out afterwards, had described me and my wife completely and by name to the merchants in Holland. And the Newlanders for the second time tried to wheedle my wife into going to America. They doubtless thought that once I had left America I would reveal their whole bag of tricks as well as the miserable condition of the great mass of unfortunate families who had gone out there, and would in this way do great harm to their transports and their trafficking in human flesh.

At this point I must mention something that I forgot to relate before. As soon as the ships transporting people from Europe have anchored at

Philadelphia, that is, the following morning, all male persons fifteen years or older are unloaded from the ship and put on to a boat. Then they are conducted two by two into town to the courthouse or city hall. There they must take the oath of allegiance to the Crown of Great Britain. When they have done this, they are taken back to the ships. Only then does the commerce in human beings begin, as I described it earlier.

I want to add only one other thing, namely, that when persons are purchased they are asked for neither discharge papers nor references. If someone has escaped the hangman and has the rope still dangling around his neck or left both his ears in Europe, there would not on that account exist any obstacles for him in Pennsylvania. If, however, he indulges in wrongdoing once again, there is no hope for him. Thus Pennsylvania is an ideal country for gallows-and-wheel customers.

# PART II

# DAILY LIFE

# Pirates in Plymouth

## *William Bradford*

About the middle of May this year [1646] came in three ships into this harbor, in warlike order. They were found to be men of war. The captain's name was Cromwell, who had taken sundry prizes from the Spaniards in the West Indies; he had a commission from the Earl of Warwick. He had aboard his vessels about 80 lusty men, but very unruly, who after they came ashore, did so distemper themselves with drink as they became like madmen, and though some of them were punished and imprisoned, yet could they hardly be restrained. Yet in the end they became more moderate and orderly. They continued here about a month or six weeks, and then went to the Massachusetts, in which time they spent and scattered a great deal of money among the people, and yet more sin I fear than money, notwithstanding all the care and watchfulness that was used towards them to prevent what might be.

In which time one sad accident fell out. A desperate fellow of the company fell a-quarreling with some of his company. His captain commanded him to be quiet and surcease his quarreling, but he would not, but reviled his captain with base language and in the end half drew his rapier and intended to run at his captain; but he closed with him and wrested his rapier from him and gave him a box on the ear. But he would not give over, but still assaulted his captain; whereupon he took the same rapier as it was in the scabbard and gave him a blow with the hilt, but it lit on his head and the small end of the bar of the rapier hilt pierced his skull, and he died a few days after. But the captain was cleared by a council of war. This fellow was so desperate a quarreler, as the captain was fain many times to chain him under hatches from hurting his fellows, as the company did testify. And this was his end.

This Captain Thomas Cromwell set forth another voyage to the West Indies from the Bay of the Massachusetts, well manned and victualed, and was out three years, and took sundry prizes and returned rich unto the Massachusetts. And there died the same summer, having got a fall from his horse, in which fall he fell on his rapier hilt and so bruised his

William Bradford: *Of Plymouth Plantation*. Edited by Samuel Eliot Morison.

body as he shortly after died thereof, with some other distempers which
brought him into a fever. Some observed that there might be something
of the hand of God herein; that as the forenamed man died of the blow
he gave him with the rapier hilt, so his own death was occasioned by a
like means.

# Thomas Morton of Merrymount
## *William Bradford*

About some three or four years before this time, there came over one
Captain Wollaston (a man of pretty parts) and with him three or four
more of some eminency, who brought with them a great many servants,
with provisions and other implements for to begin a plantation. And
pitched themselves in a place within the Massachusetts which they called
after their Captain's name, Mount Wollaston. Amongst whom was one
Mr. Morton, who it should seem had some small adventure of his own or
other men's amongst them, but had little respect amongst them, and was
slighted by the meanest servants. Having continued there some time, and
not findings things to answer their expectations nor profit to arise as they
looked for, Captain Wollaston takes a great part of the servants and
transports them to Virginia, where he puts them off at good rates, selling
their time to other men; and writes back to one Mr. Rasdall (one of his
chief partners and accounted their merchant) to bring another part of
them to Virginia likewise, intending to put them off there as he had done
the rest. And he, with the consent of the said Rasdall, appointed one
Fitcher to be his Lieutenant and govern the remains of the Plantation till
he or Rasdall returned to take further order thereabout. But this Morton
abovesaid, having more craft than honesty (who had been a kind of
pettifogger of Furnival's Inn) in the others' absence watches an opportunity (commons being but hard amongst them) and got some strong
drink and other junkets and made them a feast; and after they were
merry, he began to tell them he would give them good counsel. "You see,"
saith he, "that many of your fellows are carried to Virginia, and if you
stay till this Rasdall return, you will also be carried away and sold for
slaves with the rest. Therefore I would advise you to thrust out this
Lieutenant Fitcher, and I, having a part in the Plantation, will receive you
as my partners and consociates; so may you be free from service, and we
will converse, plant, trade, and live together as equals and support and
protect one another," or to like effect. This counsel was easily received, so
they took opportunity and thrust Lieutenant Fitcher out o' doors, and

William Bradford: *Of Plymouth Plantation.* Edited by Samuel Eliot Morison.

would suffer him to come no more amongst them, but forced him to seek
bread to eat and other relief from his neighbours till he could get passage
for England.

After this they fell to great licentiousness and led a dissolute life, pouring out themselves into all profaneness. And Morton became Lord of
Misrule, and maintained (as it were) a School of Atheism. And after they
had got some goods into their hands, and got much by trading with the
Indians, they spent it as vainly in quaffing and drinking, both wine and
strong waters in great excess (and, as some reported) £10 worth in a
morning. They also set up a maypole, drinking and dancing about it
many days together, inviting the Indian women for their consorts, dancing and frisking together like so many fairies, or furies, rather; and worse
practices. As if they had anew revived and celebrated the feasts of the
Roman goddess Flora, or the beastly practices of the mad Bacchanalians.
Morton likewise, to show his poetry composed sundry rhymes and verses,
some tending to lasciviousness, and others to the detraction and scandal
of some persons, which he affixed to this idle or idol maypole. They
changed also the name of their place, and instead of calling it Mount
Wollaston they call it Merry-mount, as if this jollity would have lasted
ever. But this continued not long, for after Morton was sent for England
(as follows to be declared) shortly after came over that worthy gentleman Mr. John Endecott, who brought over a patent under the broad seal
for the government of the Massachusetts. Who, visiting those parts, caused
that maypole to be cut down and rebuked them for their profaneness and
admonished them to look there should be better walking. So they or others
now changed the name of their place again and called it Mount Dagon.

Now to maintain this riotous prodigality and profuse excess, Morton,
thinking himself lawless, and hearing what gain the French and fishermen
made by trading of pieces, powder and shot to the Indians, he as the head
of this consortship began the practice of the same in these parts. And first
he taught them how to use them, to charge and discharge, and what
proportion of powder to give the piece, according to the size or bigness
of the same; and what shot to use for fowl and what for deer. And having
thus instructed them, he employed some of them to hunt and fowl for
him, so as they became far more active in that employment than any of
the English, by reason of their swiftness of foot and nimbleness of body,
being also quick-sighted and by continual exercise well knowing the
haunts of all sorts of game. So as when they saw the execution that a
piece would do, and the benefit that might come by the same, they
became mad (as it were) after them and would not stick to give any
price they could attain to for them; accounting their bows and arrows but
baubles in comparison of them.

And here I may take occasion to bewail the mischief that this wicked
man began in these parts, and which since, base covetousness prevailing

in men that should know better, has now at length got the upper hand and made this thing common, notwithstanding any laws to the contrary. So as the Indians are full of pieces all over, both fowling pieces, muskets, pistols, etc. They have also their moulds to make shot of all sorts, as musket bullets, pistol bullets, swan and goose shot, and of smaller sorts. Yea some have seen them have their screw-plates to make screw-pins themselves when they want them, with sundry other implements, where-with they are ordinarily better fitted and furnished than the English themselves. Yea, it is well known that they will have powder and shot when the English want it nor cannot get it; and that in a time of war or danger, as experience hath manifested, that when lead hath been scarce and men for their own defense would gladly have given a groat a pound, which is dear enough, yet hath it been bought up and sent to other places and sold to such as trade it with the Indians at 12*d* the pound. And it is like they give 3*s* or 4*s* the pound, for they will have it at any rate. And these things have been done in the same times when some of their neigh-bours and friends are daily killed by the Indians, or are in danger thereof and live but at the Indians' mercy. Yea some, as they have acquainted them with all other things, have told them how gunpowder is made, and all the materials in it, and that they are to be had in their own land; and I am confident, could they attain to make saltpeter, they would teach them to make powder.

O, the horribleness of this villainy! How many both Dutch and English have been lately slain by those Indians thus furnished, and no remedy provided; nay, the evil more increased, and the blood of their brethren sold for gain (as is to be feared) and in what danger all these colonies are in is too well known. O that princes and parliaments would take some timely order to prevent this mischief and at length to suppress it by some exemplary punishment upon some of these gain-thirsty murderers, for they deserve no better title, before their colonies in these parts be over-thrown by these barbarous savages thus armed with their own weapons, by these evil instruments and traitors to their neighbours and country! But I have forgot myself and have been too long in this digression; but now to return.

This Morton having thus taught them the use of pieces, he sold them all he could spare, and he and his consorts determined to send for many out of England and had by some of the ships sent for above a score. The which being known, and his neighbours meeting the Indians in the woods armed with guns in this sort, it was a terror unto them who lived strag-glingly and were of no strength in any place. And other places (though more remote) saw this mischief would quickly spread over all, if not pre-vented. Besides, they saw they should keep no servants, for Morton would entertain any, how vile soever, and all the scum of the country or any discontents would flock to him from all places, if this nest was not broken.

And they should stand in more fear of their lives and goods in short time from this wicked and debased crew than from the savages themselves.

So sundry of the chief of the straggling plantations, meeting together, agreed by mutual consent to solicit those of Plymouth (who were then of more strength than them all) to join with them to prevent the further growth of this mischief, and suppress Morton and his consorts before they grew to further head and strength. Those that joined in this action, and after contributed to the charge of sending him for England, were from Piscataqua, Naumkeag, Winnisimmet, Wessagusset, Nantasket and other places where any English were seated. Those of Plymouth being thus sought to by their messengers and letters, and weighing both their reasons and the common danger, were willing to afford them their help though themselves had least cause of fear or hurt. So, to be short, they first resolved jointly to write to him, and in a friendly and neighbourly way to admonish him to forbear those courses, and sent a messenger with their letters to bring his answer.

But he was so high as he scorned all advice, and asked who had to do with him, he had and would trade pieces with the Indians, in despite of all, with many other scurrilous terms full of disdain. They sent to him a second time and bade him to be better advised and more temperate in his terms, for the country could not bear the injury he did. It was against their common safety and against the King's proclamation. He answered in high terms as before; and that the King's proclamation was no law, demanding what penalty was upon it. It was answered, more than he could bear—His Majesty's displeasure. But insolently he persisted and said the King was dead and his displeasure with him, and many the like things. And threatened withal that if any came to molest him, let them look to themselves for he would prepare for them.

Upon which they saw there was no way but to take him by force; and having so far proceeded, now to give over would make him far more haughty and insolent. So they mutually resolved to proceed, and obtained of the Governor of Plymouth to send Captain Standish and some other aid with him, to take Morton by force. The which accordingly was done. But they found him to stand stiffly in his defense, having made fast his doors, armed his consorts, set divers dishes of powder and bullets ready on the table; and if they had not been over-armed with drink, more hurt might have been done. They summoned him to yield, but he kept his house and they could get nothing but scoffs and scorns from him. But at length, fearing they would do some violence to the house, he and some of his crew came out, but not to yield but to shoot; but they were so steeled with drink as their pieces were too heavy for them. Himself with a carbine, overcharged and almost half filled with powder and shot, as was after found, had thought to have shot Captain Standish; but he stepped to him and put by his piece and took him. Neither was there any hurt done to any of either side, save that one was so drunk that he ran his own nose upon the point of a sword that one held before him, as he entered the house; but he lost but a little of his hot blood.

Morton they brought away to Plymouth, where he was kept till a ship went from the Isle of Shoals for England, with which he was sent to the Council of New England, and letters written to give them information of his course and carriage. And also one was sent at their common charge to inform their Honours more particularly and to prosecute against him. But he fooled of the messenger, after he was gone from hence, and though he went for England yet nothing was done to him, not so much as re- buked, for aught was heard, but returned the next year. Some of the worst of the company were dispersed and some of the more modest kept the house till he should be heard from. But I have been too long about so unworthy a person, and bad a cause.

# The Merrymount Colony

## *Thomas Morton*

*After the dispersion of Thomas Morton and his merry men, Merrymount was renamed Mount Wollaston, although Morton suggested that a more appropriate name would be "Woefull Mount," and the unhallowed ground was sanctified by Puritan prayers. But Morton had his revenge upon his persecutors: he wrote a book entitled* The New English Canaan, *in which he held the Puritans up to ridicule and contempt. In this book, Morton attributed his troubles to the Pilgrims' jealousy of his flourishing beaver trade and the rapid progress he was making in converting the savages to the Church of England.*

*As between the Indians and the Pilgrims, he declared that he would take the redskins any day: "I have found the Massachusetts Indians more full of humanity than the Christian," he remarked. Unfortunately for Morton, much as he loathed the Puritans, he could not stay away from them even after he was arrested and shipped off to England for trial and, the Puritans devoutly hoped, hanging. Much to the Puritans' chagrin, no crime under the laws of England could be proved against him. Nevertheless, Morton was soon back again among his tormentors; again he was banished and this time he did not return. He died in Maine, railing to the end against his "bigoted oppressors."*

The Separatists, envying the prosperity and hope of the Plantation at Ma-re Mount (which they perceived began to come forward, and to be in a good way for gain in the Beaver trade), conspired together against mine Host especially (who was the owner of that Plantation), and made up a party against him; and mustered up what aid they could, accounting of him as of a great Monster.

Many threatening speeches were given out both against his person and his Habitation, which they divulged should be consumed with fire. And taking advantage of the time when his company (which seemed little to regard their threats) were gone up into the Inlands to trade with the

Thomas Morton: *New English Canaan, or New Canaan.* Edited by Charles Francis Adams.

Savages for Beaver, they set upon mine honest host at a place called Wessaguscus, where, by accident, they found him. The inhabitants there were in good hope of the subversion of the plantation at Ma-re Mount (which they principally aimed at); and the rather because mine host was a man that endeavored to advance the dignity of the Church of England, which they (on the contrary part), would labor to vilify with uncivil terms: railing against the sacred book of common prayer, and mine host that used it in a laudable manner amongst his family, as a practise of piety.

There he would be a means to bring sacks to their mill (such is the thirst after Beaver), and helped the conspirators to surprise mine host (who was there all alone). They charged him (because they would seem to have some reasonable cause against him to set a gloss upon their malice) with criminal things; which indeed had been done by such a person, but was of their conspiracy. Mine host demanded of the conspirators who it was that was author of that information, that seemed to be their ground for what they now intended. And because they answered they would not tell him, he as peremptorily replied, that he would not say whether he had, or he had not done as they had been informed.

The answer made no matter (as it seemed), whether it had been negatively or affirmatively made; for they had resolved that he should suffer, because (as they boasted) they were now become the greater number: they had shaken off their shackles of servitude, and were become Masters, and masterless people.

It appears they were like bears' whelps in former time, when mine hosts' plantation was of as much strength as theirs, but now, (theirs' being stronger), they (like overgrown bears), seemed monstrous. In brief, mine host must endure to be their prisoner until they could contrive it so that they might send him to England (as they said), there to suffer according to the merit of the fact which they intended to father upon him, supposing it would prove a heinous crime.

Much rejoicing was made that they had gotten their capital enemy (as they considered him); whom they proposed to hamper in such sort that he should not be able to uphold his plantation at Ma-re Mount.

The Conspirators sported themselves at the expense of my honest host, who meant them no hurt, and were so jocund that they feasted their bodies, and fell to tippling as if they had obtained a great prize, like the Trojans when they had the custody of Hippeus pinetree horse.

My host feigned grief and could not be persuaded either to eat or drink, because he knew emptiness would be a means to make him as watchful as the Geese kept in the Roman Capitol; whereas, for their part, the conspirators would be so drowsy that he might have an opportunity to give them the slip. Six of the conspiracy were set to watch him at Wessaguscus but he kept waking and in the dead of night, up gets mine Host and got to the second door that he was to pass, which, notwithstanding the lock, he got open and shut it after him with such violence that it affrighted some of the conspirators.

The word, which was given with an alarm was: "Oh, he's gone, he's gone, what shall we do, he's gone!" The rest (half asleep) start up in amaze and, like rams, ran their heads one at another full butt in the dark.

Their grand leader, Captain Shrimp [Myles Standish], took on most furiously and tore his clothes for anger, to see the empty nest, and their bird gone.

The rest were eager to have torn their hair from their heads but it was so short that it would give them no hold. Now Captain Shrimp thought in the loss of this prize (which he accounted his masterpiece,) all his honor would be lost for ever.

In the meantime mine Host got home to Ma-re Mount through the woods, eight miles round about the head of the river Monatoquit that parted the two Plantations [Merry Mount and Plymouth], finding his way by the help of the lightning (for it thundered as he went terribly). There he prepared powder, three pounds dried, for his present employment, and four good guns for him and the two assistants left at his house, with bullets of several sizes, three hundred or thereabouts, to be used if the conspirators should pursue him thither. These two persons promised their aid in the quarrel and confirmed that promise with health in good rosa solis.

Now Captain Shrimp, the first Captain in the Land (as he supposed), must do some new act to repair this loss. To vindicate his reputation which had sustained blemish by this oversight, he begins now to study how to repair his honor. In this manner, calling a council, the conspirators decided upon a plan of action.

He takes eight persons more to him and (like the nine Worthies of New Canaan) they embark against Ma-re Mount, where this Monster of a man, as their phrase was, had his den. The whole number, had the rest not been away from home, being but seven, would have give Captain Shrimp (a quondam Drummer) such a welcome as would have made him wish for a Drum as big as Diogenes's tub that he might have crept into it out of sight.

Now the nine Worthies approached, and mine Host prepared, having intelligence by a Savage who hastened in love from Wessaguscus to give him notice of their intent.

One of mine Host's men proved a craven: the other had drunk heavily to purchase a little valor before mine Host had observed his condition.

The nine worthies coming before the Den of this supposed Monster (this seven headed hydra, as they termed him), and began, like Don Quixote against the Windmill, to beat a parley and to offer quarter, if mine Host would yield, for they resolved to send him to England and bade him lay down his arms.

But he (who was the son of a soldier), having taken up arms in his just defense, replied that he would not lay down those arms because they were so needful at sea, if he should be sent over. Yet to save the effusion of so much worthy blood as would have issued out of the veins of these 9 worthies of New Canaan, if mine Host should have played upon them out of his port holes (for they came within danger like a flock of wild geese, as if they had been tailed one to another, as colts to be sold at a fair), mine Host was content to yield upon quarter; and did capitulate with them in what manner it should be for more certainty, because he knew what Captain Shrimp was.

He stipulated that no violence should be offered to his person, to his goods, nor to any of his Household but that he should have his arms and what else was requisite for the voyage. Their herald answered that it was agreed upon and should be performed.

But mine Host no sooner had opened the door and issued out but instantly Captain Shrimp and the rest of the worthies stepped up to him, laid hold of his arms and had him down. So eagerly was every man bent against him (not regarding as binding any agreement made with such a carnal man) that they fell upon him as if they would have eaten him. Some of them were so violent that they would have run him through, and all for haste, until an old Soldier (of the Queen's, as the Proverb is,) clapped his gun under the weapons and sharply rebuked these worthies for their unworthy practises. So the matter was taken into more deliberate consideration.

Captain Shrimp and the rest of the nine worthies made themselves (by this outrageous riot) masters of mine Host of Ma-re Mount and disposed of what he had at his plantation.

This, they knew (in the eyes of the Savages) would add to their glory and diminish the reputation of mine honest Host whom they determined to be rid of upon any terms, as zealously as if he had been the very Hydra of the time.

The nine worthies of New Canaan having now the Law in their own hands (there being no general governor in the land nor did any other Separatists regard the duty they owed their sovereign, whose natural born subjects they were, even though they had come from Holland where they had learned to work everything to their own ends and make a great show of Religion, but no humanity), for they were now to sit in Council on the case.

And much it benefited mine honest Host to be very circumspect, and to take Eacus [Governor Bradford?] to task, for his voice was more listened to than any of the others. And had not mine Host confounded all the arguments that Eacus could make in the conspirators' defense, and confounded him that swayed the rest, they would have made mine Host unable to drink in such manner of merriment any more. So that following this private counsel, given him by one that knew who ruled the roost, the hurricane ceased that otherwise would have split his pinnace.

A conclusion was made and sentence given that mine Host should be sent to England a prisoner. But when he was brought to the ship for that purpose, no man durst be so foolhardy as to undertake to carry him. So these Worthies set mine Host upon an Island, without gun, powder, or shot or dog or so much as a knife to get any thing to feed upon, or any other clothes to shelter him than a thin suit of which he had one at that time. Home he could not get to Ma-re Mount. Upon this Island he stayed a month at least, and was relieved by Savages that took notice that mine Host was a Sachem of Passonagessit, and would bring bottles of strong liquor to him, and unite themselves into a league of brotherhood with mine Host; so full of humanity are these infidels before those Christians.

From this place for England sailed mine Host in a Plymouth ship (that came into the Land to fish upon the Coast) that landed him safe in England at Plymouth. Here he stayed in England until the usual time for shipping to set forth for these parts, and then returned, no man being able to tax him with anything.

But the Worthies (in the meantime) hoped they had been rid of him.

# Edifying Incidents

## John Winthrop

*One of the "declining gentry" of England, John Winthrop decided in
1630 for religious and economic reasons to accompany the Puritans to
New England. A graduate of Cambridge University and the Inns of
Court, he was lord of Groton Manor and justice of the peace of Suffolk
County, a position to which only persons of importance were appointed.
Although his reputation has suffered at the hands of historians and novel-
ists because of his treatment of Anne Hutchinson, he was in actuality a
far more kindly and humane man than the other Puritan leaders. He took
action against Mrs. Hutchinson because he believed her to be a fomenter
of subversive ideas directed against both church and state.*

About eight persons were drowned this winter, all except three, by
adventuring upon the ice. Two of these three (one of them being far in
drink) attempted to pass from Boston to Winisemett in a small boat on
a tempestuous night. This man (accustomed to come home to Winisemett
drunk) his wife would tell him he would one day be drowned, etc. but he
made light of it. Another went aboard a ship to make merry on Saturday
night (being the beginning of the Lord's day), and returning about midnight with three of the ship's company, the boat was overset by means of
the ice, they guiding her by a rope, which went from the ship to the shore.
The seamen waded out, but the Boston man was drowned. He was a man
of good conversation and hopeful of some work of grace begun in him,
but he was drawn away by the seamens' invitation. God will be sanctified
in them that come near him. Two others were the children of one of the
church of Boston. While the parents were at the lecture, the boy (being
about seven years of age), having a small staff in his hand, ran down
upon the ice towards a boat he saw, and the ice breaking, he fell in, but
his staff kept him up till his sister, about fourteen years old, ran down to
save her brother (though there were four men at hand, and called to her
not to go, being themselves hasting to save him) and so drowned herself

*The Winthrop Papers.* Edited by Allyn B. Forbes.

and him also, being past recovery ere the men could come at them, and could easily reach ground with their feet. The parents had no more sons, and confessed that they had been too indulgent towards him and had set their hearts overmuch upon him.

This puts me in mind of another child very strangely drowned a little before winter. The parents were also members of the church of Boston. The father had undertaken to maintain the mill-dam, and being at work upon it (with some help he had hired) in the afternoon of the last day of the week, night came upon them before they had finished what they intended, and his conscience began to put him in mind of the Lord's day, and he was troubled, yet went on and wrought an hour within night. The next day, after evening exercise, and after they had supped, the mother put two children to bed in the room where they themselves did lie and they went out to visit a neighbor. When they returned, they continued about an hour in the room and missed not the child, but then the mother going to the bed, and not finding her youngest child (a daughter about five years of age), after much search she found it drowned in a well in her cellar. Which was very observable, as by a special hand of God, that the child should go out of that room in another in the dark, and then fall down a trap door or go down the stairs, and so into the well in the farther end of the cellar, the top of the well and the water being even with the ground. But the father, freely in the open congregation, did acknowledge it the righteous hand of God for his profaning his holy day against the checks of his own conscience.

# An Exemplary Christian

## *Cotton Mather*

*Cotton Mather specialized in depicting the idealized, transcendently virtuous Puritans of the first generation, the Founding Fathers of Massachusetts Bay. With these worthies, Mather felt far more at home than with his own contemporaries, most of whom, he lamented, were sadly deficient in the fervor and righteousness that had made Puritanism a driving force in the world. His sketch of Theophilus Eaton is a eulogy of humility, piety and godliness; edification rather than strict historical truth is the guiding principle. The method worked even when applied to the most unlikely characters: Mather succeeded in fitting a rough, virile old salt like William Phips, the governor of Massachusetts during the witchcraft trials, into the Puritan pattern.*

### THE CHARACTER OF THEOPHILUS EATON

So exemplary was he for a Christian that one who had been a servant unto him could many years after say, "Whatever difficulty in my daily walk I now meet withal, still something that I either saw or heard in my blessed master Eaton's conversation helps me through it all; I have reason to bless God that ever I knew him!" It was his custom when he first rose in a morning to repair unto his study, a study well perfumed with the meditations and supplications of an holy soul. After this, calling his family together, he would then read a portion of the Scripture among them; and after some devout and useful reflections upon it, he would make a prayer —not long, but extraordinary pertinent and reverent; and in the evening some of the same exercises were again attended. On the Saturday morning he would still take notice of the approaching Sabbath in his prayer and ask the grace to be remembering of it and preparing for it; and when the evening arrived, he, besides this, not only repeated a sermon but also instructed his people with putting of questions referring to the points of religion, which would oblige them to study for an answer; and if their answer were at any time insufficient, he would wisely and gently enlighten their understandings—all which he concluded with singing of a

*Selections from Cotton Mather.* Edited by Kenneth B. Murdock.

psalm. When the Lord's day came, he called his family together at the
time for the ringing of the first bell and repeated a sermon, whereunto he
added a fervent prayer especially tending unto the sanctification of the
day. At noon he sang a psalm; and at night he retired an hour into his
closet, advising those in his house to improve the same time for the good
of their own souls. He then called his family together again, and in an
obliging manner conferred with them about the things with which they
had been entertained in the house of God, shutting up all with a prayer
for the blessing of God upon them all. For solemn days of humiliation or
of thanksgiving, he took the same course and endeavored still to make
those that belonged unto him understand the meaning of the service
before them. He seldom used any recreations; but being a great reader,
all the time he could spare from company and business he commonly
spent in his beloved study, so that he merited the name which was once
given to a learned ruler of the English nation, the name of Beauclerk. In
conversing with his friends he was affable, courteous, and generally
pleasant, but grave perpetually, and so cautelous and circumspect in his
discourses and so modest in his expressions that it became a proverb for
incontestable truth, "Governor Eaton said it."

But after all, his humility appeared in having always but low expectations, looking for little regard and reward from any men after he had
merited as highly as was possible by his universal serviceableness.

His eldest son he maintained at the college until he proceeded master
of arts, and he was indeed the son of his vows and a son of great hopes.
But a severe catarrh diverted this young gentleman from the work of the
ministry whereto his father had once devoted him, and a malignant fever
then raging in those parts of the country carried off him with his wife
within two or three days of one another. This was counted the sorest of
all the trials that ever befell his father in the "days of the years of his
pilgrimage," but he bore it with a patience and composure of spirit which
was truly admirable. His dying son looked earnestly on him and said, "Sir,
what shall we do?"—whereto, with a well-ordered countenance, he replied, "Look up to God!" And when he passed by his daughter, drowned
in tears on this occasion, to her he said, "Remember the sixth command-
ment; hurt not yourself with immoderate grief. Remember Job, who said,
'The Lord hath given, and the Lord hath taken away; blessed be the
name of the Lord!' You may mark what a note the spirit of God put upon
it, 'In all this Job sinned not, nor charged God foolishly.' God accounts it
a charging of him foolishly when we don't submit unto his will patiently."
Accordingly he now governed himself as one that had attained unto the
rule of "weeping as if we wept not"; for it being the Lord's day, he repaired unto the church in the afternoon as he had been there in the forenoon, though he was never like to see his dearest son alive any more in
this world. And though before the first prayer began, a messenger came

to prevent Mr. Davenport's praying for the sick person who was now dead, yet his affectionate father altered not his course but wrote after the preacher as formerly; and when he came home, he held on his former methods of divine worship in his family, for not the excuse of Aaron omitting anything in the service of God. In like sort, when the people had been at the solemn interment of this his worthy son, he did with a very impassionate aspect and carriage then say, "Friends, I thank you all for your love and help and for this testimony of respect unto me and mine. The Lord hath given, and the Lord hath taken; blessed be the name of the Lord!" Nevertheless, retiring hereupon into the chamber where his daughter then lay sick, some tears were observed falling from him while he uttered these words, "There is a difference between a sullen silence or a stupid senselessness under the hand of God, and a child-like submission thereunto."

Thus continually he, for about a score of years, was the glory and pillar of New Haven colony. He would often say, "Some count it a great matter to die well, but I am sure 'tis a great matter to live well. All our care should be while we have our life to use it well; and so when death puts an end unto that, it will put an end unto all our cares." But having excellently managed his care to live well, God would have him to die well, without any room or time then given to take any care at all; for he enjoyed a death sudden to everyone but himself! Having worshipped God with his family after his usual manner, and upon some occasion with much solemnity charged all the family to carry it well unto their mistress, who was now confined by sickness, he supped and then took a turn or two abroad for his meditations. After that he came in to bid his wife good-night before he left her with her watchers—which, when he did, she said, "Methinks you look sad!"—whereto he replied, "The differences risen in the church of Hartford make me so." She then added, "Let us even go back to our native country again," to which he answered, "You may (and so she did), but I shall die here." This was the last word that ever she heard him speak; for now retiring unto his lodging in another chamber, he was overheard about midnight fetching a groan; and unto one sent in presently to inquire how he did, he answered the inquiry with only saying, "Very ill!" and without saying any more, he fell asleep in Jesus, in the year 1657, loosing anchor from New Haven for the better:
——*Sedes ubi Fata quietas Ostendunt.* [A throne where the Fates show themselves peaceful.]
Now let his gravestone wear at least the following

### EPITAPH

New England's glory, full of warmth and light,
Stole away (and said nothing) in the night.

# Inoculation for Smallpox

## *Cotton Mather*

*Although it never appeared in the advertising, the colonists were beset by an appalling array of death-dealing diseases: malaria, dysentery, typhoid fever, yellow fever, consumption, scurvy, influenza, typhus, measles, scarlet fever and smallpox. Against this "throng of unruly distempers," colonial physicians, still bound to the dogmas of Greek pathology, employed the standard remedies of the time: bleeding, purging, blistering and the administration of unspeakable concoctions, the basic ingredients of which were toads, vermin and offal, on the theory that if a potion could be made loathsome enough it would drive out the disease. The patients, or victims, of this therapy rightly accounted their recovery a miracle: only the strongest constitutions could survive both the disease and the cure. "The American practicioners are so rash and officious," a doctor observed in 1721, "that the saying in Ecclesiasticus may with much propriety be applied to them: 'He that sinneth before his Maker let him fall into the hands of the physician.'" Thomas Jefferson said that whenever he saw three physicians gathered together he always looked aloft for a buzzard. Some colonial publicists made the scarcity of doctors a positive merit: it was said of New York, for example, that there were so few physicians and apothecaries "that People live to a very great Age."*

*Few colonial physicians could boast a medical degree, the majority having received their training as apprentices to an established doctor. There were no medical schools, no licensing authority for physicians, no hospitals and few medical libraries. Surgeons were classed with barbers and had no high social or professional standing.*

*Medicine was Cotton Mather's second love. Under the conviction that there was an "angelic conjunction" between the practice of medicine and the study of divinity, he gladly prescribed for the bodies as well as the souls of his parishioners. He wrote, but did not publish,* The Angel of Bethesda, *the first general study of medicine written in the English colonies.*

*In 1716, having read in the* Transactions *of the Royal Society that*

*The Diary of Cotton Mather.* Edited by Worthington C. Ford.

*inoculation for smallpox had long been practiced successfully by the Turks, Mather made inquiries among the Negro slaves of Boston who, he discovered, were acquainted with the technique. When a smallpox epidemic struck Boston in 1721, he urged the Boston physicians to experiment with this new method. But Dr. William Douglass, a sincere but dogmatic man who spoke with the authority of a medical degree from the University of Edinburgh, declared that inoculation would merely spread the infection. In this opinion most of the Boston medical fraternity concurred. Only one doctor, Zabdiel Boylston, was willing to give inoculation a trial, and he was prepared to go even to the length of experimenting upon his own children. Although he stood alone among the Boston physicians, Dr. Boylston was supported by the leading clergymen, including Cotton Mather. In this instance, it was the theologians who took the lead in promoting scientific advance; the physicians were the resolute defenders of tradition.*

*As a result of Mather's and Boylston's courage and steadfastness, Boston became the scene of the first community effort in the Western world to halt the ravages of disease by immunization. In 1723, Cotton Mather was elected to the Royal Society, an honor that had been first proposed ten years before. In 1724, Dr. Boylston, having inoculated more people than any other doctor in Great Britain and the colonies went to England to lecture before the Royal College of Physicians and Surgeons. Five years later, he published* An Historical Account of the Small Pox Inoculated in New England—*the first clinical report of its kind written by an American physician.*

*May, 1721*

26. The grievous Calamity of the *Small-Pox* has now entered the Town. The Practice of conveying and suffering the *Small-pox* by *Inoculation*, has never been used in *America*, nor indeed in our Nation, But how many Lives might be saved by it, if it were practised? I will procure a Consult of our Physicians, and lay the matter before them.

27. A poor Man in Prison for Debt; some Care must be taken of him.

28. The Entrance of the *Small-pox* into the Town must awaken in me several Tempers and Actions of *Piety* relating to myself, besides a Variety of Duty to the People.

First: The glorious Lord having employ'd me a few Months ago, under an Afflatus from Heaven, to entertain the City with a Lecture on *Trouble near*, and foretel the speedy Approach of the destroying Angel: It becomes me to humble myself exceedingly, and ly in the Dust. Lest the least Vanity of mine upon seeing my poor praediction accomplished, should provoke the holy One to do some grievous Thing unto me.

Secondly: I have two Children that are liable to the Distemper; and I am at a Loss about their flying and keeping out of the Town. As I must

cry to Heaven for Direction about it, so I am on this Occasion called unto
Sacrifices; that if these dear Children must lose their Lives, the will of
my Father may be duely submitted to.

Thirdly: my own Life is likely to be extremely in danger, by the horrid
Venom of the sick Chambers, which I must look to be call'd unto; and I
would accordingly Redeem the Time to do what my hand finds to do.

30. My two Children, that have their Terrors of the Contagion breaking
in upon us; I must lay hold on the Occasion to quicken their effectual
Flights unto their SAVIOUR.

*June, 1721*

6. My *African* Servant, stands a Candidate for Baptism, and is afraid
how the Small-pox, if it spread, may handle him. I must on this Occasion
use very much Application to bring him into a thorough Christianity.

7. I have a Kinswoman at this time sick of the Small-pox; but not without hopes of Recovery. As I must now be concerned for her, so when she
is able to receive it, I must present unto her my Book of, *A perfect
Recovery.*

8. Having procured the Lecture of this Day, to be turned into a *Day
of Prayer*, because of the Calamity impending over the Town, I have an
Opportunity of speaking many things in a Sermon this day, for the Good
of the Inhabitants, and for the Advancement of that PIETY, to which the
Judgments of GOD should awaken them.

13. What shall I do? what shall I do, with regard unto *Sammy?* He
comes home, when the Small-pox begins to spread in the Neighbourhood;
and he is lothe to return unto *Cambridge.* I must earnestly look up to
Heaven for Direction.

The State of him, and of *Lizy*, who is in greater Fears than he, I must
improve with all the Contrivance I can, to make [it] subservient unto the
Interests of Piety in them.

15. The Eruption of a new *Volcano*, producing an Island in the Sea,
near *Tercera*, is a just Alarum to a secure and sleepy World. It affords
Occasion for some Thoughts which may be of use more Ways than one,
if the Minds of sensible People may be entertained with them.

22. I prepare a little Treatise on the *Small-Pox;* first awakening the
Sentiments of *Piety*, which it calls for; and then exhibiting the best
Medicines and Methods, which the world has yett had for the managing
of it; and finally, adding the new Discovery, to prevent it in the way of
Inoculation. It is possible, that this Essay may save the *Lives*, yea, and the
*Souls* of many People. Shall I give it unto the Booksellers? I am waiting
for Direction.

23. I write a Letter unto the Physicians, entreating them, to take into
consideration the important Affair of preventing the *Small-Pox*, in the
way of Inoculation.

*24.* Miserables neglected and perishing in Sickness; I must concern myself, to have them look'd after.

*27.* Lett me take Advantage from the Fear, which Distresses *Liza,* to quicken her Flights unto her SAVIOUR. And lett me give her, the little Book, which relates the Death of a young French Lady.

*July, 1721*

*10.* The various Distresses come upon the Flock, in the grievous Disease now beginning to distress the Town, must be suitably considered by me; my Prayers and Sermons must be adapted unto their Condition.

*11.* For *Sammy,* and *Liza,* Oh! what shall I do? A continual Dropping of Instructions and Awakenings.

*13.* The Supplications to be made this Day, the Testimonies to be born this Day:

Tis a Day of Humiliation thro' the Province, on the Occasion of the Calamity now upon miserable *Boston.*

*16.* At this Time, I enjoy an unspeakable Consolation. I have instructed our Physicians in the new Method used by the *Africans* and *Asiaticks,* to prevent and abate the Dangers of the *Small-Pox,* and infallibly to save the Lives of those that have it wisely managed upon them. The Destroyer, being enraged at the Proposal of any Thing, that may rescue the Lives of our poor People from him, has taken a strange Possession of the People on this Occasion. They rave, they rail, they blaspheme; they talk not only like Ideots but also like *Franticks,* And not only the Physician who began the Experiment, but I also am an Object of their Fury; their furious Obloquies and Invectives.

My Conformity to my SAVIOUR in this Thing, fills me with Joy unspeakable and full of Glory.

*17.* What shall I do for that Part of the Flock, that are fled into other Towns, to escape the Dangers of the *Small-Pox.*

Accommodate them with Books of Piety.

And unto a Number of them in the Neighbour-Town, go and preach a Lecture.

*18.* The cursed Clamour of a People strangely and fiercely possessed of the Devil, will probably prevent my saving the Lives of my two Children, from the Small-pox in the Way of Transplantation. So that I have no way left, but that of my continual and importunate Cries to Heaven for their Preservation. Accompanied with Admonitions unto them to make their own.

*21.* There being several Societies of young People, meeting for the Exercises of Religion on the Lords-day-Evenings, and they generally lying obnoxious to the Danger of the Small-Pox, I would as far as I can find Strength for it, visit them, and entertain them with Prayers and Sermons that shall be suitable for them.

This Day, I sett apart, for Supplications to the glorious Lord, especially on the behalf of my two Children, that are exposed unto the Dangers of the Small-Pox, and that I may obtain Blessings for all my Children. I also implore the Compassion of Heaven to a Town already under dreadful Judgments, but ripening for more.

And that GOD would requite me Good for all the Cursing of a People that have Satan filling of them; and yett appear to rescue and increase my Opportunities to do good, which the great Adversary is now making an hellish Assault upon.

22. Some of Neighbours are in very particular Circumstances obliging me to visit them and comfort them.

23. I have my Meditations very strongly employed on that Question:

*If I were fastened unto a* CROSS, *and under all the Circumstances of a Crucifixion, what would be my Dispositions; what my Exercises?*

My Answer to it, is written down on a separate Paper.

But I find myself so entirely brought unto such Dispositions, and such Exercises: that I have abundant Evidence that I am *crucified with* CHRIST. And now, Oh, the glorious Consequences!

24. A young Man in the Flock has made a very hopeful and joyful End, and has gloriously triumphed over Death! To animate Piety, especially among the young People in the Flock, especially now the Fire of GOD is consuming them; I preach a Sermon on this Occasion.

27. The monstrous and crying Wickedness of this Town (a Town at this time strangely possessed with the Devil), and the vile Abuse which I do myself particularly suffer from it, for nothing but my instructing our base Physicians, how to save many precious Lives; these things oblige me, in the Fear of the divine Judgments, to fall down before the Lord, with most earnest Supplications, for His Pitty and Pardon to a People so obnoxious to His Displeasure.

30. What should be my Conduct under the Outrages and Obloquies of a Town which Satan has taken a most wonderful Possession of?

I must exceedingly rejoice in my Conformity, to my admirable SAVIOUR: who was thus, and worse requited, when He saved their Lives, and came to save their Souls.

I must mightily take heed unto my own Spirit, and watch against all Ebullitions of Wrath, lest being provoked, I speak unadvisedly with my Lips.

I must give myself unto Prayer, and wait with Patience, in a full Persuasion, that my glorious Lord, will restrain and govern the Satanic Fury that is now raging; and that He will anon give me to see my Opportunities to do good strangely multiplied.

31. I must yett more particularly give to our People, a Sermon that shall most plainly and fully Instruct them, how to gett into such Terms

with Heaven, that they may be Ready, for whatever Events the Contagion that spreads in the Town may bring upon them.

*August, 1721*

*1.* Full of Distress about *Sammy;* He begs to have his Life saved, by receiving the *Small-Pox,* in the way of *Inoculation,* whereof our Neighbourhood has had no less than ten remarkable Experiments; and if he should after all dy by receiving it in the common Way, how can I answer it? On the other Side, our People, who have Satan remarkably filling their Hearts and their Tongues, will go on with infinite Prejudices against me and my Ministry, if I suffer this Operation upon the Child; and be sure, if he should happen to miscarry under it, my Condition would be insupportable.

His Grandfather advises that I keep the whole Proceeding private, and that I bring the Lad into this Method of Safety.

My GOD, I know not what to do, but my Eyes are unto Thee!

*4.* I will allow the persecuted Physician, to publish my Communications from the *Levant,* about the *Small-Pox,* and supply him with some further Armour, to conquer the Dragon.

I sett apart this Day also, as I have several Praeceeding *Friday's,* for secret Supplications; on the same Occasions, and with the same Exercises, that I have the former.

Especially, to cry unto Heaven for the Lives of my Children.

And, to cast indeed all my Burdens on the Lord.

I am sure, that I have obtained the Conduct of a good ANGEL from my GOD and SAVIOUR.

But Oh! how comprehensive a Blessing am I therein made Partaker of!

*5.* The Condition of my pious Barber, and his Family, calls for my particular Consideration.

*6.* It is the Hour and Power of Darkness on this miserable Town; and I need an uncommon Assistance from Above, that I may not miscarry by any forward or angry Impatience, or fall into any of the common Iniquities, of Lying, and Railing and Malice: or be weary of well-doing and of overcoming Evil with Good.

*7.* My clear Ideas of a *crucified Christian,* I would communicate unto the Flock, and inculcate upon them, with all Faithfulness imaginable.

*8.* What further shall I do, for my *Samuel* (Not mine, but thine, O Lord! For I offer Him up unto thee!) That he may be prepared for what is every day to be looked for!

I will much employ him in preparing of Sermons.

*9.* Some Kinsmen in continual Fears of being seized by the *Small-pox;* I lay hold on the Opportunity to press the Lessons of Piety upon them.

*10.* I rejoice in taking Opportunities to preach Lectures at the neighbouring Towns; and carry to them the Glories and Maxims of an admirable SAVIOUR.

*11.* Instigate a Neighbour-Minister to take proper Methods, for the Saving of his Life, now in extreme Danger by the Contagion spreading among us.

*12.* A poor godly Widow, has lost her only Son, by a sudden and awful Death.

*13.* I propose a particular Advantage unto Piety in me, by reading a Book newly published, on *the Employments and Services of the Blessed Spirits in Heaven.*

And prosecuting that Subject, with yett more penetrating Meditations.

*14.* And may I not be serviceable to the Flock by entertaining them, with what of this kind may be proper for them?

*15.* My dear *Sammy,* is now under the Operation of receiving the *Small-Pox* in the way of *Transplantation.* The Success of the Experiment among my Neighbours, as well as abroad in the World, and the urgent Calls of his Grandfather for it, have made me think, that I could not answer it unto God, if I neglected it. At this critical Time, how much is all Piety to be press'd upon the Child!

And it may be hoped, with the more of Efficacy, because his dearest Companion (and his Chamber-fellow at the Colledge,) dies this Day, of the Small-pox taken in the common Way.

*16.* I know not why I should not press diverse of my distressed Kinsmen, to come under the same Experiment.

*17.* The Notable Experience I now have of this New Method, for the Saving of many Lives, yea, and for the Abating and preventing of Miseries undergone by many who do live, and survive an horrible Distemper, enables me to recommend the matter so, that I hope it may be introduced into the English Nation, and a World of good may be done to the miserable Children of Men. I take the Matter into Consideration.

*18.* I may propose some agreeable Passages, to be inserted in the *News-Letters,* which may have a Notable Tendency to correct and restrain the Epidemical Follies of the Town.

*19.* Some greatly bereaved Parents must be visited and comforted.

*20.* My Soul makes a glorious Improvement in the prosecution of the Foelicity, which my SAVIOUR has in those Terms propos'd unto me, *You in me, and I in you.*

*22.* My dear *Sammy,* having received the *Small-pox* in the Way of *Inoculation,* is now under the Fever necessary to produce the Eruption. But I have Reason to fear, that he had also taken the Infection in the common Way; and he had likewise but one Insition, and one so small as to be hardly worthy of the Name of one, made upon him. If he should miscarry, besides the Loss of so hopeful a Son, I should also suffer a prodigious Clamour and Hatred from an infuriated Mob, whom the Devil has inspired with a most hellish Rage, on this Occasion. My continual Prayers and Cries, and Offerings to Heaven, must be accompanied with suitable Instructions to the Child, while our Distresses are upon us.

My little Kinsman, recovering from the Small-Pox, I will direct him, that He draw up and write down, the Returns to the Lord his Healer, which are now to be endeavored by him.

*24.* The Town is become almost an Hell upon Earth, a City full of Lies, and Murders, and Blasphemies, as far as Wishes and Speeches can render it so; Satan seems to take a strange Possession of it, in the epidemic Rage, against that notable and powerful and successful way of saving the Lives of People from the Dangers of the *Small-Pox.*

What can I do on this Occasion, to gett the miserable Town dispossessed of the evil Spirit, which has taken such an horrible Possession of it? What besides Prayer with Fasting, for it?

*25.* I will assist my Physician, in giving to the Public, some Accounts about releeving the *Small-Pox* in the way of Transplantation; which may be of great Consequence!

*25 d. vi m.* Friday. It is a very critical Time with me, a Time of unspeakable Trouble and Anguish. My dear *Sammy,* has this Week had a dangerous and threatening Fever come upon him, which is beyond what the *Inoculation* for the *Small-Pox* has hitherto brought upon any Subjects of it. In this Distress, I have cried unto the Lord; and He has answered with a Measure of Restraint upon the Fever. The Eruption proceeds, and he proves pretty full, and has not the best sort, and some Degree of his Fever holds him. His Condition is very hazardous.

I sett apart this Day, for Supplications to my glorious Lord, on this distressing Occasion. I was enabled by him to make a Sacrifice of my Son, unto Him. I submitted and consented unto it, that if He would please to kill the Lad, even in such aggravating Circumstances of Sorrow, as his Death must now be attended with, I would humbly acquiesce in His most sovereign, just and wise Dispensations. A CHRIST being left unto me, I would entirely take my whole satisfaction in Him alone, and count myself Happy enough, while I have Him to comfort me. But yett, I beg'd for the Life of the Child, that he may live to serve the Kingdome of GOD, and that the Cup which I fear may pass from me.

I have other Children also at this Time sick and weak and languishing, and in much Affliction. My SAVIOUR seems to multiply very many and heavy Loads at once upon me. Oh! may He help me to carry it well under them! Oh! may my Carriage yeeld Him a grateful Spectacle!

What can I do, but cast my Burden on the Lord!

*26.* Several poor People, sick of the common Distemper, call for my Releefs, more Ways than one unto them.

*27.* My blessed SAVIOUR, the Healer of my Soul, has at length brought me to a Blessedness, which nothing in this World, nor all the good Things of a thousand such Worlds, may be compared unto. It was not enough that I should come unto this; I am willing to be stript of all my worldly Enjoyments, and have neither Wealth, nor Health, nor Name, nor Friend left unto me, and find in a glorious CHRIST alone, all the satisfactions which People vainly promise themselves in Creatures.

But I must also come unto this; My dear, dear SAVIOUR, thou hast brought me to it! I am content, That I see no Reward of PIETY in the whole Time of my Pilgrimage upon Earth; and that none of my Prayers have such Answers here given to them, as I could have wished for. I am satisfied, in what I am sure, shall after Death be done for me, by a SAVIOUR, who, I am sure is Himself risen from the Dead. I can cheerfully take up, with what shall in a future State be done for me, by a SAVIOUR, whom I can with a strong Faith rely upon, and give Glory to God.

28. This miserable Town, is a dismal Picture and Emblem of *Hell; Fire* with *Darkness* filling of it, and a *lying Spirit* reigning there; many members of our Churches, have had a fearful Share in the false Reports, and blasphemous Speeches, and murderous Wishes in which the Town is become very guilty before the Lord. Calling upon the Flock to prepare for the Table of the Lord, I warn them to repent of whatever may have been in them offensive unto GOD, and come with suitable Dispositions of Love to GOD and CHRIST and their Neighbour, lest they provoke Him to be terrible in His holy Places.

29. The Condition of my Son *Samuel* is very singular. The Inoculation was very imperfectly performed, and scarce any more than attempted upon him; And yett for ought I know, it might be so much as to prove a Benefit unto him. He is however, endanger'd, by the ungoverned Fever that attends him. And in this Distress, I know not what to do; but, O Lord, my Eyes are unto thee!

30. That which adds to my Distress, is, that my Son-in-Law, D. W[illard] is not only languishing under an unknown Fever, but also grown delirious with it.

My Daughter *Abigail*, within a few Weeks of her Time, is very hazardously circumstanced with several Infirmities.

My Daughter *Hannah*, has a violent Feavour upon her, which extremely threatens her Life.

*September, 1721*

1. And in my Essays to live upon a CHRIST, He does quicken me and assist me wonderfully!

2. I need not now be at a Loss for particular objects of Compassion. They multiply wonderfully; they became innumerable.

3. A vast Collection of heavy Loads comes at once upon me: Some that I do not mention in these Papers, are added unto them. Full of Resignation to, and Satisfaction in, my SAVIOUR under all I am verily

perswaded, that I shall anon find the GOD of Patience, to be the GOD of Consolation.

Dear Nancy dying!

The Physicians give her over, and pronounce it, that she has not many Hours to live. I do myself also resign her; and visit her with many Prayers, in a Day for that purpose.

But I know not what well to make of it; in the midst of all my Darkness, a strange Light breaks in upon my Mind with a Perswasion, that I shall see that Word fulfilled upon the Child, *I was brought low, and He helped me.* The Child herself also returning for a few Minutes to her Sense and her Speech, told me, she had yett some Hope to see that Word fulfill'd unto her.

4. The Flock must hear me take a very solemn and bitter Notice of it, that tho the Arrows of Death are flying among us, and our young People are afraid of their Lives, yett we are not sensible that any notable Effects of Piety are produced among them. Instead thereof, there is a Rage of Wickedness among us, beyond what was ever known from the Beginning to this Day.

Dear *Nancy*, still a dying: and given over, condemned by the Physicians, to dy within a very few Hours.

5. *Sammy* recovering Strength, I must now earnestly putt him on considering, what he shall render to the Lord! Use exquisite Methods that he may come Gold out of the Fire.

*Nibby* still dangerously circumstanced.

And *Nancy* still a dying.

6. The Condition of my Sister *Maria's* Family (full of affliction) calls for my great Concern about it.

*Nancy* still a dying.

7. In the Circumstances of my dying Children, I am called unto repeated Sacrifices; I must go thro' the Duty of a Sacrificer. But shall I not exhibit unto the People of GOD, the Conduct of a Sacrificer, in such a Manner, that my Trials may be made useful to my Neighbours?

I do it this Day in the Lecture.

8. I make a Motion among the Ministers to serve the Design of Piety in the sick Families of the City.

To our Surprize, this Day, dear *Nancy* revives, and her Feaver breaks, and gives us Hopes that she may yett return unto us.

9. Still I don't want Objects for Compassion in my Neighborhood. They grow exceedingly.

10. That Word of our SAVIOUR, *If the World hate you, yee know that it hated me before it hated you;* my Soul exceedingly feeds and lives upon it. I consider the Maxims and Actions, of my SAVIOUR, which exposed Him to the Hatred of the World: I will entirely conform unto them: and if the World thereupon treat me with all the Aversion imaginable, it shall be

welcome to me, I will rejoice in it. The Joy sett before me in my SAVIOUR and in a Better World, gives me all the Satisfaction that can be wished for.

*11.* Entertain the Flock, with Meditations on the *lothsome Disease* upon us, in regard of our Sin: whereof we have a lively Emblem in the Distemper that is now raging among us.

*12.* What shall I do, that *Sammy* in his new Life may live unto God?

What shall I do, for my two feeble Daughters?

*13.* I have two kinsmen recovering of the *Small-Pox.* What shall I do, to produce in them, the grateful Improvements of serious Piety?

*15.* A Minister of the New North, having his Consort, by Death taken from him, it gives me an Opportunity, to serve him, and preach for him, and thereby to introduce a more peaceable Condition of Things in our Churches.

*16.* Alas, my Afflictions multiply upon me. I cannot number them.

I will propose one comprehensive Service for them. In moving the Selectmen to look for a seasonable Supply of Wood, for the Town; that the Poor may not suffer for want of a convenient Fuel, in the approaching Winter.

*17.* Instead of any Regrett at the Things which for the present are not joyous but grievous, I will intermix with the darkest and saddest of them, a marvelous Joy upon my Encounter with such Things, as carry on my Crucifixion to This World, and my Conformity to my crucified SAVIOUR, and the Condition of one dying on a *Cross:* because of the Joy sett before me, and the View therein given me, of my Partaking with my SAVIOUR in the heavenly Glories which He has in the future State reserved for His Followers.

*18.* How pathetically may my public Prayers represent the various Condition of the Flock in this Time of Trouble before the Lord. Lett me study and contrive to do it in the Manner that shall be most edifying for them.

*October, 1721*

*23.* The Wounds given to my Flock, in the Deaths which the Small-Pox has multiplied among us, must have a great Improvement made of them for the awakening of Piety in the Survivours.

*25.* My kinsman at *Roxbury,* I will send for him, to lodge at my House, that he may there have the *Small-Pox* in the way of *Inoculation* upon him.

*26.* Shall I not endeavour to shew our People, after what manner the Praises of the glorious GOD and His Christ, are to be copiously and affectuously celebrated? I do it this Day; which is a Day of general Thanksgiving throughout the Province.

This Day, towards the Evening, a Fever seizes me; brought on me by Colds taken in my Night-Visits, and by the Poisons of infected Chambers.

Is my Hour come? Tis welcome.

27. I have a View of speedily conquering the Fever with which I am threatened; and not suffering above three or four days Idleness and Confinement by it.

29. I am still sensible that in my Remarks on the Folly and Baseness continually expressed by our absurd and wicked People, I do not always preserve that Meekness and Wisdome, which would adorn the Doctrine of GOD my SAVIOUR. I use too bitter Terms. I will ask Wisdome of GOD for the Cure of this Distemper.

*November, 1721*

2. In the Lecture this Day, I may edify a few People of this miserable and detestable Town, with a Discourse on a lothsome Disease.

3. This abominable Town, treats me in a most malicious, and murderous Manner, for my doing as CHRIST would have me to do, in saving the Lives of the People from an horrible Death; but I will go on, in the Imitation of my admirable SAVIOUR, and overcome Evil with Good. I will address a Letter to the Lieut. Governour and other Gentlemen of New *Hampshire,* to obtain from their Charity, a considerable Quantity of Wood, for the poor of this lothsome Town, under the Necessities of the hard Winter coming on.

9. The sottish Errors, and cursed Clamours, that fill the Town and Countrey, raging against the astonishig Success of the *Small-Pox* Inoculated; makes it seasonable for me, to state the Case, and exhibit that which may silence the unreasonable People.

13. Continual Charges unto the young People of the Flock, recovered from the Small-Pox, as they come in my Way, which they do continually, to live unto GOD, and by His Goodness be led into Repentance; This will be one Article of my Conduct.

14. What an Occasion, what an Incentive, to have PIETY, more than ever quicken'd and shining in my Family, have I this morning been entertained withal!

My Kinsman, the Minister of *Roxbury,* being Entertained at my House, that he might there undergo the *Small-Pox Inoculated,* and so Return to the Service of his Flock, which have the Contagion begun among them;

Towards three a Clock in the Night, as it grew towards Morning of this Day, some unknown Hands, threw a fired Granado into the Chamber where my Kinsman lay, and which used to be my Lodging-Room. The Weight of the Iron Ball alone, had it fallen upon his Head, would have been enough to have done Part of the Business designed. But the *Granado* was charged, the upper part with dried Powder, the lower Part with a Mixture of Oil of Turpentine and Powder and what else I know not, in such a Manner, that upon its going off, it must have splitt, and have probably killed the Persons in the Room, and certainly fired the Chamber, and speedily laid the House in Ashes. But, *this Night there stood by me the Angel of the* GOD, *whose I am and whom I serve;* and the merciful Providence of GOD my SAVIOUR, so ordered it that the Granado passing thro' the Window, had by the Iron in the Middle of the Casement, such a Turn given to it, that in falling on the Floor, the fired Wild-fire in the Fuse was violently shaken out upon the Floor, without firing the Granado. When the *Granado* was taken up, there was found a Paper so tied with String about the Fuse, that it might out-Live the breaking of the Shell, which had these words in it; COTTON MATHER, *You Dog, Dam you: I'l inoculate you with this, with a Pox to you.*

*16.* Ought not the Ministers of the Town, to be called together that we may consider, what may be our Duty and most proper to be done upon the Occasion of Satan so strangely lett loose to possess the Town?

*19.* Certainly it becomes me and concerns me, to do something very considerable, in a way of Gratitude unto GOD my SAVIOUR, for the astonishing Deliverance, which He did the last Week bestow upon me, and upon what belong'd unto me.

Among other Things, I entertain the People of GOD, with a Discourse on the Services done by the good *Angels,* for the Servants of GOD. So will I bespeak more Praises to GOD my SAVIOUR for the Benefits of the angelical Ministry: which alas are not enough tho't upon.

But, behold, what my glorious Lord has brought me to.

I have been guilty of such a Crime as this. I have communicated a never-failing and most allowable Method, of preventing Death and other grievous Miseries by a terrible Distemper among my Neighbours. Every day demonstrates, that if I had been hearken'd to, many precious Lives (many Hundreds) had been saved. The Opposition to it, has been carried on, with senseless Ignorance and raging Wickedness. But the growing Triumphs of Truth over it, throw a possessed People into a Fury, which will probably cost me my Life. I have Proofs, that there are people who approve and applaud the Action of *Tuesday* Morning: and who give out Words, that tho' the first Blow miscarried, there will quickly come another, that shall doe the Business more effectually.

Now, I am so far from any melancholy Fear on this Occasion, that I am filled with unutterable Joy at the Prospect of my approaching Martyrdom. I know not what is the Meaning of it; I find, my Mouth strangely stop'd, my Heart strangely cold, if I go to ask for a Deliverance from it. But, when I think on my suffering Death for saving the Lives of dying People, it even ravishes me with a Joy unspeakable and full of Glory. I cannot help longing for the Hour, when it will be accomplished. I am even afraid almost of doing any thing for my praeservation. I have a Crown before me; and I now know by Feeling, what I formerly knew only by Reading, of the divine Consolations with which the Minds of Martyrs have been sometimes irradiated. I had much rather dy by such Hands, as now threaten my Life, than by a Feaver; and much rather dy for my Conformity to the blessed JESUS in Essays to save the Lives of Men from the Destroyer, than for some Truths, tho' precious ones, to which many Martyrs testified formerly in the Flames of *Smithfield.*

21. I must assign unto *Samuel,* such Subjects to form Discourses on, as his late Circumstances may more particularly lead unto.

22. I have some Kinsmen, (and others as dear to me) whom I will encourage to save their Lives, in the way of the *Small-Pox Inoculated.*

23. I join with my aged Father, in publishing some, SENTIMENTS ON THE SMALL-POX INOCULATED. CHRIST crowns the Cause for which I have suffered so much, with daily Victories. And Abundance of Lives may be saved by our Testimony. Truth also will be rescued and maintained.

24. I draw up the Method of Proceeding in the Inoculation of the *Small-Pox,* and communicate Copies of it, that so Physicians about the Countrey may know how to manage it.

But this Day, I likewise made an offer of my Life unto the glorious Lord. Being in daily Hazard of Death from a bloody People from no other Cause pretended but this: that I have saved the Lives of dying People, in a way by a gracious GOD revealed unto us; I declared unto my GOD and SAVIOUR, that I am unspeakably willing to dy by their Hands, and that I cannot think of my Martyrdome for Him, without unutterable Joy. I feel my Spirit not only longing for the Accomplishment of it, but even strained until it be accomplished.

29. Several Persons at this Time under the *Small-Pox Inoculated,* I must look on as my Patients, and so, my Relatives. I will do the best I can, that they may Resolve on some special Returns of Gratitude, wherein GOD their SAVIOUR may be glorified.

*December, 1721*

1. Having drawn up, the Way of Proceeding, in the *Inoculation* of the *Small-pox,* I communicate Copies of it unto the Physicians and others, in several Parts of the Countrey; that so they may be directed in the Practice of it, as there may be Occasion for it.

14. The *Small-Pox* making terrible Destruction in several Parts of *Europe,* I would hasten unto *Holland,* an account of the astonishing Success, which we have here seen of the *Small-Pox inoculated.* Who can tell, but Hundreds of Thousands of Lives, may be saved by this Communication.

# Courtship

## *Samuel Sewall*

*By 1722, when Sewall began his courtship of Madam Winthrop, he had
lost by death two wives (his first wife, Hannah Hull Sewall, had died in
1717), ten of his fourteen children and ten of his grandchildren. Nevertheless, he was still eager and fresh for marriage, but Madam Winthrop,
having been twice married, was less inclined to give matrimony a third
try. Despite his fervent prayers to Heaven for guidance, Sewall's lovelife
was not blessed. The courtship collapsed when Sewall tried to drive too
hard a bargain in the marriage settlement. Finding Madam Winthrop
obdurate, Sewall married a widow, Mary Gibbs, who outlived him.
Madam Winthrop died in 1725. One of the pallbearers was her recent
suitor—Samuel Sewall.*

*September 5* [1720]. Mary Hirst goes to board with Madam Oliver and
her mother Loyd. Going to son Sewall's, I there meet with Madam Winthrop; told her I was glad to meet her there, had not seen her a great
while; gave her Mr. Homes's sermon. . . .

*September 30.* Mr. Colman's lecture. Daughter Sewall acquaints Madam
Winthrop that if she pleased to be within at 3 P.M. I would wait on her.
She answered she would be at home.

*October 1.* Saturday, I dine at Mr. Stoddard's; from thence I went to
Madam Winthrop's just at 3. Spake to her, saying my loving wife died so
soon and suddenly 'twas hardly convenient for me to think of marrying
again. However, I came to this resolution, that I would not make my
court to any person without first consulting with her. Had a pleasant discourse about 7 single persons sitting in the fore-seat September 29th, viz.,
Madam Rebekah Dudley, Catharine Winthrop, Bridget Usher, Deliverance Legg, Rebekah Loyd, Lydia Colman, Elizabeth Bellingham. She
propounded one and another for me; but none would do; said Mrs. Loyd
was about her age.

*October 3. 2.* Waited on Madam Winthrop again; 'twas a little while
before she came in. Her daughter Noyes being there alone with me, I said

*Diary of Samuel Sewall, 1674–1729.*

I hoped my waiting on her mother would not be disagreeable to her. She answered she should not be against that that might be for her comfort. I saluted her and told her I perceived I must shortly wish her a good time (her mother had told me she was with child and within a month or two of her time). By and by in came Mr. Airs, chaplain of the Castle, and hanged up his hat, which I was a little startled at, it seeming as if he was to lodge there. At last Madam Winthrop came too. After a considerable time, I went up to her and said if it might not be inconvenient I desired to speak with her. She assented and spoke of going into another room; but Mr. Airs and Mrs. Noyes presently rose up and went out, leaving us there alone. Then I ushered in discourse from the names in the fore-seat; at last I prayed that Katharine [Mrs. Winthrop] might be the person assigned for me. She instantly took it up in the way of denial, as if she had catched at an opportunity to do it, saying she could not do it before she was asked. Said that was her mind unless she should change it, which she believed she should not; could not leave her children. I expressed my sorrow that she should do it so speedily, prayed her consideration, and asked her when I should wait on her again. She setting no time, I mentioned that day sennight. Gave her Mr. Willard's *Fountain* opened with the little print and verses, saying I hoped if we did well read that book we should meet together hereafter if we did not now. She took the book and put it in her pocket. Took leave.

*October 5.* Midweek, I dined with the court; from thence went and visited cousin Jonathan's wife, lying in with her little Betty. Gave the nurse 2 s. Although I had appointed to wait upon her, Madam Winthrop, next Monday, yet I went from my cousin Sewall's thither about 3 P.M. The nurse told me Madam dined abroad at her daughter Noyes's; they were to go out together. I asked for the maid, who was not within. Gave Katee a penny and a kiss and came away. Accompanied my son and daughter Cooper in their remove to their new house. Went to tell Joseph, and Mr. Belcher saw me by the South Meetinghouse though 'twas duskish, and said I had been at house warming (he had been at our house). Invited me to drink a glass of wine at his house at 7 and eat part of the pastry provided for the commissioner's voyage to Casco Bay. His Excellency, Madam Belcher, S.S. Col. Fitch, Mr. D. Oliver, Mr. Anthony Stoddard, Mr. Welsteed, Mr. White, Mr. Belcher sat down. At coming home gave us of the cake and gingerbread to carry away. 'Twas about ten before we got home. Mr. Oliver and I waited on the Governor at his gate, and then Mr. Oliver would wait on me home.

*October 6th.* Lecture day, Mr. Cutler, President of the Connecticut College, preached in Dr. C. Mather's turn. He made an excellent discourse from Heb. 11.14: For they that say such things declare plainly that they seek a country. Brother Odlin, son Sewall of Brooklin[e], and Mary Hirst dine with me. I asked Mary of Madana Lord, Mr. Oliver and wife,

and bid her present my service to them. October 6th a little after 6 P.M.
I went to Madam Winthrop's. She was not within. I gave Sarah Chickering, the maid, 2 s.; Juno, who brought in wood, 1 s. Afterward the nurse
came in, I gave her 18 d., having no other small bill. After awhile Dr.
Noyes came in with his mother, and quickly after his wife came in. They
sat talking, I think, till eight o'clock. I said I feared I might be some
interruption to their business. Dr. Noyes replied pleasantly he feared they
might be an interruption to me and went away. Madam seemed to harp
upon the same string: must take care of her children; could not leave that
house and neighborhood where she had dwelt so long. I told her she
might do her children as much or more good by bestowing what she laid
out in housekeeping upon them. Said her son would be of age the 7th of
August. I said it might be inconvenient for her to dwell with her daughter-
in-law, who must be mistress of the house. I gave her a piece of Mr.
Belcher's cake and gingerbread wrapped up in a clean sheet of paper.
Told her of her father's kindness to me when treasurer and I constable.
My daughter Judith was gone from me, and I was more lonesome—might
help to forward one another in our journey to Canaan. Mr. Eyre came
within the door; I saluted him, asked how Mr. Clark did, and he went
away. I took leave about 9 o'clock. I told [her] I came now to refresh her
memory as to Monday night; said she had not forgot it. In discourse with
her, I asked leave to speak with her sister; I meant to gain Madam Mico's
favor to persuade her sister. She seemed surprised and displeased, and
said she was in the same condition! . . .

*October 10th.* Examin[ed] Mr. Briggs, his account; said they could not
find Mr. Whittemore. Mr. Willard offered to answer for him. But I showed
the necessity of his being here, and appointed Wednesday 10 o'clock, and
ordered notice to be given to the auditors to pray their assistance.

In the evening I visited Madam Winthrop, who treated me with a great
deal of courtesy—wine, marmalade. I gave her a news-letter about the
thanksgiving proposals, for sake of the verses for David Jeffries. She tells
me Dr. Increase Mather visited her this day, in Mr. Hutchinson's coach.

It seems Dr. Cotton Mather's chimney fell afire yesterday, so as to
interrupt the assembly A.M. Mr. Cutler ceased preaching one quarter of
an hour.

*October 11th.* I wrote a few lines to Madam Winthrop to this purpose:
"Madam, These wait on you with Mr. Mayhew's sermon and account of
the state of the Indians on Martha's Vineyard. I thank you for your un-
merited favors of yesterday and hope to have the happiness of waiting on
you tomorrow before eight o'clock afternoon. I pray God to keep you and
give you a joyful entrance upon the two hundred and twenty-ninth year
of Christopher Columbus, his discovery; and take leave, who am, Madam,
your humble servant. S. S."

Sent this by Deacon Green, who delivered it to Sarah Chickering, her mistress not being at home.

*October 12.* Give Mr. Whittemore and Willard their oath to Dr. Mather's inventory. Visit Mr. Cooper. Go to the meeting at the widow Emon's. Mr. Manly prayed, I read half Mr. Henry's 12th chapter of the *L.Supper.*Sung 1, 2, 3, 4, 5, 10, and 12th verses of the 30th Psalm. Brother Franklin concluded with prayer. At Madam Winthrop's steps I took leave of Capt. Hill, etc.

Mrs. Anne Cotton came to door ('twas before 8), said Madam Winthrop was within, directed me into the little room where she was full of work behind a stand; Mrs. Cotton came in and stood. Madam Winthrop pointed to her to set me a chair. Madam Winthrop's countenance was much changed from what 'twas on Monday, looked dark and lowering. At last the work (black stuff or silk) was taken away; I got my chair in place, had some converse, but very cold and indifferent to what it was before. Asked her to acquit me of rudeness if I drew off her glove. Inquiring the reason, I told her it was great odds between handling a dead goat and a living lady. Got it off. I told her I had one petition to ask of her; that was that she would take off the negative she laid on me the third of October. She readily answered she could not and enlarged upon it. She told me of it so soon as she could; could not leave her house, children, neighbors, business. I told her she might do some good to help and support me. Mentioning Mrs. Gookin, Nath, the widow Weld was spoken of; said I had visited Mrs. Denison. I told her yes! Afterward I said if after a first and second vagary she would accept of me returning, her victorious kindness and good will would be very obliging. She thanked me for my book (Mr. Mayhew's sermon), but said not a word of the letter. When she insisted on the negative, I prayed there might be no more thunder and lightening, I should not sleep all night. I gave her Dr. Preston, *The Church's Marriage and the Church's Carriage,* which cost me 6 s. at the sale. The door standing open, Mr. Airs came in, hung up his hat, and sat down. After awhile, Madam Winthrop moving, he went out. John Eyre looked in. I said, "How do ye?" or "Your servant, Mr. Eyre," but heard no word from him. Sarah filled a glass of wine; she drank to me, I to her. She sent Juno home with me with a good lantern; I gave her 6 d. and bid her thank her mistress. In some of our discourse I told her I had rather go to the stone house adjoining to her than to come to her against her mind. Told her the reason why I came every other night was lest I should drink too deep draughts of pleasure. She had talked of Canary, her kisses were to me better than the best Canary. Explained the expression concerning Columbus.

*October 13.* I tell my son and daughter Sewall, that the weather was not so fair as I apprehended. Mr. Sewall preached very well in Mr. Wadsworth's turn. Mr. Williams of Weston and Mr. Odlin dine with us. Text was the "Excellency of the Knowledge of Christ." . . .

*October 17.* Monday, give Mr. Dan Willard and Mr. Pelatiah Whittemore their oaths to their accounts, and Mr. John Briggs to his, as they are attorneys to Dr. Cotton Mather, administrator to the estate of Nathan Howell, deceased. In the evening I visited Madam Winthrop, who treated me courteously, but not in clean linen as sometimes. She said she did not know whether I would come again or no. I asked her how she could so impute inconstancy to me: (I had not visited her since Wednesday night, being unable to get over the indisposition received by the treatment received that night; and *I must* in it seemed to sound like a made piece of formality.) Gave her this day's *Gazette.* Heard David Jeffries say the Lord's Prayer and some other portions of the Scriptures. He came to the door and asked me to go into chamber where his grandmother was tending little Katee, to whom she had given physic; but I chose to sit below. Dr. Noyes and his wife came in and sat a considerable time, had been visiting son and daughter Cooper. Juno came home with me.

*October 18.* Visited Madam Mico, who came to me in a splendid dress. I said, it may be you have heard of my visiting Madam Winthrop, her sister. She answered, her sister had told her of it. I asked her good will in the affair. She answered, if her sister were for it, she should not hinder her. I gave her Mr. Homes's sermon. She gave me a glass of Canary, entertained me with good discourse, and a respectful remembrance of my first wife. I took leave.

*October 19.* Midweek, visited Madam Winthrop. Sarah told me she was at Mr. Walley's, would not come home till late. I gave her Hannah 3 oranges with her duty, not knowing whether I should find her or no. Was ready to go home; but said if I knew she was there, I would go thither. Sarah seemed to speak with pretty good courage, she would be there. I went and found her there with Mr. Walley and his wife in the little room below. At 7 o'clock I mentioned going home at 8 I put on my coat and quickly waited on her home. She found occasion to speak loud to the servant, as if she had a mind to be known. Was courteous to me, but took occasion to speak pretty earnestly about my keeping a coach. I said it would cost £100 per annum; she said it would cost but £40. Spake much against John Winthrop, his falseheartedness. Mr. Eyre came in and sat a while. I offered him Dr. Incr. Mather's sermons, whereof Mr. Appleton's ordination sermon was one; said he had them already. I said I would give him another. Exit. Came away somewhat late.

*October 20.* Mr. Colman preaches from Luke 15.10: Joy among the angels. Made an excellent discourse.

At council Col. Townsend spake to me of my hood, should get a wig. I said 'twas my chief ornament, I wore it for the sake of the day. Brother Odlin and Sam, Mary, and Jane Hirst dine with us. Promised to wait on

the Governor about 7. Madam Winthrop not being at lecture, I went
thither first; found her very serene with her daughter Noyes, Mrs. Dering,
and the widow Shipreev sitting at a little table, she in her armed chair.
She drank to me, and I to Mrs. Noyes. After awhile prayed the favor to
speak with her. She took one of the candles and went into the best room,
closed the shutters, sat down upon the couch. She told me Madam Usher
had been there and said the coach must be set on wheels and not by
rusting. She spake something of my needing a wig. Asked me what her
sister said to me. I told her she said if her sister were for it, she would not
hinder it. But I told her she did not say she would be glad to have me for
her brother. Said, I shall keep you in the cold, and asked her if she would
be within tomorrow night, for we had had but a running feat. She said
she could not tell whether she should or no. I took leave. As were drinking
at the Governor's, he said, "In England the ladies minded little more than
that they might have money and coaches to ride in." I said, "And New
England brooks its name." At which Mr. Dudley smiled. Governor said
they were not quite so bad here.

   *October 21.* Friday, my son, the minister, came to me P.M. by appointment, and we pray one for another in the old chamber—more especially
respecting my courtship. About 6 o'clock I go to Madam Winthrop's;
Sarah told me her mistress was gone out, but did not tell me whither she
went. She presently ordered me a fire, so I went in, having Dr. Sibb's
*Bowels* with me to read. I read the two first sermons, still nobody came in.
At last about 9 o'clock Mr. John Eyre came in; I took the opportunity to
say to him, as I had done to Mrs. Noyes before, that I hoped my visiting
his mother would not be disagreeable to him. He answered me with much
respect. When 'twas after 9 o'clock, he of himself said he would go and
call her; she was but at one of his brothers. Awhile after I heard Madam
Winthrop's voice, inquiring something about John. After a good while
and clapping the garden door twice or thrice, she came in. I mentioned
something of the lateness, she bantered me and said I was later. She
received me courteously. I asked when our proceedings should be made
public. She said they were like to be no more public than they were
already. Offered me no wine that I remember. I rose up at 11 o'clock to
come away, saying I would put on my coat. She offered not to help me.
I prayed her that Juno might light me home; she opened the shutter and
said 'twas pretty light abroad; Juno was weary and gone to bed. So I came
home by starlight as well as I could. At my first coming in, I gave Sarah
five shillings. I wrote Mr. Eyre his name in his book with the date October
21, 1720. It cost me 8 s., Jehovah jireh! Madam told me she had visited
M. Mico, Wendell, and Wm. Clark of the South [Church].

   *October 22.* Daughter Cooper visited me before my going out of town,
stayed till about sunset. I brought her going near as far as the orange tree.
Coming back, near Leg's Corner, little David Jeffries saw me, and looking

upon me very lovingly, asked me if I was going to see his grandmother. I said, "Not tonight," gave him a penny, and bid him present my service to his grandmother.

*October 24.* I went in the hackney coach through the Common, stopped at Madam Winthrop's (had told her I would take my departure from thence). Sarah came to the door with Katee in her arms, but I did not think to take notice of the child. Called her mistress. I told her, being encouraged by David Jeffries' loving eyes and sweet words, I was come to inquire whether she could find in her heart to leave that house and neighborhood and go and dwell with me at the south end. I think she said softly, "Not yet." I told her it did not lie in my lands to keep a coach. If I should, I should be in danger to be brought to keep company with her neighbor Brooker (he was a little before sent to prison for debt). Told her I had an antipathy against those who would pretend to give themselves but nothing of their estate. I would a proportion of my estate with myself. And I supposed she would do so. As to a periwig, my best and greatest friend, I could not possibly have a greater, began to find me with hair before I was born and had continued to do so ever since; and I could not find in my heart to go to another. She commended the book I gave her, the *Church Marriage;* quoted him saying 'twas inconvenient keeping out of a fashion commonly used. I said the time and tide did circumscribe my visit. She gave me a dram of black cherry brandy and gave me a lump of the sugar that was in it. She wished me a good journey. I prayed God to keep her, and came away. Had a very pleasant journey to Salem.

*October 25.* Sent a letter of it to my son by Wakefield, who delivered it not till Wednesday; so he visited her not till Friday P.M. and then presented my service to her. . . .

*October 31.2.* . . . At night I visited Madam Winthrop about 6 P.M. They told me she was gone to Madam Mico's. I went thither and found she was gone; so returned to her house, read the Epistles to the Galatians, Ephesians in Mr. Eyre's Latin Bible. After the clock struck 8, I began to read the 103 Psalm. Mr. Wendell came in from his warehouse, asked me if I were alone. Spake very kindly to me, offered me to call Madam Winthrop. I told him she would be angry, had been at Mrs. Mico's. He helped me on with my coat, and I came home. Left the *Gazette* in the Bible, which told Sarah of, bid her present my service to Mrs. Winthrop, and tell her I had been to wait on her if she had been at home.

*November 1.* I was so taken up that I could not go if I would.

*November 2.* Midweek, went again and found Mrs. Alden there, who quickly went out. Gave her about one half pound of sugar almonds, cost 3 s. per pound. Carried them on Monday. She seemed pleased with them, asked what they cost. Spake of giving her a hundred pounds per annum if I died before her. Asked her what sum she would give me, if she should die first. Said I would give her time to consider of it. She said she heard as if I had given all to my children by deeds of gift. I told her 'twas a mistake, Point-Judith was mine, etc. That in England I owned my father's desire was that it should go to my eldest son; 'twas £20 per annum, she thought 'twas forty. I think when I seemed to excuse pressing this, she seemed to think it was best to speak of it; a long winter was coming on. Gave me a glass or two of Canary.

*November 4th.* Friday, went again about 7 o'clock; found there Mr. John Walley and his wife; sat discoursing pleasantly. I showed them Isaac Moses' writing. Madam W. served comfits to us. After awhile a table was spread, and supper was set. I urged Mr. Walley to crave a blessing, but he put it upon me. About 9 they went away. I asked Madam what fashioned necklace I should present her with. She said, "None at all." I asked her whereabout we left off last time; mentioned what I had offered to give her, asked her what she would give me. She said she could not change her condition. She had said so from the beginning, could not be so far from her children, the lecture. Quoted the Apostle Paul, affirming that a single life was better than a married. I answered that was for the present distress. Said she had not pleasure in things of that nature as formerly; I said, "You are the fitter to make me a wife." If she held in that mind, I must go home and bewail my rashness in making more haste than good speed. However, considering the supper, I desired her to be within next Monday night, if we lived so long. Assented. She charged me with saying that she must put away Juno, if she came to me. I utterly denied it; it never came in my heart; yet she insisted upon it, saying it came in upon discourse about the Indian woman that obtained her freedom this court. About 10 I said I would not disturb the good orders of her house, and came away, she not seeming pleased with my coming away. Spake to her about David Jeffries, had not seen him.

*Monday, November 7th.* My son prayed in the old chamber. Our time had been taken up by son and daughter Cooper's visit, so that I only read the 130th and 143 Psalm. 'Twas on the account of my courtship. I went to Madam Winthrop, found her rocking her little Katee in the cradle. I excused my coming so late (near eight). She set me an armed chair and cushion, and so the cradle was between her armed chair and mine. Gave her the remnant of my almonds. She did not eat of them as before, but laid them away. I said I came to inquire whether she had altered her mind since Friday, or remained of the same mind still. She said, thereabouts. I told her I loved her and was so fond as to think that she loved me. She said had a great respect for me. I told her I had made her an offer, without asking any advice; she had so many to advise with that it was a hindrance. The fire was come to one short brand besides the block, which brand was set up in end; at last it fell to pieces, and no recruit was made. She gave me a glass of wine. I think I repeated again that I would go home and bewail my rashness in making more haste than good speed. I would endeavor to contain myself and not go on to solicit her to do that which she could not consent to. Took leave of her. As came down the steps, she bid me have a care. Treated me courteously. Told her she had entered the 4th year of her widowhood. I had given her the news-letter before. I did not bid her draw off her glove as sometime I had done. Her dress was not so clean as sometime it had been, Jehovah jireh!

*Midweek, November 9th.* Dine at Brother Stoddard's; were so kind as to inquire of me if they should invite Madam Winthrop; I answered no. Thanked my sister Stoddard for her courtesy; sat down at the table Simeon Stoddard, Esq., Madam Stoddard, Samuel Sewall, Mr. Colman, Madam Colman, Mr. Cooper, Mrs. Cooper, Mrs. Hannah Cooper, Mr. Samuel Sewall of Brooklin[e], Mrs. Sewall, Mr. Joseph Sewall, Mrs. Lydia Walley, Mr. William Stoddard. Had a noble treat. At night our meeting was at the widow Belknap's. Gave each one of the meeting one of Mr. Homes's sermons, 12 in all. She sent her servant home with me with a lantern. Madam Winthrop's shutters were open as I passed by.

*November 10.* Mr. Webb preached, walk as becomes the Gospel. Dined at my son's with cousin Holman's wife.

*November 11th.* Went not to Madam Winthrop's. This is the second withdraw. . . .

*About the middle of December* Madam Winthrop made a treat for her children: Mr. Sewall, Prince, Willoughby. I knew nothing of it, but the same day abode in the Council Chamber for fear of the rain and dined alone upon Kilby's pies and good beer.

# Marriage

## *William Byrd*

*In 1706, Byrd married Lucy Parke, one of the two legitimate daughters of Colonel Parke, a Restoration rake who had made Virginia his temporary residence. Life with Lucy proved to be a succession of quarrels, recriminations and tantrums—always quickly followed, however, by reconciliations. In his diary (written in cipher and obviously never intended for publication), Byrd invariably attributes these quarrels to his wife's perverse and unpredictable temper: he is always in the right and she is always in the wrong. While it is true that Lucy had inherited the full measure of emotional instability that ran in the Parke family, it is also clear that the fault was not wholly on her side: Byrd was constantly trying to assert his superiority, even to the length of cheating when playing cards with her. Whatever the cause, Westover was the scene of some harrowing outbreaks of matrimonial strife. They ended abruptly in 1716 when Lucy Byrd died of smallpox in England.*

### April 8, 1709

I rose after 6 o'clock this morning and read a chapter in Hebrew and 150 verses in Homer's last work. I said my prayers and ate milk for breakfast. I danced my dance. My wife and I had another foolish quarrel about my saying she listened on the top of the stairs, which I suspected, in jest. However, I bore it with patience and she came soon after and begged my pardon. I settled my accounts and read some Dutch. Just before dinner Mr. Custis came and dined with us. He told us that my father Parke instead of being killed was married to his housekeeper which is more improbable. He told us that the distemper continued to rage extremely on the other side the Bay and had destroyed abundance of people. I did not keep to my rule of eating but one dish. We played at billiards and walked about the plantation. I said my prayers and had good humor, good health, and good thoughts, thanks be to God Almighty. The Indian woman died this evening, according to a dream I had last night about her.

*The Secret Diary of William Byrd of Westover, 1709–1712.* Edited by L. B. Wright and Marion Tinling.

*May 1, 1709*

I rose about 6 o'clock and read in Lucian. I recommended myself to God in a short prayer. My wife was a little indisposed and out of humor. I ate bread and butter for breakfast. We went to church over the creek and Mr. Taylor preached a good sermon. As soon as we came into church it began to rain and continued to rain all day very much. However I was not wet. When we returned my wife was something better. I ate roast beef for dinner. After dinner we were forced to keep house because of the rain. I endeavored to learn all I could from Major Burwell, who is a sensible man skilled in matters relating to tobacco. In the evening we talked about religion and my wife and her sister had a fierce dispute about the infallibility of the Bible. I neglected to say my prayers. However, I had good health, good thoughts, and good humor, thanks be to God Almighty.

*May 2, 1709*

I rose at 6 o'clock and read in Lucian. I recommended myself to God in a short prayer, and ate meat for breakfast. The women went to romping and I and my brother romped with them. About 12 o'clock my brother and sister Custis went on board their frigate in order to sail to Accomac. Then we went over the river to Carter's Creek and found Mr. Burwell indisposed with a cold and his lady ready to lie in. We ate boiled beef for supper. After supper I found myself very sleepy. About 10 o'clock we went to bed. I had good health, good humor, and good thoughts, thanks be to God Almighty.

*June 14, 1709*

I rose at 5 o'clock and read a chapter in Hebrew and some Greek in Josephus. I said my prayers and ate chocolate for breakfast. We heard guns this morning, by which we understood that the fleet was come in and I learned the same from Mr. Anderson. I ate bacon and chicken for dinner. I began to have the piles. I read some Greek in Homer. I heard guns from Swinyard's and sent my boat for my letters. In the meanwhile I walked about the plantation. In the evening the boat returned and brought some letters for me from England, with an invoice of things sent for by my wife which are enough to make a man mad. It put me out of humor very much. I neglected to say my prayers, for which God forgive me. I had good thoughts, good health, and good humor, thanks be to God Almighty.

*August 27, 1709*

I rose at 5 o'clock and read two chapters in Hebrew and some Greek in Josephus. I said my prayers and ate milk for breakfast. I danced my dance. I had like to have whipped my maid Anaka for her laziness but I forgave her. I read a little geometry. I denied my man G-r-l to go to a horse race because there was nothing but swearing and drinking there.

I ate roast mutton for dinner. In the afternoon I played at piquet with my own wife and made her out of humor by cheating her. I read some Greek in Homer. Then I walked about the plantation. I lent John H--ch £7 in his distress. I said my prayers, and had good health, good thoughts, and good humor, thanks be to God Almighty.

*October 23, 1709*

I rose at 6 o'clock and read two chapters in Hebrew and some Greek in Lucian. I said my prayers devoutly and ate milk for breakfast. Daniel came and shaved my head. About 11 o'clock I waited on the President and Colonel Harrison to church, where Mr. Cargill preached a good sermon. After church Colonel Harrison asked me to go to Mr. Blair's to dinner. I ate fish and goose for dinner. I went in the evening to Colonel Bray's where we found abundance of company and agreed to meet there the next day and have a dance. About 10 o'clock I came home and neglected to say my prayers and for that reason was guilty of uncleanness. I had bad thoughts, good health and good humor, thanks be to God Almighty.

*October 25, 1709*

I rose at 6 o'clock and read a chapter in Hebrew and then was disturbed with company. However I said my prayers and ate milk for breakfast. I went to the capitol about 10 o'clock where I found Colonel Carter. I sat about three hours and then went again to my chambers and ate a bite and did more business and came to court again. About 4 we went to dinner and I ate beef for dinner. Then we played at cards and I won £3 of Colonel Smith.

*October 26, 1709*

I went to Council, when my warrants were signed. Then we went to court about 12 o'clock and sat till 4. Then we went to dinner and I ate goose for dinner. In the evening we played at cards and I lost 40 shillings. I went home about 10 o'clock and said my prayers. . . .

*October 28, 1709*

I rose at 6 o'clock but read nothing because Colonel Randolph came to see me in the morning. I neglected to say my prayers but I ate milk for breakfast. Colonel Harrison's vessel came in from Madeira and brought abundance of letters and among the rest I had ten from Mr. Perry with a sad account of tobacco. We went to court but much time was taken up in reading our letters and not much business was done. About 3 we rose and had a meeting of the College in which it was agreed to turn Mr. Blackamore out from being master of the school for being so great a sot. . . .

*October 29, 1709*

I rose at 6 o'clock and read nothing because the governors of the College were to meet again. . . . When we met, Mr. Blackamore presented a petition in which he set forth that if the governors of the College would forgive him what was past, he would for the time to come mend his conduct. On which the governors at last agreed to keep him on, on trial, some time longer. Then we went to court where we sat till about 3 o'clock and then I learned that my sister Custis was at Mr. Bland's. I went to her and there was also Mrs. Chiswell. I went with them to Doctor B-r-t [Barret?] and ate beef for dinner. Here I stayed till 8 o'clock and then walked home. . . .

### October 31, 1709

I rose at 6 o'clock and read two chapters in Hebrew and some Greek in Lucian. I said my prayers and ate milk for breakfast. About 10 o'clock we went to court. The committee met to receive proposals for the building the College and Mr. Tullitt undertook it for £2,000 provided he might wood off the College land and all assistants from England to come at the College's risk. We sat in court till about 4 o'clock and then I rode to Green Springs to meet my wife. I found her there and had the pleasure to learn that all was well at home, thanks be to God. There was likewise Mrs. Chiswell. . . . Then we danced and were merry till about 10 o'clock. I neglected to say my prayers but had good health, good thoughts, and good humor, thanks be to God Almighty. This month I took above 400 of Colonel Quarry [or Cary] in money for bills at an allowance of 10 per cent.

### November 2, 1709

I rose at 6 o'clock and read a chapter in Hebrew and some Greek in Lucian. I said my prayers and ate milk for breakfast, and settled some accounts, and then went to court where we made an end of the business. We went to dinner about 4 o'clock and I ate boiled beef again. In the evening I went to Dr. Barret's where my wife came this afternoon. Here I found Mrs. Chiswell, my sister Custis, and other ladies. We sat and talked till about 11 o'clock and then retired to our chambers. I played at r—m with Mrs. Chiswell and kissed her on the bed till she was angry and my wife also was uneasy about it, and cried as soon as the company was gone. I neglected to say my prayers, which I should not have done, because I ought to beg pardon for the lust I had for another man's wife. However I had good health, good thoughts, and good humor, thanks be to God Almighty.

### Dec. 25, 1709

I rose at 7 o'clock and ate milk for breakfast. I neglected to say my prayers because of my company. . . . About 11 o'clock the rest of the company ate some broiled turkey for their breakfast. Then we went to church, notwithstanding it rained a little, where Mr. Anderson preached a good sermon for the occasion. I received the Sacrament with great devoutness. After church the same company went to dine with me and I ate roast beef for dinner. In the afternoon Dick Randolph and Mr. Jackson went away and Mr. Jackson rode sidelong like a woman. Then we took a walk about the plantation, but a great fog soon drove us into the house again. In the evening we were merry with nonsense and so were my servants. I said my prayers shortly and had good health, good thoughts, and good humor, thanks be to God Almighty.

*Dec. 27, 1709*

I rose at 5 o'clock and read a chapter in Hebrew and some Greek in Cassius. I said my prayers and ate milk for breakfast. I danced my dance. When the company came down I ate chocolate likewise with them. Then we played at billiards and tried some of our [tokay]. About 12 o'clock we went to Mr. Harrison's notwithstanding it was extremely cold and I ate some goose. In the afternoon we were very merry by a good fire till 5 o'clock. Then we returned home, where I found all well, thank God. In the evening we played at cards till about 10 o'clock and I lost a crown. I neglected to say my prayers and had good health, good thoughts, and good humor, thanks be to God Almighty.

*Dec. 28, 1709*

I rose at 6 o'clock and read two chapters in Hebrew and some Greek in Cassius. I said my prayers and ate milk for breakfast. I danced my dance. It continued very cold with a strong wind. About 10 o'clock I ate some chocolate with the rest of the company. Then we played at billiards and I lost. When I was beat out I read something in Dr. Day. About one we went to dinner and I ate boiled pork. In the afternoon we played again at billiards till we lost one of the balls. Then we walked about the plantation and took a slide on the ice. In the evening we played at cards till about 10 o'clock.

*Dec. 29, 1709*

I rose at 5 o'clock and read two chapters in Hebrew and some Greek in Cassius. . . . Then we took a walk and I slid on skates, notwithstanding there was a thaw. Then we returned and played at billiards till dinner. I ate boiled beef for dinner. In the afternoon we played at billiards again and in the evening took another walk and gave Mr. Isham Randolph two bits to venture on the ice. He ventured and the ice broke with him and took him up to the mid-leg. Then we came home and played a little at whisk but I was so sleepy we soon left off. . . .

*March 31, 1710*

I rose at 7 o'clock and read some Greek in bed. I said my prayers and ate milk for breakfast. Then about 8 o'clock we got a-horseback and rode to Mr. Harrison's and found him very ill but sensible. Here I met Mr. Bland, who brought me several letters from England and among the rest two from Colonel Blakiston who had endeavored to procure the government of Virginia for me at the price of £1,000 of my Lady Orkney and that my Lord [agreed] but the Duke of Marlborough declared that no one but soldiers should have the government of a plantation, so I was disappointed. God's will be done. From hence I came home where I found all well, thank God. I ate fish for dinner. In the afternoon I went again with my wife to Mr. Harrison's who continued very bad so that I resolved to stay with him all night, which I did with Mr. Anderson and Nat Burwell. He was in the same bad condition till he vomited and then he was more easy. In the morning early I returned home and went to bed. It is remarkable that Mrs. Burwell dreamed this night that she saw a person that with money scales weighed time and declared that there was no more than 18 pennies worth of time to come, which seems to be a dream with some significance either concerning the world or a sick person. In my letters from England I learned that the Bishop of Worcester was of opinion that in the year 1715 the city of Rome would be burnt to the ground, that before the year 1745 the popish religion would be routed out of the world, that before the year 1790 the Jews and Gentiles would be converted to the Christianity and then would begin the millennium.

*April 10, 1710*

I rose at 6 o'clock and wrote several letters to my overseers. I sent early to inquire after Mr. Harrison and received word that he died about 4 o'clock this morning, which completed the 18th day of his sickness, according to Mrs. Burwell's dream exactly. Just before his death he was sensible and desired Mrs. L—— with importunity to open the door because he wanted to go out and could not go till the door was open and as soon as the door was opened he died. The country has lost a very useful man and who was both an advantage and an ornament to it, and I have lost a good neighbor, but God's will be done. . . . My wife rode to Mrs. Harrison's to comfort her and to assure her that I should be always ready to do her all manner of service. My wife returned before dinner. I ate tripe for dinner. In the afternoon we played at piquet. Then I prepared my matters for the General Court. It rained, with the wind at northeast, and it was very cold, and in the night it snowed. I read news. I said my prayers and had good health, good thoughts, and good humor, thank God Almighty.

*May 14, 1710*

I rose at 6 o'clock and read some Hebrew and no Greek. I neglected to say my prayers but ate milk for breakfast, but the rest of the company ate meat. About 10 o'clock we walked to Mrs. Harrison's to the funeral, where we found abundance of company of all sorts. Wine and cake were served very plentifully. At one o'clock the corpse began to move and the ship

"Harrison" fired a gun every half minute. When we came to church the prayers were first read; then we had a sermon which was an extravagant panegyric or [eulogy]. At every turn he called him "this great man," and not only covered his faults but gave him virtues which he never possessed as well as magnified those which he had. When [the] sermon was done the funeral service was read and the poor widow trembled extremely. When all was over I put the widow, her daughter, and two sisters into my coach and Colonel Randolph, his wife, Colonel Hill, Mrs. Anderson, and the two B-r-k-s went home with us and I invited several others who would not come. . . .

*May 23, 1710*

I rose at 5 o'clock and read two chapters in Hebrew and some Greek in Anacreon. The children were a little better, thank God. . . . My daughter was very ill, but the boy had lost his fever, thank God. I settled some accounts and wrote some commonplace. I ate hashed shoat for dinner. In the afternoon Evie had a sweat that worked pretty well but not long enough, for which I was out of humor with my wife. I read some Italian and some news and then took a walk about the plantation. When I returned I had a great quarrel with my wife, in which she was to blame altogether; however I made the first step to a reconciliation, to [which] she with much difficulty consented. . . .

*May 24, 1710*

I rose at 5 o'clock and read a chapter in Hebrew and some Greek in Anacreon. . . . I sent for my cousin Harrison to let Evie blood who was ill. When she came she took away about four ounces. We put on blisters and gave her a glyster which worked very well. Her blood was extremely thick, which is common in distemper of this constitution. About 12 o'clock she began to sweat of herself, which we prompted by tincture of saffron and sage and snakeroot. This made her sweat extremely, in which she continued little or more all night. I ate some fish for dinner. In the afternoon Mr. Anderson whom I had sent for came and approved of what I had done. I persuaded him to stay all night which he agreed to. It rained in the evening. We stayed up till 12 o'clock and Bannister sat up with the child till 12 o'clock and G-r-l till break of day. . . .

*May 25, 1710*

Evie was much better, thank God Almighty, and had lost her fever. The boy was better likewise but was restless. It was very hot today. I read some Italian. I ate green peas for dinner. In the afternoon my wife and I cut some [sage] and then I read more Italian. . . . I never was more incommoded with heat in my whole life. . . .

*July 4, 1710*

I rose at 5 o'clock and read two chapters in Hebrew and some Greek in

Thucydides. . . . About 11 o'clock we went to church and had a good sermon. After church I invited nobody home because I design to break that custom that my people may go to church. I ate boiled pork for dinner. In the afternoon my wife and I had a terrible quarrel about the things she had come in but at length she submitted because she was in the wrong. For my part I kept my temper very well. . . .

### July 15, 1710

About 7 o'clock the negro boy [or Betty] that ran away was brought home. My wife against my will caused little Jenny to be burned with a hot iron, for which I quarreled with her. It was so hot today that I did not intend to go to the launching of Colonel Hill's ship but about 9 o'clock the Colonel was so kind as to come and call us. My wife would not go at first but with much entreaty she at last consented. About 12 o'clock we went and found abundance of company at the ship and about one she was launched and went off very well, notwithstanding several had believed the contrary. . . .

### September 20, 1710

I rose at 6 o'clock but read nothing because I prepared for the Governor's coming in the evening. I neglected to say my prayers but ate milk for breakfast. I settled several things in my library. All the wood was removed from the place where it used to lay to a better place. I sent John to kill some blue wing and he had good luck. I ate some boiled beef for dinner. In the afternoon all things were put into the best order because Captain Burbydge sent word that the Governor would be here at 4 o'clock but he did not come till 5. Captain Burbydge sent his boat for him and fired as he came up the river. I received at the landing with Mr. C-s and gave him 3 guns. Mr. Clayton and Mr. Robinson came with him. After he had drunk some wine he walked in the garden and in the library till it was dark. Then he went to supper and ate some blue wing. After supper we sat and talked till 9 o'clock. . . .

### September 21, 1710

I rose at 6 o'clock and read nothing but got ready to receive the company. About 8 o'clock the Governor came down. I offered him some of my fine water [?]. Then we had milk tea and bread and butter for break-fast. The Governor was pleased with everything and very complaisant. About 10 o'clock Captain Stith came and soon after him Colonel Hill, Mr. Anderson and several others of the militia officers. The Governor was extremely courteous to them. About 12 o'clock Mr. Clayton went to Mrs. Harrison's and then orders were given to bring all the men into the pasture to muster. Just as we got on our horses it began to rain hard; however this did not discourage the Governor but away we rode to the men. It rained half an hour and the Governor mustered them all the while and he presented me to the people to be their Colonel and commander-in-chief. About 3 o'clock we returned to the house and as many of the officers as could sit at the table stayed to dine with the Governor, and the rest went to take part of the hogshead [of punch] in the churchyard. We had a good dinner, well served, with which the Governor seemed to be well pleased. I ate venison for dinner. In the evening all the company went away and we took a walk and found a comic freak of a man that was drunk that hung on the pales. Then we went home and played at piquet and I won the pool. About 9 the Governor went to bed. . . .

*October 19, 1710*

About 11 o'clock I went to court, it being the day appointed for trying the criminals. After we had stayed there about 2 hours we went into Council and then came down to court again, where we stayed till 4 o'clock and then adjourned. Then I went to dine at the Governor's where I ate boiled beef for dinner. In the evening we played at cards and I lost 25 shillings. We played at basset. About 11 o'clock I returned to my lodgings. I recommended to the Governor to get some men from the men-of-war for Colonel Hill's ship. . . .

*October 20, 1710*

I went to court and gace my judgment in several cases. About one o'clock I took some sage and snakeroot. Then I returned into court again and there we sat till 3. Then I wrote a letter to my wife and after that I went to the coffeehouse where I played at hazard and lost 7 pounds and returned home very peaceful. . . .

*Dec. 25, 1710*

I rose at 5 o'clock and read a chapter in Hebrew and some Greek in Lucian. About 7 o'clock the negro woman died that was mad yesterday. I said my prayers and ate boiled milk for breakfast. The wind blew very strong and it rained exceedingly. . . . About 11 o'clock we went to church where we had prayers and the Holy Sacrament which I took devoutly. We brought nobody home to dinner. I ate boiled venison. The child was a little better. In the afternoon I took a long walk and I saw several parts of the fence blown down with the wind, which blew very hard last night. In the evening I read a sermon in Mr. Norris but a quarrel which I had with my wife hindered my taking much notice of it. However we were reconciled before we went to bed, but I made the first advance. I neglected to say my prayers but not to eat some milk. I had good health, good thoughts, and indifferent good humor, thank God Almighty.

*Feb. 5, 1711*

I rose about 8 o'clock and found my cold still worse. I said my prayers and ate milk and potatoes for breakfast. My wife and I quarreled about her pulling her brows. She threatened she would not go to Williamsburg if she might not pull them; I refused, however, and got the better of her, and maintained my authority. About 10 o'clock we went over the river and got to Colonel Duke's about 11. There I ate some toast and canary. Then we proceeded to Queen's Creek, where we found all well, thank God. We ate roast goose for supper. The women prepared to go to the Governor's the next day and my brother and I talked of old stories. My cold grew exceedingly bad so that I thought I should be sick. My sister gave me some sage tea and leaves of [s-m-n-k] which made me mad all night so that I could not sleep but was much disordered by it. I neglected to say my prayers in form but had good thoughts, good humor, and indifferent health, thank God Almighty.

*Feb. 6, 1711*

I rose about 9 o'clock but was so bad I thought I should not have been in condition to go to Williamsburg, and my wife was so kind to [say] she would stay with me, but rather than keep her from going I resolved to go if possible. I was shaved with a very dull razor, and ate some boiled milk for breakfast but neglected to say my prayers. About 10 o'clock I went to Williamsburg without the ladies. As soon as I got there it began to rain, which hindered about [sic] the company from coming. I went to the President's where I drank tea and went with him to the Governor's and found him at home. Several gentlemen were there and about 12 o'clock several ladies came. My wife and her sister came about 2. We had a short Council but more for form than for business. There was no other appointed in the room of Colonel Digges. My cold was a little better so that I ventured among the ladies, and Colonel Carter's wife and daughter were among them. It was night before we went to supper, which was very fine and in good order. It rained so that several did not come that were expected. About 7 o'clock the company went in coaches from the Governor's house to the capitol where the Governor opened the ball with a French dance with my wife. Then I danced with Mrs. Russell and then several others and among the rest Colonel Smith's son, who made a sad freak. Then we danced country dances for an hour and the company was carried into another room where was a very fine collation of sweetmeats. The Governor was very gallant to the ladies and very courteous to the gentlemen. About 2 o'clock the company returned in the coaches and because the drive was dirty the Governor carried the ladies into their coaches. My wife and I lay at my lodgings. Colonel Carter's family and Mr. Blair were stopped by the unruliness of the horses and Daniel Wilkinson was so gallant as to lead the horses himself through all the dirt and rain to Mr. Blair's house. My cold continued bad. I neglected to say my prayers and had good thoughts, good humor, but indifferent health, thank God Almighty. It rained all day and all night. The President had the worst clothes of anybody there.

*October 20, 1711*

I rose about 6 o'clock and drank tea with the Governor, who made use of this opportunity to make the Indians send some of their great men to the College, and the Nansemonds sent two, the Nottoways two, and the Meherrins two. He also demanded one from every town belonging to the Tuscaroras. About 9 the Governor mounted and we waited on him to see him exercise the horse and when all the militia was drawn up he caused the Indians to walk from one end to the other and they seemed very much afraid lest they should be killed. The Governor did nothing but wheel the foot, and Colonel Ludwell and I assisted him as well as we could. About noon the Governor ordered lists to be taken of the troops and companies that the people might make their claim to be paid, because they had been on the service five days. When this was done he gave liberty to the people to go home, except a troop and company for the guard that night. Then we went and saw the Indian boys shoot and the Indian girls run for a prize. We had likewise a war dance by the men and a love dance by the women, which sports lasted till it grew dark. Then we went to supper and I ate chicken with a good stomach. We sat with the Governor till he went to bed about 11 o'clock and then we went to Major Harrison's to supper again but the Governor ordered the sentry to keep us out and in revenge about 2 o'clock in the morning we danced a g-n-t-r dance just at the bed's head. However we called for the captain of the guard and gave him a word and then we all got in except Colonel Ludwell and we kept him out about quarter of an hour. Jenny, an Indian girl, had got drunk and made us good sport. I neglected to say my prayers and had good health, good thoughts, and good humor, thank God Almighty.

*October 21, 1711*

I rose about 6 o'clock and we began to pack up our baggage in order to return. We drank chocolate with the Governor and about 10 o'clock we took leave of the Nottoway town and the Indian boys went away with us that were designed for the College. The Governor made three proposals to the Tuscaroras: that they would join with the English to cut off those Indians that had killed the people of Carolina, that they should have 40 shillings for every head they brought in of those guilty Indians and be paid the price of a slave for all they brought in alive, and that they should send one of the chief men's sons out of every town to the College. I waited on the Governor about ten miles and then took leave of him and he went to Mr. Cargill's and I with Colonel Hill, Mr. Platt, and John Hardiman went to Colonel Harrison's where we got about 3 o'clock in the afternoon. About 4 we dined and I ate some boiled beef. My man's horse was lame for which he was let blood. At night I asked a negro girl to kiss me, and when I went to bed I was very cold because I pulled off my clothes after lying in them so long. I neglected to say my prayers but had good health, good thoughts, and good humor, thank God Almighty.

### January 9, 1712

I was a little displeased at a story somebody had told the Governor that I had said no governor ought to be trusted with £20,000. . . .

### January 15, 1712

I rose about 7 o'clock but read nothing because I wrote some letters and one especially to Will Randolph concerning what I understood the Governor had [been] informed concerning my saying no governor ought to be trusted with £20,000, and he owned he had told it because I had said it and he thought it no secret, for which I marked him as a very false friend. . . .

### January 24, 1712

I was a little perplexed what to say to the Governor to extenuate what I had said but I was resolved to say the truth, let the consequence be what it would. About 10 o'clock, I and my brother [in-law] went to town and lighted at my lodgings. Then I went to the coffeehouse where I found Mr. Clayton and he and I went to the Governor. He made us wait half an hour before he was pleased to come out to see us and when he came he looked very stiff and cold on me but did not explain himself. . . .

### March 2, 1712

I rose about 7 o'clock and read a chapter in Hebrew but no Greek because Mr. G-r-l was here and I wished to talk with him. I ate boiled milk for breakfast and danced my dance. I reprimanded him for drawing so many notes on me. However I told him if he would let me know his debts I would pay them provided he would let a mulatto of mine that is his apprentice come to work at Falling Creek the last two years of his service, which he agreed. I had a terrible quarrel with my wife concerning Jenny that I took away from her when she was beating her with the tongs. She lifted up her hands to strike me but forbore to do it. She gave me abundance of bad words and endeavored to strangle herself, but I believe in jest only. However after acting a mad woman a long time she was passive again. I ate some roast beef for dinner. In the afternoon Mr. G-r-l went away and I took a walk about the plantation. At night we drank some cider by way of reconciliation and I read nothing. I said my prayers and had health, good thoughts, and good humor, thank God Almighty. I sent Tom to Williamsburg with some fish to the Governor, and my sister Custis. My daughter was indisposed with a small fever.

### July 13, 1712

I rose about 6 o'clock and read a chapter in Hebrew. I said my prayers and had milk and hominy for breakfast. I received a letter from Dr.

Cocke in which he desired me to pay Posford 25 but in my answer I excused myself. The weather was cloudy and very hot. My wife was a little better, thank God. I read some news till dinner and then I ate some roast shoat. In the afternoon I took a nap and then my wife and I had a small dispute which put her into a foolish passion and she continued out of humor all day and would not speak to me. Then I read some news again till the evening and then I took a walk about the plantation. When I returned I spoke kindly to my wife but she would not answer me; however I considered her weakness and bore it. I said my prayers and had good health, good thoughts, and good humor, thank God Almighty.

# On Taking a Mistress

## *Benjamin Franklin*

Advice to a Young Man on Taking a Mistress *may be partly autobio-graphical—certainly it reads like a man writing out of experience. Despite the avowals of candor in his* Autobiography, *Franklin never revealed the identity of the mother of his son William, who later became a royal governor and Loyalist. It is possible that William Franklin was the result of Benjamin's failure to follow the advice he so generously handed down to young men.*

*June 25, 1745*

My dear Friend,

I know of no Medicine fit to diminish the violent natural Inclinations you mention; and if I did, I think I should not communicate it to you. Marriage is the proper Remedy. It is the most natural State of Man, and therefore the State in which you are most likely to find solid Happiness. Your Reasons against entring into it at present, appear to me not well-founded. The circumstantial Advantages you have in View by postponing it, are not only undertain, but they are small in comparison with that of the Thing itself, the being *married and settled.* It is the Man and Woman united that make the compleat human Being. Separate, she wants his Force of Body and Strength of Reason; he, her Softness, Sensibility and acute Discernment. Together they are more likely to succeed in the World. A single Man has not nearly the Value he would have in that State of Union. He is an incomplete Animal. He resembles the odd Half of a Pair of Scissars. If you get a prudent healthy Wife, your Industry in your Profession, with her good Oeconomy, will be a Fortune sufficient.

But if you will take this Councel, and persist in thinking a Commerce with the Sex inevitable, then I repeat my former Advice, that in all your Amours you should *prefer old Women to young ones.* You call this a Paradox, and demand my Reasons. They are these:

1. Because as they have more Knowledge of the World and their Minds

*The Writings of Benjamin Franklin.* Edited by Albert H. Smyth.

are better stor'd with Observations, their Conversation is more improving and more lastingly agreable.

2. Because when Women cease to be handsome, they study to be good. To maintain their Influence over Men, they supply the Diminution of Beauty by an Augmentation of Utility. They learn to do a 1000 Services small and great, and are the most tender and useful of all Friends when you are sick. Thus they continue amiable. And hence there is hardly such a thing to be found as an old Woman who is not a good Woman.

3. Because there is no hazard of Children, which irregularly produc'd may be attended with much Inconvenience.

4. Because thro' more Experience, they are more prudent and discreet in conducting an Intrigue to prevent Suspicion. The Commerce with them is therefore with regard to your Reputation. And with regard to theirs, if the Affair should happen to be known, considerable People might be rather inclin'd to excuse an old Woman who would kindly take care of a young Man, form his Manners by her good Counsels, and prevent his ruining his Health and Fortune among mercenary Prostitutes.

5. Because in every Animal that walks upright, the Deficiency of the Fluids that fill the Muscles appears first in the highest Part: The Face first grows lank and wrinkled; then the Neck; then the Breast and Arms; the lower Parts continuing to the last as plump as ever: So that covering all above with a Basket, and regarding only what is below the Girdle, it is impossible of two Women to know an old from a young one. And as in the dark all Cats are grey, the Pleasure of corporal Enjoyment with an old Woman is at least equal, and frequently superior, every Knack being by Practice capable of Improvement.

6. Because the Sin is less. The debauching of a Virgin may be her Ruin, and make her for Life unhappy.

7. Because the Compunction is less. The having made a young Girl *miserable* may give you frequent bitter Reflections; none of which can attend the making an old Woman *happy*.

8thly and Lastly. They are *so grateful!!*

Thus much for my Paradox. But still I advise you to marry directly; being sincerely

Your affectionate Friend.

# The Speech of Polly Baker

## *Benjamin Franklin*

*An inveterate literary hoaxer, Franklin produced several masterpieces of this genre. As "Silence Dogood," an opinionated, chatty country widow, he even deceived his brother James, who published Silence's letters in the* New England Courant *unaware that his brother was the author. Later, in the pages of his own* Pennsylvania Gazette, *Benjamin Franklin regaled his readers with "anecdotes, fables and fancies" presented under the guise of straight news stories. Among other things, he satirized extravagant stories about America by writing an account of "the grand Leap of the Whale in the Chace up the Fall of Niagra," which, he solemnly asserted, "is esteemed by all who have seen it, as one of the first Spectacles in Nature"—a tall story that reveals Franklin's close link with Mark Twain and other practitioners of the typically American humorous art of exaggeration. In the same vein, he offered his readers a slyly satirical version of the redeemed-Indian-captive story. In 1773, he wrote an* Edict by the King of Prussia *in which Frederick the Great made claims upon England which brought into sharp relief the injustice of Great Britain's claims upon the American colonies. During the War of Independence, he published privately a fraudulent* Supplement to the Boston Independent Chronicle, *by which it was made to appear that the Indian allies of the British government had brought in 1,062 American scalps. In the last year of his life he struck at slavery by fabricating a speech delivered in the previous century by an Algerian vindicating the practice of capturing Christians at sea and selling them into bondage.*

The Speech of Polly Baker *was Franklin's most successful hoax. Appearing first in the* London General Advertiser *in 1747 and quickly reprinted widely in Great Britain, America and France, it was long accepted as genuine. The liberal minded hailed it as a protest against the narrow prejudices of society; and in the hands of French intellectuals, Polly Baker became a symbol of the revolutionary spirit—a Joan of Arc doing battle for the emancipation of her sex.*

The Papers of Benjamin Franklin. *Edited by Leonard W. Labaree and Whitfield Bell, Jr.*

The Speech of Miss POLLY BAKER, before a Court of Judicature, at Connecticut near Boston, in New-England; where she was prosecuted the Fifth Time, for having a Bastard Child: Which influenced the Court to dispense with her Punishment, and induced one of her Judges to marry her the next Day.

May it please the Honourable Bench to indulge me in a few Words: I am a poor unhappy Woman, who have no Money to fee Lawyers to plead for me, being hard put to it to get a tolerable Living. I shall not trouble your Honours with long Speeches; for I have not the Presumption to expect, that you may, by any Means, be prevailed on to deviate in your Sentence from the Law, in my Favour. All I humbly hope is, That your Honours would charitably move the Governor's Goodness on my Behalf, that my Fine may be remitted. This is the Fifth Time, Gentlemen, that I have been dragg'd before your Court on the same Account; twice I have paid heavy Fines, and twice have been brought to Public Punishment, for want of Money to pay those Fines. This may have been agreeable to the Laws, and I don't dispute it; but since Laws are sometimes unreasonable in themselves, and therefore repealed, and others bear too hard on the Subject in particular Circumstances; and therefore there is left a Power somewhat to dispense with the Execution of them; I take the Liberty to say, That I think this Law, by which I am punished, is both unreasonable in itself, and particularly severe with regard to me, who have always lived an inoffensive Life in the Neighbourhood where I was born, and defy my Enimies (if I have any) to say I ever wrong'd Man, Woman, or Child. Abstracted from the Law, I cannot conceive (may it please your Honours) what the Nature of my Offence is. I have brought Five fine children into the World, at the Risque of my Life; I have maintained them well by my own Industry, without burthening the Township, and would have done it better, if it had not been for the heavy Charges and Fines I have paid. Can it be a Crime (in the Nature of Things I mean) to add to the Number of the King's Subjects, in a new Country that really wants People? I own it, I should think it a Praise-worthy, rather than a punishable Action. I have debauched no other Woman's Husband, nor enticed any Youth; these Things I never was charg'd with, nor has any one the least Cause of Complaint against me, unless, perhaps, the Minister, or Justice, because I have had Children without being married, by which they have missed a Wedding Fee. But, can ever this be a Fault of mine? I appeal to your Honours. You are pleased to allow I don't want Sense; but I must be stupified to the last Degree, not to prefer the Honourable State of Wedlock, to the Condition I have lived in. I always was, and still am willing to enter into it; and doubt not my behaving well in it, having all the Industry, Frugality, Fertility, and Skill in Oeconomy, appertaining to a good Wife's Character. I defy any Person to say, I ever refused an Offer of that Sort: On the contrary, I readily consented to the only Proposal of Marriage that ever was made me, which was when I was a Virgin; but too easily confiding in the Person's Sincerity that made it, I unhappily lost my own Honour, by trusting to his; for he got me with Child, and then forsook me: That very Person you all know; he is now become a Magistrate of this Country; and I had Hopes he would have appeared this Day on the Bench, and have endeavoured to moderate the Court in my Favour; then I should have scorn'd to have mention'd it; but I must now complain of it, as unjust and unequal, That my Betrayer and Undoer, the first Cause of all my Faults and Miscarriages (if they must be deemed such) should be advanc'd to Honour and Power in the Government, that punishes my Misfortunes with Stripes and Infamy. I should be told, 'tis like, That were there no Act of Assembly in the Case, the Precepts of Religion are violated by my Transgressions. If mine, then, is a religious Offense, leave it to religious Punishments. You have already excluded me from the Comforts of your Church-Communion. Is not that sufficient? You believe I have offended Heaven, and must suffer eternal Fire: Will not that be sufficient? What Need is there, then, of your additional Fines and Whipping? I own, I do not think as you do; for, if I thought what you call a Sin, was really such, I could not presumptuously commit it. But, how can it be believed, that Heaven is angry at my having Children, when to the little done by me towards it, God has been pleased to add his Divine Skill and admirable Workmanship in the Formation of their Bodies, and crown'd it, by furnishing them with rational and immortal Souls. Forgive me, Gentlemen, if I talk a little extravagantly on these Matters; I am no Divine, but if you, Gentlemen, must be making Laws, do not turn natural and useful Actions into Crimes, by your Prohibitions. But take into your wise Consideration, the great and growing Number of Batchelors in the Country, many of whom from the mean Fear of the Expences of a Family, have never sincerely and honourably courted a Woman in their Lives; and by their Manner of Living, leave unproduced (which is little better than Murder) Hundreds of their Posterity to the Thousandth Generation. Is not this a greater Offence against the Publick Good, than mine? Compel them, then, by Law, either to Marriage, or to pay double the Fine of Fornication every Year. What must poor young Women do, whom Custom have forbid to solicit the Men, and who cannot force themselves upon Husbands, when the Laws take no Care to provide them any; and yet severely punish them if they do their Duty without them; the Duty of the first and great Command of Nature, and of Nature's God, Encrease and Multiply. A Duty, from the steady Performance of which, nothing has been able to deter me; but for its Sake, I have hazarded the Loss of the Publick Esteem, and have frequently endured Publick Disgrace and Punishment; and therefore ought, in my humble Opinion, instead of a Whipping, to have a Statue erected to my Memory.

# Riding Through Virginia
## *William Byrd*

*Byrd was an avid prospector who kept his eyes open on his travels in the interior for outcroppings of ore. Although he did not turn up enough mineral wealth to make him rich, he did succeed in uncovering some highly amusing human types which he described with fine gusto. Human eccentricity never ceased to fascinate Byrd.*

*September 18.* For the pleasure of the good company of Mrs. Byrd, and her little governor, my son, I went about half way to the falls in the chariot. There we halted, not far from a purling stream, and upon the stump of a propagate oak picked the bones of a piece of roast beef. By the spirit which that gave me, I was the better able to part with the dear companions of my travels and to perform the rest of my journey on horseback by myself.

I reached Shacco's before two o'clock and crossed the river to the mills. I had the grief to find them both stand as still for the want of water as a dead woman's tongue for want of breath. It had rained so little for many weeks above the falls, that the Naiads had hardly water enough left to wash their faces. However, as we ought to turn all our misfortunes to the best advantage, I directed Mr. Booker, my first minister there, to make use of the lowness of the water for blowing up the rocks at the mouth of the canal. For that purpose I ordered iron drills to be made about two foot long, pointed with steel, chisel fashion, in order to make holes, into which we put our cartridges of powder, containing each about three ounces. There wanted skill among my engineers to choose the best parts of the stone for boring that we might blow to the most advantage. They made all their holes quite perpendicular, whereas they should have humored the grain of the stone for the more effectual execution. I ordered the points of the drills to be made chisel way, rather than the diamond, that they might need to be seldomer repaired, though in stone the diamond points would make the most despatch. The water now flowed out of the river so slowly that the miller was obliged to pond it up in the

*The Writings of William Byrd.* Edited by J. S. Bassett.

canal by setting open the flood-gates at the mouth and shutting those close at the mill. By this contrivance, he was able at any time to grind two or three bushels, either for his choice customers, or for the use of my plantations.

Then I walked to the place where they broke the flax, which is wrought with much greater ease than the hemp, and is much better for spinning. From thence I paid a visit to the weaver, who needed a little of Minerva's inspiration to make the most of a piece of cloth. Then I looked in upon my Caledonian spinster, who was mended more in her looks than in her humor. However, she promised much, though at the same time intended to perform little. She is too high-spirited for Mr. Booker, who hates to have his sweet temper ruffled, and will rather suffer matters to go a little wrong sometimes than give his righteous spirit any uneasiness. He is very honest and would make an admirable overseer where servants will do as they are bid. But eye-servants, who want abundance of overlooking, are not so proper to be committed to his care. I found myself out of order, and for that reason retired early; yet with all this precaution had a gentle fever in the night, but towards morning nature set open all her gates and drove it out in a plentiful perspiration.

19. The worst of this fever was that it put me to the necessity of taking another ounce of bark. I moistened every dose with a little brandy and filled the glass up with water, which is the least nauseous way of taking this popish medicine, and besides hinders it from purging. After I had swallowed a few poached eggs, we rode down to the mouth of the canal, and from thence crossed over to the broad Rock Island in a canoe. Our errand was to view some iron ore, which we dug up in two places. That on the surface seemed very spongy and poor, which gave us no great encouragement to search deeper, nor did the quantity appear to be very great. However, for my greater satisfaction, I ordered a hand to dig there for some time this winter. We walked from one end of the island to the other, being about half a mile in length, and found the soil very good, and too high for any flood, less than that of Deucalion, to do the least damage. There is a very wild prospect both upward and downward, the river being full of rocks, over which the stream tumbled with a murmur loud enough to drown the notes of a scolding wife. This island would make an agreeable hermitage for any good Christian who had a mind to retire from the world.

Mr. Booker told me how Dr. Ireton had cured him once of a looseness which had been upon him two whole years. He ordered him a dose of rhubarb, with directions to take twenty-five drops of laudanum so soon as he had had two physical stools. Then he rested one day, and the next he ordered him another dose of the same quantity of laudanum to be taken, also after the second stool. When this was done, he finished the cure by giving him twenty drops of laudanum every night for five nights running. The doctor insisted upon the necessity of stopping the operation of the rhubarb before it worked quite off, that what remained behind might strengthen the bowels. I was punctual in swallowing my bark, and that I might use exercise upon it, rode to Prince's Folly, and my Lord's islands, where I saw very fine corn.

In the meantime Vulcan came in order to make the drills for boring the rocks, and gave me his parole he would, by the grace of God, attend the works till they were finished, which he performed as lamely as if he had been to labor for a dead horse and not for ready money. I made a North Carolina dinner upon fresh pork, though we had a plate of green peas after it, by way of dessert, for the safety of our noses. Then my first minister and I had some serious conversation about my affairs, and I find nothing disturbed his peaceable spirit so much as the misbehavior of the spinster above-mentioned. I told him I could not pity a man who had it always in his power to do himself and her justice, and would not. If she were a drunkard, a scold, a thief, or a slanderer, we had wholesome laws that would make her back smart for the diversion of her other members, and 'twas his fault he had not put those wholesome severities in execution. I retired in decent time to my own apartment, and slept very comfortably upon my bark, forgetting all the little crosses arising from overseers and Negroes.

20. I continued the bark, and then tossed down my poached eggs with as much ease as some good breeders slip children into the world. About nine I left the prudentest orders I could think of with my vizier and then crossed the river to Shacco's. I made a running visit to three of my quarters, where, besides finding all the people well, I had the pleasure to see better crops than usual both of corn and tobacco. I parted there with my intendant, and pursued my journey to Mr. Randolph's, at Tuckahoe, without meeting with any adventure by the way. Here I found Mrs. Fleming, who was packing up her baggage with design to follow her husband the next day, who was gone to a new settlement in Goochland. Both he and she have been about seven years persuading themselves to remove to that retired part of the country, though they had the two strong arguments of health and interest for so doing. The widow smiled graciously upon me and entertained me very handsomely. Here I learned all the tragical story of her daughter's humble marriage with her uncle's overseer. Besides the meanness of this mortal's aspect, the man has not one visible qualification, except impudence, to recommend him to a female's inclinations. But there is sometimes such a charm in that Hibernian endowment, that frail woman can't withstand it, though it stand alone without any other recommendation. Had she run away with a gentleman or a pretty fellow, there might have been some excuse for her, though he were of inferior fortune: but to stoop to a dirty plebeian, without any kind of merit, is the lowest prostitution. I found the family

justly enraged at it; and though I had more good nature than to join in
her condemnation, yet I could devise no excuse for so senseless a prank as
this young gentlewoman had played. Here good drink was more scarce
than good victuals, the family being reduced to the last bottle of wine,
which was therefore husbanded very carefully. But the water was excellent. The heir of the family did not come home till late in the evening. He
is a pretty young man, but had the misfortune to become his own master
too soon. This puts young fellows upon wrong pursuits, before they have
sense to judge rightly for themselves. Though at the same time they have
a strange conceit of their own sufficiency when they grow near twenty
years old, especially if they happen to have a small smattering of learning. 'Tis then they fancy themselves wiser than all their tutors and
governors, which makes them headstrong to all advice, and above all
reproof and admonition.

21. I was sorry in the morning to find myself stopped in my career by
bad weather brought upon us by a northeast wind. This drives a world of
raw unkindly vapors upon us from Newfoundland, laden with blight,
coughs, and pleurisies. However, I complained not, lest I might be suspected to be tired of the good company. Though Mrs. Fleming was not
so much upon her guard, but mutinied strongly at the rain that hindered
her from pursuing her dear husband. I said what I could to comfort a
gentlewoman under so sad a disappointment. I told her a husband that
stayed so much at home as hers did, could be no such violent rarity, as for
a woman to venture her precious health to go daggling through the rain
after him, or to be miserable if she happened to be prevented. That it was
prudent for married people to fast sometimes from one another, that they
might come together again with the better stomach. That the best things
in this world, if constantly used, are apt to be cloying, which a little
absence and abstinence would prevent. This was strange doctrine to a
fond female, who fancies people should love with as little reason after
marriage as before.

In the afternoon Monsieur Marij, the minister of the parish, came to
make me a visit. He had been a Romish priest, but found reasons, either
spiritual or temporal, to quit that gay religion. The fault of this new convert is that he looks for as much respect from his Protestant flock as is
paid to the popish clergy, which our ill-bred Huguenots do not understand. Madam Marij had so much curiosity as to want to come too; but
another horse was wanting, and she believed it would have too vulgar an
air to ride behind her husband. This woman was of the true exchange
breed, full of discourse but void of discretion, and married a parson, with
the idle hopes he might some time or other come to be His Grace of
Canterbury. The gray mare is the better horse in that family, and the
poor man submits to her wild vagaries for peace' sake. She has just
enough of the fine lady to run in debt and be of no signification in her

household. And the only thing that can prevent her from undoing her loving husband will be that nobody will trust them beyond the sixteen thousand, which is soon run out in a Goochland store. The way of dealing there is for some small merchant or peddler to buy a Scots pennyworth of goods, and clap 150 per cent upon that. At this rate the parson can't be paid much more for his preaching than 'tis worth. No sooner was our visitor retired, but the facetious widow was so kind as to let me into all this secret history, but was at the same time exceedingly sorry that the woman should be so indiscreet and the man so tame as to be governed by an unprofitable and fantastical wife.

22. We had another wet day to try both Mrs. Fleming's patience and my good breeding. The northeast wind commonly sticks by us three or four days, filling the atmosphere with damps, injurious both to man and beast. The worst of it was, we had no good liquor to warm our blood and fortify our spirits against so strong a malignity. However, I was cheerful under all these misfortunes, and expressed no concern but a decent fear lest my long visit might be troublesome. Since I was like to have thus much leisure, I endeavored to find out what subject a dull married man could introduce that might best bring the widow to the use of her tongue. At length I discovered she was a notable quack, and therefore paid that regard to her knowledge as to put some questions to her about the bad distemper that raged then in the country. I mean the bloody flux, that was brought us in the Negro-ship consigned to Col. Braxton. She told me she made use of very simple remedies in that case, with very good success. She did the business either with hartshorn drink that had plantain leaves boiled in it, or else with a strong decoction of St. Andrew's Cross, in new milk instead of water. I agreed with her that those remedies might be very good, but would be more effectual after a dose or two of Indian physic.

But for fear this conversation might be too grave for a widow, I turned the discourse and began to talk of plays, and finding her taste lay most towards comedy, I offered my service to read one to her, which she kindly accepted. She produced the second part of *The Beggar's Opera,* which had diverted the town for forty nights successively and gained four thousand pounds to the author. This was not owing altogether to the wit or humor that sparkled in it, but to some political reflections that seemed to hit the ministry. But the great advantage of the author was that his interest was solicited by the Duchess of Queensbury, which no man could refuse who had but half an eye in his head, or half a guinea in his pocket. Her Grace, like death, spared nobody, but even took my Lord Selkirk in for two guineas, to repair which extravagance he lived upon Scots herrings two months afterwards. But the best story was, she made a very smart officer in His Majesty's guards give her a guinea, who swearing at the same time 'twas all he had in the world, she sent him fifty for it the next day, to reward his obedience. After having acquainted my company with the history of the play, I read three acts of it and left Mrs. Fleming and Mr. Randolph to finish it, who read as well as most actors do at a rehearsal. Thus we killed the time and triumphed over the bad weather.

23. The clouds continued to drive from the northeast and to menace us with more rain. But as the lady resolved to venture through it, I thought it a shame for me to venture to flinch. Therefore, after fortifying myself with two capacious dishes of coffee, and making my compliments to the ladies, I mounted, and Mr. Randolph was so kind as to be my guide.

At the distance of about three miles, in a path as narrow as that which leads to heaven, but much more dirty, we reached the homely dwelling of the Reverend Mr. Marij. His land is much more barren than his wife, and needs all Mr. Bradley's skill in agriculture to make it bring corn.

Thence we proceeded five miles farther, to a mill of Mr. Randolph's that is apt to stand still when there falls but little rain, and to be carried away when there falls a great deal.

Then I came into the main county road, that leads from Fredericksburg to Germanna, which last place I reached in ten miles more. This famous town consists of Col. Spotswood's enchanted castle on one side of the street, and a baker's dozen of ruinous tenements on the other, where so many German families had dwelt some years ago, but are now removed ten miles higher, in the fork of Rappahannock, to land of their own. There had also been a chapel about a bow-shot from the Colonel's house at the end of an avenue of cherry trees, but some pious people had lately burnt it down, with intent to get another built nearer to their own homes. Here I arrived about three o'clock and found only Mrs. Spotswood at home, who received her old acquaintance with many a gracious smile. I was carried into a room elegantly set off with pier glasses, the largest of which came soon after to an odd misfortune. Amongst other favorite animals that cheered this lady's solitude, a brace of tame deer ran familiarly about the house, and one of them came to stare at me as a stranger. But unluckily spying his own figure in the glass, he made a spring over the tea table that stood under it and shattered the glass to pieces, and falling back upon the tea table, made a terrible fracas among the china. This exploit was so sudden, and accompanied with such a noise, that it surprised me and perfectly frightened Mrs. Spotswood. But it was worth all the damage to show the moderation and good humor with which she bore this disaster.

In the evening the noble Colonel came home from his mines, who saluted me very civilly, and Mrs. Spotswood's sister, Miss Theky, who had been to meet him *en cavalier*, was so kind too as to bid me welcome. We talked over a legend of old stories, supped about nine, and then prattled with the ladies till it was time for a traveler to retire.

In the meantime I observed my old friend to be very uxorious, and exceedingly fond of his children. This was so opposite to the maxims he used to preach up before he was married, that I could not forbear rubbing up the memory of them. But he gave a very good-natured turn to his change of sentiments, by alleging that whoever brings a poor gentle-woman into so solitary a place, from all her friends and acquaintance, would be ungrateful not to use her and all that belongs to her with all possible tenderness.

28. We all kept snug in our several apartments till nine, except Miss Theky, who was the housewife of the family. At that hour we met over a pot of coffee, which was not quite strong enough to give us the palsy. After breakfast the Colonel and I left the ladies to their domestic affairs and took a turn in the garden, which has nothing beautiful but three terrace walks that fall in slopes one below another. I let him understand that besides the pleasure of paying him a visit, I came to be instructed by so great a master in the mystery of making of iron, wherein he had led the way, and was the Tubal Cain of Virginia. He corrected me a little there, by assuring me he was not only the first in this country, but the first in North America, who had erected a regular furnace. That they ran altogether upon bloomeries in New England and Pennsylvania, till his example had made them attempt greater works. But in this last colony, they have so few ships to carry their iron to Great Britain, that they must be content to make it only for their own use, and must be obliged to manufacture it when they have done. That he hoped he had done the country very great service by setting so good an example. That the four furnaces now at work in Virginia circulated a great sum of money for provisions and all other necessaries in the adjacent counties. That they took off a great number of hands from planting tobacco, and employed them in works that produced a large sum of money in England to the persons concerned, whereby the country is so much the richer. That they are besides a considerable advantage to Great Britain, because it lessens the quantity of bar iron imported from Spain, Holland, Sweden, Denmark and Muscovy, which used to be no less than twenty thousand tons yearly, though at the same time no sow iron is imported thither from any country but only from the plantations. For most of this bar iron they do not only pay silver, but our friends in the Baltic are so nice, they even expect to be paid all in crown pieces. On the contrary, all the iron they receive from the plantations, they pay for it in their own manufactures, and send for it in their own shipping.

Then I inquired after his own mines, and hoped, as he was the first that engaged in this great undertaking, that he had brought them to the most perfection. He told me he had iron in several parts of his great tract of land, consisting of forty-five thousand acres. But that the mine he was at work upon was thirteen miles below Germanna. That his ore (which was very rich) he raised a mile from his furnace, and was obliged to cart the iron when it was made, fifteen miles to Massaponux, a plantation he had upon Rappahannock River; but that the road was exceeding good, gently declining all the way, and had no more than one hill to go up in the whole journey. For this reason his loaded carts went it in a day without difficulty. He said it was true his works were of the oldest standing: but that his long absence in England, and the wretched management of Mr. Greame, whom he had entrusted with his affairs, had put him back very much. That what with neglect and severity, above eighty of his slaves were lost while he was in England, and most of his cattle starved. That his furnace stood still great part of the time, and all his plantations ran to ruin. That indeed he was rightly served for committing his affairs to the care of a mathematician, whose thoughts were always among the stars. That nevertheless, since his return, he had applied himself to rectify his steward's mistakes and bring his business again into order. That now he had contrived to do everything with his own people, except raising the mine and running the iron, by which he had contracted his expense very much. Nay, he believed that by his directions he could bring sensible Negroes to perform those parts of the work tolerably well. But at the same time he gave me to understand that his furnace had done no great feats lately, because he had been taken up in building an air furnace at Massaponux, which he had now brought to perfection, and should be thereby able to furnish the whole country with all sorts of cast iron, as cheap and as good as ever came from England. I told him he must do one thing more to have a full vent for those commodities, he must keep a shallop running into all the rivers, to carry his wares home to people's own doors. And if he would do that I would set a good example and take off a whole ton of them.

Our conversation on this subject continued till dinner, which was both elegant and plentiful. The afternoon was devoted to the ladies, who showed me one of their most beautiful walks. They conducted me through a shady lane to the landing, and by the way made me drink some very fine water that issued from a marble fountain and ran incessantly. Just behind it was a covered bench, where Miss Theky often sat and bewailed her virginity. Then we proceeded to the river, which is the south branch of Rappahannock, about fifty yards wide, and so rapid that the ferry boat is drawn over by a chain, and therefore called the Rapidan. At night we drank prosperity to all the Colonel's projects in a bowl of rack punch, and then retired to our devotions.

# PART III

# GOD AND THE DEVIL

# Religious Tolerance
## *Roger Williams*

*From the privileged sanctuary of Rhode Island, where alone in New England religious freedom prevailed, Roger Williams carried on a war of the books with the Reverend John Cotton, the foremost divine in Massachusetts Bay. A redoubtable Biblical scholar, Cotton drew most of his arguments against toleration from that source. Cotton opened the campaign in 1643 with* A Letter . . . to Mr. Williams *to which Williams responded in 1644 in* Mr. Cotton's Letter Lately Printed, Examined and Answered *and* The Bloudy Tenent of Persecution for Cause of Conscience Discussed. *Cotton answered Williams in* The Bloudy Tenent, Washed, and Made White in the Bloud of the Lambe. *Not to be outdone by such tactics, Williams published in 1652* The Bloudy Tenent Yet More Bloudy by Mr. Cotton's Efforts to Wash It White.

For his much honored, kind friend, Mrs. Anne Sadleir, at Sondon, in Hartforshire, near Puckridge. [No Date]

My much honored, kind friend, Mrs. Sadleir,

My humble respects premised to your much honored self, and Mr. Sadleir, humbly wishing you the saving knowledge and assurance of that life which is eternal, when this poor minute's dream is over. In my poor span of time, I have been oft in the jaws of death, sickening at sea, shipwrecked on shore, in danger of arrows, swords, and bullets. And yet, methinks, the most high and most holy God hath reserved me for some service to his most glorious and eternal majesty.

I think, sometimes, in this common shipwreck of mankind, wherein we all are either floating or sinking, despairing or struggling for life, why should I ever faint in striving, as Paul saith, in hopes to save myself, to save others—to call, and cry, and ask, what hope of saving, what hope of life, and of the eternal shore of mercy? Your last letter, my honored friend, I received as a bitter sweetening—as all that is under the sun, is— sweet in that I hear from you, and that you continue striving for life

*The Writings of Roger Williams.*

eternal; bitter, in that we differ about the way, in the midst of the dangers and distresses.

O blessed be the hour that ever we saw the light, and came into this vale of tears, if yet, at last, in any way, we may truly see our woeful loss and shipwreck, and gain the shore of life and mercy. You were pleased to direct me to divers books for my satisfaction. I have carefully endeavoured to get them, and some I have gotten; and upon my reading, I purpose, with God's help, to render you an ingenuous and candid account of my thoughts, results, etc. At present, I am humbly bold to pray your judicious and loving eye to one of mine.

'Tis true, I cannot but expect your distaste of it; and yet my cordial desire of your soul's peace here, and eternal, and of contributing the least mite toward it, and my humble respects to that blessed root of which you spring, force me to tender my acknowledgments, which if received or rejected, my cries shall never cease that one eternal life may give us meeting, since this present minute hath such bitter partings.

For the scope of this rejoinder, if it please the Most High to direct your eye to a glance on it, please you to know, that at my last being in England, I wrote a discourse entitled, *The Bloudy Tenent of Persecution for Cause of Conscience.* I bent my charge against Mr. Cotton especially, your standard bearer of New English ministers. That discourse he since answered, and calls his book, *The Bloudy Tenent Made White in the Bloud of the Lambe.* This rejoinder of mine, as I humbly hope, unwasheth his washings, and proves that in soul matters no weapons but soul weapons are reaching and effectual.

I am your most unworthy servant, yet unfeignedly respective,

ROGER WILLIAMS

FROM THE BLOUDY TENENT:

Truth: Sweet Peace, what hast thou there?

Peace: Arguments against persecution for cause of conscience.

Truth: And what there?

Peace: An answer to such arguments, contrarily maintaining such persecution for cause of conscience.

Truth: These arguments against such persecution, and the answer pleading for it, written (as love hopes) from godly intentions, hearts, and hands, yet in a marvellous different style and manner. The arguments against persecution in milk, the answer for it (as I may say) in blood.

The author of these arguments against persecution (as I have been informed) being committed by some then in power, close prisoner to Newgate, for the witness of some truths of Jesus, and having not the use of pen and ink, wrote these arguments in milk, in sheets of paper, brought to him by the woman his keeper, from a friend in London, as the stopples of his milk bottle.

In such paper written with milk nothing will appear, but the way of reading it by fire being known to this friend who received the papers, he transcribed and kept together the papers, although the author himself could not correct, nor view what himself had written.

It was in milk, tending to soul nourishment, even for babes and sucklings in Christ.

It was in milk, spiritually white, pure and innocent, like those white horses of the word of truth and meekness, and the white linen or armor of righteousness, in the army of Jesus. Rev. 6. and 19.

It was in milk, soft, meek, peaceable and gentle, tending both to the peace of souls, and the peace of States and Kingdoms.

Peace: The answer (though I hope out of milky pure intentions) is returned in blood: bloody and slaughterous conclusions; bloody to the souls of all men, forced to the religion and worship which every civil state or common-weal agrees on, and compels all subjects to in a dissembled uniformity.

Bloody to the bodies, first of the holy witnesses of Christ Jesus, who testify against such invented worships.

Secondly, of the nation and people slaughtering each other for their several respective religions and consciences.

### FROM THE BLOUDY TENENT YET MORE BLOUDY:

And for myself I must proclaim, before the most holy God, Angels and Men, that (whatever other white and heavenly Tenets Mr. Cotton holds) yet this is a foul, a black, and a bloody Tenet.

A Tenet of high Blasphemy against the God of Peace, the God of Order, who hath of one Blood made all Mankind to dwell upon the face of the Earth, now, all confounded and destroyed in their Civil Being and Substance, by mutual flames of war from their several respective Religions and Conscience.

A Tenet warring against the Prince of Peace, Christ Jesus, denying his Appearance and Coming in the Flesh, to put an end to and abolish the shadows of that ceremonial and typical Land of Canaan.

A Tenet fighting against the sweet end of his coming, which was not to destroy mens' lives for their Religions, but to save them, by the meek and peaceable Invitations and persuasions of his peaceable wisdoms' Maidens.

A Tenet fouly charging his Wisdom, Faithfulness, and Love, in so poorly providing such Magistrates and Civil Powers all the World over, as might effect so great a charge pretended to be committed to them.

A Tenet lamentably guilty of his most precious Blood, shed in the blood of so many hundred thousand of his poor servants by the civil powers of the World, pretending to suppress Blasphemies, Heresies, Idolatries, Superstition, &c.

A Tenet fighting with the Spirit of Love, Holiness and Meekness by kindling fiery Spirits of false zeal and Fury when yet such Spirits know not of what Spirit they are. . . .

A Tenet which no Uncleanness, no Adultery, Incest, Sodomy, or Bestiality can equal, this ravishing and forcing (explicitly or implicitly) the very Souls and Consciences of all the Nations and Inhabitants of the World.

A Tenet that put out the very eye of all true Faith, which cannot but be as free and voluntary as any Virgin in the World, in refusing or embracing any spiritual offer or object.

A Tenet loathsome and ugly (in the eyes of the God of Heaven, and serious sons of men) I say, loathsome with the palpable filths of gross dissimulation and hypocrisy. Thousands of Peoples and whole Nations, compelled by this Tenet to put on the foul vizard of Religious hypocrisy for fear of Laws, losses and punishments and for the keeping and hoping for of favour, liberty, worldly commodity &c.

A Tenet woefully guilty of hardening all false and deluded Consciences (of whatsoever Sect, Faction, Heresy, or Idolatry, though never so horrid and blasphemous) by cruelties and violences practised against them: all false Teachers and their Followers (ordinarily) contracting a Brawny and steely hardness from their sufferings for their Consciences. . . .

A Tenet that fights against the common principles of all Civility and the very civil being and combinations of men in Nations, Cities &c. by mixing (explicitly or implicitly) a spiritual and civil State together, and so confounding and overthrowing the purity and strength of both.

A Tenet that kindles the devouring flames of combustions and wars in most Nations of the World and (if God were not infinitely gracious) had almost ruined the English, French, the Scotch and Irish, and many other Nations, German, Poles, Hungarian, Bohemian, &c. . . .

A Tenet that renders the highest civil Magistrates and Ministers of Justice (the Fathers and Gods of their Countries) either odious or lamentably grievous unto the very best Subjects by either clapping or keeping on, the iron yokes of cruellest oppression. No yoke or bondage is comparably so grievous as that upon the Souls' neck of mens' Religion and Consciences.

A Tenet, all besprinkled with the bloody murders, stabs, poisonings, pistolings, powder-plots, &c. against many famous Kings, Princes, and States, either actually performed or attempted in France, England, Scotland, Low-Countries and other Nations.

A Tenet all red and bloody with those most barbarous and Tiger-like Massacres of so many thousand and ten thousands formerly in France and other parts, and so lately and so horribly in Ireland: of which, whatever causes be assigned, this chiefly will be found the true cause, and while this continues (to wit, violence against Conscience) this bloody

Issue, sooner or later, must break forth again (except God wonderfully stop it) in Ireland and other places too.

A Tenet that stunts the growth and flourishing of the most likely and hopefullest Common-weals and Countries, whilst Consciences, the best and best deserving Subjects are forced to fly (by enforced or voluntary Banishment) from their native Countries. The lamentable proof whereof England hath felt in the flight of so many worthy English into the Low Countries, New England, and from New England into Old again and other foreign parts.

A Tenet whose gross partiality denies the Principles of common Justice while Men weigh out to the Consciences of all others that which they judge not fit nor right to be weighed out to their own: Since the persecutors' Rule is to take and persecute all Consciences, only himself must not be touched.

A Tenet that is but Machiavellianism and makes a Religion but a cloak or stalking horse to policy and private Ends. . . .

A Tenet that corrupts and spoils the very Civil Honesty and Natural Conscience of a Nation. Since Conscience to God violated proves (without Repentance) ever after a very Jade, a Drug, loose and unconscionable in all converse with men.

Lastly, a Tenet in England most unseasonable, as pouring Oil upon those Flames which the high Wisdom of the Parliament (by easing the yokes of Mens' Consciences) had begun to quench.

In the sad Consideration of all which (Dear Peace) let Heaven and Earth judge of the washing and colour of this Tenet. For thee (sweet heavenly Guest) go lodge thee in the breasts of the peaceable and humble Witnesses of Jesus, that love the Truth in peace! Hide thee from the Worlds' Tumults and Combustions, in the breasts of thy truly noble children who profess and endeavour to break the iron and insupportable yokes upon the Souls and Consciences of any of the sons of Men.

## TO THE TOWN OF PROVIDENCE:

Providence, January 1655

That ever I should speak or write a tittle that tends to such an infinite liberty of conscience is a mistake, and which I have ever disclaimed and abhorred. To prevent such mistakes, I shall at present only propose this case: There goes many a ship to sea, with many hundred souls in one ship, whose weal and woe is common, and is a true picture of a commonwealth, or a human combination or society. It hath fallen out sometimes that both papists and protestants, Jews and Turks, may be embarked in one ship, upon which supposal I affirm that all the liberty of conscience that ever I pleaded for, turns upon these two hinges—that none of the papists, protestants, Jews, or Turks, be forced to come to the ship's prayers or worship, nor compelled from their own particular prayers or worship, if they practice any. I further add, that I never denied, that notwithstanding this liberty, the commander of this ship ought to command the ship's course, yea, and also command that justice, peace and sobriety, be kept and practiced, both among the seamen and all the passengers. If any of the seamen refuse to perform their services, or passengers to pay their freight; if any refuse to help, in person or purse, towards the common charges or defence; if any refuse to obey the common laws and orders of the ship, concerning their common peace or preservation; if any shall mutiny and rise up against their commanders and officers; if any should preach or write that there ought to be no commanders or officers, because all are equal in Christ, therefore no masters nor officers, no laws nor orders, no corrections nor punishments;—I say, I never denied, but in such cases, whatever is pretended, the commander or commanders may judge, resist, compel, and punish such transgressors, according to their deserts and merits. This if seriously and honestly minded, may, if it so please the Father of lights, let in some light to such as willingly shut not their eyes.

I remain studious of your common peace and liberty.

ROGER WILLIAMS

# In Defence of Intolerance
## *Nathaniel Ward*

*In condemning toleration, Nathaniel Ward found himself in good company in Puritan New England. Virtually every magistrate and clergyman in the colony took his stand upon the principles hammered out by the Simple Cobbler. Nor did the spirit of persecution abate after Ward left New England to carry his message of sectarian bigotry to Old England. In 1676, the Reverend William Hubbard declared that speaking or writing in favor of toleration ought to be prohibited and its advocates punished. "God never appointed a Sanctuary for Satan, nor City of Refuge for presumptuous offenders," he declared; and the president of Harvard lambasted "an unbounded toleration as the first born of all abominations."*

Either I am in an apoplexy, or that man is in a lethargy who does not now sensibly feel God shaking the heavens over his head and the earth under his feet—the heavens so as the sun begins to turn into darkness, the moon into blood, the stars to fall down to the ground so that little light of comfort or counsel is left to the sons of men; the earth so as the foundations are failing, the righteous scarce know where to find rest, the inhabitants stagger like drunken men; it is in a manner dissolved both in religions and relations, and no marvel, for they have defiled it by transgressing the laws, changing the ordinances, and breaking the everlasting Covenant. The truths of God are the pillars of the world whereon states and churches may stand quiet if they will; if they will not, He can easily shake them off into delusions and distractions enough.

Satan is now in his passions, he feels his passions approaching, he loves to fish in roiled waters. Though that dragon cannot sting the vitals of the elect mortally, yet that Beelzebub can fly-blow their intellectuals miserably. The finer religion grows, the finer he spins his cobweb; he will hold pace with Christ so long as his wits will serve him. He sees himself beaten out of gross idolatries, heresies, ceremonies, where the light breaks forth with power. He will, therefore, bestir him to prevaricate evangelical truths and ordinances, that if they will needs be walking yet they shall

*The Simple Cobbler of Aggawam in America.* Edited by Lawrence C. Wroth.

*laborare varicibus* [work at cross purposes] and not keep their path, he will put them out of time and place, assassinating for his engineers men of Paracelsian parts, well complexioned for honesty; for such are fittest to mountebank his chemistry into sick churches and weak judgments.

Nor shall he need to stretch his strength overmuch in this work. Too many men, having not laid their foundations sure nor ballasted their spirits deep with humility and fear, are pressed enough of themselves to evaporate their own apprehensions. Those that are acquainted with story know it has ever been so in new editions of churches: such as are least able are most busy to pudder in the rubbish and to raise dust in the eyes of more steady repairers. Civil commotions make room for uncivil practices—religious mutations, for irreligious opinions; change of air discovers corrupt bodies—reformation of religion, unsound minds. He that has any well-faced fancy in his crown and does not vent it now, fears the pride of his own heart will dub him dunce forever. Such a one will trouble the whole Israel of God with his most untimely births, though he makes the bones of his vanity stick up, to the view and grief of all that are godly wise. The devil desires no better sport than to see light heads handle their heels and fetch their careers in a time when the roof of liberty stands open.

The next perplexed question with pious and ponderous men will be, What should be done for the healing of these comfortless exulcerations? I am the unablest adviser of a thousand, the unworthiest of ten thousand; yet I hope I may presume to assert what follows without just offence.

First, such as have given or taken any unfriendly reports of us New English should do well to recollect themselves. We have been reputed a colluvies of wild opinionists, swarmed into a remote wilderness to find elbow room for our fanatic doctrines and practices. I trust our diligence past and constant sedulity against such persons and courses will plead better things for us. I dare take upon me to be the herald of New England so far as to proclaim to the world, in the name of our colony, that all Familists, Antinomians, Anabaptists, and other enthusiasts shall have free liberty to keep away from us; and such as will come to be gone as fast as they can, the sooner the better.

Secondly, I dare aver that God does nowhere in His word tolerate Christian states to give toleration to such adversaries of His truth, if they have power in their hands to suppress them.

Here is lately brought us an extract of a Magna Carta, so called, compiled between the sub-planters of a West Indian island, whereof the first article of constipulation firmly provides free stableroom and litter for all kind of consciences, be they never so dirty or jadish, making it actionable —yea, treasonable—to disturb any man in his religion or to discommend it, whatever it be. We are very sorry to see such professed profaneness in English professors as industriously to lay their religious foundations on the ruin of true religion, which strictly binds every conscience *to contend earnestly for the truth; to preserve unity of spirit, faith, and ordinances; to be all like minded, of one accord, every man to take his brother into his Christian care, to stand fast with one spirit, with one mind, striving together for the faith of the Gospel;* and by no means to permit heresies or erroneous opinions. But God, abhorring such loathsome beverages, has in His righteous judgment blasted that enterprize, which might otherwise have prospered well, for aught I know; I presume their case is generally known ere this.

If the devil might have his free option, I believe he would ask nothing else but liberty to enfranchise all false religions and to embondage the true; nor should he need. It is much to be feared that lax tolerations upon state pretences and planting necessities will be the next subtle stratagem he will spread to dista[s]te the truth of God and supplant the peace of the churches. Tolerations in things tolerable, exquisitely drawn out by the lines of the Scripture and pencil of the spirit, are the sacred favors of truth, the due latitudes of love, the fair compartments of Christian fraternity; but irregular dispensations, dealt forth by the facilities of men, are the frontiers of error, the redoubts of schism, the perilous irritaments of carnal and spiritual enmity.

My heart has naturally detested four things: the standing of the Apocrypha in the Bible; foreigners dwelling in my country to crowd out native subjects into the corners of the earth; alchemized coins; tolerations of divers religions, or of one religion in segregant shapes. He that willingly assents to the last, if he examines his heart by daylight, his conscience will tell him he is either an atheist or a heretic or a hypocrite, or at best a captive to some lust. Poly-piety is the greatest impiety in the world. True religion is *ignis probationis* [fire of proving], which doth *congregare homogenea & segregare heterogenea* [gather together the homogeneous and separate the heterogeneous].

Not to tolerate things merely indifferent to weak consciences argues a conscience too strong; pressed uniformity in these causes much disunity. To tolerate more than indifferents is not to deal indifferently with God; he that does it takes His scepter out of His hand and bids Him stand by. Who hath to do to institute religion but God? The power of all religion and ordinances lies in their purity, their purity in their simplicity; then are mixtures pernicious. I lived in a city where a Papist preached in one church, a Lutheran in another, a Calvinist in a third; a Lutheran one part of the day, a Calvinist the other, in the same pulpit. The religion of that place was but motley and meager, their affections leopard-like.

If the whole creature should conspire to do the Creator a mischief or offer Him an insolency, it would be in nothing more than in erecting untruths against His truth, or by sophisticating His truths with human medleys. The removing of some one iota in Scripture may draw out all the life and traverse all the truth of the whole Bible; but to authorize an untruth by a toleration of state is to build a sconce against the walls of heaven, to batter God out of His chair. To tell a practical lie is a great sin, but yet transient; but to set up a theoretical untruth is to warrant every lie that lies from its root to the top of every branch it hath, which are not a few.

I would willingly hope that no member of the Parliament has skilfully ingratiated himself into the hearts of the House that he might watch a time to midwife out some ungracious toleration for his own turn; and for the sake of that, some other, I would also hope that a word of general caution should not be particularly misapplied. I am the freer to suggest it because I know not one man of that mind. My aim is general, and I desire may be so accepted. Yet, good gentlemen, look well about you and remember how Tiberius played the fox with the senate of Rome and how Fabius Maximus cropped his ears for his cunning.

# Witchcraft in Salem
## *Increase Mather*

*Salem witchcraft was merely an episode in the history of a venerable superstition. In the seventeenth century, to doubt the existence of the devil was almost as heinous a sin as to doubt the existence of God. Science had not as yet cast doubt upon the reality of either God or the devil: God was in His heaven, the Evil One was in his subterranean pit and the world was a battleground between these two inveterate adversaries. Of course, the Puritans believed that in the end God would win, but, in the meantime, for His own inscrutable purposes, God permitted Satan to seize upon the souls of men. In this predatory sport, the devil employed witches and wizards as his "Hounds of Hell."*

*Of all the English colonists, the New England Puritans were the most conditioned by their religious beliefs to engage in witchhunts. Being a "City upon a Hill," the headquarters of righteousness in a sinful world, New England was thought to be particularly exposed to the hatred of Satan, who, it was presumed, had issued orders that this troublespot be wiped out forthwith. While the Puritans did not doubt that they had God on their side, they knew that they had driven an exposed salient into the infernal kingdom. With prayers and fasting they braced themselves for D-day. It came in 1692 at Salem Village.*

*The people were alerted to their danger by the publication in 1684 of Increase Mather's An Essay for the Recording of Illustrious Providences and in 1689 of Cotton Mather's Memorable Providences Relating to Witchcraft and Possessions. Cotton Mather believed that he had been specially commissioned by God to fight witchcraft and to "countermine the whole Plot of the Devil against New England in every branch of it." When the "woeful Witchcraft" made its appearance in Salem Village, Mather regarded it as part of the personal quarrel between himself and the devil: "this Assault of the evil Angels upon the Country," he said, "was intended by Hell, as a particular Defiance unto my poor Endeavours, to bring the Souls of Men unto Heaven."*

As there have been several persons vexed with evil spirits, so divers

Increase Mather: *Remarkable Providence*. Edited by George Offor.

houses have been woefully haunted by them. In the year 1679, the house of William Morse, in Newberry in New England, was strangely disquieted by a demon. After those troubles began, he did, by the advice of friends, write down the particulars of those unusual accidents. And the account which he giveth thereof is as followeth:—

On December 3, in the night time, he and his wife heard a noise upon the roof of their house, as if sticks and stones had been thrown against it with great violence; whereupon he rose out of his bed, but could see nothing. Locking the doors fast, he returned to bed again. About midnight they heard an hog making a great noise in the house, so that the man rose again and found a great hog in the house, the door being shut; but upon the opening of the door it ran out.

On December 8, in the morning, there were five great stones and bricks by an invisible hand thrown in at the west end of the house while the man's wife was making the bed; the bedstead was lifted up from the floor, and the bedstaff flung out of the window, and a cat was hurled at her; a long staff danced up and down in the chimney; a burnt brick and a piece of weather-board were thrown in at the window. The man, at his going to bed, put out his lamp, but in the morning found that the save-all of it was taken away, and yet it was unaccountably brought into its former place. On the same day the long staff but now spoken of was hanged up by a line and swung to and fro; the man's wife laid it in the fire, but she could not hold it there, inasmuch as it would forcibly fly out; yet after much ado, with joint strength they made it to burn. A shingle flew from the window, though nobody near it; many sticks came in at the same place, only one of these was so scragged that it could enter the hole but a little way, whereupon the man pushed it out; a great rail likewise was thrust in at the window so as to break the glass.

At another time an iron crook that was hanged on a nail violently flew up and down; also a chair flew about and at last lighted on the table where victuals stood ready for them to eat, and was likely to spoil all; only by a nimble catching they saved some of their meal with the loss of the rest and the overturning of their table.

People were sometimes barricaded out of doors, when as yet there was nobody to do it; and a chest was removed from place to place, no hand touching it. Their keys being tied together, one was taken from the rest, and the remaining two would fly about making a loud noise by knocking against each other. But the greatest part of this devil's feats were his mischievous ones, wherein indeed he was sometimes antic enough too, and therein the chief sufferers were the man and his wife, and his grandson. The man especially had his share in these diabolical molestations. For one while they could not eat their suppers quietly but had the ashes on the hearth before their eyes thrown into their victuals, yea, and upon their heads and clothes, insomuch that they were forced up into their chamber, and yet they had no rest there; for one of the man's shoes being left below, 'twas filled with ashes and coals and thrown up after them. Their light was beaten out, and they being laid in their bed with their little boy between them, a great stone (from the floor of the loft) weighing above three pounds was thrown upon the man's stomach, and he turning it down upon the floor, it was once more thrown upon him. A box and a board were likewise thrown upon them all; and a bag of hops was taken out of their chest, wherewith they were beaten till some of the hops were scattered on the floor, where the bag was then laid and left.

In another evening, when they sat by the fire, the ashes were so whirled at them that they could neither eat their meat nor endure the house. A peel struck the man in the face. An apron hanging by the fire was flung upon it, and singed before they could snatch it off. The man being at prayer with his family, a besom gave him a blow on his head behind and fell down before his face.

On another day, when they were winnowing of barley, some hard dirt was thrown in, hitting the man on the head and both the man and his wife on the back; and when they had made themselves clean, they essayed to fill their half-bushel; but the foul corn was in spite of them often cast in amongst the clean, and the man, being divers times thus abused, was forced to give over what he was about.

On January 23 (in particular), the man had an iron pin twice thrown at him, and his inkhorn was taken away from him while he was writing; and when by all his seeking it he could not find it, at last he saw it drop out of the air down by the fire. A piece of leather was twice thrown at him; and a shoe was laid upon his shoulder, which he catching at, was suddenly rapt from him. An handful of ashes was thrown at his face and upon his clothes; and the shoe was then clapt upon his head, and upon it he clapt his hand, holding it so fast that somewhat unseen pulled him with it backward on the floor.

On the next day at night, as they were going to bed, a lost ladder was thrown against the door and their light put out; and when the man was abed, he was beaten with an heavy pair of leather breeches, and pulled by the hair of his head and beard, pinched and scratched, and his bed-board was taken away from him. Yet more: in the next night, when the man was likewise abed, his bed-board did rise out of its place, notwithstanding his putting forth all his strength to keep it in; one of his awls was brought out of the next room into his bed and did prick him; the clothes wherewith he hoped to save his head from blows were violently plucked from thence. Within a night or two after, the man and his wife received both of them a blow upon their heads, but it was so dark that they could not see the stone which gave it. The man had his cap pulled off from his head while he sat by the fire.

The night following, they went to bed undressed because of their late disturbances, and the man, wife, boy presently felt themselves pricked, and upon search found in the bed a bodkin, a knitting needle, and two sticks picked at both ends; he received also a great blow, as on his thigh, so on his face, which fetched blood; and while he was writing, a candle-stick was twice thrown at him; and a great piece of bark fiercely smote him; and a pail of water turned up without hands. . . .

*February 2.* While he and his boy were eating of cheese, the pieces which he cut were wrested from them, but they were afterwards found upon the table under an apron and a pair of breeches; and also from the fire arose little sticks and ashes, which flying upon the man and his boy brought them into an uncomfortable pickle. But as for the boy, which the last passage spoke of, there remains much to be said concerning him and a principal sufferer in these afflictions; for on the 18th of December he, sitting by his grandfather, was hurried into great motions, and the man thereupon took him and made him stand between his legs; but the chair danced up and down and had like to have cast both man and boy into the fire; and the child was afterwards flung about in such a manner as that they feared that his brains would have been beaten out; and in the evening he was tossed as afore, and the man tried the project of hold-ing him, but ineffectually. The lad was soon put to bed, and they pres-ently heard an huge noise and demanded what was the matter, and he answered that his bedstead leaped up and down; and they (i.e., the man and his wife) went up and at first found all quiet, but before they had been there long they saw the board by his bed trembling by him and the bedclothes flying off him; the latter they laid on immediately, but they were no sooner on than off; so they took him out of his bed for quietness.

*December 29.* The boy was violently thrown to and fro, only they car-ried him to the house of a doctor in the town, and there he was free from disturbances; but returning home at night, his former trouble began, and the man taking him by the hand, they were both of them almost tripped into the fire. They put him to bed, and he was attended with the same iterated loss of his clothes, shaking of his bed-board, and noises that he had in his last conflict; they took him up, designing to sit by the fire, but the doors clattered and the chair was thrown at him; wherefore they carried him to the doctor's house, and so for that night all was well. The next morning he came home quiet; but as they were doing somewhat, he cried out that he was pricked on the back; they looked, and found a three-tined fork sticking strangely there, which being carried to the doctor's house, not only the doctor himself said that it was his, but also the doc-tor's servant affirmed it was seen at home after the boy was gone. The boy's vexations continuing, they left him at the doctor's, where he re-mained well till awhile after, and then he complained he was pricked; they looked and found an iron spindle sticking below his back. He complained he was pricked still; . . . they looked, and found there a long iron, a bowl of a spoon, and a piece of pan-shard. They lay down by him on the bed, with the light burning, but he was twice thrown from them, and the second time thrown quite under the bed. In the morning the bed was tossed about with such a creaking noise as was heard to the neighbour's. In the afternoon their knives were, one after another, brought, and put into his back, but pulled out by the spectators; only one knife, which was missing, seemed to the standers by to come out of his mouth. He was bidden to read; his book was taken and thrown about several times, at last hitting the boy's grandmother on the head. Another time he was thrust out of his chair and rolled up and down, with outcries that all things were on fire; yea, he was three times very dangerously thrown into the fire, and preserved by his friends with much ado. The boy also made, for a long time together, a noise like a dog, and like an hen with her chickens, and could not speak rationally.

Particularly on December 26, he barked like a dog, and clucked like an hen; and after long distraining to speak, said: "There's Powel, I am pinched." His tongue likewise hung out of his mouth so as that it could by no means be forced in till his fit was over, and then he said 'twas forced out by Powel. He and the house also after this had rest till the ninth of January; at which time the child, because of his intolerable ravings, and because the child lying between the man and his wife was pulled out of bed, and knocked so vehemently against the bedstead boards, in a manner very perilous and amazing. In the day-time he was carried away beyond all possibility of their finding him. His grandmother at last saw him creeping on one side, and dragged him in, where he lay miserable lame; but recovering his speech, he said that he was carried above the doctor's house, and that Powel carried him, and that the said Powel had him into the barn, throwing him against the cartwheel there and then thrusting him out at an hole; and accordingly they found some of the remainders of the threshed barley, which was on the barnfloor, hanging to his clothes.

At another time he fell into a swoon; they forced somewhat refreshing into his mouth, and it was turned out as fast as they put it in; ere long he came to himself and expressed some willingness to eat, but the meat would forcibly fly out of his mouth; and when he was able to speak, he said Powel would not let him eat. Having found the boy to be best at a neighbor's house, the man carried him to his daughter's, three miles from his own. The boy was growing antic as he was on the journey, but before the end of it he made a grievous hollowing; and when he lighted he threw a great stone at a maid in the house and fell on eating of ashes. Being at home afterwards, they had rest awhile; but on the 19 of January in the morning he swooned, and coming to himself he roared terribly and did eat ashes, sticks, rug-yarn. . . .

All this while the devil did not use to appear in any visible shape, only they would think they had hold of the hand that sometimes scratched them; but it would give them the slip. And once the man was discernibly beaten by a fist, and an hand got hold of his wrist, which he saw but could not catch; and the likeness of a blackamoor child did appear from under the rug and blanket where the man lay, and it would rise up, fall down, nod, and slip under the clothes when they endeavoured to clasp it, never speaking anything.

Neither were there many words spoken by Satan all this time; only once, having put out their light, they heard a scraping on the boards and then a piping and drumming on them, which was followed with a voice singing, "Revenge! Revenge! Sweet is revenge!" And they, being well terrified with it, called upon God—the issue of which was that suddenly, with a mournful note, there were six times over uttered such expressions as, "Alas! me knock no more! Me knock no more!" and now all ceased.

The man does, moreover, affirm that a seaman (being a mate of a ship) coming often to visit him told him that they wronged his wife who suspected her to be guilty of witchcraft, and that the boy (his grandchild) was the cause of this trouble; and that if he would let him have the boy one day, he would warrant him his house should be no more troubled as it had been—to which motion he consented. The mate came the next day betimes, and the boy was with him until night—after which his house, he saith, was not for some time molested with evil spirits.

Thus far is the relation concerning the demon at William Morse's house in Newberry. The true reason of these strange disturbances is as yet not certainly known; some (as has been hinted) did suspect Morse's wife to be guilty of witchcraft.

One of the neighbors took apples which were brought out of that house, and put them into the fire—upon which, they say, their houses were much disturbed. Another of the neighbors caused an horseshoe to be nailed before the doors; and as long as it remained so, they could not persuade the suspected person to go into the house; but when the horseshoe was gone, she presently visited them. I shall not here enlarge upon the vanity and superstition of those experiments, reserving that for another place; all that I shall say at present is that the demons, whom the blind Gentiles of old worshipped, told their servants that such things as these would very much affect them, yea, and that certain characters, signs, and charms would render their power ineffectual, and accordingly they would become subject when their own directions were obeyed. It is sport to the devils when they see silly men thus deluded and made fools of by them. Others were apt to think that a seaman, by some suspected to be a conjurer, set the devil on work thus to disquiet Morse's family; or it may be some other thing, as yet kept hid in the secrets of Providence, might be the true original of all this trouble.

# Witchcraft in Salem
## *Cotton Mather*

*Even for an expert in demonology like Cotton Mather, the outbreak of witchcraft at Salem Village raised some knotty problems. Many witnesses at the trials, for example, testified that they had been plagued by demons who assumed the form of citizens of blameless reputation. Was this "spectral evidence" conclusive or merely presumptive proof that these persons had sold their souls to the devil. The perplexed judges turned to the clergy for advice. Meeting in solemn conclave, the ministers drafted a reply to the effect that "spectral evidence" ought to be considered in the context of evidence but not as final proof of guilt. Satan, they declared, "may, by God's permission appear in the shape of an innocent man," but this was a comparatively rare occurrence and could not be regarded as conclusive unless other and more damning evidence was forthcoming.*

*Acting on the advice of the clergy, Governor Phips halted the trials. It was none to soon: twenty persons had been executed and over a hundred others were awaiting trial or death by hanging.*

The New Englanders are a people of God settled in those which were once the devil's territories, and it may easily be supposed that the devil was exceedingly disturbed when he perceived such a people here accomplishing the promise of old made unto our blessed Jesus—that he should have the utmost parts of the earth for his possession. There was not a greater uproar among the Ephesians when the gospel was first brought among them than there was among the powers of the air (after whom those Ephesians walked) when first the silver trumpets of the gospel here made the joyful sound. The devil, thus irritated, immediately tried all sorts of methods to overturn this poor plantation; and so much of the church as was fled into this wilderness immediately found the serpent cast out of his mouth a flood for the carrying of it away. I believe that never were more satanical devices used for the unsettling of any people under the sun than what have been employed for the extirpation of the

Cotton Mather: *The Wonders of the Invisible World.* Edited by George L. Burr.

vine which God has here planted, casting out the heathen and preparing a room before it and causing it to take deep root and fill the land, so that it sent its boughs unto the Atlantic sea eastward, and its branches unto the Connecticut River westward, and the hills were covered with the shadow thereof. But all those attempts of hell have hitherto been abortive; many an ebenezer has been erected unto the praise of God by his poor people here; and having obtained help from God, we continue to this day. Wherefore the devil is now making one attempt more upon us —an attempt more difficult, more surprising, more snarled with unintelligible circumstances than any that we have hitherto encountered—an attempt so critical that if we get well through, we shall soon enjoy halcyon days with all the vultures of hell trodden under our feet. He has wanted his incarnate legions to persecute us as the people of God have in the other hemisphere been persecuted. He has therefore drawn forth his more spiritual ones to make an attack upon us. We have been advised by some credible Christians yet alive that a malefactor, accused of witchcraft as well as murder, and executed in this place more than forty years ago, did then give notice of an horrible plot against the country by witchcraft and a foundation of witchcraft then laid, which if it were not seasonably discovered would probably blow up and pull down all the churches in the country. And we have now with horror seen the discovery of such a witchcraft! An army of devils is horribly broke in upon the place which is the center and, after a sort, the first-born of our English settlements; and the houses of the good people there are filled with the doleful shrieks of their children and servants, tormented by invisible hands with tortures altogether preternatural. After the mischiefs here endeavored, and since in part conquered, the terrible plague of evil angels hath made its progress into some other places where other persons have been in like manner diabolically handled. These, our poor afflicted neighbors, quickly after they become infected and infested with these demons, arrive to a capacity of discerning those which they conceive the shapes of their troublers; and notwithstanding the great and just suspicion that the demons might impose the shapes of innocent persons in their spectral exhibitions upon the sufferers (which may perhaps prove no small part of the witch plot in the issue), yet many of the persons thus represented being examined, several of them have been convicted of a very damnable witchcraft. Yea, more than one twenty have confessed that they have signed unto a book which the devil showed them and engaged in his hellish design of bewitching and running our land. We know not, at least I know not, how far the delusions of Satan may be interwoven into some circumstances of the confessions; but one would think all the rules of understanding human affairs are at an end if, after so many most voluntary, harmonious confessions, made by intelligent persons of all ages, in sundry towns, at several times, we must not believe the main strokes wherein those confessions all agree, especially when we have a thousand preternatural things every day before our eyes wherein the confessors do acknowledge their concernment and give demonstration of their being so concerned. If the devils now can strike the minds of men with any poisons of so fine a composition and operation that scores of innocent people shall unite in confessions of a crime which we see actually committed, it is a thing prodigious, beyond the wonders of the former ages; and it threatens no less than a sort of a dissolution upon the world. Now, by these confessions 'tis agreed that the devil has made a dreadful knot of witches in the country, and by the help of witches has dreadfully increased that knot; that these witches have driven a trade of commissioning their confederate spirits to do all sorts of mischiefs to the neighbors, whereupon there have ensued such mischievous consequences upon the bodies and estates of the neighborhood as could not otherwise be accounted for; yea, that at prodigious witch meetings the wretches have proceeded so far as to concert and consult the methods of rooting out the Christian religion from this country, and setting up instead of it perhaps a more gross diabolism than ever the world saw before. And yet it will be a thing little short of miracle if in so spread a business as this, the devil should not get in some of his juggles to confound the discovery of all the rest.

Martha Carrier was indicted for the bewitching of certain persons, according to the form usual in such cases, pleading not guilty to her indictment. There were first brought in a considerable number of the bewitched persons, who not only made the court sensible of an horrid witchcraft committed upon them, but also deposed that it was Martha Carrier or her shape that grievously tormented them by biting, pricking, pinching, and choking of them. It was further deposed that while this Carrier was on her examination before the magistrates, the poor people were so tortured that everyone expected their death upon the very spot, but that upon the binding of Carrier they were eased. Moreover the look of Carrier then laid the afflicted people for dead; and her touch, if her eye at the same time were off them, raised them again—which things were also now seen upon her trial. And it was testified that upon the mention of some having their necks twisted almost round by the shape of this Carrier, she replied, "It's no matter though their necks had been twisted quite off."

Before the trial of this prisoner several of her own children had frankly and fully confessed not only that they were witches themselves, but that this, their mother, had made them so. This confession they made with great shows of repentance and with much demonstration of truth. They related place, time, occasion; they gave an account of journeys, meetings, and mischiefs by them performed, and were very credible in what they said. Nevertheless, this evidence was not produced against the prisoner at the bar, inasmuch as there was other evidence enough to proceed upon.

Benjamin Abbot gave in his testimony that last March was a twelve-month this Carrier was very angry with him upon laying out some land near her husband's. Her expressions in this anger were that she would stick as close to Abbot as the bark stuck to the tree, and that he should repent of it afore seven years came to an end so as Doctor Prescot should never cure him. These words were heard by others besides Abbot himself, who also heard her say she would hold his nose as close to the grindstone as ever it was held since his name was Abbot. Presently after this he was taken with a swelling in his foot, and then with a pain in his side, and exceedingly tormented. It bred unto a sore, which was lanced by Doctor Prescot, and several gallons of corruption ran out of it. For six weeks it continued very bad; and then another sore bred in his groin, which was also lanced by Doctor Prescot. Another sore then bred in his groin, which was likewise cut, and put him to very great misery. He was brought unto death's door and so remained until Carrier was taken and carried away by the constable, from which very day he began to mend and so grew better every day and is well ever since.

Sarah Abbot also, his wife, testified that her husband was not only all this while afflicted in his body, but also that strange, extraordinary, and unaccountable calamities befell his cattle—their death being such as they could guess at no natural reason for.

Allin Toothaker testified that Richard, the son of Martha Carrier, having some difference with him, pulled him down by the hair of the head. When he rose again, he was going to strike at Richard Carrier, but fell down flat on his back to the ground and had not power to stir hand or foot until he told Carrier he yielded; and then he saw the shape of Martha Carrier go off his breast.

This Toothaker had received a wound in the wars, and he now testified that Martha Carrier told him he should never be cured. Just afore the apprehending of Carrier, he could thrust a knitting needle into his wound, four inches deep; but presently after her being seized he was thoroughly healed.

He further testified that when Carrier and he sometimes were at variance she would clap her hands at him and say he should get nothing by it—whereupon he several times lost his cattle by strange deaths, whereof no natural causes could be given.

John Rogger also testified that upon the threatening words of this malicious Carrier his cattle would be strangely bewitched, as was more particularly then described.

Samuel Preston testified that about two years ago, having some difference with Martha Carrier, he lost a cow in a strange, preternatural, unusual manner; and about a month after this, the said Carrier having again some difference with him, she told him he had lately lost a cow and it should not be long before he lost another—which accordingly came to pass; for he had a thriving and well-kept cow which without any known cause quickly fell down and died.

Phebe Chandler testified that about a fortnight before the apprehension of Martha Carrier, on a Lord's day while the psalm was singing in the church, this Carrier then took her by the shoulder and shaking her asked her where she lived. She made no answer, although as Carrier, who lived next door to her father's house, could not in reason but know who she was. Quickly after this, as she was at several times crossing the fields, she heard a voice that she took to be Martha Carrier's; and it seemed as if it was over her head. The voice told her she should within two or three days be poisoned. Accordingly, within such a little time, one half of her right hand became greatly swollen and very painful, as also part of her face—whereof she can give no account how it came. It continued very bad for some days, and several times since she has had a greater pain in her breast and been so seized on her legs that she has hardly been able to go. She added that lately, going well to the house of God, Richard, the son of Martha Carrier, looked very earnestly upon her; and immediately her hand, which had formerly been poisoned, as is above said, began to pain her greatly; and she had a strange burning at her stomach, but was then struck deaf so that she could not hear any of the prayer or singing till the two or three last words of the psalm. . . .

One Lacy, who likewise confessed her share in this witchcraft, now testified that she and the prisoner were once bodily present at a witch meeting in Salem village, and that she knew the prisoner to be a witch and to have been at a diabolical sacrament, and that the prisoner was the undoing of her and her children by enticing them into the snare of the devil.

Another Lacy, who also confessed her share in this witchcraft, now testified that the prisoner was at the witch meeting in Salem village, where they had bread and wine administered unto them.

In the time of this prisoner's trial, one Susanna Sheldon in open court had her hands unaccountably tied together with a wheel band so fast that without cutting it could not be loosed. It was done by a specter, and the sufferer affirmed it was the prisoner's.

Memorandum: This rampant hag, Martha Carrier, was the person of whom the confessions of the witches and of her own children among them are agreed that the devil had promised her she should be queen of hell.

# Witchcraft in Salem
## *Samuel Sewall*

*In 1692, despite the fact that he had no legal training, Sewall was ap-*
*pointed to the Court of Oyer and Terminer commissioned by Governor*
*Phips to try those accused of witchcraft in Salem Village. Sewall knew*
*and liked George Burroughs and yet, as a judge, he condemned Bur-*
*roughs to death as a wizard. Fearful that innocent blood had been shed*
*at Salem, Sewall interpreted the death of his daughter Sarah in 1696 to*
*mean that God was displeased with him. To avert further punishment*
*and to ease his conscience of the burden of guilt, he confessed before*
*the congregation of his church that as a judge of the Court of Oyer and*
*Terminer he committed the sin of condemning innocent people to death.*

*April 11th, 1692.* Went to Salem, where, in the Meeting-house, the persons accused of Witchcraft were examined; was a very great Assembly;
'twas awful to see how the afflicted persons were agitated. Mr. Noyes
pray'd at the beginning, and Mr. Higginson concluded. . . .
*August 19, 1692.* Doleful Witchcraft. George Burroughs, John Willard,
Jno Proctor, Martha Carrier and George Jacobs were executed at Salem,
a very great number of Spectators being present. Mr. Cotton Mather was
there, Mr. Sims, Hale, Noyes, Cheever, etc. All of them said they were
innocent, Carrier and all. Mr. Mather says they all died by a Righteous
Sentence. Mr. Burroughs, by his Speech, Prayer, protestation of his
Innocence, did much move unthinking persons, which occasions their
speaking hardly concerning his being executed.
*August 25, 1692.* Fast at the old Church, respecting the Witchcraft,
Drought, etc.
*September 19, 1692.* About noon, at Salem, Giles Cory was press'd to
death for standing Mute; much pains was used with him two days, one
after another, by the Court and Capt. Gardner of Nantucket who had
been of his acquaintance: but all in vain.
*September 20, 1692.* Now I hear from Salem that about 18 years ago, he
was suspected to have attempted and press'd a man to death, but was

*Diary of Samuel Sewall, 1674–1729.*

cleared. 'Twas not remembered till Ann Putnam was told of it by said Cory's Specter the Sabbath-day night before the Execution.

*September 21, 1692.* A petition is sent to Town in behalf of Dorcas Hoar, who now confesses; Accordingly an order is sent to the Sheriff to forbear her Execution, notwithstanding her being in the Warrant to die tomorrow. This is the first condemned person who has confess'd.

*October 15, 1692.* Went to Cambridge and visited Mr. Danforth, and discoursed with Him about the Witchcraft; thinks there cannot be a procedure in the Court except there be some better consent of Ministers and People. Told me of the woman's coming into his house last Sabbath-day sennight at Even.

*October 26, 1692.* A Bill is sent in about calling a Fast, and Convocation of Ministers, that may be led in the right way as to the Witchcrafts. The season and manner of doing it, is such, that the Court of Oyer and Terminer count themselves thereby dismissed. . . .

*October 28, 1692.* Lieut. Governor coming over the Causeway is, by reason of the high Tide, so wet, that is fain to go to bed till sends for dry clothes to Dorchester; In the Afternoon, as had done several times before, desired to have the advice of the Governor and Council as to the sitting of the Court of Oyer and Terminer next week said should move it no more; great silence, as if should say do not go.

*October 29, 1692.* Mr. Russell asked whether the Court of Oyer and Terminer should sit, expressing some fear of Inconvenience by its fall. Governor said it must fall. . . .

*November 22, 1692.* I prayed that God would pardon all my Sinful Wanderings, and direct me for the future. That God would bless the Assembly in their debates, and that would choose and assist our Judges, etc., and save New England as to Enemies and Witchcrafts, and vindicate the late Judges, consisting with his Justice and Holiness, etc., with Fasting.

*December 21, 1696.* This day I remove poor little Sarah into my Bedchamber, where about Break of Day, December 23, she gives up the Ghost in Nurse Cowell's Arms. Born, November 21, 1694. . . . Thus this very fair day is rendered foul to us by reason of the general Sorrow and Tears in the family. Master Cheever was here the evening before, I desir'd him to pray for my daughter. The Chapter read in course on Dec. 23 m. was Deut. 22, which made me sadly reflect that I had not been so thoroughly tender of my daughter; nor so effectually careful of her Defence and preservation as I should have been. The good Lord pity and pardon and help for the future as to those God has still left me.

*December 24.* Sam. recites to me in Latin, Mat. 12. from the 6th to the end of the 12th verse.* The 7th verse did awfully bring to mind the Salem Tragedy.

---

* "If ye had known what this meaneth, I will have mercy and not sacrifice, ye would not have condemned the guiltless."

PETITION PUT UP BY MR. SEWALL ON THE FAST DAY,
JANUARY 14, 1697

Copy of the Bill I put up on the Fast day; giving it to Mr. Willard as he pass'd by, and standing up at the reading of it, and bowing when finished; in the Afternoon.

Samuel Sewall, sensible of the reiterated strokes of God upon himself, and family; and being sensible, that as to the Guilt contracted upon the opening of the late Commission of Oyer and Terminer at Salem (to which the order for this Day relates) he is, upon many accounts, more concerned than any that he knows of, Desires to take the Blame and shame of it, Asking pardon of men, And especially desiring prayers that God, who has an Unlimited Authority, would pardon that sin and all other his sins; personal and Relative: And according to his infinite Benignity, and Sovereignty, Not Visit the sin of him, or of any other, upon himself or any of his, nor upon the Land: But that He would powerfully defend him against all Temptations to Sin, for the future; and vouchsafe him the efficacious, saving Conduct of his Word and Spirit.

# The Devil in the Shape of a Woman

## Cotton Mather

*Being one of the chosen few was not, Mather discovered, wholly a cause for singing hosannas. For the devil, too, took an extraordinary interest in Cotton Mather and his affairs. Mather called Satan "my Great Adversary," and he did not doubt that the Prince of Darkness accorded him an equally high place among his adversaries. Being the foremost enemy of hell, Mather was exposed to the full force of Satan's malice. As was his wont, the devil did not fight fair: he assailed Mather with lascivious thoughts, tempted him to blaspheme against the Christian religion and caused him to be plagued by enemies. In 1703, having suffered for many years from these stratagems, Mather determined to take "an exemplary Revenge upon the Devil." Characteristically, his revenge took the form of a sermon which he later published under the title:* The Wiles of the Divil. *As a precaution against the "fiery Darts" of the Old Deluder, certain to be thrown into a rage by having his favorite tricks exposed, Mather fasted and prayed with special fervor—and to such good effect that he escaped without a scratch.*

*February, 1702–03*
  *February* begins with a very astonishing Trial.
  There is a young Gentlewoman of incomparable Accomplishments. No Gentlewoman in the English *America* has had a more polite Education. She is one of rare Witt and Sense; and of a comely Aspect; and extremely Winning in her Conversation, and she has a Mother of an extraordinary Character for her Piety.
  This young Gentlewoman first Addresses me with diverse Letters, and then makes me a Visit at my House; wherein she gives me to understand, that she has long had a more than ordinary Value for my Ministry; and that since my present Condition has given her more of Liberty to think of me, she must confess herself charmed with my Person, to such a

*The Diary of Cotton Mather.* Edited by Worthington C. Ford.

Degree, that she could not but break in upon me, with her most importunate Requests, that I would make her mine; and that the highest consideration she had in it, was her eternal Salvation, for if she were mine, she could not but hope the Effect of it would be, that she should also be Christ's.

I endeavoured faithfully to sett before her, all the discouraging Circumstances attending me, that I could think of. She told me, that she had weigh'd all those Discouragements, but was fortified and resolved with a strong Faith in the mighty God, for to encounter them all. And whereas I had mention'd my way of living, in continual Prayers, Tears, Fasts, and macerating Devotions and Reservations, to divert her from her Proposal, she told me, that this very Consideration was that which animated her; for she desired nothing so much as a Share in my way of Living.

I was in a great Strait, how to treat so polite a Gentlewoman, thus applying herself unto me. I plainly told her, that I feared, whether her Proposal would not meet with unsurmountable Oppositions from those who had a great Interest in disposing of me. However I desired, that there might be Time taken, to see what would be the wisest and fittest Resolution.

In the mean Time, if I could not make her my own, I should be glad of being any way Instrumental, to make her the Lord's.

I turned my Discourse, and my Design into that Channel; and with as exquisite Artifice as I could use, I made my Essayes to engage her young Soul into Piety.

She is not much more than twenty years old. I know she has been a very aiery Person. Her Reputation has been under some Disadvantage.

What Snares may be laying for me, I know not. Much Prayer with Fasting and Patience, must be my way to encounter them.

I think, how would my Lord Jesus Christ Himself treat a returning Sinner.

I shall shortly see more into the Meaning of this odd Matter.


*February, 1702* [1703]

My sore Distresses and Temptations, I this day carried unto the Lord; with Hope of His Compassions, to his tempted Servant.

The cheef of them lies in this. The well accomplished Gentlewoman, mention'd, (tho' not by Name) in the Close of the former Year; one whome everybody does with Admiration confess to be, for her charming Accomplishments, an incomparable Person; addressing me to make her mine; and professing a Disposition unto the most Holy Flights of Religion to ly at the Bottom of her Addresses: I am in the greatest Straits imaginable, what Course to steer. Nature itself causes in me, a mighty Tenderness for a person so very amiable. Breeding requires me to treat her with Honour and Respect, and very much of Deference, to all that she shall at any time ask of me. But Religion, above all, obliges me, instead of a rash rejecting her Conversation, to contrive rather, how I may imitate the Goodness of the Lord Jesus Christ, in His Dealing with such as are upon a Conversion unto Him.

On the other side; I cannot but fear a fearful Snare, and that I may soon fall into some Error in my Conversation, if the Point proposed unto me, be found, after all, unattaineable, thro' the violent Storm of Opposition, which I cannot but foresee and suspect will be made unto it.

The dreadful Confusions, which I behold Heaven, even *devising* for me, do exceedingly break and wast my spirit. I should recover a wondrous Degree of Health, if I were not broken by these Distresses, and grievous Temptations. But these things cause me to spend more Time than ordinary for the most part every Day, in Prayers and in Tears, prostrate on my Study-floor before the Lord. Yea, and they cause me by Night also sometimes to hold my *Vigils*, in which I cry to God, until, and after, the Middle of the Night, that He would look down upon me, and help me, and save me, and not cast me off.

*18.* This Day was kept as a Fast, thro' the Province. I enjoy'd great Assistences, in the services of the Day.

As for my special soul-harassing Point: I did some Dayes ago, under my Hand, vehemently beg, as for my Life, that it might be desisted from, and that I might not be kill'd by hearing any more of it. Yett such was my flexible Tenderness, as to be conquered by the Importunities of several, to allow some further Interviewes. But I resolved, that I would make them turn chiefly upon the most glorious Design in the World. I did, accordingly; and once especially, I did, with all the Charms I could imagine, draw that witty Gentlewoman unto tearful Expressions of her Consent, unto all the Articles in the Covenant of Grace, the Articles of her Marriage and Union with the Great L[ord] Redeemer. I had abundance of Satisfaction in this Action; whatever may be the Issue of our Conversation.

*20.* My grievous Distresses (occasion'd especially by the late Addresses made unto me, by the person formerly mentioned, and the Opposition of her Enemies) cause me to fall down before the Lord, with Prayers and with Tears continually. And because my Heart is sore pained within me, to think, what I shall do, or what will be the Issue of my distressing Affayr, I think it proper to multiply my *Vigils* before the Lord. One of them I kept this Night; and as it grew towards the Morning, after I had cried unto the Lord, for my Releef and Succour, under the Temptations now harassing of me, I did again throw myself prostrate in the Dust, before the Lord; beseeching of Him, that if He would not hear my cries for myself, He would yett hear my cries for my Flock; and hereupon I wrestled with the Lord for my great Congregation, that the Interests of Religion might prevail mightily among them, and especially in the young People of my Congregation.

It was a Consolation unto me, to think, that when my People were all asleep in their Beds, their poor Pastor should be watching, and praying and weeping for them.

The Lord, in His holy Sovereignity orders it, that I am left unto great Vexations from Satan, about this Time; who fills me with fears, that I am a man rejected and abhorred of God, and given up to the worst of Delusions; and that the Lord will make no more use of me to glorify Him. I am scarce able to live under these doleful Disconsolations.

And that I may be left utterly destitute of all humane Support, my Relatives, thro' their extreme Distaste at the Talk of my Respects for the Person, above mentioned; and fear lest I should over-value her; do treat me with unsupportable Strangeness and Harshness.

*Lord, I am oppressed; undertake for me!*

27. I sett apart this Day for Prayer and Fasting in my study; especially to commend my distressing Affayr unto the Lord.

As for the ingenious Child, that solicits my Respects unto her, I cry to the Lord, with Fervency and Agony and Floods of Tears, that she may be the Lord's; and that her Union and Marriage to the Lord Jesus Christ, may be the Effect of the Discourses I have had with her. But I also resign her, and offer her up unto the Lord; and earnestly profess unto Him, that tho' I sett a great Value upon her, yett I can deny myself every thing in the World, that the Glory of His Name, and my Service to His Name, shall oblige me to part withal. Wherefore, I continually beg of the Lord, that Hee will show me my Duty and bring my Distress to a comfortable Issue.

*March, 1703*

3. My dreadful Distresses continue upon me.

For which Cause, I sett apart this Day, for the Duties of a secret Fast before the Lord; that I may obtain Direction in, and Deliverance from, the Distresses which do so exceedingly harass and buffet my Mind, and break my Soul to Peeces.

As also, that I may obtain the Presence of the Lord with me, in the Lecture to morrow, when I am to do a special Service, for His Interests.

6. Tho' I have kept one Fast in my Study this Week already, yett I must this Day keep another.

I am a most miserable Man.

That young Gentlewoman of so fine Accomplishments (that there is none in this Land in those Respects comparable to her), who has with such repeated Importunity and Ingenuity pressed my Respects to her, that I have had much ado to steer clear of great Inconveniences, hath by the Disadvantages of the Company which has continually resorted unto her unhappy Father's House, gott but a bad Name among the Generality of the People; and there appears no Possibility of her speedy Recovery of it, be her Carriage never so vertuous, and her Conversion never so notorious. By an unhappy Coincidence of some Circumstances, there is a Noise, and a mighty Noise it is, made about the Town, that I am engaged in a Courtship to that young Gentlewoman; and tho' I am so very innocent (and have so much aimed at a Conformity to my Lord Jesus Christ, and Serviceableness to Him, in my treating of her), yett it is not easy persently to confute the Rumour.

I am now under incredible Disadvantages. The Design of Satan, to entangle me in a Match that might have proved ruinous to my Family, or my Ministry, is defeated, by my Resolution totally to reject the Addresses of the young Gentlewoman to me; which I do, for the sake of the Lord Jesus Christ, whose Name, I see will suffer, if I accept her; and I do it cheerfully, tho' she be so very charming a Person.

But then, Satan has raised an horrid Storm of Reproach upon me, both for my Earliness in courting a Gentlewoman, and especially for my Courting of a Person whom they generally apprehend so disagreeable to my Character. And there is hazard, lest my Usefulness be horribly Ruined, by the Clamour of the rash People on this Occasion, before there can be due Measures taken to quiet them; and my Civility to the Person who has address'd me, will not lett me utter what would most effectually quiet them.

I am a man greatly assaulted by Satan. Is it because I have done much against the Enemy? or, are the Judgments of God incessantly pursuing of me, for my Miscarriages!

My Spirit is excessively broken. There is Danger of my dying suddenly, with smothered Griefs and Fears. I know not what to do, but to pour out my Soul unto the Lord, and submitt unto His dreadful Sovereignity and Righteousness; but my precious Opportunities to glorify the L[ord] Jesus Christ (the Apple of my Eye,) from the Mischiefs which do threaten them.

15. And now, being after all due Deliberation, fully satisfied, that my Countenancing the Proposals of coming one Day to a Marriage, with the Gentlewoman so often mentioned in these Papers, will not be consistent with my public Serviceableness; but that the Prejudices in the Minds of the People of God against it, are insuperable, and little short of universal: I sett myself to make unto the L[ord] Jesus Christ, a Sacrifice of a Person, who, for many charming Accomplishments, has not many aequals in the *English America*. In making of my Sacrifice, I have not gone upon any inferiour Considerations, nor have I minded, but sleighted, the defamatory Stories, which have been uttered concerning her, as knowing how little weight there is to be laid upon popular Slanders. But I have been

acted purely, by a religious Respect unto the Holy Name of the L[ord] Jesus Christ, and my Serviceableness to His precious Interests; which I had a thousand Times rather dy, than damnify. My Victory over Flesh and Blood in this Matter, was no unhappy Symptom, I hope, of Regeneration in my Soul. I encouraged myself with Hopes, that God would carry me well thro' my Sacrifice, in preserving the Person addressing me from any Damage by her Fondness for me; (but I must continue praying for her)! And that I should one Day meet with some wonderful Recompences.

I struck my knife, into the Heart of my Sacrifice, by a Letter to her Mother.

27. Was ever man more tempted, than the miserable *Mather!* Should I tell, in how many Forms the Divel has assaulted me, and with what Subtility and Energy, his Assaults have been carried on, it would strike my Friends with Horrour.

Sometimes, Temptations to *Impurities;* and sometimes to Blasphemy, and Atheism, and the Abandonment of all Religion, as a meer Delusion; and sometimes, to self-Destruction itself. These, even these, O miserable *Mather,* do follow thee, with an astonishing Fury. But I fall down into the Dust, on my Study-floor, with Tears before the Lord; and then they quickly vanish: tis fair Weather again. *Lord! what will thou do with me!*

*April, 1703*

3. I am under singular Distresses. What I would on many Accounts prefer, as the most eligible and honourable Condition, would be to continue all the rest of my little Time, in an unspotted Widowhood.

But my Family suffers by it, in several Instances. And yett I could concoct and conquer this Inconvenience, much easier than some other Circumstances.

My Father presses me frequently and fervently, that I would by no means take up Resolutions to continue in my Widowhood. My flexible Temper makes it not easy for me to resist his Exhortations.

But I foresee, and already suffer, a worse Encumbrance. The Applications, which the Gentlewoman formerly mentioned in these Papers, has made unto me, have occasioned very many Misrepresentations of me, among a foolish People. The coarse, tho' just, Usage that she has had from me, will also putt her upon a thousand Inventions. I shall be continually every Week, persecuted with some Noise and Nonsense carried about the Town concerning me. The Persecution of the Lyes daily invented about me, will be, I see insupportable. All the Friends I have in the World, perswade me, that I shall have no Way to gett from under these Confusions, but by proceeding unto another Marriage.

Lord, help me, what shall I do? I am a miserable man.

*13, 14, 15.* The Dispensations of Heaven towards me, in and since, the Death of my lovely Consort, have been very awful.

I have lately waded thro' dreadful Temptations, and I tremble to think, what may be the next Storm, that will be raised upon me.

About eleven Months having passed since the Lord began to take away from me the Desire of my Eyes, my Friends begin to press my Thoughts of returning to the married State. This is a Point of terrible Consequence. I had need use more than ordinary Humiliations, and Supplications, and Resignations, upon an Occasion so full of Agony.

Tho' I have rarely lett a Week pass me, without setting apart a Day for *Prayer with Fasting,* for now many, many Months together; and I have ever now and then had my *Vigils,* for a Conversation with Heaven; and every Day for the most Part, I have had one *secret Prayer* more than I use to have, and lain prostrate, in the Dust, with Tears before the Lord, because of my Distresses: Yett I thought it necessary to do something more than all of this. I resolved upon doing a thing, which I do not know to have been done, by any Man living in the World. I took up a Resolution, to spend no less than THREE DAYES together, in *Prayer with Fasting* in my Study; and *beseech the Lord thrice,* knocking at the Door of Heaven for *three Dayes* together.

Astonishing Entertainments from Heaven, were granted me, in and from this Action. God opened Heaven to me, after a Manner, that I may not, and indeed cannot express in any Writing. All I will here insert is, that now the Thought of Dying (and going to the heavenly World) was become the most easy and pleasant Thing in the World unto me. I am now advised from Heaven, that God is mine, and I am His; and He has wonderful Things to do for me.

Extraordinary Things were again done for me, that cannot be related. I will only say, the Angels of Heaven are at work for me. And I have *my own Angel,* who is a better Friend unto me, than any I have upon Earth.

The great Point of my Return to the *married State,* I did on each of the three Dayes, with a Variety of tearful Supplications plead before the Lord. I have submitted unto all the Inconveniences of a *single State,* if the Lord will confine me to it; only I have begg'd of Him, the Gifts of Purity and Patience. But I have left the Matter entirely unto the Lord; who will *withhold no good Thing* from me. I have putt my Mind over into the Hands of the Holy Spirit, that it may be disposed aright in the Matter. I have committed unto my Lord Jesus Christ, the Care of providing an agreeable Consort for me, if my support in the Service of His Church (which I am daily espousing unto Him) render it necessary or convenient. I know, that some surprising Thing will be done for me.

My three Dayes left me, in a very desireable Frame, very fearful of sinning against God; very raised in my Thoughts of Christ and Heaven; very watchful to do good, and bring forth much Fruit unto the Lord.

But because an Admission to extraordinarily Intimate Communion with Heaven, uses in my Experience to be followed with sore Buffetings from Satan, either by internal Impressions, or by external Occurrences, I had a trembling Expectation of what might follow upon that Intercourse with Heaven, whereto I had newly been admitted.

I found within two Dayes, my Mind begun to be horribly agitated, with Vexations, which did somewhat renew an Experience, that I had so often mett withal.

*May, 1703*

8. I enjoyed some Assurances, which I thought from Heaven, that God would be very merciful and wonderful in the Dispensations of His Providence, about my Return to the *married State;* and that for the sake of the Lord Jesus Christ, whose I am, a desireable Consort should be bestow'd upon me; and a glorious Angel of the Lord, should be concerned for me (as for *Isaac* of old), in this important Matter.

13. One Day, after Prayers, and Floods of Tears before the Lord, and astonishing Resignations to and Satisfactions in His glorious Will, I was just overperswaded unto the taking of a Step, towards my Return unto the married State. But a marvellous Providence of God, overruled it. I was diverted from doing a Thing, whereto my Friends, and such Friends as have a mighty Ascendant over me, had mightily urged me. I knew, that I might on every hand, meet with great Encouragements unto a matter, and yett it might prove a wrong Matter, if it should be prosecuted. So, I saw that the best of my Friends on Earth, are not much to be relied upon. My pliable and flexible Temper, will expose me to Ruines, in following the Conduct of my wisest Friends, if I don't watch exceedingly. I will wait until my heavenly Friend and Father, do more plainly show me, what He would have me to do. I will be satisfied in what the Lord shall order for me, tho' to me at the Present, there may seem a grievous Disappointment in it.

15. I sett apart this Day, for the Duties of Prayer, with Fasting, in my Study, partly that I might obtain the Presence of the Lord with me, in several important Actions, which are the next Week before me: But chiefly, that I might bespeak a good Issue, unto that very great Affayr, namely my Return into the married State.

It was a Day full of astonishing Enjoyments; a Day filled with Resignations, and Satisfactions, and heavenly Astonishments. Heaven has been opened unto me this Day. Never did I so long to dy, and fly away into Heaven. I have seen and felt unutterable Things. I have tasted that the Lord is gracious, I can by no means relate the Communications with Heaven, whereto I have been this Day admitted. I am now sure, that the

Great God is my God; that I stand before God in the Righteousness of my Lord Jesus Christ; that no good Thing shall be withheld from me; that God will make an amazing use of me to glorify Him; and that I shall be an object for the everlasting Triumphs of sovereign and infinite Grace.

I was not able to bear the Extasies of the Divine Love, into which I was raptured; They exhausted my Spirits; they made me faint and sick; they were insupportable; I was forced, even to withdraw from them, lest I should have swoon'd away under the Raptures.

19. I preached both parts of the Lord's-Day, at *Salem;* and on *Monday* returned home.

In my Absence the young Gentlewoman, to whom I have been so unkind many Weeks or Months ago, writes and comes to my Father, and brings her good Mother with her and charms the Neighbours into her Interests; and renewes her Importunities (both before and after my Journey) that I would make her mine. My Apprehension of Damage to arise therefrom unto the holy Interests of Religion, fixes me still in an unalterable Resolution, that I must never hearken to her Proposals, whatever may be the Consequence of my being so resolved. I am hereupon threatened by some with exquisite Revenges and Reproaches from her defeated Love; and the Hazards of her coming to Mischief. Some sett the Town into a new Storm of Obloquy upon me; and threaten me with an horrid Encumbrance upon all my Intentions elsewhere to return unto the married State.

Satan makes these Rebukes of Heaven upon me, after all my Prayers, and Tears, and Fasts and Resignations, to be an Occasion of sore Temptation unto me.

*June, 1703*

12. A lying Spirit is gone forth, and the People of the Town, are strangely under the Influences of it.

I have the Inconvenience of being a Person, whom the Eye and the Talk of the People is very much upon. My present Circumstances give them Opportunities to invent and report Abundance of disadvantageous Falsehoods, of my being engaged in such and such Courtships, wherein I am really unconcerned. But the Addresses which I have had from the young Gentlewoman so often mentioned in these Papers, and the Discourses thereby raised among the dissatisfied People, afford the greatest Theme for their mischievous and malicious Lying to turn upon. When all Assaults upon me from that Quarter, have been hitherto unsuccessful, at last, I am unhappily persecuted with Insinuations that I had proceeded so far in Countenancing that matter, I could not with Honour and Justice now steer clear of it, as I have done. God strangely appears for me, in this Point also, by disposing the young Gentlewoman, with her Mother, to furnish me with their Assertions, *That I have never done any unworthy*

*Thing; but acted most honourably and righteously towards them, and as became a Christian, and a Minister; and they will give all the World leave to censure them after the hardest Manner in the World, if ever they should speak the Contrary;* Yea, they have proceeded so far beyond all Bounds in my Vindication, as to say, *They verily look upon* Mr M—r *to be as great a Saint of God, as any upon Earth.* Nevertheless, the Divel owes me a Spite, and he inspires his People in this Town, to whisper impertinent Stories, which have a Tendency to make me Contemptible, and hurt my Serviceableness, and strike at, yea, strike out the Apple of my Eye. My Spirit is on this Occasion too much disturbed: I am encountring an *Hour and Power of Darkness.* My Temptations from the Clamour of many People, among whom I hear the Defaming of many; the desolate Condition of my Family, not likely to be provided for; and the Desertions which my Soul suffers, while I behold the dreadful Frown of God upon my Prayers, my Fasts, my Fears, my Resignations and all my Endeavours to glorify Him: these things do exceedingly unhinge me; and cause me sometimes to *speak unadvisedly with my Lips.* Tis well, if they do not perfectly kill me.

23. The Day before my Lecture, apply myself to Prayer with Fasting; for to obtain Help against my Temptations, and a blessed Issue of the Storms, and Fears, and Cares that are now upon me.

Then, and the Morning following, and all the Time of my Prayer before my Lecture, I was very sick (as well as otherwise horribly buffeted): but in the Time of singing the Psalm, I lifted up my Eyes and my Cries, unto my Lord Jesus Christ, that He would rate off Satan, and strengthen me for, and carry me thro' His work now before me. He did it wonderfully! I preached with mighty Assistences, on Eph. 6. 11. *The wiles of the Divel.* The Lord was wonderfully present with me.

After this, I found the Tempest of Clamour, which the Gentlewoman, defeated of her exquisite Contrivances to obtain me, had occasioned, by the Help of some evil Women against me, strangely going off. One passage I am willing to mention: A Person of principal Quality (and one who was not of principal Piety) among us, told me, on Friday, that I was the most beloved man in all the Countrey; and that I had a few Enemies but they were miserable and contemptible People; and that all the late Impertinences that had vexed me, would never do me any Damage at all.

*July, 1703*

10. In my Request for a good Servant, I received an immediate Answer, God most mercifully answered me, by sending into the Family, the Servant, which had for so many Years been a Blessing unto me and mine, and unto whom I had been so much a Father, until the Small-Pox, and the Distraction which it left upon her, the last Winter, had made her uncapable of serving me.

But God is going to build up my Family, in a far more important and illustrious Instance.

He showes me a Gentlewoman within two Houses of my own; a Gentlewoman of Piety and Probity, and a most unspotted Reputation; a Gentlewoman of good Witt and Sense, and Discretion at ordering an Household; a Gentlewoman of incomparable Sweetness in her Temper, and Humour; a Gentlewoman honourably descended and related; and a very comely person. Her Name, is Mrs. ELIZABETH HUBBARD. She is the Daughter of Dr. *John Clark*, deceased. She was married, and quickly left a Widow about four years ago, and is now near thirty Years of Age.

She has one Son, about the Age of my own. But I often urged my departed Consort to take a Fatherless child into my Family, and feed it, and cloathe it, that God might bless my Children. Why then should I think much to educate the Son of a Gentlewoman from whom I expect so much service to mine?

I am satisfied, if the Spirit of my departed Consort now in the King-dome of God, were advized, that her children were falling into the Hands of this Gentlewoman, it would be a Consolation unto her.

And, I perceive, that it would be a more than ordinary Satisfaction unto the people of my vast Flock, more than an hundred to one, for me, to seek an Acquaintance with this Gentlewoman.

Finding my Spirit much disposed unto it, (and being hastened by a Coincidence of many uneasy Circumstances), I did.

On *14 d.* 5 *m. Wednesday,* give my first Visit, unto that lovely Gentle-woman. I was entertained with more than ordinary Civility, Affection, and Veneration. And I found her to be an abundantly more agreeable Person, than ever I imagined. I see, she will be a great Gift of Heaven unto me, an astonishing Reparation of my Loss, and Compensation of all the Grief I have mett withal. If I may live to see her illuminating my Family, I shall reap a rich Harvest of the Prayers, the Tears, the Fasts, and the Resignations, with which I have been so long addressing Heaven, under the deplorable Circumstances, of about fifteen Months together.

17. I sett apart this Day, for Prayer with Fasting, in my Study, to obtain a good Progress and Success of the affayr, which I am now man-aging; and a Deliverance from any further Vexation, Temptation, or Encumbrance by the young Gentlewoman, that has vexed me with so many of her Wiles, and by such exquisite Methods been trying to ensnare or trouble me.

The Rage of that young Gentlewoman, whom out of obedience to God, I have rejected (and never more pleased God than in rejecting of her Addresses to me) is transporting her, to threaten that she will be a Thorn in my Side, and contrive all possible Wayes to vex me, affront me, dis-grace me, in my Attempting a Return to the married State with another Gentlewoman. Instead of using other Contrivances, to quell the Rage of a Person, who is of so rare a Witt, but so little Grace, that I may expect unknown Damages from her, I carried her to the Lord Jesus Christ. I pleaded, that my Lord Jesus Christ is able to do every thing; that He can restrain Satan, and all Satanic Influences at His Pleasure; that my Temptations had already proceeded a great Way; and His Name would suffer and His poor Servant would sink, if He should permitt them to proceed any further; and that I had out of Obedience unto Him, exposed myself unto the Rage, by which I was now likely to be incommoded. And I concluded still, with a triumphant Faith in my Lord Jesus Christ, for my Victory over the Mischiefs which threatened me.

Behold, within a few Dayes, the Gentlewoman without my seeking it, sent me a Letter, with a Promise under her Hand, that she would offer me none of those Disquietments, which in her Passion she had threatened. I was astonished at this work of Heaven; and with the Tears of a raptured Soul, I offered up a Sacrifice of Love and Praise unto the Lord.

My Conversation with the lovely Person, to whom Heaven has directed me, goes on, with pure, chast, noble Strokes, and the Smiles of God upon it.

And the Universal Satisfaction which it has given to the People of God, thro' town and Countrey, proclames itself, to a Degree which perfectly amazes me.

The extreme Heat of the Weather (with some other Inconveniences, by the Carpenters making some Addition to my Habitation) putt me by, from keeping a Fast this Week, as I might else have done. But,

31. I sett apart for such exercises.

About this Time, I was for two or three Dayes followed with a strong Fancy, that I should be taken away by Death, before my Return to the married State. I concluded, this Fancy to be ordered for my Trial, whether I could submitt unto such a Dispensation of Heaven. Accordingly, tho' I have a Prospect of arriving speedily to the Enjoyment of a most lovely Creature, and of astonishing Mercies to my Family in and with that lovely Person, yett when I thought of going away to my Lord Jesus Christ, in the heavenly World, I found my Soul swallow'd up in Triumphs and Raptures of Resignation unto the Will of God, if He will so order my Condition for me. I did with Tears of Joy consent unto such a Dispensation!

From hence I gathered several comfortable Things; whereof one was, that I am in very deed passed from Death to Life.

The horrible Storm of Temptations that has been of late harassing of me, is after a strange Manner calm'd and Ceas'd; and I am now speedily returning to the married State, in more happy Circumstances, than I could have imagined. I was desirous, that my Lord JESUS CHRIST, should have some special Revenues of Glory, from the *Temptations* (and all the Afflictions) that have befallen me. Wherefore I fitted for the Press, a

Discourse, which I entitled; GREAT CONSOLATIONS: *or, A brief Essay upon the Joy of a Tempted Christian, triumphing over his Temptations*. And I gave it unto the Printer.

*August, 1703*

14. Designing the next Week, to return unto the married State, I sett apart this Day, by Prayer with Fasting to seek the Blessing of God, upon me, in that Affayr; that all my Sins may be pardoned, and that no Guilt may accompany me, to procure me Chastisements from Heaven in the State whereinto I am entring; and that all the Circumstances of the next Week, may be mercifully directed and ordered by the Lord.

The dreadful Calamities of our poor Plantations, upon which the Indians are now committing their cruel Depredations, did also call me, and cause me, to ly in the Dust before the Lord.

18. THIS is the Day, the joyful Day, wherein my glorious Lord JESUS CHRIST brings me, to the rich Harvest of my Prayers, my Tears, my Resignations. I am in the Evening of this Day, to receive a most lovely Creature, and such a Gift of Heaven unto me, and mine, that the Sense thereof almost as often as I ponder thereon, dissolves me into Tears of Joy.

I resolved, that I would spend the Day in Heaven, if the Lord would please to open unto me His Heaven. I spent the whole Day in my Study, devoting it as a solemn THANKSGIVING unto the Lord. I gave Thanks for the various and marvellous mercies of God unto me, and I sang His Praises, with a Repetition of Devotions, wherein my Soul melted into Tears, felt the Love of God unto me, in all that has befallen me. But I gave Thanks very particularly, for my astonishing Preservations, from undoing myself, my Ministry, and my Family, under the amazing Temptations, which in the Time of my Widowhood, I have mett withal; and for my being brought at length, so near to the Enjoyment of a most amiable Person, and the most agreeable Consort (all things considered) that all *America* could have afforded me. The forming and finding of this excellent Creature, hath been a signal Work of my Lord Jesus Christ; and His glorious Angel has doubtless been employ'd about it!

God made this Day, to be unto me, a Day of more than ordinary Entertainments from the heavenly World. I was this Day in the Spirit, filled with the Love and Joy of the Lord. I now know, that God has loved me with an everlasting Love, and hath yett great Things to do for me, and by me.

In the Evening, my Father married me, unto a Wife, in finding of whom, I have to my Astonishment found Favour of the Lord.

I thought I should glorify my Lord Jesus Christ, and approve myself an exemplary Man, if, as I never declined any Service unto the Lord, for any Affliction, so neither should I for any Enjoyment. Wherefore, I preached the Lecture on Thursday, the Day after my Marriage; and as I preached to a vast Assembly, so I preached with a great Assistence; I had a more than usual presence of the Lord with me, in all the Service before me.

Returning Home, as I was alone, I had my Soul even ravished with the Thoughts of the Divine Favour to me; resolving hereupon to lay myself out in the Service of my dear L[ord] Jesus Christ, and of His Churches, unto the uttermost.

# Sinners in the Hands of an
# Angry God
## *Jonathan Edwards*

*When Edwards preached his message of man's infinite depravity and God's infinite power and pictured mankind dangling over the pit of hell, precariously suspended by the "forbearance of an incensed God," the blood of his auditors congealed in their veins. One member of Edwards' congregation declared he confidently expected that as soon as the sermon was finished, the trumpets would sound to proclaim the Last Judgment. The air seemed to reek of sulphur, the flames licked close and the shrieks of the damned were audible. Overwhelmed by a consciousness of sin, reprobacy and the imminence of divine retribution, Edwards' more impressionable parishioners fell to shrieking, jerking and frothing.*

*Edwards produced this effect by speaking in even, measured tones. Instead of gesturing, he simply "looked on the bell rope until he looked it off." His manner was that of a scientist methodically demonstrating the truth of a theorem by dissecting a worm. In this case, the theorem was the absolute sovereignty of God; the worm was man.*

Deut. 32.35, "Their foot shall slide in due time."

In this verse is threatened the vengeance of God on the wicked unbelieving Israelites, who were God's visible people, and who lived under the means of grace; but who, notwithstanding all God's wonderful works towards them, remained (as ver. 28) void of counsel, having no understanding in them. Under all the cultivations of heaven, they brought forth bitter and poisonous fruit; as in the two verses next preceding the text.—The expression I have chosen for my text, *Their foot shall slide in due time*, seems to imply the following things, relating to the punishment and destruction to which these wicked Israelites were exposed.

Jonathan Edwards: *Representative Selections*. Edited by Clarence H. Faust and Thomas H. Johnson.

1. That they were always exposed to *destruction;* as one that stands or walks in slippery places is always exposed to fall. This is implied in the manner of their destruction coming upon them, being represented by their foot sliding. The same is expressed, Psalm 73.18: "Surely thou didst set them in slippery places; thou castedst them down into destruction."

2. It implies, that they were always exposed to sudden unexpected destruction. As he that walks in slippery places is every moment liable to fall, he cannot foresee one moment whether he shall stand or fall the next; and when he does fall, he falls at once without warning: which is also expressed in Psalm 73.18, 19: "Surely thou didst set them in slippery places; thou castedst them down into destruction. How are they brought into desolation as in a moment!"

3. Another thing implied is, that they are liable to fall *of themselves,* without being thrown down by the hand of another; as he that stands or walks on slippery ground needs nothing but his own weight to throw him down.

4. That the reason why they are not fallen already, and do not fall now, is only that God's appointed time is not come. For it is said, that when that due time, or appointed time comes, *their foot shall slide.* Then they shall be left to fall, as they are inclined by their own weight. God will not hold them up in these slippery places any longer, but will let them go; and then, at that very instant, they shall fall into destruction; as he that stands on such slippery declining ground, on the edge of a pit, he cannot stand alone, when he is let go he immediately falls and is lost.

The observation from the words that I would now insist upon is this—"There is nothing that keeps wicked men at any one moment out of hell, but the mere pleasure of God."—By the *mere* pleasure of God, I mean his *sovereign* pleasure, his arbitrary will, restrained by no obligation, hindered by no manner of difficulty, any more than if nothing else but God's mere will had in the least degree, or in any respect whatsoever, any hand in the preservation of wicked men one moment. . . .

### APPLICATION

The use of this awful subject may be for awakening unconverted persons in this congregation. This that you have heard is the case of every one of you that are out of Christ.—That world of misery, that lake of burning brimstone, is extended abroad under you. There is the dreadful pit of the glowing flames of the wrath of God; there is hell's wide gaping mouth open; and you have nothing to stand upon, nor any thing to take hold of; there is nothing between you and hell but the air; it is only the power and mere pleasure of God that holds you up.

You probably are not sensible of this; you find you are kept out of hell, but do not see the hand of God in it; but look at other things, as the good state of your bodily constitution, your care of your own life, and the means you use for your own preservation. But indeed these things are nothing; if God should withdraw his hand, they would avail no more to keep you from falling, than the thin air to hold up a person that is suspended in it.

Your wickedness makes you as it were heavy as lead, and to tend downwards with great weight and pressure towards hell; and if God should let you go, you would immediately sink and swiftly descend and plunge into the bottomless gulf, and your healthy constitution, and your own care and prudence, and best contrivance, and all your righteousness, would have no more influence to uphold you and keep you out of hell, than a spider's web would have to stop a fallen rock. Were it not for the sovereign pleasure of God, the earth would not bear you one moment; for you are a burden to it; the creation groans with you; the creature is made subject to the bondage of your corruption, not willingly; the sun does not willingly shine upon you to give you light to serve sin and Satan; the earth does not willingly yield her increase to satisfy your lusts; nor is it willingly a stage for your wickedness to be acted upon; the air does not willingly serve you for breath to maintain the flame of life in your vitals, while you spend your life in the service of God's enemies. God's creatures are good, and were made for men to serve God with, and do not willingly subserve to any other purpose, and groan when they are abused to purposes so directly contrary to their nature and end. And the world would spew you out, were it not for the sovereign hand of him who hath subjected it in hope. There are black clouds of God's wrath now hanging directly over your heads, full of the dreadful storm, and big with thunder; and were it not for the restraining hand of God, it would immediately burst forth upon you. The sovereign pleasure of God, for the present, stays his rough wind; otherwise it would come with fury, and your destruction would come like a whirlwind, and you would be like the chaff of the summer threshing floor.

The wrath of God is like great waters that are dammed for the present; they increase more and more, and rise higher and higher, till an outlet is given; and the longer the stream is stopped, the more rapid and mighty is its course, when once it is let loose. It is true, that judgment against your evil works has not been executed hitherto; the floods of God's vengeance have been withheld; but your guilt in the mean time is constantly increasing, and you are every day treasuring up more wrath; the waters are constantly rising, and waxing more and more mighty; and there is nothing but the mere pleasure of God, that holds the waters back, that are unwilling to be stopped, and press hard to go forward. If God should only withdraw his hand from the flood-gate, it would immediately fly open, and the fiery floods of the fierceness and wrath of God, would rush forth with inconceivable fury, and would come upon you with omnipotent power; and if your strength were ten thousand times greater than it is, yea, ten thousand times greater than the strength of the stoutest, sturdiest devil in hell, it would be nothing to withstand or endure it.

The bow of God's wrath is bent, and the arrow made ready on the string, and justice bends the arrow at your heart, and strains the bow, and it is nothing but the mere pleasure of God, and that of an angry God, without any promise or obligation at all, that keeps the arrow one moment from being made drunk with your blood. Thus all you that never passed under a great change of heart, by the mighty power of the Spirit of God upon your souls; all you that were never born again, and made new creatures, and raised from being dead in sin, to a state of new, and before altogether unexperienced light and life, are in the hands of an angry God. However you may have reformed your life in many things, and may have had religious affections, and in the house of God, it is nothing but his mere pleasure that keeps you from being this moment swallowed up in everlasting destruction. However unconvinced you may now be of the truth of what you hear, by and by you will be fully convinced of it. Those that are gone from being in the like circumstances with you, see that it was so with them; for destruction came suddenly upon most of them; when they expected nothing of it, and while they were saying, Peace and safety: now they see, that those things on which they depended for peace and safety, were nothing but thin air and empty shadows.

The God that holds you over the pit of hell, much as one holds a spider, or some loathsome insect over the fire, abhors you, and is dreadfully provoked: his wrath towards you burns like fire; he looks upon you as worthy of nothing else, but to be cast into the fire; he is of purer eyes than to bear to have you in his sight; you are ten thousand times more abominable in his eyes, than the most hateful venomous serpent is in ours. You have offended him infinitely more than ever a stubborn rebel did his prince; and yet it is nothing but his hand that holds you from falling into the fire every moment. It is to be ascribed to nothing else, that you did not go to hell the last night; that you was suffered to awake again in this world, after you closed your eyes to sleep. And there is no other reason to be given, why you have not dropped into hell since you arose in the morning, but that God's hand has held you up. There is no other reason to be given why you have not gone to hell, since you have sat here in the house of God, provoking his pure eyes by your sinful wicked manner of attending his solemn worship. Yea, there is nothing else that is to be given as a reason why you do not this very moment drop down into hell.

O sinner! Consider the fearful danger you are in: it is a great furnace of wrath, a wide and bottomless pit, full of the fire of wrath, that you are held over in the hand of that God, whose wrath is provoked and incensed as much against you, as against many of the damned in hell. You hang by a slender thread, with the flames of divine wrath flashing about it, and ready every moment to singe it, and burn it asunder; and you have no interest in any Mediator, and nothing to lay hold of to save yourself, nothing to keep off the flames of wrath, nothing of your own, nothing that you ever have done, nothing that you can do, to induce God to spare you one moment.

# Personal Narrative
## *Jonathan Edwards*

*This fragment of autobiography deals almost wholly with Edwards'
spiritual tribulations. It tells more of his concept of God than does his
often-printed sermon,* Sinners in the Hands of an Angry God. *Edwards'
message was of the joys of heaven, not the terrors of hell; to him, love
was the "essence of all true religion." When he pictured mankind walking
upon "a rotten covering" over the pit of hell, his purpose was to use the
threat of hellfire to promote the cause of the Kingdom of Heaven. "I
think it is a reasonable thing," he said, "to fright persons away from hell.
They stand upon the brink, and are just ready to fall into it, and are
senseless of their danger. Is it not a reasonable thing to fright a person
out of a house on fire?"*

I had a variety of concerns and exercises about my soul, from my
childhood; but I had two more remarkable seasons of awakening, before
I met with that change, by which I was brought to those new dispositions, and that new sense of things, that I have since had. The first time
was when I was a boy, some years before I went to college, at a time of
remarkable awakening in my father's congregation. I was then very
much affected for many months, and concerned about the things of
religion, and my soul's salvation; and was abundant in religious duties.
I used to pray five times a day in secret, and to spend much time in
religious conversation with other boys; and used to meet with them
to pray together. I experienced I know not what kind of delight in
religion. My mind was much engaged in it, and had much self-righteous
pleasure; and it was my delight to abound in religious duties. I, with
some of may school-mates, joined together and built a booth in a
swamp, in a very retired spot, for a place of prayer.—And besides, I
had particular secret places of my own in the woods, where I used to
retire by myself; and was from time to time much affected. My affections seemed to be lively and easily moved, and I seemed to be in my

Jonathan Edwards: *Representative Selections.* Edited by Clarence H. Faust and
Thomas H. Johnson.

element, when engaged in religious duties. And I am ready to think, many are deceived with such affections, and such a kind of delight as I then had in religion, and mistake it for grace.

But, in process of time, my convictions and affections wore off; and I entirely lost all those affections and delights, and left off secret prayer, at least as to any constant preference of it; and returned like a dog to his vomit, and went on in the ways of sin. Indeed, I was at times very uneasy, especially towards the latter part of my time at college; when it pleased God, to seize me with a pleurisy; in which he brought me nigh to the grave, and shook me over the pit of hell. And yet, it was not long after my recovery, before I fell again into my old ways of sin. But God would not suffer me to go on with any quietness; I had great and violent inward struggles, till, after many conflicts with wicked inclinations, repeated resolutions, and bonds that I laid myself under by a kind of vows to God, I was brought wholly to break off all former wicked ways and all ways of known outward sin, and to apply myself to seek salvation, and practice many religious duties; but without that kind of affection and delight which I had formerly experienced. My concern now wrought more, by inward struggles, and conflicts, and self-reflections. I made seeking my salvation, the main business of my life. But yet, it seems to me, I sought it after a miserable manner; which has made me sometimes since to question, whether ever it issued in that which was saving; being ready to doubt, whether such miserable seeking ever succeeded. I was indeed brought to seek salvation, in a manner that I never was before; I felt a spirit to part with all things in the world, for an interest in Christ. My concern continued and prevailed, with many exercising thoughts and inward struggles; but yet it never seemed to be proper, to express that concern by the name of terror.

From my childhood up, my mind had been full of objections against the doctrine of God's sovereignty, in choosing whom he would to eternal life, and rejecting whom he pleased; leaving them eternally to perish, and be everlastingly tormented in hell. It used to appear like a horrible doctrine to me. But I remember the time very well, when I seemed to be convinced, and fully satisfied, as to this sovereignty of God, and his justice in thus eternally disposing of men, according to his sovereign pleasure. But never could give an account, how, or by what means, I was thus convinced, not in the least imagining at the time, nor a long time after, that there was any extraordinary influence of God's Spirit in it; but only that now I saw further and my reason apprehended the justice and reasonableness of it. However, my mind rested in it; and it put an end to all those cavils and objections. And there has been a wonderful alteration in my mind, with respect to the doctrine of God's sovereignty, from that day to this; so that I scarce ever have found so much as the rising of an objection against it, in the most absolute sense, in God shewing mercy to whom he will shew mercy, and hardening whom he will. God's absolute sovereignty and justice, with respect to salvation and damnation, is what my mind seems to rest assured of, as much as of any thing that I see with my eyes; at least it is so at times. But I have often, since that first conviction, had quite another kind of sense of God's sovereignty than I had then. I have often since had not only a conviction, but a *delightful* conviction. The doctrine has very often appeared exceedingly pleasant, bright, and sweet. Absolute sovereignty is what I love to ascribe to God. But my first conviction was not so.

The first instance that I remember of that sort of inward, sweet delight in God and divine things that I have lived much in since was on reading those words, 1 Tim. 1.17: *Now unto the King eternal, immortal, invisible, the only wise God, be honour and glory for ever and ever. Amen.* As I read the words, there came into my soul, and was as it were diffused through it, a sense of the glory of the Divine Being; a new sense, quite different from any thing I ever experienced before. Never any words of Scripture seemed to me as these words did. I thought with myself, how excellent a Being that was, and how happy I should be, if I might enjoy that God, and be rapt up to him in heaven and be as it were swallowed up in him for ever! I kept saying, and as it were singing, over these words of Scripture to myself; and went to pray to God that I might enjoy him, and prayed in a manner quite different from what I used to do; with a new sort of affection. But it never came into my thought that there was any thing spiritual, or of a saving nature in this.

From about that time, I began to have a new kind of apprehensions and ideas of Christ, and the work of redemption, and the glorious way of salvation by him. An inward, sweet sense of these things, at times, came into my heart; and my soul was led away in pleasant views and contemplations of them. And my mind was greatly engaged to spend my time in reading and meditating on Christ, on the beauty and excellency of his person, and the lovely way of salvation by free grace in him. I found no books so delightful to me, as those that treated of these subjects. Those words Cant. 2.1 used to be abundantly with me, *I am the rose of Sharon, and the lily of the valleys.* The words seemed to me, sweetly to represent the loveliness and beauty of Jesus Christ. The whole book of Canticles used to be pleasant to me, and I used to be much in reading it, about that time; and found, from time to time, an inward sweetness, that would carry me away, in my contemplations. This I know not how to express otherwise, than by a calm, sweet abstraction of soul from all the concerns of this world; and sometimes a kind of vision, or fixed ideas and imaginations, of being alone in the mountains, or some solitary wilderness, far from all mankind, sweetly conversing with Christ, and wrapt and swallowed up in God.

The sense I had of divine things, would often of a sudden kindle up, as it were, a sweet burning in my heart; an ardour of soul, that I know not how to express.

Not long after I first began to experience these things, I gave an account to my father of some things that had passed in my mind. I was pretty much affected by the discourse we had together; and when the discourse was ended, I walked abroad alone, in a solitary place in my father's pasture, for contemplation. And as I was walking there, and looking upon the sky and clouds, there came into my mind so sweet a sense of the glorious *majesty* and *grace* of God, as I know not how to express.—I seemed to see them both in a sweet conjunction; majesty and meekness joined together: it was a sweet, and gentle, and holy majesty; and also a majestic meekness; an awful sweetness; a high, and great, and holy gentleness.

After this my sense of divine things gradually increased, and became more and more lively, and had more of that inward sweetness. The appearance of every thing was altered; there seemed to be, as it were, a calm, sweet, cast, or appearance of divine glory, in almost every thing. God's excellency, his wisdom, his purity and love, seemed to appear in every thing; in the sun, moon, and stars; in the clouds and blue sky; in the grass, flowers, trees; in the water and all nature; which used greatly to fix my mind. I often used to sit and view the moon for a long time; and in the day, spent much time in viewing the clouds and sky, to behold the sweet glory of God in these things: in the meantime, singing forth, with a low voice, my contemplations of the Creator and Redeemer. And scarce any thing, among all the works of nature, was so sweet to me as thunder and lightning; formerly nothing had been so terrible to me. Before, I used to be uncommonly terrified with thunder, and to be struck with terror when I saw a thunderstorm rising; but now, on the contrary, it rejoiced me. I felt God, if I may so speak, at the first appearance of a thunder-storm; and used to take the opportunity, at such times, to fix myself in order to view the clouds, and see the lightnings play, and hear the majestic and awful voice of God's thunder, which oftentimes was exceedingly entertaining, leading me to sweet contemplations of my great and glorious God. While thus engaged, it always seemed natural for me to sing, or chant forth my meditations; or, to speak my thoughts in soliloquies with a singing voice.

I felt then great satisfaction, as to my good estate, but that did not content me. I had vehement longings of soul after God and Christ, and after more holiness, wherewith my heart seemed to be full, and ready to break; which often brought to my mind the words of the Psalmist, Psal. 119.28: *My soul breaketh for the longing it hath.* I often felt a mourning and lamenting in my heart, that I had not turned to God sooner, that I might have had more time to grow in grace. My mind was greatly fixed on divine things; almost perpetually in the contemplation of them. I spent most of my time in thinking of divine things, year after year; often walking alone in the woods, and solitary places, for meditation, soliloquy, and prayer, and converse with God; and it was always my manner, at such times, to sing forth my contemplations. I was almost constantly in ejaculatory prayer, wherever I was. Prayer seemed to be natural to me, as the breath by which the inward burnings of my heart had vent. The delights which I now felt in the things of religion, were of an exceedingly different kind from those before-mentioned, that I had when a boy; and what then I had no more notion of, than one born blind has of pleasant and beautiful colours. They were of a more inward, pure, soul-animating and refreshing nature. Those former delights never reached the heart; and did not arise from any sight of the divine excellency of the things of God; or any taste of the soul-satisfying and life-giving good there is in them.

My sense of divine things seemed gradually to increase, till I went to preach at New York; which was about a year and a half after they began; and while I was there, I felt them very sensibly, in a much higher degree, than I had done before. My longings after God, and holiness, were much increased. Pure and humble, holy and heavenly, christianity appeared exceedingly amiable to me. I felt a burning desire to be, in every thing, a complete christian; and, conformed to the blessed image of Christ; and that I might live, in all things, according to the pure, sweet, and blessed rules of the gospel. I had an eager thirsting after progress in these things; which put me upon pursuing and pressing after them. It was my continual strife day and night, and constant inquiry, how I should *be* more holy and *live* more holily, and more becoming a child of God, and a disciple of Christ. I now sought an increase of grace and holiness, and a holy life, with much more earnestness than ever I sought grace before I had it. I used to be continually examining myself, and studying and contriving for likely ways and means, how I should live holily, with far greater diligence and earnestness, than ever I pursued any thing in my life; but yet with too great a dependence on my own strength; which afterwards proved a great damage to me. My experience had not then taught me, as it has done since, my extreme feebleness and impotence, every manner of way; and the bottomless depths of secret corruption and deceit, there was in my heart. However, I went on with my eager pursuit after more holiness, and conformity to Christ.

The heaven I desired was a heaven of holiness; to be with God, and to spend my eternity in divine love and holy communion with Christ. My mind was very much taken up with contemplations on heaven, and the enjoyments there; and living there in perfect holiness, humility, and love: and it used at that time to appear a great part of the happiness

of heaven, that there the saints could express their love to Christ. It
appeared to me a great clog and burden, that what I felt within, I
could not express as I desired. The inward ardour of my soul, seemed
to be hindered and pent up, and could not freely flame out as it would.
I used often to think, how in heaven this principle should freely and
fully vent and express itself. Heaven appeared exceedingly delightful,
as a world of love; and that all happiness consisted in living in pure,
humble, heavenly, divine love.

I remember the thoughts I used then to have of holiness; and said
sometimes to myself, "I do certainly know that I love holiness, such as
the gospel prescribes." It appeared to me, that there was nothing in it
but what was ravishingly lovely; the highest beauty and amiableness—
a *divine* beauty; far purer than any thing here upon earth; and that
every thing else was like mire and defilement, in comparison of it.

Holiness, as I then wrote down some of my contemplations on it,
appeared to me to be of a sweet, pleasant, charming, serene, calm
nature; which brought an inexpressible purity, brightness, peacefulness
and ravishment to the soul. In other words, that it made the soul like
a field or garden of God, with all manner of pleasant flowers, enjoying
a sweet calm, and the gently vivifying beams of the sun. The soul of a
true christian, as I then wrote my meditations, appeared like such a
little white flower as we see in the spring of the year; low and humble
on the ground, opening its bosom, to receive the pleasant beams of the
sun's glory; rejoicing, as it were, in a calm rapture; diffusing around
a sweet fragrancy; standing peacefully and lovingly, in the amidst of
other flowers round about; all in like manner opening their bosoms,
to drink in the light of the sun. There was no part of creature-holiness,
that I had so [great a] sense of its loveliness, as humility, brokenness of
heart, and poverty of spirit; and there was nothing that I so earnestly
longed for. My heart panted after this—to lie low before God, as in
the dust; that I might be nothing, and that God, might be ALL, that I
might become as a little child.

While at New York, I sometimes was much affected with reflections
on my past life, considering how late it was before I began to be truly
religious; and how wickedly I had lived till then: and once so as to
weep abundantly, and for a considerable time together.

On January 12, 1723, I made a solemn dedication of myself to God,
and wrote it down; giving up myself, and all that I had to God; to be
for the future, in no respect, my own; to act as one that had no right to
himself, in any respect. And solemnly vowed, to take God for my whole
portion and felicity; looking on nothing else, as any part of my happiness, nor acting as if it were; and his law for the constant rule of my
obedience: engaging to fight, with all my might, against the world, the
flesh, and the devil, to the end of my life. But I have reason to be

infinitely humbled, when I consider, how much I have failed, of answering my obligation.

I had then abundance of sweet religious conversation, in the family where I lived, with Mr. John Smith, and his pious mother. My heart was knit in affection, to those, in whom were appearances of true piety; and I could bear the thoughts of no other companions, but such as were holy, and the disciples of the blessed Jesus. I had great longings, for the advancement of Christ's kingdom in the world; and my secret prayer used to be, in great part, taken up in praying for it. If I heard the least hint, of any thing that happened, in any part of the world, that appeared, in some respect or other, to have a favourable aspect, on the interests of Christ's kingdom, my soul eagerly catched at it; and it would much animate and refresh me. I used to be eager to read public newsletters, mainly for that end; to see if I could not find some news, favourable to the interest of religion in the world.

I very frequently used to retire into a solitary place, on the banks of Hudson's River, at some distance from the city, for contemplation on divine things and secret converse with God: and had many sweet hours there. Sometimes Mr. Smith and I walked there together, to converse on the things of God; and our conversation used to turn much on the advancement of Christ's kingdom in the world, and the glorious things that God would accomplish for his church in the latter days. I had then, and at other times, the greatest delight in the holy scriptures, of any book whatsoever. Oftentimes in reading it, every word seemed to touch my heart. I felt a harmony between something in my heart, and those sweet and powerful words. I seemed often to see so much light exhibited by every sentence, and such a refreshing food communicated, that I could not get along in reading; often dwelling long on one sentence, to see the wonders contained in it; and yet almost every sentence seemed to be full of wonders.

I came away from New York in the month of April, 1723, and had a most bitter parting with Madam Smith and her son. My heart seemed to sink within me, at leaving the family and city, where I had enjoyed so many sweet and pleasant days. I went from New York to Wethersfield, by water; and as I sailed away, I kept sight of the city as long as I could. However, that night after this sorrowful parting, I was greatly comforted in God at Westchester, where we went ashore to lodge: and had a pleasant time of it all the voyage to Saybrook. It was sweet to me to think of meeting dear christians in heaven, where we should never part more. At Saybrook we went ashore to lodge on Saturday, and there kept the Sabbath; where I had a sweet and refreshing season, walking alone in the fields.

After I came home to Windsor, I remained much in a like frame of mind, as when at New York; only sometimes I felt my heart ready to sink, with the thoughts of my friends at New York. My support was in contemplations on the heavenly state; as I find in my Diary of May 1, 1723. It was a comfort to think of that state, where there is fulness of joy; where reigns heavenly, calm, and delightful love, without alloy; where there are continually the dearest expressions of this love; where is the enjoyment of the persons loved, without ever parting; where those persons who appear so lovely in this world will really be inexpressibly more lovely, and full of love to us. And how sweetly will the mutual lovers join together, to sing the praises of God and the Lamb! How will it fill us with joy to think, that this enjoyment, these sweet exercises, will never cease, but will last to all eternity.

# PART IV

# THE INDIANS

# The Indians in Virginia

## Captain John Smith

*John Smith's interest in the Virginia Indians did not proceed from mere curiosity: during the early years of the Jamestown settlement, its survival depended upon preserving friendly relations with the neighboring savages. During his governorship, Smith conducted a forceful policy toward the Indians: he later boasted that he had compelled them to contribute to the food supply of Jamestown and he planned to reduce them to the position of agricultural laborers working for the benefit of the whites. Smith played a lone hand in a dangerous game and on several occasions he came close to losing his life. Nevertheless, as a result of his expeditions into the interior and along the shores of the Chesapeake he was easily the best-informed man in Virginia concerning the Indians' methods of waging war, their customs and their religious beliefs.*

The land is not populous, for the men be few; the far greater number is of women and children. Within 60 miles of Jamestown there are about some 5000 people, but of able men fit for their wars scarcely 1500. To nourish so many together they have yet no means, because they make so small a benefit of their land, be it never so fertile.

6 or 700 have been the most hath been seen together, when they gathered themselves to have surprised Captain Smith at Pamaunke, he having but 15 to withstand the worst of their fury. As small as the proportion of ground that hath yet been discovered, is in comparison of that yet unknown. The people differ very much in stature, especially in language, as before is expressed.

Some being very great as the Sasquesahanocks, others very little as the Wighcocomocoes, but generally tall and straight, of a comely proportion, and of a colour brown when they are of any age, but they are born white. Their hair is generally black; but few have any beards. The men wear half their heads shaven, the other half long. For Barbers they use their women, who with 2 shells will grate away the hair of any

*Travels and Works of Captain John Smith.* Edited by Edward Arber.

fashion they please. The women are cut in many fashions agreeable to their years, but always some part remaineth long.

They are very strong, of an able body and full of agility, able to endure and to lie in the woods under a tree by the fire in the worst of winter, or in the weeds and grass, in *Ambuscado* in the Summer. They are inconstant in every thing, but what fear constraineth them to keep. Crafty, timerous, quick of apprehension and very ingenuous. Some are of disposition fearful, some bold, most cautious, all *Savage*. Generally covetous of copper, beads, and such like trash. They are soon moved to anger and so malicious that they seldom forget an injury; they seldom steal one from another, lest their conjurors should reveal it and so they be pursued and punished. That they are thus feared is certain but that any can reveal their offenses by conjuration I am doubtful. Their women are careful not to be suspected of dishonesty without the leave of their husbands. Each household possesses their own lands and gardens, and most live of their own labours.

For their apparel, they are some time covered with the skins of wild beasts, which in winter are dressed with the hair but in summer without. The better sort use large mantels of deer skin not much differing in fashion from the Irish mantels. Some are embroidered with white beads, some with copper, others painted after their manner. But the common sort have scarce to cover their nakedness but with grass, the leaves of trees, or such like. We have seen some use mantels made of Turkey feathers, so prettily wrought and woven with threads and nothing could be discerned but the feathers, that was exceeding warm and very handsome. But the women are always covered about their middles with a skin and very shamefaced to be seen bare. They adorn themselves most with copper beads and paintings. Their women some have their legs, hands, breasts and faces cunningly embroidered with diverse works, as beasts, serpents, artificially wrought into their flesh with black spots. In each ear they commonly have 3 great holes, whereat they hang chains, bracelets or copper. Some of their men wear in those holes small green and yellow coloured snake, near half a yard in length, which crawling and lapping herself about his neck often times familiarly would kiss his lips. Others wear a dead Rat tied by the tail. Some on their heads wear the wing of a bird or some large feather with a Rattle. Those Rattles are somewhat like the metal trimming of a Rapier but less, which they take from the tail of a snake. Many have the whole skin of a hawk or some strange fowl stuffed with wings spread. Others a broad piece of copper, and some the hand of their enemy dried. Their heads and shoulders are painted red with root *Pocone* braided with powder mixed with oil. This they hold in summer to preserve them from the heat and in winter from the cold. Many other use forms of painting, but he is the most gallant that is the most monstrous to behold.

Their buildings and habitations are for the most part by the rivers or not far distant from some fresh spring. Their houses are built like our Arbors of small young springs bowed and tied and so close covered with mats or the bark of trees very handsomely, that notwithstanding either wind, rain or weather, they are as warm as stoves but very smoky, yet at the top of the house there is a hole made for the smoke to go into right over the fire. Against the fire they lie on little hurdles of Reeds covered with a mat, borne from the ground a foot and more by a bundle of wood. On these round about the house they lie heads and points one by thother against the fire, some covered with mats, some with skins, and some stark naked lie on the ground from 6 to 20 in a house. Their houses are in the midst of their fields or gardens which are small plots of ground, some 20, some 40, some 100, some 200, some more, some less. Sometimes from 2 to 100 of those houses together, or but a little separated by groves of trees. Near their habitations is little small wood or old trees on the ground, by reason of their burning of them for fire. So that a man may gallop a horse amongst these woods any way but where the creeks or Rivers shall hinder.

Men, women and children have their several names according to the several humors of their Parents. Their women (they say) are easily delivered of child, yet do they love children very dearly. To make them hardy, in the coldest mornings they wash them in the rivers and by painting and ointments so tan their skins, that after a year or two no weather will hurt them.

The men bestow their time in fishing, hunting, wars and such man-like exercises, scorning to be seen in any woman-like exercise, which is the cause that the womens' labor be very painful and the men often idle. The women and children do the rest of the work. They make mats, baskets, pots, mortars, pound their corn, make their bread, prepare their victuals, plant their corn, gather their corn, bear all kind of burdens, and such like.

Their fire they kindle presently by chafing a dry pointed stick in a hole of a little square piece of wood, that firing itself, will so far fire moss, leaves, or any such like dry thing that will quickly burn.

In March and April they live much upon their fishing gear and feed on fish, Turkeys and squirrels. In May and June they plant their fields and live most on Acorns, walnuts and fish. But to mend their diet, some disperse themselves in small companies and live upon fish, beasts, crabs, oysters, land tortoises, strawberries, mulberries and such like. In June, July and August they feed upon the roots of *Tocknough* berries, fish and green wheat. It is strange to see how their bodies alter with their diet, even as the deer and wild beasts, they seem fat and lean, strong

and weak. *Powhatan,* their great king, and some others that are provident, roast their fish and flesh upon hurdles as earlier has been
described, and keep it until scarce times.

For fishing and hunting and wars they use much their bow and
arrows. They bring their bows to the form of ours by the scraping of a
shell. Some of their arrows are made of straight young springs which
they head with bone, some 2 or 3 inches long. These they use to shoot
at squirrels on trees. Another sort of arrow they use is made of reeds.
These are pieced with wood, headed with splinters of chrystal or some
sharp stone, the spurs of a Turkey or the bill of some bird. For his knife
he hath the splinter of a reed to cut his feathers in form. With this knife
also, he will joint a Deer or any beast, shape his shoes, buskins, mantels,
&c. To make the notch of his arrow he hath the tooth of a Beaver, set
in a stick, wherewith he grateth it by degrees. His arrow head he
quickly maketh with a little bone, which he ever weareth at his bracer,
of any plint of a stone, or glass in the form of a heart; and these they
glue to the end of their arrows. With the sinews of a Deer and the
tops of Deers' horns boiled to a jelly, they make a glue that will not
dissolve in cold water. For their wars also they use Targets that are
round and made of the bark of trees, and a sword of wood at their
backs, but oftentimes they use for swords the horn of a Deer put
through a piece of wood in the form of a Pickaxe. Sometimes a long
stone sharpened at both ends is used in the same manner. This they were
wont to use also for hatchets but now by trafficking they have plenty
of the same form made of iron. And those are their chief instruments
and arms.

Their fishing is much in Boats. These they make of one tree by
bowing and scratching away the coals with stones and shells till they
have made it in the form of a Trough. Some of them are an elne deep
and 40 or 50 foot in length and some will bear 40 men. But the most
ordinary are smaller and will bear 10, 20, or 30, according to their bigness. Instead of oars, they use paddles and sticks with which they will
row faster than our Barges.

Betwixt their hands and thighs, their women spin the barks of trees,
deer sinews or a kind of grass they call *Pemmenow;* of these they make
a thread very even and readily. This thread serveth for many uses, as
about their housing, apparel, as also they make nets for fishing, for the
quantity as expertly braided as ours. They make also with it lines for
angling. Their hooks are either a bone grated as they notch their arrows,
in the form of a crooked pin or fishhook, or of the splinter of a bone
tied to the clift of a little stick. With the end of the line they tie on the
bait. They use also long arrows tied in a line wherewith they shoot at
fish in the rivers. But they of *Accawmack* use staves like unto Javelins

headed with bone. With these they dart fish swimming in the water. They have also many artificial weirs in which they get abundance of fish.

In their hunting and fishing they take extreme pains; yet it being their ordinary exercise from their infancy, they esteem it a pleasure and are very proud to be expert therein. And by their continual ranging and travel, they know all the advantages and places most frequented with Deer, Beasts, Fish, Fowl, Roots and Berries. At their huntings they leave their habitations and reduce themselves into companies, as the Tartars do, and go to the most desert places with their families, where they spend their time in hunting and fowling up towards the mountains by the heads of their rivers where there is plenty of game. For betwixt the rivers, the grounds are so narrow that little cometh there which they devour not. It is a marvel they can so directly pass these deserts, some 3 or 4 days journey without habitation. Their hunting houses are like unto Arbours covered with mats. These their women bear after them, with Corn, Acorns, Mortars and all bag and baggage they use. When they come to the place of exercise, every man doth his best to show his dexterity, for by their excelling in those qualities they get their wives. Forty yards will they shoot level, or very near the mark, and 120 is their best at Random. At their huntings in the deserts, they are commonly 2 or 300 together. Having found the Deer, they environ them with many fires and betwixt the fires they place themselves. And some take their stands in the midst. The Deer being thus frightened by the fires and their voices, they chase them so long within that circle that many times they kill 6, 8, 10, or 15 at a hunting. They use also to drive them into some narrow point of land when they find that advantageous; and so force them into the river where with their boats they have *Ambuscadoes* to kill them. When they have shot a Deer by land they follow him like blood hounds by the blood and stain and oftentimes so take them. Hares, Partridges, Turkeys, or Eggs, fat or lean, young or old, they devour all they can catch in their power.

In one of these huntings, they found Captain Smith in the exploration of the head of the river of *Chickahamania,* where they slew his men and took him prisoner in a Bogmire. This is where he saw those exercises and gathered these observations.

One Savage hunting alone, useth the skin of a Deer slit on the one side and so put on his arm, through the neck, so that his hand comes to the head which is stuffed, and the horns, head eyes, ears and every part as artificially counterfeited as they can devise. Thus shrouding his body in the skin, by stalking he approacheth the Deer, also gazing and licking himself. So watching his best advantage to approach, having shot him, he chaseth him by his blood and stain till he get him.

When they intend any wars, the *Werowances* usually have the advice of their Priests and Conjurers and their Allies and ancient friends but chiefly the Priests determine their resolution. Every *Werowance,* or some lusty fellow they appoint Captain over every nation. They seldom make war for lands or goods but for women and children, and principally for revenge. They have many enemies, namely all their westernly Countries beyond the mountains and the heads of the rivers. Upon the head of the Powhatans are the *Monacans,* whose chief habitation is at *Russawmeake,* unto whom the *Mouhemenchughes,* the *Massingnacks,* and *Monahassnuggs,* and other nations, pay tribute. . . .

Beyond the mountains from whence is the head of the river *Patawomeke,* the Savages report, inhabit their most mortal enemies, the *Massawomekes* upon a great salt water which by all likelihood is either some part of Canada, some great lake, or some inlet of some sea that falleth into the South sea. The *Massawomekes* are a great nation and very populous. For the heads of all those rivers, especially the *Pattawomekes,* the *Pautuxuntes,* the *Sasquesahanocks,* the *Tockwoughes,* are continually tormented by them; of whose cruelty they generally complained and were very importunate with Captain Smith and his company to free them from these tormentors. To this purpose, they offered food, conduct, assistance and continual subjection. To which he confluded to effect. But the Council then present at Jamestown, emulating his success, would not think it fit to spare him 40 men to be hazarded in those unknown regions, Smith having passed (as before was spoken of) but with 12 men, and so was lost that opportunity.

Seven boats full of these *Massawomekes* the discoverers encountered at the head of the *Bay.* Their Targets, Baskets, Swords, Tobacco pipes, Platters, Bows and Arrows, everything showed, they much exceeded them of our parts. And their dexterity in their small boats made of the bark of trees sewn with bark and well caulked with gum, argueth that they are seated upon some great river.

Against all these enemies the *Powhatans* are constrained sometimes to fight. Their chief attempts are by Stratagems, treacheries or surprises. Yet the *Werowances,* women and children, they put not to death but keep them Captives. They have a method in war and for our pleasures they shewed it us, and it was in this manner performed at *Mattapanient.*

Having painted and disguised themselves in the fiercest manner they could devise, they divided themselves into two Companies, near a 100 in a company. The one company called *Monacans,* the other *Powhatans.* Either army had their Captain. These as enemies took their stands a musket shot one from another ranked themselves 15 abreast, and each rank from another 4 or 5 yards; not in file but in the opening betwixt their files, so as the Rear could shoot as conveniently as the Front.

Having thus pitched the fields, from either part went a Messenger with these conditions: that whomsoever were vanquished, such after, should live, but their wives and children should be prize for the Conquerors.

The messengers were no sooner returned, but they approached in their orders. On each flank a Sergeant and in Rear an officer for lieutenant, all duly keeping their orders, yet leaping and singing after their accustomed tune, which they use only in wars. Upon the first flight of arrows they gave such horrible shouts and screeches as though so many infernal hellhounds could not have made them more terrible.

When they had spent their arrows, they joined together prettily, charging and retiring, every rank seconding the other. As they got advantage, they catched their enemies by the hair of the head and down he came that was taken. His enemy with his wooden sword seemed to beat out his brains and still they crept to the Rear to maintain the skirmish. The *Monacans* decreasing, the *Powhatans* charged them in the form of a half moon. They, unwilling to be enclosed, fled all in a troop to their *Ambuscadoes*, on which they led them very cunningly. The *Monacans* dispersed themselves among the fresh men, whereupon the *Powhatans* retired with all speed to their seconds; which the *Monacans* seeing, took that advantage to retire again to their own battle, and so each returned to their own quarter.

All their actions, voices and gestures, both in charging and retiring, were so strained to the height of their quality and nature, that the strangeness thereof made it seem very delightful.

For their music they use a thick cane on which they pipe as on a Recorder. For their wars, they have a great deep platter of wood. They cover the mouth thereof with a skin, at each corner they tie a walnut, which meeting on the backside near the bottom, with a small rope they twitch them together till it be so taut and stiff that they may beat upon it as upon a drum. But their chief instruments are Rattels made of small gourds or Pumpion (pumpkin) shells. Of these they have Bass, Tenor, Counter-tenor, Mean and Treble. These mingled with their voices sometimes 20 or 30 together, make such a terrible noise as would rather affright than delight any man.

If any great commander arrive at the habitation of a *Werowance*, they spread a mat as the Turks do a carpet for him to sit upon. Upon an other right opposite they sit themselves. Then do all with a tunable voice of shouting bid him welcome. After this do 2 or more of their chiefest men make an oration, testifying their love. Which they do with such vehemency and so great passions, that they sweat till they drop and are so out of breath they can scarce speak. So that a man would take them to be exceeding angry or stark mad. Such victuals as they have they spend freely; and at night where his lodging is appointed, they set a woman fresh painted red with *Pocones* and oil, to be his bedfellow.

Their manner of trading is for copper, beads and such like, for which they give such commodities as they have, as skins, fowl, fish, flesh and their country corn. But their victuals is their chiefest riches.

Every spring they make themselves sick with drinking the juice of a root they call *wighsacan* and water; whereof they pour so great a quantity that it purgeth them in a very violent manner, so that in 3 or 4 days after, they scarce recover their former health.

Sometimes they are troubled with dropsies, swellings, aches, and such like diseases, for cure whereof they build a stove in the form of a dove-house with mats so close that a few coals therein covered with a pot, will make the patient sweat extremely. For swellings also they use small pieces of touchwood in the form of cloves, which pricking on the sore, they burn close to the flesh and from thence draw the corruption with their mouth. With this root *wighsacan* they can ordinarily heal green wounds but to scarify a swelling or make incision, their best instruments are some splinted stone. Old ulcers or putrified hurts are seldom seen cured amongst them.

They have many professed Physicians who with their charms and Rattels, with an infernal rout of words and actions, will seem to suck their inward grief from their navels or their grieved places. But of our Surgeons they were so enamoured that they believed any Plaster would heal any hurt.

# Pocahontas
## *Captain John Smith*

*Smith's story of his rescue by Pocahontas, together with his account of his exploits against the Turks in Hungary, have prompted some historians to accuse him of being an errant liar. Not until 1622–24, did Smith see fit to make public an event which he alleged had occurred almost fourteen years previously. But in 1608, when Smith wrote his first description of Virginia, he had good reason for concealing the hostility of the Indians and he certainly took no pride in having been rescued by a twelve-year-old girl. After Pocahontas' marriage to John Rolfe and her subsequent sensational popularity in England, Smith found it to his advantage to speak out. Suffering the pangs of an unrequited thirst for fame, Smith was now eager to associate his name with a celebrity like Pocahontas, even though she had been dead for six years.*

CAPT. SMITH'S PETITION TO HER MAJESTY, IN BEHALF OF
POCAHONTAS, DAUGHTER TO THE INDIAN EMPEROR POWHATAN.

To the most High and Virtuous Princess,
Queen ANNE, of *Great Britain.*

Most Admir'd Madam;

The Love I bear my God, my King and Country, hath so often embolden'd me in the worst of extreme Dangers, that now Honesty doth constrain me to presume thus far beyond myself, to present your Majesty this short Discourse. If Ingratitude be a deadly Poison to all honest Virtues, I must be guilty of that Crime, if I should omit any Means to be thankful.

So it was,

That about Ten Years ago, being in *Virginia,* and taken Prisoner by the Power of *Powhatan,* their chief King, I receiv'd from this great Savage exceeding great Courtesy, especially from his Son *Nantaquaus;* the manliest, comeliest, boldest Spirit I ever saw in a Savage; and his

*Travels and Works of Captain John Smith.* Edited by Edward Arber.

Sister *Pocahontas,* the King's most dear and well beloved Daughter, being but a Child of Twelve or Thirteen Years of Age, whose compassionate pitiful Heart of my desperate Estate gave me much Cause to respect her. I being the first *Christian* this proud King and his grim Attendants ever saw, and thus enthrall'd in their barbarous Power; I cannot say I felt the least Occasion of Want, that was in the Power of those my mortal Foes to prevent, notwithstanding all their Threats. After some Six Weeks Fatting amongst those Savage Courtiers, at the Minute of my Execution she hazarded the Beating out of her own Brains to save mine, and not only that, but so prevail'd with her Father, that I was safely conducted to *James-Town,* where I found about Eight and Thirty miserable, poor and sick Creatures to keep Possession for all those large Territories of *Virginia.* Such was the Weakness of this poor Commonwealth, as had not the Savages fed us, we directly had starv'd.

And this Relief, *most Gracious Queen,* was commonly brought us by this Lady *Pocahontas,* notwithstanding all these Passages, when unconstant Fortune turn'd our Peace to War, this tender Virgin would still not spare to dare to visit us; and by her our Jars have been oft appeased, and our Wants still supplied. Were it the Policy of her Father thus to employ her, or the Ordinance of God thus to make her His Instrument, or her extraordinary Affection to our Nation, I know not: But of this I am sure, when her Father, with the utmost of his Policy and Power, sought to surprise me, having but Eighteen with me, the dark Night could not affright her from coming through the irksome Woods, and, with water'd Eyes, give me Intelligence, with her best Advice to escape his Fury; which had he known, he had surely slain her.

*James-Town,* with her wild Train, she as freely frequented as her Father's Habitation; and during the time of Two or Three Years, she, next under God, was still the Instrument to preserve this Colony from Death, Famine, and utter Confusion, which if, in those Times, had once been dissolv'd, *Virginia* might have lain, as it was at our first Arrival, till this Day. Since then, this Business having been turn'd and varied by many Accidents from what I left it, it is most certain, after a long and troublesome War, since my Departure, betwixt her Father and our Colony, all which Time she was not heard of, about Two Years after she herself was taken Prisoner, being so detain'd near Two Years longer, the Colony by that Means was reliev'd, Peace concluded, and at last, rejecting her barbarous Condition, she was married to an *English* Gentleman, with whom at this Present she is in *England.* The first *Christian* ever of that Nation: The first *Virginian* ever spake *English,* or had a Child in Marriage by an *English* Man. A Matter surely, if my Meaning be truly consider'd and well understood, worthy a Prince's Information.

Thus, *most Gracious Lady,* I have related to your Majesty what at your best Leisure our approv'd Histories will recount to you at large, as done in the Time of your Majesty's Life: And, however this might be presented you from a more worthy Pen, it cannot from a more honest Heart.

As yet I never begg'd any thing of the State, or any; and it is my want of Ability, and her exceeding Desert; your Birth, Means and Authority; her Birth, Virtue, Want and Simplicity, doth make me thus bold, humbly to beseech your Majesty to take this Knowledge of her, tho' it be from one so unworthy to be the Reporter as my self: Her Husband's Estate not being able to make her fit to attend your Majesty.

The most and least I can do, is to tell you this, and the rather because of her being of so great a Spirit, however her Stature. If she should not be well receiv'd, seeing this Kingdom may rightly have a Kingdom by her Means; her present Love to us, and Christianity, might turn to such Scorn and Fury, as to divert all this Good to the worst of Evil: Where finding that so Great a Queen should do her more Honour than she can imagine, for having been kind to her Subjects and Servants, 'twou'd so ravish her with Content, as to endear her dearest Blood to effect that your Majesty and all the King's honest Subjects most earnestly desire. And so I humbly kiss your gracious Hands, &c.

(Sign'd)

*Dated June, 1616*                                      JOHN SMITH

### POCAHONTAS RESCUES CAPTAIN SMITH

But our comedies never endured long without a tragedy; some idle exceptions being muttered against Captain Smith, for not discovering the head of Chickahamania River, and taxed by the council, to be too slow in so worthy an attempt. The next voyage he proceeded so far that with much labor by cutting of trees insunder he made his passage; but when his barge could pass no farther, he left her in a broad bay out of danger of shot, commanding none should go ashore till his return. Himself, with two English and two savages went up higher in a canoe: but he was not long absent, but his men went ashore, whose want of government gave both occasion and opportunity to the savages to surprise one George Cassen, whom they slew, and much failed not to have cut off the boat and all the rest.

Smith little dreaming of that accident, being got to the marshes at the river's head, twenty miles in the desert, had his two men slain, as is supposed, sleeping by the canoe, whilst himself by fowling sought them victual; who, finding he was beset with 200 savages, two of them he slew, still defending himself with the aid of a savage, his guide, whom he bound to his arm with his garters, and used him as a buckler. Yet he was shot in his thigh a little, and had many arrows that stuck in his clothes but no great hurt, till at last they took him prisoner.

When this news came to Jamestown, much was their sorrow for his loss, few expecting what ensued.

Six or seven weeks those barbarians kept him prisoner; many strange triumphs and conjurations they made of him, yet he so demeaned himself amongst them, as he not only diverted them from surprising the fort, but procured his own liberty, and got himself and his company such estimation amongst them that those savages admired him more than their own Quiyouckosucks [Indian god].

The manner how they used and delivered him, is as followeth:

The savages having drawn from George Cassen whither Captain Smith was gone, prosecuting that opportunity they followed him with 300 bowmen conducted by the King of Pamaunkee, who in divisions searching the turnings of the river, found Robinson and Emry by the fireside: those they shot full of arrows and slew. Then finding the Captain, as is said, that used the savage that was his guide as his shield (three of them being slain and divers other so galled), all the rest would not come near him. Thinking thus to have returned to his boat, regarding them, as he marched, more than his way, slipped up to the middle in an oasie [oozy] creek and his savage with him; yet durst they not come to him till, being near dead with cold, he threw away his arms. Then according to their composition they drew him forth and led him to the fire, where his men were slain. Diligently they chafed his benumbed limbs.

He demanding for their Captain, they showed him Opechankanough, King of Pamaunkee, to whom he gave a round, ivory double compass dial. Much they marvelled at the playing of the fly and needle, which they could see so plainly, and yet not touch it, because of the glass that covered them. But when he demonstrated by that globelike jewel, the roundness of the earth, and skies, the sphere of the sun, moon, and stars, and how the sun did chase the night round about the world continually; the greatness of the land and sea, the diversity of nations, variety of complexions, and how we were to them Antipodes, and many other such like matters, they all stood as amazed with admiration.

Notwithstanding, within an hour after they tied him to a tree, and as many as could stand about him, prepared to shoot him: but the King holding up the compass in his hand, they all laid down their bows and arrows, and in a triumphant manner led him to Orapaks, where he was after their manner kindly feasted, and well used.

Their order in conducting him was thus: drawing themselves all in file, the King in the midst had all their pieces and swords borne before him. Captain Smith was led after him by three great savages, holding him fast by each arm; and on each side six went in file with their arrows nocked. But arriving at the town (which was only thirty or forty hunting houses made of mats, which they remove as they please, as we our tents), all the women and children staring to behold him, the soldiers first all in file performed the form of a bissone [a military formation] so well as could be; and on each flank, officers as sergeants to see them keep their orders. A good time they continued this exercise, and then cast themselves in a ring, dancing in such several postures, and singing and yelling out such hellish notes and screeches; being strangely painted, every one his quiver of arrows, and at his back a club; on his arm a fox or an otter's skin, or some such matter for his vambrace [leather guard]; their heads and shoulders painted red, with oil and pocones [bloodroot] mingled together, which scarlet-like color made an exceeding handsome show; his bow in his hand, and the skin of a bird with her wings abroad dried, tied on his head, a piece of copper, a white shell, a long feather, with a small rattle growing at the tails of their snakes tied to it, or some such like toy. All this while Smith and the King stood in the midst guarded, as before is said; and after three dances they all departed. Smith they conducted to a long house, where thirty or forty tall fellows did guard him; and ere long more bread and venison was brought him than would have served twenty men. I think his stomach at that time was not very good; what he left they put in baskets and tied over his head. About midnight they set the meat again before him. All this time not one of them would eat a bite with him, till the next morning they brought him as much more; and then did they eat all the old, and reserved the new as they had done the other, which made him think they would fat him to eat him. Yet in this desperate estate, to defend him from the cold, one Maocassater brought him his gown, in requital of some beads and toys Smith had given him at his first arrival in Virginia.

Two days after a man would have slain him (but that the guard prevented it) for the death of his son, to whom they conducted him to recover the poor man then breathing his last. Smith told them that at Jamestown he had a water would do it, if they would let him fetch it, but they would not permit that; but made all the preparations they could to assault Jamestown, craving his advice, and for recompense he should have life, liberty, land, and women. In part of a table-book he writ his mind to them at the fort, what was intended, how they should follow that direction to affright the messengers, and without fail send him such things as he writ for, and an inventory with them. The difficulty and danger, he told the savages, of the mines, great guns, and other engines exceedingly affrighted them, yet according to his request they went to Jamestown, in as bitter weather as could be of frost and snow, and within three days returned with an answer.

But when they came to Jamestown, seeing men sally out as he had told them they would, they fled; yet in the night they came again to the same place where he had told them they should receive an answer, and such things as he had promised them; which they found accordingly, and with which they returned with no small expedition, to the wonder of them all that heard it, that he could either divine, or the paper could speak.

Then they led him to the Youthtanunds, the Mattapanients, the Payankatanks, the Nantaughtacunds, and Onawmanients upon the rivers of Rapahanock, and Patawomek; over all those rivers, and back again by divers other several nations, to the King's habitation at Pamaunkee: where they entertained him with most strange and fearful conjurations:

> As if near led to hell,
> Amongst the devils to dwell.

Not long after, early in a morning a great fire was made in a long house, and a mat spread on the one side, as on the other; on the one they caused him to sit, and all the guard went out of the house, and presently came skipping in a great grim fellow: all painted over with coal, mingled with oil, and many snakes' and weasels' skins stuffed with moss, and all their tails tied together, so as they met on the crown of his head in a tassel; and round about the tassel was as a coronet of feathers, the skins hanging round about his head, back, and shoulders, and in a manner covered his face; with a hellish voice, and a rattle in his hand. With most strange gestures and passions he began his invocation, and environed the fire with a circle of meal; which done, three more such like devils came rushing in with the like antique tricks, painted half black, half red; but all their eyes were painted white, and some red strokes like mutchatos [mustachios] along their cheeks. Round about him those fiends danced a pretty while, and then came in three more as ugly as the rest; with red eyes, and white strokes over their black faces. At last they all sat down right against him, three of them on the one hand of the chief priest, and three on the other. Then all with their rattles began a song; which ended, the chief priest laid down five wheat corns, then straining his arms and hands with such violence that he sweat, and his veins swelled, he began a short oration. At the conclusion they all gave a short groan, and then laid down three grains more. After that, began their song again, and then another oration, ever laying down so many corns as before, till they had twice encircled the fire. That done, they took a bunch of little sticks prepared for that purpose, continuing still their devotion, and at the end of every song and oration, they laid down a stick betwixt the divisions of corn. Till night, neither he nor they did either eat or drink; and then they feasted merrily, with the best provisions they could make. Three days they used this ceremony; the meaning whereof they told him, was to know if he intended them well or no. The circle of meal signified their country, the circles of corn the bounds of the sea, and the sticks his country. They imagined the world to be flat and round, like a trencher, and they in the midst.

After this they brought him a bag of gunpowder, which they carefully preserved till the next spring, to plant as they did their corn, because they would be acquainted with the nature of that seed.

Opitchapam, the King's brother, invited him to his house, where, with as many platters of bread, fowl, and wild beasts, as did environ him, he bid him welcome; but not any of them would eat a bite with him, but put up all the remainder in baskets.

At his return to Opechankanough's, all the King's women, and their children, flocked about him for their parts; as a due by custom, to be merry with such fragments.

> But his waking mind in hideous dreams did oft see wondrous shapes,
> Of bodies strange, and huge in growth, and of stupendous makes.

At last they brought him to Meronocomoco, where was Powhatan, their emperor. Here more than two hundred of those grim courtiers stood wondering at him, as he had been a monster, till Powhatan and his train had put themselves in their greatest braveries. Before a fire upon a seat like a bedstead, he sat covered with a great robe, made of rarowcun [raccoon] skins, and all the tails hanging by. On either hand did sit a young wench of 16 or 18 years, and along on each side of the house, two rows of men, and behind them as many women, with all their heads and shoulders painted red; many of their heads bedecked with the white down of birds, but everyone with something, and a great chain of white beads about their necks.

At his entrance before the King, all the people gave a great shout. The Queen of Appamatuck was appointed to bring him water to wash his hands, and another brought him a bunch of feathers, instead of a towel to dry them: having feasted him after their best barbarous manner they could, a long consultation was held, but the conclusion was, two great stones were brought before Powhatan. Then as many as could laid hands on him, dragged him to them, and thereon laid his head, and being ready with their clubs, to beat out his brains, Pocahontas, the King's dearest daughter, when no entreaty could prevail, got his head in her arms, and laid her own upon his to save him from death: whereat the emperor was contented he should live to make him hatchets, and her bells, beads, and copper; for they thought him as well of all occupations as themselves. For the King, himself, will make his own robes, shoes, bows, arrows, pots; plant, hunt, or do anything so well as the rest.

They say he bore a pleasant show,
But sure his heart was sad.
For who can pleasant be, and rest,
That lives in fear and dread,
And having life suspected, doth
It still suspected lead?

Two days after, Powhatan, having disguised himself in the most fear-ful manner he could, caused Captain Smith to be brought forth to a great house in the woods, and there upon a mat by the fire to be left alone. Not long after, from behind a mat that divided the house, was made the most doleful noise he ever heard, then Powhatan, more like a devil than a man, with some two hundred more as black as himself, came unto him and told him now they were friends, and presently he should go to Jamestown, to send him two great guns, and a grindstone, for which he would give him the country of Capahowosick, and for ever esteem him as his son Nantaquoud.

So to Jamestown with 12 guides Powhatan sent him. That night they quartered in the woods, he still expecting (as he had done all this long time of his imprisonment) every hour to be put to one death or other—for all their feasting. But Almighty God (by his divine providence) had mollified the hearts of these stern barbarians with compassion. The next morning betimes they came to the fort, where Smith having used the savages with what kindness he could, he showed Rawhunt, Pow-hatan's trusty servant, two demiculverings and a millstone to carry Powhatan. They found them somewhat too heavy, but when they did see him discharge them, being loaded with stones, among the boughs of a great tree loaded with icicles, the ice and branches came so tumbling down, that the poor savages ran away half dead with fear. But at last we regained some conference with them, and gave them such toys, and sent to Powhatan, his women, and children such presents, as gave them in general full content.

# The Pequot War
## *William Bradford*

In the year 1634 the Pequots (a stout and warlike people) who had made wars with sundry of their neighbours and, puffed up with many victories, grew now at variance with the Narragansetts, a great people bordering upon them there. These Narragansetts held correspondence and terms of friendship with the English of the Massachusetts. Now the Pequots, being conscious of the guilt of Captain Stone's death, whom they knew to be an Englishman, as also those that were with him, and being fallen out with the Dutch, lest they should have overmany enemies at once, sought to make friendship with the English of the Massachusetts. And for that end sent both messengers and gifts unto them, as appears by some letters sent from the Governor hither.

DEAR AND WORTHY SIR, *etc.* To let you know somewhat of our affairs, you may understand that the Pequots have sent some of theirs to us, to desire our friendship, and offered much wampum and beaver, etc. The first messengers were dismissed without answer. With the next we had divers days' conference; and taking the advice of some of our ministers and seeking the Lord in it, we concluded a peace and friendship with them, upon these conditions: That they should deliver up to us those men who were guilty of Stone's death, etc. And if we desired to plant in Connecticut, they should give up their right to us, and so we would send to trade with them as our friends—which was the chief thing we aimed at, [they] being now in war with the Dutch and the rest of their neighbours.

To this they readily agreed, and that we should mediate a peace between them and the Narragansetts, for which end they were content we should give the Narragansetts part of that present they would bestow on us. For they stood so much on their honour as they would not be seen to give anything of themselves. As for Captain Stone, they told us there were but two left of those who had any hand in his death, and that they killed him in a just quarrel. For, say they, he surprised two of our men and bound them to make them by force to show him the way up the river; and he with two other coming on shore, nine Indians watched him, and

William Bradford: *Of Plymouth Plantation.* Edited by Samuel Eliot Morison.

when they were asleep in the night, they killed them to deliver their own men. And some of them going afterwards to the pinnace, it was suddenly blown up. We are now preparing to send a pinnace unto them, etc.

In another of his, dated the 12th of the first month, he hath this:

Our pinnace is lately returned from the Pequots; they put off but little commodity, and found them a very false people, so as they mean to have no more to do with them. I have divers other things to write unto you, etc.

Yours ever assured,

*Boston, 12 of the 1st month, 1634*          JOHN WINTHROP

After these things, and as I take this year, John Oldham (of whom much is spoken before) being now an inhabitant of the Massachusetts, went with a small vessel and slenderly manned a-trading into these south parts, and upon a quarrel between him and the Indians, was cut off by them (as hath been before noted) at an island called by the Indians Munisses, but since by the English, Block Island. This, with the former about the death of Stone, and the baffling of the Pequots with the English of the Massachusetts, moved them to set out some to take revenge and require satisfaction for these wrongs. But it was done so superficially, and without their acquainting those of Connecticut and other neighbours with the same, as they did little good, but their neighbours had more hurt done. For some of the murderers of Oldham fled to the Pequots, and though the English went to the Pequots and had some parley with them, yet they did but delude them, and the English returned without doing anything to purpose, being frustrate of their opportunity by the others' deceit.

After the English were returned, the Pequots took their time and opportunity to cut off some of the English as they passed in boats and went on fowling, and assaulted them the next spring at their habitations, as will appear in its place. I do but touch these things, because I make no question they will be more fully and distinctly handled by themselves who had more exact knowledge of them and whom they did more properly concern.

### ANNO DOM: 1637

In the fore part of this year, the Pequots fell openly upon the English at Connecticut, in the lower parts of the river, and slew sundry of them as they were at work in the fields, both men and women, to the great terrour of the rest, and went away in great pride and triumph, with many high threats. They also assaulted a fort at the river's mouth, though strong and well defended; and though they did not there prevail, yet it struck them with much fear and astonishment to see their bold attempts in the face of danger. Which made them in all places to stand upon their guard and to prepare for resistance, and earnestly to solicit their friends and confederates in the Bay of Massachusetts to send them speedy aid, for they looked for more forcible assaults. Mr. Vane, being then Governor, writ from their General Court to them here to join with them in this war. To which they were cordially willing, but took opportunity to write to them about some former things, as well as present, considerable hereabout.

In the meantime, the Pequots, especially in the winter before, sought to make peace with the Narragansetts, and used very pernicious arguments to move them thereunto: so that the English were strangers and began to overspread their country, and would deprive them thereof in time, if they were suffered to grow and increase. And if the Narragansetts did assist the English to subdue them, they did but make way for their own overthrow, for if they were rooted out, the English would soon take occasion to subjugate them. And if they would hearken to them they should not need to fear the strength of the English, for they would not come to open battle with them but fire their houses, kill their cattle, and lie in ambush for them as they went abroad upon their occasions; and all this they might easily do without any or little danger to themselves. The which course being held, they well saw the English could not long subsist but they would either be starved with hunger or be forced to forsake the country. With many the like things; insomuch that the Narragansetts were once wavering and were half minded to have made peace with them, and joined against the English. But again, when they considered how much wrong they had received from the Pequots, and what an opportunity they now had by the help of the English to right themselves; revenge was so sweet unto them as it prevailed above all the rest, so as they resolved to join with the English against them, and did.

The Court here agreed forthwith to send fifty men at their own charge; and with as much speed as possibly they could, got them armed and had made them ready under sufficient leaders, and provided a bark to carry them provisions and tend upon them for all occasions. But when they were ready to march, with a supply from the Bay, they had word to stay; for the enemy was as good as vanquished and there would be no need.

I shall not take upon me exactly to describe their proceedings in these things, because I expect it will be fully done by themselves who best know the carriage and circumstances of things. I shall therefore but touch them in general. From Connecticut, who were most sensible of the hurt sustained and the present danger, they set out a party of men, and another party met them from the Bay, at Narragansetts', who were to join with them. The Narragansetts were earnest to be gone before the English were well rested and refreshed, especially some of them which came last. It should seem their desire was to come upon the enemy suddenly and undiscovered. There was a bark of this place, newly put in there, which was come from Connecticut, who did encourage them to lay hold of the Indians' forwardness, and to show as great forwardness as they, for it would encourage them, and expedition might prove to their great advantage. So they went on, and so ordered their march as the Indians brought them to a fort of the enemy's (in which most of their chief men were) before day. They approached the same with great silence and surrounded it both with English and Indians, that they might not break out; and so assaulted them with great courage, shooting amongst them, and entered the fort with all speed. And those that first entered found sharp resistance from the enemy who both shot at and grappled with them; others ran into their houses and brought out fire and set them on fire, which soon took in their mat; and standing close together, with the wind all was quickly on a flame, and thereby more were burnt to death than was otherwise slain; It burnt their bowstrings and made them unserviceable; those that scaped the fire were slain with the sword, some hewed to pieces, others run through with their rapiers, so as they were quickly dispatched and very few escaped. It was conceived they thus destroyed about 400 at this time. It was a fearful sight to see them thus frying in the fire and the streams of blood quenching the same, and horrible was the stink and scent thereof; but the victory seemed a sweet sacrifice, and they gave the praise thereof to God, who had wrought so wonderfully for them, thus to enclose their enemies in their hands and give them so speedy a victory over so proud and insulting an enemy.

The Narragansett Indians all this while stood round about, but aloof from all danger and left the whole execution to the English, except it were the stopping of any that broke away. Insulting over their enemies in this their ruin and misery, when they saw them dancing in the flames, calling them by a word in their own language, signifying "O brave Pequots!" which they used familiarly among themselves in their own praise in songs of triumph after their victories. After this service was thus happily accomplished, they marched to the waterside where they met with some of their vessels, by which they had refreshing with victuals and other necessaries. But in their march the rest of the Pequots drew into a body and accosted them, thinking to have some advantage against them by reason of a neck of land. But when they saw the English prepare for them they kept aloof, so as they neither did hurt nor could receive any.

After their refreshing, and repair together for further counsel and directions, they resolved to pursue their victory and follow the war against the rest. But the Narragansett Indians, most of them, forsook them, and such of them as they had with them for guides or otherwise, they found them very cold and backward in the business, either out of envy, or that they saw the English would make more profit of the victory than they were willing they should; or else deprive them of such advantage as themselves desired, by having them become tributaries unto them, or the like.

For the rest of this business, I shall only relate the same as it is in a letter which came from Mr. Winthrop to the Governor here, as followeth.

That I may make an end of this matter, this Sassacus (the Pequots' chief sachem) being fled to the Mohawks, they cut off his head, with some other of the chief of them, whether to satisfy the English or rather the Narragansetts (who, as I have since heard, hired them to do it) or for their own advantage, I well know not; but thus this war took end. The rest of the Pequots were wholly driven from their place, and some of them submitted themselves to the Narragansetts and lived under them. Others of them betook themselves to the Mohegans under Uncas, their sachem, with the approbation of the English of Connecticut, under whose protection Uncas lived; and he and his men had been faithful to them in this war and done them very good service. But this did so vex the Narragansetts, that they had not the whole sway over them, as they have never ceased plotting and contriving how to bring them under; and because they cannot attain their ends, because of the English who have protected them, they have sought to raise a general conspiracy against the English, as will appear in another place.

# The Pequot War

## *Edward Johnson*

*The massacre of the Pequot Indians in 1636 was a favorite theme among New England writers because it seemed to be irrefutable proof that God was on their side. Edward Johnson extracted the last ounce of moralizing, religious exaltation and sheer delight in bloodshed from this incident of the Pequot War.*

After the Ministers of Christ had, through the grace that was given them, exhorted and encouraged these Soldiers appointed for the work, the Indian guides with whom they had been provided brought them at the close of day to a small river where they could perceive many persons had been dressing fish. Upon the sight thereof, the Indian guides concluded they were now a feasting it at their fort which was hard at hand. The English, calling a Council of war, being directed by the speciallist providence of the most high God, they concluded to storm the fort a little before break of day, at which time they supposed the Indians being up late in their jolly feasting, would be in their deepest sleep. And surely so it was, for they now slept their last. The English, keeping themselves as covertly as they could, approached the fort at the time appointed. The fort was builded of whole Trees set in the ground fast and standing upon end about twelve foot high, very large. The Indians, having pitched their Wigwams within it, the entrance being on two sides, with intricate Meanders to enter. The chief Leaders of the English made some little stand before they offered to enter, but yet boldly they rushed on, and found the passages guarded at each place with an Indian Bow-man, ready on the string. They soon let fly and wounded the foremost of the English in the shoulder. Yet, having dispatched the Porters, they found the winding way in without a Guide, where they soon placed themselves round the Wigwams and, according to direction, they made their first shot with muzzle of their Muskets down to the

Edward Johnson: *The Wonder-Working Providence of Sions Saviour in New England*. Edited by J. F. Jameson.

ground, knowing the Indian manner is to lie on the ground to sleep, from which they being in this terrible manner awakened, unless it were such as were slain with the shot.

After this some of the English entered the Wigwams where they received some shot with their Arrows, yet catching up the firebrands they began to fire them and others of the English Soldiers with powder did the same. The day now began to break, the Lord intending to have these murderers know he would look out of the cloudy pillar upon them. And now these women and children set up a terrible out-cry; the men were smitten down and slain as they came forth with a great slaughter, the Squaws crying out, oh much winn it Englishmen, who moved with pity toward them, saved their lives. And hereupon some young youth cried, I squaw, I squaw, thinking to find the like mercy. There were some of these Indians, as is reported, whose bodies were not to be pierced by their sharp rapiers or swords of a long time, which made some of the Soldiers think the Devil was in them, for there were some Powwows among them, which work strange things with the help of Satan. But this was very remarkable, one of them being wounded to death and thrust through the neck with a Halbert yet, after all, lying groaning upon the ground, he caught the halbert's spear in his hand and wound it quite round.

After the English were thus possessed of this first victory, they sent their prisoners to the pinnaces and prosecuted the war in hand to the next Battalia of the Indians which lay on a hill about two miles distant. And indeed their stoutest Soldiers were at this place and not yet come to the fort. The English, being weary with their night work and wanting such refreshing as the present work required, began to grow faint. Yet, having obtained one victory, they were very desirous of another and, further, they knew right well till this cursed crew were utterly rooted out, they should never be at peace. Therefore they marched on toward them. Now assuredly, had the Indians known how much weakened our Soldiers were at present, they might have borne them down with their multitude, they being very strong and agile of body, had they come to hand-grips. But the Lord (who would have his people know their work was his and he only must order their Counsels and war-like work for them) did bring them timely supply from the vessels and also gave them a second victory wherein they slew many more of their enemies, the residue flying into a very thick swamp, being unaccessible by reason of the boggy holes of water and thick bushes. The English, drawing up their company, beleaguered the swamp, and the Indians in the meantime skulking up and down and as they saw opportunity they made shot with their Arrows at the English and then suddenly they would fall flat along in the water to defend themselves from the retaliation of the Soldiers' Muskets. This lasted not long for our English being but a small number had parted themselves far asunder. But by the providence of the most high God, some of them spied an Indian with a kettle at his back going more inwardly into the swamp, by which they perceived there was some place of firm land in the midst thereof. This caused them to make way for the passage of their Soldiers which brought this war to a period for, although many got away, yet were they no such considerable number as ever to raise war any more. The slain or wounded of the English were (through the mercy of Christ) but a few. One of them being shot through the body, near about the breast, regarding it not till a long time after, which caused the blood to dry and thicken on either end of the arrow so that it could not be drawn forth his body without great difficulty and much pain, yet did he escape with his life and the wound healed.

Thus the Lord was pleased to assist his people in this war and deliver them out of the Indians' hands, who were very lusty proper men of their hands, most of them, as may appear by one passage which I shall here relate: thus it came to pass, as the Soldiers were upon their march, close by a great thicket, where no eye could penetrate far, as it often falls out in such wearisome ways, where neither men nor beast have beaten out a path, some Soldiers were lingering behind their fellows. Two Indians, watching their opportunity, much like a hungry hawk, when they supposed the last man was come up, who kept a double double distance in his march, they suddenly and swiftly snatched him up in their talons, hoisting him upon their shoulders and ran into the swamp with him. The Soldier, being unwilling to be made a Pope by being borne on men's shoulders, strove with them all he could to free himself from their hands but, like a careful Commander, one Captain Davenport, then Lieutenant of this company, being diligent in his place to bring up the rear, coming up with them followed with speed into the swamp after him. Having a very sharp cutlass tied to his wrist and being well able to make it bite sore when he set it on, he resolved to make it fall foul on the Indians' bones. He soon overtook them but was prevented by the buckler they held up from hitting them, the buckler being the man they had taken. It was matter of much wonder to see with what dexterity they hurled the poor Soldier about as if they had been handling a Lacedaemonian shield, so that the nimble Captain Davenport could not, for a long time, fasten one stroke upon them. Yet, at last, dying their tawny skin into a crimson colour, the cast down their prey and hasted through the thickets for their lives. The Soldier thus redeemed had no such hard usage but that he is alive, as I suppose, at this very day.

The Lord in mercy toward his poor Churches, having thus destroyed these bloody barbarous Indians, he returns his people in safety to their vessels where they take account of their prisoners. The Squaws and some young youths they brought home with them and, finding the men to be deeply guilty of the crimes they undertook the war for, they brought away only their heads as a token of their victory. By this means the Lord struck a trembling terror into all the Indians round about, even to this very day.

# Indian Customs and Manners
## *Robert Beverley*

*Beverley's attitude toward the Indians was rarely encountered among the colonists: he praised them for resisting the white man's civilization and for trying to preserve their own way of life. Despite his admiration of the Indians, he described them not as noble savages but as human beings, and he studied their customs and religious beliefs in the spirit of an anthropologist. Since these natives seemed to possess so many estimable qualities, Beverley wished that more settlers had followed John Rolfe's example and married Indian girls. How much bloodshed would have been spared, Beverley exclaimed, if an enlightened policy of racial amalgamation had been adopted in the early years of settlement.*

### OF THE PERSONS OF THE INDIANS, AND THEIR DRESS

1. The *Indians* are of the middling and largest stature of the *English:* They are straight and well proportioned, having the cleanest and most exact Limbs in the World: They are so perfect in their outward frame, that I never heard of one single *Indian,* that was either dwarfish, crooked, bandy-legged, or otherwise misshapen. But if they have any such practice among them, as the *Romans* had, of exposing such Children till they died, as were weak and misshapen at their Birth, they are very shy of confessing it, and I could never yet learn that they had.

Their Color, when they are grown up, is a Chestnut brown and tawny; but much clearer in their Infancy. Their Skin comes afterwards to harden and grow blacker, by greasing and Sunning themselves. They have generally coal black Hair, and very black Eyes, which are most commonly graced with that sort of Squint which many of the *Jews* are observed to have. Their Women are generally Beautiful, possessing an uncommon delicacy of Shape and Features, and wanting no Charm, but that of a fair Complexion.

2. The Men wear their Hair cut after several fanciful Fashions, sometimes greased, and sometimes painted. The Great Men, or better

Robert Beverley: *The History and Present State of Virginia.* Edited by Louis B. Wright.

sort, preserve a long Lock behind for distinction. They pull their Beards up by the roots with a Muscle-shell; and both Men and Women do the same by the other parts of their Body for Cleanliness sake. The Women wear the Hair of the Head very long, either hanging at their Backs, or brought before in a single Lock, bound up with a Fillet of Peak, or Beads; sometimes also they wear it neatly tied up in a Knot behind. It is commonly greased, and shining black, but never painted.

The People of Condition of both Sexes, wear a sort of Coronet on their Heads, from 4 to 6 inches broad, open at the top, and composed of Peak, or Beads, or else of both interwoven together, and worked into Figures, made by a nice mixture of the Colors. Sometimes they wear a Wreath of Died Furrs; as likewise Bracelets on their Necks and Arms. The Common People go bareheaded, only sticking large shining Feathers about their Heads, as their fancies lead them.

3. Their Cloths are a large Mantle, carelessly wrapped about their Bodies, and sometimes girt close in the middle with a Girdle. The upper part of this Mantle is drawn close upon the Shoulders, and the other hangs below their Knees. When that's thrown off, they have only for Modesty sake a piece of Cloth, or a small Skin, tied round their Waste, which reaches down to the middle of the Thigh. The common sort tie only a String round their Middle, and pass a piece of Cloth or Skin around between their Thighs, which they turn at each end over the String.

Their Shoes, when they wear any, are made of an entire piece of Buck-Skin; except when they sow a piece to the bottom, to thicken the Soal. They are fasten'd on with running Strings, the Skin being drawn together like a Purse on the top of the Foot, and tied round the Ankle. The *Indian* name of this kind of Shoe is *Moccasin*.

4. I don't find that the *Indians* have any other distinction in their dress, or the fashion of their Hair, than only what a greater degree of Riches enables them to make; except it be their Religious persons, who are known by the particular cut of the Hair, and the unusual figure of their Garments; as our Clergy are distinguished by their Canonical Habit.

The Habit of the *Indian* Priest, is a Cloak made in the form of a Woman's Petticoat; but instead of tying it about their middle, they fasten the gatherings about their Neck, and tie it upon the Right Shoulder, always keeping one Arm out to use upon occasion. This Cloak hangs even at the bottom, but reaches no lower than the middle of the Thigh; but what is most particular in it, is, that it is constantly made of a skin dressed soft, with the Pelt or Fur on the outside, and reversed; insomuch, that when the Cloak has been a little worn, the hair falls down in flakes, and looks very shagged, and frightful.

The cut of their Hair is likewise peculiar to their Function; for 'tis all shaven close except a thin Crest, like a Cockscomb which stands bristling up, and runs in a semi-circle from the Forehead up along the Crown to the nape of the Neck. They likewise have a border of Hair over the Forehead, which by its own natural strength, and by the stiffening it receives from Grease and Paint, will stand out like the peak of a Bonnet.

5. The dress of the Women is little different from that of the Men, except in the tying of their Hair. The Ladies of Distinction wear deep Necklaces, Pendants and Bracelets, made of small Cylinders of the *Conque* shell, which they call *Peak:* They likewise keep their Skin clean, and shining with Oil, while the Men are commonly bedaubed all over with Paint.

They are remarkable for having small round Breasts, and so firm, that they are hardly ever observed to hang down, even in old Women. They commonly go naked as far as the Navel downward, and upward to the middle of the Thigh, by which means they have the advantage of discovering their fine Limbs, and complete Shape.

### OF THE MARRIAGES AMONGST THE INDIANS, AND MANAGEMENT OF THEIR CHILDREN

6. The *Indians* have their solemnities of Marriage, and esteem the Vows made at that time, as most sacred and inviolable. Notwithstanding they allow both the Man and the Wife to part upon disagreement; yet so great is the disreputation of a Divorce, that Married people, to avoid the Character of Inconstant and Ungenerous, very rarely let their Quarrels proceed to a Separation. However, when it does so happen, they reckon all the ties of Matrimony dissolved, and each hath the liberty of marrying another. But Infidelity is accounted the most unpardonable of all Crimes in either of the Parties, as long as the Contract continues.

In these Separations, the Children go, according to the affection of the Parent, with the one or the other; for Children are not reckoned a Charge among them, but rather Riches, according to the blessing of the Old Testament; and if they happen to differ about dividing their Children, their method is then, to part them equally, allowing the Man the first choice.

7. Tho the young *Indian* Women are said to prostitute their bodies for *Wampom* Peak, Runtees, Beads, and other such like fineries; yet I never could find any ground for the accusation, and believe it only to be an unjust scandal upon them. This I know, that if ever they have a Child while they are single, it is such a disgrace to them, that they never after get Husbands. Besides, I must do 'em the justice to say, I never heard of a Child any of them had before Marriage, and the *Indians* themselves disown any such custom; tho they acknowledge at the same time, that the Maidens are entirely at their own disposal, and may manage their persons as they think fit.

Indeed I believe this Story to be an aspersion cast on those innocent Creatures, by reason of the freedom they take in Conversation, which uncharitable Christians interpret as Criminal, upon no other ground, than the guilt of their own Consciences.

The *Indian* Damsels are full of spirit, and from thence are always inspired with Mirth and good Humor. They are extremely given to laugh, which they do with a Grace not to be resisted. The excess of Life and Fire, which they never fail to have, makes them frolicksome, but without any real imputation to their Innocence. However, this is ground enough for the English, who are not very nice in distinguishing betwixt guilt, and harmless freedom, to think them Incontinent: Tho it be with as little justice, as the jealous *Spaniards* condemn the liberty used by the Women of *France,* which are much more chaste than their own Ladies, which they keep under the strictest confinement.

8. The manner of the *Indians* treating their young Children is very strange, for instead of keeping them warm, at their first entry into the World, and wrapping them up, with I don't know how many Cloths, according to our own fond custom; the first thing they do, is to dip the Child over the Head and Ears in cold Water, and then to bind it naked to a convenient Board, having a hole fitly placed for evacuation; but they always put Cotton, Wool, Fur, or other soft thing, for the Body to rest easy on, between the Child and the Board. In this posture they keep it several months, till the Bones begin to harden, the Joints to knit, and the Limbs to grow strong; and then they let it loose from the Board, suffering it to crawl about, except when they are feeding, or playing with it.

While the Child is thus at the Board, they either lay it flat on its back, or set it leaning on one end, or else hang it up by a string fasten'd to the upper end of the Board for that purpose. The Child and Board being all this while carried about together. As our Women undress their Children to clean them and shift their Linen, so they do theirs to wash and grease them.

The method the Women have of carrying their Children after they are suffered to crawl about, is very particular; they carry them at their backs in Summer, taking one Leg of the Child under their Arm, and the Counter-Arm of the Child in their Hand over their Shoulder; the other Leg hanging down, and the Child all the while holding fast with its other Hand; but in Winter they carry them in the hollow of their Match-coat at their back, leaving nothing but the Child's Head out.

### OF THE TOWNS, BUILDINGS AND FORTIFICATIONS
### OF THE INDIANS

9. The method of the *Indian* Settlements is altogether by Cohabitation, in Townships, from fifty to five hundred Families in a Town, and each of these Towns is commonly a Kingdom. Sometimes one King has the

command of several of these Towns, when they happen to be united in his Hands, by Descent or Conquest; but in such cases there is always a Viceregent appointed in the dependent Town, who is at once Governour, Judge, Chancellor, and has the same Power and Authority which the King himself has in the Town where he resides. This Viceroy is obliged to pay to his Principal some small Tribute, as an acknowledgment of his submission, as likewise to follow him to his Wars, whenever he is required.

10. The manner the Indians have of building their Houses, is very slight and cheap; when they would erect a *Wigwang*, which is the *Indian* name for a House, they stick Saplings into the ground by one end, and bend the other at the top, fastening them together by strings made of fibrous Roots, the rind of Trees, or of the green Wood of the white Oak, which will rive into Thongs. The smallest sort of these Cabins are conical like a Beehive; but the larger are built in an oblong form, and both are cover'd with the Bark of Trees, which will rive off into great flakes. Their Windows are little holes left open for the passage of the Light, which in bad weather they stop with Shutters of the same Bark, opening the Leeward Windows for Air and Light. Their Chimney, as among the true Born *Irish*, is a little hole in the top of the House, to let out the smoke, having no sort of Funnel, or any thing within, to confine the Smoke from ranging through the whole Roof of the Cabins, if the vent will not let it out fast enough. The Fire is always made in the middle of the Cabin. Their Door is a Pendent Mat, when they are near home; but when they go abroad, they barricade it with great Logs of Wood set against the Mat, which are sufficient to keep out Wild Beasts. There's never more than one Room in a House, except in some Houses of State, or Religion, where the Partition is made only by Mats, and loose Poles.

11. Their Houses or Cabins, as we call them, are by this ill method of Building, continually Smokey, when they have Fire in them; but to ease that inconvenience, and to make the Smoke less troublesome to their Eyes, they generally burn Pine, or Lightwood (that is, the fat knots of dead Pine), the Smoke of which does not offend the Eyes, but smuts the Skin exceedingly, and is perhaps another occasion of the darkness of their Complexion.

12. Their Seats, like those in the Eastern part of the World, are the ground itself; and as the People of Distinction amongst them used Carpets, so cleanliness has taught the better sort of these, to spread Match-coats and Mats, to sit on.

They take up their Lodging in the sides of their Cabins upon a Couch made of Board, Sticks, or Reeds, which are raised from the Ground upon Forks, and cover'd with Mats or Skins. Sometimes they lie upon a Bear Skin, or other thick Pelt dressed with the Hair on, and laid upon the

Ground near a Fire, covering themselves with their Match-coats. In warm weather a single Mat is their only Bed, and another rolled up, their Pillow. In their Travels, a Grass-plat under the covert of a shady Tree, is all the lodgings they require, and is as pleasant and refreshing to them, as a Down Bed and fine *Holland* Sheets are to us.

*13.* Their Fortifications consist only of a Palisade of about ten or twelve feet high; and when they would make themselves very safe, they treble the Pale. They often encompass their whole Town: But for the most part only their Kings Houses, and as many others as they judge sufficient to harbor all their People, when an Enemy comes against them. They never fail to secure within their Palisade, all their Religious Reliques, and the Remains of their Princes. Within this Inclosure, they likewise take care to have a supply of Water, and to make a place for a Fire, which they frequently dance round with great solemnity.

### OF THE TRAVELLING, RECEPTION, AND ENTERTAINMENT OF THE INDIANS

*19.* Their Travels they perform altogether on foot, the fatigue of which they endure to admiration. They make no other provision for their Journey, but their Gun or Bow, to supply them with Food for many hundreds miles together. If they carry any Flesh in their marches, they barbicue it, or rather dry it by degrees, at some distance, over the clear Coals of a Wood fire; just as the *Charibees* are said, to preserve the Bodies of their Kings and Great men from Corruption. Their Sauce to this dry meat (if they have any besides a good Stomach) is only a little Bears Oil, or Oil of Acorns; which last they force out, by boiling the Acorns in a strong Lye. Sometimes also in their Travels, each man takes with him a pint or quart of *Rockahomonie*, that is, the finest *Indian* corn, parched, and beaten to powder. When they find their Stomach empty (and cannot stay for the tedious Cookery of other things), they put about a spoonful of this into their Mouths, and drink a draught of Water upon it, which stays their Stomachs, and enables them to pursue their Journey without delay. But their main dependance is upon the Game they kill by the way, and the natural Fruits of the Earth. They take no care about Lodging in these Journeys: but content themselves with the shade of a Tree, or a little High Grass.

When they fear being discover'd, or follow'd by an Enemy in their Marches; they, every morning, having first agreed where they shall rendezvous at night, disperse themselves into the Woods, and each takes a several way, that so the Grass or Leaves being but singly pressed, may rise again, and not betray them. For the *Indians* are very artful in following a track, even where the Impressions are not visible to other People, especially if they have any advantage from the looseness of the Earth, from the stiffness of the Grass, or the stirring of the Leaves, which in the Winter Season lie very thick upon the ground; and likewise afterwards, if they do not happen to be burned.

When in their Travels, they meet with any Waters, which are not fordable, they make Canoes of Birch Bark, by slipping it whole off the Tree, in this manner. First, they gash the Bark quite round the Tree, at the length they would have the Canoe of, then slit down the length from end to end; when that is done, they with their *Tomahawks* easily open the Bark, and strip it whole off. Then they force it open with Sticks in the middle, slope the underside of the ends, and sow them up, which helps to keep the Belly open; or if the Birch trees happen to be small, they sew the Bark of two together; The Seams they dawb with Clay or Mud, and then pass over in these Canoes, by two, three, or more at a time, according as they are in bigness. By reason of the lightness of these Boats, they can easily carry them over Land, if they foresee that they are like to meet with any more Waters, that may impede their March; or else they leave them at the Water side, making no farther account of them; except it be to repass the same Waters in their return.

20. They have a peculiar way of receiving Strangers, and distinguishing whether they come as Friends or Enemies; tho they do not understand each others Language: and that is by a singular method of smoking Tobacco; in which these things are always observed.

1. They take a Pipe much larger and bigger than the common Tobacco Pipe, expressly made for that purpose, with which all Towns are plentifully provided; they call them the Pipes of Peace.

2. This Pipe they always fill with Tobacco, before the Face of the Strangers, and light it.

3. The chief Man of the *Indians*, to whom the Strangers come, takes two or three Whiffs, and then hands it to the chief of the Strangers.

4. If the Stranger refuses to Smoke in it, 'tis a sign of War.

5. If it be Peace, the chief of the Strangers takes a Whiff or two in the Pipe, and presents it to the next Great Man of the Town, they come to visit; he, after taking two or three Whiffs, gives it back to the next of the Strangers, and so on alternately, until they have past all the persons of Note on each side, and then the Ceremony is ended.

After a little discourse, they march together in a friendly manner into the Town, and then proceed to explain the Business upon which they came. This Method is as general a Rule among all the *Indians* of those parts of *America*, as the Flag of Truce is among the *Europeans*. And tho the fashion of the Pipe differ, as well as the ornaments on it, according to the humor of the several Nations, yet 'tis a general Rule, to make these Pipes remarkably bigger, than those for common use, and to adorn them with beautiful Wings, and Feathers of Birds, as likewise with Peak, Beads, or other such Foppery. Father *Lewis Henepin* gives a particular description of one, that he took notice of, among the *Indians*, upon the Lakes wherein he Travell'd. He describes it by the name of *Calumet* of Peace, and his words are these. Book I. Chap. 24.

"This *Calumet* is the most mysterious thing in the World, among the Salvages of the Continent of the Northern *America;* for it is used in all their important transactions: However, it is nothing else but a large Tobacco pipe, made of red, black or white Marble: The Head is finely polished, and the Quill, which is commonly two foot and a half long, is made of a pretty strong Reed, or Cane, adorned with Feathers of all Colors, interlaced with Locks of Womens' Hair. They tie it to two Wings of the most curious Birds they can find, which makes their *Calumet* not much unlike *Mercury's* Wand, or that Staff Ambassadors did formerly carry, when they went to treat of Peace. They sheath that Reed into the Neck of Birds they call *Huars*, which are as big as our Geese, and spotted with black and white; or else of a sort of Ducks, which make their Nest upon Trees, tho the Water be their ordinary element; and whose Feathers be of many different colours. However, every Nation adorns their Calumet as they think fit, according to their own genius, and the Birds they have in their Country.

"Such a Pipe is a Pass and Safe Conduct among all the Allies of the Nation who has given it. And in all Embassies, the Ambassador carries that *Calumet*, as the symbol of Peace, which is always respected: For, the Salvages are generally persuaded, that a great misfortune would befall them, if they violated the Public Faith of the *Calumet*.

"All their Enterprises, Declarations of War, or Conclusions of Peace, as well as all the rest of their Ceremonies, are Sealed (if I may be permitted to say so) with this *Calumet:* They fill that Pipe with the best Tobacco they have, and then present it to those, with whom they have concluded any great affair; and Smoke out of the same after them."

*21.* They have a remarkable way of entertaining all Strangers of Condition, which is performed after the following manner. First, the King or Queen, with a Guard, and a great Retinue, march out of the Town, a quarter or half a mile, and carry Mats for their accommodation; when they meet the Strangers, they invite them to sit down upon those Mats. Then they pass the Ceremony of the Pipe, and afterwards, having spent about half an hour in grave discourse, they get up all together, and march into the Town. Here the first Compliment, is to wash the Courteous Travellers' Feet; then he is treated at a Sumptuous Entertainment, served up by a great number of Attendants. After which he is diverted with Antique *Indian* Dances, performed both by Men and Women, and accompanied with great variety of Wild Music. At this rate he is regaled till Bed time; when a Brace of young Beautiful Virgins are chosen to wait upon him that night, for his particular refreshment. These Damsels are to Undress this happy Gentleman, and as soon as he is in Bed, they gently lay themselves down by him, one on one side of him, and the

other on the other. They esteem it a breach of Hospitality, not to submit
to every thing he desires of them. This kind Ceremony is used only to
Men of great Distinction: And the Young Women are so far from suffering in their Reputation for this Civility, that they are envied for it by
all the other Girls, as having had the greatest Honor done them in the
World.

After this manner perhaps many of the Heroes were begotten in old
time, who boasted themselves to be the Sons of some Wayfaring God.

#### OF THE LEARNING, AND LANGUAGES OF THE INDIANS

22. These *Indians* have no sort of Letters to express their words by,
but when they would communicate any thing, that cannot be delivered
by Message, they do it by a sort of Hieroglyphic, or representation of
Birds, Beasts or other things, showing their different meaning, by the
various forms described, and by the different position of the Figures.

The *Indians* when they travel never so small a way, being much em-
broiled in War one with another, use several marks painted upon their
Shoulders, to distinguish themselves by, and show what Nation they are
of. The usual mark is one, two or three Arrows: one Nation paints these
Arrows upwards, another downwards, a third sideways, and others
again use other distinctions, from whence it comes to pass, that the
*Virginia* Assembly took up the humor, of making Badges of Silver,
Copper or Brass, of which they gave a sufficient number, to each Nation
in amity with the *English,* and then made a Law, that the *Indians*
should not travel among the *English* Plantations, without one of these
Badges in their Company to show that they are Friends. And this is
all the Heraldry, that I know is practised among the *Indians*.

23. Their Language differs very much, as anciently in the several
parts of *Britain;* so that Nations at a moderate distance, do not understand one another. However, they have a sort of general Language, like
what *Lahontan* calls the *Algonquin,* which is understood by the Chief
men of many Nations, as *Latin* is in most parts of *Europe,* and *Lingua
Franca* quite thro the *Levant.*

The general Language here used, is said to be that of the *Occaneeches,*
tho they have been but a small Nation, ever since those parts were
known to the *English:* but in what this Language may differ from that
of the *Algonquin* I am not able to determine.

# Captured by Indians

## Mrs. Mary Rowlandson

*The most famous of the narratives of Indian captivity is Mrs. Mary Row-landson's* The Sovereignty and Goodness of God, together with the Faith-fulness of His Promises Displayed. *Her book has been called "one of the most widely read pieces of seventeeth-century prose": first published in London in 1682 it has gone through more than thirty editions. Despite the formidable title, Mrs. Rowlandson told her story with verve and an eye for colorful detail, but the book is above all a tale of indomitable courage and perseverance sustained by religious faith. Writing for the instruction of her children, Mrs. Rowlandson's purpose was to celebrate the virtues of plain living, high ideals and trust in God. She believed that God had permitted her to be carried into captivity in order to test her faith: "For whom the Lord loveth he chasteneth." As a result of her har-rowing experiences in the wilderness, she gave up smoking on the ground that it was a trap set by the devil to tempt thoughtless people to waste their time. "Surely," she said, "there are many who may be better em-ployed than by sucking a stinking Tobacco pipe."*

*Mrs. Rowlandson, the wife of the Reverend Joseph Rowlandson, was living at Lancaster, Massachusetts, a town of fifty families about thirty-five miles from Boston, when the Indians struck on February 10, 1675 (1676 New Style). Since her husband had gone to Boston to urge the colonial authorities to send soldiers to protect the frontier, Mrs. Rowland-son was alone with her three children. Living nearby were her two sisters and their families. Half a dozen of the houses in Lancaster were fortified but the Indians were too well armed to be kept at bay. Mrs. Rowlandson describes what happened in Lancaster on that "doleful day."*

On the tenth of February, 1675, came the Indians with great numbers upon Lancaster. Their first coming was about sunrising. Hearing the noise of some guns, we looked out; several houses were burning, and the smoke ascending to heaven. There were five persons taken in one house; the father and the mother and a sucking child they knocked on

*Narratives of the Indian Wars, 1675–1699.* Edited by Charles H. Lincoln.

the head; the other two they took and carried away alive. There were two others, who being out of their garrison upon some occasion were set upon; one was knocked on the head, the other escaped. Another there was who running along was shot and wounded, and fell down; he begged of them his life, promising them money (as they told me), but they would not hearken to him but knocked him on the head, and stripped him naked, and split open his bowels. Another, seeing many of the Indians about his barn, ventured and went out, but was quickly shot down. There were three others belonging to the same garrison who were killed; the Indians, getting up upon the roof of the barn, had advantage to shoot down upon them over their fortification. Thus these murderous wretches went on, burning and destroying before them.

At length they came and beset our own house, and quickly it was the dolefulest day that ever mine eyes saw. The house stood upon the edge of a hill; some of the Indians got behind the hill, others into the barn, and others behind anything that could shelter them; from all which places they shot against the house, so that the bullets seemed to fly like hail. And quickly they wounded one man among us, then another, and then a third. About two hours (according to my observation, in that amazing time) they had been about the house before they prevailed to fire it which they did with flax and hemp which they brought out of the barn, and there being no defense about the house, only two flankers at two opposite corners and one of them not finished. They fired it once and one ventured out and quenched it, but they quickly fired it again, and that took.

Now is the dreadful hour come that I have often heard of (in time of war, as it was the case of others), but now mine eyes see it. Some in our house were fighting for their lives, others wallowing in their blood, the house on fire over our heads, and the bloody heathen ready to knock us on the head if we stirred out. Now might we hear mothers and children crying out for themselves, and one another, "Lord, what shall we do?" Then I took my children (and one of my sisters, hers) to go forth and leave the house; but as soon as we came to the door and appeared, the Indians shot so thick that the bullets rattled against the house as if one had taken an handful of stones and threw them, so that we were fain to give back. We had six stout dogs belonging to our garrison, but none of them would stir, though another time, if any Indian had come to the door, they were ready to fly upon him and tear him down. The Lord hereby would make us the more to acknowledge his hand, and to see that our help is always in him.

But out we must go, the fire increasing and coming along behind us, roaring, and the Indians gaping before us with their guns, spears and hatchets to devour us. No sooner were we out of the house but my brother-in-law (being before wounded, in defending the house, in or near the throat) fell down dead, whereat the Indians scornfully shouted, and hallooed, and were presently upon him, stripping off his clothes. The bullets flying thick, one went through my side, and the same (as would seem) through the bowels and hand of my dear child in my arms. One of my elder sister's children, named William, had then his leg broken, which the Indians perceiving, they knocked him on the head. Thus were we butchered by those merciless heathen, standing amazed, with the blood running down to our heels.

My eldest sister being yet in the house, and seeing those woeful sights, the infidels hauling mothers one way and children another, and some wallowing in their blood, and her elder son telling her that her son William was dead, and myself was wounded, she said, "And, Lord, let me die with them." Which was no sooner said, but she was struck with a bullet, and fell down dead over the threshold. I hope she is reaping the fruit of her good labors, being faithful to the service of God in her place. In her younger years she lay under much trouble upon spiritual accounts, till it pleased God to make that precious Scripture take hold of her heart, 2 Corinthians 12:9. *And he said unto me, my grace is sufficient for thee.* More than twenty years after I have heard her tell how sweet and comfortable that place was to her.

But to return. The Indians laid hold of us, pulling me one way and the children another, and said, "Come go along with us." I told them they would kill me. They answered, if I were willing to go along with them, they would not hurt me.

Oh, the doleful sight that now was to behold at this house! *Come, behold the works of the Lord, what desolations he hath made in the earth.* Of thirty-seven persons who were in this one house, none escaped either present death or a bitter captivity, save only one, who might say as he, Job 1:15, *And I only am escaped alone to tell the news.* There were twelve killed, some shot, some stabbed with their spears, some knocked down with their hatchets. When we are in prosperity, oh, the little that we think of such dreadful sights, and to see our dead friends and relations lie bleeding out their heart blood upon the ground. There was one who was chopped into the head with a hatchet, and stripped naked, and yet was crawling up and down. It is solemn sight to see so many Christians lying in their blood, some here and some there, like a company of sheep torn by wolves, all of them stripped naked by a company of hellhounds, roaring, singing, ranting, and insulting, as if they would have torn our very hearts out; yet the Lord by his Almighty power preserved a number of us from death, for there were twenty-four of us taken alive and carried captive.

I had often before this said that if the Indians should come, I should choose rather to be killed by them than taken alive. But when it came to the trial my mind changed; their glittering weapons so daunted my spirit that I chose rather to go along with those (as I may say) ravenous beasts than that moment to end my days. And that I may the better declare what happened to me during that grievous captivity, I shall particularly speak of the several removes we had up and down the wilderness.

### THE FIRST REMOVE

Now away we must go with those barbarous creatures, with our bodies wounded and bleeding, and our hearts no less than our bodies. About a mile we went that night, up upon a hill within sight of the town, where they intended to lodge. There was hard by a vacant house (deserted by the English before, for fear of the Indians). I asked them whether I might not lodge in the house that night, to which they answered, "What, will you love Englishmen still?" This was the dolefulest night that ever my eyes saw. Oh, the roaring and singing and dancing and yelling of those black creatures in the night, which made the place a lively resemblance of hell! And as miserable was the waste that was there made, of horses, cattle, sheep, swine, calves, lambs, roasting pigs, and fowl (which they had plundered in the town), some roasting, some lying and burning, and some boiling to feed our merciless enemies; who were joyful enough though we were disconsolate. To add to the dolefulness of the former day and the dismalness of the present night, my thoughts ran upon my losses and sad bereaved condition. All was gone, my husband gone (at least separated from me, he being in the Bay; and to add to my grief the Indians told me they would kill him as he came homeward), my children gone, my relations and friends gone, our house and home and all our comforts within door and without, all was gone (except my life), and I knew not but the next moment that might go too. There remained nothing to me but one poor wounded babe, and it seemed at present worse than death that it was in such a pitiful condition, bespeaking compassion, and I had no refreshing for it, nor suitable things to revive it. Little do many think what is the savageness and brutishness of this barbarous enemy, ay, even those that seem to profess more than others among them, when the English have fallen into their hands.

### THE SECOND REMOVE

But now, the next morning, I must turn my back upon the town, and travel with them into the vast and desolate wilderness, I know not whither. It is not my tongue or pen can express the sorrows of my heart and bitterness of my spirit that I had at this departure; but God was with me, in a wonderful manner carrying me along and bearing up my spirit, that it did not quite fail. One of the Indians carried my poor wounded babe upon a horse; it went moaning all along, "I shall die, I shall die." I went on foot after it, with sorrow that cannot be expressed. At length I took it off the horse, and carried it in my arms till my strength failed, and I fell down with it. Then they set me upon a horse with my wounded child in my lap, and there being no furniture upon the horse's back, as we were going down a steep hill we both fell over the horse's head, at which they like inhumane creatures laughed and rejoiced to see it, though I thought we should there have ended our days, as overcome with so many difficulties. But the Lord renewed my strength still and carried me along, that I might see more of his power; yea, so much that I could never have thought of, had I not experienced it.

After this it quickly began to snow, and when night came on they stopped. And now down I must sit in the snow, by a little fire, and a few boughs behind me, with my sick child in my lap calling much for water, being now (through the wound) fallen into a violent fever. My own wound also was growing so stiff that I could scarce sit down or rise up; yet so it must be that I must sit all this cold winter night upon the cold snowy ground, with my sick child in my arms, looking that every hour would be the last of its life, and having no Christian friend near me, either to comfort or help me. Oh, I may see the wonderful power of God, that my spirit did not utterly sink under my affliction. Still the Lord upheld me with his gracious and merciful spirit, and we were both alive to see the light of the next morning.

### THE THIRD REMOVE

The morning being come, they prepared to go on their way. One of the Indians got up upon a horse, and they set me up behind him, with my poor sick babe in my lap. A very wearisome and tedious day I had of it, what with my own wound, and my child being so exceeding sick and in a lamentable condition with her wound. It may be easily judged what a poor feeble condition we were in, there being not the least crumb of refreshment that came within either of our mouths, from Wednesday night to Saturday night, except only a little cold water.

This day in the afternoon, about an hour by sun, we came to the place where they intended, viz., an Indian town called Menameset, north of Quabaug. When we were come, oh, the number of pagans (now merciless enemies) that there came about me, that I may say as David, Psalm 27:13, *I had fainted, unless I had believed,* etc. The next day was the Sabbath. I then remembered how careless I had been of God's holy time, how many Sabbaths I had lost and misspent, and how evilly I had walked in God's sight; which lay so close unto my spirit, that it was easy for me to see how righteous it was with God to cut off the thread of my life and cast me out of his presence for ever. Yet the Lord still showed mercy to me and upheld me; and as he wounded me with one hand, so he healed me with the other.

This day there came to me one Robert Pepper (a man belonging to Roxbury), who was taken in Captain Beers's fight, and had been now a considerable time with the Indians and up with them almost as far as Albany to see King Philip, as he told me, and was now very lately come into these parts. Hearing, I say, that I was in this Indian town, he obtained leave to come and see me. He told me he himself was wounded in the leg at Captain Beers's fight, and was not able some time to go; but as they carried him, and as he took oaken leaves and laid them to his wound, through the blessing of God he was able to travel again. Then I took oaken leaves and laid to my side, and with the blessing of God it cured me also; yet before the cure was wrought, I may say, as it is in Psalm 38:5,6, *My wounds stink and are corrupt. . . . I am troubled; I am bowed down greatly; I go mourning all the day long.*

I sat much alone with a poor wounded child in my lap, which moaned night and day, having nothing to revive the body or cheer the spirits of her. But instead of that, sometimes one Indian would come and tell me one hour, "Your master will knock your child in the head," and then a second, and then a third, "Your master will quickly knock your child in the head." This was the comfort I had from them, miserable comforters are ye all, as he said. Thus nine days I sat upon my knees, with my babe in my lap, till my flesh was raw again. My child being even ready to depart this sorrowful world, they bade me carry it out to another wigwam (I suppose because they would not be troubled with such spectacles), whither I went with a very heavy heart, and down I sat with the picture of death in my lap. About two hours in the night, my sweet babe like a lamb departed this life, on February 18, 1675, it being about six years and five months old. It was nine days from the first wounding in this miserable condition, without any refreshing of one nature or other except little cold water.

I cannot but take notice how at another time I could not bear to be in the room where any dead person was, but now the case is changed; I must and could lie down by my dead babe, side by side all the night after. I have thought since of the wonderful goodness of God to me, in preserving me in the use of my reason and senses in that distressed time, that I did not use wicked and violent means to end my own miserable life.

In the morning, when they understood that my child was dead, they sent for me home to my master's wigwam. (By my master in this writing must be understood Quanopin, who was a Sagamore, and married King Philip's wife's sister; not that he first took me, but I was sold to him by another Narragansett Indian, who took me when first I came out of the garrison.) I went to take up my dead child in my arms to carry it with me, but they bid me let it alone; there was no resisting, but go I must and leave it. When I had been at my master's wigwam, I took the first opportunity I could get to go look after my dead child; when I came I asked them what they had done with it. They told me it was upon the hill. Then they went and showed me where it was, where I saw the ground was newly digged, and there they told me they had buried it. There I left that child in the wilderness, and must commit it, and myself also, in this wilderness condition to him who is above all.

God having taken away this dear child, I went to see my daughter Mary, who was at this same Indian town, at a wigwam not very far off, though we had little liberty or opportunity to see one another. She was about ten years old, and taken from the door at first by a Praying Indian and afterward sold for a gun. When I came in sight she would fall a-weeping, at which they were provoked, and would not let me come near her, but bade me be gone; which was a heart-cutting word to me. I had one child dead, another in the wilderness I knew not where, the third they would not let me come near to: *Me* (as he said) *have ye bereaved of my children; Joseph is not, and Simeon is not, and ye will take Benjamin also, all these things are against me.*

I could not sit still in this condition, but kept walking from one place to another. And as I was going along, my heart was even overwhelmed with the thoughts of my condition, and that I should have children and a nation which I knew not ruled over them. Whereupon I earnestly entreated the Lord that he would consider my low estate and show me a token for good and, if it were his blessed will, some sign and hope of some relief. And indeed quickly the Lord answered, in some measure, my poor prayers. For as I was going up and down mourning and lamenting my condition, my son came to me and asked me how I did. I had not seen him before since the destruction of the town, and I knew not where he was till I was informed by himself that he was amongst a smaller parcel of Indians, whose place was about six miles off. With tears in his eyes he asked me whether his sister Sarah was dead, and told me he had seen his sister Mary, and prayed me that I would not be troubled in reference to himself. The occasion of his coming to see me at this time was this. There was, as I said, about six miles from us a small plantation of Indians, where it seems he had been during his captivity; and at this time there were some forces of the Indians gathered out of our company and some also from them (among whom was my son's master) to go to assault and burn Medfield. In this time of the absence of his master, his dame brought him to see me. I took this to be some gracious answer to my earnest and unfeigned desire.

The next day, viz., to this, the Indians returned from Medfield, all the company, for those that belonged to the other small company came through the town that now we were at. But before they came to us, oh, the outrageous roaring and whooping that there was. They began their din about a mile before they came to us. By their noise and whooping they signified how many they had destroyed (which was at that time twenty-three). Those that were with us at home were gathered together as soon as they heard the whooping, and every time that the other went over their number, those at home gave a shout, that the very earth rung again. And thus they continued till those that had been upon the expedition were come up to the sagamore's wigwam, and then, oh, the hideous insulting and triumphing that there was over some Englishmen's scalps that they had taken (as their manner is) and brought with them.

I cannot but take notice of the wonderful mercy of God to me in those afflictions, in sending me a Bible. One of the Indians that came from Medfield fight had brought some plunder and came to me and asked me if I would have a Bible, he had got one in his basket. I was glad of it, and asked him whether he thought the Indians would let me read? He answered, yes. So I took the Bible, and in that melancholy time it came into my mind to read first the 28th chapter of Deuteronomy, which I did, and when I had read it, my dark heart wrought on this manner. That there was no mercy for me, that the blessings were gone, and the curses come in their room, and that I had lost my opportunity. But the Lord helped me still to go on reading till I came to Chapter 3 the seven first verses, where I found, There was mercy promised again, if we would return to him by repentance; and though we were scattered from one end of the earth to the other yet the Lord would gather us together, and turn all those curses upon our enemies. I do not desire to live to forget this Scripture, and what comfort it was to me.

Now the Indians began to talk of removing from this place, some one way and some another. There were now besides myself nine English captives in this place (all of them children, except one woman). I got an opportunity to go and take my leave of them; they being to go one way and I another, I asked them whether they were earnest with God for deliverance. They told me they did as they were able, and it was some comfort to me that the Lord stirred up children to look to him. The woman, viz., Goodwife Joslin, told me she would never see me again, and that she could find in her heart to run away. I wished her not to run away by any means, for we were near thirty miles from any English town, and she very big with child, and had but one week to reckon, and another child in her arms, two years old, and bad rivers there were to go over, and we were feeble, with our poor and coarse entertainment. I had my Bible with me; I pulled it out and asked her whether she would read; we opened the Bible and lighted on Psalm 27, in which psalm we especially took notice of that, *ver. ult., Wait on the*

*Lord: be of good courage, and he shall strengthen thine heart: wait, I say, on the Lord.*

### THE FOURTH REMOVE

And now I must part with that little company I had. Here I parted from my daughter Mary (whom I never saw again till I saw her in Dorchester, returned from captivity), and from four little cousins and neighbors, some of which I never saw afterward; the Lord only knows the end of them. Amongst them also was that poor woman before-mentioned, who came to a sad end, as some of the company told me in my travel. She having much grief upon her spirit, about her miserable condition, being so near her time, she would be often asking the Indians to let her go home. They not being willing to that, and yet vexed with her impor- tunity, gathered a great company together about her, and stripped her naked, and set her in the midst of them, and when they had sung and danced about her (in their hellish manner) as long as they pleased, they knocked her on the head, and the child in her arms with her. When they had done that, they made a fire and put them both into it, and told the other children that were with them that if they attempted to go home they would serve them in like manner. The children said she did not shed one tear, but prayed all the while.

But to return to my own journey. We traveled about half a day or little more, and came to a desolate place in the wilderness, where there were no wigwams or inhabitants before. We came about the middle of the afternoon to this place, cold and wet and snowy and hungry and weary, and no refreshing for man but the cold ground to sit on, and our poor Indian cheer.

Heartaching thoughts here I had about my poor children, who were scattered upon down among the wild beasts of the forest. My head was light and dizzy (either through hunger or hard lodging or trouble, or all together), my knees feeble, my body raw by sitting double night and day, that I cannot express to man the affliction that lay upon my spirit; but the Lord helped me at that time to express it to himself. I opened my Bible to read, and the Lord brought that precious Scripture to me, Jeremiah 31:16. *Thus saith the Lord, Refrain thy voice from weeping, and thine eyes from tears, for thy work shall be rewarded . . . and they shall come again from the land of the enemy.* This was a sweet cordial to me, when I was ready to faint; many and many a time have I sat down and wept sweetly over this Scripture. At this place we continued about four days.

### THE FIFTH REMOVE

The occasion (as I thought) of their moving at this time was the English Army, it being near and following them. For they went as if they had

gone for their lives, for some considerable way, and then they made a
stop, and chose some of their stoutest men and sent them back to hold
the English Army in play whilst the rest escaped. And then, like Jehu,
they marched on furiously, with their old and with their young; some
carried their old decrepit mothers, some carried one and some another.
Four of them carried a great Indian upon a bier, but going through a
thick wood with him they were hindered and could make no haste,
whereupon they took him upon their back and carried him, one at a
time, till they came to Baquaug River. Upon a Friday a little after noon
we came to this river. When all the company was come up and were
gathered together, I thought to count the number of them, but they
were so many, and being somewhat in motion, it was beyond my skill.
In this travel, because of my wound, I was somewhat favored in my
load; I carried only my knitting work and two quarts of parched meal.
Being very faint, I asked my mistress to give me one spoonful of the
meal, but she would not give me a taste.

They quickly fell to cutting dry trees, to make rafts to carry them
over the river, and soon my turn came to go over. By the advantage of
some brush which they had laid upon the raft to sit upon, I did not wet
my foot (though many of themselves at the other end were mid-leg
deep), which cannot but be acknowledged as a favor of God to my
weakened body, it being a very cold time. I was not before acquainted
with such kind of doings or dangers. *When thou passest through the
waters I will be with thee; and through the rivers, they shall not overflow thee,* Isaiah, 43:2. A certain number of us got over the river that
night, but it was the night after the Sabbath before all the company was
got over. On the Saturday they boiled an old horse's leg which they had
got, and so we drank of the broth, as soon as they thought it was ready,
and when it was almost all gone they filled it up again.

The first week of my being among them I hardly ate anything. The
second week I found my stomach grow very faint for want of something, and yet it was very hard to get down their filthy trash. But the
third week, though I could think how formerly my stomach would turn
against this or that, and I could starve and die before I could eat such
things, yet they were sweet and savory to my taste.

I was at this time knitting a pair of white cotton stockings for my
mistress, and had not yet wrought upon a Sabbath day; when the Sabbath came they bade me go to work. I told them it was the Sabbath
day and desired them to let me rest, and told them I would do as much
more tomorrow; to which they answered me they would break my face.
And here I cannot but take notice of the strange providence of God in
preserving the heathen. They were many hundred, old and young, some
sick and some lame, many had papooses at their backs, the greatest
number at this time with us were squaws, and they traveled with all

they had, bag and baggage, and yet they got over this river aforesaid; and on Monday they set their wigwams on fire, and away they went. On that very day came the English Army after them to this river, and saw the smoke of their wigwams, and yet this river put a stop to them. God did not give them courage or activity to go over after us; we were not ready for so great a mercy as victory and deliverance; if we had been, God would have found out a way for the English to have passed this river, as well as for the Indians with the squaws and children and all their luggage. *Oh that my people had hearkened to me, and Israel had walked in my ways! I should soon have subdued their enemies, and turned my hand against their adversaries.* Psalm 81:13, 14.

### THE SIXTH REMOVE

On Monday (as I said) they set their wigwams on fire and went away. It was a cold morning, and before us there was a great brook with ice on it. Some waded through it, up to the knees and higher, but others went till they came to a beaver dam, and I amongst them, where through the good providence of God I did not wet my foot. I went along that day mourning and lamenting, leaving farther my own country, and traveling into the vast and howling wilderness, and I understood something of Lot's wife's temptation when she looked back. We came that day to a great swamp, by the side of which we took up our lodging that night. When I came to the brow of the hill that looked toward the swamp, I thought we had been come to a great Indian town (though there were none but our own company). The Indians were as thick as the trees: it seemed as if there had been a thousand hatchets going at once; if one looked before one, there was nothing but Indians, and behind one, nothing but Indians, and so on either hand, I myself in the midst, and no Christian soul near me. And yet how hath the Lord preserved me in safety? Oh, the experience that I have had of the goodness of God, to me and mine!

### THE SEVENTH REMOVE

After a restless and hungry night there, we had a wearisome time of it the next day. The swamp by which we lay was, as it were, a deep dungeon, and an exceeding high and steep hill before it. Before I got to the top of the hill I thought my heart and legs and all would have broken and failed me. What through faintness and soreness of body, it was a grievous day of travel to me. As we went along I saw a place where English cattle had been; that was comfort to me, such as it was. Quickly after that we came to an English path, which so took with me that I thought I could have freely lain down and died. That day, a little after noon, we came to Squakeag, where the Indians quickly spread themselves over the deserted English fields, gleaning what they could find; some picked up ears of wheat that were trickled down, some found ears of corn, some found groundnuts, and others sheaves of wheat that were frozen together in the shock, and went to threshing of them out. Myself got two ears of Indian corn, and whilst I did but turn my back one of them was stolen from me, which much troubled me.

There came an Indian to them at that time with a basket of horse liver. I asked him to give me a piece. "What," says he, "can you eat horse liver?" I told him I would try, if he would give a piece, which he did, and I laid it on the coals to roast. But before it was half ready they got half of it away from me, so that I was fain to take the rest and eat it as it was, with the blood about my mouth, and yet a savory bit it was to me. For to the hungry soul every bitter thing is sweet. A solemn sight methought it was, to see fields of wheat and Indian corn forsaken and spoiled, and the remainders of them to be food for our merciless enemies. That night we had a mess of wheat for our supper.

### THE EIGHTH REMOVE

On the morrow morning we must go over the river, i.e., Connecticut, to meet with King Philip. Two canoes full they had carried over; the next turn I myself was to go, but as my foot was upon the canoe to step in there was a sudden outcry among them, and I must step back; and instead of going over the river, I must go four or five miles up the river farther northward. Some of the Indians ran one way and some another. The cause of this rout was, as I thought, their espying some English scouts who were thereabout. In this travel up the river, about noon the company made a stop and sat down, some to eat and others to rest them.

As I sat amongst them, musing of things past, my son Joseph unexpectedly came to me. We asked of each other's welfare, bemoaning our doleful condition and the change that had come upon us. We had husband and father and children and sisters and friends and relations and house and home and many comforts of this life; but now we may say, as Job, *Naked came I out of my mother's womb, and naked shall I return thither: The Lord gave, and the Lord hath taken away; blessed be the name of the Lord.* I asked him whether he would read; he told me he earnestly desired it. I gave him my Bible, and he lighted upon that comfortable Scripture, Psalm 118:17, 18. *I shall not die, but live, and declare the works of the Lord. The Lord hath chastened me sore, yet he hath not given me over to death.* "Look here, Mother," says he, "did you read this?" And here I may take occasion to mention one principal ground of my setting forth these lines: even as the Psalmist says, to declare the works of the Lord and his wonderful power in carrying us along, preserving us in the wilderness, while under the enemy's hand, and returning of us in safety again, and his goodness in bringing to my hand so many comfortable and suitable Scriptures in my distress.

But to return, we traveled on till night, and in the morning we must go over the river to Philip's crew. When I was in the canoe I could not but be amazed at the numerous crew of pagans that were on the bank on the other side. When I came ashore they gathered all about me, I sitting alone in the midst. I observed they asked one another questions, and laughed and rejoiced over their gains and victories. Then my heart began to fail, and I fell a-weeping, which was the first time to my remembrance that I wept before them. Although I had met with so much affliction, and my heart was many times ready to break, yet could I not shed one tear in their sight, but rather had been all this while in a maze, and like one astonished; but now I may say, as Psalm 137:1, *By the rivers of Babylon, there we sat down, yea, we wept when we remembered Zion.*

There one of them asked me why I wept. I could hardly tell what to say, yet I answered, they would kill me. "No," said he, "none will hurt you." Then came one of them and gave me two spoonfuls of meal to comfort me, and another gave me half a pint of peas; which was more worth than many bushels at another time.

Then I went to see King Philip. He bade me come in and sit down, and asked me whether I would smoke it (a usual compliment nowadays among saints and sinners), but this no way suited me. For though I had formerly used tobacco, yet I had left it ever since I was first taken. It seems to be a bait the Devil lays to make men lose their precious time. I remember with shame how formerly when I had taken two or three pipes I was presently ready for another, such a bewitching thing it is. But I thank God, he has now given me power over it; surely there are many who may be better employed than to lie sucking a stinking tobacco pipe.

Now the Indians gather their forces to go against Northampton. Overnight one went about yelling and hooting to give notice of the design. Whereupon they fell to boiling of groundnuts and parching of corn (as many as had it) for their provision; and in the morning away they went.

During my abode in this place, Philip spake to me to make a shirt for his boy, which I did, for which he gave me a shilling. I offered the money to my master, but he bade me keep it, and with it I bought a piece of horseflesh. Afterwards he asked me to make a cap for his boy, for which he invited me to dinner. I went, and he gave me a pancake, about as big as two fingers; it was made of parched wheat, beaten and fried in bear's grease, but I thought I never tasted pleasanter meat in my life. There was a squaw who spake to me to make a shirt for her sannup [husband], for which she gave me a piece of bear. Another asked me to knit a pair of stockings, for which she gave me a quart of peas. I boiled my peas and bear together, and invited my master and mistress to dinner, but the proud gossip, because I served them both in one dish, would eat nothing, except one bit that he gave her upon the point of his knife.

Hearing that my son was come to this place, I went to see him, and found him lying flat upon the ground. I asked him how he could sleep so. He answered me that he was not asleep but at prayer, and lay so, that they might not observe what he was doing.

### THE NINTH REMOVE

But instead of either going to Albany or homeward, we must go five miles up the river, and then go over it. Here we abode a while. Here lived a sorry Indian, who spake to me to make him a shirt; when I had done it he would pay me nothing for it. But he living by the river-side, where I often went to fetch water, I would often be putting him in mind, and calling for my pay; at last he told me, if I would make another shirt for a papoose not yet born, he would give me a knife, which he did when I had done it. I carried the knife in, and my master asked me to give it him, and I was not a little glad that I had anything that they would accept of and be pleased with. When we were at this place, my master's maid came home: she had been gone three weeks into the Narragansett country to fetch corn, where they had stored up some in the ground. She brought home about a peck and a half of corn. This was about the time that their great captain, *Naonanto*, was killed in the Narragansett country.

My son being now about a mile from me, I asked liberty to go and see him. They bid me go, and away I went; but quickly lost myself, travelling over hills and through swamps, and could not find the way to him. And I cannot but admire at the wonderful power and goodness of God to me, in that though I was gone from home and met with all sorts of Indians, and those I had no knowledge of, and there being no Christian soul near me, yet not one of them offered the least imaginable miscarriage to me. I turned homeward again, and met with my master, and he showed me the way to my son. When I came to him, I found him not well; and withal he had a boil on his side which much troubled him. We bemoaned one another a while, as the Lord helped us, and then I returned again. When I was returned, I found myself as unsatisfied as I was before. I went up and down mourning and lamenting, and my spirit was ready to sink with the thoughts of my poor children. My son was ill, and I could not but think of his mournful looks, having no Christian friend near him, to do any office of love to him, either for soul or body. And my poor girl, I knew not where she was, nor whether she was sick or well, alive or dead. I repaired under these thoughts to my Bible (my great comforter in that time), and that scripture came to my hand, *"Cast thy burden upon the Lord, and he shall sustain thee."*—Psal. 55:22.

But I was fain to go look after something to satisfy my hunger; and going among the wigwams, I went into one, and there found a squaw who showed herself very kind to me, and gave me a piece of bear. I put it into my pocket and came home; but could not find an opportunity to broil it, for fear they should get it from me. And there it lay all the day and night in my stinking pocket. In the morning, I went again to the same squaw, who had a kettle of groundnuts boiling. I asked her to let me boil my piece of bear in the kettle, which she did, and gave me some groundnuts to eat with it; and I cannot but think how pleasant it was to me. I have sometimes seen bear baked handsomely amongst the English, and some liked it, but the thoughts that it was bear made me tremble. But now, that was savory to me that one would think was enough to turn the stomach of a brute creature.

One bitter cold day, I could find no room to sit down before the fire. I went out, and could not tell what to do, but I went into another wigwam, where they were also sitting around the fire; but the squaw laid a skin for me, and bid me sit down, and gave me some groundnuts, and bid me come again, and told me they would buy me if they were able. And yet these were strangers to me that I never knew before.

### THE TENTH REMOVE

That day a small part of the company removed about three quarters of a mile, intending farther the next day. When they came to the place they intended to lodge, and had pitched their wigwams, being hungry, I went again back to the place we were before at, to get something to eat; being encouraged by the squaw's kindness, who bid me come again. When I was there, there came an Indian to look after me; who, when he had found me, kicked me all along. I went home and found venison roasting that night, but they would not give me one bit of it. Sometimes I met with favor and sometimes with nothing but frowns.

### THE ELEVENTH REMOVE

The next day in the morning, they took their travel, intending a day's journey up the river; I took my load at my back, and quickly we came to wade over a river, and passed over tiresome and wearisome hills. One hill was so steep, that I was fain to creep up upon my knees, and to hold by the twigs and bushes to keep myself from falling backward. But I hope all those wearisome steps that I have taken are but a forwarding of me to the heavenly rest. *"I know, O Lord, that thy judgments are right, and that thou in faithfulness hath afflicted me."*—Psalm 119:75.

### THE TWELFTH REMOVE

It was upon a Sabbath-day morning that they prepared for their travel. This morning I asked my master whether he would sell me to my husband; he answered, *nux;* which did much rejoice my spirits. My mistress, before we went, was gone to the burial of a papoos, and returning, she found me sitting and reading my Bible. She snatched it hastily out of my hand and threw it out of doors. I ran out and caught it up, and put it in my pocket, and never let her see it afterwards. Then they packed up their things to be gone, and gave me my load; I complained it was too heavy, whereupon she gave me a slap on the face and bid me be gone. I lifted up my heart to God, hoping that redemption was not far off; and the rather because their insolence grew worse and worse.

But thoughts of my going homeward, for so we bent our course, much cheered my spirit, and made my burden seem light, and almost nothing at all. But, to my amazement and great perplexity, the scale was soon turned; for when we had got a little way, on a sudden my mistress gave out she would go no further, but turn back again, and said I must go back again with her; and she called her sannup, and would have had him go back also, but he would not, but said he would go on, and come to us again in three days. My spirit was upon this, I confess, very impatient, and almost outrageous. I thought I could as well have died as went back. I cannot declare the trouble that I was in about it; back again I must go. As soon as I had an opportunity, I took my Bible to read, and that quieting scripture came to my hand, Psalm 46:10,— *"Be still, and know that I am God,"* which stilled my spirit for the present; but a sore time of trial I concluded I had to go through; my master being gone, who seemed to me the best friend I had of an Indian, both in cold and hunger, and quickly so it proved. Down I sat, with my heart as full as it could hold, and yet so hungry that I could not sit neither. But going out to see what I could find, and walking among the trees, I found six acorns and two chestnuts, which were some refreshment to me. Towards night I gathered me some sticks for my own comfort, that I might not lie cold; but when we came to lie down, they bid me go out and lie somewhere else, for they had company, they said come in more than their own. I told them I could not tell where to go; they bid me go look; I told them if I went to another wigwam they would be angry and send me home again. Then one of the company drew his sword and told me he would run me through if I did not go presently. Then was I fain to stoop to this rude fellow, and go out in the night I knew not whither. Mine eyes hath seen that fellow afterwards walking up and down in Boston, under the appearance of a friendly Indian, and several others of the like cut. I went to one wigwam, and they told me they had no room. Then I went to another, and they said the same. At last, an old Indian bid me come to him, and his squaw gave me some groundnuts; she gave me also something to lay under my head, and a good fire we had; through the good providence of God, I had a comfortable lodging that night. In the morning, another Indian bid me come at night and he would give me six groundnuts, which I did. We were at this place and time about two miles from Connecticut river. We went in the morning, to gather groundnuts, to the river, and went back again at night. I went with a great load at my back for they when they went, though but a little way, would carry all their frumpery with them. I told them the skin was off my back, but I had no other comforting answer from them than this, that it would be no matter if my head was off too.

## THE THIRTEENTH REMOVE

Instead of going towards the bay, which was what I desired, I must go with them five or six miles down the river, into a mighty thicket of brush; where we abode almost a fortnight. Here one asked me to make a shirt for her papoos, for which she gave me a meal of broth, which was thickened with meal made of the bark of a tree; and to make it better she had put into it about a handful of peas, and a few roasted groundnuts. I had not seen my son a pretty while, and here was an Indian of whom I made enquiry after him, and asked him when he saw him. He answered me, that such a time his master roasted him, and that himself did eat a piece of him as big as his two fingers, and that he was very good meat. But the Lord upheld my spirit under this discouragement; and I considered their horrible addictedness to lying, and that there is not one of them that makes the least conscience of speaking the truth.

In this place, one cold night, as I lay by the fire, I removed a stick which kept the heat from me; a squaw moved it down again, at which I looked up, and she threw an handful of ashes in my eyes; I thought I should have been quite blinded and never have seen more; but, lying down, the water ran out of my eyes, and carried the dirt with it, that by the morning I recovered my sight again. Yet upon this, and the like occasions, I hope it is not too much to say with Job, *"Have pity upon me, have pity upon me, O ye my friends, for the hand of the* LORD *has touched me."* And here, I cannot but remember how many times, sitting in their wigwams, and musing on things past, I should suddenly leap up and run out, as if I had been at home, forgetting where I was, and what my condition was; but when I was without, and saw nothing but wilderness and woods, and a company of barbarous heathen, my mind quickly returned to me, which made me think of that spoken concerning Samson, who said, *"I will go out and shake myself as at other times, but he wist not that the Lord was departed from him."*

About this time I began to think that all my hopes of restoration would come to nothing. I thought of the English Army, and hoped for their coming, and being retaken by them, but that failed. I hoped to be carried to Albany, as the Indians had discoursed, but that failed also. I thought of being sold to my husband, as my master spake; but instead of that, my master himself was gone, and I left behind, so that my spirit was now quite ready to sink. I asked them to let me go out and pick up some sticks, that I might get alone, and pour out my heart unto the Lord. Then also I took my Bible to read, but I found no comfort here neither; yet, I can say in all my sorrows and afflictions, God did not leave me to have any impatient work toward himself, as if his ways were unrighteous; but I knew that he laid upon me less than I deserved. Afterward, before this doleful time ended with me, I was turning the leaves of my Bible, and the Lord brought to me some scripture which did a little revive me; as that, Isa. 55:8,—*"For my thoughts are not your thoughts, neither are my ways your ways, saith the Lord."* And also that, Psalm 35:5,—*"Commit thy ways unto the Lord, trust also in him, and he shall bring it to pass."*

About this time, they came yelping from Hadley, having there killed three Englishmen, and brought one captive with them, viz. Thomas Reed. They all gathered about the poor man, asking him many questions. I desired also to go and see him; and when I came, he was crying bitterly, supposing they would quickly kill him. Whereupon I asked one of them whether they intended to kill him; he answered me they would not. He being a little cheered with that, I asked him about the welfare of my husband; he told me he saw him such a time in the Bay, and he was well, but very melancholy. By which I certainly understood, though I suspected it before, that whatsoever the Indians told me respecting him was vanity and lies. Some of them told me he was dead, and they had killed him; some said he was married again, and that the governor wished him to marry, and told him that he should have his choice; and that all persuaded him that I was dead. So like were these barbarous creatures to him who was a liar from the beginning.

As I was sitting once in the wigwam here, Philip's maid came with the child in her arms, and asked me to give her a piece of my apron to make a flap for it. I told her I would not; then my mistress bid me give it, but I still said no; the maid told me if I would not give her a piece, she would tear a piece off it. I told her I would tear her coat then: with that my mistress rises up, and takes a stick big enough to have killed me, and struck at me with it, but I stept out, and she struck the stick into the mat of the wigwam. But while she was pulling it out, I ran to the maid, and gave her all my apron; and so that storm went over.

Hearing that my son was come to this place, I went to see him, and told him his father was well, but very melancholy. He told me he was as much grieved for his father as for himself. I wondered at his speech, for I thought I had enough upon my spirit, in reference to myself, to make me mindless of my husband and every one else, they being safe among their friends. He told me also, that a while before, his master, together with other Indians, were going to the French for powder; but by the way the Mohawks met with them, and killed four of their company, which made the rest turn back again; for which I desire that myself and he may ever bless the Lord: for it might have been worse with him had he been sold to the French, than it proved to be in his remaining with the Indians.

I went to see an English youth in this place, one John Gilbert, of Springfield. I found him laying without doors upon the ground. I asked him how he did; he told me he was very sick of a flux with eating so much blood. They had turned him out of the wigwam, and with him an Indian papoos, almost dead, (whose parents had been killed), in a bitter cold day, without fire or clothes; the young man himself had nothing on but his shirt and waistcoat. This sight was enough to melt a heart of flint. There they lay quivering in the cold, the youth round like a dog, the papoos stretched out, with his eyes, nose, and mouth full of dirt, and yet alive, and groaning. I advised John to go and get to some fire; he told me he could not stand, but I persuaded him still, lest he should lie there and die. And with much ado I got him to a fire, and went myself home. As soon as I was got home, his master's daughter came after me, to know what I had done with the Englishman; I told her I had got him to a fire in such a place. Now had I need to pray Paul's prayer, 2 Thess. 3:2,—*"that we may be delivered from unreasonable and wicked men."* For her satisfaction I went along with her, and brought her to him; but before I got home again, it was noised about that I was running away, and getting the English youth along with me, that as soon as I came in, they began to rant and domineer, asking me where I had been, and what I had been doing, and saying they would knock me on the head. I told them I had been seeing the English youth, and that I would not run away. They told me I lied, and getting up a hatchet, they came to me and said they would knock me down if I stirred out again; and so confined me to the wigwam. Now may I say with David, 2 Sam. 24:14,—*"I am in a great strait."* If I keep in, I must die with hunger; and if I go out, I must be knocked on the head. This distressed condition held that day, and half the next; and then the Lord remembered me, whose mercies are great. Then came an Indian to me with a pair of stockings which were too big for him, and he would have me ravel them out and knit them fit for him. I showed myself willing, and bid him ask my mistress if I might go along with him a little way.

She said yes, I might; but I was not a little refreshed with that news, that I had my liberty again. Then I went along with him, and he gave me some roasted groundnuts, which did again revive my feeble stomach.

Being got out of her sight, I had time and liberty again to look into my Bible, which was my guide by day, and my pillow by night. Now that comfortable scripture presented itself to me, Isa. 45:7,—"*For a small moment have I forsaken thee, but with great mercies will I gather thee.*" Thus the Lord carried me along from one time to another, and made good to me this precious promise and many others. Then my son came to see me, and I asked his master to let him stay a while with me, that I might comb his head and look over him, for he was almost over-come with lice. He told me when I had done that he was very hungry, but I had nothing to relieve him, but bid him go into the wigwams as he went along, and see if he could get any thing among them; which he did, and, it seems, tarried a little too long, for his master was angry with him, and beat him, and then sold him. Then he came running to tell me he had a new master, and that he had given him some groundnuts already. Then I went along with him to his new master, who told me he loved him, and he should not want. So his master carried him away; and I never saw him afterward, till I saw him at Piscataqua, in Portsmouth.

That night they bid me go out of the wigwam again; my mistress's papoos was sick, and it died that night; and there was one benefit in it, that there was more room. I went to a wigwam and they bid me come in, and gave me a skin to lie upon, and a mess of venison and ground-nuts, which was a choice dish among them. On the morrow they buried the papoos; and afterward, both morning and evening, there came a company to mourn and howl with her; though I confess I could not much condole with them. Many sorrowful days I had in this place; often getting alone, "*like a crane or a swallow, so did I chatter; I did mourn as a dove; mine eyes fail with looking upward. O Lord, I am oppressed, undertake for me.*"—Isa. 38:14. I could tell the Lord as Hezekiah, ver. 3, "*Remember now, O Lord, I beseech thee, how I have walked before thee in truth.*" Now had I time to examine all my ways. My conscience did not accuse me of unrighteousness towards one or another; yet I saw how in my walk with God I had been a careless creature. As David said, "*against thee only have I sinned.*" And I might say with the poor publican, "*God be merciful unto me a sinner.*" Upon the Sabbath days I could look upon the sun, and think how people were going to the house of God to have their souls refreshed, and then home and their bodies also; but I was destitute of both, and might say as the poor prodigal, "*He would fain have filled his belly with the husks that the swine did eat, and no man gave unto him.*"—Luke 15:16. For I must say with him, "*Father, I have sinned against heaven and in thy*

*sight."*—Ver. 21. I remember how on the night before and after the
Sabbath, when my family was about me, and relations and neighbors
with us, we could pray, and sing, and refresh our bodies with the good
creatures of God, and then have a comfortable bed to lie down on; but
instead of all this, I had only a little swill for the body, and then, like
a swine, must lie down on the ground. I cannot express to man the
sorrow that lay upon my spirits. The Lord knows it. Yet that comfortable
scripture would often come to my mind,—*"For a small moment have
I forsaken thee, but with great mercies will I gather thee."*

## THE FOURTEENTH REMOVE

Now must we pack up and be gone from this thicket, bending our
course towards the Bay towns; I having nothing to eat by the way this
day but a few crums of cake that an Indian gave my girl the same
day we were taken. She gave it me, and I put it in my pocket. There
it lay, till it was so mouldy, for want of good baking, that one could
not tell what it was made of; it fell all into crums, and grew so dry and
hard that it was like little flints; and this refreshed me many times when
I was ready to faint. It was in my thoughts when I put it to my mouth,
that if ever I returned I would tell the world what a blessing the Lord
gave to such mean food. As we went along, they killed a deer, with a
young one in her. They gave me a piece of the fawn, and it was so
young and tender that one might eat the bones as well as the flesh, and
yet I thought it very good. When night came on we sat down. It rained,
but they quickly got up a bark wigwam, where I lay dry that night. I
looked out in the morning, and many of them had lain in the rain all
night, I knew by their reeking. Thus the Lord dealt mercifully with me
many times, and I fared better than many of them. In the morning they
took the blood of the deer, and put it into the paunch and so boiled it.
I could eat nothing of that, though they eat it sweetly. And yet they
were so nice in other things, that when I had fetched water, and had
put the dish I dipped the water with into the kettle of water which I
brought, they would say they would knock me down, for they said it
was a sluttish trick.

## THE FIFTEENTH REMOVE

We went on our travel. I having got a handful of groundnuts for my
support that day, they gave me my load, and I went on cheerfully, with
the thoughts of going homeward, having my burthen more upon my
back than my spirit. We came to Baquaug river again that day, near
which we abode a few days. Sometimes one of them would give me a
pipe, another a little tobacco, another a little salt, which I would change
for victuals. I cannot but think what a wolfish appetite persons have in
a starving condition; for many times, when they gave me that which

was hot, I was so greedy, that I should burn my mouth, that it would trouble me many hours after, and yet I should quickly do the like again. And after I was thoroughly hungry, I was never again satisfied; for though it sometimes fell out that I had got enough, and did eat till I could eat no more, yet I was as unsatisfied as I was when I began. And now could I see that scripture verified, there being many scriptures that we do not take notice of or understand till we are afflicted, Mic. 6:14,— *"Thou shalt eat and not be satisfied."* Now might I see more then ever before the miseries that sin hath brought upon us. Many times I should be ready to run out against the heathen, but that scripture would quiet me again, Amos 3:6,—*"Shall there be evil in the city, and the Lord hath not done it?"* The Lord help me to make a right improvement of his word, that I might learn that great lesson, Mic. 6:8, 9,—*"He hath showed thee, O man, what is good; and what doth the Lord require of thee, but to do justly and love mercy, and walk humbly with thy God? Hear ye the rod, and who hath appointed it."*

### THE SIXTEENTH REMOVE

We began this remove with wading over Baquaug River. The water was up to the knees, and the stream very swift, and so cold that I thought it would have cut me in sunder. I was so weak and feeble that I reeled as I went along, and thought there I must end my days at last, after my bearing and getting through so many difficulties. The Indians stood laughing to see me staggering along; but in my distress the Lord gave me experience of the truth and goodness of that promise, Isaiah 43:2: *When thou passest through the waters, I will be with thee; and through the rivers, they shall not overflow thee.* Then I sat down to put on my stockings and shoes, with the tears running down mine eyes, and many sorrowful thoughts in my heart, but I got up to go along with them.

Quickly there came up to us an Indian who informed them that I must go to Wachusett to my master, for there was a letter come from the Council to the sagamores about redeeming the captives, and that there would be another in fourteen days, and that I must be there ready. My heart was so heavy before that I could scarce speak or go in the path; and yet now so light that I could run. My strength seemed to come again and recruit my feeble knees and aching heart; yet it pleased them to go but one mile that night, and there we stayed two days. In that time came a company of Indians to us, near thirty, all on horseback. My heart skipped within me, thinking they had been Englishmen at the first sight of them, for they were dressed in English apparel, with hats, white neckcloths, and sashes about their waists, and ribbons upon their shoulders; but when they came near, there was a vast difference between the lovely faces of Christians and the foul looks of these heathens, which much damped my spirit again.

## THE SEVENTEENTH REMOVE

A comfortable remove it was to me, because of my hopes. They gave me a pack, and along we went cheerfully. But quickly my will proved more than my strength; having little or no refreshing, my strength failed me and my spirit was almost quite gone. Now may I say with David, Psalm 109:22, 23, 24, *I am poor and needy, and my heart is wounded within me. I am gone like the shadow when it declineth; I am tossed up and down like the locust. My knees are weak through fasting, and my flesh faileth of fatness.*

At night we came to an Indian town, and the Indians sat down by a wigwam discoursing, but I was almost spent and could scarce speak. I laid down my load and went into the wigwam, and there sat an Indian boiling of horses' feet (they being wont to eat the flesh first, and when the feet were old and dried, and they had nothing else, they would cut off the feet and use them). I asked him to give me a little of his broth or water they were boiling in. He took a dish and gave me one spoonful of samp, and bid me take as much of the broth as I would. Then I put some of the hot water to the samp and drank it up, and my spirit came again. He gave me also a piece of the rough or ridding of the small guts, and I broiled it on the coals; and now may I say with Jonathan, *See, I pray you, how mine eyes have been enlightened, because I tasted a little of this honey,* 1 Samuel 14:29. Now is my spirit revived again; though means be never so inconsiderable, yet if the Lord bestow his blessing upon them, they shall refresh both soul and body.

## THE EIGHTEENTH REMOVE

We took up our packs and along we went, but a wearisome day I had of it. As we went along I saw an Englishman stripped naked and lying dead on the ground, but knew not who it was. Then we came to another Indian town, where we stayed all night. In this town there were four English children, captives, and one of them my own sister's. I went to see how she did, and she was well, considering her captive condition. I would have tarried that night with her, but they that owned her would not suffer it. Then I went into another wigwam, where they were boiling corn and peas, which was a lovely sight to see, but I could not get a taste thereof. Then I went to another wigwam, where there were two of the English children; the squaw was boiling horses' feet. Then she cut me off a little piece, and gave one of the English children a piece also. Being very hungry, I had quickly eat up mine, but the child could not bite it, it was so tough and sinewy, but lay sucking, gnawing, chewing, and slobbering of it in the mouth and hand. Then I took it of the child and eat it myself, and savory it was to my taste. Then may I say as Job, Chapter 6:7, *The things that my soul refused to touch are as my sorrowful meat.* Thus the Lord made that pleasant refreshing, which another time would have been an abomination. Then I went home to my mistress's wigwam, and they told me I disgraced my master with begging, and if I did so any more they would knock me in the head. I told them they had as good knock me in the head as starve me to death.

### THE NINETEENTH REMOVE

They said, when we went out, that we must travel to Wachusett this day. But a bitter weary day I had of it, traveling now three days together, without resting any day between. At last, after many weary steps, I saw Wachusett Hills, but many miles off. Then we came to a great swamp, through which we traveled up to the knees in mud and water, which was heavy going to one tired before. Being almost spent, I thought I should have sunk down at last and never got out; but I may say, as in Psalm 94:18, *When my foot slipped, thy mercy, O Lord, held me up.*

Going along, having indeed my life but little spirit, Philip, who was in the company, came up and took me by the hand and said, "Two weeks more and you shall be mistress again." I asked him if he spake true. He answered, "Yes, and quickly you shall come to your master again" (who had been gone from us three weeks).

After many weary steps we came to Wachusett, where he was, and glad I was to see him. He asked me when I washed me. I told him not this month. Then he fetched me some water himself, and bid me wash, and gave me the glass to see how I looked, and bid his squaw give me something to eat. So she gave me a mess of beans and meat, and a little groundnut cake. I was wonderfully revived with this favor showed me, Psalm 106:46, *He made them also be pitied of all those that carried them captives.*

My master had three squaws, living sometimes with one and sometimes with another one. One was this old squaw at whose wigwam I was, and with whom my master had been those three weeks. Another was Wettimore, with whom I had lived and served all this while. A severe and proud dame she was, bestowing every day in dressing herself neat as much time as any of the gentry of the land; powdering her hair and painting her face, going with necklaces, with jewels in her ears and bracelets upon her hands. When she had dressed herself, her work was to make girdles of wampum and beads. The third squaw was a younger one, by whom he had two papooses. By that time I was refreshed by the old squaw, with whom my master was, Wettimore's maid came to call me home, at which I fell a-weeping. Then the old squaw told me, to encourage me, that if I wanted victuals I should come to her, and that I should lie there in her wigwam. Then I went with the maid, and quickly came again and lodged there. The squaw laid a mat under me and a good rug over me—the first time I had any such kindness showed me. I understood that Wettimore thought that if she should let me go and serve with the old squaw, she would be in danger to lose not only my service but the redemption pay also. And I was not a little glad to hear this, being by it raised in my hopes that in God's due time there would be an end of this sorrowful hour.

Then came an Indian and asked me to knit him three pair of stockings, for which I had a hat and a silk handkerchief. Then another asked me to make her a shift, for which she gave me an apron. Then came Tom and Peter with the second letter from the Council about the captives. Though they were Indians, I gat them by the hand and burst out into tears; my heart was so full that I could not speak to them.

But recovering myself, I asked them how my husband did, and all my friends and acquaintances. They said, "They are all very well but melancholy." They brought me two biscuits and a pound of tobacco. The tobacco I quickly gave away. When it was all gone, one asked me to give him a pipe of tobacco. I told him it was all gone. Then began he to rant and threaten. I told him when my husband came I would give him some. "Hang him rogue," says he, "I will knock out his brains if he comes here." And then again in the same breath they would say that if there should come an hundred without guns they would do them no hurt: so unstable and like mad men they were. So that fearing the worst, I durst not send to my husband, though there were some thoughts of his coming to redeem and fetch me, not knowing what might follow. For there was little more trust to them than to the master they served.

When the letter was come, the sagamores met to consult about the captives, and called me to them to inquire how much my husband would give to redeem me. When I came I sat down among them, as I was wont to do, as their manner is. Then they bade me stand up, and said they were the "General Court." They bid me speak what I thought he would give. Now knowing that all we had was destroyed by the Indians, I was in a great strait; I thought if I should speak of but a little, it would be slighted, and hinder the matter, if of a great sum, I knew not where it would be procured. At a venture, I said, "Twenty pounds," yet desired them to take less. But they would not hear of that, but sent that message to Boston, that for twenty pounds I should be redeemed. It was a Praying Indian that wrote their letter for them.

There was another Praying Indian who told me that he had a brother that would not eat horse, his conscience was so tender and scrupulous (though as large as hell for the destruction of poor Christians). Then, he said, he read that Scripture to him, 2 Kings 6:25, *There was a great famine in Samaria; and, behold, they besieged it, until an ass's head was sold for fourscore pieces of silver, and the fourth part of a cab of dove's dung for five pieces of silver.* He expounded this place to his brother and showed him that it was lawful to eat that in a famine which is not at another time. "And now," says he, "he will eat horse with any Indian of them all."

There was another Praying Indian who, when he had done all the mischief that he could, betrayed his own father into the English hands, thereby to purchase his own life. Another Praying Indian was at Sudbury fight, though, as he deserved, he was afterward hanged for it. There was another Praying Indian so wicked and cruel as to wear a string about his neck, strung with Christians' fingers. Another Praying Indian, when they went to Sudbury fight, went with them, and his squaw also with him, with her papoose at her back.

Before they went to that fight, they got a company together to powaw; the manner was as followeth. There was one that kneeled upon a deerskin, with the company round him in a ring, who all kneeled, striking upon the ground with their hands and with sticks, and muttering or humming with their mouths. Besides him who kneeled in the ring, there also stood one with a gun in his hand. Then he on the deerskin made a speech, and all manifested assent to it; and so they did many times together. Then they bade him with the gun go out of the ring, which he did, but when he was out, they called him in again; but he seemed to make a stand. Then they called the more earnestly, till he returned again. Then they all sang. Then they gave him two guns, in either hand one. And so he on the deerskin began again; and at the end of every sentence in his speaking they all assented, humming or muttering with their mouths, and striking upon the ground with their hands. Then they bade him with the two guns go out of the ring again; which he did, a little way. Then they called him in again, but he made a stand, so they called him with greater earnestness; but he stood reeling and wavering, as if he knew not whether he should stand or fall, or which way to go. Then they called him with exceeding great vehemency, all of them, one and another. After a little while he turned in, staggering as he went, with his arms stretched out, in either hand a gun. As soon as he came in, they all sang and rejoiced exceedingly awhile. And then he upon the deerskin made another speech, unto which they all assented in a rejoicing manner; and so they ended their business, and forthwith went to Sudbury fight.

To my thinking they went without any scruple but that they should prosper and gain the victory. And they went out not so rejoicing, but they came home with as great a victory. For they said they had killed two captains and almost an hundred men. One Englishman they brought along with them; and he said it was too true, for they had made sad work at Sudbury, as indeed it proved. Yet they came home without that rejoicing and triumphing over their victory which they were wont to show at other times, but rather like dogs (as they say) which have lost their ears. Yet I could not perceive that it was for their own loss of men.

They said they had not lost above five or six, but I missed none, except in one wigwam. When they went, they acted as if the Devil had told them that they should gain the victory; and now they acted as if the Devil had told them they should have a fall. Whether it were so or no I cannot tell but so it proved, for quickly they began to fall, and so it held on that summer, till they came to utter ruin. They came home on a Sabbath day, and the powaw that kneeled upon the deerskin came home (I may say, without abuse) as black as the Devil.

When my master came home, he came to me and bid me make a shirt for his papoose, of a Holland-laced pillowbere. About that time there came an Indian to me and bid me come to his wigwam at night and he would give me some pork and groundnuts. Which I did, and as I was eating, another Indian said to me, "He seems to be your good friend, but he killed two Englishmen at Sudbury, and there lie their clothes behind you." I looked behind me, and there I saw bloody clothes, with bullet holes in them; yet the Lord suffered not this wretch to do me any hurt. Yea, instead of that, he many times refreshed me; five or six times did he and his squaw refresh my feeble carcass. If I went to their wigwam at any time, they would always give me something, and yet they were strangers that I never saw before. Another squaw gave me a piece of fresh pork, and a little salt with it, and lent me her pan to fry it in; and I cannot but remember what a sweet, pleasant, and delightful relish that bit had to me, to this day. So little do we prize common mercies when we have them to the full.

### THE TWENTIETH REMOVE

It was their usual manner to remove, when they had done any mischief, lest they should be found out; and so they did at this time. We went about three or four miles, and there they built a great wigwam, big enough to hold a hundred Indians, which they did in preparation to a great day of dancing. They would say now amongst themselves that the governor would be so angry for his loss at Sudbury that he would send no more about the captives, which made me grieve and tremble. My sister being not far from the place where we now were, and hearing that I was here, desired her master to let her come and see me, and he was willing to it and would go with her; but she, being ready before him, told him she would go before, and was come within a mile or two of the place. Then he overtook her, and began to rant as if he had been mad, and made her go back again in the rain so that I never saw her till I saw her in Charlestown. But the Lord requited many of their ill doings, for this Indian her master was hanged afterwards at Boston.

The Indians now began to come from all quarters, against their merry dancing day. Among some of them came one Goodwife Kettle. I told her my heart was so heavy that it was ready to break. "So is mine too," said she, but yet said, "I hope we shall hear some good news shortly." I could hear now how earnestly my sister desired to see me, and I as earnestly desired to see her; and yet neither of us could get an opportunity. My daughter was also now about a mile off, and I had not seen her in nine or ten weeks, as I had not seen my sister since our first taking. I earnestly desired them to let me go and see them; yea, I entreated, begged, and persuaded them but to let me see my daughter, and yet so hardhearted were they that they would not suffer it. They made use of their tyrannical power whilst they had it, but through the Lord's wonderful mercy their time was now but short.

On a Sabbath day, the sun being about an hour high in the afternoon, came Mr. John Hoar (the Council permitting him, and his own forward spirit inclining him) together with the two forementioned Indians, Tom and Peter, with their third letter from the Council. When they came near, I was abroad; though I saw them not, they presently called me in and bade me sit down and not stir. Then they catched up their guns and away they ran, as if an enemy had been at hand, and the guns went off apace. I manifested some great trouble, and they asked me what was the matter. I told them I thought they had killed the Englishman (for they had in the meantime informed me that an Englishman was come). They said no, they shot over his horse and under, and before his horse, and they pushed him this way and that way, at their pleasure, showing what they could do. Then they let him come to their wigwams. I begged of them to let me see the Englishman, but they would not. But there was I fain to sit their pleasure. When they had talked their fill with him, they suffered me to go to him. We asked each other of our welfare, and I asked him how my husband did, and all my friends. He told me they were all well, and would be glad to see me. Amongst other things which my husband sent me there came a pound of tobacco, which I sold for nine shillings in money; for many of the Indians for want of tobacco smoked hemlock and ground ivy. It was a great mistake in any who thought I sent for tobacco for myself, for through the favor of God that desire was overcome.

I now asked them whether I should go home with Mr. Hoar. They answered "No," one and another of them, and, it being night, we lay down with that answer. In the morning Mr. Hoar invited the sagamores to dinner; but when we went to get it ready, we found that they had stolen the greatest part of the provision Mr. Hoar had brought, out of his bags in the night. And we may see the wonderful power of God in that one passage, in that when there was such a great number of the Indians together, and so greedy of a little good food, and no English there but Mr. Hoar and myself, that there they did not knock us in the head and take what we had; there being not only some provision but also trading cloth, a part of the twenty pounds agreed upon. But instead of doing us any mischief, they seemed to be ashamed of the fact, and said it were some "matchit" [bad] Indian that did it. Oh, that we could believe that there is no thing too hard for God! God showed his power over the heathen in this, as he did over the hungry lions when Daniel was cast into the den.

Mr. Hoar called them betimes to dinner, but they ate very little, they being so busy in dressing themselves and getting ready for their dance, which was carried on by eight of them, four men and four squaws, my master and mistress being two. He was dressed in his Holland shirt, with great laces sewed at the tail of it; he had his silver buttons, his white stockings, his garters were hung round with shillings, and he had girdles of wampum upon his head and shoulders. She had a kersey coat, and covered with girdles of wampum from the loins upward; her arms from her elbows to her hands were covered with bracelets, there were hand-fuls of necklaces about her neck, and several sorts of jewels in her ears. She had fine red stockings and white shoes, her hair powdered and face painted red that was always before black. And all the dancers were after the same manner. There were two others singing and knocking on a kettle for their music. They kept hopping up and down one after another, with a kettle of water in the midst standing warm upon some embers, to drink of when they were dry. They held on till it was almost night, throwing out wampum to the standers-by.

That night I asked them again if I should go home. They all as one said no, except my husband would come for me. When we were lain down, my master went out of the wigwam and by and by sent in an Indian called James the Printer, who told Mr. Hoar that my master would let me go home tomorrow if he would let him have one pint of liquor. Then Mr. Hoar called his own Indians, Tom and Peter, and bid them go and see whether he would promise it before all three; and if he would, he should have it; which he did, and he had it. Then Philip, smelling the business, called me to him and asked me what I would give him to tell me some good news and speak a good word for me. I told him I could not tell what to give him, I would anything I had, and asked him what he would have. He said, two coats and twenty shillings in money, and half a bushel of seed corn, and some tobacco. I thanked him for his love, but I knew the good news as well as the crafty fox.

My master after he had had his drink quickly came ranting into the wigwam again, and called for Mr. Hoar, drinking to him and saying he was a good man, and then again he would say "Hang him rogue." Being almost drunk, he would drink to him, and yet presently say he should be hanged. Then he called for me. I trembled to hear him, yet I was fain to go to him, and he drank to me, showing no incivility. He was the first Indian I saw drunk all the while that I was amongst them. At last his squaw ran out, and he after her, round the wigwam, with his money jingling at his knees. But she escaped him. But having an old squaw, he ran to her, and so through the Lord's mercy we were no more troubled that night.

Yet I had not a comfortable night's rest, for I think I can say I did not sleep for three nights together. The night before the letter came from the Council I could not rest, I was so full of fears and troubles, God many times leaving us most in the dark when deliverance is nearest; yea, at this time I could not rest night or day. The next night I was overjoyed, Mr. Hoar being come, and that with such good tidings. The third night I was even swallowed up with the thoughts of things, viz., that ever I should go home again, and that I must go leaving my children behind me in the wilderness; so that sleep was now almost departed from mine eyes.

On Tuesday morning they called their General Court (as they call it) to consult and determine whether I should go home or no. And they all as one man did seemingly consent to it that I should go home, except Philip, who would not come among them.

But to return again to my going home, where we may see a remarkable change of providence. At first they were all against it, except my husband should come for me; but afterwards they assented to it, and seemed much to rejoice in it. Some asked me to send them some bread, others some tobacco; others shaking me by the hand offered me a hood and scarf to ride in; not one moving hand or tongue against it. Thus hath the Lord answered my poor desire, and the many earnest requests of others put up unto God for me.

In my travels an Indian came to me and told me if I were willing he and his squaw would run away and go home along with me. I told him no, I was not willing to run away but desired to wait God's time, that I might go home quietly and without fear. And now God hath granted me my desire. Oh, the wonderful power of God that I have seen, and the experience that I have had! I have been in the midst of those roaring lions and savage bears, that feared neither God nor man nor the Devil, by night and day, alone and in company, sleeping all sorts together, and yet not one of them ever offered the least abuse of unchastity to me, in word or action. Though some are ready to say I speak it for my own credit, I but speak it in the presence of God, and to his glory. God's power is as great now, and as sufficient to save, as when he preserved Daniel in the lions' den, or the three children in the fiery furnace. I may well say as his Psalm 107:1, *O give thanks unto the Lord, for he is good; for his mercy endureth for ever.* Let the redeemed of the Lord say so, whom he hath redeemed from the hand of the enemy, especially that I should come away in the midst of so many hundreds of enemies quietly and peaceably, and not a dog moving his tongue.

So I took my leave of them, and in coming along my heart melted into tears, more than all the while I was with them, and I was almost swallowed up with the thoughts that ever I should go home again. About the sundown, Mr. Hoar and myself and the two Indians came to Lancaster, and a solemn sight it was to me. There had I lived many comfortable years amongst my relations and neighbors, and now not one Christian to be seen, nor one house left standing. We went on to a farmhouse that was yet standing, where we lay all night, and a comfortable lodging we had, though nothing but straw to lie on. The Lord preserved us in safety that night, and raised us up again in the morning, and carried us along, that before noon we came to Concord. Now was I full of joy, and yet not without sorrow: joy to see such a lovely sight, so many Christians together, and some of them my neighbors. There I met with my brother and my brother-in-law, who asked me if I knew where his wife was. Poor heart! He had helped to bury her, and knew it not; she, being shot down by the house, was partly burnt, so that those who were at Boston at the desolation of the town and came back afterward and buried the dead did not know her. Yet I was not without sorrow, to think how many were looking and longing, and my own children amongst the rest, to enjoy that deliverance that I had now received, and I did not know whether ever I should see them again.

Being recruited with food and raiment, we went to Boston that day, where I met with my dear husband, but the thoughts of our dear children, one being dead and the other we could not tell where, abated our comfort to each other. I was not before so much hemmed in with the merciless and cruel heathen, but now as much with pitiful, tenderhearted, and compassionate Christians. In that poor and distressed and beggarly condition I was received in, I was kindly entertained in several houses; so much love I received from several (some of whom I knew, and others I knew not) that I am not capable to declare it. But the Lord knows them all by name: the Lord reward them sevenfold into their bosoms of his spirituals, for their temporals. The twenty pounds, the price of my redemption, was raised by some Boston gentlemen and Mrs. Usher, whose bounty and religious charity I would not forget to make mention of. Then Mr. Thomas Shepard of Charlestown received us into his house, where we continued eleven weeks; and a father and mother they were to us. And many more tenderhearted friends we met with in that place.

We were now in the midst of love, yet not without much and frequent heaviness of heart for our poor children, and other relations, who were still in affliction. The week following, after my coming in, the governor and Council sent forth to the Indians again, and that not without success, for they brought in my sister and Goodwife Kettle. Their not knowing where our children were was a sore trial to us still, and yet we were not without secret hopes that we should see them again. That which was dead lay heavier upon my spirit than those which were alive and amongst the heathen; thinking how it suffered with its wounds, and I was no way able to relieve it, and how it was buried by the heathen in the wilderness, from among all Christians. We were hurried up and down in our thoughts; sometimes we should hear a report that they were gone this way and sometimes that, and that they were come in, in this place or that. We kept inquiring and listening to hear concerning them, but no certain news as yet.

About this time the Council had ordered a day of public thanksgiving. Though I thought I had still cause of mourning, and being unsettled in our minds, we thought we would ride toward the eastward, to see if we could hear anything concerning our children. And as we were riding along (God is the wise disposer of all things) between Ipswich and Rowley, we met with Mr. William Hubbard, who told us that our son Joseph was come in to Major Waldron's, and another with him, which was my sister's son. I asked him how he knew it. He said the major himself told him so. So along we went till we came to Newbury, and their minister being absent, they desired my husband to preach the thanksgiving for them. He was not willing to stay there that night, but would go over to Salisbury, to hear further, and come again in the morning; which he did, and preached there that day. At night, when he had done, one came and told him that his daughter was come in at Providence. Here was mercy on both hands. Now hath God fulfilled that precious Scripture which was such a comfort to me in my distressed condition. When my heart was ready to sink into the earth (my children being gone I could not tell whither) and my knees trembled under me and I was walking through the valley of the shadow of death, then the Lord brought, and now had fulfilled, that reviving word unto me: *Thus saith the Lord, Refrain thy voice from weeping, and thine eyes from tears; for thy work shall be rewarded . . . and they shall come again from the land of the enemy.*

Now we were between them, the one on the east, and the other on the west. Our son being nearest, we went to him first, to Portsmouth, where we met with him, and with the major also, who told us he had done what he could, but could not redeem him under seven pounds, which the good people thereabouts were pleased to pay. The Lord reward the major, and all thereat, though unknown to me, for their labor of love. My sister's son was redeemed for four pounds, which the Council gave order for the payment of. Having now received one of our children, we hastened toward the other. Going back through Newbury, my husband preached there on the Sabbath day, for which they rewarded him manyfold.

On Monday we came to Charlestown, where we heard that the Governor of Rhode Island had sent over for our daughter, to take care of her, being now within his jurisdiction: which should not pass without our acknowledgments. But she being nearer Rehoboth than Rhode Island, Mr. Newman went over and took care of her, and brought her to his own house. And the goodness of God was admirable to us in our low estate, in that he raised up compassionate friends on every side to us, when we had nothing to recompense any for their love. The Indians were now gone that way, that it was apprehended dangerous to go to her. But the carts which carried provisions to the English Army, being guarded, brought her with them to Dorchester, where we received her safe. Blessed be the Lord for it, for great is his power, and he can do whatsoever seemeth him good.

Her coming in was after this manner. She was traveling one day with the Indians, with her basket at her back. The company of Indians were got before her, and gone out of sight, all except one squaw. She followed the squaw till night, and then both of them lay down, having nothing over them but the heavens and nothing under them but the earth. Thus she traveled three days together, not knowing whither she was going, having nothing to eat or drink but water and green whortleberries. At last they came into Providence, where she was kindly entertained by several of that town. The Indians often said that I should never have her under twenty pounds. But now the Lord hath brought her in upon free cost, and given her to me the second time. The Lord make us a blessing indeed, each to others. Now have I seen that Scripture also fulfilled, Deuteronomy 30:4,7: *If any of thine be driven out to the outmost parts of heaven, from thence will the Lord thy God gather thee, and from thence will he fetch thee. And the Lord thy God will put all these curses upon thine enemies and on them that hate thee, which persecuted thee.*

Thus hath the Lord brought me and mine out of that horrible pit, and hath set us in the midst of tenderhearted and compassionate Christians. It is the desire of my soul that we may walk worthy of the mercies received, and which we are receiving.

# PART V

# THE SOUTH

# Virginia

## Robert Beverley

*As a historian, Beverley was most successful in dealing with his own times. He was not deeply concerned with the past: it was the present and future state of Virginia that engrossed his attention. Here he found much cause for satisfaction: in many respects, he considered Virginia to be an improvement over England. Contrasted with the mother country, the colony afforded better farmland, enjoyed more religious liberty and was blessed with a more equable climate. The "spring and fall afford as pleasant weather as Mahomet promised in his Paradise," he asserted; but he acknowledged that mosquitoes and chiggers were not mentioned by Mahomet in his inventory of the delights of heaven.*

### OF THE PEOPLE, INHABITANTS OF VIRGINIA

I can easily imagin with Sir *Josiah Child*, that this, as well as all the rest of the Plantations, was for the most part at first peopled by Persons of low Circumstances, and by such as were willing to seek their Fortunes in a Foreign Country. Nor was it hardly possible it should be otherwise; for 'tis not likely that any Man of a plentiful Estate, should voluntarily abandon a happy Certainty, to roam after imaginary Advantages, in a New World. Besides which incertainty, he must have propos'd to himself, to encounter the infinite Difficulties and Dangers, that attend a New Settlement. These Discouragements were sufficient to terrifie any Man, that cou'd live easy in *England*, from going to provoke his Fortune in a strange Land.

Those that went over to that Country first, were chiefly single Men, who had not the Incumbrance of Wives and Children in *England;* and if they had, they did not expose them to the fatigue and hazard of so long a Voyage, until they saw how it should fare with themselves. From hence it came to pass, that when they were setled there in a comfortable way of Subsisting a Family, they grew sensible of the Misfortune of

Robert Beverley: *The History and Present State of Virginia.* Edited by Louis B. Wright.

wanting Wives, and such as had left Wives in *England,* sent for them; but the single Men were put to their Shifts. They excepted against the *Indian* Women, on account of their being *Pagans,* and for fear they shou'd conspire with those of their own Nation, to destroy their Husbands. Under this Difficulty they had no hopes, but that the Plenty in which they liv'd, might invite Modest Women of small Fortunes, to go over thither from *England.* However, they wou'd not receive any, but such as cou'd carry sufficient Certificate of their Modesty, and good Behaviour. Those if they were but moderately qualified in all other Respects, might depend upon Marrying very well in those Days, without any Fortune. Nay, the first Planters were so far from expecting Money with a Woman, that 'twas a common thing for them to buy a deserving Wife, at the price of 100 Pound, and make themselves believe, they had a hopeful bargain.

But this way of Peopling the Colony was only at first; for after the advantages of the Climate, and the fruitfulness of the Soil were well known, and all the dangers incident to Infant Settlements were over, People of better Condition retir'd thither with their Families, either to increase the Estates they had before, or else to avoid being persecuted for their Principles of Religion, or Government.

Thus in the time of the Rebellion in *England,* several good Cavalier Families went thither with their Effects, to escape the Tyranny of the Usurper. And so again, upon the Restoration, many People of the opposite Party took Refuge there, to shelter themselves from the King's Resentment. But they had not many of these last, because that Country was famous, for holding out the longest for the Royal Family, of any of the *English* Dominions; for which reason, the Roundheads went for the most part to *New-England,* as did most of those, that in the Reign of King *Charles* II. were molested on the account of their Religion, though some of these fell likewise to the share of *Virginia.* As for Malefactors condemn'd to Transportation, they have always receiv'd very few, and for many years last past, their Laws have been severe against them.

### OF THE BUILDINGS IN VIRGINIA

There are two fine Publick Buildings in this Country, which are the most Magnificent of any in *America:* One of which is the College before spoken of, and the other the Capitol or State-House, as it was formerly call'd: That is, the House for Convention of the General Assembly, for the Setting of the General Court, for the Meeting of the Council, and for keeping of their several Offices.

Not far from this, is also built the publick Prison of the Country, which is a large and convenient Structure, with Partitions for the different Sexes, and distinct Rooms for Petty-Offenders. To this is also annexed a convenient Yard to Air the Criminals in, for preservation of their Life and Health, till the time of their Trial.

These are all erected at Middle-Plantation, now nam'd *Williamsburgh*, where Land is laid out for a new Town. The College, and Capitol are both built of Brick, and cover'd with Shingle.

The Private Buildings are of late very much improved; several Gentle-men there, having built themselves large Brick Houses of many Rooms on a Floor, and several Stories high, as also some Stone-Houses: but they don't covet to make them lofty, having extent enough of Ground to build upon; and now and then they are visited by high Winds, which wou'd incommode a towring Fabrick. They always contrive to have large Rooms, that they may be cool in Summer. Of late they have made their Stories much higher than formerly, and their Windows large, and sasht with Cristal Glass; and within they adorn their Apartments with rich Furniture.

All their Drudgeries of Cookery, Washing, Daries, &c. are perform'd in Offices detacht from the Dwelling-Houses, which by this means are kept more cool and Sweet.

Their Tobacco-Houses are all built of Wood, as open and airy as is consistent with keeping out the Rain; which sort of Building, is most convenient for the curing of their Tobacco.

Their common covering for Dwelling-Houses is Shingle, which is an Oblong Square of Cypress or Pine-Wood; but they cover their Tobacco-Houses with thin Clapboard; and tho' they have Slate enough in some particular parts of the Country, and as strong Clay as can be desired for making of Tile, yet they have very few tiled Houses; neither has any one yet thought it worth his while, to dig up the Slate, which will hardly be made use of, till the Carriage there becomes cheaper, and more common.

## OF THE TEMPERATURE OF THE CLIMATE, AND THE INCONVENIENCES ATTENDING IT

The Natural Temperature of the Inha[bit]ed part of the Country, is hot and moist: tho' this Moisture I take to be occasion'd by the abundance of low Grounds, Marshes, Creeks, and Rivers, which are every where among their lower Settlements; but more backward in the Woods, where they are now Seating, and making new Plantations, they have abundance of high and dry Land, where there are only Crystal Streams of Water, which flow gently from their Springs, and divide themselves into in-numerable Branches, to moisten and enrich the adjacent Lands.

The Country is in a very happy Situation, between the extreams of Heat and Cold, but inclining rather to the first. Certainly it must be a happy Climate, since it is very near of the same Latitude with the Land of Promise. Besides, as *Judæa* was full of Rivers, and Branches of Rivers;

So is *Virginia:* As that was seated upon a great Bay and Sea, wherein were all the conveniences for Shipping and Trade; So is *Virginia.* Had that fertility of Soil? So has *Virginia,* equal to any Land in the known World. In fine, if any one impartially considers all the Advantages of this Country, as Nature made it; he must allow it to be as fine a Place, as any in the Universe; but I confess I am asham'd to say any thing of its Improvements, because I must at the same time reproach my Country-Men with a Laziness that is unpardonable. If there be any excuse for them in this Matter, 'tis the exceeding plenty of good things, with which Nature has blest them; for where God Almighty is so Merciful as to work for People, they never work for themselves.

All the Countries in the World, seated in or near the Latitude of *Virginia,* are esteem'd the Fruitfullest, and Pleasantest of all Clymates. As for Example, *Canaan, Syria, Persia,* great part of *India, China* and *Japan,* the *Morea, Spain, Portugal,* and the Coast of *Barbary,* none of which differ many Degrees of Latitude from *Virginia.* These are reckon'd the Gardens of the World, while *Virginia* is unjustly neglected by its own Inhabitants, and abus'd by other People.

That which makes this Country most unfortunate, is, that it must submit to receive its Character from the Mouths not only of unfit, but very unequal Judges; For, all its Reproaches happen after this manner.

Many of the Merchants and others that go thither from *England,* make no distinction between a cold, and a hot Country: but wisely go sweltering about in their thick Cloaths all the Summer, because they used to do so in their *Northern* Climate; and then unfairly complain of the heat of the Country. They greedily Surfeit with their delicious Fruits, and are guilty of great Intemperance, through the exceeding Generosity of the Inhabitants; by which means they fall Sick, and then unjustly complain of the unhealthiness of the Country. In the next place, the Sailers for want of Towns there, are put to the hardship of rowling most of the Tobacco, a Mile or more, to the Water-side; this Splinters their Hands sometimes, and provokes 'em to curse the Country. Such Exercise, and a bright Sun, makes them hot, and then they imprudently fall to drinking cold Water, or perhaps New Cyder, which in its Season, they find at every Planter's House; Or else they greedily devour all the green Fruit, and unripe Trash they can meet with, and so fall into Fluxes, Fevers, and the Belly-Ach; and then, to spare their own Indiscretion, they in their Tarpawlin Language, cry, God D—— the Country. This is the true State of the case, as to the Complaints of its being Sickly; For, by the most impartial Observation I can make, if People will be perswaded to be Temperate, and take due care of themselves, I believe it is as healthy a Country, as any under Heaven: but the extraordinary pleasantness of the Weather, and the goodness of the Fruit, lead

People into many Temptations. The clearness and brightness of the
Sky, add new vigour to their Spirits, and perfectly remove all Splenetick
and sullen Thoughts. Here they enjoy all the benefits of a warm Sun,
and by their shady Groves, are protected from its Inconvenience. Here
all their Senses are entertain'd with an endless Succession of Native
Pleasures. Their Eyes are ravished with the Beauties of naked Nature.
Their Ears are Serenaded with the perpetual murmur of Brooks, and
the thorow-base which the Wind plays, when it wantons through the
Trees; the merry Birds too, join their pleasing Notes to this rural Consort, especially the Mock-birds, who love Society so well, that whenever
they see Mankind, they will perch upon a Twigg very near them, and
sing the sweetest wild Airs in the World: But what is most remarkable
in these Melodious Animals, they will frequently fly at small distances
before a Traveller, warbling out their Notes several Miles an end, and
by their Musick, make a Man forget the Fatigues of his Journey. Their
Taste is regaled with the most delicious Fruits, which without Art, they
have in great Variety and Perfection. And then their smell is refreshed
with an eternal fragrancy of Flowers and Sweets, with which Nature
perfumes and adorns the Woods almost the whole year round.

Have you pleasure in a Garden? All things thrive in it, most surprise-
ingly; you can't walk by a Bed of Flowers, but besides the entertainment
of their Beauty, your Eyes will be saluted with the charming colours
of the Humming Bird, which revels among the Flowers, and licks off
the Dew and Honey from their tender Leaves, on which it only feeds.
It's size is not half so large as an *English* Wren, and its colour is a
glorious shining mixture of Scarlet, Green, and Gold. Colonel *Byrd,* in
his Garden, which is the finest in that Country, has a Summer-House set
round with the *Indian* Honey-Suckle, which all the Summer is continually full of Sweet Flowers, in which these Birds delight exceedingly.
Upon these Flowers, I have seen ten or a dozen of these Beautiful
Creatures together, which sported about me so familiarly, that with
their little Wings they often fann'd my Face.

On the other side, all the Annoyances and Inconveniences of the
Country, may fairly be summed up, under these three Heads, Thunder,
Heat, and troublesome Vermin.

I confess, in the hottest part of Summer, they have sometimes very
loud and surprizing Thunder, but rarely any Dammage happens by it.
On the contrary, it is of such advantage to the cooling and refining of
the Air, that it is oftner wished for, than fear'd. But they have no Earth-
quakes, which the *Caribbee* Islands are so much troubled with.

Their Heat is very seldom troublesome, and then only by the accident
of a perfect Calm, which happens perhaps two or three times in a year,
and lasts but a few Hours at a time; and even that Inconvenience is

made easie by cool Shades, by open Airy rooms, Summer-Houses, Arbors, and Grottos: But the Spring and Fall, afford as pleasant Weather, as *Mahomet* promis'd in his Paradise.

All the troublesome Vermine, that ever I heard any Body complain of, are either Frogs, Snakes, Musketa's, Chinches, Seedticks, or Red-worms, by some call'd Potato-lice. Of all which I shall give an account in their Order.

Some People have been so ill inform'd, as to say, that *Virginia* is full of Toads, though there never yet was seen one Toad in it. The Marshes, Fens, and Watry Grounds, are indeed full of harmless Frogs, which do no hurt, except by the noise of their croaking Notes: but in the upper parts of the Country, where the Land is high and dry, they are very scarce. In the Swamps and running Streams, they have Frogs of an incredible bigness, which are call'd Bull-frogs, from the roaring they make. Last year I found one of these near a Stream of fresh Water, of so prodigious a Magnitude, that when I extended its Leggs, I found the distance betwixt them, to be seventeen Inches and an half. I am confident, six *French-Men* might have made a comfortable Meal of its Carcase.

Some People in *England* are startled at the very Name of the Rattle-Snake, and fancy every corner of that Province so much pestr'd with them, that a Man goes in constant danger of his Life, that walks abroad in the Woods. But this is as gross a Mistake, as most of the other ill reports of this Country. For in the first place, this Snake is very rarely seen; and when that happens, it never do's the least Mischief, unless you offer to disturb it, and thereby provoke it to bite in its own defence. But it never fails to give you fair warning, by making a noise with its Rattle, which may be heard at a convenient distance. For my own part, I have travell'd the Country as much as any Man in it of my Age, by Night and by Day, above the Inhabitants, as well as among them; and yet I never see a Rattle-Snake alive, and at liberty, in all my Life. I have seen them indeed after they have been killed, or pent up in Boxes to be sent to *England*. The bite of this Viper, without some immediate Application, is certainly Death; but Remedies are so well known, that none of their Servants are ignorant of them. I never knew any that had been hurt by these, or any other of their Snakes, although I have a general knowledge all over the Country, and have been in every part of it. They have several other Snakes which are seen more frequently, and have very little or no hurt in them, *viz.* such as they call Black-Snakes, Water-Snakes, and Corn-Snakes. The black Viper-Snake, and the Copper-bellied Snake, are said to be as Venemous as the Rattle-Snake, but they also are as seldom seen; these three poisonous Snakes, bring forth their young alive, whereas the other three sorts lay Eggs, which are hatched afterwards; and that is the distinction they make, esteeming only those

to be Venemous, which are Viviparous. They have likewise the Horn-
Snake, so call'd from a sharp Horn it carries in its Tail, with which it
assaults any thing that offends it, with that force, that it will strike its
Tail into the But-end of a Musquet, from whence it is not able to disengage it self.

All sorts of Snakes will charm both Birds, and Squirrels, and the
*Indians* pretend to charm them. Several Persons have seen Squirrels
run down a Tree, directly into a Snakes mouth; they have likewise seen
Birds fluttering up and down, and chattering at these Snakes, till at last
they have dropt down just before them.

Some few years agoe, I was a Bear-Hunting in the Woods above the
Inhabitants, and having straggled from my Companions, I was entertain'd at my return, with the Relation of a pleasant Rencounter, between
a Dog and a Rattle-Snake, about a Squirrel. The Snake had got the
Head and Shoulders of the Squirrel into his Mouth, which being something too large for his Throat, it took him up some time to moisten the
Furr of the Squirrel with his Spawl, to make it slip down. The Dog
took this Advantage, seiz'd the hinder parts of the Squirrel, and tugg'd
with all his Might. The Snake on the other side wou'd not let go his hold
for a long time, till at last, fearing he might be bruised by the Dog's
running away with him, he gave up his Prey to the Enemy, which he
eat, and we eat the Snake, which was dainty food.

Musketaes are a sort of Vermin, of less danger, but much more
troublesom, because more frequent. They are a long tail'd Gnat, such
as are in all Fens, and low Grounds in *England,* and I think, have no
other difference from them than the Name. Neither are they troubled
with 'em any where, but in their low Grounds, and Marshes. These
Insects I believe are stronger, and continue longer there, by reason of
the warm Sun, than in *England.* Whoever is persecuted with them in his
House there, may get rid of them, by this easie Remedy. Let him but set
open his Windows at Sun-set, and shut them again before the Twilight
be quite shut in, and all the Musketaes in the Room,will go out at the
Windows, and leave the Room clear.

Chinches are a sort of flat Bug, which lurks in the Beadsteads and
Bedding, and disturbs People's Rest a-nights. Every neat House-Wife
contrives there, by several Devices, to keep her Beds clear of them. But
the best way I ever heard, effectually to destroy them, is by a narrow
search among the Bedding early in the Spring, before these Vermin
begin to Nitt, and run about; for they lie snug all the Winter, and are
in the Spring large and full of the Winters Growth, having all their Seed
within them; and so they become a fair Mark to find, and may with
their whole Breed be destroy'd.

Seed-Ticks, and Red-Worms are small Insects, that annoy People by
day, as Musketaes, and Chinches do by Night: but both these keep out

of your way, if you will keep out of theirs: for Seed-Ticks are no where to be met with, but in the track of Cattle, upon which the great Ticks fasten, and fill their Skins so full of Blood, that they drop off, and where-ever they happen to fall, they produce a kind of Egg, which lies about a Fortnight, before the Seedlings are Hatched. These Seedlings run in Swarms up the next blade of Grass, that lies in their way, and then the first thing that brushes that blade of Grass, gathers off most of these Vermine, which stick like burrs, upon any thing that touches them.

Red-Worms lie only in old dead Trees, and rotten Loggs; and without sitting down upon such, a Man never meets with them, nor at any other Season, but only in the midst of Summer. A little warm Water, immediately brings off both Seed-Ticks, and Red-Worms, tho' they lie never so thick upon any part of the Body: but without some such Remedy, they are so small, that nothing will lay hold of them, but the point of a Pen-Knife, Needle, or such like. And tho' nothing be done to remove them, yet the itching they occasion, goes away after two days.

Their Winters are very short, and don't continue above three or four Months, of which they have seldom thirty days of unpleasant Weather, all the rest being blest with a clear Air, and a bright Sun. However, they have very hard Frost sometimes, but it rarely lasts above three or four days, that is, till the Wind change; for if it blow not between the *North-East,* and *North-West* Points, from the cold Appellatian Mountains, they have no Frost at all. But these Frosts are attended with a Serene Sky, and are otherwise made Delightful, by the tameness of the Wild-fowl and other Game, which by their incredible Number, afford the pleasantness Shooting in the World.

Their Rains, except in the depth of Winter, are extreamly agreeable and refreshing. All the Summer long they last but a few Hours at a time, and sometimes not above half an Hour, and then immediately succeeds clear Sun-shine again: but in that short time it rains so powerfully, that it quits the debt of a long Drought, and makes every thing green and gay.

I have heard that this Country is reproacht with suddain, and dangerous changes of Weather; but that Imputation is unjust: For tho' it be true, that in the Winter, when the Wind comes over those vast Mountains to the *North-West,* which are supposed to retain mighty Magazines of Ice, and Snow, the Weather is then very rigorous; yet in Spring, Summer, and Autumn, such Winds are only cool and pleasant Breezes, which serve to refresh the Air, and correct those Excesses of Heat, which the Situation would otherwise make that Country liable to.

### OF THE DISEASES INCIDENT TO VIRGINIA

While we are upon the Climate, and its Accidents, it will not be improper, to mention the Diseases incident to *Virginia.* Distempers come not there by choaking up the Spirits, with a foggy and thick Air, as in some *Northern* Climes; nor by a stifling Heat, that exhales the vigour of those, that dwell in a more *Southerly* Latitude: But by a wilful and foolish indulging themselves in those Pleasures, which in a warm and fruitful Country, Nature lavishes upon Mankind, for their Happiness, and not for their Destruction.

Thus I have seen Persons impatient of Heat, lie almost naked upon the cold Grass in the Shades, and there often forgetting themselves fall asleep. Nay, many are so imprudent, as to do this in an Evening, and perhaps lie so all Night; when between the Dew from Heaven, and the Damps from the Earth, such impressions are made upon the humours of their Body, as occasion fatal Distempers.

Thus also have I seen Persons put into a great heat by excessive Action, and in the midst of that Heat, strip off their Cloths, and expose their open Pores to the Air. Nay, I have known some mad enough in this hot Condition, to take huge draughts of cold Water, or perhaps of Milk and Water, which they esteem much more cold in Operation, than Water alone.

And thus likewise have I seen several People, (especially New-Comers) so intemperate in devouring the pleasant Fruits, that they have fallen into dangerous Fluxes, and Surfeits. These, and such like Disorders, are the chief occasions of their Diseases.

The first Sickness that any New-Comer happens to have there, he unfairly calls a Seasoning, be it Fever, Ague, or anything else, that his own folly, or excesses bring upon him.

Their Intermitting Fevers, as well as their Agues, are very troublesome, if a fit Remedy be not apply'd; but of late the Doctors there, have made use of the *Cortex Peruviana* with Success, and find that it seldom or never fails to remove the Fits. The Planters too, have several Roots natural to the Country, which in this case they cry up as Infallible. They have the Happiness to have very few Doctors, and those such as make use only of simple Remedies, of which their Woods afford great Plenty. And indeed, their Distempers are not many, and their Cures are so generally known, that there is not Mystery enough, to make a Trade of Physick there, as the Learned do in other Countries, to the great oppression of Mankind.

When these Damps, Colds, and Disorders, affect the Body more gently, and do not seize People violently at first; then for want of some timely Application, (the Planters abhorring all Physick, except in desperate cases,) these small Disorders are suffer'd to go on, until they grow into a *Cachexie*, by which the Body is overrun with obstinate scorbutick Humours. And this in a more fierce, and virulent Degree, I take to be the Yaws.

The Gripes is the Distemper of the *Caribbee* Islands, not of that

Country, and seldom gets footing there, and then only upon great
Provocations; Namely, by the Intemperances before mentioned, together
with an unreasonable use of filthy and unclean Drinks. Perhaps too it
may come by new and unfine Cyder, Perry, or Peach-drink, which the
People are impatient to Drink before they are ready; or by the excessive
use of Lime-Juice, and foul Sugar in Punch and Flip; or else by the
constant drinking of uncorrected Beer, made of such windy, unwholsom
things, as some People make use of in Brewing.

Thus having fairly reckon'd up all the principal Inconveniences of the
Climate, and the Distempers incident to the Country, I shall add a
Chapter of the Recreations and Amusements used there, and then proceed to the natural Benefits they enjoy. After which, I shall conclude
with some hints concerning their Trade, and Improvements.

### OF THE RECREATIONS, AND PASTIMES USED IN VIRGINIA

For their Recreation, the Plantations, Orchards, and Gardens constantly
afford 'em fragrant and delightful Walks. In their Woods and Fields,
they have an unknown variety of Vegetables, and other rarities of
Nature to discover and observe. They have Hunting, Fishing, and
Fowling, with which they entertain themselves an hundred ways. Here
is the most Good-nature, and Hospitality practis'd in the World, both
towards Friends and Strangers: but the worst of it is, this Generosity is
attended now and then, with a little too much Intemperance. The Neighbourhood is at much the same distance, as in the Country in *England*:
but with this Advantage, that all the better sort of People have been
abroad, and seen the World, by which means they are free from that
stiffness and formality, which discover more Civility, than Kindness:
And besides, the goodness of the Roads, and the fairness of the Weather,
bring People oftener together.

The *Indians*, as I have already observ'd, had in their Hunting, a way
of concealing themselves, and coming up to the Deer, under the blind
of a Stalking-Head, in imitation of which, many People have taught their
Horses to stalk it, that is, to walk gently by the Huntsman's side, to
cover him from the sight of the Deer. Others cut down Trees for the
Deer to browze upon, and lie in wait behind them. Others again set
Stakes, at a certain distance within their Fences, where the Deer have
been used to leap over into a Field of Peas, which they love extreamly;
these Stakes they so place, as to run into the Body of the Deer, when he
Pitches, by which means they Impale him.

They Hunt their Hares, (which are very numerous) a Foot, with
Mungrils or swift Dogs, which either catch them quickly, or force them
to hole in a hollow Tree, whither all their Hares generally tend, when
they are closely pursued. As soon as they are thus holed, and have

crawl'd up into the Body of the Tree, the business is to kindle a Fire, and smother them with Smoak, till they let go their hold, and fall to the bottom stifled; from whence they take them. If they have a mind to spare their Lives, upon turning them loose, they will be as fit as ever to hunt at another time; for the mischief done them by the Smoak, immediately wears off again.

They have another sort of Hunting, which is very diverting, and that they call Vermine Hunting; It is perform'd a Foot, with small Dogs in the Night, by the Light of the Moon or Stars. Thus in Summertime they find abundance of Raccoons, Opossums, and Foxes in the Corn-Fields, and about their Plantations: but at other times, they must go into the Woods for them. The Method is to go out with three or four Dogs, and as soon as they come to the place, they bid the Dogs seek out, and all the Company follow immediately. Where-ever a Dog barks, you may depend upon finding the Game; and this Alarm, draws both Men and Dogs that way. If this Sport be in the Woods, the Game by that time you come near it, is perhaps mounted to the top of an high Tree, and then they detach a nimble Fellow up after it, who must have a scuffle with the Beast, before he can throw it down to the Dogs; and then the Sport increases, to see the Vermine encounter those little Currs. In this sort of Hunting, they also carry their great Dogs out with them, because Wolves, Bears, Panthers, Wild-Cats, and all other Beasts of Prey, are abroad in the Night.

For Wolves they make Traps, and set Guns bated in the Woods, so that when he offers to seize the Bate, he pulls the Trigger, and the Gun discharges upon him. What *Elian* and *Pliny* write, of the Horses being benummed in their Legs, if they tread in the Track of a Wolf, does not hold good here; for I my self, and many others, have rid full Speed after Wolves in the Woods, and have seen live ones taken out of a Trap, and drag'd at a Horse's Tail; and yet those that follow'd on Horseback, have not perceived any of their Horses to falter in their pace.

They have many pretty devices besides the Gun, to take wild Turkeys; And among others, a Friend of mine invented a great Trap, wherein he at times caught many Turkeys, and particularly seventeen at one time, but he could not contrive it so, as to let others in after he had entrapped the first flock, until they were taken out.

The *Indian* Invention of Weirs in Fishing, is mightily improved by the English besides which, they make use of Seins, Trolls, Casting-Netts, Setting-Netts, Hand-fishing, and Angling, and in each find abundance of Diversion. I have set in the shade, at the Heads of the Rivers Angling, and spent as much time in taking the Fish off the Hook, as in waiting for their taking it. Like those of the *Euxine* Sea, they also Fish with Spil-yards, which is a long Line staked out in the River, and hung with

a great many Hooks on short strings, fasten'd to the main Line, about
three or four Foot asunder. The only difference is, our Line is supported
by Stakes, and theirs is buoyed up with Gourds.

Their Fowling is answerable to their Fishing for plenty of Game, in
its proper Season, no Plantation being so ill stored, as to be without a
great deal. They have a vast variety of it, several sorts of which, I have
not yet mention'd, as Beaver, Otter, Squirrels, Partridges, Pigeons, and
an infinite number of small Birds, &c.

The admirable Oeconomy of the Beavers, deserves to be particularly
remember'd. They cohabit in one House, are incorporated in a regular
Form of Government, something like Monarchy, and have over them
a Superintendent, which the *Indians* call *Pericu.* He leads them out to
their several Imployments, which consist in Felling of Trees, biting off
the Branches, and cutting them into certain lengths, suitable to the
business they design them for, all which they perform with their Teeth.
When this is done, the Governor orders several of his Subjects to joyn
together, and take up one of those Logs, which they must carry to their
House or Damm, as occasion requires. He walks in State by them all the
while, and sees that every one bear his equal share of the burden; while
he bites with his Teeth, and lashes with his Tail, those that lag behind,
and do not lend all their Strength. They commonly build their Houses
in Swamps, and then to raise the Water to a convenient height, they
make a Damm with Logs, and a binding sort of Clay, so firm, that
though the Water runs continually over, it cannot wash it away. Within
these Damms, they'l inclose Water enough to make a Pool, like a Mill-
pond; and if a Mill happen to be built upon the same Stream, below
their Damm, the Miller in a dry Season, finds it worth his while to cut
it, to supply his Mill with Water. Upon which Disaster, the Beavers are
so expert at their Work, that in one or two Nights time, they will repair
the breach, and make it perfectly whole again. Sometimes they build
their Houses in a broad Marsh, where the Tide ebbs and flows, and then
they make no Damm at all. The Doors into their Houses are under
Water. I have been at the Demolishing one of these Houses, that was
found in a Marsh, and was surpriz'd to find it fortify'd with Logs, that
were six Foot long, and ten Inches through, and had been carried at
least one hundred and fifty yards. This House was three Stories high,
and contain'd five Rooms, that is to say, two in the lower, and middle
Stories, and but one at the top. These Creatures have a great deal of
Policy, and know how to defeat all the Subtilty and Strategems of the
Hunter, who seldom can meet with them, tho' they are in great numbers
all over the Country.

There is yet another kind of Sport, which the young People take great
Delight in, and that is, the Hunting of wild Horses; which they pursue

sometimes with Dogs, and sometimes without. You must know they have many Horses foaled in the Woods of the Uplands, that never were in hand, and are as shy as any Savage Creature. These having no mark upon them, belong to him, that first takes them. However, the Captor commonly purchase these Horses very dear, by spoiling better in the pursuit; in which case, he has little to make himself amends, besides the pleasure of the Chace. And very often this is all he has for it, for the wild Horses are so swift, that 'tis difficult to catch them; and when they are taken, tis odds but their Grease is melted, or else being old, they are so sullen, that they can't be tam'd.

The Inhabitants are very Courteous to Travellers, who need no other Recommendation, but the being Human Creatures. A Stranger has no more to do, but to inquire upon the Road, where any Gentleman, or good House-keeper Lives, and there he may depend upon being received with Hospitality. This good Nature is so general among their People, that the Gentry when they go abroad, order their Principal Servant to entertain all Visitors, with every thing the Plantation affords. And the poor Planters, who have but one Bed, will very often sit up, or lie upon a Form or Couch all Night, to make room for a weary Traveller, to repose himself after his Journey.

If there happens to be a Churl, that either out of Covetousness, or Ill-nature, won't comply with this generous Custom, he has a mark of Infamy set upon him, and is abhorr'd by all. But I must confess, (and am heartily sorry for the occasion) that this good Neighbourhood has of late been much depraved by the present Governor, who practices, the detestable Politicks of governing by Parties; by which, Feuds and Heart-burnings have been kindled in the Minds of the People; and Friendship, Hospitality, and Good-Neighbourhood, have been extreamly discouraged.

OF THE NATURAL PRODUCT OF *Virginia*, AND THE
ADVANTAGES OF THEIR HUSBANDRY

The extream fruitfulness of that Country, has been sufficiently shewn in the Second Book, and I think we may justly add, that in that particularly it is not exceeded by any other. No Seed is Sowed there, but it thrives, and most Plants are improved, by being Transplanted thither. And yet there's very little Improvement made among them, nor any thing us'd in Traffique, but Tobacco.

Besides all the natural Productions mention'd in the Second Book, you may take notice, that Apples from the Seed, never degenerate into Crabs, or Wildings there, but produce the same, or better Fruit than the Mother-Tree, (which is not so in *England*,) and are wonderfully improved by Grafting and Managing; yet there are very few Planters that graft at all, and much fewer that take any care to get choice Fruits.

The Fruit-Trees are wonderfully quick of growth, so that in six or seven years time from the Planting, a Man may bring an Orchard to bear in great plenty, from which he may make store of good Cyder, or distill great quantities of Brandy; for the Cyder is very strong, and yields abundance of in Spirit. Yet they have very few, that take any care at all for an Orchard; nay, many that have good Orchards, are so negligent of them, as to let them go to ruine, and expose the Trees to be torn, and barked by the Catle.

Peaches, Nectarines, and Apricocks, as well as Plums and Cherries, grow there upon Standard Trees. They commonly bear in three years from the Stone, and thrive so exceedingly, that they seem to have no need of Grafting or Inoculating, if any Body would be so good a Husband; and truly I never heard of any that did Graft either Plum, Nectarine, Peach or Apricock in that Country.

Peaches and Nectarines I believe to be Spontaneous some-where or other on that Continent; for the *Indians* have, and ever had greater variety, and finer sorts of them than the *English.* The best sort of these cling to the Stone, and will not come off clear, which they call Plum-Nectarines, and Plum-Peaches, or Cling-Stones. Some of these are 12 or 13 Inches in the Girt. These sorts of Fruits are raised so easily there, that some good Husbands plant great Orchards of them, purposely for their Hogs; and others make a Drink of them, which they call Mobby, and either drink it as Cyder, or Distil it off for Brandy. This makes the best Spirit next to Grapes.

Grape-Vines of the *English* Stock, as well as those of their own Production, bear most abundantly, if they are suffered to run near the Ground, and increase very kindly by Slipping; yet very few have them at all in their Gardens, much less indeavour to improve them by cutting or laying. Indeed my Curiosity the last year, caused me to lay some of the white Muscadine, which came of a Stock removed thither from *England,* and they increased by this method to Admiration: I likewise set several Slips of the cuttings of the same Vine, and the Major part of the Sets bore Grapes in perfection the first year, I remember I had seven full Bunches from one of them.

When a single Tree happens in clearing the Ground, to be left standing with a Vine upon it, open to the Sun and Air; that Vine generally produces as much as 4 or five others, that remain in the Woods. I have seen in this case, more Grapes upon one single Vine, than wou'd load a *London* Cart. And for all this, the People never remove any of them into their Gardens, but content themselves throughout the whole Country, with the Grapes they find thus wild; much less can they be expected to attempt the making of Wine or Brandy from the Grape.

The Almond, Pomgranate and Fig, ripen there very well, and yet there are not ten People in the Country, that have any of them in their Gardens, much less endeavour to preserve any of them for future spending, or to propagate them to make a Trade.

A Garden is no where sooner made than there, either for Fruits, or Flowers. Tulips from the Seed-flower the second year at farthest. All sorts of Herbs have there a perfection in their flavour, beyond what I ever tasted in a more *Northern* Climate. And yet they han't many Gardens in the Country, fit to bear that name.

All sorts of *English* Grain thrive, and increase there, as well as in any other part of the World as for Example, Wheat, Barley, Oats, Rye, Peas, Rape, &c. And yet they don't make a Trade of any of them. Their Peas indeed, are troubled with Wivels, which eat a Hole in them: But this Hole does neither dammage the Seed, nor make the Peas unfit for Boiling. And such as are sow'd late, and gather'd after *August,* are clear of that Inconvenience.

It is thought too much for the same Man, to make the Wheat, and grind it, bolt it, and bake it himself. And it is too great a charge for every Planter, who is willing to sow Barley, to build a Malt-House, and Brew-House too, or else to have no benefit of his Barley; nor will it answer, if he wou'd be at the Charge. These things can never be expected from a single Family: But if they had cohabitations, it might be thought worth attempting. Neither as they are now settled, can they find any certain Market for their other Grain, which if they had Towns, would be quite otherwise.

Rice has been tried there, and is found to grow as well, as in *Carolina,* or in any other part of the Earth: But it labours under the same inconvenience, the want of a Community, to husk and clean it; and after all, to take it off the Planters Hands.

I have related at large in the first Book, how Flax, Hemp, Cotton, and the Silk-Worms have thriven there, in the several essays made upon them; how formerly there was Incouragement given for making of Linnen, Silk, &c. and how all Persons not performing several things towards producing of them were put under a Fine: But now all Incouragement of such things is taken away, and People are not only suffer'd to neglect them, but such as do go about them, are discouraged by their Governor, according to the Maxim laid down in the Memorials before recited.

Silk-grass is there spontaneous in many places, and may be cut several times in a Year. I need not mention what Advantage may be made of so useful a Plant, whose Fibres are as fine as Flax, and much stronger than Hemp. Mr. *Purchas* tells us, in his *Fourth Pilgrim,* Page 1786, That in the first Discovery of this part of the World, they presented Q. *Elizabeth* with a Piece of Grogram that had been made of it. And yet

to this Day they make no manner of use of this Plant, no, not so much
as the *Indians* did, before the *English* came among them, who then
made their Baskets, Fishing Nets, and Lines, of it.

The Sheep increase well, and bear good Fleeces, but they generally
are suffer'd to be torn off their Backs by Briers, and Bushes, instead of
being shorn, or else are left rotting upon the Dunghil with their Skins.

Bees thrive there abundantly, and will very easily yield to the careful
Huswife, two Crops of Honey in a Year, and besides lay up a Winter-
store sufficient to preserve their Stocks.

The Beeves, when any Care is taken of them in the Winter, come to
great Perfection. They have noble Marshes there, which, with the Charge
of draining only, would make as fine Pastures as any in the World; and
yet there is not an hundred Acres of Marsh drained throughout the
whole Country.

Hogs swarm like Vermine upon the Earth, and are often accounted
such, insomuch that when an Inventory of any considerable Man's
Estate is taken by the Executors, the Hogs are left out, and not listed
in the Appraisement. The Hogs run where they list, and find their own
Support in the Woods, without any Care of the Owner; and in many
Plantations it is well, if the Proprietor can find and catch the Pigs, or
any part of a Farrow, when they are young, to mark them; for if there
be any markt in a Gang of Hogs, they determine the Property of the
rest, because they seldom miss their Gangs; but as they are bred in
Company, so they continue to the End.

The Woods produce great Variety of Incense and sweet Gums, which
distil from several Trees; as also Trees bearing Honey, and Sugar, as
before was mention'd; Yet there's no use made of any of them, either
for Profit or Refreshment.

All sorts of Naval Stores may be produced there, as Pitch, Tar, Rosin,
Turpentine, Plank, Timber, and all sorts of Masts, and Yards, besides
Sails, Cordage, and Iron, and all these may be transported, by an easy
Water-Carriage.

These and a Thousand other Advantages that Country naturally
affords, which its Inhabitants make no manner of use of. They can
see their Naval Stores daily benefit other People, who send thither to
build Ships; while they, instead of promoting such Undertakings among
themselves, and easing such as are willing to go upon them, allow them
no manner of Encouragement, but rather the contrary. They receive no
Benefit nor Refreshment from the Sweets, and precious things they
have growing amongst them, but make use of the Industry of *England*
for all such things.

What Advantages do they see the Neighbouring Plantations make
of their Grain and Provisions, while they, who can produce them
infinitely better, not only neglect the making a Trade thereof, but even

a necessary Provision against an accidental Scarcity, contenting themselves with a supply of Food from hand to mouth, so that if it should please God, to send them an unseasonable Year, there wou'd not be found in the Country, Provision sufficient to support the People for three Months extraordinary.

By reason of the unfortunate Method of the Settlement, and want of Cohabitation, they cannot make a beneficial use of their Flax, Hemp, Cotten, Silk, Silk-grass, and Wool, which might otherwise supply their Necessities, and leave the Produce of Tobacco to enrich them, when a gainful Market can be found for it.

Thus they depend altogether upon the Liberality of Nature, without endeavouring to improve its Gifts, by Art or Industry. They spunge upon the Blessings of a warm Sun, and a fruitful Soil, and almost grutch the Pains of gathering in the Bounties of the Earth. I should be asham'd to publish this slothful Indolence of my Countrymen, but that I hope it will rouse them out of their Lethargy, and excite them to make the most of all those happy Advantages which Nature has given them; and if it does this, I am sure they will have the Goodness to forgive me.

# History of the Dividing Line
## *William Byrd*

*The History of the Dividing Line was based upon Byrd's experiences in 1727 as a member of the Virginia Commission, which surveyed and relocated the disputed boundary between North Carolina and Virginia. Byrd also wrote the Secret History of the Dividing Line, which deals with the same events as those described in the History but recounts at greater length the quarrels that occurred between the Virginia and North Carolina surveying parties. For these broils, Byrd placed the blame wholly upon the North Carolina Commissioners, whom he described as "Knights of the Rum-Cask," who devoted much of their time to tippling and to pursuing Indian women and tavernkeepers' daughters. During one especially heated imbroglio, one of the North Carolina Commissioners tried to brain a Virginian with "a Limb of our Table, big enough to knock down an Ox." Understandably, the Virginians were not sorry to see the North Carolinians go their own way but, added Byrd, "in justice to our Carolina friends, they stuck by us as long as our liquor lasted and were so kind as to drink our good journey to the mountains in the last bottle we had left."*

All the people in the neighborhood flocked to John Heath's to behold such rarities as they fancied us to be. The men left their beloved chimney corners, the good women their spinning wheels, and some, of more curiosity than ordinary, rose out of their sick beds to come and stare at us. They looked upon us as a troop of knight errants who were running this great risk of our lives, as they imagined, for the public weal; and some of the gravest of them questioned much whether we were not all criminals condemned to this dirty work for offenses against the state. What puzzled them most was what could make our men so very light-hearted under such intolerable drudgery. "Ye have little reason to be merry, my masters," said one of them, with a very solemn face, "I fancy

*William Byrd's Histories of the Dividing Line Betwixt Virginia and North Carolina.* Edited by William K. Boyd.

the pocoson you must struggle with tomorrow will make you change
your note and try what metal you are made of. Ye are, to be sure, the
first of human race that ever had the boldness to attempt it, and I dare
say will be the last. If, therefore, you have any worldly goods to dispose
of, my advice is that you make your wills this very night, for fear you
die intestate tomorrow." But, glad these frightful tales were so far from
disheartening the men, that they served only to whet their resolution.

9. The surveyors entered early upon their business this morning, and
ran the line through Mr. Eyland's plantation, as far as the banks of
North River. They passed over it in the periauga and landed in Gibbe's
marsh, which was a mile in breadth and tolerably firm. They trudged
through this marsh without much difficulty as far as the high land,
which promised more fertility than any then had seen in these lower
parts. But this firm land lasted not long before they came upon the
dreadful pocoson they had been threatened with. Nor did they find it
one jot better than it had been painted to them. The beavers and otters
had rendered it quite impassable for any creature but themselves.

Our poor fellows had much ado to drag their legs after them in this
quagmire but, disdaining to be balked, they could hardly be persuaded
from pressing forward by the surveyors, who found it absolutely necessary to make a traverse in the deepest place to prevent their sticking
fast in the mire and becoming a certain prey to the turkey buzzards.

This horrible day's work ended two miles to the northward of Mr.
Merchant's plantation, divided from Northwest River by a narrow
swamp, which is causewayed over. We took up our quarters in the open
field not far from the house, correcting, by a fire as large as a Roman
funeral pile, the aguish exhalations arising from the sunken grounds that
surrounded us.

The neck of land included betwixt North River and Northwest River,
with the adjacent marsh, belonged formerly to Governor Gibbs but since
his decease to Colonel Bladen, in right of his first lady, who was Mr.
Gibb's daughter. It would be a valuable tract of land in any country
but North Carolina, where, for want of navigation and commerce, the
best estate affords little more than a coarse subsistence.

10. The Sabbath happened very opportunely to give some ease to our
jaded people, who rested religiously from every work but that of cook-
ing the kettle. We observed very few cornfields in our walks, and those
very small, which seemed the stranger to us because we could see no
other tokens of husbandry or improvement. But upon further inquiry,
we were given to understand people only made corn for themselves and
not for their stocks, which know very well how to get their own living.
Both cattle and hogs ramble in the neighboring marshes and swamps,
where they maintain themselves the whole winter long and are not
fetched home till the spring. Thus these indolent wretches, during one

half of the year, lose the advantage of the milk of their cattle, as well as
their dung, and many of the poor creatures perish in the mire, into the
bargain, by this ill management. Some who pique themselves more upon
industry than their neighbors will now and then, in compliment to their
cattle, cut down a tree whose limbs are loaden with the moss aforemen-
tioned. The trouble would be too great to climb the tree in order to
gather this provender, but the shortest way (which in this country is
always counted the best) is to fell it, just like the lazy Indians, who
do the same by such trees as bear fruit, and so make one harvest for all.
By this bad husbandry milk is so scarce in the winter season that were
a big-bellied woman to long for it, she would lose her longing. And in
truth I believe this is often the case, and at the same time a very good
reason why so many people in this province are marked with a custard
complexion.

The only business here is raising of hogs, which is managed with the
least trouble and affords the diet they are most fond of. The truth of it
is, the inhabitants of North Carolina devour so much swine's flesh that
it fills them full of gross humours. For want, too, of a constant supply of
salt, they are commonly obliged to eat it fresh, and that begets the
highest taint of scurvy. Thus, whenever a severe cold happens to constitutions thus vitiated, 'tis apt to improve into the yaws, called there
very justly the country distemper. This has all the symptoms of the
pox, with this aggravation, that no preparation of mercury will touch
it. First it seizes the throat, next the palate, and lastly shows its spite to
the poor nose, of which 'tis apt in a small time treacherously to under-
mine the foundation. This calamity is so common and familiar here that
it ceases to be a scandal, and in the disputes that happen about beauty
the noses have in some companies much ado to carry it. Nay, 'tis said
that once, after three good pork years, a motion had like to have been
made in the house of burgesses, that a man with a nose should be in-
capable of holding any place of profit in the province; which extraordinary motion could never have been intended without some hopes of a
majority.

Thus, considering the foul and pernicious effects of eating swine's
flesh in a hot country, it was wisely forbidden and made an abomination
to the Jews, who lived much in the same latitude with Carolina.

12. We ordered the surveyors early to their business, who were blessed
with pretty dry grounds for three miles together. But they paid dear for
it in the next two, consisting of one continued frightful pocoson, which
no creatures but those of the amphibious kind ever had ventured into
before. This filthy quagmire did in earnest put the men's courage to a
trial, and though I can't say it made them lose their patience, yet they
lost their humor for joking. They kept their gravity like so many Spaniards, so that a man might then have taken his opportunity to plunge up

to the chin without danger of being laughed at. However, this unusual composure of countenance could not fairly be called complaining. Their day's work ended at the mouth of Northern's Creek, which empties itself into Northwest River; though we chose to quarter a little higher up the river, near Mossy Point. This we did for the convenience of an old house to shelter our persons and baggage from the rain which threatened us hard. We judged the thing right, for there fell an heavy shower in the night that drove the most hardy of us into the house. Though indeed our case was not much mended by retreating thither, because the tenement having not long before been used as a pork store, the moisture of the air dissolved the salt that lay scattered on the floor, and made it as wet within doors as without. However, the swamps and marshes we were lately accustomed to had made such beavers and otters of us that nobody caught the least cold.

We had encamped so early that we found time in the evening to walk near half a mile into the woods. There we came upon a family of mulattoes that called themselves free, though by the shyness of the master of the house, who took care to keep least in sight, their freedom seemed a little doubtful. It is certain many slaves shelter themselves in this obscure part of the world, nor will any of their righteous neighbors discover them. On the contrary, they find their account in settling such fugitives on some out-of-the-way corner of their land to raise stocks for a mean and inconsiderable share, well knowing their condition makes it necessary for them to submit to any terms. Nor were these worthy borderers content to shelter runaway slaves, but debtors and criminals have often met with the like indulgence. But if the government of North Carolina has encouraged this unneighborly policy in order to increase their people, it is no more than what ancient Rome did before them, which was made a city of refuge for all debtors and fugitives, and from that wretched beginning grew up in time to be mistress of a great part of the world. And considering how fortune delights in bringing great things out of small, who knows but Carolina may, one time or other, come to be the seat of some other great empire?

12. Everything had been so soaked with the rain that we were obliged to lie by a good part of the morning and dry them. However, that time was not lost, because it gave the surveyors an opportunity of platting off their work and taking the course of the river. It likewise helped to recruit the spirits of the men, who had been a little harassed with yesterday's march. Notwithstanding all this, we crossed the river before noon and advanced our line three miles. It was not possible to make more of it, by reason good part of the way was either marsh or pocoson. The line cut two or three plantations, leaving part of them in Virginia and part of them in Carolina. This was a case that happened frequently, to the great inconvenience of the owners, who were therefore

314     THE SOUTH

obliged to take out two patents and pay for a new survey in each government.

In the evening we took up our quarters in Mr. Ballance's pasture, a little above the bridge built over Northwest River. There we discharged the two periaugas, which in truth had been very serviceable in transporting us over the many waters in that dirty and difficult part of our business. Our landlord had a tolerable good house and clean furniture, and yet we could not be tempted to lodge in it. We chose rather to lie in the open field, for fear of growing too tender. A clear sky, spangled with stars, was our canopy, which being the last thing we saw before we fell asleep gave us magnificent dreams. The truth of it is, we took so much pleasure in that natural kind of lodging that I think at the foot of the account, mankind are great losers by the luxury of feather beds and warm apartments.

The curiosity of beholding so new and withal so sweet a method of encamping brought one of the Senators of North Carolina to make us a midnight visit. But he was so very clamorous in his commendations of it, that the sentinel, not seeing his quality either through his habit or behavior, had like to have treated him roughly. After excusing the unseasonableness of his visit and letting us know he was a parliament man, he swore he was so taken with our lodging that he would set fire to his house as soon as he got home and teach his wife and children to lie, like us, in the open field.

13. Early this morning our chaplain repaired to us with the men we had left at Mr. Wilson's. We had sent for them the evening before to relieve those who had the labor-oar from Currituck Inlet. But to our great surprise they petitioned not to be relieved, hoping to gain immortal reputation by being the first of mankind that ventured through the great Dismal. But the rest being equally ambitious of the same honor, it was but fair to decide their pretensions by lot. After fortune had declared herself, those which she had excluded offered money to the happy persons to go in their stead. But Hercules would have as soon sold the glory of cleansing the Augean stables, which was pretty near the same sort of work. No sooner was the controversy at an end but we sent those unfortunate fellows back to their quarters whom chance had condemned to remain upon firm land and sleep in a whole skin. In the meanwhile the surveyors carried the line three miles, which was no contemptible day's work, considering how cruelly they were entangled with briers and gall bushes. The leaf of this last shrub bespeaks it to be of the alaternus family.

Our work ended within a quarter of a mile of the Dismal abovementioned, where the ground began to be already full of sunken holes and slashes, which had, here and there, some few reeds growing in them. 'Tis hardly credible how little the bordering inhabitants were acquainted with this mighty swamp, notwithstanding they had lived their whole lives within smell of it. Yet as great strangers as they were to it they pretended to be very exact in their account of its dimensions and were positive it could not be above seven or eight miles wide, but knew no more of the matter than star-gazers know of the distance of the fixed stars. At the same time, they were simple enough to amuse our men with idle stories of the lions, panthers and alligators they were like to encounter in that dreadful place. In short, we saw plainly there was no intelligence of this terra incognita to be got but from our own experience. For that reason it was resolved to make the requisite dispositions to enter it next morning. We allotted every one of the surveyors for this painful enterprise, with twelve men to attend them. Fewer than that could not be employed in clearing the way, carrying the chain, marking the trees, and bearing the necessary bedding and provisions. Nor would the commissioners themselves have spared their persons on this occasion, but for fear of adding to the poor men's burthen while they were certain they could add nothing to their resolution.

We quartered with out friend and fellow traveler, William Wilkins, who had been our faithful pilot to Currituck and lived about a mile from the place where the line ended. Everything looked so very clean and the furniture so neat that we were tempted to lodge within doors. But the novelty of being shut up so close quite spoiled our rest, nor did we breathe so free by abundance as when we lay in the open air.

14. Before nine of the clock this morning the provisions, bedding and other necessaries were made up into packs for the men to carry on their shoulders into the Dismal. They were victualed for eight days at full allowance, nobody doubting but that would be abundantly sufficient to carry them through that inhospitable place; nor indeed was it possible for the poor fellows to stagger under more. As it was, their loads weighed from sixty to seventy pounds, in just proportion to the strength of those who were to bear them.

'Twould have been unconscionable to have saddled them with burthens heavier than that, when they were to lug them through a filthy bog, which was hardly practicable with no burthen at all. Besides this luggage at their backs, they were obliged to measure the distance, mark the trees, and clear the way for the surveyors every step they went. It was really a pleasure to see with how much cheerfulness they undertook, and with how much spirit they went through all this drudgery. For their greater safety, the commissioners took care to furnish them with Peruvian bark, rhubarb and hipocoacanah, in case they might happen in that wet journey to be taken with fevers or fluxes.

Although there was no need of example to inflame persons already so cheerful, yet to enter the people with the better grace, the author and two more of the commissioners accompanied them half a mile into the Dismal. The skirts of it were thinly planted with dwarf reeds and gall bushes, but when we got into the Dismal itself, we found the reeds grew there much taller and closer, and, to mend the matter, were so interlaced with bamboo briers that there was no scuffling through them without the help of pioneers. At the same time we found the ground moist and trembling under our feet like a quagmire, insomuch that it was an easy matter to run a ten-foot pole up to the head in it without exerting any uncommon strength to do it. Two of the men, whose burthens were the least cumbersome, had orders to march before with their tomahawks and clear the way in order to make an opening for the surveyors. By their assistance we made a shift to push the line half a mile in three hours, and then reached a small piece of firm land, about a hundred yards wide, standing up above the rest like an island. Here the people were glad to lay down their loads and take a little refreshment, while the happy man whose lot it was to carry the jug of rum began already, like Æsop's bread-carriers, to find it grow a good deal lighter.

After reposing about an hour, the commissioners recommended vigor and constancy to their fellow-travelers, by whom they were answered with three cheerful huzzas, in token of obedience. This ceremony was no sooner over but they took up their burthens and attended the motion of the surveyors, who, though they worked with all their might, could reach but one mile farther, the same obstacles still attending them which they had met with in the morning. However small this distance may seem to such as are used to travel at their ease, yet our poor men, who were obliged to work with an unwieldy load at their backs, had reason to think it a long way; especially in a bog where they had no firm footing, but every step made a deep impression which was instantly filled with water. At the same time they were laboring with their hands to cut down the reeds, which were ten feet high, their legs were hampered with the briers. Besides, the weather happened to be very warm, and the tallness of the reeds kept off every friendly breeze from coming to refresh them. And indeed it was a little provoking to hear the wind whistling among the branches of the white cedars, which grew here and there amongst the reeds, and at the same time not have the comfort to feel the least breath of it.

In the meantime the three commissioners returned out of the Dismal the same way they went in and having joined their brethren proceeded that night as far as Mr. Wilson's. This worthy person lives within sight of the Dismal, in the skirts whereof his stocks range and maintain themselves all the winter, and yet he knew as little of it as he did of Terra Australis Incognita. He told us a Canterbury tale of a North Briton whose curiosity spurred him a long way into this great desert, as he called it, near twenty years ago, but he having no compass nor seeing the sun for several days together wandered about till he was almost famished; but at last he bethought himself of a secret his countrymen make use of to pilot themselves in a dark day. He took a fat louse out of his collar and exposed it to the open day on a piece of white paper which he brought along with him for his journal. The poor insect, having no eyelids turned himself about till he found the darkest part of the heavens, and so made the best of his way towards the north. By this direction he steered himself safe out, and gave such a frightful account of the monsters he saw and the distresses he underwent that no mortal since has been hardy enough to go upon the like dangerous discovery.

15. The surveyors pursued their work with all diligence, but still found the soil of the Dismal so spongy that the water oozed up into every footstep they took. To their sorrow, too, they found the reeds and briers more firmly interwoven than they did the day before. But the greatest grievance was from large cypresses which the wind had blown down and heaped upon one another. On the limbs of most of them grew sharp snags, pointing every way like so many pikes, that required much pains and caution to avoid. These trees being evergreens, and shooting their large tops very high, are easily overset by every gust of wind, because there is no firm earth to steady their roots. Thus many of them were laid prostrate, to the great encumbrance of the way. Such variety of difficulties made the business go on heavily, insomuch that from morning till night the line could advance no farther than one mile and thirty-one poles. Never was rum, that cordial of life, found more necessary than it was in this dirty place. It did not only recruit the people's spirits, now almost jaded with fatigue, but served to correct the badness of the water, and at the same time to resist the malignity of the air. Whenever the men wanted to drink, which was very often, they had nothing more to do but to make a hole and the water bubbled up in a moment. But it was far from being either clear or well tasted, and had besides a physical effect, from the tincture it received from the roots of the shrubs and trees that grew in the neighborhood.

While the surveyors were thus painfully employed, the commissioners discharged the long score they had with Mr. Wilson for the men and horses which had been quartered upon him during our expedition to Currituck. From thence we marched in good order along the east side of the Dismal, and passed the long bridge that lies over the south branch of Elizabeth River. At the end of eighteen miles we reached Timothy Ivy's plantation, where we pitched our tent for the first time, and were furnished with everything the place afforded. We perceived the happy effects of industry in this family, in which every one looked tidy and clean and carried in their countenances the cheerful marks of plenty. We saw no drones there, which are but too common, alas, in that part of the world. Though in truth the distemper of laziness seizes the men oftener much than the women. These last spin, weave and knit, all with their own hands, while their husbands, depending on the bounty of the climate, are slothful in everything but getting of children, and in that only instance make themselves useful members of an infant colony.

There is but little wool in that province, though cotton grows very kindly, and, so far south, is seldom nipped by the frost. The good women mix this with their wool for their outer garments; though, for want of fulling, that kind of manufacture is open and sleazy. Flax likewise thrives there extremely, being perhaps as fine as any in the world, and I question not might, with a little care and pains, be brought to rival that of Egypt; and yet the men are here so intolerable lazy they seldom take the trouble to propagate it.

16. The line was this day carried one mile and a half and sixteen poles. The soil continued soft and miry, but fuller of trees, especially white cedars. Many of these, too, were thrown down and piled in heaps, high enough for a good Muscovite fortification. The worst of it was, the poor fellows began now to be troubled with fluxes, occasioned by bad water and moist lodging, but chewing of rhubarb kept that malady within bounds.

In the meantime the commissioners decamped early in the morning and made a march of twenty-five miles, as far as Mr. Andrew Mead's, who lives upon Nansemond River. They were no sooner got under the shelter of that hospitable roof but it began to rain hard and continued so to do great part of the night. This gave them much pain for their friends in the Dismal, whose sufferings spoiled their taste for the good cheer wherewith they were entertained themselves. However, late that evening, these poor men had the fortune to come upon another terra firma, which was the luckier for them, because the lower ground, by the rain that fell, was made a fitter lodging for tadpoles than men. In our journey we remarked that the north side of this great swamp lies higher than either the east or the west, nor were the approaches to it so full of sunken grounds. We passed by no less than two Quaker meeting houses, one of which had an awkward ornament on the west end of it, that seemed to ape a steeple. I must own I expected no such piece of foppery from a sect of so much outside simplicity. That persuasion prevails much in the lower end of Nansemond County, for want of ministers to pilot the people a decenter way to heaven. The ill reputation of tobacco planted in those lower parishes makes the clergy unwilling to accept of them, unless it be such whose abilities are as mean as their pay. Thus, whether the churches be quite void or but indifferently filled, the Quakers will have an opportunity of gaining proselytes. 'Tis a wonder no popish missionaries are sent from Maryland to labor in this neglected vineyard, who we know have zeal enough to traverse sea and land on the meritorious errand of making converts. Nor is it less strange that some wolf in sheep's clothing arrives not from New England to lead astray a flock that has no shepherd. People uninstructed in any religion are ready to embrace the first that offers. It is natural for helpless man to adore his Maker in some form or other, and were there any exception to this rule, I should suspect it to be among the Hottentots of the Cape of Good Hope and of North Carolina.

There fell a great deal of rain in the night, accompanied with a strong wind. The fellow-feeling we had for the poor Dismalites on account of this unkind weather rendered the down we laid upon uneasy. We fancied them half-drowned in their wet lodging, with the trees blowing down about their ears. These were the gloomy images our fears suggested; though it was so much uneasiness clear gain. They happened to come off much better, by being luckily encamped on the dry piece of ground afore-mentioned.

17. They were, however, forced to keep the Sabbath in spite of their teeth, contrary to the dispensation our good chaplain had given them. Indeed, their short allowance of provision would have justified their making the best of their way, without distinction of days. 'Twas certainly a work both of necessity and self-preservation to save themselves from starving. Nevertheless, the hard rain had made everything so thoroughly wet that it was quite impossible to do any business. They therefore made a virtue of what they could not help, and contentedly rested in their dry situation.

Since the surveyors had entered the Dismal, they had laid eyes on no living creature: neither bird nor beast, insect nor reptile came in view. Doubtless the eternal shade that broods over this mighty bog and hinders the sunbeams from blessing the ground makes it an uncomfortable habitation for anything that has life. Not so much as a Zealand frog could endure so aguish a situation. It had one beauty, however, that delighted the eye, though at the expense of all the other senses: the moisture of the soil preserves a continual verdure, and makes every plant an evergreen, but at the same time the foul damps ascend without ceasing, corrupt the air, and render it unfit for respiration. Not even a turkey buzzard will venture to fly over it, no more that the Italian vultures will over the filthy Lake Avernus, or the birds in the Holy Land over the Salt Sea where Sodom and Gomorrah formerly stood.

In these sad circumstances, the kindest thing we could do for our suffering friends was to give them a place in the Litany. Our chaplain, for his part, did his office and rubbed us up with a seasonable sermon. This was quite a new thing to our brethren of North Carolina, who live in a climate where no clergyman can breathe any more than spiders in Ireland.

For want of men in holy orders, both the members of the council and justices of the peace are empowered by the laws of that country to marry all those who will not take one another's word; but for the ceremony of christening their children, they trust that to chance. If a parson come in their way, they will crave a cast of his office, as they call it, else they are content their offspring should remain as arrant pagans as themselves. They account it among their greatest advantages that they are not priest-ridden, not remembering that the clergy is rarely guilty of bestriding such as have the misfortune to be poor. One thing may be said for the inhabitants of that province, that they are not troubled with any religious fumes and have the least superstition of any people living. They do not know Sunday from any other day, any more than Robinson Crusoe did, which would give them a great advantage were they given to be industrious. But they keep so many Sabbaths every week, that their disregard of the seventh day has no manner of cruelty in it, either to servants or cattle.

It was with some difficulty we could make our people quit the good cheer they met with at this house, so it was late before we took our departure; but to make us amends, our landlord was so good as to conduct us ten miles on our way, as far as the Cypress Swamp, which drains itself into the Dismal. Eight miles beyond that we forded the waters of the Coropeak, which tend the same way as do many others on that side. In six miles more we reached the plantation of Mr. Thomas Spight, a grandee of North Carolina. We found the good man upon his crutches, being crippled with the gout in both his knees. Here we flattered ourselves we should by this time meet with good tiding of the surveyors, but had reckoned, alas! without our host: on the contrary, we were told the Dismal was at least thirty miles wide in that place. However, as nobody could say this on his own knowledge, we ordered guns to be fired and a drum to be beaten, but received no answer, unless it was from that prating nymph Echo, who, like a loquacious wife, will always have the last word, and sometimes return three for one.

18. It was indeed no wonder our signal was not heard at that time by the people in the Dismal, because in truth, they had not then penetrated one third of their way. They had that morning fallen to work with great vigor; and finding the ground better than ordinary, drove on the line two miles and thirty-eight poles. This was reckoned an Herculean day's work, and yet they would not have stopped there, had not an impenetrable cedar thicket checked their industry. Our landlord had seated himself on the borders of this Dismal, for the advantage of the green food his cattle find there all winter, and for the rooting that supports his hogs. This, I own, is some convenience to his purse for which his whole family pay dear in their persons, for they are devoured by mosquitoes all the summer and have agues every spring and fall which corrupt all the juices of their bodies, give them a cadaverous

complexion, and besides a lazy, creeping habit, which they never get rid of.

*19.* We ordered several men to patrol on the edge of the Dismal, both towards the north and towards the south, and to fire guns at proper distances. This they performed very punctually, but could hear nothing in return, nor gain any sort of intelligence. In the meantime whole flocks of women and children flew hither to stare at us with as much curiosity as if we had lately landed from Bantam or Morocco. Some borderers, too, had a great mind to know where the line would come out, being for the most part apprehensive lest their lands should be taken into Virginia. In that case they must have submitted to some sort of order and government; whereas in North Carolina every one does what seems best in his own eyes. There were some good women that brought their children to be baptized, but brought no capons along with them to make the solemnity cheerful. In the meantime it was strange that none came to be married in such a multitude, if it had only been for the novelty of having their hands joined by one in holy orders. Yet so it was, that though our chaplain christened above an hundred, he did not marry so much as one couple during the whole expedition. But marriage is reckoned a lay contract in Carolina, as I said before, and a country justice can tie the fatal knot there as fast as an archbishop. None of our visitors could, however, tell us any news of the surveyors, nor indeed was it possible any of them should at that time, they being still laboring in the midst of the Dismal. It seems they were able to carry the line this day no further than one mile and sixty-one poles, and that whole distance was through a miry cedar bog, where the ground trembled under their feet most frightfully. In many places, too, their passage was retarded by a great number of fallen trees that lay horsing upon one another. Though many circumstances concurred to make this an unwholesome situation, yet the poor men had no time to be sick, nor can one conceive a more calamitous case than it would have been to be laid up in that uncomfortable quagmire. Never were patients more tractable or willing to take physic than these honest fellows; but it was from a dread of laying their bones in a bog that would soon spew them up again. That consideration also put them upon more caution about their lodging. They first covered the ground with square pieces of cypress bark, which now, in the spring they could easily slip off the tree for that purpose. On this they spread their bedding; but unhappily the weight and warmth of their bodies made the water rise up betwixt the joints of the bark, to their great inconvenience. Thus they lay not only moist, but also exceedingly cold, because their fires were continually going out. For no sooner was the trash upon the surface burnt away, but immediately the fire was extinguished by the moisture of the soil, insomuch that it was great part of the sentinel's business to rekindle it again in a fresh place every quarter of an hour. Nor could they indeed do their duty better because cold was the only enemy they had to guard against in a miserable morass where nothing can inhabit.

20. We could get no tidings yet of our brave adventurers, notwithstanding we despatched men to the likeliest stations to inquire after them. They were still scuffling in the mire, and could not possibly forward the line this whole day more than one mile and sixty-four chains. Every step of this day's work was through a cedar bog, where the trees were somewhat smaller and grew more into a thicket. It was now a great misfortune to the men to find their provisions grow less as their labor grew greater; they were all forced to come to short allowance, and consequently to work hard without filling their bellies. Though this was very severe upon English stomachs, yet the people were so far from being discomfited at it, that they still kept up their good humour, and merrily told a young fellow in the company, who looked very plump and wholesome, that he must expect to go first to pot, if matters should come to extremity. This was only said by way of jest, yet it made him thoughtful in earnest. However, for the present he returned them a very civil answer, letting them know that, dead or alive, he should be glad to be useful to such worthy good friends. But, after all, this humorous saying had one very good effect, for that younker, who before was a little inclined by his constitution to be lazy, grew on a sudden extremely industrious, that so there might be less occasion to carbonade him for the good of his fellow travelers. While our friends were thus embarrassed in the Dismal, the commissioners began to lie under great uneasiness for them. They knew very well their provisions must by this time begin to fall short, nor could they conceive any likely means of a supply. At this time of the year both the cattle and hogs had forsaken the skirts of the Dismal, invited by the springing grass on the firm land. All our hopes were that Providence would cause some wild game to fall in their way, or else direct them to a wholesome vegetable for subsistence. In short they were haunted with so many frights on this occasion that they were in truth more uneasy than the persons whose case they lamented.

We had several visitors from Edenton, in the afternoon, that came with Mr. Gale, who had prudently left us at Currituck, to scuffle through that dirty country by ourselves. These gentlemen, having good noses, had smelled out, at thirty miles' distance, the precious liquor with which the liberality of our good friend Mr. Mead had just before supplied us. That generous person had judged very right, that we were now got out of the latitude of drink proper for men in affliction, and, therefore was so good as to send his cart loaden with all sorts of refreshments, for which the commissioners returned him their thanks, and the chaplain his blessing.

21. The surveyors and their attendants began now in good earnest to be alarmed with apprehensions of famine, nor could they forbear looking with some sort of appetite upon a dog which had been the faithful companion of their travels. Their provisions were now near exhausted. They had this morning made the last distribution, that so each might husband his small pittance as he pleased. Now it was that the fresh colored young man began to tremble, every joint of him, having dreamed the night before that the Indians were about to barbecue him over live coals. The prospect of famine determined the people at last, with one consent, to abandon the line for the present, which advanced but slowly, and make the best of their way to firm land. Accordingly they set off very early, and by the help of the compass which they carried along with them steered a direct westwardly course. They marched from morning till night, and computed their journey to amount to about four miles, which was a great way, considering the difficulties of the ground. It was all along a cedar swamp, so dirty and perplexed that if they had not traveled for their lives they could not have reached so far. On their way they espied a turkey buzzard that flew prodigiously high to get above the noisome exhalations that ascend from that filthy place. This they were willing to understand as a good omen, according to the superstitions of the ancients, who had great faith in the flight of vultures. However, after all this tedious journey, they could yet discover no end of their toil, which made them very pensive, especially after they had eat the last morsel of their provisions. But to their unspeakable comfort, when all was hushed in the evening, they heard the cattle low and the dogs bark very distinctly, which to men in that distress was more delightful music than Faustina or Farinelli could have made. In the meantime the commissioners could get no news of them from any of their visitors, who assembled from every point of the compass. But the good landlord had visitors of another kind while we were there, that is to say, some industrious masters of ships that lay in Nansemond River. These worthy commanders came to bespeak tobacco from these parts to make up their loadings, in contempt of the Virginia law which positively forbade their taking in any made in North Carolina. Nor was this restraint at all unreasonable; because they have no law in Carolina, either to mend the quality or lessen the quantity of tobacco, or so much as to prevent the turning out of seconds, all which cases have been provided against by the laws of Virginia. Wherefore, there can be no reason why the inhabitants of that province should have the same advantage of shipping their tobacco in our parts, when they will by no means submit to the same restrictions that we do.

22. Our patrol happened not to go far enough to the northward this morning; if they had, the people in the Dismal might have heard the report of their guns. For this reason they returned without any tidings,

which threw us into a great though unnecessary perplexity. This was now the ninth day since they entered into that inhospitable swamp, and consequently we had reason to believe their provisions were quite spent. We knew they worked hard and therefore would eat heartily so long as they had wherewithal to recruit their spirits, not imagining the swamp so wide as they found it. Had we been able to guess where the line would come out, we would have sent men to meet them with a fresh supply; but as we could know nothing of that, and as we had neither compass nor surveyor to guide a messenger on such an errand, we were unwilling to expose him to no purpose; therefore, all we were able to do for them, in so great an extremity, was to recommend them to a merciful Providence. However long we might think the time, yet we were cautious of showing our uneasiness, for fear of mortifying our landlord. He had done his best for us, and therefore we were unwilling he should think us dissatisfied with our entertainment. In the midst of our concern, we were most agreeably surprised, just after dinner, with the news that the Dismalites were all safe.

24. This being Sunday, we had a numerous congregation, which flocked to our quarters from all the adjacent country. The news that our surveyors were come out of the Dismal increased the number very much, because it would give them an opportunity of guessing, at least, whereabouts the line could cut, whereby they might form some judgment whether they belonged to Virginia or Carolina. Those who had taken up land within the disputed bounds were in great pain lest it should be found to lie in Virginia; because this being done contrary to an express order of that government, the patentees had great reason to fear they should in that case have lost their land. But their apprehensions were now at an end, when they understood that all the territory which had been controverted was like to be left in Carolina. In the afternoon, those who were to reenter the Dismal were furnished with the necessary provisions, and ordered to repair the overnight to their landlord, Peter Brinkley's, that they might be ready to begin their business early on Monday morning. Mr. Irvine was excused from the fatigue, in compliment to his lungs; but Mr. Mayo and Mr. Swan were robust enough to return upon that painful service, and, to do them justice, they went with great alacrity. The truth was, they now knew the worst of it; and could guess pretty near at the time when they might hope to return to land again.

25. The air was chilled this morning with a smart northwest wind, which favored the Dismalites in their dirty march. They returned by the path they had made in coming out, and with great industry arrived in the evening at the spot where the line had been discontinued. After so long and laborious a journey, they were glad to repose themselves on their couches of cypress-bark, where their sleep was as sweet as it

would have been on a bed of Finland down. In the meantime we who stayed behind had nothing to do but to make the inconvenience that easily discourages lazy people from making this improvement: very often, in autumn, when the apples begin to ripen, they are visited with numerous flights of parakeets that bite all the fruit to pieces in a moment for the sake of the kernels. The havoc they make is sometimes so great that whole orchards are laid waste in spite of all the noises that can be made or mawkins that can be dressed up to fright them away. These ravenous birds visit North Carolina only during the warm season, and so soon as the cold begins to come on retire back towards the sun. They rarely venture so far north as Virginia, except in a very hot summer, when they visit the most southern parts of it. They are very beautiful; but like some other pretty creatures, are apt to be loud and mischievous.

27. Betwixt this and Edenton there are many thuckleberry slashes, which afford a convenient harbor for wolves and foxes. The first of these wild beasts is not so large and fierce as they are in other countries more northerly. He will not attack a man in the keenest of his hunger, but run away from him as from an animal more mischievous than himself. The foxes are much bolder, and will sometimes not only make a stand but likewise assault any one that would balk them of their prey. The inhabitants hereabouts take the trouble to dig abundance of wolfpits, so deep and perpendicular that when a wolf is once tempted into them he can no more scramble out again than a husband who has taken the leap can scramble out of matrimony.

Most of the houses in this part of the country are loghouses, covered with pine or cypress shingles three feet long and one broad. They are hung upon laths with pegs, and their doors, too, turn upon wooden hinges and have wooden locks to secure them, so that the building is finished without nails or other ironwork. They also set up their pales without any nails at all, and indeed more securely than those that are nailed. There are three rails mortised into the posts, the lowest of which serves as a sill with a groove in the middle big enough to receive the end of the pales: the middle part of the pale rests against the inside of the next rail, and the top of it is brought forward to the outside of the uppermost. Such wreathing of the pales in and out makes them stand firm, and much harder to unfix than when nailed in the ordinary way.

Within three or four miles of Edenton the soil appears to be a little more fertile, though it is much cut with slashes which seem all to have a tendency towards the Dismal. This town is situated on the north side of Albemarle Sound, which is there about five miles over. A dirty slash runs all along the back of it, which in the summer is a foul annoyance and furnishes abundance of that Carolina plague, mosquitoes. There may be forty or fifty houses, most of them small and built without expense. A citizen here is counted extravagant if he has ambition enough to aspire to a brick chimney. Justice herself is but indifferently lodged, the courthouse having much the air of a common tobacco-house. I believe this is the only metropolis in the Christian or Mohammedan world where there is neither church, chapel, mosque, synagogue, or any other place of public worship of any sect or religion whatsoever. What little devotion there may happen to be is much more private than their vices. The people seem easy without a minister as long as they are exempted from paying him. Sometimes the Society for Propagating the Gospel has had the charity to send over missionaries to this country; but unfortunately the priest has been too lewd for the people, or, which oftener happens, they too lewd for the priest. For these reasons these reverend gentlemen have always left their flocks as arrant heathen as they found them. Thus much, however, may be said for the inhabitants of Edenton, that not a soul has the least taint of hypocrisy or superstition, acting very frankly and above-board in all their excesses.

Provisions here are extremely cheap and extremely good, so that people may live plentifully at a trifling expense. Nothing is dear but law, physic, and strong drink, which are all bad in their kind, and the last they get with so much difficulty that they are never guilty of the sin of suffering it to sour upon their hands. Their vanity generally lies not so much in having a handsome dining room, as a handsome house of office: in this kind of structure they are really extravagant. They are rarely guilty of flattering or making any court to their governors, but treat them with all the excesses of freedom and familiarity. They are of opinion their rulers would be apt to grow insolent if they grew rich, and for that reason take care to keep them poorer and more dependent, if possible, than the saints in New England used to do their governors. They have very little coin, so they are forced to carry on their home traffic with paper money. This is the only cash that will tarry in the country, and for that reason the discount goes on increasing between that and real money, and will do so to the end of the chapter.

*April 1.* The surveyors, getting now upon better ground quite disengaged from underwoods, pushed on the line almost twelve miles. They left Somerton Chapel near two miles to the northwards, so that there was now no place of public worship left in the whole province of North Carolina.

The high land of North Carolina was barren and covered with a deep sand; and the low grounds were wet and boggy, insomuch that several of our horses were mired and gave us frequent opportunities to show our horsemanship.

The line cut William Spight's plantation in two, leaving little more than his dwelling house and orchard in Virginia. Sundry other plantations were split in the same unlucky manner, which made the owners accountable to both governments. Wherever we passed we constantly found the borderers laid it to heart if their land was taken into Virginia: they chose much rather to belong to Carolina, where they pay no tribute, either to God or to Cæsar. Another reason was that the government there is so loose and the laws are so feebly executed that, like those in the neighborhood of Sidon formerly, every one does just what seems good in his own eyes. If the governor's hands have been weak in that province, under the authority of the lord proprietors, much weaker in that province, under the authority of the lord proprietors, much weaker than were the hands of the magistrate, who though he might have had virtue enough to endeavor to punish offenders, which very rarely happened, yet that virtue had been quite impotent, for want of ability to put it in execution. Besides, there might have been some danger, perhaps, in venturing to be so rigorous, for fear of undergoing the fate of an honest justice in Currituck precinct. This bold magistrate, it seems, taking upon him to order a fellow to the stocks for being disorderly in his drink, was for his intemperate zeal carried thither himself, and narrowly escaped being whipped by the rabble into the bargain.

This easy day's work carried the line to the banks of Somerton Creek, that runs out of Chowan River a little below the mouth of Nottoway.

2. In less than a mile from Somerton Creek the line was carried to Blackwater, which is the name of the upper part of Chowan, running some miles above the mouth of Nottoway. It must be observed that Chowan, after taking a compass round the most beautiful part of North Carolina, empties itself into Albemarle Sound a few miles above Edenton. The tide flows seven or eight miles higher than where the river changes its name and is navigable thus high for any small vessel. Our line intersected it exactly half a mile to the northward of Nottoway. However, in obedience to His Majesty's command, we directed the surveyors to come down the river as far as the mouth of Nottoway in order to continue our true west line from thence. Thus we found the mouth of Nottoway to lie no more than half a minute farther to the northward than Mr. Lawson had formerly done. That gentleman's observations, it seems, placed it in 36° 30′, and our working made it out to be 36° 30½′ —a very inconsiderable variance.

The surveyors crossed the river over against the middle of the mouth of Nottoway, where it was about eighty yards wide. From thence they ran the line about half a mile through a dirty pocoson, as far as an Indian field. Here we took up our lodging in a moist situation, having the pocoson above mentioned on one side of us, and a swamp on the other.

In this camp three of the Meherrin Indians made us a visit. They told us that the small remains of their nation had deserted their ancient

town, situated near the mouth of Meherrin River, for fear of the Catawbas, who had killed fourteen of their people the year before; and
the few that survived that calamity had taken refuge amongst the
English on the east side of Chowan. Though, if the complaint of these
Indians were true, they are hardly used by our Carolina friends. But
they are the less to be pitied, because they have ever been reputed the
most false and treacherous to the English of all the Indians in the
neighborhood.

Not far from the place where we lay, I observed a large oak which
had been blown up by the roots, the body of which was shivered into
perfect strings, and was, in truth, the most violent effects of lightning
I ever saw.

But the most curious instance of that dreadful meteor happened at
York, where a man was killed near a pine tree in which the lightning
made a hole before it struck the man, and left an exact figure of the
tree upon his breast, with all its branches, to the wonder of all that
beheld it, in which I shall be more particular hereafter.

7. The next day being Sunday, we ordered notice to be sent to all
the neighborhood that there would be a sermon at this place, and an
opportunity of christening their children. But the likelihood of rain got
the better of their devotion, and what perhaps might still be a stronger
motive, of their curiosity. In the morning we despatched a runner to the
Nottoway town to let the Indians know we intended them a visit that
evening, and our honest landlord was so kind as to be our pilot thither,
being about four miles from his house. Accordingly in the afternoon we
marched in good order to the town, where the female scouts, stationed
on an eminence for that purpose, had no sooner spied us but they gave
notice of our approach to their fellow citizens by continual whoops and
cries, which could not possibly have been more dismal at the sight of
their most implacable enemies. This signal assembled all their great
men, who received us in a body and conducted us into the fort.

This fort was a square piece of ground inclosed with substantial
puncheons, or strong palisades, about ten feet high, and leaning a little
outwards to make a scalade more difficult. Each side of the square
might be about a hundred yards long, with loopholes at proper distances,
through which they may fire upon the enemy. Within this inclosure we
found bark cabins sufficient to lodge all their people in case they should
be obliged to retire thither. These cabins are no other but close arbors
made of saplings, arched at the top, and covered so well with bark as to
be proof against all weather. The fire is made in the middle, according
to the Hibernian fashion, the smoke whereof finds no other vent but at
the door, and so keeps the whole family warm at the expense both of
their eyes and complexion. The Indians have no standing furniture in
their cabins but hurdles to repose their persons upon which they cover

with mats or deerskins. We were conducted to the best apartments in the fort, which just before had been made ready for our reception, and adorned with new mats that were sweet and clean. The young men had painted themselves in a hideous manner, not so much for ornament as terror. In that frightful equipage they entertained us with sundry war dances wherein they endeavored to look as formidable as possible. The instrument they danced to was an Indian drum, that is, a large gourd with a skin braced taut over the mouth of it. The dancers all sang to this music, keeping exact time with their feet, while their heads and arms were screwed into a thousand menacing postures. Upon this occasion the ladies had arrayed themselves in all their finery. They were wrapped in their red and blue match coats, thrown so negligently about them that their mahogany skins appeared in several parts, like the Lacedæmonian damsels of old. Their hair was braided with white and blue peak, and hung gracefully in a large roll upon their shoulders.

This peak consists of small cylinders cut out of a conch shell, drilled through and strung like beads. It serves them both for money and jewels, the blue being of much greater value than the white, for the same reason that Ethiopian mistresses in France are dearer than French, because they are more scarce. The women wear necklaces and bracelets of these precious materials when they have a mind to appear lovely. Though their complexions be a little sad-colored, yet their shapes are very straight and well proportioned. Their faces are seldom handsome, yet they have an air of innocence and bashfulness, that with a little less dirt would not fail to make them desirable.

Such charms might have had their full effect upon men who had been so long deprived of female conversation, but that the whole winter's soil was so crusted on the skins of those dark angels that it required a very strong appetite to approach them. The bear's oil, with which they anoint their persons all over, makes their skins soft, and at the same time protects them from every species of vermin that use to be troublesome to other uncleanly people. We were unluckily so many that they could not well make us the compliment of bed-fellows, according to the Indian rules of hospitality, though a grave matron whispered one of the commissioners very civilly in the ear, that if her daughter had been but one year older, she should have been at his devotion.

It is by no means a loss of reputation among the Indians for damsels that are single to have intrigues with the men; on the contrary, they count it an argument of superior merit to be liked by a great number of gallants. However, like the ladies that game they are a little mercenary in their amours and seldom bestow their favors out of stark love and kindness. But after these women have once appropriated their charms by marriage, they are from thenceforth faithful to their vows, and will hardly ever be tempted by an agreeable gallant, or be provoked by a brutal or even by a fumbling husband to go astray. The little work that is done among the Indians is done by the poor women, while the men are quite idle, or at most employed only in the gentlemanly diversions of hunting and fishing.

In this, as well as in their wars, they use nothing but firearms, which they purchase of the English for skins. Bows and arrows are grown into disuse, except only amongst their boys. Nor is it ill policy, but on the contrary very prudent, thus to furnish the Indians with firearms, because it makes them depend entirely upon the English, not only for their trade, but even for their subsistence. Besides, they were really able to do more mischief while they made use of arrows, of which they would let silently fly several in a minute with wonderful dexterity, whereas now they hardly ever discharge their firelocks more than once, which they insidiously do from behind a tree, and then retire as nimbly as the Dutch horse used to do now and then formerly in Flanders.

We put the Indians to no expense but only of a little corn for our horses, for which in gratitude we cheered their hearts with what rum we had left, which they love better than they do their wives and children. Though these Indians dwell among the English and see in what plenty a little industry enables them to live, yet they choose to continue in their stupid idleness, and to suffer all the inconveniences of dirt, cold and want, rather than to disturb their heads with care, or defile their hands with labor.

The whole number of people belonging to the Nottoway town, if you include women and children, amount to about two hundred. These are the only Indians of any consequence now remaining within the limits of Virginia. The rest are either removed or dwindled to a very inconsiderable number, either by destroying one another or else by the smallpox and other diseases—though nothing has been so fatal to them as their ungovernable passion for rum, with which, I am sorry to say it, they have been but too liberally supplied by the English that live near them.

And here I must lament the bad success Mr. Boyle's charity has hitherto had towards converting any of these poor heathens to Christianity. Many children of our neighboring Indians have been brought up in the college of William and Mary. They have been taught to read and write, and have been carefully instructed in the principles of the Christian religion, till they came to be men. Yet after they returned home, instead of civilizing and converting the rest, they have immediately relapsed into infidelity and barbarism themselves.

And some of them, too, have made the worst use of the knowledge they acquired among the English by employing it against their benefactors. Besides, as they unhappily forget all the good they learn, and

remember the ill, they are apt to be more vicious and disorderly than
the rest of their countrymen.

I ought not to quit this subject without doing justice to the great
prudence of Colonel Spotswood in this affair. That gentleman was
lieutenant governor of Virginia when Carolina was engaged in a bloody
war with the Indians. At that critical time it was thought expedient to
to keep a watchful eye upon our tributary savages, who we knew had
nothing to keep them to their duty but their fears. Then it was that he
demanded of each nation a competent number of their great men's
children to be sent to the college, where they served as so many hostages
for the good behavior of the rest, and at the same time were themselves
principled in the Christian religion. He also placed a schoolmaster among
the Sapony Indians, at the salary of fifty pounds per annum, to instruct
their children. The person that undertook that charitable work was Mr.
Charles Griffin, a man of good family, who by the innocence of his life
and the sweetness of his temper was perfectly well qualified for that
pious undertaking. Besides he had so much the secret of mixing pleasure
with instruction that he had not a scholar who did not love him affectionately. Such talents must needs have been blest with a proportionable
success, had he had not been unluckily removed to the college, by which
he left the good work he had begun unfinished. In short, all the pains
he had taken among the infidels had no other effect but to make them
something cleanlier than other Indians are. The care Colonel Spotswood
took to tincture the Indian children with Christianity produced the
following epigram, which was not published during his administration,
for fear it might then have looked like flattery.

> Long has the furious priest essayed in vain,
> With sword and faggot, infidels to gain,
> But now the milder soldier wisely tries
> By gentler methods to unveil their eyes.
> Wonders apart, he knew 'twere vain t'engage
> The fix'd preventions of misguided age.
> With fairer hopes he forms the Indian youth
> To early manners, probity and truth.
> The lion's whelp thus, on the Libian shore,
> Is tamed and gentled by the artful Moor,
> Not the grim sire, inured to blood before.

I'm sorry I can't give a better account of the state of the poor Indians
with respect to Christianity, although a great deal of pains has been
and still continues to be taken with them. For my part, I must be of
opinion, as I hinted before, that there is but one way of converting these
poor infidels and reclaiming them from barbarity, and that is, charitably

to intermarry with them, according to the modern policy of the most Christian King in Canada and Louisiana. Had the English done this at the first settlement of the colony, the infidelity of the Indians had been worn out at this day, with their dark complexions, and the country had swarmed with people more than it does with insects. It was certainly an unreasonable nicety that prevented their entering into so good-natured an alliance. All nations of men have the same natural dignity, and we all know that very bright talents may be lodged under a very dark skin. The principal difference between one people and another proceeds only from the different opportunities of improvement. The Indians by no means want understanding, and are in their figure tall and well-proportioned. Even their copper-colored complexion would admit of blanching if not in the first, at the farthest in the second generation. I may safely venture to say, the Indian women would have made altogether as honest wives for the first planters as the damsels they used to purchase from aboard the ships. It is strange, therefore, that any good Christian should have refused a wholesome, straight bed-fellow, when he might have had so fair a portion with her as the merit of saving her soul.

8. We rested on our clean mats very comfortably, though alone, and the next morning went to the toilet of some of the Indian ladies, where, what with the charms of their persons and the smoke of their apartments, we were almost blinded. They offered to give us silkgrass baskets of their own making, which were modestly refused, knowing that an Indian present, like that of a nun, is a liberality put out to interest, and a bribe placed to the greatest advantage. Our chaplain observed with concern that the ruffles of some of our fellow travelers were a little discolored with puccoon, wherewith the good man had been told those ladies used to improve their invisible charms.

About 10 o'clock we marched out of town in good order, and the war captains saluted us with a volley of small arms. From thence we proceeded over Black-water bridge to Colonel Henry Harrison's, where we congratulated each other upon our return into Christendom.

Thus ended our progress for this season, which we may justly say was attended with all the success that could be expected. Besides the punctual performance of what was committed to us, we had the pleasure to bring back every one of our company in perfect health. And this we must acknowledge to be a singular blessing, considering the difficulties and dangers to which they had been exposed. We had reason to fear the many waters and sunken grounds through which we were obliged to wade might have thrown the men into sundry acute distempers; especially the Dismal, where the soil was so full of water, and the air so full of damps, that nothing but a Dutchman could live in them. Indeed, the foundation of all our success was the exceeding dry season.

It rained during the whole journey but rarely, and then, as when Herod built his temple, only in the night or upon the Sabbath, when it was no hindrance at all to our progress.

The tenth of September being thought a little too soon for the commissioners to meet, in order to proceed on the line, on account of snakes, it was agreed to put it off to the twentieth of the same month, of which due notice was sent to the Carolina commissioners.

*Sept. 19.* We, on the part of Virginia, that we might be sure to be punctual, arrived at Mr. Kinchin's, the place appointed, on the nineteenth, after a journey of three days, in which nothing remarkable happened. We found three of the Carolina commissioners had taken possession of the house, having come thither by water from Edenton. By the great quantity of provisions these gentlemen brought, and the few men they had to eat them, we were afraid they intended to carry the line to the South Sea. They had five hundred pounds of bacon and dried beef, and five hundred pounds of biscuit, and not above three or four men. The misfortune was, they forgot to provide horses to carry their good things, or else trusted to the incertainty of hiring them here, which, considering the place, was leaving too much to that jilt, hazard. On our part we had taken better care, being completely furnished with everything necessary for transporting our baggage and provisions. Indeed we brought no other provisions out with us but a thousand pounds of bread, and had faith enough to depend on Providence for our meat, being desirous to husband the public money as much as possible. We had no less than twenty men, besides the chaplain, the surveyors and all the servants, to be subsisted upon this bread. However, that it might hold out the better, our men had been ordered to provide themselves at home with provision for ten days, in which time we judged we should get beyond the inhabitants, where forest game of all sorts was like to be plenty at that time of the year.

*20.* This being the day appointed for our rendezvous, great part of it was spent in the careful fixing our baggage and assembling our men, who were ordered to meet us here. We took care to examine their arms, and made proof of the powder provided for the expedition. Our provision-horses had been hindered by the rain from coming up exactly at the day; but this delay was the less disappointment, by reason of the ten days' subsistence the men had been directed to provide for themselves. Mr. Moseley did not join us till the afternoon, nor Mr. Swan till several days later.

Mr. Kinchin had unadvisedly sold the men a little brandy of his own making, which produced much disorder, causing some to be too choleric, and others too loving, insomuch that a damsel who assisted in the kitchen had certainly suffered what the nuns call martyrdom, had she

not capitulated a little too soon. This outrage would have called for
some severe discipline, had she not bashfully withdrawn herself early
in the morning, and so carried off the evidence.

*Oct. 12.* We were so cruelly entangled with bushes and grapevines all
day that we could advance the line no farther than five miles and
twenty-eight poles. The vines grow very thick in these woods, twining
lovingly round the trees almost everywhere, especially to the saplings.
This makes it evident how natural both the soil and climate of this
country are to vines, though I believe most to our own vines. The
grapes we commonly met with were black, though there be two or three
kinds of white grapes that grow wild. The black are very sweet, but
small, because the strength of the vine spends itself in wood; though
without question a proper culture would make the same grapes both
larger and sweeter. But, with all these disadvantages, I have drunk
tolerably good wine pressed from them, though made without skill.
There is then good reason to believe it might admit of great improvement, if rightly managed.

Our Indian killed a bear, of two years old, that was feasting on these
grapes. He was very fat, as they generally are in that season of the year.
In the fall, the flesh of this animal has a high relish, different from that
of other creatures, though inclining nearest to that of pork, or rather of
wild boar. A true woodsman prefers this sort of meat to that of the
fattest venison, not only for the *haut gout*, but also because the fat of it
is well tasted, and never rises in the stomach. Another proof of the goodness of this meat is that it is less apt to corrupt than any other with
which we are acquainted. As agreeable as such rich diet was to the
men, yet we who were not accustomed to it tasted it at first with some
sort of squeamishness, the animal being of the dog kind; though a little
use soon reconciled us to this American venison. And that its being of
the dog kind might give us the less disgust, we had the example of that
ancient and polite people, the Chinese, who reckon dog's flesh too good
for any under the quality of a mandarin. This beast is in truth a very
clean feeder, living, while the season lasts, upon acorns, chestnuts and
chinquapins, wild honey and wild grapes. They are naturally not carnivorous, unless hunger constrain them to it after the mast is all gone,
and the product of the woods quite exhausted. They are not provident
enough to lay up any hoard, like the squirrels, nor can they, after all,
live very long upon licking their paws, as Sir John Mandeville and some
other travelers tell us, but are forced in the winter months to quit the
mountains and visit the inhabitants. Their errand is then to surprise a
poor hog at a pinch to keep from starving. And to show that they are
not flesh-eaters by trade they devour their prey very awkwardly. They
don't kill it right out and feast upon its blood and entrails, like other

ravenous beasts, but having, after a fair pursuit, seized it with their paws, they begin first upon the rump, and so devour one collop after another, till they come to the vitals, the poor animal crying all the while for several minutes together. However, in so doing, Bruin acts a little imprudently, because the dismal outcry of the hog alarms the neighborhood, and 'tis odds but he pays the forfeit with his life before he can secure his retreat.

But bears soon grow weary of this unnatural diet, and about January, when there is nothing to be gotten in the woods, they retire into some cave or hollow tree, where they sleep away two or three months very comfortably. But then they quit their holes in March, when the fish begin to run up the rivers, on which they are forced to keep Lent till some fruit or berry comes in season. But bears are fondest of chestnuts, which grow plentifully towards the mountains, upon very large trees, where the soil happens to be rich. We were curious to know how it happened that many of the outward branches of those trees came to be broke off in that solitary place, and were informed that the bears are so discreet as not to trust their unwieldy bodies on the smaller limbs of the tree, that would not bear their weight; but after venturing as far as is safe, which they can judge to an inch, they bite off the end of the branch, which falling down, they are content to finish their repast upon the ground. In the same cautious manner they secure the acorns that grow on the weaker limbs of the oak. And it must be allowed that in these instances a bear carries instinct a great way and acts more reasonably than many of his betters who indiscreetly venture upon frail projects that will not bear them.

30. In the evening one of the men knocked down an opossum, which is a harmless little beast that will seldom go out of your way, and if you take hold of it, it will only grin and hardly ever bite. The flesh was well tasted and tender, approaching nearest to pig, which it also resembles in bigness. The color of its fur was a goose gray, with a swine's snout, and a tail like a rat, but at least a foot long. By twisting this tail about the arm of a tree, it will hang with all its weight and swing to anything it wants to take hold of. It has five claws on the forefeet of equal length, but the hinder feet have only four claws, and a sort of thumb standing off at a proper distance. Their feet being thus formed qualify them for climbing up trees to catch little birds, which they are very fond of. But the greatest particularity of this creature, and which distinguishes it from most others that we are acquainted with, is the false belly of the female, into which her young retreat in time of danger. She can draw the slit, which is the inlet into this pouch, so close, that you must look narrowly to find it, especially if she happen to be a virgin. Within the false belly may be seen seven or eight teats, on which the young ones

grow from their first formation till they are big enough to fall off, like ripe fruit from a tree.

This is so odd a method of generation, that I should not have believed it without the testimony of mine own eyes. Besides a knowing and credible person has assured me he has more than once observed the embryo opossums growing to the teat before they were completely shaped, and afterwards watched their daily growth till they were big enough for birth. And all this he could the more easily pry into, because the dam was so perfectly gentle and harmless, that he could handle her just as he pleased. I could hardly persuade myself to publish a thing so contrary to the course that nature takes in the production of other animals, unless it were a matter commonly believed in all countries where that creature is produced, and has been often observed by persons of undoubted credit and understanding. They say that the leather-winged bats produce their young in the same uncommon manner. And that young sharks at sea, and the young vipers ashore, run down the throats of their dams when they are closely pursued.

The frequent crossing of Crooked Creek, and mounting the steep banks of it, gave the finishing stroke to the foundering of our horses; and no less than two of them made a full stop here, and would not advance a foot farther, either by fair means or foul. We had a dreamer of dreams amongst us, who warned me in the morning to take care of myself, or I should infallibly fall into the creek; I thanked him kindly and used what caution I could, but was not able, it seems, to avoid my destiny, for my horse made a false step and laid me down at my full length in the water. This was enough to bring dreaming into credit, and I think it much for the honor of our expedition, that it was graced not only with a priest but also with a prophet. We were so perplexed with this serpentine creek, as well as in passing the branches of the Irvine (which were swelled since we saw them before) that we could reach but five miles this whole day. In the evening we pitched our tent near Miry Creek (though an uncomfortable place to lodge in) purely for the advantage of the canes. Our hunters killed a large doe and two bears, which made all other misfortunes easy. Certainly no Tartar ever loved horseflesh, or Hottentot guts and garbage, better than woodsmen do bear. The truth of it is, it may be proper food perhaps for such as work or ride it off, but, with our chaplain's leave, who loved it much, I think it not a very proper diet for saints, because 'tis apt to make them a little too rampant.

And now, for the good of mankind and for the better peopling an infant colony which has no want but that of inhabitants, I will venture to publish a secret of importance which our Indian disclosed to me. I asked him the reason why few or none of his countrywomen were barren. To which curious question he answered, with a broad grin upon

his face, they had an infallible secret for that. Upon my being importunate to know what the secret might be, he informed me that if any
Indian woman did not prove with child at a decent time after marriage,
the husband, to save his reputation with the women, forthwith entered
into a bear-diet for six weeks, which in that time makes him so vigorous
that he grows exceedingly impertinent to his poor wife, and 'tis great
odds but he makes her a mother in nine months. And thus much I am
able to say, besides, for the reputation of the bear diet, that all the married men of our company were joyful fathers within forty weeks after
they got home, and most of the single men had children sworn to them
within the same time, our chaplain always excepted, who, with much
ado, made a shift to cast out that importunate kind of devil, by dint of
fasting and prayer.

*Nov. 1.* By the negligence of one of the men in not hobbling his horse,
he straggled so far that he could not be found. This stopped us all the
morning long; yet, because our time should not be entirely lost, we
endeavored to observe the latitude at twelve o'clock. Though our
observation was not perfect, by reason the wind blew a little too fresh,
however, by such a one as we could make, we found ourselves in
36° 20' only. Notwithstanding our being thus delayed, and the uneven-
ness of the ground over which we were obliged to walk (for most of us
served now in the infantry) we traveled no less than six miles; though,
as merciful as we were to our poor beasts, another of 'em tired by the
way and was left behind for the wolves and panthers to feast upon.

As we marched along, we had the fortune to kill a brace of bucks,
as many bears, and one wild turkey. But this was carrying sport to
wantonness because we butchered more than we were able to transport.
We ordered the deer to be quartered and divided amongst the horses
for the lighter carriage, and recommended the bears to our daily attendants, the turkey-buzzards. We always chose to carry venison along with
us rather than bear, not only because it was less cumbersome, but likewise because the people could eat it without bread, which was now
almost spent. Whereas the other, being richer food, lay too heavy upon
the stomach, unless it were lightened by something farinaceous. This is
what I thought proper to remark, for the service of all those whose
business or diversion shall oblige them to live any time in the woods.
And because I am persuaded that very useful matters may be found out
by searching this great wilderness, especially the upper parts of it about
the mountains, I conceive it will help to engage able men in that good
work, if I recommend a wholesome kind of food, of very small weight
and very great nourishment, that will secure them from starving in case
they should be so unlucky as to meet with no game. The chief discouragement at present from penetrating far into the woods is the

trouble of carrying a load of provisions. I must own famine is a frightful
monster, and for that reason to be guarded against as well as we can.
But the common precautions against it are so burthensome that people
cannot tarry long out and go far enough from home to make any effectual
discovery. The portable provisions I would furnish our foresters withal
are glue-broth and rockahominy: one contains the essence of bread, the
other of meat. The best way of making glue-broth is after the following
method: Take a leg of beef, veal, venison, or any other young meat,
because old meat will not so easily jelly. Pare off all the fat, in which
there is no nutriment, and of the lean make a very strong broth, after
the usual manner, by boiling the meat to rags till all the goodness be
out. After skimming off what fat remains, pour the broth into a wide
stew-pan, well tinned, and let it simmer over a gentle, even fire, till it
comes to a thick jelly. Then take it off and set it over boiling water,
which is an evener heat, and not so apt to burn the broth to the vessel.
Over that let it evaporate, stirring it very often till it be reduced, when
cold, into a solid substance like glue. Then cut it into small pieces, laying
them single in the cold, that they may dry the sooner. When the pieces
are perfectly dry, put them into a canister, and they will be good, if
kept dry, a whole East Indian voyage. This glue is so strong, that two
or three drams, dissolved in boiling water with a little salt, will make
half a pint of good broth, and if you should be faint with fasting or
fatigue, let a small piece of this glue melt in your mouth, and you will
find yourself surprisingly refreshed. One pound of this cookery would
keep a man in good heart above a month, and is not only nourishing
but likewise very wholesome. Particularly it is good against fluxes, which
woodsmen are very liable to by lying too near the moist ground and
guzzling too much cold water. But as it will be only used now and then,
in times of scarcity, when game is wanting, two pounds of it will be
enough for a journey of six months. But this broth will be still more
heartening, if you thicken every mess with half a spoonful of rockahominy, which is nothing but Indian corn parched without burning, and
reduced to powder. The fire drives out all the watery parts of the corn,
leaving the strength of it behind, and this being very dry, becomes
much lighter for carriage and less liable to be spoiled by the moist air.
Thus half a dozen pounds of this sprightful bread will sustain a man for
as many months, provided he husband it well, and always spare it when
he meets with venison, which, as I said before, may be very safely eaten
without any bread at all. By what I have said, a man need not encumber
himself with more than eight or ten pounds of provisions, though he
continue half a year in the woods. These and his gun will support him
very well during that time, without the least danger of keeping one
single fast. And though some of his days may be what the French call
*jours maigres,* yet there will happen no more of those than will be

necessary for his health, and to carry off the excesses of the days of plenty, when our travelers will be apt to indulge their lawless appetites too much.

7. After crossing the Dan, we made a march of eight miles over hills and dales as far as the next ford of that river. And now we were by practice become such very able footmen that we easily out-walked our horses and could have marched much farther, had it not been in pity to their weakness. Besides, here was plenty of canes, which was reason enough to make us shorten our journey. Our gunners did great execution as they went along, killing no less than two braces of deer, and as many wild turkeys.

Though practice will soon make a man of tolerable vigor an able footman, yet, as a help to bear fatigue I used to chew a root of ginseng as I walked along. This kept up my spirits, and made me trip away as nimbly in my half jack-boots as younger men could do in their shoes. This plant is in high esteem in China, where it sells for its weight in silver. Indeed it does not grow there, but in the mountains of Tartary, to which place the emperor of China sends ten thousand men every year on purpose to gather it. But it grows so scattering there, that even so many hands can bring home no great quantity. Indeed it is a vegetable of so many virtues that Providence has planted it very thin in every country that has the happiness to produce it. Nor indeed is mankind worthy of so great a blessing, since health and long life are commonly abused to ill purposes. This noble plant grows likewise at the cape of Good Hope, where it is called kanna and is in wonderful esteem among the Hottentots. It grows also on the northern continent of America, near the mountains, but as sparingly as truth and public spirit. It answers exactly both to the figure and virtue of that which grows in Tartary, so that there can be no doubt of its being the same. Its virtues are, that it gives an uncommon warmth and vigor to the blood, and frisks the spirits, beyond any other cordial. It cheers the heart even of a man that has a bad wife, and makes him look down with great composure on the crosses of the world. It promotes insensible perspiration, dissolves all phlegmatic and viscous humors that are apt to obstruct the narrow channels of the nerves. It helps the memory, and would quicken even Helvetian dullness. 'Tis friendly to the lungs, much more than scolding itself. It comforts the stomach and strengthens the bowels, preventing all colics and fluxes. In one word, it will make a man live a great while, and very well while he does live. And what is more, it will even make old age amiable, by rendering it lively, cheerful, and good-humored. However, 'tis of little use in the feats of love, as a great prince once found, who, hearing of its invigorating quality, sent as far as China for some of it, though his ladies could not boast of any advantage thereby.

*15.* About three miles from our camp we passed Great Creek, and then, after traversing very barren grounds for five miles together, we crossed the Trading Path, and soon after had the pleasure of reaching the uppermost inhabitant. This was a plantation belonging to Colonel Mumford, where our men almost burst themselves with potatoes and milk. Yet, as great a curiosity as a house was to us foresters, still we chose to lie in the tent, as being much the cleaner and sweeter lodging.

The Trading Path above mentioned receives its name from being the route the traders take with their caravans, when they go to traffic with the Catawbas and other southern Indians. The Catawbas live about two hundred and fifty miles beyond Roanoke River, and yet our traders find their account in transporting goods from Virginia to trade with them at their own town. The common method of carrying on this Indian commerce is as follows: Gentlemen send for goods proper for such a trade from England, and then either venture them out at their own risk to the Indian towns, or else credit some traders with them of substance and reputation, to be paid in skins at a certain price agreed betwixt them. The goods for the Indian trade consist chiefly in guns, powder, shot, hatchets (which the Indians call tomahawks,) kettles, red and blue planes, Duffields, Stroudwater blankets, and some cutlery wares, brass rings and other trinkets. These wares are made up into packs and carried upon horses, each load being from one hundred and fifty to two hundred pounds, with which they are able to travel about twenty miles a day, if forage happen to be plentiful. Formerly a hundred horses have been employed in one of these Indian caravans, under the conduct of fifteen or sixteen persons only, but now the trade is much impaired, insomuch that they seldom go with half that number.

The course from Roanoke to the Catawbas is laid down nearest southwest, and lies through a fine country that is watered by several beautiful rivers. Those of the greatest note are, first, Tar river, which is the upper part of Pamptico, Flat River, Little River and Eno River, all three branches of Neuse. Between Eno and Saxapahaw rivers are the Haw old fields, which have the reputation of containing the most fertile high land in this part of the world, lying in a body of about fifty thousand acres. This Saxapahaw is the upper part of Cape Fair River, the falls of which lie many miles below the Trading Path. Some mountains overlook this rich spot of land, from whence all the soil washes down into the plain, and is the cause of its exceeding fertility. Not far from thence the path crosses Aramanchy River, a branch of Saxapahaw, and about forty miles beyond that, Deep River, which is the north branch of Peedee. Then forty miles beyond that, the path intersects the Yadkin, which is there half a mile over, and is supposed to be the south branch of the same Peedee. The soil is exceedingly rich on both sides the Yadkin, abounding in rank grass and prodigiously large trees; and for plenty of fish, fowl and venison, is inferior to no part of the northern continent. There the traders commonly lie still for some days, to recruit their horses' flesh as well as to recover their own spirits.

Six miles further is Crane Creek, so named from its being the rendezvous of great armies of cranes, which wage a more cruel war at this day with the frogs and the fish than they used to do with the pigmies in the days of Homer. About three-score miles more bring you to the first town of the Catawbas, called Nauvasa, situated on the banks of Santee River. Besides this town there are five others belonging to the same nation, lying all on the same stream, within the distance of twenty miles. These Indians were all called formerly by the general name of the Usherees, and were a very numerous and powerful people. But the frequent slaughters made upon them by the northern Indians, and, what has been still more destructive by far, the intemperance and foul distempers introduced amongst them by the Carolina traders, have now reduced their numbers to a little more than four hundred fighting men, besides women and children. It is a charming place where they live, the air very wholesome, the soil fertile, and the winters ever mild and serene.

In Santee River, as in several others of Carolina, a small kind of alligator is frequently seen, which perfumes the water with a musky smell. They seldom exceed eight feet in length in these parts, whereas, near the equinoctial, they come up to twelve or fourteen. And the heat of the climate don't only make them bigger, but more fierce and voracious. They watch the cattle there when they come to drink and cool themselves in the river; and because they are not able to drag them into the deep water, they make up by stratagem what they want in force. They swallow great stones, the weight of which, being added to their strength, enables them to tug a moderate cow under water, and as soon as they have drowned her, they discharge the stones out of their maw and then feast upon the carcass.

However, as fierce and as strong as these monsters are, the Indians will surprise them napping as they float upon the surface, get astride upon their necks, then whip a short piece of wood like a truncheon into their jaws, and holding the ends with their two hands, hinder them from diving by keeping their mouths open, and when they are almost spent, they will make to the shore, where their riders knock them on the head and eat them. This amphibious animal is a smaller kind of crocodile, having the same shape exactly, only the crocodile of the Nile is twice as long, being when full grown from twenty to thirty feet. This enormous length is the more to be wondered at, because the crocodile is hatched from an egg very little larger than that of a goose. It has a long head, which it can open very wide, with very sharp and strong teeth. Their eyes are small, their legs short, with claws upon their feet. Their tail makes half the length of their body, and the whole is guarded with hard, impenetrable scales, except the belly, which is much softer and smoother. They keep much upon the land in the day time, but towards the evening retire into the water to avoid the cold dews of the night. They run pretty fast right forward, but are very awkward and slow in turning, by reason of their unwieldy length. It is an error that they have no tongue, without which they could hardly swallow their food; but in eating they move the upper jaw only, contrary to all other animals. The way of catching them in Egypt is with a strong hook fixed to the end of a chain and baited with a joint of pork, which they are very fond of. But a live hog is generally tied near, the cry of which allures them to the hook. This account of the crocodile will agree in most particulars with the alligator, only the bigness of the last cannot entitle it to the name of "leviathan," which Job gave formerly to the crocodile, and not to the whale, as some interpreters would make us believe.

So soon as the Catawba Indians are informed of the approach of the Virginia caravans, they send a detachment of their warriors to bid them welcome, and escort them safe to their town, where they are received with great marks of distinction. And their courtesies to the Virginia traders, I dare say, are very sincere, because they sell them better goods and better pennyworths than the traders of Carolina. They commonly reside among the Indians till they have bartered their goods away for skins, with which they load their horses and come back by the same path they went. There are generally some Carolina traders that constantly live among the Catawbas, and pretend to exercise a dictatorial authority over them. These petty rulers don't only teach the honester savages all sorts of debauchery, but are unfair in their dealings, and use them with all kinds of oppression. Nor has their behavior been at all better to the rest of the Indian nations among whom they reside, by abusing their women and evil-entreating their men; and by the way, this was the true reason of the fatal war which the nations roundabout made upon Carolina in the year 1713. Then it was that all the neighboring Indians, grown weary of the tyranny and injustice with which they had been abused for many years, resolved to endure their bondage no longer, but entered into general confederacy against their oppressors of Carolina. The Indians opened the war by knocking most of those little tyrants on the head that dwelt amongst them under pretense of regulating their commerce, and from thence carried their resentment so far as to endanger both North and South Carolina.

16. We gave orders that the horses should pass Roanoke River at Monisep Ford, while most of the baggage was transported in a canoe. We landed at the plantation of Cornelius Keith, where I beheld the wretchedest scene of poverty I had ever met with in this happy part of the world. The man, his wife and six small children, lived in a pen, like

so many cattle, without any roof over their heads but that of heaven. And this was their airy residence in the day time, but then there was a fodder stack not far from this inclosure, in which the whole family sheltered themselves anights and in bad weather. However, 'twas almost worth while to be as poor as this man was, to be as perfectly contented. All his wants proceeded from indolence, and not from misfortune. He had good land, as well as good health and good limbs to work it, and, besides, had a trade very useful to all the inhabitants round about. He could make and set up quern stones very well, and had proper materials for that purpose just at hand, if he could have taken the pains to fetch them. There is no other kind of mills in these remote parts, and therefore if the man would have worked at his trade he might have lived very comfortably. The poor woman had a little more industry, and spun cotton enough to make a thin covering for her own and her children's nakedness.

I am sorry to say it, but idleness is the general character of the men in the southern part of this colony as well as in North Carolina. The air is so mild, and the soil so fruitful, that very little labor is required to fill their bellies, especially where the woods afford such plenty of game. These advantages discharge the men from the necessity of killing themselves with work, and then for the other article of raiment, a very little of that will suffice in so temperate a climate. But so much as is absolutely necessary falls to the good women's share to provide. They all spin, weave and knit, whereby they make a good shift to clothe the whole family; and to their credit be it recorded, many of them do it very completely, and thereby reproach their husbands' laziness in the most inoffensive way, that is to say, by discovering a better spirit of industry in themselves.

From hence we moved forward to Colonel Mumford's other plantation, under the care of Miles Riley, where, by that gentleman's directions, we were again supplied with many good things. Here it was we discharged our worthy friend and fellow traveler, Mr. Bearskin, who had so plentifully supplied us with provisions during our long expedition. We rewarded him to his heart's content, so that he returned to his town loaden with riches and the reputation of having been a great discoverer.

17. This being Sunday, we were seasonably put in mind how much we were obliged to be thankful for our happy return to the inhabitants. Indeed, we had great reason to reflect with gratitude on the signal mercies we had received. First, that we had, day by day, been fed by the bountiful hand of Providence in the desolate wilderness, insomuch that if any of our people wanted one single meal during the whole expedition, it was entirely owing to their own imprudent management. Secondly, that not one man of our whole company had any violent distemper or bad accident befall him, from one end of the line to the

other. The very worst that happened was, that one of them gave himself a smart cut on the pan of his knee with a tomahawk, which we had the good fortune to cure in a short time, without the help of a surgeon. As for the misadventures of sticking in the mire and falling into rivers and creeks, they were rather subjects of mirth than complaint, and served only to diversify our travels with a little farcical variety. And, lastly, that many uncommon incidents have concurred to prosper our undertaking.

We had not only a dry spring before we went out, but the preceding winter, and even a year or two before, had been much drier than ordinary. This made not only the Dismal, but likewise most of the sunken grounds near the seaside, just hard enough to bear us, which otherwise had been quite impassable. And the whole time we were upon the business, which was in all about sixteen weeks, we were never catched in the rain except once, nor was our progress interrupted by bad weather above three or four days at most. Besides all this, we were surprised by no Indian enemy, but all of us brought our scalps back safe upon our heads. This cruel method of scalping of enemies is prac- ticed by all the savages in America, and perhaps is not the least proof of their original from the northern inhabitants of Asia. Among the ancient Scythians it was constantly used, who carried about these hairy scalps as trophies of victory. They served them, too, as towels at home and trappings for their horses abroad. But these were not content with the skin of their enemies' heads, but also made use of their skulls for cups to drink out of upon high festival days, and made greater ostenta- tion of them than if they had been made of gold or the purest crystal.

Besides the duties of the day, we christened one of our men who had been bred a Quaker. The man desired this of his own mere motion, with- out being tampered with by the parson, who was willing every one should go to Heaven his own way. But whether he did it by the con- viction of his own reason, or to get rid of some troublesome forms and restraints, to which the saints of that persuasion are subject, I can't positively say.

18. We proceeded over a level road twelve miles, as far as George Hix's plantation, on the south side Meherrin River, our course being for the most part northeast. By the way we hired a cart to transport our baggage, that we might the better befriend our jaded horses. Within two miles of our journey's end this day, we met the express we had sent the Saturday before to give notice of our arrival. He had been almost as expeditious as a carrier pigeon, riding in two days no less than two hundred miles.

All the grandees of the Sapony nation did us the honor to repair hither to meet us, and our worthy friend and fellow traveler, Bearskin, appeared among the gravest of them in his robes of ceremony. Four young ladies of the first quality came with them, who had more the air of cleanliness than any copper-colored beauties I had ever seen; yet we resisted all their charms, notwithstanding the long fast we had kept from the sex, and the bear diet we had been so long engaged in. Nor can I say the price they set upon their charms was at all exorbitant. A princess for a pair of red stockings can't, surely, be thought buying repentance much too dear.

The men had something great and venerable in their countenances, beyond the common mien of savages; and indeed they ever had the reputation of being the honestest, as well as the bravest Indians we have ever been acquainted with. This people is now made up of the remnants of several other nations, of which the most considerable are the Sapony, the Occaneches, and Steukenhocks, who not finding themselves separately numerous enough for their defense, have agreed to unite into one body, and all of them now go under the name of the Sapony. Each of these was formerly a distinct nation, or rather a several clan or canton of the same nation, speaking the same language, and using the same customs. But their perpetual wars against all other Indians in time reduced them so low as to make it necessary to join forces together.

They dwelt formerly not far below the mountains, upon Yadkin River, about two hundred miles west and by south from the falls of Roanoke. But about twenty-five years ago they took refuge in Virginia, being no longer in condition to make head not only against the northern Indians, who are their implacable enemies, but also against most of those to the south. All the nations round about, bearing in mind the havoc these Indians used formerly to make among their ancestors in the insolence of their power, did at length avenge it home upon them, and made them glad to apply to this government for protection. Colonel Spotswood, our then lieutenant governor, having a good opinion of their fidelity and courage, settled them at Christanna, ten miles north of Roanoke, upon the belief that they would be a good barrier on that side of the country against the incursion of all foreign Indians. And in earnest they would have served well enough for that purpose, if the white people in the neighborhood had not debauched their morals and ruined their health with rum, which was the cause of many disorders and ended at last in a barbarous murder committed by one of these Indians when he was drunk, for which the poor wretch was executed when he was sober. It was matter of great concern to them, however, that one of their grandees should be put to so ignominious a death. All Indians have as great an aversion to hanging as the Muscovites, though perhaps not for the same cleanly reason: these last believing that the soul of one that dies in this manner, being forced to sally out of the body at the postern, must needs be defiled. The Sapony took this execution so much to heart, that they soon after quitted their settlement and removed in a body to the Catawbas. The daughter of the Tetero king went away with the Sapony, but being the last of her nation, and fearing she should not be treated according to her rank, poisoned herself, like an old Roman, with the root of the trumpet plant. Her father died two years before, who was the most intrepid Indian we have been acquainted with. He had made himself terrible to all other Indians by his exploits, and had escaped so many dangers that he was esteemed invulnerable. But at last he died of a pleurisy, the last man of his race and nation, leaving only that unhappy daughter behind him, who would not long survive him.

The most uncommon circumstance in this Indian visit was that they all came on horseback, which was certainly intended for a piece of state, because the distance was but three miles, and 'tis likely they had walked afoot twice as far to catch their horses. The men rode more awkwardly than any Dutch sailor, and the ladies bestrode their palfreys à la mode de France, but were so bashful about it that there was no persuading them to mount till they were quite out of our sight. The French women used to ride a-straddle, not so much to make them sit firmer in the saddle, as from the hopes the same thing might peradventure befall them that once happened to the nun of Orleans, who, escaping out of a nunnery, took post en cavalier, and in ten miles' hard riding had the good fortune to have all the tokens of a man break out upon her. This piece of history ought to be the more credible, because it leans upon much the same degree of proof as the tale of Bishop Burnet's two Italian nuns, who, according to his lordship's account, underwent the same happy metamorphosis, probably by some other violent exercise.

*19.* From hence we despatched the cart with our baggage under a guard, and crossed Meherrin River, which was not thirty yards wide in that place. By the help of fresh horses that had been sent us, we now began to mend our pace, which was also quickened by the strong inclinations we had to get home. In the distance of five miles we forded Meherrin Creek, which was very near as broad as the river. About eight miles farther we came to Sturgeon Creek, so called from the dexterity an Occaneche Indian showed there in catching one of those royal fish, which was performed after the following manner. In the summer time 'tis no unusual thing for sturgeons to sleep on the surface of the water, and one of them having wandered up into this creek in the spring, was floating in that drowsy condition. The Indian above mentioned ran up to the neck into the creek a little below the place where he discovered the fish, expecting the stream would soon bring his game down to him. He judged the matter right, and as soon as it came within his reach, he whipped a running noose over his jowl. This waked the sturgeon, which being strong in its own element darted immediately under water and dragged the Indian after him. The man made it a point of honor to keep his hold, which he did to the apparent danger of being drowned. Sometimes both the Indian and the fish disappeared for a quarter of a minute, and then rose at some distance from where they dived. At this rate they continued flouncing about, sometimes above and sometimes under water, for a considerable time, till at last the hero suffocated his adversary and haled his body ashore in triumph.

About six miles beyond that, we passed over Wicco-quoi Creek, named so from the multitude of rocks over which the water tumbles in a fresh, with a bellowing noise. Not far from where we went over is a rock much higher than the rest, that strikes the eye with agreeable horror, and near it a very talkative echo, that, like a fluent helpmeet, will return her good man seven words for one, and after all be sure to have the last. It speaks not only the language of men, but also of birds and beasts, and often a single wild goose is cheated into the belief that some of his company are not far off, by hearing his own cry multiplied; and 'tis pleasant to see in what a flutter the poor bird is, when he finds himself disappointed. On the banks of this creek are very broad low grounds in many places, and abundance of good high land, though a little subject to floods.

We had but two miles more to Captain Embry's, where we found the housekeeping much better than the house. Our bountiful landlady had set her oven and all her spits, pots, gridirons and saucepans to work, to diversify our entertainment, though after all it proved but a Mohammedan feast, there being nothing to drink but water. The worst of it was, we had unluckily outrid the baggage, and for that reason were obliged to lodge very sociably in the same apartment with the family, where, reckoning women and children, we mustered in all no less than nine persons, who all pigged lovingly together.

20. In the morning Colonel Bolling, who had been surveying in the neighborhood, and Mr. Walker, who dwelt not far off, came to visit us; and the last of these worthy gentlemen, fearing that our drinking so much water might incline us to pleurisies, brought us a kind supply both of wine and cider. It was noon before we could disengage ourselves from the courtesies of this place, and then the two gentlemen above mentioned were so good as to accompany us that day's journey, though they could by no means approve of our Lithuanian fashion of dismounting now and then in order to walk part of the way on foot.

We crossed Nottoway River not far from our landlord's house, where it seemed to be about twenty-five yards over. This river divides the county of Prince George from that of Brunswick. We had not gone eight miles farther before our eyes were blessed with the sight of Sapony chapel, which was the first house of prayer we had seen for more than two calendar months. About three miles beyond that, we passed over Stony Creek, where one of those that guarded the baggage killed a polecat, upon which he made a comfortable repast. Those of his company were so squeamish they could not be persuaded at first to taste, as they said, of so unsavory an animal; but seeing the man smack his lips with more pleasure than usual, they ventured at last to be of his mess, and instead of finding the flesh rank and high-tasted, they owned it to be the sweetest morsel they had ever eat in their lives. The ill savor of this little beast lies altogether in its urine, which nature has made so detestably ill-scented on purpose to furnish a helpless creature with something to defend itself. For as some brutes have horns and hoofs, and others are armed with claws, teeth and tusks for their defense; and as some spit a sort of poison at their adversaries, like the paco; and others dart quills at their pursuers, like the porcupine; and as some have no weapons to help themselves but their tongue, and others none but their tails; so the poor polecat's safety lies altogether in the irresistible stench of its water; insomuch that when it finds itself in danger from an enemy, it moistens its bushy tail plentifully with this liquid ammunition, and then, with great fury, sprinkles it like a shower of rain full into the eyes of its assailant, by which it gains time to make its escape. Nor is the polecat the only animal that defends itself by a stink. At the cape of Good Hope is a little beast called a stinker, as big as a fox and shaped like a ferret, which being pursued has no way to save himself but by farting and squittering, and then such a stench ensues that none of its pursuers can possibly stand it.

At the end of thirty good miles, we arrived in the evening at Colonel Bolling's, where first, from a primitive course of life, we began to relapse into luxury. This gentleman lives within hearing of the falls of Appomattox River, which are very noisy whenever a flood happens to roll a greater stream than ordinary over the rocks. The river is navigable for small craft as high as the falls, and at some distance from thence fetches a compass, and runs nearly parallel with James River almost as high as the mountains. While the commissioners fared sumptuously here, the poor chaplain and two surveyors, stopped ten miles short at a poor planter's house, in pity to their horses, made a St. Anthony's meal, that is, they supped upon the pickings of what stuck in their teeth ever since breakfast. But to make them amends, the good man laid them in his own bed, where they all three nestled together in one cotton sheet and one of brown oznaburgs, made still something browner by two months' copious perspiration.

21. But those worthy gentlemen were so alert in the morning after their light supper, that they came up with us before breakfast, and honestly paid their stomachs all they owed them.

We made no more than a Sabbath day's journey from this to the next hospitable house, namely, that of our great benefactor, Colonel Mumford. We had already been much befriended by this gentleman, who, besides sending orders to his overseers at Roanoke to let us want for nothing, had, in the beginning of our business, been so kind as to recommend most of the men to us who were the faithful partners of our fatigue. Although in most other achievements those who command are apt to take all the honor to themselves of what perhaps was more owing to the vigor of those who were under them, yet I must be more just, and allow these brave fellows their full share of credit for the service we performed, and must declare, that it was in a great measure owing to their spirit and indefatigable industry that we overcame many obstacles in the course of our line, which till then had been esteemed insurmountable. Nor must I at the same time omit to do justice to the surveyors, and particularly to Mr. Mayo, who, besides an eminent degree of skill, encountered the same hardships and underwent the same fatigue that the forwardest of the men did, and that with as much cheerfulness as if pain had been his pleasure, and difficulty his real diversion. Here we discharged the few men we had left, who were all as ragged as the Gibeonite ambassadors, though, at the same time, their rags were very honorable by the service they had so vigorously performed in making them so.

22. A little before noon we all took leave and dispersed to our several habitations, where we were so happy as to find all our families well. This crowned all our other blessings, and made our journey as prosperous as it had been painful. Thus ended our second expedition, in which we extended the line within the shadow of the Cherokee Mountains, where we were obliged to set up our pillars, like Hercules, and return home. We had now, upon the whole, been out sixteen weeks, including going and returning, and had traveled at least six hundred miles, and no small part of that distance on foot. Below, towards the seaside, our course lay through marshes, swamps, and great waters, and above, over steep hills, craggy rocks, and thickets, hardly penetrable. Notwithstanding this variety of hardships, we may say, without vanity, that we faithfully obeyed the King's orders, and performed the business effectually in which we had the honor to be employed.

Nor can we by any means reproach ourselves of having put the Crown to any exorbitant expense in this difficult affair, the whole charge, from beginning to end, amounting to no more than one thousand pounds. But let no one concerned in this painful expedition complain of the scantiness of his pay, so long as His Majesty has been graciously pleased to add to our reward the honor of his royal approbation, and to declare, notwithstanding the desertion of the Carolina commissioners, that the line by us run shall hereafter stand as the true boundary betwixt the governments of Virginia and North Carolina.

# PART VI

# LITERATURE

# Anne Bradstreet

As "Contemplations" and "To My Dear and Loving Husband" make
abundantly clear, Anne Bradstreet had the gift of true poetic feeling and
expression. For the most part, however, her work is burdened with a
highly artificial style, replete with quirks, puns, fantastic imagery and
labored ingenuities derived from her first love among poets, the French
Huguenot Du Bartas. Equally unfortunate for her poetry, she was fond
of writing from books rather than from experience: she set down not
what she strongly felt but what other poets had told her she ought to feel.
Nevertheless, when she broke the spell cast by "Great Bartas sugar'd
lines" and forgot the didacticism that the Puritans often confused with
poetry, she wrote simply and directly. On those occasions, she reached
heights of feeling and controlled expression not attained by an American
poetess prior to Emily Dickinson.

### TO MY DEAR AND LOVING HUSBAND

If ever two were one, then surely we.
If ever man were lov'd by wife, then thee;
If ever wife was happy in a man,
Compare with me ye women if you can.
I prize thy love more than whole Mines of gold,
Or all the riches that the East doth hold.
My love is such that Rivers cannot quench,
Nor ought but love from thee, give recompense.
Thy love is such I can no way repay,
The heavens reward thee manifold I pray.
Then while we live, in love lets so persever,
That when we live no more, we may live ever.

### CONTEMPLATIONS

Some time now past in the Autumnal Tide,
When Phoebus wanted but one hour to bed,
The trees all richly clad, yet void of pride,
Where gilded o're by his rich golden head.
Their leaves & fruits seem'd painted, but was true

The Poems of Mrs. Anne Bradstreet. Together with Her Prose Remains. Edited
by Charles Eliot Norton.

Of green, or red, of yellow, mixed hue,
Rapt were my senses at this delectable view.

### 2.

I wist not what to wish, yet sure thought I,
If so much excellence abide below;
How excellent is he that dwells on high?
Whose power and beauty by his works we know.
Sure he is goodness, wisdome, glory, light,
That hath this under world so richly dight:
More Heaven then Earth was here no winter & no night.

### 3.

Then on a stately Oak I cast mine Eye,
Whose ruffling top the Clouds seem'd to aspire;
How long since thou wast in thine Infancy?
Thy strength, and stature, more thy years admire,
Hath hundred winters past since thou wast born?
Or thousand since thou brakest thy shell of horn,
If so, all these as nought, Eternity doth scorn.

### 4.

Then higher on the glistering Sun I gaz'd,
Whose beams was shaded by the leavie Tree,
The more I look'd, the more I grew amaz'd,
And softly said, what glory's like to thee?
Soul of this world, this Universes Eye,
No wonder, some made thee a Deity:
Had I not better known (alas), the same had I.

### 5.

Thou as a Bridegroom from thy Chamber rushes,
And as a strong man, joyes to run a race,
The morn doth usher thee, with smiles & blushes,
The Earth reflects her glances in thy face.
Birds, insects, Animals with Vegetative,
Thy heart from death dulness doth revive:
And in the darksome womb of fruitful nature dive.

### 7.

Art thou so full of glory, that no Eye
Hath strength, thy shining Rayes once to behold?
And is thy splendid Throne erect so high?
As to approach it, can no earthly mould.
How full of glory then must thy Creator be?
Who gave this bright light luster unto thee:
Admir'd ador'd for ever, be that Majesty.

### 9.

I heard the merry grasshopper then sing,
The black clad Cricket, bear a second part,
They kept one tune, and plaid on the same string;
Seeming to glory in their little Art.
Shall Creatures abject; thus their voices raise?
And in their kind resound their makers praise:
Whilst I as mute, can warble forth no higher layes.

### 21.

Under the cooling shadow of a stately Elm
Close sate I by a goodly Rivers side,
Where gliding streams the Rocks did overwhelm;
A lonely place, with pleasures dignifi'd.
I once that lov'd the shady woods so well,
Now thought the rivers did the trees excel,
And if the sun would ever shine, there would I dwell.

### 22.

While on the stealing stream I fixt mine eye,
Which to the long'd for Ocean held its course,
I markt, nor crooks, nor rubs that there did lye
Could hinder ought, but still augment its force:
O happy Flood, quoth I, that holds thy race
Till thou arrive at thy beloved place,
Nor is it rocks or shoals that can obstruct thy pace.

### 23.

Nor is't enough, that thou alone may'st slide,
But hundred brooks in thy clear waves do meet,
So hand in hand along with thee they glide
To *Thetis* house, where all imbrace and greet:
Thou Emblem true, of what I count the best,
O could I lead my Rivolets to rest,
So may we press to that vast mansion, ever blest.

### 29.

Man at the best a creature frail and vain,
In knowledg ignorant, in strength but weak,
Subject to sorrows, losses, sickness, pain,
Each storm his state, his mind, his body break,
From some of these he never finds cessation,
But day or night, within, without, vexation,
Troubles from foes, from friends, from dearest, near'st Relation.

### 30.

And yet this sinfull creature, frail and vain,

This lump of wretchedness, of sin and sorrow,
This weather-beaten vessel wrackt with pain,
Joyes not in hope of an eternal morrow;
Nor all his losses, crosses, and vexation,
In weight, in frequency and long duration
Can make him deeply groan for that divine Translation.

### 33.

O Time the fatal wrack of mortal things,
That draws oblivions curtains over kings,
Their sumptuous monuments, men know them not,
Their names without a Record are forgot,
Their parts, their ports, their pomp's all laid in th'dust
Nor wit nor gold, nor buildings scape times rust;
But he whose name is graved in the white stone
Shall last and shine when all of these are gone.

# Michael Wigglesworth

*Michael Wigglesworth was born in England of "godly parents," who lived in a wicked village. Shortly after they moved out, God destroyed the village by fire. This incident set the pattern for young Wigglesworth's life: always try to keep one jump ahead of God's vengeance. Emigrating to New England, a holy place where the chances of avoiding wholesale chastisement seemed better than in Old England, Wigglesworth entered* Harvard College, received a degree in divinity and became a minister at Malden, Massachusetts. In 1662, at a time of severe drought, he wrote God's Controversy with New England, *a Jeremiad in which he attributed the crop failures to God's anger at the backsliding of His saints. "New England planted, prospered, declining, threatened, punished"—a succinct but awful tale. Having thus set the stage, he wrote* The Day of Doom, or Poetical Description of the Great and Last Judgment. *Here in jingling, dog-trot meter, Wigglesworth expounded the tenets of Puritanical Calvinism—original sin, damnation for the many and salvation for the few.*

*In marked contrast to the brooding, implacable and vengeful Jehovah he worshiped, Wigglesworth was a mere wisp of a man: a mild, inoffensive, dyspeptic little invalid who would have fainted at the sight of even a small part of the violence he described so vividly and so lovingly in* The Day of Doom. *(Valetudinarianism apparently agreed with him: he was the father of eight children and at the time of his death in 1705, at the age of seventy-four, he had recently become a bridegroom for the third time.) His own spiritual life, however, was anything but placid; as he said, he walked through "a howling wilderness of fiery temptations" and he fell prey to agonies of mind that would have shattered the health of a far stronger man. Accustomed to taking constant inventory of his thoughts and acts, he discovered, among other things, that he was guilty of pride, slothfulness, sensuality, "fleshy lusts," vain thoughts, carnality, wantonness, "an unthankful impenitent heart" and addiction to the pursuit of "earthy contentments." He was even assailed by momentary doubts as to the infallibility of the Scriptures, the existence of God and the divinity of Christ. Harboring such "an Ocean of deadly poison" in his heart, he could only conclude that he was destined to land in the hottest spot in*

Michael Wigglesworth: *The Day of Doom.* Edited by Kenneth B. Murdoch.

hell, and so lively was his imagination that even in his quiet country parsonage he felt the searing flames and heard the shrieks of the damned.

Kindly and sweet-tempered as he was, Wigglesworth could never resist an opportunity to deliver rebukes, homilies and admonitions to his fellow men. As a tutor at Harvard, he experienced no lack of such occasions: students guilty of "playing musick," indulging in games or merrymaking of any kind always found Wigglesworth ready with a reproof and a warning of imminent punishment by the Almighty. "Laughter and merriment" seemed to him to be closely akin to sin; he prayed that he might "rather live a melancholy life . . . than by merriment run into a course of provoking God." When his students balked at studying Hebrew, Wigglesworth was moved to deplore the "spirit of unbridled licentiousness" that had taken possession of Harvard.

Thus, besides worrying about the state of his own soul he took the spiritual welfare of the student body upon his conscience. No man, he concluded, carried a heavier burden than he.

The Day of Doom was the most popular poem written in colonial America. Many generations of New England schoolchildren learned it by heart with their catechisms; it went through many editions and it fixed in the minds of thousands of Americans an indelible picture of God and the hereafter. Cotton Mather declared that it would continue to be read until the Day of Doom itself compelled readers to put it aside for the more pressing business of settling accounts with their Maker.

### GOD'S CONTROVERSY WITH NEW ENGLAND: EPILOGUE

Ah dear New England! dearest land to me;
    Which unto God hath hitherto been dear,
And mayst be still more dear than formerly,
    If to his voice thou wilt incline thine ear.

Consider well and wisely what the rod,
    Wherewith thou art from year to year chastized,
Instructeth thee. Repent, & turn to God,
    Who will not have his nurture be despised.

Thou still hast in thee many praying saints,
    Of great account, and precious with the Lord,
Who daily pour out unto him their plaints,
    And strive to please him both in deed & word.

Cheer on, sweet souls, my heart is with you all,
    And shall be with you, maugre Satan's might:
And whereso'ere this body be a Thrall,
    Still in New-England shall be my delight.

### THE DAY OF DOOM: SELECTIONS

Still was the night, serene and bright,
  when all men sleeping lay;
Calm was the season, and carnal reason
  thought it would last for ay.
Soul, take thine ease, let sorrow cease,
  much good thou hast in store;
This was their song, their cups among,
  the evening before.

Wallowing in all kind of sin,
  vile wretches lay secure;
The best of men had scarcely then
  their lamps kept in good ure;
Virgins unwise, who through disguise
  amongst the best were numbered,
Had closed their eyes; yea, and the wise
  through sloth and frailty slumbered.

Like as of old, when men grow bold,
  God's threatenings to contemn,
Who stopped their ear and would not hear
  when mercy warnèd them,
But took their course without remorse
  till God began to pour
Destruction the world upon
  in a tempestuous shower.

They put away the evil day,
  and drowned their cares and fears,
Til drowned were they and swept away
  by vengeance unawares.
So at the last, whilst men slept fast
  in their security,
Surprised they are in such a snare
  as cometh suddenly.

For at midnight broke forth a light,
  which turned the night to day,
And speedily a hideous cry
  did all the world dismay.
Sinners awake, their hearts do ache,
  trembling their loins surpriseth,
Amazed with fear by what they hear,
  each one of them ariseth.

They rush from beds with giddy heads,
   and to their windows run,
Viewing this light which shone more bright
   than doth the noonday sun.
Straightway appears (they see't with tears)
   the Son of God most dread,
Who with his train comes on amain
   to judge both quick and dead.

Before his face the heavens give place,
   and skies are rent asunder,
With mighty voice and hideous noise,
   more terrible than thunder.
His brightness damps heaven's glorious lamps,
   and makes them hide their heads;
As if afraid and quite dismayed,
   they quit their wonted steads.

Ye sons of men that durst contemn
   the threat'nings of God's word,
How cheer you now? your hearts, I trow,
   are thrilled as with a sword.
Now atheist blind, whose brutish mind
   a God could never see,
Dost thou perceive, dost thou believe·
   that Christ thy judge shall be?

Stout courages, whose hardiness
   could death and hell outface,
Are you as bold, now you behold
   your judge draw near apace?
They cry, "No, no, alas and woe,
   our courage all is gone;
Our hardiness, foolhardiness,
   hath us undone, undone."

No heart so bold but now grows cold
   and almost dead with fear,
No eye so dry but now can cry
   and pour out many a tear.
Earth's potentates and pow'rful states,
   captains and men of might,
Are quite abashed, their courage dashed
   at this most dreadful sight.

Mean men lament, great men do rent
   their robes and tear their hair;

They do not spare their flesh to tear
  through horrible despair.
All kindreds wail; their hearts do fail;
  horror the world doth fill
With weeping eyes and loud outcries,
  yet knows not how to kill.

Some hide themselves in caves and delves
  and places under ground,
Some rashly leap into the deep
  to 'scape by being drowned,
Some to the rocks (O senseless blocks!)
  and woody mountains run,
That there they might this fearful sight
  and dreaded presence shun.

In vain do they to mountains say,
  "Fall on us and hide
From Judge's ire, more hot than fire,
  for who may it abide?"
No hiding place can from his face
  sinners at all conceal,
Whose flaming eye hid things does spy
  and darkest things reveal.

The judge draws nigh, exalted high
  upon a lofty throne,
Amidst the throng of angels strong,
  like Israel's holy one.
The excellence of whose presence
  and awful majesty
Amazeth Nature and every creature
  doth more than terrify.

The mountains smoke, the hills are shook,
  the earth is rent and torn,
As if she should be clean dissolved
  or from her center borne.
The sea doth roar, forsake the shore,
  and shrinks away for fear.
The wild beast flee into the sea,
  so soon as he draws near.

Whose glory bright, whose wondrous might,
  whose power imperial
So far surpass whatever was
  in realms terrestrial,

That tongues of men (nor angels' pen)
    cannot the same express,
And therefore I must pass it by,
    lest speaking should transgress.

Before his throne a trump is blown,
    proclaiming the day of doom,
Forthwith he cries, "Ye dead, arise,
    and unto judgment come."
No sooner said but 'tis obeyed;
    supulchers opened are;
Dead bodies all rise at his call,
    and's mighty power declare.

Both sea and land, at his command,
    their dead at once surrender;
The fire and air constrained are
    also their dead to tender.
The mighty word of this great lord
    links body and soul together,
Both of the just and the unjust,
    to part no more forever.

The same translates from mortal states
    to immortality
All that survive and be alive,
    i' th' twinkling of an eye;
That so they may abide for aye
    to endless weal or woe,
Both the renate and reprobate
    are made to die no more.

His wingèd hosts fly through all coasts
    together gathering
Both good and bad, both quick and dead,
    and all to judgment bring,
Out of their holes these creeping moles
    that hid themselves for fear
By force they take and quickly make
    before the Judge appear.

Thus every one before the throne
    of Christ the Judge is brought,
Both righteous and impious
    that good or ill had wrought,
A separation and diff'ring station
    by Christ appointed is

(To sinners sad) 'twixt good and bad,
    'twixt heirs of woe and bliss.

## PLEA OF THE INFANTS

Then to the bar all they drew near
    who died in infancy
And never had no good or bad
    effected personally.
But from the womb unto the tomb
    were straightway carrièd,
Or at the least e'er they transgressed,
    who thus began to plead.

"If for our own transgression
    or disobedience
We here did stand at thy left hand,
    just were the recompense.
But Adam's guilt our souls hath spilt,
    his fault is chargèd on us,
And that alone hath overthrown
    and utterly undone us.

"Not we, but he, ate of the tree
    whose fruit was interdicted;
Yet on us all of his sad fall
    the punishment's inflicted.
How could we sin that had not been,
    or how is his sin our
Without consent, which to prevent
    we never had a power?

"O great Creator, why was our nature
    depravèd and forlorn,
Why so defiled and made so vile
    whilst we were yet unborn?
If it be just, and needs we must
    transgressors reckoned be,
Thy mercy, Lord, to us afford,
    which sinners hath set free.

"Behold we see Adam set free
    and saved from his trespass,
Whose sinful fall has spilt us all
    and brought us to this pass.
Canst thou deny us once to try
    or grace to us to tender,
When he finds grace before thy face,
    that was the chief offender?"

Then answerèd the Judge most dread,
  "God doth such doom forbid,
That men should die eternally
  for what they never did,
But what you call old Adam's fall,
  and only his trespass,
You call amiss to call it his;
  both his and yours it was.

"He was designed of all mankind
  to be a public head,
A common root, whence all should shoot,
  and stood in all their stead;
He stood or fell, did ill or well,
  not for himself alone,
But for you all, who now his fall
  and trespass would disown.

"If he had stood, then all his brood
  had been establishèd
In God's true love, never to move,
  nor once awry to tread:
Then all his race my Father's grace
  should have enjoyed forever,
And wicked sprights by subtle sleights
  could them have harmed never.

"Would you have grieved to have received
  through Adam so much good,
As had been your for evermore,
  if he at first had stood?
Would you have said, 'We ne'er obeyed,
  nor did thy laws regard;
It ill befits with benefits
  us, Lord, so to reward'?

"Since then to share in his welfare
  you could have been content,
You may with reason share in his treason,
  and in the punishment.
Hence you were born in state forlorn,
  with natures so depraved,
Death was your due, because that you
  had so yourself behaved.

"You think if we had been as he
  whom God did so betrust,

We to our cost would ne'er have lost
  all for a paltry lust.
Had you been made in Adam's stead,
  you would like things have wrought,
And so into the selfsame woe
  yourselves and yours have brought.

"I may deny you once to try
  or grace to you to tender,
Though he find grace before my face,
  who was the chief offender;
Else should my grace cease to be grace,
  for it should not be free,
If to release whom I should please
  I have no liberty.

"If upon one what's due to none,
  I frankly shall bestow,
And on the rest shall not think best
  compassion's skirts to throw,
Whom injure I? Will you envy
  and grudge at others' weal,
Or me accuse, who did refuse
  yourselves to help and heal?

"Am I alone of what's my own
  no master or no lord?
Or if I am, how can you claim
  what I to some afford?
Will you demand grace at my hand,
  and challenge what is mine?
Will you teach me whom to set free,
  and thus my grace confine?

"You sinners are, and such a share
  as sinners may expect,
Such you shall have, for I do save
  none but my own elect.
Yet to compare your sin with their
  who lived a longer time,
I do confess yours is much less,
  though every sin's a crime.

"A crime it is; therefore, in bliss
  you may not hope to dwell;
But unto you I shall allow
  the easiest room in hell."

The glorious King thus answering,
    they cease and plead no longer;
Their consciences must needs confess
    his reasons are the stronger.

Thus all men's pleas the Judge with ease
    does answer and confute,
Until that all, both great and small,
    are silencèd and mute.
Vain hopes are cropped, all mouths are stopped
    sinners have nought to say
But that 'tis just and equal most
    they should be damned for aye.

# Edward Taylor

*One of the distinguishing marks of Taylor's verse was his practice of developing a single metaphor or figure throughout a poem. Sometimes this method broke down in grotesquely strained analogies, but often it produced a poem of rare and consistent imagery. Whether successful or not, it is clear that Taylor's poetry was always inspired by an overpowering feeling of love for Christ that did not desert him even in his frequent bereavements.*

### HUSWIFERY

Make me, O Lord, thy Spinning Wheele compleat;
   Thy Holy Worde my Distaff make for mee.
Make mine Affections thy Swift Flyers neate,
   And make my Soule thy holy Spoole to bee.
   My Conversation make to be thy Reele,
   And reele the yarn thereon spun of thy Wheele.

Make me thy Loome then, knit therein this Twine:
   And make thy Holy Spirit, Lord, winde quill:
Then weave the Web thyselfe. The yarn is fine.
   Thine Ordinances make my Fulling Mills.
   Then dy the same in Heavenly Colours Choice,
   All pinkt with Varnish't Flowers of Paradise.

Then cloath therewith mine Understanding, Will,
   Affections, Judgment, Conscience, Memory;
My Words and Actions, that their shine may fill
   My wayes with glory and thee glorify.
   Then mine apparell shall display before yee
   That I am Cloathed in Holy robes for glory.

### UPON WEDLOCK AND DEATH OF CHILDREN

A curious Knot God made in Paradise,
   And drew it out inamled neatly Fresh.
It was the True-Love Knot, more sweet than spice,
   And set with all the flowers of Graces dress.
   Its Weddens Knot, that ne're can be unti'de:
   No Alexanders Sword can it divide.

*The Poetical Works of Edward Taylor.* Edited by Thomas H. Johnson.

The slips here planted, gay and glorious grow:
  Unless an Hellish breath do sindge their Plumes.
Here Primrose, Cowslips, Roses, Lilies blow,
    With Violets and Pinkes that voide perfumes:
    Whose beautious leaves are lac'd with Honey Dew,
    And Chanting birds Chirp out Sweet Musick true.

When in this Knot I planted was, my Stock
  Soon knotted, and a manly flower out brake.
And after it my branch again did knot:
    Brought out another Flower: its sweet breath'd mate.
    One knot gave tother and tothers place;
    Thence Checkling Smiles fought in each others face.

But oh' a glorious hand from glory came,
  Guarded with Angells, soon did Crop this flower,
Which almost tore the root up of the same,
    At that unlookt for, Dolesome, darksome houre.
    In Pray're to Christ perfum'de it did ascent,
    And Angells bright did it to heaven tend.

But pausing on't this Sweet perfum'd my thought,
    Christ would in Glory have a Flower, Choice, Prime.
And having Choice, chose this my branch forth brought.
    Lord, take' I thanke thee, thou takst ought of mind;
    It is my pledg in glory; part of mee
    It now in it, Lord, glorifi'de with thee.

But praying o're my branch, my branch did sprout,
  And bore another manly flower, and gay,
And after another, sweet brake out,
    The which the former hand soon got away.
    But oh! the torture, Vomit, screechings, groans!
    And six weeks fever would pierce hearts like stones.

Griefe o're doth flow: and nature fault would finde
  Were not thy Will my Spell, Charm, Joy, and Gem:
That as I said, I say, take, Lord, they're thine:
    I piecemeale pass to Glory bright in them.
    I joy may I sweet Flowers for Glory breed,
    Whether thou getst them green, or lets them seed.

### MEDITATION EIGHTY-TWO
#### SECOND SERIES

John VI: 53: Except ye eat the flesh of the Son of man, and drink his blood,
ye have no life in you.
    Some Life with Spoon, or Trencher do mentaine

Or Suck its food through a Small Quill or Straw:
But make me, Lord, this Life thou givst, Sustain
   With thy Sweet Flesh and Blood, by Gospell Law.
   Feed it on Zions Pasty Plate-Delights:
   I'de suck it from her Candlesticks Sweet Pipes.

Need makes the Oldwife trot; Necessity
   Saith, I must eate this Flesh, and drinke this blood
If not, no Life's in mee that's worth a Fly;
   This mortall Life, while here, eats mortall Foode
   That sends out influences to mentaine,
   A little while, and then holds back the same.

But Soule Sweet Bread is in God's Backhouse made
   On Heavens high Dresser Boarde and throughly bakd:
On Zions Gridiron, sapt in'ts dripping trade,
   That all do live that on it do partake,
   Its Flesh and Blood even of the Deity:
   None that do eat and Drinke it, ever dy.

Have I vitall Sparke even of this Fire?
   How Dull am I? Lord let thy Spirit blow
Upon my Coale, untill its heart is higher,
   And I be quickned by the same, and Glow.
   Here's Manna, Angell food, to fatten them,
   That I must eate or be a wither'd stem.

Lord, make my Faith thy golden Quill wherethrough
   I vitall Spirits from thy blood may suck.
Make Faith my Grinders, thy Choice Flesh to chew,
   My Withered Stock shall with frim Fruits be Stuck.
   My Soule shall then in Lively Notes forth ring
   Upon her Virginalls, praise for this thing.

# Bacon's Epitaph

# *(Anonymous)*

*Nathaniel Bacon, a young man who had recently arrived in Virginia, led the revolt that broke out in 1676 against the authority of Governor William Berkeley, whom a large part of the people held responsible for the Indian forays on the frontier and the economic and political ills of the colony. At the head of a considerable body of armed farmers and frontiersmen, Bacon seemed on the point of conquering the province when he was struck down by disease. Restored temporarily to power, Governor Berkeley took heavy vengeance upon the disorganized Baconians by confiscations of property and executions.*

*The author of this elegy on Bacon is unknown. To have inspired the kind of devotion that animated this poem, Bacon must have possessed magnetic powers of leadership. Some historians regard him as a mere opportunist while others have acclaimed him a fighting democrat, a true precursor of Thomas Jefferson.*

### BACON'S EPITAPH MADE BY HIS MAN

Death why so cruel! what no other way  
To manifest thy spleen, but thus to slay  
Our hopes of safety; liberty, our all  
Which, through thy tyranny, with him must fall  
To its late Chaos? Had thy rigid force  
Been dealt by retail, and not thus in gross  
Grief had been silent: Now we must complain  
Since thou, in him, hast more than thousand slain  
Whose lives and safeties did so much depend  
On him their life, with him their lives must end.  

If't be a sin to think Death brib'd can be  
We must be guilty: say twas bribery  
Guided the fatal shaft. Virginia's foes  
To whom for secret crimes, just vengeance owes  
Deserved plagues, dreading their just desert  

*The Burwell Papers.*

Corrupted Death by Parasscellcian art
Him to destroy; whose well tried courage such
Their heartless hearts, nor arms, nor strength could touch.
   Who now must heal those wounds, or stop that blood
The Heathen made, and drew into a flood?
Who i'st must plead our Cause? nor Trump nor Drum
Nor Deputations; these alas are dumb
And cannot speak. Our Arms (though nere so strong)
Will want the aid of his Commanding tongue,
Which Conquer'd more than Caesar: He orethrew
Only the outward frame; this Could subdue
The rugged works of nature. Souls replete
With dull chilled cold, he'd animate with heat
Drawn forth of reasons Lymbick. In a word
*Mars* and *Minerva*, both in him Concurred
For arts, for arms, whose pen and sword alike
As Cato's did, may admiration strike
Into his foes; while they confess with all
It was their guilt styl'd him a Criminal.
Only this difference doth from truth proceed
They in the guilt, he in the name must bleed
While none shall dare his Obsequies to sing
In deserved measures; until time shall bring
Truth Crown'd with freedom, and from danger free
To sound his praises to posterity.
   Here let him rest; while we this truth report
He's gone from hence unto a higher Court
To plead his Cause: where he by this doth know
WHETHER TO CAESAR HE WAS FRIEND, OR FOE.

# Ebenezer Cook

*After pouring out his wrath against Maryland in* The Sot-Weed Factor, *Cook returned to the colony. Styling himself "E. Cook, Laureat," he became the leader of the first literary group to emerge in the South. Having experienced a change of heart toward the colony, he revised* The Sot-Weed Factor, *softening its more caustic passages. He is also credited with the authorship of the* Maryland Muse, *a satirical account in rhyme of Bacon's Rebellion. In 1730, he (or someone bearing the initials E. C.) published the* Sot-Weed Redivivus, or the Planter's Looking Glass.

### THE SOT-WEED FACTOR, OR A VOYAGE TO MARYLAND, A SATIRE: SELECTIONS

Condemned by fate to wayward curse,
Of friends unkind, and empty purse—
Plagues worse than filled Pandora's box—
I took my leave of Albion's rocks
With heavy heart, concerned that I
Was forced my native soil to fly,
And the Old World must bid goodbye.
But heaven ordained it should be so,
And to repine is vain, we know.
Freighted with fools from Plymouth found
To Maryland our ship was bound,
Where we arrived in dreadful pain,
Shocked by the terrors of the main;
For full three months our wavering boat
Did through the surly ocean float,
And furious storms and threatening blasts
Both tore our sails and sprung our masts.
Wearied, yet pleased we did escape
Such ills, we anchored at the cape;
But weighing soon, we ploughed the bay,
To cove it in Piscataway.
Intending there to open store,
I put myself and goods ashore:
Where soon repaired a numerous crew,

Ebenezer Cook: *The Sot-Weed Factor.* Edited by Bernard C. Steiner.

In shirts and drawers of Scotch-cloth blue
With neither stockings, hat nor shoe.
These sot-weed planters crowd the shore,
In hue as tawny as a Moor:
Figures so strange, no god designed
To be a part of human kind:
But wanton nature, void of rest,
Moulded the brittle clay in jest.
At last a fancy very odd
Took me, this was the Land of Nod;
Planted at first, when vagrant Cain,
His brother had unjustly slain;
Then conscious of the crime he'd done,
From vengeance dire he hither run,
And in a hut supinely dwelt,
The first in furs and sot-weed dealt
And ever since his time, the place
Has harboured a detested race;
Who when they could not live at home,
For refuge to these worlds did roam;
In hopes by flight they might prevent
The devil and his fell intent,
Obtain from triple-tree reprieve,
And heaven and hell alike deceive;
But ere their manner I display,
I think it fit I open lay
My entertainment by the way:
That strangers well may be aware on,
What homely diet they must fare on.
To touch that shore where no good sense is found,
But conversation's lost, and manners drowned,
I crossed unto the other side
A river whose impetuous tide
The savage borders does divide;
In such a shining odd invention,
I scarce can give its due dimension.
The Indians call this watery wagon
Canoe, a vessel none can brag on;
Cut from a poplar tree or pine,
And fashioned like a trough for swine:
In this most noble fishing boat
I boldly put myself afloat;
Standing erect, with legs stretched wide,
We paddled to the other side:
Where being landed safe by hap,
As Sol fell into Thetis' lap,
A ravenous gang bent on the stroll,
Of wolves for prey, began to howl;

This put me in a panic fright,
Lest I should be devourèd quite:
But as I there a-musing stood,
And quite benighted in a wood,
A female voice pierced through my ears,
Crying, "You rogue, drive home the steers."
I listened to the attractive sound,
And straight a herd of cattle found
Drove by a youth, and homeward bound;
Cheered with the sight, I straight thought fit
To ask where I a bed might get.
The surly peasant bid me stay,
And asked from whom I'd run away.
Surprised at such a saucy word,
I instantly lugged out my sword;
Swearing I was no fugitive,
But from Great Britain did arrive,
In hopes I better there might thrive.
To which he mildly made reply,
"I beg your pardon, sir, that I
Should talk to you unmannerly;
But if you please to go with me,
To yonder house, you'll welcome be."
Encountering soon the smoky seat,
The planter old did thus me greet:
"Whether you come from gaol or college,
You're welcome to my certain knowledge;
And if you please all night to stay,
My son shall put you in the way."
Which offer I most kindly took,
And for a seat did round me look;
When presently amongst the rest
He placed his unknown English guest,
Who found them drinking for a whet
A cask of cider on the fret,
Till supper came upon the table,
On which I fed whilst I was able.
So after hearty entertainment
Of drink and victuals without payment
(For planters tables, you must know,
Are free for all that come and go),
While pone and milk, with mush well stored,
In wooden dishes graced the board,
With hominy and cider-pap
(Which scarce a hungry dog would lap),
Well stuffed with fat from bacon fried,
Or with molasses dulcified,
Then out our landlord pulls a pouch,

As greasy as the leather couch
On which he sat, and straight begun
To load with weed his Indian gun;
In length, scarce longer than one's finger.
His pipe smoked out with awful grace,
With aspect grave and solemn pace,
The reverend sire walks to a chest,
Of all his furniture the best,
Closely confined within a room
Which seldom felt the weight of broom,
From thence he lugs a cag of rum,
And nodding to me, thus begun:
"I find," says he, "you don't much care
For this our Indian country fare;
But let me tell you, friend of mine,
You may be glad of it in time,
Though now your stomach is so fine;
And if within this land you stay,
You'll find it true what I do say."
This said, the roundlet up he threw,
And bending backwards strongly drew:
I plucked as stoutly for my part,
Although it made me sick at heart,
And got so soon into my head
I scarce could find my way to bed.

Where all things were in such Confusion,
I thought the World at its conclusion:
A Herd of Planters on the ground,
O'er-whelm'd with Punch, dead drunk we found:
Others were fighting and contending,
Some burnt their Cloaths to save the mending.
A few whose Heads by frequent use,
Could better bare the potent Juice,
Gravely debated State Affairs.
Whilst I most nimbly trip'd up Stairs;
Leaving my Friend discoursing oddly,
And mixing things Prophane and Godly:
Just then beginning to be Drunk,
As from the Company I slunk,
To every Room and Nook I crept,
In hopes I might have somewhere slept;
But all the bedding was possest
By one or other drunken Guest:

I met a *Quaker, Yea* and *Nay;*
A Pious Conscientious Rogue,
As e'er woar Bonnet or a Brogue,

Who neither Swore nor kept his Word
But cheated in the Fear of God;
And when his Debts he would not pay,
By Light within he ran away.

St. *Mary's* once was in repute,
Now here the Judges try the Suit,
And Lawyers twice a Year dispute
As oft the Bench most gravely meet,
Some to get Drunk, and some to eat,
A swinging share of Country Treat.
But as for Justice right or wrong,
Not one amongst the numerous throng,
Knows what they mean, or has the Heart,
To give his Verdict on a Stranger's part:
Now Court being call'd by beat of Drum,
The Judges left their Punch and Rum,

The Byast Court without delay,
Adjudg'd by Debt in Country Pay;
In Pipe Staves, Corn, or Flesh of Boar,
Rare Cargo for the *English* Shoar:
Raging with Grief, full speed I ran,
To joyn the Fleet at *Kicketan;*
Embarqu'd and waiting for a Wind,
I left this dreadful Curse behind.

May Canniballs transported o'er the Sea
Prey on these Slaves, as they have done on me;
May never Merchant's, trading Sails explore
This Cruel, this Inhospitable Shoar;
But left abandon'd by the World to starve
May they sustain the Fate they well deserve:
May they turn Savage, or as *Indians* wild,
From Trade, Converse, and Happiness exil'd;
Recreant to Heaven, may they adore the Sun,
And into Pagan Superstitions run
For Vengeance ripe——
May Wrath Divine then lay those Regions wast
Where no Man's Faithful, nor a Woman Chast.

# Benjamin Franklin

Poor Richard's Almanac *was the most successful almanac published in colonial America. From it, Franklin culled the most sententious maxims which he published under the title:* The Way to Wealth. *It was the first and the most famous of a long line of self-help books dedicated to the proposition that the most important function of the American male was making money and otherwise getting on in the world. Unlike some of his successors in this field, Franklin did not promise quick, effortless riches through speculation; there was no room for unearned increment in his philosophy. Instead, he emphasized the qualities required for success in a frontier community where capital accumulation was a vital need: self-reliance, prudence, plain living and thrift. The way to wealth, as Franklin pictured it, was a hard, stony path of self-denial and hard work at the end of which lay the haven: security based upon a lifetime devoted to labor and accumulation.*

## THE WAY TO WEALTH

Courteous Reader

I have heard that nothing gives an author so great pleasure, as to find his works respectfully quoted by other learned authors. This pleasure I have seldom enjoyed; for though I have been, if I may say it without vanity, an *eminent author* of almanacks annually now a full quarter of a century, my brother authors in the same way, for what reason I know not, have ever been very sparing in their applauses, and no other author has taken the least notice of me, so that did not my writings produce me some some solid *pudding*, the great deficiency of *praise* would have quite discouraged me.

I concluded at length, that the people were the best judges of my merit; for they buy my works; and besides, in my rambles where I am not personally known, I have frequently heard one or other of my adages repeated, with *as Poor Richard says* at the end on 't; this gave me some satisfaction, as it showed not only that my instructions were regarded, but discovered likewise some respect for my authority; and I own that

*The Writings of Benjamin Franklin.* Edited by Albert H. Smyth.

to encourage the practice of remembering and repeating those wise sentences, I have sometimes *quoted myself* with great gravity.

Judge, then, how much I must have been gratified by an incident I am going to relate to you. I stopped my horse lately where a great number of people were collected at a vendue of merchant goods. The hour of sale not being come, they were conversing on the badness of the times and one of the company called to a plain clean old man, with white locks, "Pray, Father Abraham, what think you of the times? Won't these heavy taxes quite ruin the country? How shall we be ever able to pay them? What would you advise us to?" Father Abraham stood up, and replied, "If you'd have my advice, I'll give it to you in short, for *A word to the wise is enough,* and *Many words won't fill a bushel,* as Poor Richard says." They joined in desiring him to speak his mind, and gathering round him, he proceeded as follows:

"Friends," says he, "and neighbours, the taxes are indeed very heavy, and if those laid on by the government were the only ones we had to pay, we might more easily discharge them; but we have many others, and much more grievous to some of us. We are taxed as much by our idleness, three times as much by our pride, and four times as much by our folly; and from these taxes the commissioners cannot ease or deliver us by allowing an abatement. However, let us hearken to good advice and something may be done for us; *God helps them that help themselves,* as Poor Richard says, in his Almanac of 1733.

"It would be thought a hard government that should tax its people one-tenth part of their time, to be employed in its service. But idleness taxes many of us much more, if we reckon all that is spent in absolute sloth, or doing of nothing, with that which is spent in idle employment or amusements, that amount to nothing. Sloth, by bringing on diseases, absolutely shortens life. *Sloth, like rust, consumes faster than labour wears; while the used key is always bright,* as Poor Richard says. *But dost thou love life, then do not squander time, for that is the stuff life is made of,* as Poor Richard says. How much more than is necessary do we spend in sleep, forgetting that *The sleeping fox catches no poultry* and that *There will be sleeping enough in the grave,* as Poor Richard says.

"If *time be of all things the most precious, wasting time must be,* as Poor Richard says, *the greatest prodigality;* since, as he elsewhere tells us, *Lost time is never found again; and what we call time enough, always proves little enough.* Let us then up and be doing, and doing to the purpose; so by diligence shall we do more with less perplexity. *Sloth makes all things difficult, but industry all easy,* as Poor Richard says, and *He that riseth late must trot all day, and shall scarce overtake his business at night;* while *Laziness travels so slowly, that poverty soon overtakes him,* as we read in Poor Richard, who adds, *Drive thy business, let not that drive thee;* and *Early to bed, and early to rise, makes a man healthy, wealthy, and wise.*

"So what signifies wishing and hoping for better times? We may make these times better, if we bestir ourselves. *Industry need not wish,* as Poor Richard says, *and he that lives upon hope will die fasting. There are no gains without pains; then help hands, for I have no lands,* or if I have, they are smartly taxed. And, as Poor Richard likewise observes, *He that hath a trade hath an estate; and he that hath a calling, hath an office of profit and honour;* but then the trade must be worked at, and the calling well followed, or neither the estate nor the office will enable us to pay our taxes. If we are industrious, we shall never starve; for as Poor Richard says, *At the working man's house hunger looks in, but dares not enter.* Nor will the bailiff or the constable enter, for *industry pays debts, while despair encreaseth them,* says Poor Richard. What though you have found no treasure, nor has any rich relation left you a legacy, *Diligence is the mother of good-luck,* as Poor Richard says, *and God gives all things to industry. Then plough deep, while sluggards sleep, and you shall have corn to sell and to keep,* says Poor Dick. Work while it is called to-day, for you know not how much you may be hindered to-morrow, which makes Poor Richard say, *One to-day is worth two to-morrows,* and farther, *Have you somewhat to do tomorrow, do it to-day.* If you were a servant, would you not be ashamed that a good master should catch you idle? Are you then your own master, *Be ashamed to catch yourself idle,* as Poor Dick says. When there is so much to be done for yourself, your family, your country, and your gracious King, be up by peep of day; *Let not the sun look down and say, Inglorious here he lies.* Handle your tools without mittens; remember that *The cat in gloves catches no mice,* as Poor Richard says. 'Tis true there is much to be done, and perhaps you are weak-handed, but stick to it steadily; and you will see great effects, for *Constant dropping wears away stones,* and *By diligence and patience the mouse ate in two the cable;* and *Little strokes fell great oaks,* as Poor Richard says in his Almanack, the year I cannot just now remember.

"Methinks I hear some of you say, 'Must a man afford himself no leisure?' I will tell thee, my friend, what Poor Richard says, *Employ thy time well, if thou meanest to gain leisure; and, since thou are not sure of a minute, throw not away an hour.* Leisure is time for doing something useful; this leisure the diligent man will obtain, but the lazy man never; so that, as Poor Richard says, *A life of leisure and a life of laziness are two things.* Do you imagine that sloth will afford you more comfort than labour? No, for as Poor Richard says, *Trouble springs from idleness, and grievous toil from needless ease. Many without labour would live by their wits only, but they break for want of stock.* Whereas industry gives comfort, and plenty, and respect: *Fly pleasures, and they'll follow you. The diligent spinner has a large shift;* and *Now I have a sheep and a cow, everybody bids me good morrow;* all which is well said by Poor Richard.

"But with our industry we must likewise be steady, settled, and careful, and oversee our own affairs with our own eyes, and not trust too much to others; for as Poor Richard says,

> *I never saw an oft-removèd tree,*
> *Nor yet an oft-removèd family,*
> *That throve so well as those that settled be.*

And again, *Three removes is as bad as a fire;* and again, *Keep thy shop, and thy shop will keep thee;* and again, *If you would have your business done, go; if not, send.* And again,

> *He that by the plough would thrive,*
> *Himself must either hold or drive.*

And again, *The eye of a master will do more work than both his hands;* and again, *Want of care does us more damage than want of knowledge;* and again, *Not to oversee workmen, is to leave them your purse open.* Trusting too much to others' care is the ruin of many; for, as the Almanack says, *In the affairs of this world, men are saved, not by faith, but by the want of it;* but a man's own care is profitable; for, saith Poor Dick, *Learning is to the studious,* and *riches to the careful,* as well as *Power to the bold,* and *heaven to the virtuous.* And farther, *If you would have a faithful servant, and one that you like, serve yourself.* And again, he adviseth to circumspection and care, even in the smallest matters, because sometimes *A little neglect may breed great mischief;* adding, *For want of a nail the shoe was lost; for want of a shoe the horse was lost; and for want of a horse the rider was lost, being overtaken and slain by the enemy; all for want of care about a horse-shoe nail.*

"So much for industry, my friends, and attention to one's own business; but to these we must add frugality, if we would make our industry more certainly successful. A man may, if he knows not how to save as he gets, keep his nose all his life to the grindstone, and die not worth a groat at last. *A fat kitchen makes a lean will,* as Poor Richard says, and

> *Many estates are spent in the getting,*
> *Since women for tea forsook spinning and knitting,*
> *And men for punch forsook hewing and splitting.*

*If you would be wealthy,* says he, in another Almanack, *think of saving as well as of getting: The Indies have not made Spain rich, because her outgoes are greater than her incomes.*

"Away then with your expensive follies, and you will not then have so much cause to complain of hard times, heavy taxes, and chargeable families; for, as Poor Dick says,

*Women and wine, game and deceit,*
*Make the wealth small and the wants great.*

And farther, *What maintains one vice, would bring up two children.*
You may think perhaps, that a *little* tea, or a *little* punch now and then,
diet a *little* more costly, clothes a *little* finer, and a *little* entertainment
now and than, can be no *great* matter; but remember what Poor Richard
says, *Many a little makes a mickle;* and farther, *Beware of little expenses; a small leak will sink a great ship;* and again, *Who dainties
love, shall beggars prove;* and moreover, *Fools make feasts, and wise
men eat them.*

"Here you are all got together at this vendue of fineries and knick-
knacks. You call them *goods;* but if you do not take care, they will prove
*evils* to some of you. You expect they will be sold *cheap,* and perhaps
they may for less than they cost; but if you have no occasion for them,
they must be *dear* to you. Remember what Poor Richard says: *Buy what
thou hast need of, and ere long thou shalt sell thy necessaries.* And again,
*At a great pennyworth pause a while.* He means that perhaps the cheap-
ness is *apparent* only, and not *real;* or the bargain, by straitening thee
in thy business, may do thee more harm than good. For in another place
he says, *Many have been ruined by buying good pennyworths.* Again,
Poor Richard says, *'Tis foolish to lay out money in a purchase of repentance;* and yet this folly is practiced every day at vendues, for want of
minding the Almanack. *Wise men,* as Poor Dick says, *learn by others'
harms, fools scarcely by their own;* but *felix quem faciunt aliena pericula
cautum.* Many a one, for the sake of finery on the back, have gone with
a hungry belly, and half-starved their families. *Silks and satins, scarlet
and velvets,* as Poor Richard says, *put out the kitchen fire.*

"These are not the necessaries of life; they can scarcely be called the
conveniences; and yet only because they look pretty, how many want
to have them! The artificial wants of mankind thus become more
numerous than the natural; and, as Poor Dick says, *For one poor person,
there are an hundred indigent.* By these, and other extravagancies, the
genteel are reduced to poverty, and forced to borrow of those whom
they formerly despised, but who through industry and frugality have
maintained their standing; in which case it appears plainly, that *A
ploughman on his legs is higher than a gentleman on his knees,* as Poor
Richard says. Perhaps they have had a small estate left them, which they
knew not the getting of; they think, *'tis day, and will never be night;*
that a little to be spent out of so much, is not worth minding; *A child
and a fool,* as Poor Richard says, *imagine twenty shillings and twenty
years can never be spent,* but, *Always taking out of the meal-tub, and
never putting in, soon comes to the bottom;* as Poor Dick says, *When
the well's dry, they know the worth of water.* But this they might have
known before, if they had taken his advice; *If you would know the value*

*of money, go and try to borrow some; for, he that goes a borrowing goes a sorrowing;* and indeed so does he that lends to such people, when he goes to get it in again. Poor Dick further advises, and says,

> *Fond pride of dress is sure a very curse;*
> *Ere fancy you consult, consult your purse.*

And again, *Pride is as loud a beggar as want, and a great deal more saucy.* When you have bought one fine thing, you must buy ten more, that your appearance may be all of a piece; but Poor Dick says, *'Tis easier to suppress the first desire, than to satisfy all that follow it.* And 'tis as truly folly for the poor to ape the rich, as for the frog to swell in order to equal the ox.

> *Great estates may venture more,*
> *But little boats should keep near shore.*

'Tis, however, a folly soon punished; for *Pride that dines on vanity, sups on contempt,* as Poor Richard says. And in another place, *Pride breakfasted with plenty, dined with poverty, and supped with infamy.* And after all, of what use is this pride of appearance, for which so much is risked, so much is suffered? It cannot promote health, or ease pain; it makes no increase of merit in the person, it creates envy, it hastens misfortune.

> *What is a butterfly? At best*
> *He's but a caterpillar drest.*
> *The gaudy fop's his picture just,*

as Poor Richard says.

"But what madness must it be to run in debt for these superfluities! We are offered, by the terms of this vendue, six months' credit; and that perhaps has induced some of us to attend it, because we cannot spare the ready money, and hope now to be fine without it. But, ah, think what you do when you run in debt; you give to another power over your liberty. If you cannot pay at the time, you will be ashamed to see your creditor; you will be in fear when you speak to him; you will make poor pitiful sneaking excuses, and by degrees come to lose your veracity, and sink into base downright lying; for, as Poor Richard says, *The second vice is lying, the first is running in debt.* And again, to the same purpose, *Lying rides upon debt's back.* Whereas a free-born Englishman ought not to be ashamed or afraid to see or speak to any man living. But poverty often deprives a man of all spirit and virtue: *'Tis hard for an empty bag to stand upright,* as Poor Richard truly says.

"What would you think of that prince, or that government, who should issue an edict forbidding you to dress like a gentleman or a gentlewoman, on pain of imprisonment or servitude? Would you not say, that you were free, have a right to dress as you please, and that such an edict would be a breach of your privileges, and such a government tyrannical? And yet you are about to put yourself under that tyranny, when you run in debt for such dress! Your creditor has authority, at his pleasure to deprive you of your liberty, by confining you in gaol for life, or to sell you for a servant, if you should not be able to pay him! When you have got your bargain, you may, perhaps, think little of payment; but *Creditors*, Poor Richard tells us, *have better memories than debtors;* and in another place says, *Creditors are a superstitious sect, great observers of set days and times.* The day comes round before you are aware, and the demand is made before you are prepared to satisfy it; or if you bear your debt in mind, the term which at first seemed so long will, as it lessens, appear extremely short. Time will seem to have added wings to his heels as well as shoulders. *Those have a short Lent,* saith Poor Richard, *who owe money to be paid at Easter.* Then since, as he says, *The borrower is a slave to the lender, and the debtor to the creditor,* disdain the chain, preserve your freedom; and maintain your independency: be industrious and free; be frugal and free. At present, perhaps, you may think yourself in thriving circumstances, and that you can bear a little extravagance without injury; but,

> *For age and want save while you may;*
> *No morning sun lasts a whole day,*

as Poor Richard says. Gain may be temporary and uncertain, but ever while you live, expense is constant and certain; and *'Tis easier to build two chimneys, than to keep one in fuel,* as Poor Richard says. So, *Rather go to bed supperless than rise in debt.*

> *Get what you can, and what you get hold;*
> *'Tis the stone that will turn all your lead into gold,*

as Poor Richard says. And when you have got the philosopher's stone, sure you will no longer complain of bad times, or the difficulty of paying taxes.

"This doctrine, my friends, is reason and wisdom; but after all, do not depend too much upon your own industry, and frugality, and prudence, though excellent things, for they may all be blasted without the blessing of Heaven; and therefore, ask that blessing humbly, and be not uncharitable to those that at present seem to want it, but comfort and help them. Remember, Job suffered, and was afterwards prosperous.

"And now to conclude, *Experience keeps a dear school, but fools will learn in no other, and scarce in that;* for it is true, *We may give advice, but we cannot give conduct,* as Poor Richard says. However, remember this, *They that won't be counselled, can't be helped,* as Poor Richard says: and farther, that, *If you will not hear reason, she'll surely rap your knuckles.*"

Thus the old gentleman ended his harangue. The people heard it, and approved the doctrine, and immediately practiced the contrary, just as if it had been a common sermon; for the vendue opened, and they began to buy extravagantly, notwithstanding his cautions and their own fear of taxes. I found the good man had thoroughly studied my Almanacks, and digested all I had dropt on these topics during the course of five and twenty years. The frequent mention he made of me must have tired any one else, but my vanity was wonderfully delighted with it, though I was conscious that not a tenth part of the wisdom was my own, which he ascribed to me, but rather the gleanings I had made of the sense of all ages and nations. However, I resolved to be the better for the echo of it; and though I had at first determined to buy stuff for a new coat, I went away resolved to wear my old one a little longer. Reader, if thou wilt do the same, thy profit will be as great as mine. I am, as ever, thine to serve thee,

RICHARD SAUNDERS.

### ADVICE TO A YOUNG TRADESMAN

To My Friend, A. B.:

As you have desired it of me, I write the following hints, which have been of service to me, and may, if observed, be so to you.

Remember, that *time* is money. He that can earn ten shillings a day by his labour, and goes abroad, or sits idle, one half of that day, though he spends but sixpence during his diversion or idleness, ought not to reckon *that* the only expense; he has really spent, or rather thrown away, five shillings besides.

Remember, that *credit* is money. If a man lets his money lie in my hands after it is due, he gives me the interest, or so much as I can make of it during that time. This amounts to a considerable sum where a man has good and large credit, and makes good use of it.

Remember, that money is of the prolific, generating nature. Money can beget money, and its offspring can beget more, and so on. Five shillings turned is six, turned again it is seven and three-pence, and so on till it becomes an hundred pounds. The more there is of it, the more it produces every turning, so that the profits rise quicker and quicker. He that kills a breeding sow, destroys all her offspring to the thousandth generation. He that murders a crown, destroys all that it might have produced, even scores of pounds.

Remember, that six pounds a year is but a groat a day. For this little sum (which may be daily wasted either in time or expense unperceived) a man of credit may, on his own security, have the constant possession and use of an hundred pounds. So much in stock, briskly turned by an industrious man, produces great advantage.

Remember this saying, *The good paymaster is lord of another man's purse.* He that is known to pay punctually and exactly to the time he promises, may at any time, and on any occasion, raise all the money his friends can spare. This is sometimes of great use. After industry and frugality, nothing contributes more to the raising of a young man in the world than punctuality and justice in all his dealings; therefore never keep borrowed money an hour beyond the time you promised, lest a disappointment shut up your friend's purse for ever.

The most trifling actions that affect a man's credit are to be regarded. The sound of your hammer at five in the morning, or nine at night, heard by a creditor, makes him easy six months longer; but, if he see you at a billiard table, or hears your voice at a tavern, when you should be at work, he sends for his money the next day; demands it, before he can receive it, in a lump.

It shows, besides, that you are mindful of what you owe; it makes you appear a careful as well as an honest man, and that still increases your credit.

Beware of thinking all your own that you possess, and of living accordingly. It is a mistake that many people who have credit fall into. To prevent this, keep an exact account for some time, both of your expenses and your income. If you take the pains at first to mention particulars, it will have this good effect: you will discover how wonderfully small, trifling expenses mount on to large sums, and will discern what might have been, and may for the future be saved, without occasioning any great inconvenience.

In short, the way to wealth, if you desire it, is as plain as the way to market. It depends chiefly on two words, *industry* and *frugality;* that is, waste neither *time* nor *money,* but make the best use of both. Without industry and frugality nothing will do, and with them every thing. He that gets all he can honestly, and saves all he gets (necessary expenses excepted), will certainly become *rich,* if that Being who governs the world, to whom all should look for a blessing on their honest endeavors, doth not, in his wise providence, otherwise determine.

AN OLD TRADESMAN.

# PART VII

# FOUR COLONIAL
# VIEWS

# Itinerarium

## Dr. Alexander Hamilton

*The best travel account written during the colonial period was the* Itinerarium *of Dr. Alexander Hamilton. Born in Scotland in 1712, Hamilton was a graduate of the medical school of Edinburgh University. In 1739, he came to Annapolis, Maryland, where an older brother had preceded him, to practice medicine. A successful physician, he suffered from chronic illness, which in 1744 prompted him to undertake a tour of the Northern colonies in the hope of restoring his health. In the course of his travels, he visited Philadelphia, New York, Albany, Newport, Boston and Portsmouth, New Hampshire.*

*Mounted on his horse, accompanied by his Negro manservant, and dressed in fine clothes, laced hat and wearing a sword, Dr. Hamilton was obviously a person of quality, a conspicuous member of what was called in the eighteenth century "the better sort." From this vantage point, he looked down upon the "ignorant vulgar," the "rabble of clowns," "the many headed beast" and impudent parvenus he encountered on his journey. His contempt for "the lower orders" was intensified by their susceptibility to the evangelical preaching of the Reverend George Whitfield and other revivalists. For this was the era of the Great Awakening when religious fervor, having long lain dormant, erupted in screaming, convulsions and hysteria. As an eighteenth-century rationalist, Dr. Hamilton could not endure "enthusiasm" in any form: it was emphatically not the way a gentleman of culture and refinement behaved.*

*But Dr. Hamilton's lively sense of humor saved him from being merely a class-conscious aristocrat sourly surveying from the top of the social scale the antics of humanity. He delighted in "characters"—the more outlandish the more he relished them—and he had the gift of describing incisively a person or an event in a sentence. Moreover, he was a sociable, affable, generally good-humored man who rejoiced in an opportunity to spend an evening over a bottle of wine with men of education, culture and wit. Since he carried letters of introduction to gentlemen in the*

Gentleman's Progress: The Itinerarium of Dr. Alexander Hamilton. Edited by Carl Bridenbaught.

*Northern cities, he was welcomed into their social gatherings and clubs.*
*Here Dr. Hamilton was in his element: few men in the American colonies*
*were more "clubable" than he. The eighteenth century was the Age of*
*Clubs: there were clubs for the improvement of useful knowledge, clubs*
*for the study of natural philosophy, clubs for the discussion of literature,*
*clubs for the performance of chamber music and clubs for virtually every*
*other purpose that could bring men together for a sociable evening. It*
*was a very masculine world, but Dr. Hamilton, a bachelor, had an eye,*
*appraising and highly critical, for the ladies as well.*

*Dr. Hamilton's impressions of the domestic manners—and the lack of*
*them—of the Americans were set down with humor, irony and sarcasm.*
*In his book, the comic spirit triumphed over ill health and pain. But not*
*for long: he died a few years after his return to Annapolis and his mar-*
*riage. His* Itinerarium, *his only book, was not published until 1907.*

Just as I dismounted at Tradaway's, I found a drunken club dismiss-
ing. Most of them had got upon their horses and were seated in an
oblique situation, deviating much from a perpendicular to the horizontal
plan[e], a posture quite necessary for keeping the center of gravity within
its propper base for the support of the superstructure; hence we deduce
the true physicall reason why our heads overloaded with liquor become
too ponderous for our heels. Their discourse was as oblique as their
position; the only thing intelligible in it was oaths and God dammes;
the rest was an inarticulate sound like Rabelais' frozen words a thawing,
interlaced with hiccupings and belchings. I was uneasy till they were
gone, and my landlord, seeing me stare, made that trite apology—that
indeed he did not care to have such disorderly fellows come about his
house; he was always noted far and near for keeping a quiet house and
entertaining only gentlemen or such like, but these were country
people, his neighbours, and it was not prudent to disoblige them upon
slight occasions. "Alas, sir!" added he, "we that entertain travelers must
strive to oblige everybody, for it is our dayly bread." While he spoke
thus, our Bacchanalians, finding no more rum in play, rid off helter
skelter as if the devil had possessed them, every man sitting his horse in
a see-saw manner like a bunch of rags tyed upon the saddle.

I found nothing particular or worth notice in my landlord's character
or conversation, only as to his bodily make. He was a fat pursy man
and had large bubbies like a woman. I supped upon fried chickens and
bacon, and after supper the conversation turned upon politicks, news,
and the dreaded French war; but it was so very lumpish and heavy that
it disposed me mightily to sleep. This learned company consisted of the
landlord, his overseer and miller, and another greasy thumb'd fellow
who, as I understood, professed physick and particularly surgery. In the
drawing of teeth, he practiced upon the housemaid, a dirty piece of

lumber, who made such screaming and squalling as made me imagine
there was murder going forwards in the house. However, the artist got
the tooth out att last with a great clumsy pair of blacksmith's forceps;
and indeed it seemed to require such an instrument, for when he showed
it to us, it resembled a horsenail more than a tooth.

The miller, I found, professed musick and would have tuned his crowd
to us, but unfortunately the two middle strings betwixt the bass and
treble were broke. This man told us that he could play by the book. After
having had my fill of this elegant company, I went to bed att 10 o'clock.

*Friday, June 1st.* The sun rose in a clear horizon, and the air in these
highlands was, for two hours in the morning, very cool and refreshing.
I breakfasted upon some dirty chocolate, but the best that the house
could afford, and took horse about half an hour after six in the morning.
For the first thirteen miles the road seemed gravelly and hilly, and the
land but indifferent.

## SUSQUEHANNA FERRY

When I came near Susquehanna, I looked narrowly in the bottoms for
the gensing but could not discover it. The lower ferry of Susquehanna,
which I crossed, is above a mile broad. It is kept by a little old man
whom I found att vittles with his wife and family upon a homely dish
of fish without any kind of sauce. They desired me to eat, but I told
them I had no stomach. They had no cloth upon the table, and their
mess was in a dirty, deep, wooden dish which they evacuated with their
hands, cramming down skins, scales, and all. They used neither knife,
fork, spoon, plate, or napkin because, I suppose, they had none to use.
I looked upon this as a picture of that primitive simplicity practiced by
our forefathers long before the mechanical arts had supplyed them with
instruments for the luxury and elegance of life. I drank some of their
cider, which was very good, and crossed the ferry in company with a
certain Scots-Irishman by the name Thomas Quiet. The land about
Susquehanna is pretty high and woody, and the channell of the river
rockey.

Mr. Quiet rid a little scrub bay mare which he said was sick and
ailing and could not carry him, and therefore he 'lighted every half mile
and ran a couple of miles att a footman's pace to spell the poor beast
(as he termed it). He informed me he lived att Monocosy and had been
out three weeks in quest of his creatures (horses), four of which had
strayed from his plantation. I condoled his loss and asked him what his
mare's distemper was, resolving to prescribe for her, but all that I could
gett out of him was that the poor silly beast had choaked herself in eating her oats; so I told him that if she was choaked, she was past my art
to recover.

This fellow, I observed, had a particular down-hanging look which made me suspect he was one of our New Light biggots. I guessed right, for he introduced a discourse concerning Whitfield and enlarged pretty much and with some warmth upon the doctrines of that apostle, speaking much in his praise. I took upon me, in a ludicrous manner, to impungn some of his doctrines, which, by degrees, put Mr. Quiet in a passion. He told me flatly that I was damnd without redemption. I replyed that I thought his name and behaviour were very incongruous and desired him to change it with all speed, for it was very improper that such an angry, turbulent mortall as he should be called by the name of Thomas Quiet.

### PRINCIPIO IRON WORKS—NORTH EAST

In the height of this fool's passion, I overtook one Mr. B[axte]r, a proprietor in the iron works there, and, after mutual salutation, the topic of discourse turned from religious controversy to politicks; so putting on a little faster, we left this inflamed bigot and his sick mare behind. This gentleman accompanied me to North East and gave me directions as to the road.

### ELK FERRY

I crossed Elk Ferry att 3 in the afternoon. One of the ferry men, a young fellow, plyed his tongue much faster than his oar. He characterized some of the chief dwellers in the neighbourhood, particularly some young merchants, my countrymen, for whom he had had the honour to stand pimp in their amours. He let me know that he understood some scraps of Latin and repeated a few hexameter lines out of Lilly's Grammar. He told me of a clever fellow of his name who had composed a book for which he would give all the money he was master of to have the pleasure of reading it. I asked him who this namesake of his was. He replied it was one Terence, and, to be sure, he must have been an arch dog, for he never knew one of the name but he was remarkable for his parts.

### BOHEMIA

Thus entertained, I got over the ferry and rode to Bohemia, and calling att the manor house there, I found nobody att home. I met here a reverend parson who was somewhat inquisitive as to where I came from and the news, but I was not very communicative. I understood afterwards it was Parson Wye.

### BOHEMIA FERRY

I crossed Bohemia Ferry and lodged at the ferry house. The landlord's name I cannot remember, but he seemed to be a man of tollerable parts for one in his station. Our conversation ran chiefly upon religion. He gave me a short account of the spirit of enthusiasm that had lately possessed the inhabitants of the forrests there and informed me that it had been a common practice for companies of 20 or 30 hare-brained fanaticks to ride thro' the woods singing of psalms. I went to bed att 9 att night; my landlord, his wife, daughters, and I lay all in one room.

*Saturday, June 2d.* In the morning there was a clear sky overhead but a foggy horizon and the wind att south, which presaging heat, I set out very early.

## SASSAFRAX FERRY

I took the road to Newtown upon Chester River, crossed Sassafrax Ferry at 7 o'clock in the morning, where I found a great concourse of people att a fair. The roads here are exceeding good and even, but dusty in the summer and deep in the winter season. The day proved very hot. I encountered no company, and I went three or four miles out of my way.

## NEWTOWN

I reached Newtown at 12 o'clock and put up att Dougherty's, a publick house there. I was scarce arrived when I met severall of my acquaintance. I dined with Dr. Anderson and spent the rest of the day in a sauntering manner. The northern post arrived att night. I read the papers but found nothing of consequence in them; so after some comicall chat with my landlord, I went to bed at eleven o'clock att night.

*Sunday, June 3d.* I stayed all this day att Newtown and breakfasted with Th. Clay, where I met with one W——b, a man of the law, to appearance a civil, good natured man but set up for a kind of connoisseur in many things. I went to visit some friends and dined att the taveren where I was entertained by the tricks of a female baboon in the yard. This lady had more attendants and hangers-on att her levee than the best person (of quality as I may say) in town. She was very fond of the compliments and company of the men and boys but expressed in her gestures an utter aversion att women and girls, especially negroes of that sex—the lady herself being of a black complexion; yet she did not att all affect her countrywomen.

At night I was treated by Captain Binning of Boston with a bowl of lemmon punch. He gave me letters for his relations att Boston. Whiele we put about the bowl, a deal of comicall discourse pass'd in which the landlord, a man of a particular talent att telling comic storys, bore the chief part.

*Monday, June 4th.* The morning being clear and somewhat cool, I got up before 5 o'clock and soon mounted horse. I had a solitary route to Bohemia and went very much out of my way by being too particular and nice in observing directions.

## SASSAFRAX AND BOHEMIA FERRIES

I reached Mr. Alexander's house on the mannor att 12 o'clock. There I
stayed and dined and drank tea with Miss C[ours]ey. After some talk
and laugh, I took my leave att 5 o'clock designing 12 miles farther to
one Vanbibber's that keeps a house upon the Newcastle road, but
instead of going there, I went out of my way and lay att one Hollings-
worth's att the head of Elk.

## HEAD OF ELK

There is a great marsh upon the left hand of his house, which I passed
in the night, thro' the middle of which runs Elk. The multitude of fire-
flys glittering in the dark upon the surface of this marshe makes it
appear like a great plain scattered over with spangles.

In this part of the country I found they chiefly cultivated British
grain, as wheat, barley, and oats. They raise, too, a great deal of flax,
and in every house here the women have two or three spinning wheels
a going. The roads up this way are tollerably levell but, in some places,
stoney. After a light supper I went to bed att 10 o'clock.

## PENNSYLVANIA—NEWCASTLE

*Tuesday, June 5th.* I took horse a little after 5 in the morning, and after
a solitary ride thro' stoney, unequall road, where the country people
stared att me like sheep when I inquired of them the way, I arrived att
Newcastle upon Delaware att 9 o'clock in the morning and baited my
horses att one Curtis's att the Sign of the Indian King, a good house of
entertainment.

This town stands upon stoney ground just upon the water, there being
from thence a large prospect eastward towards the Bay of Delaware and
the province of the Jerseys. The houses are chiefly brick, built after the
Dutch modell, the town having been originally founded and inhabited
by the Dutch when it belonged to New York government. It consists
chiefly of one great street which makes an elbow att right angles. A
great many of the houses are old and crazy. There is in the town two
publick buildings, viz., a court house and church.

Att Curtis's I met company going to Philadelphia and was pleased att
it, being myself an utter stranger to the roads. This company consisted of
three men: Thomas Howard, Timothy Smith, and William Morison. I
treated them with some lemmon punch and desired the favour of their
company. They readily granted my request and stayed some time for me
till I had eat breakfast. Smith, in his hat and coat, had the appearance
of a Quaker, but his discourse was purged of thee's and thou's tho' his
delivery seemed to be solemn and slow paced. Howard was a talkative
man, abounding with words and profuse in compliments which were

generally blunt and came out in an awkward manner. He bestowed much panegyrick upon his own behaviour and conduct.

Morison (who, I understood, had been att the Land Office in Annapolis inquiring about a title he had to some land in Maryland) was a very rough-spun, forward, clownish blade, much addicted to swearing, att the same time desirous to pass for a gentleman; notwithstanding which ambition, the conscientiousness of his naturall boorishness obliged him frequently to frame ill-tim'd apologys for his misbehaviour, which he termed frankness and freeness. It was often, "Damn me, gentlemen, excuse me; I am a plain, honest fellow; all is right down plain dealing, by God." He was much affronted with the landlady att Curtis's who, seeing him in a greasy jacket and breeches and a dirty worsted cap, and withall a heavy, forward, clownish air and behaviour, I suppose took him for some ploughman or carman and so presented him with some scraps of cold veal for breakfast, he having declared he could not drink "your damned washy tea." As soon as he saw his mess he swore, "Damn him, if it wa'nt out of respect to the gentleman in company" (meaning me) he would throw her cold scraps out at the window and break her table all to pieces should it cost him 100 pounds for dammages. Then taking off his worsted nightcap, he pulled a linnen one out of his pocket and clapping it upon his head, "Now," says he, "I'm upon the borders of Pennsylvania and must look like a gentleman; 'tother was good enough for Maryland, and damn my blood if ever I come into that rascally province again if I don't procure a leather jacket that I may be in a trim to box the saucy jacks there and not run the hazard of tearing my coat." This showed, by the bye, that he paid more regard to his coat than his person, a remarkable instance of modesty and self denyall.

He then made a transition to politicks and damned the late Sr. R[obert] W[alpole] for a rascall. We asked him his reasons for cursing Sir Robert, but he would give us no other but this, that he was certainly informed by some very good gentlemen, who understood the thing right well, that he said Sr. Robert was a damnd rogue. And att the conclusion of each rodomontade, he told us that tho' he seemed to be but a plain, homely fellow, yet he would have us know that he was able to afford better than many that went finer: he had good linnen in his bags, a pair of silver buckles, silver clasps, and gold sleeve buttons, two Holland shirts, and some neat nightcaps; and that his little woman att home drank tea twice a day; and he himself lived very well and expected to live better so soon as that old rogue B——t dyed and he could secure a title to his land.

The chief topic of conversation among these three Pennsylvanian dons upon the road was the insignificancy of the neighbouring province of Maryland when compared to that of Pennsylvania. They laid out all the advantages of the latter which their bungling judgement could suggest and displayed all the imperfections and disadvantages of the first. They enlarged upon the immorality, drunkenness, rudeness and immoderate swearing so much practiced in Maryland and added that no such vices were to be found in Pennsylvania. I heard this and contradicted it not, because I knew that the first part of the proposition was pretty true. They next fell upon the goodness of the soil as far more productive of pasturage and grain. I was silent here likewise, because the first proposition was true, but as to the other relating to grain, I doubted the truth of it. But what appeared most comical in their criticisms was their making a merit of the stonnyness of the roads. "One may ride," says Howard, "50 miles in Maryland and not see as many stones upon the roads as in 50 paces of road in Pennsylvania." This I knew to be false, but as I thought there was no advantage in stony roads, I even let them take the honour of it to themselves and did not contradict them.

Att Newcastle I heard news of Mr. Hasel, my intended fellow traveler. They told me he was att Willmington upon Cristin River.

### CRISTIN FERRY—WILLMINGTON—BRANDYWINE

We crossed that ferry att twelve o'clock and saw Willmington about a mile to the left hand. It is about the largeness of Annapolis but seemingly more compactly built, the houses all brick. We rid seven miles farther to one Foord's, passing over a toll bridge in bad repair att a place called Brandywine. Att Foord's we dined and baited our horses. There one Usher, a clergyman, joined our company, a man seemingly of good natural parts and civil behaviour but not overlearned for the cloth. While dinner was getting ready, a certain Philadelphian merchant called on Mr. Howard, and with him we had a dish of swearing and loud talking.

After dinner we fell upon politicks, and the expected French war naturally came in, whence arose a learned dispute in company which was about settling the meaning of the two words, declaration and proclamation. Mr. Smith asserted that a proclamation of war was an impropper phrase, and that it ought to be a declaration of war, and on the other hand, a proclamation of peace. Mr. Morison affirmed with a bloody oath that there might be such a thing as a proclamation of a declaration and swore heartily that he knew it to be true both by experience and hearsay. They grew very loud upon it as they put about the bowl, and I retired into a corner of the room to laugh a little, handkerchief fashion, pretending to be busied in blowing my nose; so I slurded laugh with nose-blowing as people sometimes do a fart with coughing.

At last the parson determined all by a learned definition to this purpose: that a proclamation was a publication of anything by authority, and a declaration only a simple declaring of anything without any authority, at all but the bare assertion of a certain fact, as if I should declare that such a one was drunk att such a time, or that such a person swore so and so.

This dispute ended, we took our horses and rode moderately, it being excessive hot. I observed the common stile of salutation upon the road here was How d'ye? and How is 't?

The people all along the road were making of hay which, being green and piled up in rucks, cast a very sweet and agreeable smell. There are here as fine meadows and pasture grounds as any ever I saw in England. The country here is not hilly, nor are the woods very tall or thick. The people in generall follow farming and have very neat, brick dwelling houses upon their farms.

### CHESTER

We passed thro' Chester att 7 o'clock att night, where we left Morison, Smith, and Howard, and the parson and I jogged on intending to reach Darby, a town about 9 or 10 miles from Chester. Chester is a pretty, neat, and large village, built chiefly of brick, pleasantly situated upon a small river of the same name that discharges itself into Delaware about half a mile below where the village stands. Over this river is a wooden bridge built with large rafters and plank in form of an arch. The State House is a pretty enough building. This put me in mind of Chelsea near London, which it resembles for neatness but is not near so large.

### DARBY

The parson and I arrived att Darby, our resting place, att half an hour after eight att night. This village stands in a bottom and partly upon the ascent of a hill which makes it have a dull, melancholly appearance. We put up att a publick house kept by one Thomas where the landlady looked after everything herself, the landlord being drunk as a lord. The liquor had a very strange effect upon him, having deprived him of the use of his tongue. He sat motionless in a corner smoking his pipe and would have made a pretty good figure upon arras.

We were entertained with an elegant dispute between a young Quaker and the boatswain of a privateer concerning the lawfullness of using arms against an enemy. The Quaker thee'd and thou'd it thro' the nose to perfection, and the privateer's boatswain swore just like the boatswain of a privateer, but they were so far from settling the point that the Quaker had almost acted contrary to his principles, clenching his fist att his antagonist to strike him for bidding God damn him. Att nine Mr. Usher and I went to bed.

### SKUYLKILL FERRY

*Wednesday, June 6th.* We mounted horse att 5 in the morning, crossed

Skuylkill Ferry att 6, and in half an hour more put up our horses att one Cockburn's att the Sign of the Three Tons in Chestnut Street.

## PHILADELPHIA

The country round the city of Philadelphia is level and pleasant, having a prospect of the large river of Delaware and the province of East Jersey upon the other side. You have an agreeable view of this river for most of the way betwixt Philadelphia and Newcastle. The plan or platform of the city lyes betwixt the two rivers of Delaware and Skuylkill, the streets being laid out in rectangular squares which makes a regular, uniform plan, but upon that account, altogether destitute of variety.

Att my entering the city, I observed the regularity of the streets, but att the same time the majority of the houses mean and low and much decayed, the streets in generall not paved, very dirty, and obstructed with rubbish and lumber, but their frequent building excuses that. The State House, Assembly House, the great church in Second Street, and Whitefield's church are good buildings.

I observed several comicall grotesque phizzes in the inn where I put up which would have afforded variety of hints for a painter of Hogarth's turn. They talked there upon all subjects—politicks, religion, and trade —some tollerably well, but most of them ignorantly. I discovered two or three chaps very inquisitive, asking my boy who I was, whence come, and whither bound.

I was shaved by a little, finicall, humpbacked old barber who kept dancing round me and talking all the time of the operation and yet did his job lightly and to a hair. He abounded in compliments and was a very civil fellow in his way. He told me he had been a journeyman to the business for 40 odd years, notwithstanding which, he understood how to trim gentlemen as well (thank God) as the best masters and despaired not of preferment before he dyed.

I delivered my letters, went to dine with Collector Alexander, and visited severall people in town. In the afternoon I went to the coffee house where I was introduced by Dr. Thomas Bond to severall gentlemen of the place, where the ceremony of shaking of hands, an old custom peculiar to the English, was performed with great gravity and the usuall compliments. I took private lodgings att Mrs. Cume's in Chestnut Street.

*Thursday, June 7th.* I remarked one instance of industry as soon as I got up and looked out att my chamber window, and that was the shops open att 5 in the morning. I breakfasted with Mrs. Cume and dined by invitation with Dr. Thomas Bond where, after some talk upon physicall matters, he showed me some pretty good anatomical preparations of the muscles and blood vessels injected with wax.

After dinner Mr. Venables, a Barbadian gentleman, came in who, when we casually had mentioned the free masons, began to rail bitterly against that society as an impudent, assuming, and vain caball pretending to be wiser than all mankind besides, an *imperium in imperio,* and therefor justly to be discouraged and suppressed as they had lately been in some foreign countrys. Tho' I am no free mason myself, I could not agree with this gentleman, for I abhorr all tyrannicall and arbitrary notions. I believe the free masons to be an innocent and harmless society that have in their constitution nothing mysterious or beyond the verge of common human understanding, and their secret which has made such a noise, I imagine is just no secret att all.

In the evening att the coffee house, I met Mr. Hasell, and inquiring how he did and how he had fared on his way, he replied as to health he was pretty well, but he had almost been devoured with bugs and other vermin and had met with mean, low company which had made him very uneasy. He added that he had heard good news from Barbadoes concerning his friends there—from one, who he imagined called himself Captain Scrotum, a strange name indeed, but this gentleman had always some comicall turn in his discourse. I parted with him and went to the tavern with Mr. Currie and some Scots gentlemen where we spent the night agreeably and went home sober att eleven o'clock.

*Friday, June 8.* I read Montaign's Essays in the forenoon which is a strange medley of subjects and particularly entertaining.

I dined att a tavern with a very mixed company of different nations and religions. There were Scots, English, Dutch, Germans, and Irish; there were Roman Catholicks, Church men, Presbyterians, Quakers, Newlightmen, Methodists, Seventh-day men, Moravians, Anabaptists, and one Jew. The whole company consisted of 25 planted round an oblong table in a great hall well stoked with flys. The company divided into committees in conversation; the prevailing topick was politicks and conjectures of a French war. A knott of Quakers there talked only about selling of flour and the low price it bore. They touch a little upon religion, and high words arose among some of the sectaries, but their blood was not hot enough to quarrell, or, to speak in the canting phraze, their zeal wanted fervency. A gentleman that sat next me proposed a number of questions concerning Maryland, understanding I had come from thence. In my replys I was reserved, pretending to know little of the matter as being a person whose business did not lye in the way of history and politicks.

In the afternoon I went to see some ships that lay in the river. Among the rest were three vessels a fitting out for privateers—a ship, a sloop, and a schooner. The ship was a large vessel, very high and full rigged; one Capt. Mackey intended to command her upon the cruise. Att 6 o'clock I went to the coffee house and drank a dish of coffee with Mr. Hasell.

After staying there an hour or two, I was introduced by Dr. Phineas Bond into the Governour's Club, a society of gentlemen that met at a taveren every night and converse on various subjects. The Governour gives them his presence once a week, which is generally upon Wednesday, so that I did not see him there. Our conversation was entertaining; the subject was the English poets and some of the foreign writers, particularly Cervantes, author of Don Quixote, whom we loaded with elogiums due to his character. Att eleven o'clock I left this club and went to my lodging.

*Saturday, June 9th.* This morning there fell a light rain which proved very refreshing, the weather having been very hot and dry for severall days. The heat in this city is excessive, the sun's rays being reflected with such power from the brick houses and from the street pavement which is brick. The people commonly use awnings of painted cloth or duck over their shop doors and windows and, att sunset, throw buckets full of water upon the pavement which gives a sensible cool. They are stocked with plenty of excellent water in this city, there being a pump att almost every 50 paces distance. There are a great number of balconies to their houses where sometimes the men sit in a cool habit and smoke.

The market in this city is perhaps the largest in North America. It is kept twice a week upon Wednesdays and Saturdays. The street where it stands, called Market Street, is large and spacious, composed of the best houses in the city.

They have but one publick clock here which strikes the hour but has neither index nor dial plate. It is strange they should want such an ornament and conveniency in so large a place, but the chief part of the community consisting of Quakers, they would seem to shun ornament in their publick edifices as well as in their apparrell or dress.

The Quakers here have two large meetings, the Church of England one great church in Second Street, and another built for Whitefield in which one Tennent, a fanatick, now preaches, the Romans one chapell, the Anabaptists one or two meetings, and the Presbyterians two.

The Quakers are the richest and the people of greatest interest in this government; of them their House of Assembly is chiefly composed. They have the character of an obstinate, stiff-necked generation and a perpetuall plague to their governours. The present governour, Mr. Thomas, has fallen upon a way to manage them better than any of his predecessors did and, att the same time, keep pretty much in their good graces and share some of their favours. However, the standing or falling of the Quakers in the House of Assembly depends upon their making sure the interest of the Palatines in this province, who of late have turned so numerous that they can sway the votes which way they please.

Here is no publick magazine of arms nor any method of defense, either for city or province, in case of the invasion of an enemy. This is owing to the obstinacy of the Quakers in maintaining their principle of non-resistance. It were a pity but they were put to a sharp triall to see whether they would act as they profess.

I never was in a place so populous where the *goût* for publick gay diversions prevailed so little. There is no such things as assemblys of the gentry among them, either for dancing or musick; these they have had an utter aversion to ever since Whitefield preached among them. Their chief employ, indeed, is traffick and mercantile business which turns their thoughts from these levitys. Some Virginia gentlemen that came here with the Commissioners of the Indian Treaty were desirous of having a ball but could find none of the female sex in a humour for it. Strange influence of religious enthusiasm upon human nature to excite an aversion at these innocent amusements, for the most part so agreeable and entertaining to the young and gay, and indeed, in the opinion of moderate people, so conducive to the improvement of politeness, good manners, and humanity.

I was visited this morning by an acquaintance from Annapolis of whom, inquiring the news, I could not learn anything material.

I dined att the taveren, and returning home after dinner I read part of a book lately written by Fielding entitled *The Adventures of Joseph Andrews*, a masterly performance of its kind and entertaining; the characters of low life here are naturally delineated, and the whole performance is so good that I have not seen anything of that kind equal or excel it.

This proved a rainy afternoon which, because it abated the sultry heat, was agreeable. I drank tea with Collector Alexander, where I saw Mr. Hasell. Their conversation turned upon the people in Barbadoes, and as I knew nothing of the private history of that island, I only sat and heard, for they went upon nothing but private characters and persons. This is a trespass on good manners which many well-bred people fall into thro' inadvertency, two engrossing all the conversation upon a subject which is strange and unknown to a third person there.

At six in the evening I went to my lodging, and looking out att the window, having been led there by a noise in the street, I was entertained by a boxing match between a master and his servant. The master was an unwieldly, pott-gutted fellow, the servant muscular, rawbon'd, and tall; therefore tho' he was his servant in station of life, yet he would have been his master in single combat had not the bystanders asisted the master and help him up as often as the fellow threw him down. The servant, by his dialect, was a Scotsman; the names he gave his master were no better than little bastard, and shitten elf, terms ill apply'd to such a pursy load of flesh. This night proved very rainy.

*Sunday, June 10th.* This proved a very wet morning, and there was a

strange and surprising alteration of the temperature of the air from hot
and dry (to speak in the style of that elegant and learned physician, Dr.
Salmon and some other ancient philosophers) to cold and moist.

I intended to have gone to church, or meeting, to edify by the Word
but was diverted from my good purpose by some polite company I fell
into who were all utter strangers to churches and meetings. But I
understood that my negro Dromo very piously stepped into the Lutheran
church to be edified with a sermon preached in High Dutch, which, I
believe, when dressed up in the fashion of a discourse, he understood
every bit as well as English and so might edify as much with the one as
he could have done with the other.

I dined att a private house with some of my countrymen, but our
table chat was so trivial and trifling that I mention it not. After dinner
I read the second volume of *The Adventures of Joseph Andrews* and
thought my time well spent.

I drank tea with Mrs. Cume at 5 o'clock. There was a lady with her
who gave us an elegant dish of scandal to relish our tea. At 6 o'clock
I went to the coffee house where I saw the same faces I had seen before.
This day we had expresses from N. York which brought instructions to
proclaim war against France, and there was an express immediately
dispatched to Annapolis in Maryland for the same purpose.

*Monday, June 11th.* The morning proved clear, and the air cool and
refreshing, which was a great relaxation and relief after the hot weather
that had preceded. I read Montaigne's Essays in the morning and was
visited by Dr. Lloyd Zachary, a physician in this place.

I dined with Collector Alexander and went in the afternoon in the
company of some gentlemen to attend the Governour to the Court
House stairs where war was publickly to be proclaimed against France.
There were about 200 gentlemen attended Governour Thomas. Coll. Lee
of Virginia walked att his right hand, and Secretary Peters upon his left;
the procession was led by about 30 flags and ensigns taken from
privateer vessels and others in the harbour, which were carried by a
parcell of roaring sailors. They were followed by 8 or 10 drums that
made a confounded martiall noise, but all the instrumental musick they
had was a pitifull scraping negroe fiddle which followed the drums and
could not be heard for the noise and clamour of the people and the rattle
of the drums. There was a rabble of about 4,000 people in the street and
great numbers of ladies and gentlemen in the windows and balconies.
Three ploclamations were read: 1st, the King of England's proclamation
of war against the French king; 2nd, a proclamation for the encouragement of such as should fit out privateers against the enemy; 3rd, the
Governour of Pennsylvania's proclamation for that province in particular, denouncing war and hostility against France.

When Secretary Peters had read these, the Governour, with a very audible voice, desired all such persons as were fit to carry arms to provide themselves—every man with a good musket, cartouche box, powder and shot, and such implements as were requisite either to repel or annoy the enemy if there should be any necessity or occasion—adding that he should surely call upon each of them to see that they were provided. "For depend upon it," says he, "this Province shall not be lost by any neglect or oversight of mine."

The Governour having thus spoke, a certain bold fellow in the crowd with a stentorian voice made this reply. "Please your Honour," says he, "what you say is right, but I and many others here, poor men, have neither money nor credit to procure a musket or the third part of a musket, so that unless the publick takes care to proivde us, the bulk of the people must go unfurnished, and the country be destitute of defense." The Governour made no reply but smiled; so went into his chariot with Coll. Lee and the Secretary and drove homewards.

In the evening I drank tea with Mrs. Cume and went to the coffee house. Att 7 o'clock I went to the Governour's Club where were a good many strangers, among the rest Captain Macky, commander of the privateer ship. The conversation ran chiefly upon trade and the late expedition at Cartagene. Severall toasts were drunk, among which were some celebrated ones of the female sex.

*Tuesday, June 12.* This seemed to me an idle kind of a day, and the heat began to return. I prepared my baggage, intending tomorrow to proceed on my journey towards New York, which city I proposed to be my next resting place. I breakfasted abroad and dined att the taveren where I met another strange medley of company and, among the rest, a trader from Jamaica, a man of an inquisitive disposition who seized me for half an hour, but I was upon the reserve.

I drank tea with Mrs. Cume att 5 o'clock. There was with her a masculine-faced lady, very much pitted with the smallpox. I soon found she was a Presbyterian, and a strait-laced one too. She discovered my religion before I spoke. "You, sir," said she, "was educated a Presbyterian, and I hope you are not like most of your countrymen of that perswasion who, when they come abroad in the world, shamefully leave the meeting and go to church." I told her that I had dealt impartially betwixt both since I came to the place, for I had gone to neither. "That is still worse," said she.

I found this lady pretty well versed in the church history of Maryland. "I am surprized," said she, "how your goverment can suffer such a rascally clergy. Maryland has become a receptacle and, as it were, a common shore for all the filth and scum of that order. I am informed that taylors, cobblers, blacksmiths, and such fellows, when they cannot live like gentlemen by their trade in that place, go home to take orders of some latitudinarian bishop and return learned preachers, setting up for teachers of the people, that have more need of schooling themselves; but that might bear some excuse if their lives were exemplary and their morals good, but many of them are more compleatly wicked than the most profligate and meanest of the laity. It is a shame that such fellows should be inducted into good livings without any further ceremony or inquiry about them than a recommendation from Lord Baltimore.

"The English think fit sometimes to be very merry upon the ignorance and stupidity of our Presbyterian clerks. I am sorry indeed that it is too true that many of them have exposed themselves in ridiculous colours, but, notwithstanding this, can the generality of their clergy, as wise and learned as they are, show such good behaviour and moral life? Besides, generally speaking, in Scotland where the Presbyterian constitution is the national church, they admitt none now to holy orders who have not had a college education, studied divinity regularly, and undergone a thorough examination before a presbytery of clerks. Do the English do so? No, their inferior clergy are rascally fellows who have neither had a fit education nor had their knowledge put to the tryall by examination, but undergoing some foolish ceremony or farce from a bishop, commence teachers presently and prove afterwards inferior to none for ignorance and vice. Such are your Maryland clerks."

I heard this long harangue with patience and attempted to speak in defense of our clergy, but this lady's instructions bore such credit with her that she would not be contradicted. I quoted the maxim of Constantine the Great who used to say that when a clergyman offended, he would cover him with his cloak; but her charity for the order, I found, did not extend so far; so I allowed her to run on in this kind of criticall declamation till her stock was exhausted.

I must make a few remarks before I leave this place. The people in generall are inquisitive concerning strangers. If they find one comes there upon the account of trade or traffic, they are fond of dealing with him and cheating him if they can. If he comes for pleasure or curiosity, they take little or no notice of him unless he be a person of more than ordinary rank; then they know as well as others how to fawn and cringe. Some persons there were inquisitive about the state of religion in Maryland. My common reply to such questions was that I studied their constitutions more than their consciences so knew something of the first but nothing of the latter.

They have in generall a bad notion of their neighbouring province, Maryland, esteeming the people a sett of cunning sharpers; but my notion of the affair is that the Pennsylvanians are not a whit inferior to them in the science of chicane, only their method of tricking is different. A Pennsylvanian will tell a lye with a sanctified, solemn face; a Marylander, perhaps, will convey his fib in a volley of oaths; but the effect and point in view is the same tho' the manner of operating be different.

In this city one may live tollerably cheap as to the articles of eating and drinking, but European goods here are extravagantly dear. Even goods of their own manufacture such as linnen, woolen, and leather bear a high price. Their government is a kind of anarchy (or no government), there being perpetual jarrs betwixt the two parts of the legislature. But that is no strange thing, the ambition and avarice of a few men in both partys being the active springs in these dissentions and altercations, tho' a specious story about the good and interest of the country is trumpt up by both; yet I would not be so severe as to say so of all in generall.

Mr. Thomas, the present governour, I believe is an upright man and has the interest of the province really att heart, having done more for the good of that obstinate generation, the Quakers, than any of his predecessours have done. Neither are they so blind as not to see it, for he shares more of their respect than any of their former governours were wont to do.

There is polite conversation here among the better sort, among whom there is no scarcity of men of learning and good sense. The ladies, for the most part, keep att home and seldom appear in the streets, never in publick assemblies except att the churches or meetings; therefor I cannot with certainty enlarge upon their charms, having had little or no opportunity to see them either congregated or separate, but to be sure the Philadelphian dames are as handsome as their neighbours.

The staple of this province is bread, flower, and pork. They make no tobacco but a little for their own use. The country is generally plain and levell, fruitfull in grain and fruits, pretty well watered, and abounding in woods backward. It is upon the growing hand, more than any of the provinces of America. The Germans and high Dutch are of late become very numerous here.

*Wednesday, June 13.* Early in the morning I set out from Philadelphia, being willing to depart that city where, upon account of the excessive heat, it was a pain to live and breathe. Two gentlemen of the city, Mr. Currie and Mr. Wallace, complimented me with their company 5 miles of the road. I remarked in the neighbourhood of Philadelphia some stone bridges, the first that I had seen in America. The country people whom I met asked in generall whether war had been proclaimed against France.

#### SHAMANY FERRY—BRISTO

About 9 in the morning I crossed Shamany Ferry and half an hour after rested at Bristo, a small town 20 miles N. East of Philadelphia situated upon Delaware River, opposite to which upon the other side of the river stands Burlington, the chief town in the East Jerseys.

I put up my horses in Bristo and breakfasted att Malachi Walton's att the Sign of the Crown, intending to tarry till the cool of the evening and then proceed to Trenton about 10 miles farther. Bristo is pleasantly situated and consists of one street that runs upon a descent towards the river and then, making an angle or elbow, runs parallel to the river for about a quarter of a mile. Here are some wharfs, pretty commodious, for small vessels to load and unload. The houses in the town are chiefly brick, and the adjacent land pretty levell and woody.

## DELAWARE FERRY—JERSEY GOVERNMENT—TRENTON

I took horse about 5 in the afternoon, crossed the ferry of Delaware about 7 o'clock, and a little after arrived att Trenton in East Jersey. Upon the left hand near the river on the Jersey side is a pretty box of a house, the propperty of Governour Thomas of Pennsylvania, in which Coll. Morris, the present Governour of the Jerseys, lives. Upon the right hand close upon the town is a fine water mill belonging likewise to Collonell Thomas, with a very pretty cascade that falls over the dam like a transparent sheet about 30 yards wide.

I was treated att my entry into the town with a dish of staring and gaping from the shop doors and windows, and I observed two or three people laying hold of Dromo's stirrups, inquiring, I suppose, who I was and whence I came.

I put up att one Eliah Bond's att the Sign of the Wheat Sheaf. Two gentlemen of the town came there and invited me into their company. One was named Cadwaller, a doctor in the place and, as I understood, a fallen-off Quaker. We supped upon cold gammon and a salad. Our discourse was mixed and rambling; att first it was politicall; then Cadwaller gave me the character of the constitution and government. The House of Assembly here, he told me, was chiefly composed of mechanicks and ignorant wretches, obstinate to the last degree; that there were a number of proprietors in the government, and a multitude of Quakers. He enlarged a little in the praise of Governour Morris, who is now a very old man. From politicks the discourse turned to religion and then to physick.

Cadwaller asked me concerning severall people in Maryland, and among the rest (not yet knowing me) he came across myself, asking me if Hamilton att Annapolis was dead or alive. "Here he is," says I, "bodily and not spiritually."

## PERTH AMBOY

At nine in the morning we stoped att the Sign of the King's Arms in Amboy where I breakfasted. As I sat in the porch I observed an antick figure pass by having an old plaid banyan, a pair of thick worsted stockings, ungartered, a greasy worsted nightcap, and no hat. "You see that originall," said the landlord. "He is an old batchellor, and it is his humour to walk the street always in that dress. Tho he makes but a pitifull appearance, yet is he proprietor of most of the houses in town. He is very rich, yet for all that, has no servant but milks his own cow, dresses his own vittles, and feeds his own poultry himself."

Amboy is a small town (it is a very old American city, being older than the city of New York) being a chartered city, much less than our Annapolis, and here frequently the Supream Court and Assembly sit. It has in it one Presbyterian meeting and a pretty large market house, lately built. It is the principall town in New Jersey and appears to be laid out in the shape of a St. George's cross, one main street cutting the other at right angles. 'Tis a seaport, having a good harbour but small trade. They have here the best oysters I have eaten in America. It lyes close upon the water, and the best houses in town are ranged along the water side.

In the Jerseys the people are chiefly Presbyterians and Quakers, and there are so many proprietors that share the lands in New Jersey, and so many doubtfull titles and rights that it creates an inexhaustible and profitable pool for the lawyers.

### AMBOY FERRY—NEW YORK GOVERNMENT—STATEN ISLAND

Att ten o'clock I crossed the ferry to Staten Island where are some miles of pretty stony, sandy, and uneven road. I took notice of one entire stone there about 10 foot high, 12 foot long, and 6 or 7 foot thick. At one end of it grew an oak tree, the trunk of which seemed to adhere or grow to the stone. It lay close by a little cottage which it equalld pretty near in dimensions. I remarked this stone because I had not seen so large a one any where but in the Highlands of Scotland. A great many of the trees here are hung thick with long, hairy, grey moss which, if handsomly oild and powdered and tyed behind with a bag or ribbon, would make a tollerable beau-periwig. In this island are a great many poor, thatched cottages. It is about 18 miles long and 6 or 7 miles broad. It seems to abound with good pasture and is inhabited by farmers. There are in or near it some towns, the chief of which are Kathrin's Town, Cuckold's Town, and Woodbridge.

### NARROWS FERRY

I came to the Narrows att two o'clock and dined att one Corson's that keeps the ferry. The landlady spoke both Dutch and English. I dined upon what I never had eat in my life before—a dish of fryed clams, of which shellfish there is abundance in these parts. As I sat down to dinner I observed a manner of saying grace quite new to me. My landlady and her two daughters put on solemn, devout faces, hanging down their heads and holding up their hands for half a minute. I, who had grace-lessly fallen to without remembering that duty according to a wicked custom I had contracted, sat staring att them with my mouth choak full, but after this short meditation was over, we began to lay about us and stuff down the fryed clams with rye bread and butter. They took such a deal of chawing that we were long att dinner, and the dish began to cool before we had eaten enough. The landlady called for the bedpan. I could not guess what she intended to do with it unless it was to warm her bed to go to sleep after dinner, but I found that it was used by way of a chafing dish to warm our dish of clams. I stared att the novelty for some time, and reaching over for a mug of beer that stood on the opposite side of the table, my bag sleeve catched hold of the handle of the bedpan and unfortunately overset the clams, at which the landlady was a little ruffled and muttered a scrape of Dutch of which I understood not a word except *mynheer*, but I suppose she swore, for she uttered her speech with an emphasis.

After dinner I went on board the ferry boat and, with a pretty good breeze, crossed the Narrows in half an hour to Long Island.

## LONG ISLAND

Att the entry of this bay is a little craggy island about one or two miles long called Coney Island. Before I came to New York Ferry, I rode a byway where, in seven miles' riding, I had 24 gates to open. Dromo, being about 20 paces before me, stopped att a house where, when I came up, I found him discoursing a negroe girl who spoke Dutch to him. "Dis de way to York?" says Dromo. "Yaw, dat is Yarikee," said the wench, pointing to the steeples. "What devil you say?" replies Dromo. "Yaw, *mynheer*," said the wench. "Damme you, what you say?" said Dromo again. "Yaw, yaw," said the girl. "You a damn black bitch," said Dromo and so rode on. The road here for several miles is planted thick upon each side with rows of cherry trees, like hedges, and the lots of land are mostly enclosed with stone fences.

## YORK FERRY

Att 5 in the afternoon I called att one Baker's that keeps the York Ferry where, while I sat waiting for a passage, there came in a man and his wife that were to go over. The woman was a beauty, having a fine complexion and good features, black eyes and hair, and an elegant shape. She had an amorous look, and her eyes, methought, spoke a language which is universally understood. While she sat there her tongue never lay still, and tho' her discourse was of no great importance, yet methought her voice had musick in it, and I was fool enough to be highly pleased to see her smiles att every little impertinence she uttered. She talked of a neighbour of hers that was very ill and said she was sure she would dye, for last night she had dreamt of nothing but white horses and washing of linnen. I heard this stuff with as much pleasure as if Demosthenes or Cicero had been exerting their best talents, but meantime was not so stupid but I knew that it was the fine face and eyes and not the discourse that charmed me. Att six o'clock in the evening I landed att New York.

## NEW YORK

This city make a very fine appearance for above a mile all along the river, and here lyes a great deal of shipping. I put my horses up att one Waghorn's att the Sign of the Cart and Horse. There I fell in with a company of toapers. Among the rest was an old Scotsman, by name Jameson, sheriff of the city, and two aldermen whose names I know not. The Scotsman seemed to be dictator to the company; his talent lay in history, having a particular knack att telling a story. In his narratives he interspersed a particular kind of low wit well known to vulgar under-standings. And having a homely carbuncle kind of a countenance with a hideous knob of a nose, he screwd it into a hundred different forms while he spoke and gave such a strong emphasis to his words that he merely spit in one's face att three or four feet distance, his mouth being plentifully bedewed with salival juice, by the force of the liquor which he drank and the fumes of the tobacco which he smoaked. The com-pany seemed to admire him much, but he set me a staring.

After I had sat some time with this polite company, Dr. Colchoun, surgeon to the fort, called in, to whom I delivered letters, and he carried me to the taveren which is kept by one Todd, an old Scotsman, to supp with the Hungarian Club of which he is a member and which meets there every night. The company were all strangers to me except Mr. Home, Secretary of New Jersey, of whom I had some knowledge, he having been att my house att Annapolis. They saluted me very civilly, and I, as civilly as I could, returned their compliments in neat short speeches such as, "Your very humble servant," "I'm glad to see you," and the like commonplace phrazes used upon such occasions. We went to supper, and our landlord Todd entertained us as he stood waiting with quaint saws and jack pudding speeches. "Praised be God," said he, "as to cuikry, I defaa ony French cuik to ding me, bot a haggis is a dish I wadna tak the trouble to mak. Look ye, gentlemen, there was anes a Frenchman axed his frind to denner. His frind axed him "What ha' ye gotten till eat?' 'Four an' twenty legs of mutton,' quo' he, 'a' sae differently cuiked that ye winna ken whilk is whilk.' Sae whan he gaed there, what deel was it, think ye, but four and twenty sheep's trotters, be God.'" He was going on with this tale of a tub when, very seasonably for the company, the bell, hastily pulled, called him to another room, and a little after we heard him roaring att the stair head, "Damn ye bitch, wharefor winna ye bring a canle?"

After supper they set in for drinking, to which I was averse and there-for sat upon nettles. They filled up bumpers att each round, but I would drink only three which were to the King, Governour Clinton, and Governour Bladen, which last was my own. Two or three toapers in the company seemed to be of opinion that a man could not have a more sociable quality or endowment than to be able to pour down seas of liquor and remain unconquered while others sunk under the table. I heard this philosophical maxim but silently dissented to it. I left the company att 10 att night pretty well flushed with my three bumpers and, ruminating on my folly, went to my lodging att Mrs. Hogg's in Broadstreet.

*Saturday, June 16.* I breakfasted with my landlady's sister, Mrs. Boswall. In the morning Dr. Colchoun called to see me, and he and I made an appointment to dine att Todd's. In the afternoon I took a turn thro' severall of the principall streets in town, guarding against staring about me as much as possible for fear of being remarked for a stranger gaping and staring being the true criterion or proof of rustick strangers in all places.

The following observations occurred to me: I found this city less in extent but, by the stir and frequency upon the streets, more populous than Philadelphia; I saw more shipping in the harbour; the houses are more compact and regular and, in generall, higher built, most of them after the Dutch model with their gravell ends fronting the street. There are a few built of stone, more of wood, but the greatest number of brick, and a great many covered with pan tile and glazed tile with the year of God when built figured out with plates of iron upon the fronts of severall of them. The streets, in generall, are but narrow and not regularly disposed. The best of them run parallell to the river, for the city is built all along the water. In generall this city has more of an urban appearance than Philadelphia. Their wharfs are mostly built with logs of wood piled upon a stone foundation. In the city are severall large public buildings. There is a spacious church belonging to the English congregation with a pretty high but heavy, clumsy steeple built of freestone fronting the street called Broadway. There are two Dutch churches, severall other meetings, and a pretty large Town House at the head of Broadstreet. The Exchange stands near the water and is a wooden structure, going to decay. From it a pier runs into the water, called the Long Bridge, about 50 paces long, covered with plank and supported with large wooden posts. The Jews have one synagogue in this city. The women of fashion here appear more in publick than in Philadelphia and dress much gayer. They come abroad generally in the cool of the evening and go to the Promenade.

I returned to my lodging att 4 o'clock, being pretty much tired with my walk. I found with Mrs. Boswall a handsome young Dutch woman. We drank tea and had a deal of trifling chat, but the presence of a pretty lady, as I hinted before, makes even triffling agreeable. In the evening

I wrote letters to go by the post to Annapolis and att night went and supped with the Hungarian Club att Todd's, where, after the bumpers began to go round according to their laudable custom, we fell upon various conversation in which Todd, standing by, mixed a deal of his clumsy wit which, for the mere stupidity of it, sometimes drew a laugh from the company. Our conversation ended this night with a piece of criticism upon a poem in the newspaper, where one of the company, Mr. Moore, a lawyer, showed more learning than judgment in a disquisition he made upon nominatives and verbs, and the necessity there was for a verb to each nominative in order to make sense.

*Sunday, June 17th.* At breakfast, I found with Mrs. Boswall some gentlemen, among whom was Mr. Jefferys, an officer of the customs in New York. To me he seemed a man of an agreeable conversation and spirit. He had been in Maryland some years agoe and gave me an account of some of his adventures with the planters there. He shewed me a deal of civility and complaisance, carried me to church, and provided me with a pew. The minister who preached to us was a stranger. He gave us a good discourse upon the Christian virtues. There was a large congregation of above a thousand, among which was a number of dressed ladies. This church is above 100 foot long and 80 wide. Att the east end of it is a large semicircular area in which stands the altar, pretty well ornamented with painting and gilding. The gallerys are supported with wooden pillars of the Ionick order with carved work of foliage and cherubs' heads gilt betwixt the capitals. There is a pretty organ att the west end of the church consisting of a great number of pipes handsomly gilt and adorned, but I had not the satisfaction of hearing it play, they having at this time no organist, but the vocall musick of the congregation was very good.

Mr. Jefferys carried me to Mr. Bayard's to dine, and att 4 o'clock we went to the coffee house. I drank tea att a gentlewoman's house, whose name I know not, being introduced there by Mr. Jefferys. There was an old lady and two young ones, her daughters I suppose. The old lady's discourse run upon news and politicks, but the young women sat mute, only now and then smiled att what was said, and Mr. Jefferys enlivened the conversation with repartee.

Att six o'clock I went to see the fort and battery. The castle, or fort, is now in ruins, having been burnt down three or four years ago by the conspirators but they talk of repairing it again. The Lieutenant Governour had here a house and a chapell, and there are fine gardens and walks from which one has a very pretty view of the city. In the fort are severall guns, some of them brass and cast in a handsome mould. The new battery is raised with ramparts of turf, and the guns upon it are in size from 12 to 18 pounders. The main battery is a great half moon or semicircular rampart bluff upon the water, being turf upon a

stone foundation about 100 paces in length, the platform of which is
laid in some places with plank, in others with flagstone. Upon it there
are 56 great iron guns, well mounted, most of them being 32 pounders.
Mr. Jefferys told me that to walk out after dusk upon this platform
was a good way for a stranger to fit himself with a courtezan, for that
place was the generall rendezvous of the fair sex of that profession after
sunset. He told me there was a good choice of pretty lasses among them,
both Dutch and English. However, I was not so abandoned as to go
among them but went and supped with the Club at Todd's.

It appeared that our landlord was drunk, both by his words and
actions. When we called for anything he hastily pulled the bell rope,
and when the servants came up, Todd had by that time forgot what was
called for. Then he gave us a discourse upon law and gospell and swore
by God that he would prove that law was founded upon gospell and
gospell upon law, and that reason was depending upon both, and therefore to be a good lawyer it was substituted to be a good gospeller. We
asked him what such a wicked dog as he had to do with gospell: He
swore by God that he had a soul to be saved as well as the King, and
he would not be hanged for all the Kings in Christendome. After some
taggs of incoherent arguments, he departed the room in wrath, calling
us heathens and infidels. I went home att 12 o'clock.

*Monday, June 18.* Most of this day proved rainy, and therefore I
could not stir much abroad. I dined att Todd's with Dr. Colchoun and a
young gentleman, a stranger. After dinner the doctor and I went to
the coffee house and took a hitt att backgammon. He beat me two
games. Att 5 in the afternoon I drank tea with Mrs. Boswall and went
to the coffee house again, where I looked on while they played att chess.
It continued to rain very hard. This night I shunned company and went
to bed att nine.

*Tuesday, June 19th.* At breakfast with my landlady, I found two
strange gentlemen that had come from Jamaica. They had just such
cloudy countenances as are commonly worn the morning after a
debauch in drinking. Our conversation was a medley, but the chief
subject we went upon was the differences of climates in the American
provinces with relation to the influence they had upon human bodies.
I gave them as just an account as I could of Maryland—the air and
temperature of that province, and the distempers incident to the people
there.

The people of New York att the first appearance of a stranger are
seemingly civil and courteous, but this civility and complaisance soon
relaxes if he be not either highly recommended or a good toaper. To
drink stoutly with the Hungarian Club, who are all bumper men, is
the readiest way for a stranger to recommend himself, and a sett among
them are very fond of making a stranger drunk. To talk bawdy and to

have a knack att punning passes among some there for good sterling wit. Govr. Clinton himself is a jolly toaper and gives good example and, for that one quality, is esteemed among these dons.

The staple of New York is bread flower and skins. It is a very rich place, but it is not so cheap living here as att Philadelphia. They have very bad water in the city, most of it being hard and brackish. Ever since the negroe conspiracy, certain people have been appointed to sell water in the streets, which they carry on a sledge in great casks and bring it from the best springs about the city, for it was when the negroes went for tea water that they held their caballs and consultations, and therefor they have a law now that no negroe shall be seen upon the streets without a lanthorn after dark.

In this city are a mayor, recorder, aldermen, and common council. The goverment is under the English law, but the chief places are possessed by Dutchmen, they composing the best part of the House of Assembly. The Dutch were the first settlers of this province, which is very large and extensive, the States of Holland having purchased the country of one Hudson, who pretended first to have discovered it, but they att last exchanged it with the English for Saranam, and ever since there have been a great number of Dutch here, tho' now their language and customs begin pretty much to wear out and would very soon die were it not for a parcell of Dutch domines here who, in the education of their children, endeavour to preserve the Dutch customs as much as possible. There is as much jarring here betwixt the powers of the legislature as in any of the other American provinces.

They have a diversion here, very common, which is the barbecuing of a turtle, to which sport the chief gentry in town commonly go once or twice a week.

There are a great many handsome women in this city. They appear much more in publick than att Philadelphia. It is customary here to ride thro' the street in light chairs. When the ladys walk the streets in the daytime, they commonly use umbrellas, prettily adorned with feathers and painted.

There are two coffee houses in this city, and the northern and southeren posts go and come here once a week. I was tired of nothing here but their excessive drinking, for in this place you may have the best of company and conversation as well as att Philadelphia.

### BOSTON

I need scarce take notice that Boston is the largest town in North America, being much above the same extent as the city of Glasgow in Scotland and having much the same number of inhabitants, which is between 20 and 30 thousand. It is considerably larger than either Philadelphia or New York, but the streets are irregularly disposed and, in

generall, too narrow. The best street in the town is that which runs
down towards the Long Wharf which goes by the name of King's Street.
This town is a considerable place for shipping and carrys on a great
trade in time of peace. There were now above 100 ships in the harbour
besides a great number of small craft tho' now, upon account of the
war, the times are very dead. The people of this province chiefly follow
farming and merchandise. Their staples are shipping, lumber, and fish.
The goverment is so far democratic as that the election of the Governour's Council and the great officers is made by the members of the
Lower House, or representatives of the people. Mr. Shirly, the present
Governour, is a man of excellent sense and understanding and is very
well respected there. He understands how to humour the people and,
att the same time, acts for the interest of the Government. Boston is
better fortified against an enemy than any port in North America, not
only upon account of the strength of the Castle but the narrow passage
up into the harbour, which is not above 160 foot wide in the channell
att high water.

There are many different religions and perswasions here, but the chief
sect is that of the Presbyterians. There are above 25 churches, chapells
and meetings in the town, but the Quakers here have but a small remnant, having been banished from the province att the first settlement
upon account of some disturbances they raised. The people here have
lately been, and indeed are now, in great confusion and much infested
with enthusiasm from the preaching of some fanaticks and New Light
teachers, but now this humour begins to lessen. The people are generally
more captivated with speculative than with practicall religion. It is not
by half such a flagrant sin to cheat and cozen one's neighbour as it is to
ride about for pleasure on the sabbath day or to neglect going to church
and singing of psalms.

The middling sort of people here are to a degree disingenuous and
dissembling, which appears even in their common conversation in which
their indirect and dubious answers to the plainest and fairest questions
show their suspicions of one another. The better sort are polite, man-
nerly, and hospitable to strangers, such strangers, I mean, as come not
to trade among them (for of them they are jealous). There is more
hospitality and frankness showed here to strangers than either at York
or at Philadelphia. And in the place there is abundance of men of learning and parts; so that one is att no loss for agreeable conversation nor
for any sett of company he pleases. Assemblys of the gayer sort are
frequent here; the gentlemen and ladys meeting almost every week att
concerts of musick and balls. I was present att two or three such and
saw as fine a ring of ladys, as good dancing, and heard musick as elegant
as I had been witness to anywhere. I must take notice that this place
abounds with pretty women who appear rather more abroad than they

do att York and dress elegantly. They are, for the mots part, free and affable as well as pretty. I saw not one prude while I was here.

The paper currency of these provinces is now very much depreciated, and the price or value of silver rises every day, their money being now 6 for one upon sterling. They have a variety of paper currencys in the provinces; viz., that of New Hampshire, the Massachusetts, Rhode Island, and Connecticut, all of different value, divided and subdivided into old and new tenors so that it is a science to know the nature and value of their moneys, and what will cost a stranger some study and application. Dr. Dowglass has writ a compleat treatise upon all the different kinds of paper currencys in America, which I was att the pains to read. It was the expense of the Canada expedition that first brought this province in debt and put them upon the project of issuing bills of credit. Their money is chiefly founded upon land security, but the reason of its falling so much in value is their issuing from time to time such large summs of it and their taking no care to make payments att the expiration of the stated terms. They are notoriously guilty of this in Rhode Island colony so that now it is dangerous to pass their new moneys in the other parts of New England, it being a high penalty to be found so doing. This fraud must light heavy upon posterity. This is the only part ever I knew where gold and silver coin is not uncommonly current.

*Friday, August 17.* I left Boston this mornnig att half an hour after nine o'clock, and nothing I regretted so much as parting with La Moinnerie, the most lively and merry companion ever I had met with, always gay and cheerfull, now dancing and then singing tho' every day in danger of being made a prisoner. This is the peculiar humour of the French in prosperity and adversity. Their temper is always alike, far different from the English, who, upon the least misfortune, are for the most part cloggd and overclouded with melancholly and vapours and, giving way to hard fortune, shun all gaiety and mirth. La Moinnerie was much concerned att my going away and wished me again and again *une bon voyage* and *bon santé,* keeping fast hold of my stirrup for about a quarter of an hour.

### SEABROOK FERRY—SEABROOK

I crossed the ferry att 5 o'clock. This river of Connecticut is navigable for 50 miles up the country. Upon it are a good many large trading towns, but the branches of the river run up above 200 miles. We could see the town of Seabrook below us on the westeren side of the river. I lodged this night att one Mrs. Lay's, a widow woman, who keeps a good house upon the road about 6 miles from Seabrook. I had much difficulty to find the roads upon this side Connecticut River. They wind and turn so much and are divided into such a number of small paths.

I find they are not quite so scrupulous about bestowing titles here as in Maryland. My landlady goes here by the name of Madam Lay. I cannot tell for what, for she is the homeliest piece both as to mein, make, and dress that ever I saw, being a little round-shouldered woman, pale faced and wrinkly, clothed in the coarsest homespun cloth; but it is needless to dispute her right to the title since we know many upon whom it is bestowed who have as little right as she.

*Tuesday, August 28.* I departed Lay's att seven in the morning and rid some miles thro' a rocky highland, the wind blowing pretty sharp and cool att northwest.

## KILLINGSWORTH

A little after eight o'clock I passed thro' Killingsworth, a small town pleasantly situated. I breakfasted att one Scran's about halfway betwixt Killingsworth and Gilfoord. This is a jolly old man, very fat and pursy, and very talkative and full of history. He had been an American soldier in Q. Anne's War and had traveled thro' most of the continent of North America. He inquired of me if poor Dick of Noye was alive, which question I had frequently put to me in my travells.

## GILFOORD

Going from this house I passed thro' Gilfoord att eleven o'clock in company of an old man whom I overtook upon the road. He showed me a curious stone bridge within a quarter of a mile of this town. It lay over a small brook and was one entire stone about 10 foot long, 6 broad, and 8 or 10 inches thick, being naturally bent in the form of an arch without the help of a chisell to cut it into that shape. "Observe here, sir," says the old man, "you may ride 1000 miles and not meet with such a stone." Gilfoord is a pretty town built upon a pleasant plain. In it there is a meeting, upon the steeple of which is a publick clock.

## BRANFOORD

I came to Branfoord, another scattered town built upon high rocky ground, a little after one o'clock, where I dined att the house of one Frazer. Going from thence I passed thro' a pleasant, delightfull part of the country, being a medley of fine green plains, and little rocky and woody hills, capped over, as it were, with bushes.

## NEWHAVEN FERRY—NEWHAVEN

I crossed Newhaven Ferry betwixt 4 and 5 o'clock in the afternoon. This is a pleasant navigable river than runs thro' a spacious green plain into the Sound. I arrived in Newhaven att 5 o'clock, where I put up att one Monson's att the Sign of the Half Moon. There is but little good liquor to be had in the publick houses upon this road. A man's horses are better provided for than himself, but he pays dear for it. The publick house keepers seem to be somewhat wild and shy when a stranger calls. It is with difficulty you can get them to speak to you, show you a room, or ask you what you would have, but they will gape and stare when you speak as if they were quite astonished.

*Wednesday, September 12.* I was waked this morning before sunrise with a strange bawling and hollering without doors. It was the landlord ordering his negroes with an imperious and exalted voice. In his orders the known term or epithet, son of a bitch, was often repeated.

I came downstairs and found one Mr. White, a Philadelphian, and the loggerheaded fellow that supped with us last night ordering some tea for breakfast. Mr. Mason, among other judicious questions, asked me how cheeses sold in Maryland. I told him I understood nothing of that kind of merchandize but if he wanted to know the price of cathar-ticks and emeticks there, I could inform him. He asked me what sort of commoditys these were. I replied that it was a particular kind of truck which I dealt in. When our tea was made it was such abominable stuff that I could not drink of it but drank a porringer of milk.

### PITSCATUAY

We set off att seven o'clock and before nine passed thro' a place called Pitscatuay about 3 miles from Brunswick. I have observed that severall places upon the American main go by that name. The country here is pleasant and levell, intermixed with skirts of woods and meadow ground, the road in generall good but stony in some places.

*Wednesday, September 19.* Today I resolved to take my departure from this town. In the morning my barber came to shave me and almost made me sick with his Irish brogue and stinking breath. He told me that he was very glad to see that I was after being of the right religion. I asked him how he came to know what religion I was of. "Ohon! and sweet Jesus now!" said he, "As if I had not seen your Honour at the Roman Catholic chapell coming upon Sunday last." Then he run out upon a blundering encomium concerning the Catholicks and their prin-ciples. I dined with Mr. Alexander, and taking my leave of him and his wife, I went to Mr. Strider's in Front Street where I had some commis-sions to deliver to Mr. Tasker att Annapolis, and taking horse att half an hour after three o'clock, I left Philadelphia and crossed Skuylkill Ferry at a quarter after four. I passed thro' the town of Darby about an hour before sunset.

### CHESTER

About the time of the sun's going down, the air turned very sharp, it being a degree of frost. I arrived in Chester about half an hour after seven, riding into town in company with an Irish teague who overtook me on the road. Here I put up att one Mather's, an Irishman att the Sign of the Ship.

Att my seeing of the city of Philadelphia, I conceived a quite different notion of both city and inhabitants from that which I had before from the account or description of others. I could not apprehend this city to be so very elegant or pretty as it is commonly represented. In its present situation it is much like one of our country market towns in England. When you are in it the majority of the buildings appear low and mean, the streets unpaved, and therefor full of rubbish and mire. It makes but an indifferent appearance att a distance, there being no turrets or steeples to set it off to advantage, but I believe that in a few years hence it will be a great and a flourishing place and the chief city in North America. The people are much more polite, generally speaking, than I apprehended them to be from the common account of travelers. They have that accomplishment peculiar to all our American colonys, viz., subtlety and craft in their dealings. They apply themselves strenuously to business, having little or no turn towards gaiety (and I know not indeed how they should since there are few people here of independent fortunes or of high luxurious taste). Drinking here is not att all in vogue, and in the place there is pretty good company and conversation to be had. It is a degree politer than New York tho' in its fabrick not so urban, but Boston excels both for politeness and urbanity tho' only a town.

*Thursday, September 20th.* I set out att nine o'clock from Mather's and about two miles from Chester was overtaken by a Quaker, one of the politest and best behaved of that kidney ever I had met with. We had a deal of discourse about news and politicks, and after riding 4 miles together we parted. I now entered the confines of the three notched road by which I knew I was near Maryland. Immediately upon this something ominous happened, which was my man's tumbling down, flump, two or three times, horse and baggage and all, in the middle of a plain road. I likewise could not help thinking that my state of health was changed for the worse upon it.

# Autobiography

## *Benjamin Franklin*

*Probably no American perfected a literary style comparable to Franklin's and yet produced so few books. Franklin wrote an impressive number of sketches, newspaper articles, letters and scientific papers, but he is a man of only one book: his* Autobiography—*and it was never finished. It consists of three parts: the first written in 1771, the second in 1784 and the third part in 1788. The first section, dealing with his early years of struggle, was written for the instruction of his illegitimate son, William Franklin. The second part, written after Franklin had become world famous, was intended for the public: here the emphasis is upon the self-conscious preaching of virtue and the methods of "arriving at moral perfection." In the final section, begun a few years before Franklin's death, the effects of age are apparent: the old spontaneity and wit are lacking.*

*Franklin was a natural autobiographer. Carl Van Doren has made a large volume by piecing together the autobiographical portions of Franklin's writings. Fragment though it is, Franklin's* Autobiography *is the most widely read work of its kind in literature. Few men, including the great religious teachers, have left a more deeply etched and finely drawn impress of their personality.*

TWYFORD, AT THE BISHOP OF ST. ASAPH'S, 1771

Dear Son: I have ever had pleasure in obtaining any little anecdotes of my ancestors. You may remember the inquiries I made among the remains of my relations when you were with me in England, and the journey I undertook for that purpose. Imagining it may be equally agreeable to you to know the circumstances of my life, many of which you are yet unacquainted with, and expecting the enjoyment of a week's uninterrupted leisure in my present country retirement, I sit down to write them for you. To which I have besides some other inducements. Having emerged from the poverty and obscurity in which I was born

*The Writings of Benjamin Franklin.* Edited by Albert H. Smyth.

and bred, to a state of affluence and some degree of reputation in the world, and having gone so far through life with a considerable share of felicity, the conducing means I made use of, which with the blessing of God so well succeeded, my posterity may like to know, as they may find some of them suitable to their own situations, and therefore fit to be imitated.

That felicity, when I reflected on it, has induced me sometimes to say that, were it offered to my choice, I should have no objection to a repetition of the same life from its beginning, only asking the advantages authors have in a second edition to correct some faults of the first. So I might, besides correcting the faults, change some sinister accidents and events of it for others more favorable. But, though this were denied, I should still accept the offer. Since such a repetition is not to be expected, the next thing most like living one's life over again seems to be a recollection of that life, and to make that recollection as durable as possible by putting it down in writing.

Hereby, too, I shall indulge the inclination so natural in old men to be talking of themselves and their own past actions; and I shall indulge it without being tiresome to others, who, through respect to age, might conceive themselves obliged to give me a hearing, since this may be read or not as anyone pleases. And, lastly (I may as well confess it, since my denial of it will be believed by nobody), perhaps I shall a good deal gratify my own *vanity*. Indeed, I scarce ever heard or saw the introductory words, "Without vanity I may say," etc., but some vain thing immediately followed. Most people dislike vanity in others, whatever share they have of it themselves; but I give it fair quarter wherever I meet with it, being persuaded that it is often productive of good to the possessor and to others that are within his sphere of action; and therefore, in many cases, it would not be altogether absurd if a man were to thank God for his vanity among the other comforts of life. . . .

Josiah, my father, married young, and carried his wife with three children into New England, about 1682. The conventicles having been forbidden by law, and frequently disturbed, induced some considerable men of his acquaintance to remove to that country, and he was prevailed with to accompany them thither, where they expected to enjoy their mode of religion with freedom. By the same wife he had four children more born there, and by a second wife ten more, in all seventeen; of which I remember thirteen sitting at one time at his table, who all grew up to be men and women, and married; I was the youngest son, and the youngest child but two, and was born in Boston, New England. My mother, the second wife, was Abiah Folger, daughter of Peter Folger, one of the first settlers of New England, of whom honorable mention is made by Cotton Mather in his church history of that country, entitled *Magnalia Christi Americana*, as "a godly, learned

Englishman," if I remember the words rightly. I have heard that he wrote sundry small occasional pieces, but only one of them was printed, which I saw now many years since. It was written in 1675, in the home-spun verse of that time and people, and addressed to those then concerned in the government there. It was in favor of liberty of conscience, and in behalf of the Baptists, Quakers, and other sectaries that had been under persecution, ascribing the Indian wars, and other distresses that had befallen the country, to that persecution, as so many judgments of God to punish so heinous an offense, and exhorting a repeal of those uncharitable laws. The whole appeared to me as written with a good deal of decent plainness and manly freedom. The six concluding lines I remember, though I have forgotten the two first of the stanza; but the purport of them was that his censures proceeded from good-will, and, therefore, he would be known to be the author.

> Because to be a libeler (says he)
>   I hate it with my heart;
> From Sherburne town, where now I dwell
>   My name I do put here;
> Without offense your real friend,
>   It is Peter Folgier.

My elder brothers were all put apprentices to different trades. I was put to the grammar school at eight years of age, my father intending to devote me, as the tithe of his sons, to the service of the Church. My early readiness in learning to read (which must have been very early, as I do not remember when I could not read), and the opinion of all his friends, that I should certainly make a good scholar, encouraged him in this purpose of his. My uncle Benjamin, too, approved of it, and proposed to give me all his shorthand volumes of sermons, I suppose as a stock to set up with, if I would learn his character. I continued, however, at the grammar school not quite one year, though in that time I had risen gradually from the middle of the class of that year to be head of it, and farther was removed into the next class above it, in order to go with that into the third at the end of the year. But my father, in the meantime, from a view of the expense of a college education, which, having so large a family, he could not well afford, and the mean living many so educated were afterwards able to obtain—reasons that he gave to his friends in my hearing—altered his first intention, took me from the grammar school, and sent me to a school for writing and arithmetic, kept by a then famous man, Mr. George Brownell, very successful in his profession generally, and that by mild, encouraging methods. Under him I acquired fair writing pretty soon, but I failed in the arithmetic, and made no progress in it. At ten years old I was taken home to assist my father in his business, which was that of a tallow chandler and soap-boiler, a business he was not bred to, but had assumed on his arrival in New England and on finding his dyeing trade would not maintain his family, being in little request. Accordingly, I was employed in cutting wick for the candles, filling the dipping mold and the molds for cast candles, attending the shop, going of errands, etc.

I disliked the trade, and had a strong inclination for the sea, but my father declared against it; however, living near the water, I was much in and about it, learnt early to swim well, and to manage boats; and when in a boat or canoe with other boys, I was commonly allowed to govern, especially in any case of difficulty; and upon other occasions I was generally a leader among the boys, and sometimes led them into scraps, of which I will mention one instance, as it shows an early projecting public spirit, though not then justly conducted.

There was a salt marsh that bounded part of the mill pond, on the edge of which, at high water, we used to stand to fish for minnows. By much ramping we had made it a mere quagmire. My proposal was to build a wharf there fit for us to stand upon, and I showed my comrades a large heap of stones, which were intended for a new house near the marsh, and which would very well suit our purpose. Accordingly, in the evening, when the workmen were gone, I assembled a number of my playfellows, and, working with them diligently like so many emmets, sometimes two or three to a stone, we brought them all away and built our little wharf. The next morning the workmen were surprised at missing the stones, which were found in our wharf. Inquiry was made after the removes; we were discovered and complained of; several of us were corrected by our fathers; and, though I pleaded the usefulness of the work, mine convinced me that nothing was useful which was not honest. . . .

From a child I was fond of reading, and all the little money that came into my hands was ever laid out in books. Pleased with the *Pilgrim's Progress,* my first collection was of John Bunyan's works in separate little volumes. I afterward sold them to enable me to buy R. Burton's *Historical Collections;* they were small chapmen's books, and cheap, 40 or 50 in all. My father's little library consisted chiefly of books in polemic divinity, most of which I read, and have since often regretted that, at a time when I had such a thirst for knowledge, more proper books had not fallen in my way, since it was now resolved I should not be a clergyman. Plutarch's *Lives* there was in which I read abundantly, and I still think that time spent to great advantage. There was also a book of Defore's, called an *Essay on Projects,* and another of Dr. Mather's, called *Essays to Do Good,* which perhaps gave me a turn of thinking that had an influence on some of the principal future events of my life.

This bookish inclination at length determined my father to make me a printer, though he had already one son (James) of that profession. In 1717 my brother James returned from England with a press and letters to set up his business in Boston. I liked it much better than that of my father, but still had a hankering for the sea. To prevent the apprehended effect of such an inclination, my father was impatient to have me bound to my brother. I stood out some time, but at last was persuaded, and signed the indentures when I was yet but twelve years old. I was to serve as an apprentice till I was twenty-one years of age, only I was to be allowed journeyman's wages during the last year. In a little time I made great proficiency in the business, and became a useful hand to my brother. I now had access to better books. An acquaintance with the apprentices of booksellers enabled me sometimes to borrow a small one, which I was careful to return soon and clean. Often I sat up in my room reading the greatest part of the night, when the book was borrowed in the evening and to be returned early in the morning, lest it should be missed or wanted.

And after some time an ingenious tradesman, Mr. Matthew Adams, who had a pretty collection of books, and who frequented our printing house, took notice of me, invited me to his library, and very kindly lent me such books as I chose to read. I now took a fancy to poetry, and made some little pieces; my brother, thinking it might turn to account, encouraged me, and put me on composing occasional ballads. One was called "The Lighthouse Tragedy," and contained an account of the drowning of Captain Worthilake, with his two daughters; the other was a sailor's song, on the taking of Teach (or Blackbeard) the pirate. They were wretched stuff, in the Grub-street-ballad style; and when they were printed he sent me about the town to sell them. The first sold wonderfully, the event being recent, having made a great noise. This flattered my vanity; but my father discouraged me by ridiculing my performances, and telling me verse-makers were generally beggars. So I escaped being a poet, most probably a very bad one; but, as prose writing has been of great use to me in the course of my life, and was a principal means of my advancement, I shall tell you how, in such a situation, I acquired what little ability I have in that way.

There was another bookish lad in the town, John Collins by name, with whom I was intimately acquainted. We sometimes disputed, and very fond we were of argument, and very desirous of confuting one another, which disputatious turn, by the way, is apt to become a very bad habit, making people often extremely disagreeable in company by the contradiction that is necessary to bring it into practice; and thence, besides souring and spoiling the conversation, is productive of disgusts and perhaps enmities where you may have occasion for friendship. I had caught it by reading my father's books of dispute about religion. Persons of good sense, I have since observed, seldom fall into it, except lawyers, university men, and men of all sorts that have been bred at Edinburgh.

A question was once, somehow or other, started between Collins and me, of the propriety of educating the female sex in learning, and their abilities for study. He was of opinion that it was improper, and that they were naturally unequal to it. I took the contrary side, perhaps a little for dispute's sake. He was naturally more eloquent, had a ready plenty of words; and sometimes, as I thought, bore me down more by his fluency than by the strength of his reasons. As we parted without settling the point, and were not to see one another again for some time, I sat down to put my arguments in writing, which I copied fair and sent to him. He answered, and I replied. Three or four letters of a side had passed, when my father happened to find my papers and read them. Without entering into the discussion, he took occasion to talk to me about the manner of my writing; observed that, though I had the advantage of my antagonist in correct spelling and pointing (which I owed to the printing house), I fell far short in elegance of expression, in method, and in perspicuity, of which he convinced me by several instances. I saw the justice of his remarks, and thence grew more attentive to the manner in writing, and determined to endeavor at improvement.

About this time I met with an odd volume of the *Spectator*. It was the third. I had never before seen any of them. I bought it, read it over and over, and was much delighted with it. I thought the writing excellent, and wished, if possible, to imitate it. With this view I took some of the papers, and, making short hints of the sentiment in each sentence, laid them by a few days, and then, without looking at the book, tried to complete the papers again, by expressing each hinted sentiment at length, and as fully as it had been expressed before, in any suitable words that should come to hand. Then I compared my *Spectator* with the original, discovered some of my faults, and corrected them. But I found I wanted a stock of words, or a readiness in recollecting and using them, which I thought I should have acquired before that time if I had gone on making verses; since the continual occasion for words of the same import, but of different length, to suit the measure, or of different sound for the rhyme, would have laid me under a constant necessity of searching for variety, and also have tended to fix that variety in my mind, and make me master of it. Therefore I took some of the tales and turned them into verse; and, after a time, when I had pretty well forgotten the prose, turned them back again. I also sometimes jumbled my collections of hints into confusion, and after some weeks endeavored to reduce them into the best order, before I began to form the full sentences and complete the paper. This was to teach me method in the arrangement of thoughts. By comparing my work afterwards with the original, I discovered many faults and amended them; but I sometimes had the pleasure of fancying that, in certain particulars of small import, I had been lucky enough to improve the method or the language, and this encouraged me to think I might possibly in time come to be a tolerable English writer, of which I was extremely ambitious. My time for these exercises and for reading was at night, after work or before it began in the morning, or on Sundays, when I contrived to be in the printing house alone, evading as much as I could the common attendance on public worship which my father used to exact on me when I was under his care, and which indeed I still thought a duty, though I could not, as it seemed to me, afford time to practice it.

When about sixteen years of age I happened to meet with a book, written by one Tryon, recommending a vegetable diet. I determined to go into it. My brother, being yet unmarried, did not keep house, but boarded himself and his apprentices in another family. My refusing to eat flesh occasioned an inconveniency, and I was frequently chid for my singularity. I made myself acquainted with Tryon's manner of preparing some of his dishes, such as boiling potatoes or rice, making hasty pudding, and a few others, and then proposed to my brother that if he would give me, weekly, half the money he paid for my board, I would board myself. He instantly agreed to it, and I presently found that I could save half what he paid me. This was an additional fund for buying books. But I had another advantage in it. My brother and the rest going from the printing house to their meals, I remained there alone, and, dispatching presently my light repast, which often was no more than a biscuit or a slice of bread, a handful of raisins or a tart from the pastry cook's, and a glass of water, had the rest of the time till their return for study, in which I made the greater progress from that greater clearness of head and quicker apprehension which usually attend temperance in eating and drinking.

And now it was that, being on some occasion made ashamed of my ignorance in figures, which I had twice failed in learning when at school, I took Cocker's book of arithmetic, and went through the whole by myself with great ease. I also read Seller's and Shermy's books of navigation, and became acquainted with the little geometry they contain; but never proceeded far in that science. And I read about this time Locke *On Human Understanding*, and the *Art of Thinking* by Messrs. du Port Royal.

While I was intent on improving my language, I met with an English grammar (I think it was Greenwood's), at the end of which there were two little sketches of the arts of rhetoric and logic, the latter finishing with a specimen of a dispute in the Socratic method; and soon after I procured Xenophon's *Memorable Things of Socrates*, wherein there are many instances of the same method. I was charmed with it, adopted it, dropped my abrupt contradiction and positive argumentation, and put on the humble inquirer and doubter. And being then, from reading Shaftesbury and Collins, become a real doubter in many points of our religious doctrine, I found this method safest for myself and very embarrassing to those against whom I used it; therefore I took a delight in it, practiced it continually, and grew very artful and expert in drawing people, even of superior knowledge, into concessions the consequences of which they did not foresee, entangling them in difficulties out of which they could not extricate themselves, and so obtaining victories that neither myself nor my cause always deserved. I continued this method some few years, but gradually left it, retaining only the habit of expressing myself in terms of modest diffidence; never using, when I advanced anything that may possibly be disputed, the words *certainly*, *undoubtedly*, or any others that give the air of positiveness to an opinion; but rather say, I conceive or apprehend a thing to be so and so; it appears to me, or *I should think it so or so*, for such and such reasons; or *I imagine it to be so;* or *it is so, if I am not mistaken*. This habit, I believe, has been of great advantage to me when I have had occasion to inculcate my opinions, and persuade men into measures that I have been from time to time engaged in promoting; and, as the chief ends of conversation are to *inform* or to *be informed*, to *please* or to *persuade*, I wish well-meaning, sensible men would not lessen their power of doing good by a positive, assuming manner, that seldom fails to disgust, tends to create opposition, and to defeat every one of those purposes for which speech was given to us, to wit, giving or receiving information or pleasure. For, if you would inform, a positive and dogmatical manner in advancing your sentiments may provoke contradiction and prevent a candid attention. If you wish information and improvement from the knowledge of others, and yet at the same time express yourself as firmly fixed in your present opinions, modest, sensible men, who do not love disputation, will probably leave you undisturbed in the possession of your error. And by such a manner you can seldom hope to recommend yourself in *pleasing* your hearers, or to persuade those whose concurrence you desire. . . .

My brother had, in 1720 or 1721, begun to print a newspaper. It was the second that appeared in America, and was called the *New England Courant*. The only one before it was the *Boston News-Letter*. I remember his being dissuaded by some of his friends from the undertaking, as not likely to succeed, one newspaper being, in their judgment, enough for America. At this time (1771) there are not less than five-and-twenty. He went on, however, with the undertaking, and, after having worked in composing the types and printing of the sheets, I was employed to carry the papers through the streets to the customers.

He had some ingenious men among his friends who amused themselves by writing little pieces for this paper, which gained it credit and made it more in demand, and these gentlemen often visited us. Hearing their conversations and their accounts of the approbation their papers were received with, I was excited to try my hand among them; but, being still a boy, and suspecting that my brother would object to printing anything of mine in his paper if he knew it to be mine, I contrived to disguise my hand, and, writing an anonymous paper, I put it in at night under the door of the printing house. It was found in the morning, and communicated to his writing friends, when they called in as usual. They read it, commented on it in my hearing, and I had the exquisite pleasure of finding it met with their approbation, and that, in their different guesses at the author, none were named but men of some character among us for learning and ingenuity. I suppose now that I was rather lucky in my judges, and that perhaps they were not really so very good ones as I then esteemed them.

Encouraged, however, by this, I wrote and conveyed in the same way to the press several more papers, which were equally approved, and I kept my secret till my small fund of sense for such performances was pretty well exhausted, and then I discovered it, when I began to be considered a little more by my brother's acquaintance, and in a manner that did not quite please him, as he thought, probably with reason, that it tended to make me too vain. And, perhaps, this might be one occasion of the differences that we began to have about this time. Though a brother, he considered himself as my master, and me as his apprentice, and, accordingly, expected the same services from me as he would from another, while I thought he demeaned me too much in some he required of me, who from a brother expected more indulgence. Our disputes were often brought before our father, and I fancy I was either generally in the right, or else a better pleader, because the judgment was generally in my favor. But my brother was passionate, and had often beaten me, which I took extremely amiss; and, thinking my apprenticeship very tedious, I was continually wishing for some opportunity of shortening it, which at length offered in a manner unexpected.*

One of the pieces in our newspaper on some political point, which I have now forgotten, gave offense to the Assembly. He was taken up, censured, and imprisoned for a month, by the speaker's warrant, I suppose because he would not discover his author. I too was taken up and examined before the council; but, though I did not give them any satisfaction, they contented themselves with admonishing me, and dismissed me, considering me, perhaps, as an apprentice, who was bound to keep his master's secrets.

During my brother's confinement, which I resented a good deal, not-

* I fancy his harsh and tyrannical treatment of me might be a means of impressing me with that aversion to arbitrary power that has stuck to me through my whole life.

withstanding our private differences, I had the management of the paper; and I made bold to give our rulers some rubs in it, which my brother took very kindly, while others began to consider me in an unfavorable light, as a young genius that had a turn for libeling and satire. My brother's discharge was accompanied with an order of the House (a very odd one) that "James Franklin should no longer print the paper called the *New England Courant*."

There was a consultation held in our printing house among his friends, what he should do in this case. Some proposed to evade the order by changing the name of the paper; but, my brother seeing inconveniences in that, it was finally concluded on, as a better way, to let it be printed for the future under the name of BENJAMIN FRANKLIN; and, to avoid the censure of the Assembly, that might fall on him as still printing it by his apprentice, the contrivance was that my old indenture should be returned to me, with a full discharge on the back of it, to be shown on occasion; but, to secure to him the benefit of my service, I was to sign new indentures for the remainder of the term, which were to be kept private. A very flimsy scheme it was; however, it was immediately executed, and the paper went on accordingly, under my name, for several months.

At length, a fresh difference arising between my brother and me, I took upon me to assert my freedom, presuming that he would not venture to produce the new indentures. It was not fair in me to take this advantage, and this I therefore reckon one of the first errata of my life; but the unfairness of it weighed little with me when under the impressions of resentment for the blows his passion too often urged him to bestow upon me, though he was otherwise not an ill-natured man: perhaps I was too saucy and provoking.

When he found I would leave him, he took care to prevent my getting employment in any other printing house of the town, by going round and speaking to every master, who accordingly refused to give me work. I then thought of going to New York, as the nearest place where there was a printer; and I was rather inclined to leave Boston when I reflected that I had already made myself a little obnoxious to the governing party, and, from the arbitrary proceedings of the Assembly in my brother's case, it was likely I might, if I stayed, soon bring myself into scrapes; and further, that my indiscreet disputations about religion began to make me pointed at with horror by good people as an infidel or atheist. I determined on the point, but, my father now siding with my brother, I was sensible that, if I attempted to go openly, means would be used to prevent me. My friend Collins, therefore, undertook to manage a little for me. He agreed with the captain of a New York sloop for my passage, under the notion of my being a young acquaintance of his that had got a naughty girl with child, whose friends would compel me to marry her, and therefore I could not appear or come away publicly. So I sold some of my books to raise a little money, was taken on board privately, and, as we had a fair wind, in three days I found myself in New York, near three hundred miles from home, a boy of but seventeen, without the least recommendation to, or knowledge of, any person in the place, and with very little money in my pocket.

My inclinations for the sea were by this time worn out, or I might now have gratified them. But, having a trade, and supposing myself a pretty good workman, I offered my service to the printer in the place, old Mr. William Bradford, who had been the first printer in Pennsylvania, but removed from thence upon the quarrel of George Keith. He could give me no employment, having little to do, and help enough already; but says he, "My son at Philadelphia has lately lost his principal hand, Aquila Rose, by death; if you go thither, I believe he may employ you." Philadelphia was a hundred miles farther; I set out, however, in a boat for Amboy, leaving my chest and things to follow me round by sea. . . .

It was about this time I conceived the bold and arduous project of arriving at moral perfection. I wished to live without committing any fault at any time; I would conquer all that either natural inclination, custom, or company might lead me into. As I knew, or thought I knew, what was right and wrong, I did not see why I might not always do the one and avoid the other. But I soon found I had undertaken a task of more difficulty than I had imagined. While my care was employed in guarding against one fault, I was often surprised by another; habit took the advantage of inattention; inclination was sometimes too strong for reason. I concluded, at length, that the mere speculative conviction that it was our interest to be completely virtuous was not sufficient to prevent our slipping; and that the contrary habits must be broken, and good ones acquired and established, before we can have any dependence on a steady, uniform rectitude of conduct. For this purpose I therefore contrived the following method.

In the various enumerations of the moral virtues I had met with in my reading, I found the catalogue more or less numerous, as different writers included more or fewer ideas under the same name. Temperance, for example, was by some confined to eating and drinking, while by others it was extended to mean the moderating every other pleasure, appetite, inclination, or passion, bodily or mental, even to our avarice and ambition. I proposed to myself, for the sake of clearness, to use rather more names, with fewer ideas annexed to each, than a few names with more ideas; and I included under thirteen names of virtues all that at that time occurred to me as necessary or desirable, and annexed to each a short precept, which fully expressed the extent I gave to its meaning.

These names of virtues, with their precepts, were:

### 1. Temperance
Eat not to dullness; drink not to elevation.

### 2. Silence
Speak not but what may benefit others or yourself; avoid trifling conversation.

### 3. Order
Let all your things have their places; let each part of your business have its time.

### 4. Resolution
Resolve to perform what you ought, perform without fail what you resolve.

### 5. Frugality
Make no expense but to do good to others or yourself; i.e., waste nothing.

### 6. Industry
Lose no time; be always employed in something useful; cut off all unnecessary actions.

### 7. Sincerity
Use no hurtful deceit; think innocently and justly, and, if you speak, speak accordingly.

### 8. Justice
Wrong none by doing injuries, or omitting the benefits that are your duty.

### 9. Moderation
Avoid extremes; forbear resenting injuries so much as you think they deserve.

### 10. Cleanliness
Tolerate no uncleanliness in body, clothes, or habitation.

### 11. Tranquillity
Be not disturbed at trifles, or at accidents common or unavoidable.

### 12. Chastity
Rarely use venery but for health or offspring, never to dullness, weakness, or the injury of your own or another's peace or reputation.

### 13. Humility
Imitate Jesus and Socrates.

My intention being to acquire the *habitude* of all these virtues, I judged it would be well not to distract my attention by attempting the whole at once, but to fix it on one of them at a time; and, when I should be master of that, then to proceed to another, and so on, till I should have gone through the thirteen; and, as the previous acquisition of some might facilitate the acquisition of certain others, I arranged them with that view, as they stand above. Temperance first, as it tends to procure that coolness and clearness of head which is so necessary where constant vigilance was to be kept up, and guard maintained against the unremitting attraction of ancient habits and the force of perpetual temptations. This being acquired and established, Silence would be more easy; and, my desire being to gain knowledge at the same time that I improved in virtue, and considering that in conversation it was obtained rather by the use of the ears than of the tongue, and therefore wishing to break a habit I was getting into of prattling, punning, and joking, which only made me acceptable to trifling company, I gave *Silence* the second place. This and the next, *Order*, I expected would allow me more time for attending to my project and my studies. *Resolution*, once become habitual, would keep me firm in my endeavors to obtain all the subsequent virtues; *Frugality* and *Industry*, freeing me from my remaining debt, and producing affluence and independence, would make more easy the practice of *Sincerity* and *Justice*, etc., etc. Conceiving then, that, agreeably to the advice of Pythagoras in his Golden Verses, daily examination would be necessary, I contrived the following method for conducting that examination.

I made a little book, in which I allotted a page for each of the virtues. I ruled each page with red ink, so as to have seven columns, one for each day of the week, marking each column with a letter for the day. I crossed these columns with thirteen red lines, marking the beginning of each line with the first letter of one of the virtues, on which line, and in its proper column, I might mark, by a little black spot, every fault I found upon examination to have been committed respecting that virtue upon that day.

I determined to give a week's strict attention to each of the virtues successively. Thus, in the first week, my great guard was to avoid every the least offense against *Temperance*, leaving the other virtues to their ordinary chance, only marking every evening the faults of the day. Thus, if in the first week I could keep my first line, marked T, clear of spots, I supposed the habit of that virtue so much strengthened, and its opposite weakened, that I might venture extending my attention to include the next, and for the following week keep both lines clear of spots. Proceeding thus to the last, I could go through a course complete in thirteen weeks, and four courses in a year. And like him who, having a garden to weed, does not attempt to eradicate all the bad herbs at once, which would exceed his reach and his strength, but works on one of the beds at a time, and, having accomplished the first, proceeds to a

*Form of the pages*

| TEMPERANCE | | | | | | |
|---|---|---|---|---|---|---|
| EAT NOT TO DULLNESS, DRINK NOT TO ELEVATION. | | | | | | |

|     | S. | M. | T. | W. | T. | F. | S. |
|-----|----|----|----|----|----|----|----|
| T.  |    |    |    |    |    |    |    |
| S.  | ✻  | ✻  |    | ✻  |    | ✻  |    |
| O.  | ✻✻ | ✻  | ✻  |    | ✻  | ✻  | ✻  |
| R.  |    |    | ✻  |    |    | ✻  |    |
| F.  |    | ✻  |    |    | ✻  |    |    |
| I.  |    |    | ✻  |    |    |    |    |
| S.  |    |    |    |    |    |    |    |
| J.  |    |    |    |    |    |    |    |
| M.  |    |    |    |    |    |    |    |
| C.  |    |    |    |    |    |    |    |
| T.  |    |    |    |    |    |    |    |
| C.  |    |    |    |    |    |    |    |
| H.  |    |    |    |    |    |    |    |

second, so I should have, I hoped, the encouraging pleasure of seeing on my pages the progress I made in virtue, by clearing successively my lines of their spots, till in the end, by a number of courses, I should be happy in viewing a clean book, after a thirteen weeks' daily examination. . . .

In 1739 arrived among us from Ireland the Reverend Mr. Whitefield, who had made himself remarkable there as an itinerant preacher. He was at first permitted to preach in some of our churches; but the clergy, taking a dislike to him, soon refused him their pulpits, and he was obliged to preach in the fields. The multitudes of all sects and denominations that attended his sermons were enormous, and it was matter of speculation to me, who was one of the number, to observe the extraordinary influence of his oratory on his hearers, and how much they admired and respected him, notwithstanding his common abuse of them by assuring them they were naturally *half beasts and half devils*. It was wonderful to see the change soon made in the manners of our inhabitants. From being thoughtless or indifferent about religion, it seemed as if all the world were growing religious, so that one could not walk through the town in an evening without hearing psalms sung in different families of every street.

And, it being found inconvenient to assemble in the open air, subject to its inclemencies, the building of a house to meet in was no sooner proposed, and persons appointed to receive contributions, but sufficient sums were soon received to procure the ground and erect the building, which was one hundred feet long and seventy broad, about the size of Westminster Hall; and the work was carried on with such spirit as to be finished in a much shorter time than could have been expected. Both house and ground were vested in trustees, expressly for the use of any preacher of any religious persuasion who might desire to say something to the people at Philadelphia; the design in building not being to accommodate any particular sect, but the inhabitants in general; so that even if the Mufti of Constantinople were to send a missionary to preach Mohammedanism to us, he would find a pulpit at his service.

Mr. Whitefield, in leaving us, went preaching all the way through the colonies to Georgia. The settlement of that province had lately been begun, but, instead of being made with hardy, industrious husbandmen, accustomed to labor, the only people fit for such an enterprise, it was with families of broken shopkeepers and other insolvent debtors, many of indolent and idle habits, taken out of the jails, who, being set down in the woods, unqualified for clearing land, and unable to endure the hardships of a new settlement, perished in numbers, leaving many helpless children unprovided for. The sight of their miserable situation inspired the benevolent heart of Mr. Whitefield with the idea of building an orphan house there, in which they might be supported and educated. Returning northward, he preached up this charity, and made large collections, for his eloquence had a wonderful power over the hearts and purses of his hearers, of which I myself was an instance.

I did not disapprove of the design, but, as Georgia was then destitute of materials and workmen, and it was proposed to send them from Philadelphia at a great expense, I thought it would have been better to have built the house there, and brought the children to it. This I advised; but he was resolute in his first project, rejected my counsel, and I therefore refused to contribute. I happened soon after to attend one of his sermons, in the course of which I perceived he intended to finish with a collection, and I silently resolved he should get nothing from me. I had in my pocket a handful of copper money, three or four silver dollars, and five pistoles in gold. As he proceeded, I began to soften, and concluded to give the coppers. Another stroke of his oratory made me ashamed of that, and determined me to give the silver; and he finished so admirably that I emptied my pocket wholly into the collector's dish, gold and all. At this sermon there was also one of our club, who, being of my sentiments respecting the building in Georgia, and suspecting a collection might be intended, had, by precaution, emptied his pockets before he came from home. Towards the conclusion of the discourse, however, he felt a strong desire to give, and applied to a neighbor, who stood near him, to borrow some money for the purpose. The application was unfortunately to perhaps the only man in the company who had the firmness not to be affected by the preacher. His answer was, "At any other time, Friend Hopkinson, I would lend to thee freely; but not now, for thee seems to be out of thy right senses." . . .

In 1746, being at Boston, I met there with a Dr. Spence, who was lately arrived from Scotland, and showed me some electric experiments. They were imperfectly performed, as he was not very expert; but, being on a subject quite new to me, they equally surprised and pleased me. Soon after my return to Philadelphia, our library company received from Mr. P. Collinson, Fellow of the Royal Society of London, a present of a glass tube, with some account of the use of it in making such experiments. I eagerly seized the opportunity of repeating what I had seen at Boston; and, by much practice, acquired great readiness in performing those, also, which we had an account of from England, adding a number of new ones. I say much practice, for my house was continually full, for some time, with people who came to see these new wonders.

To divide a little this incumbrance among my friends, I caused a number of similar tubes to be blown at our glass house, with which they furnished themselves, so that we had at length several performers. Among these, the principal was Mr. Kinnersley, an ingenious neighbor, who, being out of business, I encouraged to undertake showing the experiments for money, and drew up for him two lectures, in which the experiments were ranged in such order, and accompanied with such explanations in such method, as that the foregoing should assist in comprehending the following. He procured an elegant apparatus for the purpose, in which all the little machines that I had roughly made for myself were nicely formed by instrument-makers. His lectures were well attended, and gave great satisfaction; and after some time he went through the colonies, exhibiting them in every capital town, and picked up some money. In the West India islands, indeed, it was with difficulty the experiments could be made, from the general moisture of the air.

Obliged as we were to Mr. Collinson for his present of the tube, etc., I thought it right he would be informed of our success in using it, and wrote him several letters containing accounts of our experiments. He got them read in the Royal Society, where they were not at first thought worth so much notice as to be printed in their transactions. One paper, which I wrote for Mr. Kinnersley, on the sameness of lightning with electricity, I sent to Dr. Mitchel, an acquaintance of mine, and one of the members also of that society, who wrote me word that it had been read, but was laughed at by the connoisseurs. The papers, however, being shown to Dr. Fothergill, he thought them of too much value to be stifled, and advised the printing of them. Mr. Collinson then gave them to Cave for publication in his *Gentleman's Magazine;* but he chose to print them separately in a pamphlet, and Dr. Fothergill wrote the preface. Cave, it seems, judged rightly for his profit, for by the additions that arrived afterward they swelled to a quarto volume, which has had five editions, and cost him nothing for copy money.

It was, however, some time before those papers were much taken notice of in England. A copy of them happening to fall into the hands of the Count de Buffon, a philosopher deservedly of great reputation in France, and, indeed, all over Europe, he prevailed with M. Dalibard to translate them into French, and they were printed at Paris. The publication offended the Abbé Nollet, preceptor in natural philosophy to the royal family, and an able experimenter, who had formed and published a theory of electricity, which then had the general vogue. He could not at first believe that such a work came from America, and said it must have been fabricated by his enemies at Paris, to decry his system. Afterwards, having been assured that there really existed such a person as Franklin at Philadelphia, which he had doubted, he wrote and published a volume of letters, chiefly addressed to me, defending his theory, and denying the verity of my experiments and of the positions deduced from them.

I once purposed answering the abbé, and actually began the answer; but, on consideration that my writings contained a description of experiments which anyone might repeat and verify, and, if not to be verified, could not be defended; or of observations offered as conjectures, and not delivered dogmatically, therefore not laying me under any obligation to defend them; and reflecting that a dispute between two persons, writing in different languages, might be lengthened greatly by mistranslations, and thence misconceptions of one another's meaning, much of one of the abbé's letters being founded on an error in the translation, I concluded to let my papers shift for themselves, believing it was better to spend what time I could spare from public business in making new experiments than in disputing about those already made. I therefore never answered M. Nollet, and the event gave me no cause to repent my silence; for my friend M. le Roy, of the Royal Academy of Sciences, took up my cause and refuted him; my book was translated into the Italian, German, and Latin languages; and the doctrine it contained was by degrees universally adopted by the philosophers of Europe, in preference to that of the abbé; so that he lived to see himself the last of his sect, except Monsieur B——, of Paris, his élève and immediate disciple.

What gave my book the more sudden and general celebrity was the success of one of its proposed experiments, made by Messrs. Dalibard and de Lor at Marly, for drawing lightning from the clouds. This engaged the public attention everywhere. M. de Lor, who had an apparatus for experimental philosophy, and lectured in that branch of science, undertook to repeat what he called the *Philadelphia experiments;* and, after they were performed before the king and court, all the curious of Paris flocked to see them. I will not swell this narrative with an account of that capital experiment, nor of the infinite pleasure I received in the success of a similar one I made soon after with a kite at Philadelphia, as both are to be found in the histories of electricity.

Dr. Wright, an English physician, when at Paris, wrote to a friend, who was of the Royal Society, an account of the high esteem my experiments were in among the learned abroad, and of their wonder that my writings had been so little noticed in England. The society, on this, resumed the consideration of the letters that had been read to them; and the celebrated Dr. Watson drew up a summary account of them, and of all I had afterwards sent to England on the subject, which he accompanied with some praise of the writer. This summary was then printed in their *Transactions;* and, some members of the society in London, particularly the very ingenious Mr. Canton, having verified the experiment of procuring lightning from the clouds by a pointed rod, and acquainting them with the success, they soon made me more than amends for the slight with which they had before treated me. Without my having made any application for that honor, they chose me a member, and voted that I should be excused the customary payments, which would have amounted to twenty-five guineas, and ever since have given me their *Transactions* gratis. They also presented me with the gold medal of Sir Godfrey Copley for the year 1753, the delivery of which was accompanied by a very handsome speech of the president, Lord Macclesfield, wherein I was highly honored.

# Journal

## *John Woolman*

*As a stylist, Woolman had few peers in colonial America. He wrote simply and directly, always seeking the colorless and always finding the right word.*

*His* Journal *is both a mirror of the man and of the Society of Friends in the "Golden Age of Quakerism."*

CHAPTER I.

1720–1742.

His Birth and Parentage. — Some Account of the Operations of Divine Grace on his Mind in his Youth. — His first Appearance in the Ministry. — And his Considerations, while Young, on the Keeping of Slaves.

I have often felt a motion of love to leave some hints in writing of my experience of the goodness of God, and now, in the thirty-sixth year of my age, I begin this work.

I was born in Northampton, in Burlington County, West Jersey, in the year 1720. Before I was seven years old I began to be acquainted with the operations of Divine love. Through the care of my parents, I was taught to read nearly as soon as I was capable of it; and as I went from school one day, I remember that while my companions were playing by the way, I went forward out of sight, and, sitting down, I read the twenty-second chapter of Revelation: "He showed me a pure river of water of life, clear as crystal, proceeding out of the throne of God and of the Lamb, &c." In reading it, my mind was drawn to seek after that pure habitation which I then believed God had prepared for his servants. The place where I sat, and the sweetness that attended my mind, remain fresh in my memory. This, and the like gracious visitations, had such an effect upon me that when boys used ill language it troubled me; and, through the continued mercies of God, I was preserved from that evil.

*The* Journal *and Other Writings of John Woolman.* Edited by Vida D. Scudder.

The pious instructions of my parents were often fresh in my mind, when I happened to be among wicked children, and were of use to me. Having a large family of children, they used frequently, on first-days, after meeting, to set us one after another to read the Holy Scriptures, or some religious books, the rest sitting by without much conversation; I have since often thought it was a good practice. From what I had read and heard, I believed there had been, in past ages, people who walked in uprightness before God in a degree exceeding any that I knew or heard of now living: and the apprehension of there being less steadiness and firmness amongst people in the present age often troubled me while I was a child.

I may here mention a remarkable circumstance that occurred in my childhood. On going to a neighbor's house, I saw on the way a robin sitting on her nest, and as I came near she went off; but having young ones, she flew about, and with many cries expressed her concern for them. I stood and threw stones at her, and one striking her she fell down dead. At first I was pleased with the exploit, but after a few minutes was seized with horror, at having, in a sportive way, killed an innocent creature while she was careful for her young. I beheld her lying dead, and thought those young ones, for which she was so careful, must now perish for want of their dam to nourish them. After some painful considerations on the subject, I climbed up the tree, took all the young birds, and killed them, supposing that better than to leave them to pine away and die miserably. In this case I believed that Scripture proverb was fulfilled, "The tender mercies of the wicked are cruel." I then went on my errand, and for some hours could think of little else but the cruelties I had committed, and was much troubled. Thus He whose tender mercies are over all his works hath placed a principle in the human mind, which incites to exercise goodness towards every living creature; and this being singly attended to, people become tender-hearted and sympathizing; but when frequently and totally rejected, the mind becomes shut up in a contrary disposition.

About the twelfth year of my age, my father being abroad, my mother reproved me for some misconduct, to which I made an undutiful reply. The next first-day, as I was with my father returning from meeting, he told me that he understood I had behaved amiss to my mother, and advised me to be more careful in future. I knew myself blamable, and in shame and confusion remained silent. Being thus awakened to a sense of my wickedness, I felt remorse in my mind, and on getting home I retired and prayed to the Lord to forgive me, and I do not remember that I ever afterwards spoke unhandsomely to either of my parents, however foolish in some other things.

Having attained the age of sixteen years, I began to love wanton company; and though I was preserved from profane language or scandalous conduct, yet I perceived a plant in me which produced much wild grapes; my merciful Father did not, however, forsake me utterly, but at times, through his grace, I was brought seriously to consider my ways; and the sight of my backslidings affected me with sorrow, yet for want of rightly attending to the reproofs of instruction, vanity was added to vanity, and repentance to repentance. Upon the whole, my mind became more and more alienated from the truth, and I hastened toward destruction. While I meditate on the gulf towards which I travelled, and reflect on my youthful disobedience, for these things I weep, mine eye runneth down with water.

Advancing in age, the number of my acquaintance increased, and thereby my way grew more difficult. Though I had found comfort in reading the Holy Scriptures and thinking on heavenly things, I was now estranged therefrom. I knew I was going from the flock of Christ and had no resolution to return, hence serious reflections were uneasy to me, and youthful vanities and diversions were my greatest pleasure. In this road I found many like myself, and we associated in that which is adverse to true friendship.

In this swift race it pleased God to visit me with sickness, so that I doubted of recovery; then did darkness, horror, and amazement with full force seize me, even when my pain and distress of body were very great. I thought it would have been better for me never to have had being, than to see the day which I now saw. I was filled with confusion, and in great affliction, both of mind and body, I lay and bewailed myself. I had not confidence to lift up my cries to God, whom I had thus offended; but in a deep sense of my great folly I was humbled before him. At length that word which is as a fire and a hammer broke and dissolved my rebellious heart; my cries were put up in contrition; and in the multitude of his mercies I found inward relief, and a close engagement that if he was pleased to restore my health I might walk humbly before him.

After my recovery this exercise remained with me a considerable time, but by degrees giving way to youthful vanities, and associating with wanton young people, I lost ground. The Lord had been very gracious, and spoke peace to me in the time of my distress, and I now most ungratefully turned again to folly; at time I felt sharp reproof, but I did not get low enough to cry for help. I was not so hardy as to commit things scandalous, but to exceed in vanity and to promote mirth was my chief study. Still I retained a love and esteem for pious people, and their company brought an awe upon me. My dear parents several times admonished me in the fear of the Lord, and their admonition entered into my heart and had a good effect for a season; but not getting deep enough to pray rightly, the tempter, when he came, found entrance. Once having spent a part of the day in wantonness, when I went to bed at night there lay in a window near my bed a Bible, which I opened, and first cast my eye on the text, "We lie down in our shame, and our confusion covereth us." This I knew to be my case, and meeting with so unexpected a reproof I was somewhat affected with it, and went to bed under remorse of conscience, which I soon cast off again.

Thus time passed on; my heart was replenished with mirth and wantonness, while pleasing scenes of vanity were presented to my imagination, till I attained the age of eighteen years, near which time I felt the judgments of God in my soul, like a consuming fire, and looking over my past life the prospect was moving. I was often sad, and longed to be delivered from those vanities; then again my heart was strongly inclined to them, and there was in me a sore conflict. At times I turned to folly, and then again sorrow and confusion took hold of me. In a while I resolved totally to leave off some of my vanities, but there was a secret reserve in my heart of the more refined part of them, and I was not low enough to find true peace. Thus for some months I had great troubles; my will was unsubjected, which rendered my labors fruitless. At length, through the merciful continuance of heavenly visitations, I was made to bow down in spirit before the Lord. One evening I had spent some time in reading a pious author, and walking out alone I humbly prayed to the Lord for his help, that I might be delivered from all those vanities which so ensnared me. Thus being brought low, he helped me, and as I learned to bear the cross I felt refreshment to come from his presence, but not keeping in that strength which gave victory I lost ground again, the sense of which greatly affected me. I sought deserts and lonely places, and there with tears did confess my sins to God and humbly craved his help. And I may say with reverence, he was near to me in my troubles, and in those times of humiliation opened my ear to discipline. I was now led to look seriously at the means by which I was drawn from the pure truth, and learned that if I would live such a life as the faithful servants of God lived, I must not go into company as heretofore in my own will, but all the cravings of sense must be governed by a Divine principle. In times of sorrow and abasement these instructions were sealed upon me, and I felt the power of Christ prevail over selfish desires, so that I was preserved in a good degree of steadiness, and being young, and believing at that time that a single life was best for me, I was strengthened to keep from such company as had often been a snare to me.

I kept steadily to meetings; spent first-day afternoons chiefly in reading the Scriptures and other good books, and was early convinced in my mind that true religion consisted in an inward life, wherein the heart doth love and reverence God the Creator, and learns to exercise true justice and goodness, not only toward all men, but also toward the brute creatures; that, as the mind was moved by an inward principle to love God as an invisible, incomprehensible Being, so, by the same principle, it was moved to love him in all his manifestations in the visible world; that, as by his breath the flame of life was kindled in all animal sensible creatures, to say we love God as unseen, and at the same time exercise cruelty toward the least creature moving by his life, or by life derived from him, was a contradiction in itself. I found no narrowness respecting sects and opinions, but believed that sincere, upright-hearted people, in every society, who truly love God, were accepted of him.

As I lived under the cross, and simply followed the opening of truth, my mind, from day to day, was more enlightened, my former acquaintance were left to judge of me as they would, for I found it safest for me to live in private, and keep these things sealed up in my own breast. While I silently ponder on that change wrought in me, I find no language equal to convey to another a clear idea of it. I looked upon the works of God in this visible creation, and an awfulness covered me. My heart was tender and often contrite, and universal love to my fellow-creatures increased in me. This will be understood by such as have trodden in the same path. Some glances of real beauty may be seen in their faces who dwell in true meekness. There is a harmony in the sound of that voice to which Divine love gives utterance, and some appearance of right order in their temper and conduct whose passions are regulated; yet these do not fully show forth that inward life to those who have not felt it; this white stone and new name is only known rightly by such as receive it.

Now, though I had been thus strengthened to bear the cross, I still found myself in great danger, having many weaknesses attending me, and strong temptations to wrestle with; in the feeling whereof I frequently withdrew into private places, and often with tears besought the Lord to help me, and his gracious ear was open to my cry.

All this time I lived with my parents, and wrought on the plantation; and having had schooling pretty well for a planter, I used to improve myself in winter evenings, and other leisure times. Being now in the twenty-first year of my age, with my father's consent I engaged with a man, in much business as a shop-keeper and baker, to tend shop and keep books. At home I had lived retired; and now having a prospect of being much in the way of company, I felt frequent and fervent cries in my heart to God, the Father of Mercies, that he would preserve me from all taint and corruption; that, in this more public employment, I might serve him, my gracious Redeemer, in that humility and self-denial which I had in a small degree exercised in a more private life.

The man who employed me furnished a shop in Mount Holly, about five miles from my father's house, and six from his own, and there I lived alone and tended his shop. Shortly after my settlement here I was visited by several young people, my former acquaintance, who supposed that vanities would be as agreeable to me now as ever. At these times I cried to the Lord in secret for wisdom and strength; for I felt myself encompassed with difficulties, and had fresh occasion to bewail the follies of times past, in contracting a familiarity with libertine people; and as I had now left my father's house outwardly, I found my Heavenly Father to be merciful to me beyond what I can express.

By day I was much amongst people, and had many trials to go through; but in the evenings I was mostly alone, and I may with thankfulness acknowledge, that in those times the spirit of supplication was often poured upon me; under which I was frequently exercised, and felt my strength renewed.

After a while, my former acquaintance gave over expecting me as one of their company, and I began to be known to some whose conversation was helpful to me. And now, as I had experienced the love of God, through Jesus Christ, to redeem me from many pollutions, and to be a succor to me through a sea of conflicts, with which no person was fully acquainted, and as my heart was often enlarged in this heavenly principle, I felt a tender compassion for the youth who remained entangled in snares like those which had entangled me. This love and tenderness increased, and my mind was strongly engaged for the good of my fellow-creatures. I went to meetings in an awful frame of mind, and endeavored to be inwardly acquainted with the language of the true Shepherd. One day, being under a strong exercise of spirit, I stood up and said some words in a meeting; but not keeping close to the Divine opening, I said more than was required of me. Being soon sensible of my error, I was afflicted in mind some weeks, without any light or comfort even to that degree that I could not take satisfaction in anything. I remembered God, and was troubled, and in the depth of my distress he had pity upon me, and sent the Comforter. I then felt forgiveness for my offence; my mind became calm and quiet, and I was truly thankful to my gracious Redeemer for his mercies. About six weeks after this, feeling the spring of Divine love opened, and a concern to speak, I said a few words in a meeting, in which I found peace. Being thus humbled and disciplined under the cross, my understanding became more strengthened to distinguish the pure spirit which inwardly moves upon the heart, and which taught me to wait in silence sometimes many weeks toegther, until I felt that rise which prepares the creature to stand like a trumpet, through which the Lord speaks to his flock.

From an inward purifying, and steadfast abiding under it springs a lively operative desire for the good of others. All the faithful are not called to the public ministry; but whoever are, are called to minister of that which they have tasted and handled spiritually. The outward modes of worship are various; but whenever any are true ministers of Jesus

Christ, it is from the operation of his Spirit upon their hearts, first purifying them, and thus giving them a just sense of the conditions of others.
This truth was early fixed in my mind, and I was taught to watch the
pure opening, and to take heed lest, while I was standing to speak, my
own will should get uppermost, and cause me to utter words from
worldly wisdom, and depart from the channel of the true gospel ministry.

In the management of my outward affairs, I may say with thankfulness, I found truth to be my support; and I was respected in my master's
family, who came to live in Mount Holly within two years after my
going there.

In a few months after I came here, my master bought several Scotchmen servants, from on board a vessel, and brought them to Mount Holly
to sell, one of whom was taken sick and died. In the latter part of his
sickness, being delirious, he used to curse and swear most sorrowfully;
and the next night after his burial I was left to sleep alone in the chamber where he died. I perceived in me a timorousness; I knew, however,
I had not injured the man, but assisted in taking care of him according
to my capacity. I was not free to ask any one on that occasion to sleep
with me. Nature was feeble; but every trial was a fresh incitement to
give myself up wholly to the service of God, for I found no helper like
him in times of trouble.

About the twenty-third year of my age, I had many fresh and heavenly openings, in respect to the care and providence of the Almighty
over his creatures in general, and over man as the most noble amongst
those which are visible. And being clearly convinced in my judgment
that to place my whole trust in God was best for me, I felt renewed
engagements that in all things I might act on an inward principle of
virtue, and pursue worldly business no further than as truth opened
my way.

About the time called Christmas I observed many people, both in
town and from the country, resorting to public-houses, and spending
their time in drinking and vain sports, tending to corrupt one another;
on which account I was much troubled. At one house in particular there
was much disorder; and I believed it was a duty incumbent on me to
speak to the master of that house. I considered I was young, and that
several elderly friends in town had opportunity to see these things;
but though I would gladly have been excused, yet I could not feel my
mind clear.

The exercise was heavy; and as I was reading what the Almighty said
to Ezekiel, respecting his duty as a watchman, the matter was set home
more clearly. With prayers and tears I besought the Lord for his assistance, and He, in loving-kindness, gave me a resigned heart. At a suitable opportunity I went to the public-house; and seeing the man
amongst much company, I called him aside, and in the fear and dread

of the Almighty expressed to him what rested on my mind. He took it
kindly, and afterwards showed more regard to me than before. In a
few years afterwards he died, middle-aged; and I often thought that
had I neglected my duty in that case it would have given me great
trouble; and I was humbly thankful to my gracious Father, who had
supported me herein.

My employer, having a negro woman, sold her, and desired me to
write a bill of sale, the man being waiting who bought her. The thing
was sudden; and though I felt uneasy at the thoughts of writing an
instrument of slavery for one of my fellow-creatures, yet I remembered
that I was hired by the year, that it was my master who directed me to
do it, and that it was an elderly man, a member of our Society, who
bought her; so through weakness I gave way, and wrote it; but at the
executing of it I was so afflicted in my mind, that I said before my
master and the Friend that I believed slave-keeping to be a practice
inconsistent with the Christian religion. This, in some degree, abated
my uneasiness; yet as often as I reflected seriously upon it I thought I
should have been clearer if I had desired to be excused from it, as a
thing against my conscience; for such it was. Some time after this a
young man of our Society spoke to me to write a conveyance of a slave
to him, he having lately taken a negro into his house. I told him I was
not easy to write it; for, though many of our meeting and in other places
kept slaves, I still believed the practice was not right, and desired to be
excused from the writing. I spoke to him in good-will; and he told me
that keeping slaves was not altogether agreeable to his mind; but that
the slave being a gift made to his wife he had accepted her.

CHAPTER IV.

1757, 1758.

Visit to the Families of Friends at Burlington. — Journey to Pennsylvania,
Maryland, Virginia, and North Carolina. — Considerations on the State of
Friends there, and the Exercise he was under in Travelling among those
so generally concerned in keeping Slaves, with some Observations on this
Subject. — Epistle to Friends at New Garden and Crane Creek. — Thoughts
on the Neglect of a Religious Care in the Education of the Negroes.

Thirteenth fifth month, 1757. — Being in good health, and abroad with
Friends visiting families, I lodged at a Friend's house in Burlington.
Going to bed about the time usual with me, I awoke in the night, and
my meditations, as I lay, were on the goodness and mercy of the Lord,
in a sense whereof my heart was contrited. After this I went to sleep
again; in a short time I awoke; it was yet dark, and no appearance of
day or moonshine, and as I opened mine eyes I saw a light in my

chamber, at the apparent distance of five feet, about nine inches in diameter, of a clear, easy brightness, and near its centre the most radiant. As I lay still looking upon it without any surprise, words were spoken to my inward ear, which filled my whole inward man. They were not the effect of thought, nor any conclusion in relation to the appearance, but as the language of the Holy One spoken in my mind. The words were, CERTAIN EVIDENCE OF DIVINE TRUTH. They were again repeated exactly in the same manner, and then the light disappeared.

Feeling the exercise in relation to a visit to the Southern Provinces to increase upon me, I acquainted our Monthly Meeting therewith, and obtained their certificate. Expecting to go alone, one of my brothers who lived in Philadelphia, having some business in North Carolina, proposed going with me part of the way; but as he had a view of some outward affairs, to accept of him as a companion was some difficulty with me, whereupon I had conversation with him at sundry times. At length feeling easy in my mind, I had conversation with several elderly Friends of Philadelphia on the subject, and he obtaining a certificate suitable to the occasion, we set off in the fifth month, 1757. Coming to Nottingham week-day meeting, we lodged at John Churchman's, where I met with our friend, Benjamin Buffington, from New England, who was returning from a visit to the Southern Provinces. Thence we crossed the river Susquehanna, and lodged at William Cox's in Maryland.

Soon after I entered this province a deep and painful exercise came upon me, which I often had some feeling of, since my mind was drawn toward these parts, and with which I had acquainted my brother before we agreed to join as companions. As the people in this and the Southern Provinces live much on the labor of slaves, many of whom are used hardly, my concern was that I might attend with singleness of heart to the voice of the true Shepherd, and be so supported as to remain unmoved at the faces of men.

As it is common for Friends on such a visit to have entertainment free of cost, a difficulty arose in my mind with respect to saving my money by kindness received from what appeared to me to be the gain of oppression. Receiving a gift, considered as a gift, brings the receiver under obligations to the benefactor, and has a natural tendency to draw the obliged into a party with the giver. To prevent difficulties of this kind, and to preserve the minds of judges from any bias, was that Divine prohibition: "Thou shalt not receive any gift; for a gift blindeth the wise, and perverteth the words of the righteous." (Exod. xxiii. 8.) As the disciples were sent forth without any provision for their journey, and our Lord said the workman is worthy of his meat, their labor in the gospel was considered as a reward for their entertainment, and therefore not received as a gift; yet, in regard to my present journey, I could not see my way clear in that respect. The difference appeared thus: the entertainment the disciples met with was from them whose hearts God had opened to receive them, from a love to them and the truth they published; but we, considered as members of the same religious society, look upon it as a piece of civility to receive each other in such visits; and such reception, at times, is partly in regard to reputation, and not from an inward unity of heart and spirit. Conduct is more convincing than language, and where people, by their actions, manifest that the slave-trade is not so disagreeable to their principles but that it may be encouraged, there is not a sound uniting with some Friends who visit them.

The prospect of so weighty a work, and of being so distinguished from many whom I esteemed before myself, brought me very low, and such were the conflicts of my soul that I had a near sympathy with the Prophet, in the time of his weakness, when he said: "If thou deal thus with me, kill me, I pray thee, if I have found favor in thy sight." (Num. xi. 15.) But I soon saw that this proceeded from the want of a full resignation to the Divine will. Many were the afflictions which attended me, and in great abasement, with many tears, my cries were to the Almighty for his gracious and fatherly assistance, and after a time of deep trial I was honored to understand the state mentioned by the Psalmist more clearly than ever I had done before; To wit: "My soul is even as a weaned child." (Psalm cxxxi. 2.) Being thus helped to sink down unto resignation, I felt a deliverance from that tempest in which I had been sorely exercised, and in calmness of mind went forward, trusting that the Lord Jesus Christ, as I faithfully attended to him, should be a counsellor to me in all difficulties, and that by his strength I should be enabled even to save money with the members of society where we had entertainment, when I found that omitting it would obstruct that work to which I believed he had called me. As I copy this after my return, I may here add, that oftentimes I did so under a sense of duty. The way in which I did it was thus: when I expected soon to leave a Friend's house where I had entertainment, if I believed that I should not keep clear from the gain of oppression without leaving money,I spoke to one of the heads of the family privately, and desired them to accept of those pieces of silver, and give them to such of their negroes as they believed would make the best use of them; and at other times I gave them to the negroes myself, as the way looked clearest to me. Before I came out, I had provided a large number of small pieces for this purpose and thus offering them to some who appeared to be wealthy people was a trial both to me and them. But the fear of the Lord so covered me at times that my way was made easier than I expected; and few, if any, manifested any resentment at the offer, and most of them, after some conversation, accepted of them.

Ninth of fifth month. — A Friend at whose house we breakfasted setting us a little on our way, I had conversation with him, in the fear of the Lord, concerning his slaves, in which my heart was tender; I used much plainness of speech with him, and he appeared to take it kindly. We pursued our journey without appointing meetings, being pressed in my mind to be at the Yearly Meeting in Virginia. In my travelling on the road, I often felt a cry rise from the centre of my mind, thus: "O Lord, I am a stranger on the earth, hide not thy face from me." On the 11th, we crossed the rivers Patowmack and Rapahannock, and lodged at Port Royal. On the way we had the company of a colonel of the militia, who appeared to be a thoughtful man. I took occasion to remark on the difference in general betwixt a people used to labor moderately for their living, training up their children in frugality and business, and those who live on the labor of slaves; the former, in my view, being the most happy life. He concurred in the remark, and mentioned the trouble arising from the untoward, slothful disposition of the negroes, adding that one of our laborers would do as much in a day as two of their slaves. I replied, that free men, whose minds were properly on their business, found a satisfaction in improving, cultivating, and providing for their families; but negroes, laboring to support others who claim them as their property, and expecting nothing but slavery during life, had not the like inducement to be industrious.

After some further conversation I said, that men having power too often misapplied it; that though we made slaves of the negroes, and the Turks made slaves of the Christians, I believed that liberty was the natural right of all men equally. This he did not deny, but said the lives of the negroes were so wretched in their own country that many of them lived better here than there. I replied, "There is great odds in regard to us on what principle we act; and so the conversation on that subject ended. I may here add that another person, some time afterwards, mentioned the wretchedness of the negroes, occasioned by their intestine wars, as an argument in favor of our fetching them away for slaves. To which I replied, if compassion for the Africans, on account of their domestic troubles, was the real motive of our purchasing them, that spirit of tenderness being attended to, would incite us to use them kindly, that, as strangers brought out of affliction, their lives might be happy among us. And as they are human creatures, whose souls are as precious as ours, and who may receive the same help and comfort from the Holy Scriptures as we do, we could not omit suitable endeavors to instruct them therein; but that while we manifest by our conduct that our views in purchasing them are to advance ourselves, and while our buying captives taken in war animates those parties to push on the war, and increase desolation amongst them, to say they live unhappily in Africa is far from being an argument in our favor. I further said, the present circumstances of these provinces to me appear difficult; the slaves look like a burdensome stone to such as burden themselves with them; and that if the white people retain a resolution to prefer their outward prospects of gain to all other considerations, and do not act conscientiously toward them as fellow-creatures, I believe that burden will grow heavier and heavier, until times change in a way disagreeable to us. The person appeared very serious, and owned that in considering their condition and the manner of their treatment in these provinces he had sometimes thought it might be just in the Almighty so to order it.

Having travelled through Maryland, we came amongst Friends at Cedar Creek in Virginia, on the 12th; and the next day rode, in company with several of them, a day's journey to Camp Creek. As I was riding along in the morning, my mind was deeply affected in a sense I had of the need of Divine aid to support me in the various difficulties which attended me, and in uncommon distress of mind I cried in secret to the Most High, "O Lord be merciful, I beseech thee, to thy poor afflicted creature!" And some time, I felt inward relief, and, soon after, a Friend in company began to talk in support of the slave-trade, and said the negroes were understood to be the offspring of Cain, their blackness being the mark which God sent upon him after he murdered Abel his brother; that it was the design of Providence they should be slaves, as a condition proper to the race of so wicked a man as Cain was. Then another spake in support of what had been said. To all which I replied in substance as follows: that Noah and his family were all who survived the flood, according to Scripture; and as Noah was of Seth's race, the family of Cain was wholly destroyed. One of them said that after the flood Ham went to the land of Nod and took a wife; that Nod was a land far distant, inhabited by Cain's race, and that the flood did not reach it; and as Ham was sentenced to be a servant of servants to his brethren, these two families, being thus joined, were undoubtedly fit only for slaves. I replied, the flood was a judgment upon the world for their abominations, and it was granted that Cain's stock was the most wicked, and therefore unreasonable to suppose that they were spared. As to Ham's going to the land of Nod for a wife, no time being fixed, Nod might be inhabited by some of Noah's family before Ham married a second time; moreover the text saith "That all flesh died that moved upon the earth." (Gen. vii. 21.) I further reminded them how the prophets repeatedly declare "that the son shall not suffer for the iniquity of the father, but every one be answerable for his own sins." I was troubled to perceive the darkness of their imaginations, and in some pressure of spirit said, "The love of ease and gain are the motives in general of keeping slaves, and men are wont to take hold of weak arguments to support a cause which is unreasonable. I have no interest on either side, save only the interest which I desire to have in the truth.

I believe liberty is their right, and as I see they are not only deprived of it, but treated in other respects with inhumanity in many places, I believe He who is a refuge for the oppressed will, in his own time, plead their cause, and happy will it be for such as walk in uprightness before him." And thus our conversation ended.

Fourteenth of fifth month. — I was this day at Camp Creek Monthly Meeting, and then rode to the mountains up James River, and had a meeting at a Friend's house, in both which I felt sorrow of heart, and my tears were poured out before the Lord, who was pleased to afford a degree of strength by which way was opened to clear my mind amongst Friends in those places. From thence I went to Fork Creek, and so to Cedar Creek again, at which place I now had a meeting. Here I found a tender seed, and as I was preserved in the ministery to keep low with the truth, the same truth in their hearts answered it, that it was a time of mutual refreshment from the presence of the Lord. I lodged at James Standley's, father of William Standley, one of the young men who suffered imprisonment at Winchester last summer on account of their testimony against fighting, and I had some satisfactory conversation with him concerning it. Hence I went to the Swamp Meeting, and to Wayanoke Meeting, and then crossed James River, and lodged near Burleigh. From the time of my entering Maryland I have been much under sorrow, which of late so increased upon me that my mind was almost overwhelmed, and I may say with the Psalmist, "In my distress I called upon the Lord, and cried to my God," who, in infinite goodness, looked upon my affliction, and in my private retirement sent the Comforter for my relief, for which I humbly bless his holy name.

The sense I had of the state of the churches brought a weight of distress upon me. The gold to me appeared dim, and the fine gold changed, and though this is the case too generally, yet the sense of it in these parts hath in a particular manner borne heavy upon me. It appeared to me that through the prevailing of the spirit of this world the minds of many were brought to an inward desolation, and instead of the spirit of meekness, gentleness, and heavenly wisdom, which are the necessary companions of the true sheep of Christ, a spirit of fierceness and the love of dominion too generally prevailed. From small beginnings in error great buildings by degrees are raised, and from one age to another are more and more strengthened by the general concurrence of the people; and as men obtain reputation by their profession of the truth, their virtues are mentioned as arguments in favor of general error; and those of less note, to justify themselves, say, such and such good men did the like. By what other steps could the people of Judah arise to that height in wickedness as to give just ground for the Prophet Isaiah to declare, in the name of the Lord, "that none calleth for justice, nor any pleadeth for truth" (Isa. lix. 4), or for the Almighty to call upon the great city of Jerusalem just before the Babylonish captivity, "If ye can find a man, if there be any who executeth judgment, that seeketh the truth, and I will pardon it"? (Jer. v. 1.)

The prospect of a way being open to the same degeneracy, in some parts of this newly settled land of America, in respect to our conduct towards the negroes, hath deeply bowed my mind in this journey, and though briefly to relate how these people are treated is no agreeable work, yet, after often reading over the notes I made as I travelled, I find my mind engaged to preserve them. Many of the white people in those provinces take little or no care of negro marriages; and when negroes marry after their own way, some make so little account of those marriages that with views of outward interest they often part men from their wives by selling them far asunder, which is common when estates are sold by executors at vendue. Many whose labor is heavy being followed at their business in the field by a man with a whip, hired for that purpose, have in common little else allowed but one peck of Indian corn and some salt for one week, with a few potatoes; the potatoes they commonly raise by their labor on the first day of the week. The correction ensuing on their disobedience to overseers, or slothfulness in business, is often very severe, and sometimes desperate.

Men and women have many times scarcely clothes sufficient to hide their nakedness, and boys and girls ten and twelve years old are often quite naked amongst their master's children. Some of our Society, and some of the society called Newlights, use some endeavors to instruct those they have in reading; but in common this is not only neglected, but disapproved. These are the people by whose labor the other inhabitants are in a great measure supported, and many of them in the luxuries of life. These are the people who have made no agreement to serve us, and who have not forfeited their liberty that we know of. These are the souls for whom Christ died, and for our conduct towards them we must answer before Him who is no respecter of persons. They who know the only true God, and Jesus Christ whom he hath sent, and are thus acquainted with the merciful, benevolent, gospel spirit, will therein perceive that the indignation of God is kindled against oppression and cruelty, and in beholding the great distress of so numerous a people will find cause for mourning.

From my lodgings I went to Burleigh Meeting, where I felt my mind drawn in a quiet, resigned state. After long silence I felt an engagement to stand up, and through the powerful operation of Divine love we were favored with an edifying meeting. The next meeting we had was at Black-Water, and from thence went to the Yearly Meeting at the Western Branch. When business began, some queries were introduced by some of their members for consideration, and, if approved, they were to be answered hereafter by their respective Monthly Meetings.

They were the Pennsylvania queries, which had been examined by a committee of Virginia Yearly Meeting appointed the last year, who made some alterations in them, one of which alterations was made in favor of a custom which troubled me. The query was, "Are there any concerned in the importation of negroes, or in buying them after imported?" which was thus altered, "Are there any concerned in the importation of negroes, or buying them to trade in?" As one query admitted with unanimity was, "Are any concerned in buying or vending goods unlawfully imported, or prize goods?" I found my mind engaged to say that as we profess the truth, and were there assembled to support the testimony of it, it was necessary for us to dwell deep and act in that wisdom which is pure, or otherwise we could not prosper. I then mentioned their alteration, and referring to the last-mentioned query, added, that as purchasing any merchandise taken by the sword was always allowed to be inconsistent with our principles, so negroes being captives of war, or taken by stealth, it was inconsistent with our testimony to buy them; and their being our fellow-creatures, and sold as slaves, added greatly to the iniquity. Friends appeared attentive to what was said; some expressed a care and concern about their negroes; none made any objection, by way of reply to what I said, but the query was admitted as they had altered it.

As some of their members have heretofore traded in negroes, as in other merchandise, this query being admitted will be one step further than they have hitherto gone, and I did not see it my duty to press for an alteration, but felt easy to leave it all to Him who alone is able to turn the hearts of the mighty, and make way for the spreading of truth on the earth, by means agreeable to his infinite wisdom. In regard to those they already had, I felt my mind engaged to labor with them, and said that as we believe the Scriptures were given forth by holy men, as they were moved by the Holy Ghost, and many of us know by experience that they are often helpful and comfortable, and believe ourselves bound in duty to teach our children to read them; I believed that if we were divested of all selfish views, the same good spirit that gave them forth would engage us to teach the negroes to read, that they might have the benefit of them. Some present manifested a concern to take more care in the education of their negroes.

Twenty-ninth fifth month. — At the house where I lodged was a meeting of ministers and elders. I found an engagement to speak freely and plainly to them concerning their slaves; mentioning how they as the first rank in the society, whose conduct in that case was much noticed by others, were under the stronger obligations to look carefully to themselves. Expressing how needful it was for them in that situation to be thoroughly divested of all selfish views; that, living in the pure truth, and acting conscientiously towards those people in their education and otherwise, they might be instrumental in helping forward a work so exceedingly necessary, and so much neglected amongst them. At the twelfth hour the meeting of worship began, which was a solid meeting.

The next day, about the tenth hour, Friends met to finish their business, and then the meeting for worship ensued, which to me was a laborious time; but through the goodness of the Lord, truth, I believed, gained some ground, and it was a strengthening opportunity to the honest-hearted.

About this time I wrote an epistle to Friends in the back settlements of North Carolina, as follows: —

To Friends at their Monthly Meeting at New Garden and Cane Creek, in North Carolina:—

Dear Friends,—It having pleased the Lord to draw me forth on a visit to some parts of Virginia and Carolina, you have often been in my mind; and though my way is not clear to come in person to visit you, yet I feel it in my heart to communicate a few things, as they arise in the love of truth. First, my dear friends, dwell in humility; and take heed that no views of outward gain get too deep hold of you, that so your eyes being single to the Lord, you may be preserved in the way of safety. Where people let loose their minds after the love of outward things, and are more engaged in pursuing the profits and seeking the friendships of this world than to be inwardly acquainted with the way of true peace, they walk in a vain shadow, while the true comfort of life is wanting. Their examples are often hurtful to others; and their treasures thus collected do many times prove dangerous snares to their children.

But where people are sincerely devoted to follow Christ, and dwell under the influence of his Holy Spirit, their stability and firmness, through a Divine blessing, is at times like dew on the tender plants round about them, and the weightiness of their spirits secretly works on the minds of others. In this condition, through the spreading influence of Divine love, they feel a care over the flock, and way is opened for maintaining good order in the Society. And though we may meet with opposition from another spirit, yet, as there is a dwelling in meekness, feeling our spirits subject, and moving only in the gentle, peaceable wisdom, the inward reward of quietness will be greater than all our difficulties. Where the pure life is kept to, and meetings of discipline are held in the authority of it, we find by experience that they are comfortable, and tend to the health of the body.

While I write, the youth come fresh in my way. Dear young people, choose God for your portion; love his truth, and be not ashamed of it; choose for your company such as serve him in uprightness; and shun as most dangerous the conversation of those whose lives are of an ill savor; for by frequenting such company some hopeful young people have come to great loss, and been drawn from less evils to greater, to their utter ruin. In the bloom of youth no ornament is so lovely as that of virtue, nor any enjoyment equal to those which we partake of in fully resigning ourselves to the Divine will. These enjoyments add sweetness to all other comforts, and give true satisfaction in company and conversation, where people are mutually acquainted with it; and as your minds are thus seasoned with the truth, you will find strength to abide steadfast to the testimony of it, and be prepared for services in the church.

And now, dear friends and brethren, as you are improving a wilderness, and may be numbered amongst the first planters in one part of a province, I beseech you, in the love of Jesus Christ, wisely to consider the force of your examples, and think how much your successors may be thereby affected. It is a help in a country, yea, and a great favor and blessing, when customs first settled are agreeable to sound wisdom; but when they are otherwise the effect of them is grievous; and children feel themselves encompassed with difficulties prepared for them by their predecessors.

As moderate care and exercise, under the direction of true wisdom, are useful both to mind and body, so by these means in general the real wants of life are easily supplied, our gracious Father having so proportioned one to the other that keeping in the medium we may pass on quietly. Where slaves are purchased to do our labor numerous difficulties attend it. To rational creatures bondage is uneasy, and frequently occasions sourness and discontent in them; which affects the family and such as claim the mastery over them. Thus people and their children are many times encompassed with vexations, which arise from their applying to wrong methods to get a living.

I have been informed that there is a large number of Friends in your parts who have no slaves; and in tender and most affectionate love I beseech you to keep clear from purchasing any. Look, my dear friends, to Divine Providence, and follow in simplicity that exercise of body, that plainness and frugality, which true wisdom leads to; so may you be preserved from those dangers which attend such as are aiming at outward ease and greatness.

Treasures, though small, attained on a true principle of virtue, are sweet; and while we walk in the light of the Lord there is true comfort and satisfaction in the possession; neither the murmurs of an oppressed people, nor a throbbing, uneasy conscience, nor anxious thoughts about the events of things, hinder the enjoyment of them.

When we look towards the end of life, and think on the division of our substance among our successors, if we know that it was collected in the fear of the Lord, in honesty, in equity, and in uprightness of heart before him, we may consider it as his gift to us, and, with a single eye to his blessing, bestow it on those we leave behind us. Such is the happiness of the plain ways of true virtue. "The work of righteousness shall be peace; and the effect of righteousness, quietness and assurance for ever." (Isa. xxxii. 17.)

Dwell here, my dear friends; and then in remote and solitary deserts you may find true peace and satisfaction. If the Lord be our God, in truth and reality, there is safety for us; for he is a stronghold in the day of trouble, and knoweth them that trust in him.

*Isle of Wight County, in Virginia,*
*20th of the 5th month, 1757*

From the Yearly Meeting in Virginia I went to Carolina, and on the 1st of sixth month was at Wells Monthly Meeting, where the spring of the gospel ministry was opened, and the love of Jesus Christ experienced among us; to his name be the praise.

Here my brother joined with some Friends from New Garden who were going homeward; and I went next to Simons Creek Monthly Meeting, where I was silent during the meeting for worship. When business came on, my mind was exercised concerning the poor slaves, but I did not feel my way clear to speak. In this condition I was bowed in spirit before the Lord, and with tears and inward supplication besought him so to open my understanding that I might know his will concerning me; and, at length, my mind was settled in silence. Near the end of their business a member of their meeting expressed a concern that had some time lain upon him, on account of Friends so much neglecting their duty in the education of their slaves, and proposed having meetings sometimes appointed for them on a week day, to be attended only by some Friends to be named in their Monthly Meetings. Many present appeared to unite with the proposal. One said he had often wondered that they, being our fellow-creatures, and capable of religious understanding, had been so exceedingly neglected; another expressed the like concern, and appeared zealous that in future it might be more closely considered. At length a minute was made, and the further consideration of it referred to their next Monthly Meeting. The Friend who made this proposal hath negroes; he told me that he was at New Garden, about two hundred and fifty miles from home, and came back alone; that in this solitary journey this exercise, in regard to the education of their negroes, was from time to time renewed in his mind. A Friend of some note in Virginia, who hath slaves, told me that he being far from home on a lonesome journey had many serious thoughts about them; and his mind was so impressed therewith that he believed he saw a time coming when Divine Providence would alter the circumstances of these people, respecting their condition as slaves.

From hence I went to a meeting at Newbegun Creek, and sat a considerable time in much weakness; then I felt truth open the way to speak a little in much plainness and simplicity, till at length, through the increase of Divine love amongst us, we had a seasoning opportunity. This was also the case at the head of Little River, where we had a crowded meeting on a first-day. I went thence to the Old Neck, where I was led into a careful searching out of the secret workings of the mystery of iniquity, which, under a cover of religion, exalts itself against that pure spirit which leads in the way of meekness and self-denial. Pineywoods was the last meeting I was at in Carolina; it was large, and my heart being deeply engaged, I was drawn forth into a fervent labor amongst them.

When I was at Newbegun Creek a Friend was there who labored for his living, having no negroes, and who had been a minister many years. He came to me the next day, and as we rode together, he signified that he wanted to talk with me concerning a difficulty he had been under, which he related nearly as follows. That as moneys had of late years been raised by a tax to carry on the wars, he had a scruple in his mind in regard to paying it, and chose rather to suffer distraint of his goods; but as he was the only person who refused it in those parts, and knew not that any one else was in the like circumstances, he signified that it had been a heavy trial to him, especially as some of his brethren had been uneasy with his conduct in that case. He added, that from a sympathy he felt with me yesterday in meeting, he found freedom thus to open the matter in the way of querying concerning Friends in our parts; I told him the state of Friends amongst us as well as I was able, and also that L had for some time been under the like scruple. I believed him to be one who was concerned to walk uprightly before the Lord, and esteemed it my duty to preserve this note concerning him, Samuel Newby.

From hence I went back into Virginia, and had a meeting near James Cowpland's; it was a time of inward suffering, but through the goodness of the Lord I was made content; at another meeting, through the renewings of pure love, we had a very comfortable season.

Travelling up and down of late, I have had renewed evidences that to be faithful to the Lord, and content with his will concerning me, is a most necessary and useful lesson for me to be learning; looking less at the effects of my labor than at the pure motion and reality of the concern, as it arises from heavenly love. In the Lord Jehovah is everlasting strength; and as the mind, by humble resignation, is united to Him, and we utter words from an inward knowledge that they arise from the heavenly spring, though our way may be difficult, and it may require close attention to keep in it, and though the manner in which we may be led may tend to our own abasement; yet, if we continue in patience and meekness, heavenly peace will be the reward of our labors.

I attended Curles Meeting, which, though small, was reviving to the honest-hearted. Afterwards I went to Black Creek and Caroline Meetings, from whence, accompanied by William Standley before mentioned, I rode to Goose Creek, being much through the woods, and about one hundred miles. We lodged the first night at a public-house; the second in the woods; and the next day we reached a Friend's house at Goose Creek. In the woods we were under some disadvantage, having no fireworks nor bells for our horses, but we stopped a little before night and let them feed on the wild grass, which was plentiful, in the mean time cutting with our knives a store against night. We then secured our horses, and gathering some bushes under an oak we lay down; but the mosquitoes being numerous and the ground damp I slept but little. Thus lying in the wilderness, and looking at the stars, I was led to contemplate on the condition of our first parents when they were sent forth from the garden; how the Almighty, though they had been disobedient, continued to be a father to them, and showed them what tended to their felicity as intelligent creatures, and was acceptable to him. To provide things relative to our outward living, in the way of true wisdom, is good, and the gift of improving in things useful is a good gift, and comes from the Father of Lights. Many have had this gift; and from age to age there have been improvements of this kind made in the world. But some, not keeping to the pure gift, have in the creaturely cunning and self-exaltation sought out many inventions. As the first motive to these inventions of men, as distinct from that uprightness in which man was created, was evil, so the effects have been and are evil. It is, therefore, as necessary for us at this day constantly to attend on the heavenly gift, to be qualified to use rightly the good things in this life amidst great improvements, as it was for our first parents when they were without any improvements, without any friend or father but God only.

I was at a meeting at Goose Creek, and next at a Monthly Meeting at Fairfax, where, through the gracious dealing of the Almighty with us, his power prevailed over many hearts. From thence I went to Monoquacy and Pipe Creek in Maryland; at both places I had cause humbly to adore Him who had supported me through many exercises, and by whose help I was enabled to reach the true witness in the hearts of others. There were some hopeful young people in those parts. I had meetings afterwards at John Everit's, in Monalen, and at Huntingdon, and I was made humbly thankful to the Lord, who opened my heart amongst the people in these new settlements, so that it was a time of encouragement to the honest-minded.

At Monalen a Friend gave me some account of a religious society among the Dutch, called Mennonists, and amongst other things related a passage in substance as follows: One of the Mennonists having acquaintance with a man of another society at a considerable distance, and being with his wagon on business near the house of his said acquaintance, and night coming on, he had thoughts of putting up with him, but passing by his fields, and observing the distressed appearance of his slaves, he kindled a fire in the woods hard by, and lay there that night. His said acquaintance hearing where he lodged, and afterward meeting the Mennonist, told him of it, adding he should have been heartily welcome at his house, and from their acquaintance in former time wondered at his conduct in that case. The Mennonist replied, "Ever since I lodged by thy field I have wanted an opportunity to speak with thee. I had intended to come to thy house for entertainment, but seeing thy slaves at their work, and observing the manner of their dress, I had no liking to come to partake with thee." He then admonished him to use them with more humanity, and added, "As I lay by the fire that night, I thought that as I was a man of substance thou wouldst have received me freely; but if I had been as poor as one of thy slaves, and had no power to help myself, I should have reecived from thy hand no kinder usage than they."

In this journey I was out about two months, and travelled about eleven hundred and fifty miles. I returned home under an humbling sense of the gracious dealings of the Lord with me, in preserving me through many trials and afflictions.

CHAPTER VIII.

1761, 1762.

Visits Pennsylvania, Shrewsbury, and Squan. — Publishes the Second part of his Considerations on keeping Negroes. — The Grounds of his appearing in some Respects singular in his Dress. — Visit to the Families of Friends of Ancocas and Mount Holly Meetings. — Visits to the Indians at Wehaloosing on the River Susquehanna.

Having felt my mind drawn towards a visit to a few meetings in Pennsylvania, I was very desirous to be rightly instructed as to the time of setting off. On the 10th of fifth month, 1761, being the first day of the week, I went to Haddonfield Meeting, concluding to seek for heavenly instruction, and come home, or go on, as I might then believe best for me, and there through the springing up of pure love I felt encouragement, and so crossed the river. In this visit I was at two quarterly and three monthly meetings, and in the love of truth I felt my way open to labor with some noted Friends who kept negroes. As I was favored to keep to the root, and endeavor to discharge what I believed was required of me, I found inward peace therein, from time to time, and thankfulness of heart to the Lord, who was graciously pleased to be a guide to me.

Eighth month, 1961. — Having felt drawings in my mind to visit Friends in and about Shrewsbury, I went there, and was at their Monthly Meeting, and their first-day meeting; I had also a meeting at Squan, and another at Squanquam, and, as way opened, had conversation with some noted Friends concerning their slaves. I returned home in a thankful sense of the goodness of the Lord.

From the concern I felt growing in me for some years, I wrote part the second of a work entitled "Considerations on keeping Negroes," which was printed this year, 1762. When the overseers of the press had done with it, they offered to get a number printed, to be paid for out of the Yearly Meeting's stock, to be given away; but I being most easy to publish it at my own expense, and offering my reasons, they appeared satisfied.

This stock is the contribution of the members of our religious society in general, among whom are some who keep negroes, and, being inclined to continue them in slavery, are not likely to be satisfied with such books being spread among a people, especially at their own expense, many of whose slaves are taught to read, and such, receiving them as a gift, often conceal them. But as they who make a purchase generally buy that which they have a mind for, I believed it best to sell them, expecting by that means they would more generally be read with attention. Advertisements were signed by order of the overseers of the press, and directed to be read in the Monthly Meetings of business within our own Yearly Meeting, informing where the books were, and that the price was no more than the cost of printing and binding them. Many were taken off in our parts; some I sent to Virginia, some to New York, some to my acquaintance at Newport, and some I kept, intending to give part of them away, where there appeared a prospect of service.

In my youth I was used to hard labor, and though I was middling healthy, yet my nature was not fitted to endure so much as many others. Being often weary, I was prepared to sympathize with those whose circumstances in life, as free men, required constant labor to answer the demands of their creditors, as well as with others under oppression. In the uneasiness of body which I have many times felt by too much labor, not as a forced but a voluntary oppression, I have often been excited to think on the original cause of that oppression which is imposed on many in the world. The latter part of the time wherein I labored on our plantation, my heart, through the fresh visitations of heavenly love, being often tender, and my leisure time being frequently spent in reading the life and doctrines of our blessed Redeemer, the account of the sufferings of martyrs, and the history of the first rise of our Society, a belief was gradually settled in my mind, that if such as had great estates generally lived in that humility and plainness which belong to a Christian life, and laid much easier rents and interests on their lands and moneys, and thus led the way to a right use of things, so great a number of people might be employed in things useful, that labor both for men and other creatures would need to be no more than an agreeable employ, and divers branches of business, which serve chiefly to please the natural inclinations of our minds, and which at present seem necessary to circulate that wealth which some gather, might, in this way of pure wisdom, be discontinued. As I have thus considered these things, a query at times hath arisen: Do I, in all my proceedings, keep to that use of things which is agreeable to universal righteousness? And then there hath some degree of sadness at times come over me, because I accustomed myself to some things which have occasioned more labor than I believe Divine wisdom intended for us.

From my early acquaintance with truth I have often felt an inward distress, occasioned by the striving of a spirit in me against the operation of the heavenly principle; and in this state I have been affected with a sense of my own wretchedness, and in a mourning condition have felt earnest longings for that Divine help which brings the soul into true liberty. Sometimes, on retiring into private places, the spirit of supplication hath been given me, and under a heavenly covering I have asked my gracious Father to give me a heart in all things resigned to the direction of his wisdom; in uttering language like this, the thought of my wearing hats and garments dyed with a dye hurtful to them, has made lasting impression on me.

In visiting people of note in the Society who had slaves, and laboring with them in brotherly love on that account, I have seen, and the sight has affected me, that a conformity to some customs distinguishable from pure wisdom has entangled many, and that the desire of gain to support these customs has greatly opposed the work of truth. Sometimes when the prospect of the work before me has been such that in bowedness of spirit I have been drawn into retired places, and have besought the Lord with tears that he would take me wholly under his direction, and show me the way in which I ought to walk, it hath revived with strength of conviction that if I would be his faithful servant I must in all things attend to his wisdom, and be teachable, and so cease from all customs contrary thereto, however used among religious people.

As he is the perfection of power, of wisdom, and of goodness, so I believe he hath provided that so much labor shall be necessary for men's support in this world as would, being rightly divided, be a suitable employment of their time; and that we cannot go into superfluities, or grasp after wealth in a way contrary to his wisdom, without having connection with some degree of oppression, and with that spirit which leads to self-exaltation and strife and which frequently brings calamities on countries by parties contending about their claims.

Being thus fully convinced, and feeling an increasing desire to live in the spirit of peace, I have often been sorrowfully affected with thinking on the unquiet spirit in which wars are generally carried on, and with the miseries of many of my fellow-creatures engaged therein; some suddenly destroyed; some wounded, and after much pain remaining cripples; some deprived of all their outward substance and reduced to want; and some carried into captivity. Thinking often on these things, the use of hats and garments dyed with a dye hurtful to them, and wearing more clothes in summer than are useful, grew more uneasy to me, believing them to be customs which have not their foundation in pure wisdom. The apprehension of being singular from my beloved friends was a strait upon me, and thus I continued in the use of some things contrary to my judgment.

On the 31st of fifth month, 1761, I was taken ill of a fever, and after it had continued near a week I was in great distress of body. One day there was a cry raised in me that I might understand the cause of my affliction, and improve under it, and my conformity to some customs which I believed were not right was brought to my remembrance. In the continuance of this exercise I felt all the powers in me yield themselves up into the hands of Him who gave me being, and was made thankful that he had taken hold of me by his chastisements. Feeling the necessity of further purifying, there was now no desire in me for health until the design of my correction was answered. Thus I lay in abasement and brokenness of spirit, and as I felt a sinking down into a calm resignation, so I felt, as in an instant, an inward healing in my nature; and from that time forward I grew better.

Though my mind was thus settled in relation to hurtful dyes, I felt easy to wear my garments heretofore made, and continued to do so about nine months. Then I thought of getting a hat the natural color of the fur, but the apprehension of being looked upon as one affecting singularity felt uneasy to me. Here I had occasion to consider that things, though small in themselves, being clearly enjoined by Divine authority, become great things to us; and I trusted that the Lord would support me in the trials that might attend singularity, so long as singularity was only for his sake. On this account I was under close exercise of mind in the time of our General Spring Meeting, 1762, greatly desiring to be rightly directed; when, being deeply bowed in spirit before the Lord, I was made willing to submit to what I apprehended was required of me, and when I returned home got a hat of the natural color of the fur.

In attending meetings this singularity was a trial to me, and more especially at this time, as white hats were used by some who were fond of following the changeable modes of dress, and as some Friends who knew not from what motives I wore it grew shy of me, I felt my way for a time shut up in the exercise of the ministry. In this condition, my mind being turned toward my Heavenly Father with fervent cries that I might be preserved to walk before him in the meekness of wisdom, my heart was often tender in meetings, and I felt an inward consolation which to me was very precious under these difficulties.

I had several dyed garments fit for use which I believed it best to wear till I had occasion for new ones. Some Friends were apprehensive that my wearing such a hat savored of an affected singularity; those who spoke with me in a friendly way I generally informed, in a few words, that I believed my wearing it was not in my own will. I had at times been sensible that a superficial friendship had been dangerous to me; and many Friends being now uneasy with me, I had an inclination to acquaint some with the manner of my being led into these things; yet upon a deeper thought I was for a time most easy to omit it, believing the present dispensation was profitable, and trusting that if I kept my place the Lord in his own time would open the hearts of Friends towards me. I have since had cause to admire his goodness and loving-kindness in leading about and instructing me, and in opening and enlarging my heart in some of our meetings.

In the eleventh month this year, feeling an engagement of mind to visit some families in Mansfield, I joined my beloved friend Benjamin Jones, and we spent a few days together in that service. In the second month, 1763, I joined, in company with Elizabeth Smith and Mary Noble, in a visit to the families of Friends at Ancocas. In both these visits, through the baptizing power of truth, the sincere laborers were often comforted, and the hearts of Friends opened to receive us. In the fourth month following, I accompanied some Friends in a visit to the families of Friends in Mount Holly; during this visit my mind was often drawn into an inward awfulness, wherein strong desires were raised for the everlasting welfare of my fellow-creatures, and through the kindness of our Heavenly Father our hearts were at times enlarged, and Friends were invited, in the flowings of Divine love, to attend to that which would settle them on the sure foundation.

Having for many years felt love in my heart towards the natives of this land who dwell far back in the wilderness, whose ancestors were formerly the owners and possessors of the land where we dwell, and who for a small consideration assigned their inheritance to us, and being at Philadelphia in the 8th month, 1761, on a visit to some Friends who had slaves, I fell in company with some of those natives who lived on the east branch of the river Susquehanna, at an Indian town called Wehaloosing, two hundred miles from Philadelphia. In conversation with them by an interpreter, as also by observations on their countenances and conduct, I believed some of them were measurably acquainted with that Divine power which subjects the rough and froward will of the creature. At times I felt inward drawings towards a visit to that place, which I mentioned to none except my dear wife until it came to some ripeness. In the winter of 1762 I laid my prospects before my friends at our Monthly and Quarterly, and afterwards at our General Spring Meeting; and having the unity of Friends, and being thoughtful about an Indian pilot, there came a man and three women from a little beyond that town to Philadelphia on business. Being informed thereof by letter, I met them in town in the 5th month, 1763; and after some conversation, finding they were sober people, I, with the concurrence of Friends in that place, agreed to join them as companions in their return, and we appointed to meet at Samuel Foulk's, at Richland, in Bucks County, on the 7th of sixth month. Now, as this visit felt weighty, and was performed at a time when travelling appeared perilous, so the dispensations of Divine Providence in preparing my mind for it have been memorable, and I believe it good for me to give some account thereof.

After I had given up to go, the thoughts of the journey were often attended with unusual sadness; at which times my heart was frequently turned to the Lord with inward breathings for his heavenly support, that I might not fail to follow him wheresoever he might lead me. Being at our youth's meeting at Chesterfield, about a week before the time I expected to set off, I was there led to speak on that prayer of our Redeemer to the Father: "I pray not that thou shouldest take them out of the world, but that thou shouldest keep them from the evil." And in attending to the pure openings of truth, I had to mention what he elsewhere said to his Father: "I know that thou hearest me at all times"; so, as some of his followers kept their places, and as his prayer was granted, it followed necessarily that they were kept from evil; and as some of those met with great hardships and afflictions in this world, and at last suffered death by cruel men, so it appears that whatsoever befalls men while they live in pure obedience to God certainly works for their good, and may not be considered an evil as it relates to them. As I spake on this subject my heart was much tendered, and great awfulness came over me. On the first day of the week, being at our own afternoon meeting, and my heart being enlarged in love, I was led to speak on the care and protection of the Lord over his people, and to make mention of that passage where a band of Syrians, who were endeavoring to take captive the prophet, were disappointed; and how the Psalmist said, "The angel of the Lord encampeth round about them that fear him." Thus, in true love and tenderness, I parted from Friends, expecting the next morning to proceed on my journey. Being weary I went early to bed. After I had been asleep a short time I was awoke by a man calling at my door, and inviting me to meet some Friends at a public-house in our town, who came from Philadelphia so late that Friends were generally gone to bed. These Friends informed me that an express had arrived the last morning from Pittsburg, and brought news that the Indians had taken a fort from the English westward, and had slain and scalped some English people near the said Pittsburg, and in divers places. Some elderly Friends in Philadelphia, knowing the time of my intending to set off, had conferred together, and thought good to inform me of these things before I left home, that I might consider them and proceed as I believed best. Going to bed again, I told not my wife till morning. My heart was turned to the Lord for his heavenly instruction; and it was an humbling time to me. When I told my dear wife, she appeared to be deeply concerned about it; but in a few hours' time my mind became settled in a belief that it was my duty to proceed on my journey, and she bore it with a good degree of resignation. In this conflict of spirit there were great searchings of heart and strong cries to the Lord, that no motion might in the least degree be attended to but that of the pure spirit of truth.

The subjects before mentioned, on which I had so lately spoken in public, were now fresh before me, and I was brought inwardly to commit myself to the Lord, to be disposed of as he saw best. I took leave of my family and neighbors in much bowedness of spirit, and went to our Monthly Meeting at Burlington. After taking leave of Friends there, I crossed the river, accompanied by my friends, Israel and John Pemberton; and parting the next morning with Israel, John bore me company to Samuel Foulk's, where I met the before-mentioned Indians; and we were glad to see each other. Here my friend Benjamin Parvin met me, and proposed joining me as a companion, — we had before exchanged some letters on the subject, — and now I had a sharp trial on his account; for, as the journey appeared perilous, I thought if he went chiefly to bear me company, and we should be taken captive, my having been the means of drawing him into these difficulties would add to my own afflictions; so I told him my mind freely, and let him know that I was resigned to go alone; but after all, if he really believed it to be his duty to go on, I believed his company would be very comfortable to me. It was, indeed, a time of deep exercise, and Benjamin appeared to be so fastened to the visit that he could not be easy to leave me; so we went on, accompanied by our friends John Pemberton and William Lightfoot of Pikeland. We lodged at Bethlehem, and there parting with John, William and we went forward on the 9th of the sixth month, and got lodging on the floor of a house, about five miles from Fort Allen. Here we parted with William, and at this place we met with an Indian trader lately come from Wyoming. In conversation with him, I perceived that many white people often sell rum to the Indians, which I believe is a great evil. In the first place, they are thereby deprived of the use of reason, and, their spirits being violently agitated, quarrels often arise which end in mischief, and the bitterness and resentment occasioned hereby are frequently of long continuance. Again, their skins and furs, gotten through much fatigue and hard travels in hunting, with which they intended to buy clothing, they often sell at a low rate for more rum, when they become intoxicated; and afterward, when they suffer for want of the necessaries of life, are angry with those who, for the sake of gain, took advantage of their weakness. Their chiefs have often complained of this in their treaties with the English. Where cunning people pass counterfeits and impose on others that which is good for nothing, it is considered as wickedness; but for the sake of gain to sell that which we know does people harm, and which often works their ruin, manifests a hardened and corrupt heart, and is an evil which demands the care of all true lovers of virtue to suppress. While my mind this evening was thus employed, I also remembered that the people on the frontiers, among whom this evil is too common, are often poor; and that they venture to the outside of a colony in order to live more independently of the wealthy, who often set high rents on their land. I was renewedly confirmed in a belief, that if all our inhabitants lived according to sound wisdom, laboring to promote universal love and righteousness, and ceased from every inordinate desire after wealth, and from all customs which are tinctured with luxury, the way would be easy for our inhabitants, though they might be much more numerous than at present, to live comfortably on honest employments, without the temptation they are so often under of being drawn into schemes to make settlements on lands which have not been purchased of the Indians, or of applying to that wicked practice of selling rum to them.

Tenth of sixth month. — We set out early this morning and crossed the western branch of Delaware, called the Great Lehie, near Fort Allen. The water being high, we went over in a canoe. Here we met an Indian, had friendly conversation with him, and gave him some biscuit; and he, having killed a deer, gave some of it to the Indians with us. After travelling some miles, we met several Indian men and women with a cow and horse, and some household goods, who were lately come from their dwelling at Wyoming, and were going to settle at another place. We made them some small presents, and, as some of them understood English, I told them my motive for coming into their country, with which they appeared satisfied. One of our guides talking awhile with an ancient woman concerning us, the poor old woman came to my companion and me and took her leave of us with an appearance of sincere affection. We pitched our tent near the banks of the same river, having labored hard in crossing some of those mountains called the Blue Ridge. The roughness of the stones and the cavities between them, with the steepness of the hills, made it appear dangerous. But we were preserved in safety, through the kindness of Him whose works in these mountainous deserts appeared awful, and towards whom my heart was turned during this day's travel.

Near our tent, on the sides of large trees peeled for that purpose, were various representations of men going to and returning from the wars, and of some being killed in battle. This was a path heretofore used by warriors, and as I walked about viewing those Indian histories, which were painted mostly in red or black, and thinking on the innumerable afflictions which the proud, fierce spirit produceth in the world, also on the toils and fatigues of warriors in travelling over mountains and deserts; on their miseries and distresses when far from home and wounded by their enemies; of their bruises and great weariness in chasing one another over the rocks and mountains; of the restless, unquiet state of mind of those who live in this spirit, and of the hatred which mutually grows up in the minds of their children, — the desire to cherish the spirit of love and peace among these people arose very fresh in me. This was the first night that we lodged in the woods, and being wet with travelling in the rain, as were also our blankets, the ground, our tent, and the bushes under which we purposed to lay, all looked discouraging; but I believed that it was the Lord who had thus far brought me forward, and that he would dispose of me as he saw good, and so I felt easy. We kindled a fire, with our tent open to it, then laid some bushes next the ground, and put our blankets upon them for our bed, and, lying down, got some sleep. In the morning, feeling a little unwell, I went into the river; the water was cold, but soon after I felt fresh and well. About eight o'clock we set forward and crossed a high mountain supposed to be upward of four miles over, the north side being the steepest. About noon we were overtaken by one of the Moravian brethren going to Wehaloosing, and an Indian man with him who could talk English; and we being together while our horses ate grass had some friendly conversation; but they, travelling faster than we, soon left us. This Moravian, I understood, had this spring spent some time at Wehaloosing, and was invited by some of the Indians to come again.

Twelfth of sixth month being the first of the week and a rainy day, we continued in our tent, and I was led to think on the nature of the exercise which hath attended me. Love was the first motion, and thence a concern arose to spend some time with the Indians, that I might feel and understand their life and the spirit they live in, if haply I might receive some instruction from them, or they might be in any degree helped forward by my following the leadings of truth among them; and as it pleased the Lord to make way for my going at a time when the troubles of war were increasing, and when, by reason of much wet weather, travelling was more difficult than usual at that season, I looked upon it as a more favorable opportunity to season my mind, and to bring me into a nearer sympathy with them. As mine eye was to the great Father of Mercies, humbly desiring to learn his will concerning me, I was made quiet and content.

Our guide's horse strayed, though hoppled, in the night, and after searching some time for him his footsteps were discovered in the path going back, whereupon my kind companion went off in the rain, and after about seven hours returned with him. Here we lodged again, tying up our horses before we went to bed, and loosing them to feed about break of day.

Thirteenth of sixth month.—The sun appearing, we set forward, and as

I rode over the barren hills my meditations were on the alterations in the circumstances of the natives of this land since the coming in of the English. The lands near the sea are conveniently situated for fishing; the lands near the rivers, where the tides flow, and some above, are in many places fertile, and not mountainous, while the changing of the tides makes passing up and down easy with any kind of traffic. The natives have in some places, for trifling considerations, sold their inheritance so favorably situated, and in other places have been driven back by superior force; their way of clothing themselves is also altered from what it was, and they being far removed from us have to pass over mountains, swamps, and barren deserts, so that travelling is very troublesome in bringing their skins and furs to trade with us. By the extension of English settlements, and partly by the increase of English hunters, the wild beasts on which the natives chiefly depend for subsistence are not so plentiful as they were, and people too often, for the sake of gain, induce them to waste their skins and furs in purchasing a liquor which tends to the ruin of them and their families.

My own will and desires were now very much broken, and my heart was with much earnestness turned to the Lord, to whom alone I looked for help in the dangers before me. I had a prospect of the English along the coast for upwards of nine hundred miles, where I travelled, and their favorable situation and the difficulties attending the natives as well as the negroes in many places were open before me. A weighty and heavenly care came over my mind, and love filled my heart towards all mankind, in which I felt a strong engagement that we might be obedient to the Lord while in tender mercy he is yet calling to us, and that we might so attend to pure universal righteousness as to give no just cause of offence to the gentiles, who do not profess Christianity, whether they be the blacks from Africa, or the native inhabitants of this continent. Here I was led into a close and laborious inquiry whether I, as an individual, kept clear from all things which tended to stir up or were connected with wars, either in this land or in Africa; my heart was deeply concerned that in future I might in all things keep steadily to the pure truth, and live and walk in the plainness and simplicity of a sincere follower of Christ. In this lonely journey I did greatly bewail the spreading of a wrong spirit, believing that the prosperous, convenient situation of the English would require a constant attention in us to Divine love and wisdom, in order to their being guided and supported in a way answerable to the will of that good, gracious, and Almighty Being, who hath an equal regard to all mankind. And here luxury and covetousness, with the numerous oppressions and other evils attending them, appeared very afflicting to me, and I felt in that which is immutable that the seeds of great calamity and desolation are sown and growing fast on this continent. Nor have I words sufficient to set forth the longing I then felt, that we who are placed along the coast, and have tasted the love and goodness of God, might arise in the strength thereof, and like faithful messengers labor to check the growth of these seeds, that they may not ripen to the ruin of our posterity.

On reaching the Indian settlement at Wyoming, we were told that an Indian runner had been at that place a day or two before us, and brought news of the Indians having taken an English fort westward, and destroyed the people, and that they were endeavoring to take another; also that another Indian runner came there about the middle of the previous night from a town about ten miles from Wehaloosing, and brought the news that some Indian warriors from distant parts came to that town with two English scalps, and told the people that it was war with the English.

Our guides took us to the house of a very ancient man. Soon after we had put in our baggage there came a man from another Indian house some distance off. Perceiving there was a man near the door I went out; the man had a tomahawk wrapped under his match-coat out of sight. As I approached him he took it in his hand; I went forward, and, speaking to him in a friendly way, perceived he understood some English. My companion joining me, we had some talk with him concerning the nature of our visit in these parts; he then went into the house with us, and, talking with our guides, soon appeared friendly, sat down and smoked his pipe. Though taking his hatchet in his hand at the instant I drew near to him had a disagreeable appearance, I believe he had no other intent than to be in readiness in case any violence were offered to him.

On hearing the news brought by these Indian runners, and being told by the Indians where we lodged, that the Indians about Wyoming expected in a few days to move to some larger towns, I thought, to all outward appearance, it would be dangerous travelling at this time. After a hard day's journey I was brought into a painful exercise at night, in which I had to trace back and view the steps I had taken from my first moving in the visit; and though I had to bewail some weakness which at times had attended me, yet I could not find that I had ever given way to wilful disobedience. Believing I had, under a sense of duty, come thus far, I was now earnest in spirit, beseeching the Lord to show me what I ought to do. In this great distress I grew jealous of myself, lest the desire of reputation as a man firmly settled to persevere through dangers, or the fear of disgrace from my returning without performing the visit, might have some place in me. Full of these thoughts, I lay great part of the night, while my beloved companion slept by me, till the Lord, my gracious Father, who saw the conflicts of my soul, was pleased to give quietness. Then I was again strengthened to commit my life, and all things relating thereto, into his heavenly hands, and got a little sleep towards day.

Fourteenth of sixth month.—We sought out and visited all the Indians hereabouts that we could meet with, in number about twenty. They were chiefly in one place, about a mile from where we lodged. I expressed to them the care I had on my mind for their good, and told them that true love had made me willing thus to leave my family to come and see the Indians and speak with them in their houses. Some of them appeared kind and friendly. After taking leave of them, we went up the river Susquehanna about three miles, to the house of an Indian called Jacob January. He had killed his hog, and the women were making store of bread and preparing to move up the river. Here our pilots had left their canoe when they came down in the spring, and lying dry it had become leaky. This detained us some hours, so that we had a good deal of friendly conversation with the family; and, eating dinner with them, we made them some small presents. Then putting our baggage into the canoe, some of them pushed slowly up the stream, and the rest of us rode our horses. We swam them over a creek called Lahawahamunk, and pitched our tent above it in the evening. In a sense of God's goodness in helping me in my distress, sustaining me under trials, and inclining my heart to trust in him, I lay down in an humble, bowed frame of mind, and had a comfortable night's lodging.

Fifteenth of sixth month.—We proceeded forward till the afternoon, when, a storm appearing, we met our canoe at an appointed place and stayed all night, the rain continuing so heavy that it beat through our tent and wet both us and our baggage. The next day we found abundance of trees blown down by the storm yesterday, and had occasion reverently to consider the kind dealings of the Lord, who provided a safe place for us in a valley while this storm continued. We were much hindered by the trees which had fallen across our path, and in some swamps our way was so stopped that we got through with extreme difficulty. I had this day often to consider myself as a sojourner in this world. A belief in the all-sufficiency of God to support his people in their pilgrimage felt comfortable to me, and I was industriously employed to get to a state of perfect resignation.

We seldom saw our canoe but at appointed places, by reason of the path going off from the river. This afternoon Job Chilaway, an Indian from Wehaloosing, who talks good English and is acquainted with several people in and about Philadelphia, met our people on the river. Understanding where we expected to lodge, he pushed back about six miles, and came to us after night; and in a while our own canoe arrived, it being hard work pushing up the stream. Job told us than an Indian came in haste to their town yesterday and told them that three warriors from a distance lodged in a town above Wehaloosing a few nights past, and that these three men were going against the English at Juniata. Job was going down the river to the province-store at Shamokin. Though I was so far favored with health as to continue travelling, yet, through the various difficulties in our journey, and the different way of living from which I had been used to, I grew sick. The news of these warriors being on their march so near us, and not knowing whether we might not fall in with them, was a fresh trial of my faith; and though, through the strength of Divine love, I had several times been enabled to commit myself to the Divine disposal, I still found the want of a renewal of my strength, that I might be able to persevere therein; and my cries for help were put up to the Lord, who, in great mercy, gave me a resigned heart, in which I found quietness.

Parting from Job Chilaway on the 17th, we went on and reached Wehaloosing about the middle of the afternoon. The first Indian that we saw was a woman of a modest countenance, with a Bible, who spake first to our guide, and then with an harmonious voice expressed her gladness at seeing us, having before heard of our coming. By the direction of our guide we sat down on a log while he went to the town to tell the people we were come. My companion and I, sitting thus together in a deep inward stillness, the poor woman came and sat near us; and great awfulness coming over us, we rejoiced in a sense of God's love manifested to our poor souls. After a while we heard a conch-shell blow several times, and then came John Curtis and another Indian man, who kindly invited us into a house near the town, where we found about sixty people sitting in silence. After sitting with them a short time I stood up, and in some tenderness of spirit acquainted them, in a few short sentences, with the nature of my visit, and that a concern for their good had made me willing to come thus far to see them; which some of them understanding interpreted to the others, and there appeared gladness among them. I then showed them my certificate, which was explained to them; and the Moravian who overtook us on the way, being now here, bade me welcome. But the Indians knowing that this Moravian and I were of different religious societies, and as some of their people had encouraged him to come and stay awhile with them, they were, I believe, concerned that there might be no jarring or discord in their meetings; and having, I suppose, conferred together, they acquainted me that the people, at my request, would at any time come together and hold meetings. They also told me that they expected the Moravian would speak in their settled meetings, which are commonly held in the morning and near evening. So finding liberty in my heart to speak to the Moravian, I told him of the care I felt on my mind for the good of these people, and my belief that no ill effects would follow if I sometimes spake in their meetings when love engaged me thereto, without calling them together at times when they did not meet of course. He expressed his good-will towards my speaking at any time all that I found in my heart to say.

On the evening of the 18th I was at their meeting, where pure gospel love was felt, to the tendering of some of our hearts. The interpreters endeavored to acquaint the people with what I said, in short sentences, but found some difficulty, as none of them were quite perfect in the English and Delaware tongues, so they helped one another, and we labored along, Divine love attending. Afterwards, feeling my mind covered with the spirit of prayer, I told the interpreters that I found it in my heart to pray to God, and believed, if I prayed aright, he would hear me; and I expressed my willingness for them to omit interpreting; so our meeting ended with a degree of Divine love. Before the people went out, I observed Papunehang (the man who had been zealous in laboring for a reformation in that town, being then very tender) speaking to one of the interpreters, and I was afterwards told that he said in substance as follows: "I love to feel where words come from."

Nineteenth of sixth month and first of the week.—This morning the Indian who came with the Moravian, being also a member of that society, prayed in the meeting, and then the Moravian spake a short time to the people. In the afternoon, my heart being filled with a heavenly care for their good, I spake to them awhile by interpreters; but none of them being perfect in the work, and I feeling the current of love run strong, told the interpreters that I believed some of the people would understand me, and so I proceeded without them; and I believe the Holy Ghost wrought on some hearts to edification where all the words were not understood. I looked upon it as a time of Divine favor, and my heart was tendered and truly thankful before the Lord. After I sat down, one of the interpreters seemed spirited to give the Indians the substance of what I said.

Before our first meeting this morning, I was led to meditate on the manifold difficulties of these Indians who, by the permission of the Six Nations, dwell in these parts. A near sympathy with them was raised in me, and, my heart being enlarged in the love of Christ, I thought that the affectionate care of a good man for his only brother in affliction does not exceed what I then felt for that people. I came to this place through much trouble; and though through the mercies of God I believed that if I died in the journey it would be well with me, yet the thoughts of falling into the hands of Indian warriors were, in times of weakness, afflicting to me; and being of a tender constitution of body, the thoughts of captivity among them were also grievous; supposing that as they were strong and hardy they might demand service of me beyond what I could well bear. But the Lord alone was my keeper, and I believed that if I went into captivity it would be for some good end. Thus, from time to time, my mind was centred in resignation, in which I always found quietness. And this day, though I had the same dangerous wilderness between me and home, I was inwardly joyful that the Lord had strengthened me to come on this visit, and had manifested a fatherly care over me in my poor lowly condition, when, in mine own eyes, I appeared inferior to many among the Indians.

When the last-mentioned meeting was ended, it being night, Papunehang went to bed; and hearing him speak with an harmonious voice, I suppose for a minute or two, I asked the interpreter, who told me that he was expressing his thankfulness to God for the favors he had received that day, and prayed that he would continue to favor him with the same, which he had experienced in that meeting. Though Papunehang had before agreed to receive the Moravian and join with them, he still appeared kind and loving to us.

I was at two meetings on the 20th, and silent in them. The following morning, in meeting, my heart was enlarged in pure love among them, and in short plain sentences I expressed several things that rested upon me, which one of the interpreters gave the people pretty readily. The meeting ended in supplication, and I had cause humbly to acknowledge the loving kindness of the Lord towards us; and then I believed that a door remained open for the faithful disciples of Jesus Christ to labor among these people. And now, feeling my mind at liberty to return, I took my leave of them in general at the conclusion of what I said in meeting, and we then prepared to go homeward. But some of their most active men told us that when we were ready to move the people would choose to come and shake hands with us. Those who usually came to meeting did so; and from a secret draught in my mind I went among some who did not usually go to meeting, and took my leave of them also. The Moravian and his Indian interpreter appeared respectful to us at parting. This town, Wehaloosing, stands on the bank of the Susquehanna, and consists, I believe, of about forty houses, mostly compact together, some about thirty feet long and eighteen wide,—some bigger, some less. They are built mostly of split plank, one end being set in the ground, and the other pinned to a plate on which rafters are laid, and then covered with bark. I understand a great flood last winter overflowed the greater part of the ground where the town stands, and some were now about moving their houses to higher ground.

We expected only two Indians to be of our company, but when we were ready to go we found many of them were going to Bethlehem with skins and furs, and chose to go in company with us. So they loaded two canoes in which they desired us to go, telling us that the waters were so raised with the rains that the horses should be taken by such as were better acquainted with the fording-places. We, therefore, with several Indians, went in the canoes, and others went on horses, there being seven besides ours. We met with the horsemen once on the way by appointment, and at night we lodged a little below a branch called Tankhannah, and some of the young men, going out a little before dusk with their guns, brought in a deer.

Through diligence we reached Wyoming before night, the 22d, and understood that the Indians were mostly gone from this place. We went up a small creek into the woods with our canoes, and, pitching our tent, carried out our baggage, and before dark our horses came to us. Next morning, the horses being loaded and our baggage prepared, we set forward, being in all fourteen, and with diligent travelling were favored to get near half-way to Fort Allen. The land on this road from Wyoming to our frontier being mostly poor, and good grass being scarce, the Indians chose a piece of low ground to lodge on, as the best for grazing. I had sweat much in travelling, and, being weary, slept soundly. In the night I perceived that I had taken cold, of which I was favored soon to get better.

Twenty-fourth of sixth month.—This day we passed Fort Allen and lodged near it in the woods. We forded the westerly branch of the Delaware three times, which was a shorter way than going over the top of the Blue Mountains called the Second Ridge. In the second time of fording where the river cuts through the mountain, the waters being rapid and pretty deep, my companion's mare, being a tall, tractable animal, was sundry times driven back through the river, being laden with the burdens of some small horses which were thought unable to come through with their loads. The troubles westward, and the difficulty for Indians to pass through our frontier, was, I apprehend, one reason why so many came, expecting that our being in company would prevent the outside inhabitants being surprised. We reached Bethlehem on the 25th, taking care to keep foremost, and to acquaint people on and near the road who these Indians were. This we found very needful, for the frontier inhabitants were often alarmed at the report of the English being killed by Indians westward. Among our company were some whom I did not remember to have seen at meeting, and some of these at first were very reserved; but we being several days together, and behaving in a friendly manner towards them, and making them suitable return for the services they did us, they became more free and sociable.

Twenty-sixth of sixth month.—Having carefully endeavored to settle all affairs with the Indians relative to our journey, we took leave of them, and I thought they generally parted from us affectionately. We went forward to Richland and had a very comfortable meeting among our friends, it being the first day of the week. Here I parted with my kind friend and companion Benjamin Parvin, and, accompanied by my friend Samuel Foulk, we rode to John Cadwallader's, from whence I reached home the next day, and found my family tolerably well. They and my

friends appeared glad to see me return from a journey which they apprehended would be dangerous; but my mind, while I was out, had been
so employed in striving for perfect resignation, and had so often been
confirmed in a belief, that, whatever the Lord might be pleased to allot
for me, it would work for good, that I was careful lest I should admit
any degree of selfishness in being glad overmuch, and labored to improve
by those trials in such a manner as my gracious Father and Protector
designed. Between the English settlements and Wehaloosing we had
only a narrow path, which in many places is much grown up with
bushes, and interrupted by abundance of trees lying across it. These,
together with the mountain swamps and rough stones, make it a difficult
road to travel, and the more so because rattlesnakes abound here, of
which we killed four. People who have never been in such places have
but an imperfect idea of them; and I was not only taught patience, but
also made thankful to God, who thus led about and instructed me, that
I might have a quick and lively feeling of the afflictions of my fellow-
creatures, whose situation in life is difficult.

CHAPTER XI.

1772.

Embarks at Chester, with Samuel Emlen, in a Ship bound for London. —
Exercise of Mind respecting the Hardships of the Sailors. — Considerations
on the Dangers of training Youth to a Seafaring Life. — Thoughts during
a Storm at Sea. — Arrival in London.

Having been some time under a religious concern to prepare for crossing
the seas, in order to visit Friends in the northern parts of England, and
more particularly in Yorkshire, after consideration I thought it expedient
to inform Friends of it at our Monthly Meeting at Burlington, who,
having unity with me therein, gave me a certificate. I afterwards communicated the same to our Quarterly Meeting, and they likewise certi-
fied their concurrence. Some time after, at the General Spring Meeting
of ministers and elders, I thought it my duty to acquaint them with the
religious exercise which attended my mind; and they likewise signified
their unity therewith by a certificate, dated the 24th of third month,
1772, directed to Friends in Great Britain.

In the fourth month following I thought the time was come for me to
make some inquiry for a suitable conveyance; and as my concern was
principally towards the northern parts of England, it seemed most
proper to go in a vessel bound to Liverpool or Whitehaven. While I was
at Philadelphia deliberating on this subject I was informed that my
beloved friend Samuel Emlen, junior, intended to go to London, and had
taken a passage for himself in the cabin of the ship called the Mary and

Elizabeth, of which James Sparks was master, and John Head, of the city of Philadelphia, one of the owners; and feeling a draught in my mind towards the steerage of the same ship, I went first and opened to Samuel the feeling I had concerning it.

My beloved friend wept when I spake to him, and appeared glad that I had thoughts of going in the vessel with him, though my prospect was toward the steerage; and he offering to go with me, we went on board, first into the cabin,—a commodious room,—and then into the steerage, where we sat down on a chest, the sailors being busy about us. The owner of the ship also came and sat down with us. My mind was turned towards Christ, the Heavenly Counsellor, and feeling at this time my own will subjected, my heart was contrite before him. A motion was made by the owner to go and sit in the cabin, as a place more retired; but I felt easy to leave the ship, and, making no agreement as to a passage in her, told the owner if I took a passage in the ship I believed it would be in the steerage; but did not say much as to my exercise in that case.

After I went to my lodgings, and the case was a little known in town, a Friend laid before me the great inconvenience attending a passage in the steerage, which for a time appeared very discouraging to me.

I soon after went to bed, and my mind was under a deep exercise before the Lord, whose helping hand was manifested to me as I slept that night, and his love strengthened my heart. In the morning I went with two Friends on board the vessel again, and after a short time spent therein, I went with Samuel Emlen to the house of the owner, to whom, in the hearing of Samuel only, I opened my exercise in relation to a scruple I felt with regard to a passage in the cabin, in substance as follows:—

"That on the outside of that part of the ship where the cabin was I observed sundry sorts of carved work and imagery; that in the cabin I observed some superfluity of workmanship of several sorts; and that according to the ways of men's reckoning, the sum of money to be paid for a passage in that apartment has some relation to the expense of furnishing it to please the minds of such as give way to a conformity to this world; and that in this, as in other cases, the moneys received from the passengers are calculated to defray the cost of these superfluities, as well as the other expenses of their passage. I therefore felt a scruple with regard to paying my money to be applied to such purposes."

As my mind was now opened, I told the owner that I had, at several times, in my travels, seen great oppressions on this continent, at which my heart had been much affected and brought into a feeling of the state of the sufferers; and having many times been engaged in the fear and love of God to labor with those under whom the oppressed have been borne down and afflicted, I have often perceived that with a view to get riches and to provide estates for children, that they may live conformably to the customs and honors of this world, many are entangled in the spirit of oppression, and the exercise of my soul had been such that I could not find peace in joining in anything which I saw was against that wisdom which is pure.

After this I agreed for a passage in the steerage; and hearing that Joseph White had desired to see me, I went to his house, and next day home, where I tarried two nights. Early the next morning I parted with my family under a sense of the humbling hand of God upon me, and, going to Philadelphia, had an opportunity with several of my beloved friends, who appeared to be concerned for me an account of the unpleasant situation of that part of the vessel in which I was likely to lodge. In these opportunities my mind, through the mercies of the Lord, was kept low in an inward waiting for his help; and Friends having expressed their desire that I might have a more convenient place than the steerage, did not urge it, but appeared disposed to leave me to the Lord.

Having stayed two nights at Philadelphia, I went the next day to Derby Monthly Meeting, where through the strength of Divine love my heart was enlarged towards the youth there present, under which I was helped to labor in some tenderness of spirit. I lodged at William Horn's and afterwards went to Chester, where I met with Samuel Emlen, and we went on board 1st of fifth month, 1772. As I sat alone on the deck I felt a satisfactory evidence that my proceedings were not in my own will, but under the power of the cross of Christ.

Seventh of fifth month. — We have had rough weather mostly since I came on board, and the passengers, James Reynolds, John Till Adams, Sarah Logan and her hired maid, and John Bispham, all sea-sick at times; from which sickness, through the tender mercies of my Heavenly Father, I have been preserved, my afflictions now being of another kind. There appeared an openness in the minds of the master of the ship and in the cabin passengers towards me. We are often together on the deck, and sometimes in the cabin. My mind, through the merciful help of the Lord, hath been preserved in a good degree watchful and quiet, for which I have great cause to be thankful.

As my lodging in the steerage, now near a week, hath afforded me sundry opportunities of seeing, hearing, and feeling with respect to the life and spirit of many poor sailors, an exercise of soul hath attended me in regard to placing out children and youth where they may be likely to be exampled and instructed in the pure fear of the Lord.

Being much among the seamen I have, from a motion of love, taken sundry opportunities with one of them at a time, and have in free conversation labored to turn their minds towards the fear of the Lord. This day we had a meeting in the cabin, where my heart was contrite under a feeling of Divine love.

I believe a communication with different parts of the world by sea is at times consistent with the will of our Heavenly Father, and to educate some youth in the practice of sailing, I believe may be right; but how lamentable is the present corruption of the world! How impure are the channels through which trade is conducted! How great is the danger to which poor lads are exposed when placed on shipboard to learn the art of sailing! Five lads training up for the seas were on board this ship. Two of them were brought up in our Society, and the other, by name James Naylor, is a member, to whose father James Naylor, mentioned in Sewel's history, appears to have been uncle. I often feel a tenderness of heart towards these poor lads, and at times look at them as though they were my children according to the flesh.

O that all may take heed and beware of covetousness! O that all may learn of Christ, who was meek and lowly of heart. Then in faithfully following him he will teach us to be content with food and raiment without respect to the customs or honors of this world. Men thus redeemed will feel a tender concern for their fellow-creatures, and a desire that those in the lowest stations may be assisted and encouraged, and where owners of ships attain to the perfect law of liberty and are doers of the Word, these will be blessed in their deeds.

A ship at sea commonly sails all night, and the seamen take their watches four hours at a time. Rising to work in the night, it is not commonly pleasant in any case, but in dark rainy nights it is very disagreeable, even though each man were furnished with all conveniences. If, after having been on deck several hours in the night, they come down into the steerage soaking wet, and are so closely stowed that proper convenience for change of garments is not easily come at, but for want of proper room their wet garments are thrown in heaps, and sometimes, through much crowding, are trodden under foot in going to their lodgings and getting out of them, and it is difficult at times for each to find his own. Here are trials for the poor sailors.

Now, as I have been with them in my lodge, my heart hath often yearned for them, and tender desires have been raised in me that all owners and masters of vessels may dwell in the love of God and therein act uprightly, and by seeking less for gain and looking carefully to their ways they may earnestly labor to remove all cause of provocation from the poor seamen, so that they may neither fret nor use excess of strong drink; for, indeed, the poor creatures, in the wet and cold, seem to apply at times to strong drink to supply the want of other convenience. Great reformation is wanting in the world, and the necessity of it among those who do business on great waters hath at this time been abundantly opened before me.

Eighth of fifth month.—This morning the clouds gathered, the wind blew strong from the southeast, and before noon so increased that sailing appeared dangerous. The seamen then bound up some of their sails and took down others, and the storm increasing they put the dead-lights, so called, into the cabin windows and lighted a lamp as at night. The wind now blew vehemently, and the sea wrought to that degree that an awful seriousness prevailed in the cabin, in which I spent, I believe, about seventeen hours, for the cabin passengers had given me frequent invitations, and I thought the poor wet toiling seamen had need of all the room in the crowded steerage. They now ceased from sailing and put the vessel in the posture called lying to.

My mind during this tempest, through the gracious assistance of the Lord, was preserved in a good degree of resignation; and at times I expressed a few words in his love to my shipmates in regard to the all-sufficiency of Him who formed the great deep, and whose care is so extensive that a sparrow falls not without his notice; and thus in a tender frame of mind I spoke to them of the necessity of our yielding in true obedience to the instructions of our Heavenly Father, who sometimes through adversities intendeth our refinement.

About eleven at night I went out on the deck. The sea wrought exceedingly, and the high, foaming waves round about had in some sort the appearance of fire, but did not give much if any light. The sailor at the helm said he lately saw a corposant at the head of the mast. I observed that the master of the ship ordered the carpenter to keep on the deck; and, though he said little, I apprehended his care was that the carpenter with his axe might be in readiness in case of any extremity. Soon after this the vehemency of the wind abated, and before morning they again put the ship under sail.

Tenth of fifth month.—It being the first day of the week and fine weather, we had a meeting in the cabin, at which most of the seamen were present; this meeting was to me a strengthening time. 13th.—As I continue to lodge in the steerage I feel an openness this morning to express something further of the state of my mind in respect to poor lads bound apprentice to learn the art of sailing. As I believe sailing is of use in the world, a labor of soul attends me that the pure counsel of truth may be humbly waited for in this case by all concerned in the business of the seas. A pious father whose mind is exercised for the everlasting welfare of his child may not with a peaceable mind place him out to an employment among a people whose common course of life is manifestly corrupt and profane. Great is the present defect among seafaring men in regard to virtue and piety; and, by reason of an abundant traffic and many ships being used for war, so many people are employed on the sea that the subject of placing lads to this employment appears very weighty.

When I remember the saying of the Most High through his prophet, "This people have I formed for myself; they shall show forth my praise," and think of placing children among such to learn the practice of sailing, the consistency of it with a pious education seems to me like that mentioned by the prophet, "There is no answer from God."

Profane examples are very corrupting and very forcible. And as my mind day after day and night after night hath been affected with a sympathizing tenderness towards poor children who are put to the employment of sailors, I have sometimes had weighty conversation with the sailors in the steerage, who were mostly respectful to me and became more so the longer I was with them. They mostly appeared to take kindly what I said to them; but their minds were so deeply impressed with the almost universal depravity among sailors that the poor creatures in their answers to me have revived in my remembrance that of the degenerate Jews a little before the captivity, as repeated by Jeremiah the prophet, "There is no hope."

# Letters From an American Farmer
## *Michel-Guillaume Jean de Crèvecoeur*

*In the best of all possible worlds that was the English colonies, Crève-coeur did not understand why Americans should be restive under British rule and why they should seek to break the connection with their mother country. Caught unawares by the American Revolution, Crèvecoeur became a Loyalist and took refuge within the British lines. His book,* Letters from an American Farmer, *describing the idyllic conditions that had existed prior to the Revolution, did not appear until 1782. It was first published in London. In 1783, Crèvecoeur became French consul in New York. Seven years later he returned to France. His last trip to America was made in 1800–1801.*

### WHAT IS AN AMERICAN

I wish I could be acquainted with the feelings and thoughts which must agitate the heart and present themselves to the mind of an enlightened Englishman, when he first lands on this continent. He must greatly rejoice that he lived at a time to see this fair country discovered and settled; he must necessarily feel a share of national pride, when he views the chain of settlements which embellishes these extended shores. When he says to himself, this is the work of my countrymen, who, when convulsed by factions, afflicted by a variety of miseries and wants, restless and impatient, took refuge here.They brought along with them their national genius, to which they principally owe what liberty they enjoy, and what substance they possess. Here he sees the industry of his native country displayed in a new manner, and traces in their works the embryos of all the arts, sciences, and ingenuity which flourish in Europe. Here he beholds fair cities, substantial villages, extensive fields, an immense country filled with decent houses, good roads, orchards, meadows, and bridges, where an hundred years ago all was wild, woody, and uncultivated! What a train of pleasing ideas this fair spectacle must suggest; it is a prospect which must inspire a good citizen with the most

Crèvecoeur (J. Hector St.-John): *Letters from an American Farmer.* Edited by William Barton Blake.

heartfelt pleasure. The difficulty consists in the manner of viewing so extensive a scene. He is arrived on a new continent; a modern society offers itself to his contemplation, different from what he had hitherto seen. It is not composed, as in Europe, of great lords who possess everything, and of a herd of people who have nothing. Here are no aristocratical families, no courts, no kings, no bishops, no ecclesiastical dominion, no invisible power giving to a few a very visible one; no great manufacturers employing thousands, no great refinements of luxury. The rich and the poor are not so far removed from each other as they are in Europe. Some few towns excepted, we are all tillers of the earth, from Nova Scotia to West Florida. We are a people of cultivators, scattered over an immense territory, communicating with each other by means of good roads and navigable rivers, united by the silken bands of mild government, all respecting the laws, without dreading their power, because they are equitable. We are all animated with the spirit of an industry which is unfettered and unrestrained, because each person works for himself. If he travels through our rural districts he views not the hostile castle, and the haughty mansion, contrasted with the clay-built hut and miserable cabin, where cattle and men help to keep each other warm, and dwell in meanness, smoke, and indigence. A pleasing uniformity of decent competence appears throughout our habitations. The meanest of our log-houses is a dry and comfortable habitation. Lawyer or merchant are the fairest titles our towns afford; that of a farmer is the only appellation of the rural inhabitants of our country. It must take some time ere he can reconcile himself to our dictionary, which is but short in words of dignity, and names of honour. There, on a Sunday, he sees a congregation of respectable farmers and their wives, all clad in neat homespun, well mounted, or riding in their own humble waggons. There is not among them an esquire, saving the unlettered magistrate. There he sees a parson as simple as his flock, a farmer who does not riot on the labour of others. We have no princes, for whom we toil, starve, and bleed: we are the most perfect society now existing in the world. Here man is free as he ought to be; nor is this pleasing equality so transitory as many others are. Many ages will not see the shores of our great lakes replenished with inland nations, nor the unknown bounds of North America entirely peopled. Who can tell how far it extends? Who can tell the millions of men whom it will feed and contain? for no European foot has as yet travelled half the extent of this mighty continent!

The next wish of this traveller will be to know whence came all these people? they are a mixture of English, Scotch, Irish, French, Dutch, Germans, and Swedes. From this promiscuous breed, that race now called Americans have arisen. The eastern provinces must indeed be excepted, as being the unmixed descendants of Englishmen. I have heard many wish that they had been more intermixed also: for my part, I am no wisher, and think it much better as it has happened. They exhibit a most conspicuous figure in this great share in the pleasing perspective displayed in these thirteen provinces. I know it is fashionable to reflect on them, but I respect them for what they have done; for the accuracy and wisdom with which they have settled their territory; for the decency of their manners; for their love of letters; their ancient college, the first in this hemisphere; for their industry; which to me who am but a farmer, is the criterion of everything. There never was a people, situated as they are, who with so ungrateful a soil have done more in so short a time. Do you think that the monarchical ingredients which are more prevalent in other governments, have purged them from all foul stains? Their histories assert the contrary.

In this great American asylum, the poor of Europe have by some means met together, and in consequences of various causes; to what purpose should they ask one another what countrymen they are? Alas, two thirds of them had no country. Can a wretch who wanders about, who works and starves, whose life is a continual scene of sore affliction or pinching penury; can that man call England or any other kingdom his country? A country that had no bread for him, whose fields procured him no harvest, who met with nothing but the frowns of the rich, the severity of the laws, with jails and punishments; who owned not a single foot of the extensive surface of this planet? No! urged by a variety of motives, here they came. Every thing has tended to regenerate them; new laws, a new mode of living, a new social system; here they are become men: in Europe they were as so many useless plants, wanting vegetative mould, and refreshing showers; they withered, and were mowed down by want, hunger, and war; but now by the power of transplantation, like all other plants they have taken root and flourished! Formerly they were not numbered in any civil lists of their country, except in those of the poor; here they rank as citizens. By what invisible power has this surprising metamorphosis been performed? By that of the laws and that of their industry. The laws, the indulgent laws, protect them as they arrive, stamping on them the symbol of adoption; they receive ample rewards for their labours; these accumulated rewards procure them lands; those lands confer on them the title of freemen, and to that title every benefit is affixed which men can possibly require. This is the great operation daily performed by our laws. From whence proceed these laws? From our government. Whence the government? It is derived from the original genius and strong desire of the people ratified and confirmed by the crown. This is the great chain which links us all, this is the picture which every province exhibits, Nova Scotia excepted.

There the crown has done all; either there were no people who had genius, or it was not much attended to: the consequence is, that the province is very thinly inhabited indeed; the power of the crown in conjunction with the musketos has prevented men from settling there. Yet some parts of it flourished once, and it contained a mild harmless set of people. But for the fault of a few leaders, the whole were banished. The greatest political error the crown ever committed in America, was to cut off men from a country which wanted nothing but men!

What attachment can a poor European emigrant have for a country where he had nothing? The knowledge of the language, the love of a few kindred as poor as himself, were the only cords that tied him: his country is now that which gives him land, bread, protection, and consequence: *Ubi panis ibi patria,* is the motto of all emigrants. What then is the American, this new man? He is either an European, or the descendant of an European, hence that strange mixture of blood, which you will find in no other country. I could point out to you a family whose grandfather was an Englishman, whose wife was Dutch, whose son married a French woman, and whose present four sons have now four wives of different nations. *He* is an American, who, leaving behind him all his ancient prejudices and manners, receives new ones from the new mode of life he has embraced, the new government he obeys, and the new rank he holds. He becomes an American by being received in the broad lap of our great *Alma Mater.* Here individuals of all nations are melted into a new race of men, whose labours and posterity will one day cause great changes in the world. Americans are the western pilgrims, who are carrying along with them that great mass of arts, sciences, vigour, and industry which began long since in the east; they will finish the great circle. The Americans were once scattered all over Europe; here they are incorporated into one of the finest systems of population which has ever appeared, and which will hereafter become distinct by the power of the different climates they inhabit. The American ought therefore to love this country much better than that wherein either he or his forefathers were born. Here the rewards of his industry follow with equal steps the progress of his labour; his labour is founded on the basis of nature, *self-interest;* can it want a stronger allurement? Wives and children, who before in vain demanded of him a morsel of bread, now, fat and frolicsome, gladly help their father to clear those fields whence exuberant crops are to arise to feed and to clothe them all; without any part being claimed, either by a despotic prince, a rich abbot, or a mighty lord. Here religion demands but little of him; a small voluntary salary to the minister, and gratitude to God; can he refuse these? The American is a new man, who acts upon new principles; he must therefore entertain new ideas, and form new opinions. From involuntary idleness, servile dependence, penury, and useless labour, he has passed to toils of a very different nature, rewarded by ample sub-sistence.—This is an American.

British America is divided into many provinces, forming a large as-sociation, scattered along a coast 1500 miles extent and about 200 wide. This society I would fain examine, at least such as it appears in the middle provinces; if it does not afford that variety of tinges and grada-tions which may be observed in Europe, we have colours peculiar to ourselves. For instance, it is natural to conceive that those who live near the sea, must be very different from those who live in the woods; the intermediate space will afford a separate and distinct class.

Men are like plants; the goodness and flavour of the fruit proceeds from the peculiar soil and exposition in which they grow. We are nothing but what we derive from the air we breathe, the climate we inhabit, the government we obey, the system of religion we profess, and the nature of our employment. Here you will find but few crimes; these have acquired as yet no root among us. I wish I was able to trace all my ideas; if my ignorance prevents me from describing them properly, I hope I shall be able to delineate a few of the outlines, which are all I propose.

Those who live near the sea, feed more on fish than on flesh, and often encounter that boisterous element. This renders them more bold and enterprising; this leads them to neglect the confined occupations of the land. They see and converse with a variety of people; their intercourse with mankind becomes extensive. The sea inspires them with a love of traffic, a desire of transporting produce from one place to another; and leads them to a variety of resources which supply the place of labour. Those who inhabit the middle settlements, by far the most numerous, must be very different; the simple cultivation of the earth purifies them, but the indulgences of the government, the soft remonstrances of re-ligion, the rank of independent freeholders, must necessarily inspire them with sentiments, very little known in Europe among people of the same class. What do I say? Europe has no such class of men; the early knowledge they acquire, the early bargains they make, give them a great degree of sagacity. As freemen they will be litigious; pride and ob-stinacy are often the cause of law suits; the nature of our laws and governments may be another. As citizens it is easy to imagine, that they will carefully read the newspapers, enter into every political disquisition, freely blame or censure governors and others. As farmers they will be careful and anxious to get as much as they can, because what they get is their own. As northern men they will love the cheerful cup. As Christians, religion curbs them not in their opinions; the general indul-gence leaves every one to think for themselves in spiritual matters; the laws inspect our actions, our thoughts are left to God. Industry, good living, selfishness, litigiousness, country politics, the pride of freemen, religious indifference, are their characteristics. If you recede still farther from the sea, you will come into more modern settlements; they exhibit the same strong lineaments, in a ruder appearance. Religion seems to have still less influence, and their manners are less improved.

Now we arrive near the great woods, near the last inhabited districts; there men seem to be placed still farther beyond the reach of government, which in some measure leaves them to themselves. How can it pervade every corner; as they were driven there by misfortunes, necessity of beginnings, desire of acquiring large tracts of land, idleness, frequent want of economy, ancient debts; the re-union of such people does not afford a very pleasing spectacle. When discord, want of unity and friendship; when either drunkenness or idleness prevail in such remote districts; contention, inactivity, and wretchedness must ensue. There are not the same remedies to these evils as in a long established community. The few magistrates they have, are in general little better than the rest; they are often in a perfect state of war; that of man against man, sometimes decided by blows, sometimes by means of the law; that of man against every wild inhabitant of these venerable woods, of which they are come to dispossess them. There men appear to be no better than carnivorous animals of a superior rank, living on the flesh of wild animals when they can catch them, and when they are not able, they subsist on grain. He who would wish to see America in its proper light, and have a true idea of its feeble beginnings and barbarous rudiments, must visit our extended line of frontiers where the last settlers dwell, and where he may see the first labours of settlement, the mode of clearing the earth, in all their different appearances; where men are wholly left dependent on their native tempers, and on the spur of uncertain industry, which often fails when not sanctified by the efficacy of a few moral rules. There, remote from the power of example and check of shame, many families exhibit the most hideous parts of our society. They are a kind of forlorn hope, preceding by ten or twelve years the most respectable army of veterans which come after them. In that space, prosperity will polish some, vice and the law will drive off the rest, who uniting again with others like themselves will recede still farther; making room for more industrious people, who will finish their improvements, convert the loghouse into a convenient habitation, and rejoicing that the first heavy labours are finished, will change in a few years that hitherto barbarous country into a fine fertile, well regulated district. Such is our progress, such is the march of the Europeans toward the interior parts of this continent. In all societies there are off-casts; this impure part serves as our precursors or pioneers; my father himself was one of that class, but he came upon honest principles, and was therefore one of the few who held fast; by good conduct and temperance, he transmitted to me his fair inheritance, when not above one in fourteen of his contemporaries had the same good fortune.

Forty years ago this smiling country was thus inhabited; it is now purged, a general decency of manners prevails throughout, and such has been the fate of our best countries.

Exclusive of those general characteristics, each province has its own, founded on the government, climate, mode of husbandry, customs, and peculiarity of circumstances. Europeans submit insensibly to these great powers, and become, in the course of a few generations, not only Americans in general, but either Pennsylvanians, Virginians, or provincials under some other name. Whoever traverses the continent must easily observe those strong differences, which will grow more evident in time. The inhabitants of Canada, Massachusetts, the middle provinces, the southern ones will be as different as their climates; their only points of unity will be those of religion and language.

As I have endeavoured to show you how Europeans become Americans; it may not be disagreeable to show you likewise how the various Christian sects introduced, wear out, and how religious indifference becomes prevalent. When any considerable number of a particular sect happen to dwell contiguous to each other, they immediately erect a temple, and there worship the Divinity agreeably to their own peculiar ideas. Nobody disturbs them. If any new sect springs up in Europe it may happen that many of its professors will come and settle in America. As they bring their zeal with them, they are at liberty to make proselytes if they can, and to build a meeting and to follow the dictates of their consciences; for neither the government nor any other power interferes. If they are peaceable subjects, and are industrious, what is it to their neighbours how and in what manner they think fit to address their prayers to the Supreme Being? But if the sectaries are not settled close together, if they are mixed with other denominations, their zeal will cool for want of fuel, and will be extinguished in a little time. Then the Americans become as to religion, what they are as to country, allied to all. In them the name of Englishman, Frenchman, and European is lost, and in like manner, the strict modes of Christianity as practised in Europe are lost also. This effect will extend itself still farther hereafter, and though this may appear to you as a strange idea, yet it is a very true one. I shall be able perhaps hereafter to explain myslf better; in the meanwhile, let the following example serve as my first justification.

Let us suppose you and I to be travelling; we observe that in this house, to the right, lives a Catholic, who prays to God as he has been taught, and believes in transubstantiation; he works and raises wheat, he has a large family of children, all hale and robust; his belief, his prayers offend nobody. About one mile farther on the same road, his next neighbour may be a good honest plodding German Lutheran, who addresses himself to the same God, the God of all, agreeably to the modes he has been educated in, and believes in consubstantiation; by so doing he scandalises nobody; he also works in his fields, embellishes the earth, clears swamps, etc. What has the world to do with his Lutheran principles? He persecutes nobody, and nobody persecutes him, he visits his neighbours, and his neighbours visit him. Next to him lives a seceder, the most enthusiastic of all sectaries; his zeal is hot and fiery, but separated as he is from others of the same complexion, he has no congregation of his own to resort to, where he might cabal and mingle religious pride with worldly obstinacy. He likewise raises good crops, his house is handsomely painted, his orchard is one of the fairest in the neighbourhood. How does it concern the welfare of the country, or of the province at large, what this man's religious sentiments are, or really whether he has any at all? He is a good farmer, he is a sober, peaceable, good citizen: William Penn himself would not wish for more. This is the visible character, the invisible one is only guessed at, and is nobody's business. Next again lives a Low Dutchman, who implicitly believes the rules laid down by the synod of Dort. He conceives no other idea of a clergyman than that of an hired man; if he does his work well he will pay him the stipulated sum; if not he will dismiss him, and do without his sermons, and let his church be shut up for years. But notwithstanding this coarse idea, you will find his house and farm to be the neatest in all the country; and you will judge by his waggon and fat horses, that he thinks more of the affairs of this world than of those of the next. He is sober and laborious, therefore he is all he ought to be as to the affairs of this life; as for those of the next, he must trust to the great Creator. Each of these people instruct their children as well as they can, but these instructions are feeble compared to those which are given to the youth of the poorest class in Europe. Their children will therefore grow up less zealous and more indifferent in matters of religion than their parents. The foolish vanity, or rather the fury of making Proselytes, is unknown here; they have no time, the seasons call for all their attention, and thus in a few years, this mixed neighbourhood will exhibit a strange religious medley, that will be neither pure Catholicism nor pure Calvinism. A very perceptible indifference even in the first generation, will become apparent; and it may happen that the daughter of the Catholic will marry the son of the seceder, and settle by themselves at a distance from their parents. What religious education will they give their children? A very imperfect one. If there happens to be in the neighbourhood any place of worship, we will suppose a Quaker's meeting; rather than not show their fine clothes, they will go to it, and some of them may perhaps attach themselves to that society. Others will remain in a perfect state of indifference; the children of these zealous parents will not be able to tell what their religious principles are, and their grandchildren still less. The neighbourhood of a place of worship generally leads them to it, and the action of going thither, is the strongest evidence they can give of their attachment to any sect. The Quakers are the only people who retain a fondness for their own mode of worship; for be they ever so far separated from each other, they hold a sort of communion with the society, and seldom depart from its rules, at least in this country. Thus all sects are mixed as well as all nations; thus religious indifference is imperceptibly disseminated from one end of the continent to the other; which is at present one of the strongest characteristics of the Americans. Where this will reach no one can tell, perhaps it may leave a vacuum fit to receive other systems. Persecution, religious pride, the love of contradiction, are the food of what the world commonly calls religion. These motives have ceased here; zeal in Europe is confined; here it evaporates in the great distance it has to travel; there it is a grain of powder inclosed, here it burns away in the open air, and consumes without effect.

But to return to our back settlers, I must tell you, that there is something in the proximity of the woods, which is very singular. It is with men as it is with the plants and animals that grow and live in the forests; they are entirely different from those that live in the plains. I will candidly tell you all my thoughts but you are not to expect that I shall advance any reasons. By living in or near the woods, their actions are regulated by the wildness of the neighbourhood. The deer often come to eat their grain, the wolves to destroy their sheep, the bears to kill their hogs, the foxes to catch their poultry. This surrounding hostility immediately puts the gun into their hands; they watch these animals, they kill some; and thus by defending their property, they soon become professed hunters; this is the progress; once hunters, farewell to the plough. The chase renders them ferocious, gloomy, and unsociable; a hunter wants no neighbour, he rather hates them, because he dreads the competition. In a little time their success in the woods makes them neglect their tillage. They trust to the natural fecundity of the earth, and therefore do little; carelessness in fencing often exposes what little they sow to destruction; they are not at home to watch; in order therefore to make up the deficiency, they go oftener to the woods. That new mode of life brings along with it a new set of manners, which I cannot easily describe. These new manners being grafted on the old stock, produces a strange sort of lawless profligacy, the impressions of which are indelible. The manners of the Indian natives are respectable, compared with this European medley. Their wives and children live in sloth and inactivity; and having no proper pursuits, you may judge what education the latter receive. Their tender minds have nothing else to contemplate but the example of their parents; like them they grow up a mongrel breed, half civilised, half savage, except nature stamps on them some constitutional propensities. That rich, that voluptuous sentiment is gone that struck them so forcibly; the possession of their freeholds no longer conveys to their minds the same pleasure and pride. To all these reasons you must add, their lonely situation, and you cannot imagine what an effect on manners the great distances they live from each other has! Consider one of the last settlements in its first view: of what is it composed? Europeans who have not that sufficient share of knowledge they ought to have, in order to prosper; people who have suddenly passed from oppression, dread of government, and fear of laws, into the unlimited freedom of the woods. This sudden change must have a very great effect on most men, and on that class particularly. Eating of wild meat, whatever you may think, tends to alter their temper; though all the proof I can adduce, is, that I have seen it: and having no place of worship to resort to, what little society this might afford is denied them. The Sunday meetings, exclusive of religious benefits, were the only social bonds that might have inspired them with some degree of emulation in neatness. Is it then surprising to see men thus situated, immersed in great and heavy labours, degenerate a little? It is rather a wonder the effect is not more diffusive. The Moravians and the Quakers are the only instances in exception to what I have advanced. The first never settle singly, it is a colony of the society which emigrates; they carry with them their forms, worship, rules, and decency: the others never begin so hard, they are always able to buy improvements, in which there is a great advantage, for by that time the country is recovered from its first barbarity. Thus our bad people are those who are half cultivators and half hunters; and the worst of them are those who have degenerated altogether into the hunting state. As old ploughmen and new men of the woods, as Europeans and new made Indians, they contract the vices of both; they adopt the moroseness and ferocity of a native, without his mildness, or even his industry at home. If manners are not refined, at least they are rendered simple and inoffensive by tilling the earth; all our wants are supplied by it, our time is divided between labour and rest, and leaves none for the commission of great misdeeds. As hunters it is divided between the toil of the chase, the idleness of repose, or the indulgence of inebriation. Hunting is but a licentious idle life, and if it does not always pervert good dispositions; yet, when it is united with bad luck, it leads to want: want stimulates that propensity to rapacity and injustice, too natural to needy men, which is the fatal gradation. After this explanation of the effects which follow by living in the woods, shall we yet vainly flatter ourselves, with the hope of converting the Indians? We should rather begin with converting our back-settlers; and now if I dare mention the name of religion, its sweet accents would be lost in the immensity of these woods. Men thus placed are not fit either to receive or remember its mild instructions; they want temples and ministers, but as soon as men cease to remain at home, and begin to lead an erratic life, let them be either tawny or white, they cease to be its disciples.

Thus have I faintly and imperfectly endeavoured to trace our society from the sea to our woods! yet you must not imagine that every person who moves back, acts upon the same principles, or falls into the same degeneracy. Many families carry with them all their decency of conduct, purity of morals, and respect of religion; but these are scarce, the power of example is sometimes irresistable. Even among these back-settlers, their depravity is greater or less, according to what nation or province they belong. Were I to adduce proofs of this, I might be accused of partiality. If there happens to be some rich intervals, some fertile bottoms, in those remote districts, the people will there prefer tilling the land to hunting, and will attach themselves to it; but even on these fertile spots you may plainly perceive the inhabitants to acquire a great degree of rusticity and selfishness.

It is in consequence of this straggling situation, and the astonishing power it has on manners, that the back-settlers of both the Carolinas, Virginia, and many other parts, have been long a set of lawless people; it has been even dangerous to travel among them. Government can do nothing in so extensive a country, better it should wink at these irregularities, than that it should use means inconsistent with its usual mildness. Time will efface those stains: in proportion as the great body of population approaches them they will reform, and become polished and subordinate. Whatever has been said of the four New England provinces, no such degeneracy of manners has ever tarnished their annals; their back-settlers have been kept within the bounds of decency, and government, by means of wise laws, and by the influence of religion. What a detestable idea such people must have given to the natives of the Europeans! They trade with them, the worst of people are permitted to do that which none but persons of the best characters should be employed in. They get drunk with them, and often defraud the Indians. Their avarice, removed from the eyes of their superiors, knows no bounds; and aided by the little superiority of knowledge, these traders deceive them, and even sometimes shed blood. Hence those shocking violations, those sudden devastations which have so often stained our frontiers, when hundreds of innocent people have been sacrificed for the crimes of a few. It was in consequence of such behaviour, that the Indians took the hatchet against the Virginians in 1774. Thus are our first steps trod, thus are our first trees felled, in general, by the most vicious of our people; and thus the path is opened for the arrival of a second and better class, the true American freeholders; the most respectable set of people in this part of the world: respectable for their industry, their happy independence, the great share of freedom they possess, the good

regulation of their families, and for extending the trade and the dominion of our mother country.

Europe contains hardly any other distinctions but lords and tenants;
this fair country alone is settled by freeholders, the possessors of the
soil they cultivate, members of the government they obey, and the
framers of their own laws, by means of their representatives. This is a
thought which you have taught me to cherish; our difference from
Europe, far from diminishing, rather adds to our usefulness and consequence as men and subjects. Had our forefathers remained there, they
would only have crowded it, and perhaps prolonged those convulsions
which had shook it so long. Every industrious European who transports
himself here, may be compared to a sprout growing at the foot of a great
tree; it enjoys and draws but a little portion of sap; wrench it from the
parent roots, transplant it, and it will become a tree bearing fruit also.
Colonists are therefore entitled to the consideration due to the most
useful subjects; a hundred families barely existing in some parts of
Scotland, will here in six years, cause an annual exportation of 10,000
bushels of wheat: 100 bushels being but a common quantity for an
industrious family to sell, if they cultivate good land. It is here then
that the idle may be employed, the useless become useful, and the poor
become rich; but by riches I do not mean gold and silver, we have but
little of those metals; I mean a better sort of wealth, cleared lands,
cattle, good houses, good clothes, and an increase of people to enjoy
them.

There is no wonder that this country has so many charms, and presents
to Europeans so many temptations to remain in it. A traveller in Europe
becomes a stranger as soon as he quits his own kingdom; but it is otherwise here. We know, properly speaking, no strangers; this is every
person's country; the variety of our soils, situations, climates, governments, and produce, hath something which must please everybody. No
sooner does an European arrive, no matter of what condition, than his
eyes are opened upon the fair prospect; he hears his language spoke, he
retraces many of his own country manners, he perpetually hears the
names of families and towns with which he is acquainted; he sees
happiness and prosperity in all places disseminated; he meets with
hospitality, kindness, and plenty everywhere; he beholds hardly any
poor, he seldom hears of punishments and executions; and he wonders
at the elegance of our towns, those miracles of industry and freedom.
He cannot admire enough our rural districts, our convenient roads, good
taverns, and our many accommodations; he involuntarily loves a country
where everything is so lovely. When in England, he was a mere Englishman; here he stands on a larger portion of the globe, not less than its
fourth part, and may see the productions of the north, in iron and naval
stores; the provisions of Ireland, the grain of Egypt, the indigo, the rice

of China. He does not find, as in Europe, a crowded society, where every place is over-stocked; he does not feel that perpetual collision of parties, that difficulty of beginning, that contention which oversets so many. There is room for everybody in America; has he any particular talent, or industry? he exerts it in order to procure a livelihood, and it succeeds. Is he a merchant? the avenues of trade are infinite; is he eminent in any respect? he will be employed and respected. Does he love a country life? pleasant farms present themselves; he may purchase what he wants, and thereby become an American farmer. Is he a labourer, sober and industrious? he need not go many miles, nor receive many informations before he will be hired, well fed at the table of his employer, and paid four or five times more than he can get in Europe. Does he want uncultivated lands? thousands of acres present themselves, which he may purchase cheap. Whatever be his talents or inclinations, if they are moderate, he may satisfy them. I do not mean that every one who comes will grow rich in a little time; no, but he may procure an easy, decent maintenance, by his industry. Instead of starving he will be fed, instead of being idle he will have employment; and these are riches enough for such men as come over here. The rich stay in Europe, it is only the middling and the poor that emigrate. Would you wish to travel in independent idleness, from north to south, you will find easy access, and the most cheerful reception at every house; society without ostentation, good cheer without pride, and every decent diversion which the country affords, with little expense. It is no wonder that the European who has lived here a few years, is desirous to remain; Europe with all its pomp, is not to be compared to this continent, for men of middle stations, or labourers.

An European, when he first arrives, seems limited in his intentions, as well as in his views; but he very suddenly alters his scale; two hundred miles formerly appeared a very great distance, it is now but a trifle; he no sooner breathes our air than he forms schemes, and embarks in designs he never would have thought of in his own country. There the plenitude of society confines many useful ideas, and often extinguishes the most laudable schemes which here ripen into maturity. Thus Europeans become Americans.

But how is this accomplished in that crowd of low, indigent people, who flock here every year from all parts of Europe? I will tell you; they no sooner arrive than they immediately feel the good effects of that plenty of provisions we possess: they fare on our best food, and they are kindly entertained; their talents, character, and peculiar industry are immediately inquired into; they find countrymen everywhere disseminated, let them come from whatever part of Europe. Let me select one as an epitome of the rest; he is hired, he goes to work, and works moderately; instead of being employed by a haughty person, he finds himself with his equal, placed at the substantial table of the farmer, or else at an inferior one as good; his wages are high, his bed is not like that bed of sorrow on which he used to lie: if he behaves with propriety, and is faithful, he is caressed, and becomes as it were a member of the family. He begins to feel the effects of a sort of resurrection; hitherto he had not lived, but simply vegetated; he now feels himself a man, because he is treated as such; the laws of his own country had overlooked him in his insignificancy; the laws of this cover him with their mantle. Judge what an alteration there must arise in the mind and thoughts of this man; he begins to forget his former servitude and dependence, his heart involuntarily swells and glows; this first swell inspires him with those new thoughts which constitute an American. What love can he entertain for a country where his existence was a burthen to him; if he is a generous good man, the love of this new adoptive parent will sink deep into his heart. He looks around, and sees many a prosperous person, who but a few years before was as poor as himself. This encourages him much, he begins to form some little scheme, the first, alas, he ever formed in his life. If he is wise he thus spends two or three years, in which time he acquires knowledge, the use of tools, the modes of working the lands, felling trees, etc. This prepares the foundation of a good name, the most useful acquisition he can make. He is encouraged, he has gained friends; he is advised and directed, he feels bold, he purchases some land; he gives all the money he has brought over, as well as what he has earned, and trusts to the God of harvests for the discharge of the rest. His good name procures him credit. He is now possessed of the deed, conveying to him and his posterity the fee simple and absolute property of two hundred acres of land, situated on such a river. What an epocha in this man's life! He is become a freeholder, from perhaps a German boor — he is now an American, a Pennsylvanian, an English subject. He is naturalised, his name is enrolled with those of the other citizens of the province. Instead of being a vagrant, he has a place of residence; he is called the inhabitant of such a county, or of such a district, and for the first time in his life counts for something; for hitherto he has been a cypher. I only repeat what I have heard many say, and no wonder their hearts should glow, and be agitated with a multitude of feelings, not easy to describe. From nothing to start into being; from a servant to the rank of a master; from being the slave of some despotic prince, to become a free man, invested with lands, to which every municipal blessing is annexed! What a change indeed! It is in consequence of that change that he becomes an American. This great metamorphosis has a double effect, it extinguishes all his European prejudices, he forgets that mechanism of subordination, that servility of disposition which poverty had taught him; and sometimes he is apt to forget too much, often passing from one extreme to the other. If he is a good man, he forms schemes of future prosperity, he proposes to educate his children better than he has been educated himself; he thinks of future modes of conduct, feels an ardour to labour he never felt before. Pride steps in and leads him to everything that the laws do not forbid: he respects them; with a heart-felt gratitude he looks toward the east, toward that insular government from whose wisdom all his new felicity is derived, and under whose wings and protection he now lives. These reflections constitute him the good man and the good subject. Ye poor Europeans, ye, who sweat, and work for the great—ye, who are obliged to give so many sheaves to the church, so many to your lords, so many to your government, and have hardly any left for yourselves—ye, who are held in less estimation than favourite hunters or useless lap-dogs—ye, who only breathe the air of nature, because it cannot be withheld from you; it is here that ye can conceive the possibility of those feelings I have been describing; it is here the laws of naturalisation invite every one to partake of our great labours and felicity, to till unrented, untaxed lands! Many, corrupted beyond the power of amendment, have brought with them all their vices, and disregarding the advantages held to them, have gone on in their former career of iniquity, until they have been overtaken and punished by our laws. It is not every emigrant who succeeds; no, it is only the sober, the honest, and industrious: happy those to whom this transition has served as a powerful spur to labour, to prosperity, and to the good establishment of children, born in the days of their poverty; and who had no other portion to expect but the rags of their parents, had it not been for their happy emigration. Others again, have been led astray by this enchanting scene; their new pride, instead of leading them to the fields, has kept them in idleness; the idea of possessing lands is all that satisfies them—though surrounded with fertility, they have mouldered away their time in inactivity, misinformed husbandry, and ineffectual endeavours. How much wiser, in general, the honest Germans than almost all other Europeans; they hire themselves to some of their wealthy landsmen, and in that apprenticeship learn everything that is necessary. They attentively consider the prosperous industry of others, which imprints in their minds a strong desire of possessing the same advantages. This forcible idea never quits them, they launch forth, and by dint of sobriety, rigid parsimony, and the most persevering industry, they commonly succeed. Their astonishment at their first arrival from Germany is very great—it is to them a dream; the contrast must be powerful indeed; they observe their countrymen flourishing in every place; they travel through whole counties where not a word of English is spoken; and in the names and the language of the people, they retrace Germany. They have been an useful acquisition to this continent, and to Pennsylvania in particular; to them it owes some share of its prosperity: to their mechanical knowledge and patience it owes the finest mills in all America, the best teams of horses, and many other advantages. The recollection of their former poverty and slavery never quits them as long as they live.

The Scotch and the Irish might have lived in their own country perhaps as poor, but enjoying more civil advantages, the effects of their new situation do not strike them so forcibly, nor has it so lasting an effect. From whence the difference arises I know not, but out of twelve families of emigrants of each country, generally seven Scotch will succeed, nine German, and four Irish. The Scotch are frugal and laborious, but their wives cannot work so hard as German women, who on the contrary vie with their husbands, and often share with them the most severe toils of the field, which they understand better. They have therefore nothing to struggle against, but the common casualties of nature. The Irish do not prosper so well; they love to drink and to quarrel; they are litigious, and soon take to the gun, which is the ruin of everything; they seem beside to labour under a greater degree of ignorance in husbandry than the others; perhaps it is that their industry had less scope, and was less exercised at home. I have heard many relate, how the land was parcelled out in that kingdom; their ancient conquest has been a great detriment to them, by over-setting their landed property. The lands possessed by a few, are leased down *ad infinitum,* and the occupiers often pay five guineas an acre. The poor are worse lodged there than anywhere else in Europe; their potatoes, which are easily raised, are perhaps an inducement to laziness: their wages are too low, and their whisky too cheap.

There is no tracing observations of this kind, without making at the same time very great allowances, as there are everywhere to be found, a great many exceptions. The Irish themselves, from different parts of that kingdom, are very different. It is difficult to account for this surprising locality, one would think on so small an island an Irishman must be an Irishman: yet it is not so, they are different in their aptitude to, and in their love of labour.

The Scotch on the contrary are all industrious and saving; they want nothing more than a field to exert themselves in, and they are commonly sure of succeeding. The only difficulty they labour under is, that technical American knowledge which requires some time to obtain; it is not easy for those who seldom saw a tree, to conceive how it is to be felled, cut up, and split into rails and posts.

As I am fond of seeing and talking of prosperous families, I intend to finish this letter by relating to you the history of an honest Scotch Hebridean, who came here in 1774, which will show you in epitome what the Scotch can do, wherever they have room for the exertion of their industry. Whenever I hear of any new settlement, I pay it a visit once or twice a year, on purpose to observe the different steps each settler takes, the gradual improvements, the different tempers of each family, on which their prosperity in a great nature depends; their different modifications of industry, their ingenuity, and contrivance; for being all poor, their life requires sagacity and prudence. In the evening I love to hear them tell their stories, they furnish me with new ideas; I sit still and listen to their ancient misfortunes, observing in many of them a strong degree of gratitude to God, and the government. Many a well meant sermon have I preached to some of them. When I found laziness and inattention to prevail, who could refrain from wishing well to these new countrymen, after having undergone so many fatigues. Who could withhold good advice? What a happy change it must be, to descend from the high, sterile, bleak lands of Scotland, where everything is barren and cold, to rest on some fertile farms in these middle provinces! Such a transition must have afforded the most pleasing satisfaction.

The following dialogue passed at an out-settlement, where I lately paid a visit:

Well, friend, how do you do now; I am come fifty odd miles on purpose to see you; how do you go on with your new cutting and slashing? Very well, good Sir, we learn the use of the axe bravely, we shall make it out; we have a belly full of victuals every day, our cows run about, and come home full of milk, our hogs get fat of themseves in the woods: Oh, this is a good country! God bless the king, and William Penn; we shall do very well by and by, if we keep our healths. Your log-house looks neat and light, where did you get these shingles? One of our neighbours is a New-England man, and he showed us how to split them out of chestnut-trees. Now for a barn, but all in good time, here are fine trees to build with. Who is to frame it, sure you don't understand that work yet ?A countryman of ours who has been in America these ten years, offers to wait for his money until the second crop is lodged in it. What did you give for your land? Thirty-five shillings per acre, payable in seven years. How many acres have you got? An hundred and fifty. That is enough to begin with; is not your land pretty hard to clear? Yes, Sir, hard enough, but it would be harder still if it were ready cleared, for then we should have no timber, and I love the woods much; the land is nothing without them. Have not you found out any bees yet? No, Sir; and if we had we should not know what to do with them. I will tell you by and by. You are very kind. Farewell, honest man, God prosper you; whenever you travel toward ———, inquire for J. S. He will entertain you kindly, provided you bring him good tidings from your family and farm. In this manner I often visit them, and carefully examine their houses, their modes of ingenuity, their different ways; and make them all relate all they know, and describe all they feel. These are scenes which I believe you would willingly share with me.

I well remember your philanthropic turn of mind. Is it not better to contemplate under these humble roofs, the rudiments of future wealth and population, than to behold the accumulated bundles of litigious papers in the office of a lawyer? To examine how the world is gradually settled, how the howling swamp is converted into a pleasing meadow, the rough ridge into a fine field; and to hear the cheerful whistling, the rural song, where there was no sound heard before, save the yell of the savage, the screech of the owl or the hissing of the snake? Here an European, fatigued with luxury, riches, and pleasures, may find a sweet relaxation in a series of interesting scenes, as affecting as they are new. England, which now contains so many domes, so many castles, was once like this; a place woody and marshy; its inhabitants, now the favourite nation for arts and commerce, were once painted like our neighbours. The country will flourish in its turn, and the same observations will be made which I have just delineated. Posterity will look back with avidity and pleasure, to trace, if possible, the era of this or that particular settlement.

Pray, what is the reason that the Scots are in general more religious, more faithful, more honest, and industrious than the Irish? I do not mean to insinuate national reflections, God forbid! It ill becomes any man, and much less an American; but as I know men are nothing of themselves, and that they owe all their different modifications either to government or other local circumstances, there must be some powerful causes which constitute this great national difference.

Agreeable to the account which several Scotchmen have given me of the north of Britain, of the Orkneys, and the Hebride Islands, they seem, on many accounts, to be unfit for the habitation of men; they appear to be calculated only for great sheep pastures. Who then can blame the inhabitants of these countries for transporting themselves hither? This great continent must in time absorb the poorest part of Europe; and this will happen in proportion as it becomes better known; and as war, taxation, oppression, and misery increase there. The Hebrides appear to be fit only for the residence of malefactors, and it would be much better to send felons there than either to Virginia or Maryland. What a strange compliment has our mother country paid to two of the finest provinces in America! England has entertained in that respect very mistaken ideas; what was intended as a punishment, is become the good fortune of several; many of those who have been transported as felons, are now rich, and strangers to the stings of those wants that urged them to violations of the law: they are become industrious, exemplary, and useful citizens. The English government should purchase the most northern and barren of those islands; it should send over to us the honest, primitive Hebrideans, settle them here on good lands, as a reward for their virtue and ancient poverty; and replace them with a colony of her wicked sons. The severity of the climate, the inclemency of the seasons, the sterility of the soil, the tempestuousness of the sea, would afflict and punish enough. Could there be found a spot better adapted to retaliate the injury it had received by their crimes? Some of those islands might be considered as the hell of Great Britain, where all evil spirits should be sent. Two essential ends would be answered by this simple operation. The good people, by emigration, would be rendered happier; the bad ones would be placed where they ought to be. In a few years the dread of being sent to that wintry region would have a much stronger effect than that of transportation.—This is no place of punishment; were I a poor hopeless, breadless Englishman, and not restrained by the power of shame, I should be very thankful for the passage. It is of very little importance how, and in what manner an indigent man arrives; for if he is but sober, honest, and industrious, he has nothing more to ask of heaven. Let him go to work, he will have opportunities enough to earn a comfortable support, and even the means of procuring some land; which ought to be the utmost wish of every person who has health and hands to work. I knew a man who came to this country, in the literal sense of the expression, stark naked; I think he was a Frenchman, and a sailor on board an English man-of-war. Being discontented, he had stripped himself and swam ashore; where, finding clothes and friends, he settled afterwards at Maraneck, in the county of Chester, in the province of New York: he married and left a good farm to each of his sons. I knew another person who was but twelve years old when he was taken on the frontiers of Canada, by the Indians; at his arrival at Albany he was purchased by a gentleman, who generously bound him apprentice to a tailor. He lived to the age of ninety, and left behind him a fine estate and a numerous family, all well settled; many of them I am acquainted with.—Where is then the industrious European who ought to despair?

After a foreigner from any part of Europe is arrived, and become a citizen; let him devoutly listen to the voice of our great parent, which says to him, "Welcome to my shores, distressed European; bless the hour in which thou didst see my verdant fields, my fair navigable rivers, and my green mountains!—If thou wilt work, I have bread for thee; if thou wilt be honest, sober, and industrious, I have greater rewards to confer on thee—ease and independence. I will give thee fields to feed and clothe thee; a comfortable fireside to sit by, and tell thy children by what means thou hast prospered; and a decent bed to repose on. I shall endow thee beside with the immunities of a freeman. If thou wilt carefully educate thy children, teach them gratitude to God, and reverence to that government, that philanthropic government, which has collected here so many men and made them happy. I will also provide for thy progeny; and to every good man this ought to be the most holy, the most powerful, the most earnest wish he can possibly form, as well as the most consolatory prospect when he dies. Go thou and work and till; thou shalt prosper, provided thou be just, grateful, and industrious."

# Bibliography

Anonymous. "Bacon's Epitaph." *The Burwell Papers*. Proceedings of the Massachusetts Historical Society. Boston, 1866–67.

———. *Narratives of the Insurrections, 1675–1690*. Edited by Charles M. Andrews. New York, 1948.

Beverley, Robert. *The History and Present State of Virginia*. Edited by Louis B. Wright. Chapel Hill, North Carolina, 1947.

Bradford, William. *Of Plymouth Plantation*. Edited by Samuel Eliot Morison. New York, 1952.

Bradstreet, Anne. *The Poems of Mrs. Anne Bradstreet. Together with Her Prose Remains*. Edited by Charles Eliot Norton. New York, 1897.

Byrd, William. *William Byrd's Histories of the Dividing Line Betwixt Virginia and North Carolina*. Edited by William K. Boyd. Raleigh, North Carolina, 1929.

———. *The Writings of "Colonel William Byrd, of Westover in Virginia, Esq."* Edited by John S. Bassett. New York, 1901.

———. *The Secret Diary of William Byrd of Westover, 1709–1712*. Edited and decoded by Louis B. Wright and Marion Tingling. Richmond, Virginia, 1941.

———. *Another Secret Diary of William Byrd of Westover, 1739–1741, with Letters and Literary Exercises, 1696–1726*. Decoded and edited by Marion Tingling. Richmond, Virginia, 1942.

———. *The London Diary, and Other Writings*. Edited by Louis B. Wright and Marion Tingling. New York, 1958.

Cook, Ebenezer. *The Sot-Weed Factor*. Edited by Bernard C. Steiner. Baltimore, 1900.

Crèvecoeur, pseud., (J. Hector St. John). *Letters from an American Farmer*. Edited by William Barton Blake. London, 1912.

Edwards, Jonathan. *Representative Selections*, with Introduction, Bibliography, and Notes. Edited by Clarence H. Faust and Thomas H. Johnson. New York, 1935.

Franklin, Benjamin. *The Writings of Benjamin Franklin*. Edited by Albert H. Smyth, 10 vols. New York, 1905–07.

———. *The Papers of Benjamin Franklin*. Edited by Leonard W. Labaree and Whitfield Bell, Jr. Vols. I–III. New Haven, 1959–61.

Hamilton, Alexander. *Gentleman's Progress: The Itinerarium of Dr.*

*Alexander Hamilton.* Edited by Carl Bridenbaught. Chapel Hill, North Carolina, 1948.

Johnson, Edward. *The Wonder-Working Providence of Sions Saviour in New England.* Edited by J. F. Jameson. New York, 1910.

Mather, Cotton. *The Diary of Cotton Mather.* Edited by Worthington C. Ford. Collections of the Massachusetts Historical Society, Seventh Series, Vols. 7–8. Boston, 1911–12.

———. *Selections from Cotton Mather.* Edited by Kenneth B. Murdock. New York, 1926.

———. *The Wonders of the Invisible World.* (*Narratives of the Witchcraft Cases*). Edited by George L. Burr. New York, 1914.

Mather, Increase. *Remarkable Providence.* Edited by George Offor. London, 1890.

Mittelberger, Gottfried. *Gottfried Mittelberger's Journey to Pennsylvania.* Translated by Carl Theo. Eben. Philadelphia, 1898.

———. *Journey to Pennsylvania. By Gottfried Mittelberger.* Edited and Translated by Oscar Handlin and John Clive. Cambridge, Massachusetts, 1960.

Morton, Thomas. *New English Canaan, or New Canaan.* Edited by Charles Francis Adams. Boston, 1883.

Rowlandson, Mary. *Narratives of the Indian Wars, 1675–1699.* Edited by Charles H. Lincoln. New York, 1913. Original Narratives of American History Series.

Sewall, Samuel. *Diary of Samuel Sewall, 1674–1729.* Collections of the Massachusetts Historical Society, Fifth Series. Vols. 5–7. Boston, 1878–82.

Smith, John. *Travels and Works of Captain John Smith.* Edited by Edward Arber, 2 vols. Birmingham, England, 1884.

Taylor, Edward. *The Poetical Works of Edward Taylor.* Edited by Thomas H. Johnson. Princeton, 1939.

———. *Poems; edited by Donald E. Stanford.* New Haven, 1960.

Ward, Nathaniel. *The Simple Cobbler of Aggawam in America.* Edited by Lawrence C. Wroth. New York, 1937.

Wigglesworth, Michael. *The Day of Doom.* Edited by Kenneth B. Murdock. New York, 1929.

Williams, Roger. *The Writings of Roger Williams, Providence, Rhode Island,* 6 vols. Providence, 1866–74.

Winthrop, John. *The Winthrop Papers.* Edited by Allyn B. Forbes. Collections of the Massachusetts Historical Society. Boston, 1931–44.

——— and Margaret. *Some Old Puritan Love-Letters.* Edited by Joseph H. Twichell. New York, 1893.

Woolman, John. *The Journal and other Writings of John Woolman.* Edited by Vida D. Scudder. London, 1910.

———. *The Journal of John Woolman and a Plea for the Poor.* Edited by Frederick B. Tolles. New York, 1961.